HJT
TRAINING PROFESSIONALS

HJT Training Immigration Manual

© 2010 HJT Training

IMMIGRATION DEPARTMENT
Parker Rhodes, Solicitors
14 & 22 Moorgate Street
ROTHERHAM
S60 2DA

No part of this book may be reproduced or utilised in any form or by any electronic or mechanical, including photocopying, recording or by any information storage and retrieval system without permission in writing.

Further information and copies of this manual can be obtained from:

HJT Training Ltd
1 Liverpool Street,
London EC2M 7QD

t +44 (0) 20 7956 2000
f +44 (0) 20 7956 2001
e enquiries@hjt-training.co.uk

HJT Training is a company limited by guarantee. Registered in England and Wales. Reg no. 4891943

ISBN: 978-0-9554356-3-8

Version 9-2

Contents

INTRODUCTION 1
    THE HJT IMMIGRATION MANUAL 3
    THE LSC ACCREDITATION SCHEME 3
    THE OISC REGISTRATION SCHEME 4
    SOURCES OF INFORMATION ON IMMIGRATION LAW 5

CHAPTER 1: IMMIGRATION CONTROL 7
    WHO IS SUBJECT TO IMMIGRATION CONTROL? 9
    ENTERING THE UK 11
    REMAINING IN THE UK 12
    SOURCES OF LAW 14
    MAKING AN APPLICATION 21

CHAPTER 2: IMMIGRATION CATEGORIES AND POLICIES 31
    POINTS BASED SYSTEM 34
    NAVIGATING THE RULES 34
    COMMON REQUIREMENTS OF THE RULES 36
    VISITORS: R.40 TO 56 47
    STUDENTS AND THEIR FAMILIES: R.57 TO 87 54
    SHORT-TERM EMPLOYMENT CATEGORIES: R.88 TO 127 55
    LONG RESIDENCE: R.276A TO 276D 56
    SPOUSES AND CIVIL PARTNERS: R.277 TO 289C 59
    FIANCÉ(E)S AND PROPOSED CIVIL PARTNERS: R.289AA TO 295 69
    UNMARRIED PARTNERS: R.295AA TO 295O 69
    CHILDREN: R.296 TO 316 70
    OTHER FAMILY MEMBERS: R.317 TO 319 74
    RETURNING RESIDENTS: R.18 TO 20 77
    GENERAL GROUNDS FOR REFUSAL 79
    POLICIES AND CONCESSIONS 85

CHAPTER 3: INTERNATIONAL PROTECTION 101
    REFUGEE LAW AND HUMANITARIAN PROTECTION 103
    THE REFUGEE CONVENTION 103
    WELL FOUNDED FEAR 105
    BEING PERSECUTED 121
    THE CONVENTION REASONS 129
    PROTECTION AND RELOCATION 133
    NON REFOULEMENT 138
    CESSATION CLAUSES 138
    EXCLUSION CLAUSES 140
    HUMANITARIAN PROTECTION 145

CHAPTER 4: ASYLUM PROCESS AND PRACTICE 151
    CLAIMING ASYLUM 153

Age disputes 156
  Fast-track appeals 159
  Third Country Cases 161
  'Clearly unfounded' certificates 168
  Fresh claims 169
  Benefits of recognition as a refugee 183
  Benefits of Humanitarian Protection 187

CHAPTER 5: HUMAN RIGHTS LAW 189

  Human Rights Act 1998 191
  European Convention on Human Rights 193
  ECHR and immigration law 196
  Article 2 196
  Article 3 197
  Article 4 207
  Article 5 207
  Article 6 209
  Article 8 210
  Article 14 226
  Discretionary Leave 226
  Travel documents 228

CHAPTER 6: EUROPEAN COMMUNITY LAW 231

  Principle of free movement 233
  Countries to which free movement law applies 233
  Interaction of UK and EC law 236
  Who benefits? 240
  Benefits of the exercise of Treaty rights 251
  Excluding and removing EEA nationals from UK 257
  Rights of appeal 260
  Accession States 261
  The Ankara Agreement 264

CHAPTER 7: BRITISH NATIONALITY LAW 273

  A brief history of nationality law 275
  Birth or adoption in the UK 278
  Birth outside the UK 282
  Acquisition by registration as an adult 285
  Naturalisation 286
  Challenging nationality decisions 290
  Stopping being British 291
  Checklist for Nationality 293

CHAPTER 8: POINTS BASED SYSTEM 295

  Introduction 297
  Sponsorship under the points-based system 298
  Documentary evidence and Home Office guidance 301
  Overstaying and extension applications 303

- Tier 1: highly skilled 304
- Tier 2: skilled workers 317
- Tier 4: students 325
- Tier 5: youth mobility and temporary workers 335
- Dependants of PBS migrants 343
- Right of appeal 344
- Right of review 345

CHAPTER 9: ENFORCEMENT: DETENTION AND DEPORTATION 347
- Detention 349
- Release and bail 358
- Administrative removal 366
- Deportation 367

CHAPTER 10: RACE DISCRIMINATION 379
- Race relations and immigration law and practice 381
- Race Relations Act 1976 (as amended) 382
- Race discrimination in immigration cases 389

CHAPTER 11: THE LAW OF APPEALS 393
- Right of appeal 395
- Grounds of appeal 401
- Appeals structure 403
- First Tier Tribunal 410
- Seeking permission to appeal from the FTT 425
- Seeking permission to appeal from the UT 430
- Pursuing an Upper Tribunal appeal 431
- Onward appeal 436
- Tribunal determinations as precedents 438

CHAPTER 12: CRIMINAL OFFENCES 441
- Introduction 443
- Immigration officers and police powers 443
- Effects of a criminal conviction 444
- Article 31 defence against prosecution 446
- Trafficking 446
- Offences under the Immigration Act 1971 447
- Offences under the 2004 Act 452
- Offences in Nationality Acts 453
- Employer and financial institution offences 453
- Giving immigration advice: The OISC 454
- Offences connected with support 455

CHAPTER 13: PROFESSIONAL ETHICS 457
- General duties 458
- Basic principles 458
- False representations 459
- Appeals 459

Costs and client care	460
Supervision	461
Liens – retention of documents	462
Standard of work	462
Supervision of staff	463
Conflict of interest	463
Confidentiality	467
Money Laundering	470
Duties to the Court	471
Complaints procedures	474

CHAPTER 14: PRACTICAL SKILLS 477

Asylum applications	478
Professional Conduct Regarding Asylum Claims	484
Expert evidence practice direction	485
Commissioning medical evidence	487
Commissioning country expert evidence	491

Introduction

THE HJT IMMIGRATION MANUAL 3
THE LSC ACCREDITATION SCHEME 3
THE OISC REGISTRATION SCHEME 4

The HJT immigration manual

This manual was originally devised and written with a view to training practitioners for the immigration accreditation scheme run by the Legal Services Commission and the Solicitor Regulation Authority. Since the first edition, the manual has been extensively rewritten and revised to reflect changes in the law and to improve the delivery of the information the manual contains. This latest edition continues that tradition of continual improvement.

The manual is now accompanied by specially designed complementary training materials, namely a set of Powerpoint slides based on the graphics boxes, examples and tips that have gradually been introduced into the manual and an extensive set of questions and model answers structured around the chapters of this manual. Contact HJT Training if you are interested in making use of these materials.

During its short lifetime, the manual has evolved to become the leading introductory text for new immigration practitioners and for students of immigration law. Hundreds of new immigration lawyers have been trained by HJT Training using this manual.

The original contributors included Gail Elliman, David Jones, David Robinson, Mark Symes and Colin Yeo. Later editions have been extensively re-written and updated by Colin Yeo. Thanks go to Vincent Fox for invaluable assistance with updating and correcting, to Androulla Demetriou for her design expertise and to Natasha Knight for her patience and hard work in producing the printed edition.

The LSC accreditation scheme

The Legal Services Commission (LSC) requires any contributor to a legal aid contract in immigration law to be accredited under the accreditation scheme. There are three levels to this scheme. This manual is suitable for training for levels 1 and 2.

It is beyond the scope of the manual to describe the requirements of the accreditation scheme and the nature of the examinations at levels 1 and 2. HJT Training runs revision courses before each round of examinations which address these issues.

Information on the LSC accreditation scheme is, unfortunately, not necessarily easy to obtain. Responsibility for the scheme is divided between a number of organisations, as follows:

- **Legal Services Commission**. The LSC requires those billing work under an immigration legal aid contract to be accredited under a Law Society scheme that the LSC persuaded the Law Society to institute. The LSC website is notoriously almost impossible to navigate but is the place to look for information about the requirement to be accredited (or reaccredited).

- **The Law Society**. The accreditation scheme belongs to the Law Society even if it is effectively imposed by the LSC. The Law Society had transferred responsibility for the immigration accreditation scheme to the Solicitors Regulation Authority but it seems to have been transferred back to the Law Society some time in 2009. The Law Society website is the place to look for information about the requirements of the scheme.

    See www.lawsociety.org.uk > Member Services > Accreditation schemes > Immigration and Asylum

    The most useful documents for an aspirant accredited caseworker are the standards and guidance documents for levels 1 and 2. For some reason each document is divided into standards, which tell one very little about what one is expected to know, and then much more specific guidance, which is far more helpful in providing direction for a potential examinee. The guidance constitutes essential reading for anyone seeking to sit the exams. At the time of writing it had last been updated in July 2009.

- **Central Law Training**. CLT administer the examinations and their website is the place to look for information about when the next round of examinations is scheduled.

Past examination papers are not publicly available. HJT has created a major resource of questions in the same style and of the same approximate level of difficulty to those that will be faced in the examinations. The HJT examination pack, available from HJT Training, includes questions and model answers and model mark schemes.

The OISC registration scheme

The Office of the Immigration Services Commissioner (OISC) was created by the Immigration Act 1999 and regulates immigration advisers who are not exempted from the scheme by virtue of their professional status (primarily solicitors and barristers). In short, those who are not solicitors (or working under the supervision of a solicitor) or barristers are not permitted to give immigration advice, unless they are properly regulated by the OISC.

Again, it is beyond the scope of the manual to describe the OISC scheme in detail. As with the LSC scheme, there are knowledge and skills examinations and assessments that must be completed in order to register with the OISC. The OISC scheme also requires a successful applicant to show knowledge of the OISC Code of Practice and the existence of certain minimum best practice business practices. Unlike the LSC scheme, these are administered and run directly by the OISC itself.

See www.oisc.gov.uk for further details.

Neither HJT Training nor any other training provider can provide OISC accreditation or registration as this lies with the OISC alone. However, HJT Training does offer training that will assist a person seeking registration with the

OISC and is an OISC Continuing Professional Development (CPD) training provider.

The levels of the OISC and LSC schemes broadly correspond as follows:

LSC	OISC
Probationer	Level 1 (signposting only)
Level 1 (accredited caseworker)	Level 2
Level 2 (senior caseworker)	Level 3
Level 3 (advanced caseworker)	No equivalent

Sources of information on immigration law

Immigration law changes on a very frequent basis. As will be seen in the following chapter, new immigration Acts of Parliament are now passed on an annual basis, and immigration law is cursed by a complex plethora of secondary legislation, rules and European directives and regulations. It is an extremely complex subject. Mastering it is difficult, and staying up to date is even harder.

As well as this manual, HJT can recommend the following as sources of information on immigration law and practice:

- **ILPA**. Membership of the Immigration Law Practitioners Association is essential for any serious immigration lawyer. The monthly ILPA mailing to members, ILPA emails and sub-committee email lists are invaluable and unrivalled sources of information. The various ILPA best practice guides are essential reading for any new immigration lawyer aspiring to become a good immigration lawyer.

- **JCWI**. The Joint Council for the Welfare of Refugees publishes the famous JCWI Handbook every few years and this is one of the standard reference works for immigration lawyers.

- **Macdonald**, *Immigration Law and Practice*. This is the gold standard immigration law reference book.

- **Symes and Jorro**, *Asylum and Human Rights Law and Practice*. This is the gold standard asylum, human rights and international protection reference book.

- **Refugee Legal Group**. The RLG was formerly an informal group of asylum lawyers who met on a monthly basis. In recent years it has morphed into a members-only internet forum of around 900 members administered by Asylum Aid. It is an invaluable source of information. Be warned, though: asking unintelligent questions on the group exposes one's ignorance to a very wide field indeed.

- **Update websites**. There are various websites that provide updates on immigration and asylum law, including:

    Garden Court Chambers immigration update:
    www.gardencourtchambers.co.uk

    Free Movement blog: http://freemovement.wordpress.com

    NCADC (National Coalition of Anti Deportation Campaigns): www.ncadc.org.uk)

    ICAR (Information Centre about Asylum and Refugees): www.icar.org.uk)

Chapter 1: Immigration control

WHO IS SUBJECT TO IMMIGRATION CONTROL? 9

ENTERING THE UK 11

REMAINING IN THE UK 12

SOURCES OF LAW 14

    PRIMARY LEGISLATION 15

    SECONDARY LEGISLATION 19

    POLICIES AND CONCESSIONS 20

MAKING AN APPLICATION 21

    TIMING 21

        Automatic extension of leave 22

        Effect of an invalid application 22

    APPLICATION FORMS AND FEES 22

        Out-of-country applications 22

        In-country immigration status applications 24

    PRESCRIBED FORM OF APPLICATIONS 26

    APPLICATION FEES 27

    ROLE OF FURTHER REPRESENTATIONS 28

Who is subject to immigration control?

The fundamental rule of immigration control is that it is exclusive in nature. Everyone is excluded from lawful entry or residence unless they are either exempted from control or have permission.

General rule
- Everyone is excluded

Unless
- Not subject to immigration control
- Permission ('leave') is granted

Those not subject to immigration control include British citizens and others with what is called the 'right of abode' and also EEA nationals and others who can rely on European Community law.

This basic rule, the founding principle of immigration law, is derived from s.1 Immigration Act 1971, still the framework Act for immigration control, despite heavy amendments over the intervening years:

> s.1(1) All those who are in this Act expressed to have the right of abode in the United Kingdom shall be free to live in and to come and go into and from, the United Kingdom...
>
> (2) Those not having that right may live, work and settle in the United Kingdom by permission and subject to such regulation and control of their entry into, stay in and departure from the United Kingdom as is imposed by this Act...

The right of abode is therefore an extremely important form of status, as it exempts the possessor from immigration controls. However, immigration officers can detain and examine possessors of the right of abode to establish that they do indeed hold that status.

Being subject to immigration control means, with an important exception regarding a form of temporary status called 'temporary admission', that a person must always possess leave to enter or remain in the UK to be lawfully present in the UK. Temporary admission is discussed in further detail at Chapter 10. The different circumstances in which a person may apply for leave from outside the UK and from inside the UK (for example, switching from one immigration category to another or extending one's leave in the same category) are set out in the Immigration Rules, HC395. The Immigration Rules are the principal reference point when advising a person on their immigration options.

> **Example**
>
> Alia is from Bangladesh. She has family in the UK (her grandfather went to work in the UK in the 1960s and some of the family stayed and some returned to Bangladesh) and would like to visit them and perhaps do a course at college.
>
> An experienced immigration adviser would recognise that Alia needs to be asked further questions to determine whether she is entitled to British citizenship. Depending on the outcome of those enquiries, there are two ways she might travel to the UK:
>
> (i) It may transpire that she is exempt from immigration control due to an entitlement to citizenship, and can come and go from the UK as she pleases and study, work or live there if she chooses. However, if she simply got on a plane and flew to Heathrow, she would have serious difficulty convincing an Immigration Officer of her claim to citizenship. She would be well advised to apply in Bangladesh for a 'certificate of entitlement' which demonstrates that she has the right of abode in the UK.
>
> (ii) If she is not entitled to British citizenship, she will need to apply for permission to enter the UK for a specific purpose. The UK has immigration laws allowing entry to both visitors and students if they meet certain requirements, but Alia will have to make up her mind which to apply under before travelling. As will be discussed below, she would need to apply for 'entry clearance' before travelling, because Bangladeshis require a visa before setting off for the UK.

Entering the UK

As stated above, in order to enter the UK in a legal sense, all persons subject to immigration control must possess leave to enter. Leave to enter is granted (or refused) by Immigration Officers, usually at a port of entry, such as Heathrow airport.

However, some immigrants must even before applying for leave to enter apply for a document called an entry clearance. This is known colloquially as a visa and until recently took the form of a sticker (also known as a vignette) placed in the holder's passport or travel document. This has now been replaced with the Identity card for Foreign Nationals (ICFN), which is an identity card carried by the migrant in conjunction with his or her passport. The terminology has recently changed on UKBA application forms and practitioners will encounter the ICFN referred to as a Biometric Residence Permit (BRP).

If a person who is required by law to possess entry clearance before applying for leave to enter arrives in the UK and attempts to apply for leave to enter, that person must be refused: immigration rule 320(5).

The rules on who does and does not require entry clearance are as follows:

Visa nationals
- Always required: Appendix 1

6 months +
- Always required: Rule 24

Rule says so
- Always required: check individual rules

A non-visa national can, optionally, apply for entry clearance prior to travel, and if refused on arrival at port will then potentially have an in-country right of appeal. This would be very useful advice to give to a person who is at risk of refusal on arrival, for example because of a poor immigration history which is discernable by an Immigration Officer from his or her current passport.

As can probably be deduced from the proceeding passages, this part of immigration control takes place abroad. An application for entry clearance is made to an Entry Clearance Officer, usually referred to by immigration lawyers as an ECO. ECOs are based abroad at British embassies, High Commissions (the same as an embassy except based in a Commonwealth country) or consulates. These venues are increasingly being referred to as Visa Application Centres.

Usually, because of the Immigration (Leave to Enter and Remain) Order 2000, an entry clearance will also include the grant of leave to enter, which becomes effective on entry to the UK. However, on arrival an Immigration Officer may examine the leave to enter and has the power to cancel the entry clearance which contains the leave to enter under certain limited circumstances:

> False representations or material facts not disclosed, with or without knowledge, in writing or orally

> Change in circumstances since entry clearance issued

> Restricted returnability, medical grounds, criminal record, subject to a deportation order or exclusion conducive to public good

See 1971 Act, Schedule 2, paragraph 2A and also the immigration rules at r.321).

There are a number of other relevant provisions relating to entry clearance:

- Entry clearance applications for any purpose other than a visit must be made in the overseas post where the applicant resides or the nearest designated post if there is none

- Entry clearance can be revoked if the Entry Clearance Officer or an Immigration Officer decides that is been obtained through false representations or if material facts were not disclosed or if a change of circumstances since its issue removes the basis of the person's claim to enter (unless that change of circumstances is that someone is over the minimum age requirement when they met that requirement at the time the application was made: see immigration rule r.27).

Many of the busiest entry clearance posts now employ an agent or courier firm to accept and process applications before forwarding them to the entry clearance post for decision.

Remaining in the UK

Once present legally in the UK, a person subject to immigration control who has been granted limited leave to enter can apply to remain for longer. If no such application is made, the person will must either leave the UK or will become an overstayer, which is a criminal act (see chapter on criminal offences).

An application to stay for longer once already present in the UK is described in the immigration rules as an application for an 'extension of leave' or 'extension of stay' and if successful 'leave to remain' will be granted.

There is no other difference between leave to enter and leave to remain than that the former is granted before legal entry to the UK and the latter after legal entry to the UK. Leave to enter is therefore usually obtained from Immigration Officers at ports of entry and leave to remain is usually obtained from immigration caseworkers working at the UK Border Agency, based at Croydon, Liverpool or another office.

> **Top tip**
>
> When immigration lawyers refer to extensions of leave, they are often referring to an extension of leave in the same immigration category. For example, a student will often be granted one year of leave to enter initially and then have to apply for further periods of leave to remain if on a course of longer than one years' duration. Immigration lawyers often refer to an application for an extension of leave in a different immigration category as a variation application or as 'switching'. For example, a student might meet the love of his or her life, get married and want to apply for leave to remain as a spouse.

The following flowcharts provide examples of how the different processes discussed above fit together into actual applications for entry and stay. The examples all assume that everything goes according to plan for the potential immigrant – refusals, appeals and removals are not dealt with here. The employment column is based on the general procedure but the introduction of the points based system means that specific reference to Tiers 1, 2 and 5 should be made dependant on the applicant's circumstances. See Chapter 9 for more information on this category.

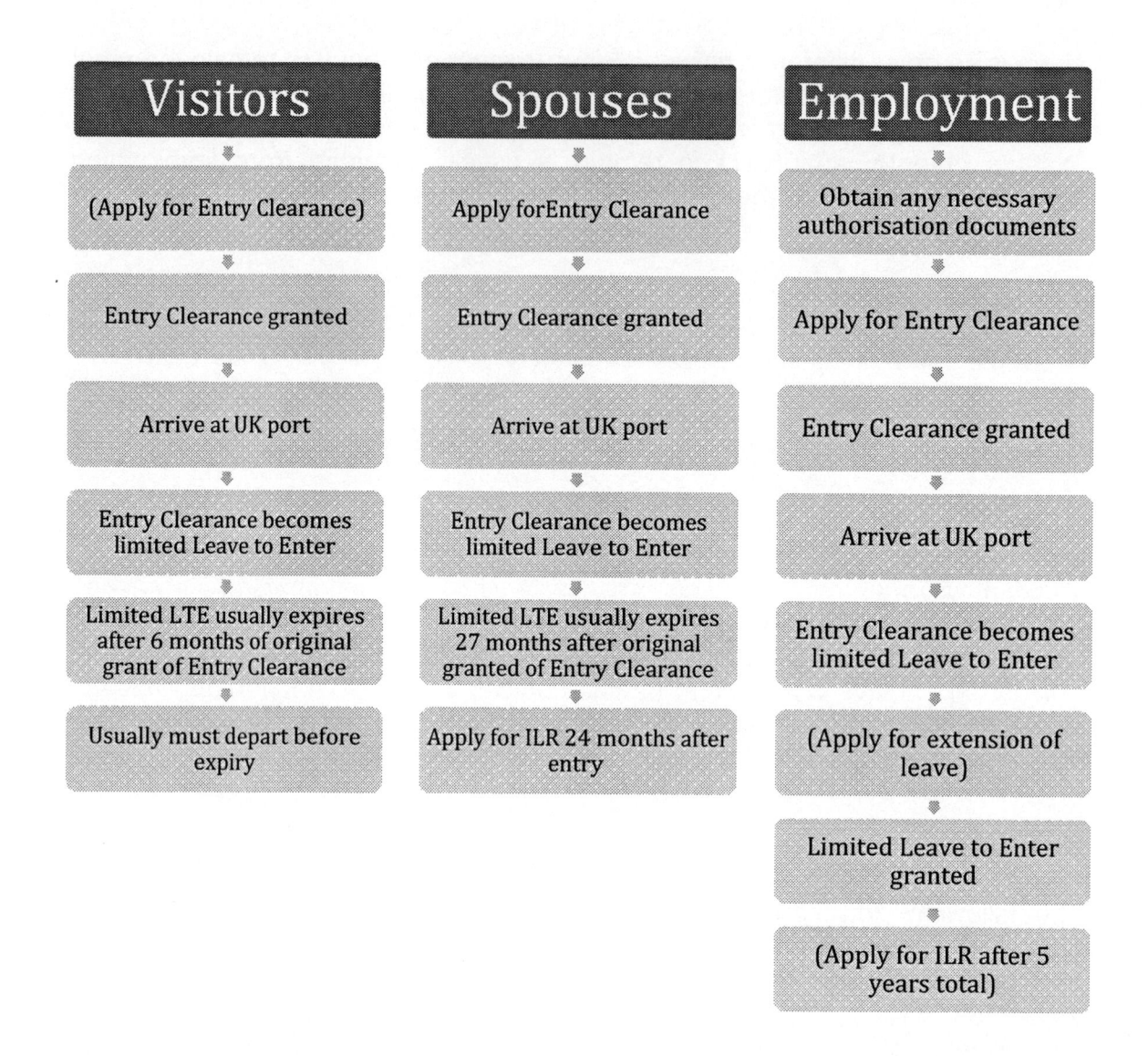

Visitors	Spouses	Employment
(Apply for Entry Clearance)	Apply for Entry Clearance	Obtain any necessary authorisation documents
Entry Clearance granted	Entry Clearance granted	Apply for Entry Clearance
Arrive at UK port	Arrive at UK port	Entry Clearance granted
Entry Clearance becomes limited Leave to Enter	Entry Clearance becomes limited Leave to Enter	Arrive at UK port
Limited LTE usually expires after 6 months of original grant of Entry Clearance	Limited LTE usually expires 27 months after original granted of Entry Clearance	Entry Clearance becomes limited Leave to Enter
Usually must depart before expiry	Apply for ILR 24 months after entry	(Apply for extension of leave)
		Limited Leave to Enter granted
		(Apply for ILR after 5 years total)

Brackets have been used around the visitor entry clearance application boxes because some visitors require entry clearance (referred to as 'visa nationals') and others do not (referred to as 'non visa nationals').

Sources of law

It is essential as a practitioner and for the accreditation examinations to be able to navigate with ease around the various pieces of legislation that govern immigration and asylum law. Immigration control is maintained through primary legislation, secondary legislation, Home Office policy, commitment to our obligations under international conventions and the ultimate discretion of the Secretary of State which can override all the rules and legislation.

Primary legislation

Immigration Act 1971

- Continues to provide the framework of immigration control
- All persons without a right of abode are subject to immigration control (s.1)
- Defines who has a right of abode (amended by other legislation) (s.2)
- Provides that entry/stay is regulated by the grant of leave to enter or remain for either a limited or indefinite period (s.3)
- Provides for regulation and control of entry into and stay in the UK by the Secretary of State through powers (delegated to entry clearance officers and immigration officers and under-secretaries at the Home Office) to grant (s.4):
  - Entry clearance
  - Leave to enter
  - Leave to remain/further leave to remain
  - Make a decision to remove
  - Make a decision to deport
  - Make a decision to revoke a deportation order
- Provides for when a person may become liable for deportation (s.3(5))
- Gives the power to remove only to certain countries or territories – specified in para 8 of Schedule 2
- Defines various terms including illegal entrant (s.33)
- Provides for the power to examine passengers and detain passengers (Schedule 2)
- Provides for the grant of bail (Schedule 2)

British Nationality Act 1983

- Redefined nationality and citizenship and limited 'right of abode' to newly created British citizens (replacing Citizens of the United Kingdom and Commonwealth with six new categories of nationality and citizenship). While the Act may at first glance appear indecipherable, patience will be rewarded:
- s.1 defines acquisition by birth or adoption
- s.2 defines acquisition by descent
- s.3 sets out the provisions for the registration of minors born outside the UK
- s.6 and Schedule 1 set out the criteria for acquisition by naturalisation
- s.4 to s.4C sets out other registration provisions
- s.11 defines who acquired citizenship on commencement of the Act
- s.14 defines a 'British citizen by descent' and, in effect, also 'otherwise than by descent'. The distinction is important, as will be seen in the nationality law chapter.

Immigration Act 1988

- Introduced carrier liabilities for the first time but now of little ongoing significance

Asylum and Immigration Appeals Act 1993

- Incorporated UN Convention Relating to the Status of Refugees 1951 and 1967 Protocol into UK law for first time. Gave right of appeal on refugee grounds to illegal entrants.

Asylum and Immigration Act 1996

- Includes s.8, the criminal offence of employing a person with no right to work (recently amended through 2002 Act enabling provision). On commencement of the relevant provisions of the 2006 Act (see below) this will be superseded.

Special Immigration Appeals Commission Act 1997

- Created SIAC for security-sensitive appeals

Human Rights Act 1998

- Incorporated ECHR into UK law. However, the HRA was 'enabled' in immigration and asylum appeals in immigration cases by the 1999 Act and the 2002 Act. Separate remedies are available directly under the HRA, though, given the right factual situation.

Immigration and Asylum Act 1999

- Came into force between November 1999 and October 2000. It provided a new framework for immigration control but has been largely superseded except in certain important respects:
  - amends IA 1971 to provide for entry clearance to have effect as leave to enter (s.3)
  - provides powers of administrative removal for persons (s.10)
  - provides for the registration of immigration advisors through the Office of the Immigration Services Commissioner (OISC), including the introduction of related criminal offences and enforcement powers
  - provides for the dispersal of asylum seekers
  - provides for suspicious marriages to be reported
  - creates new offences relating to facilitating/harbouring illegal entrants and increases powers of arrest and power to search premises and persons

Nationality, Immigration and Asylum Act 2002

- Came into force largely on 1 April 2003, although some provisions were introduced as early as November 2002. Changes include:
  - sets out powers of the Immigration tribunal
  - provides for certain asylum claims to be certified as manifestly unfounded and that the right to challenge such decisions is to be exercised from abroad only (commonly but rather obscurely referred to as non-suspensive appeals because removal is not suspended) (s.94)
  - extends immigration offences and penalties
  - brings in a power to revoke British Citizenship (s.4 amending s.40 British Nationality Act 1981)
  - provides for establishment of accommodation centres and removal centres (ss.16-42)
  - allows for revocation of indefinite leave to remain (s.76)
  - introduces a new framework of appeal rights and specific grounds of appeal (ss.81-83)
  - grounds of appeal (s.84)
  - limitations on appeal rights (ss.88-99)
  - gives domestic life to Article 33(2) of the Refugee Convention (s.72)
  - introduces provisions for juxtaposed controls with EEA countries

Asylum and Immigration (Treatment of Claimants, etc) Act 2004

- Radically changed the old system of appeals via the introduction of the 'single' tier, replacing the Immigration Appellate Authority system of Adjudicators and the Immigration Appeal Tribunal with the now also defunct Asylum and Immigration Tribunal, populated by Immigration Judges, Designated Immigration Judges and Senior Immigration Judges. This came into effect in April 2005. Other provisions included:
  - a controversial permission to marry requirement for overseas nationals which was successfully challenged in the House of Lords case of SSHD v Baiai & Ors (s.19-25)
  - introduced important new immigration criminal offences, including arriving without an immigration document (s.2), not co-operating with removal (s.35) and trafficking (s.4)
  - introduced statutory negative presumptions about the assessment of credibility in asylum cases (s.8)
  - abolished back payments of income support and other benefits for those recognised as refugees, as well as numerous other provisions relating to welfare and asylum support
  - introduced various regulation-making powers (not yet used at time of writing), including to partially designate countries or groups for 'non-suspensive' appeals
  - introduced powers for electronic monitoring, or 'tagging', as a form of reporting restriction for those on bail or temporary admission

Immigration, Asylum and Nationality Act 2006

- The major change introduced in this legislation was the abolition of appeal rights against entry clearance decisions for students and employment categories, but this has come into effect gradually in line with the Points Based System (s.4). Most other changes were relatively minor:
  - amended appeal rights for those recognised as refugees where a decision is made that they no longer qualify for international protection (s.1)
  - adjustments to s.104 of the 2002 Act to prevent the statutory abandonment of certain types of appeal ('upgrade' appeals for full refugee status and racial discrimination claims) (s.9)
  - introduces a new regime of civil penalty notices and fines for employers who employ immigrants without permission to work as well as a new criminal offence to replace s.8 1996 Act (s.15 to 26)
  - various provisions relating to information sharing and other enforcement powers (s.27 to 42)
  - removes registration as a British citizen as of right by introducing a good character requirement (s.58)

UK Borders Act 2007

- The changes instituted under the Act generally have little impact on day to day casework:
  - the exception to this are the new provisions on automatic deportations, subject to a human rights exemption and other exemptions
  - provision for biometric immigration documents
  - provision for imposing conditions on reporting and residence on those granted limited leave
  - enhanced powers of detention for immigration officers

Criminal Justice and Immigration Act 2008

- Sections 130-137 of this Act provide for a special immigration status for individuals who cannot be removed to their country of origin because of human rights concerns, but who have committed crimes falling under s.72 NIAA 2002 or are excluded from refugee status by virtue of Article 1F of the Refugee Convention. Spouses, civil partners and children may also be subjected to the same status. The status can prohibit the person from working, subject them to heavy reporting and residence conditions and leaves them on a reduced welfare support package.

Tribunals, Courts and Enforcement Act 2007

- This legislation has amended and revised the procedures at the Asylum and Immigration Tribunal. The system has been replaced with the Immigration and Asylum Chamber, First Tier Tribunal and Upper Tribunal. Administrative procedures remain principally the same as they were under the old system. The most radical change is the capacity for the Upper Tribunal to hear applications for Judicial Review.

Borders, Citizenship and Immigration Act 2009

- Little of this Act is in force at the time of writing but provisions include:
  - Makes more difficult the requirements for becoming a British citizen (but not before July 2011)
  - Introduces the 'probationary citizenship' scheme
  - Power to transfer fresh claim judicial reviews to the Upper Tier of the two Tier Tribunals Service
  - Powers to restrict what studies a person can undertake in the UK
  - A new duty to safeguard and promote the welfare of children

Secondary legislation

Immigration Rules (HC395)

- Regulates who may and may not be granted entry clearance and/or leave to enter or remain.
- HC395 is not actually law or secondary legislation as such and the SSHD retains discretion to allow entry outside HC395. SSHD cannot act more restrictively than is set out in HC395 as, assuming there is a right of appeal, the decision will be overturned on appeal or failing that would be susceptible to judicial review. The Immigration Rules are made under section 3(5) of the 1971 Act and are subject to the 'scrutiny-lite' negative resolution procedure in Parliament: statements of changes are made in Parliament and if no objections are raised within 40 days, the statements take legal effect.

Asylum and Immigration Tribunal (Procedure) Rules 2005

- Regulates the appeal system, including time limits for lodging appeals. This is the place to start your search when look for anything relating to appeals procedure.
- In February 2010 when the appeal system was reformed by the Tribunals, Courts and Enforcement Act 2007 (TCEA) these rules became the rules for the Immigration and Asylum Chamber of the First Tier Tribunal.
- Appeals in the Immigration and Asylum Chamber of the Upper Tribunal are governed by the general Upper Tribunal rules, the Tribunal Procedure (Upper Tribunal) Rules 2008.
- See the chapter on appeals law for more information

Asylum and Immigration Tribunal (Fast Track Procedure) Rules 2005

- Applies specifically to Harmondsworth and Yarl's Wood super-fast-track cases. Also to be replaced in early 2010.
- As with the general rules, these became the rules for fast track appeals in the IAC of the First Tier Tribunal in February 2010

Immigration (European Economic Area) Regulations 2006

- Enables EC freedom of movement law and regulates appeal rights and residence rights for EEA nationals and related 3rd country nationals.

Immigration Orders

- There are many Orders made under secondary legislation powers that can have a major effect on immigration law. To take but one example, the Immigration (Leave to Enter and Remain) Order 2000 simplified immigration control for persons with visas. Under this Order, entry clearance takes effect as leave to enter if it specifies the purpose for which the holder wishes to enter the country and if it is endorsed with the conditions to which it is subject. Visit visas operate as leave to enter on an unlimited number of occasions for so long as they are valid (for six months if six months or more remain of the visa's period of validity; or for the visa's remaining period of validity, if less than six months. Leave given for more than six months, or which was conferred by entry clearance (other than visit visas), does not normally lapse when a person leaves the Common Travel Area.
- There are many, many other orders, the most useful of which are included in the secondary legislation section of Phelan and Gillespie's Immigration Law Handbook.

Commencement Orders

- Bring into force the specific provisions of primary and sometimes secondary legislation.

Policies and concessions

The UK Border Agency publishes policies on how the Immigration Rules and other provisions will be interpreted by UKBA staff and on discretionary entry outside the rules. Concessions usually relate to entry outside the rules (which is possible because of the Secretary of State's discretion to allow entry outside the Rules). Examples to be found at the UKBA website are Immigration Directorate Instructions (IDI), Asylum Policy Instructions (API), Entry Clearance Guidance (ECG) and Nationality Instructions (NI).

This subject is dealt with more fully in a later chapter.

Making an application

Applications can be categorised into two broad types. Those made at an entry clearance post (out-of-country) and those made at the Port of Entry or with the Home Office (in-country).

There are a number of elements to making a valid application:

- Timing
- Correct application form
- Correct fee
- Necessary documents (e.g. photos)
- Evidence in support

Timing

Most immigration rules for in-country extensions of stay (whether one is applying in the same category or a different category to one's existing category) require that the applicant possess current leave to enter or remain. An illegal entrant or overstayer is thereby prevented from regularising his or her position by, for example, applying for leave to remain as a spouse.

This is not always the case, though, and an astute and effective immigration lawyer will realise that some immigration rules are silent on this issue, which means that regularisation is possible by certain routes.

Leave required
- e.g. rules 248(vii), 284(i) and 295D(i)

Leave not required
- e.g. rules 289A and 317
- See also the Points Based System

As more fully discussed in the chapter on the Points Based System, PBS switching provisions require that an applicant 'must have, or have last been granted, entry clearance, leave to enter or remain'.

Note also that some rules require not only that the applicant possess current leave but also that the leave was 'given in accordance with any provisions of these Rules', which prevents those in possession of Discretionary Leave or other leave outside the rules from applying in such a category.

Automatic extension of leave

The Home Office will not normally consider applications for extension of leave until shortly before a person's leave runs out. Given that the Home Office sometimes takes several weeks or even longer to make a decision, this often results in the persons leave apparently expiring while the application is under consideration at the Home Office.

A further difficulty arises with negative decisions by the Home Office where the person appeals. If the Home Office has refused leave, does this mean that while the person is appealing he or she is left with no leave and is an overstayer?

Section 3C of the Immigration Act 1971 was enacted to deal with these problems. It automatically extends leave while an in-time and valid application is pending and then also if an appeal is lodged and remains pending. It also extends the conditions attached to the previous grant of leave.

Effect of an invalid application

Rejection of an invalid application is not treated as a refusal of leave. This can have very serious consequences. The effect of the rejection of an application as invalid is that no application has been made. If the application is resubmitted after leave expires and is rejected, the right of appeal is lost and the applicant has become an overstayer – potentially a criminal offence and also something that can cause problems later under the general grounds for refusal. The decision on whether an application is valid is made by the Initial Consideration Unit or, for those attending in person, the Public Enquiry Office. The forms and accompanying documents are checked for compliance, and the merits of the application are disregarded at that stage. Invalid applications are returned to applicants or their advisers, endorsed with the defects which need remedying, or enclosing appropriate forms if the application was incorrectly made by letter. Clearly, it is vitally important that the application is validly made to the satisfaction of the Initial Consideration Unit or Public Caller Unit.

These serious consequences are somewhat mitigated by the judgment in *JH (Zimbabwe) v SSHD* [2009] EWCA Civ 78. The Court of Appeal held that an application made on the wrong form (e.g. on a SET rather than an FLR form) was in fact a valid immigration application, even if it was ultimately doomed to fail. The Court went on to find that it is possible to vary an application by applying for a different form of immigration status on a different application form, up until the time that a decision is made by the Secretary of State on the application. It had previously been thought that once leave was extended automatically by section 3C Immigration Act 1971, it was not possible to vary an application.

Application forms and fees

Out-of-country applications

Neither the legislation nor the rules prescribe any specific form of application for entry clearance. This means that a letter containing sufficient details for an application could in theory be accepted. However, in practice the correct form should be used, otherwise it is highly likely that the application will be returned, as r.34 of HC395 requires that the correct form is used. Confusingly, many entry clearance posts continue to use old forms until they are exhausted, even though newer forms have been introduced. Note an application is not legally made unless accompanied by the appropriate fee in local currency: r.30 of HC395. On-line applications are becoming increasingly utilised by Visa Application Centres (VAC). An applicant should check the application procedure for the specific VAC that they wish to apply to for specific guidance. Where online facilities are available, it is usual that the application is completed online and then printed for despatch, either by post or in person to the VAC, accompanied by the supporting documentation.

The entry clearance application forms change regularly and are available free from the Foreign and Commonwealth Office website: http://www.ukvisas.gov.uk

- VAF1A-K: different types of visitor
- VAF2: employment
- VAF3A: student
- VAF3B: student dependent
- VAF4A: settlement
- VAF4B: returning resident
- VAF5: EEA family permit
- VAF6: Direct Airside Transit
- VAF7: right of abode
- VAF8A: Overseas Territories Visa (for visits to OTs)
- VAF8B: Commonwealth Country Visa (for visits)
- VAF9: Points Based System Migrant (plus one of the relevant PBS appendices relating to a specific category)
- VAF10: Points Based System Dependent

The fees for the principal types of entry clearance application as of 1 October 2010 are as follows (some in fact effective as of November 2010):

Visa	Fee

Short term visit	£70
Settlement	£750
Dependent relative	£1680
Certificate of Entitlement	£245
Tier 1	£750
Tier 1 Post Study Work	£344
Tier 2	£350
Tier 4	£220
Tier 5	£130

The above list is not comprehensive and reduced fees sometimes apply for CESC nationals. EEA nationals and their family members do not need to pay a fee for immigration applications, nor do the pre-existing families of refugees.

In-country immigration status applications

The current non-business, non-EEA forms are as follows:

Form LTR (multiple)

- For multiple applications where the same person is paying: Up to 25 people may be included. It is intended for use by legal representatives or advisers (e.g. student or school advisers) but can be used by anyone wanting to make multiple leave to remain applications and make one payment. It is not to be used in work permit applications where there are already arrangements for multiple applications, nor for dependents.

Form NTL (No Time Limit)

- Use this form to apply for an indefinite leave stamp (No Time Limit) to be endorsed in a new passport or travel document of a person who already has indefinite leave to enter, or to remain in the United Kingdom

Form FLR (M)

- Use this form to apply for an extension of stay in the United Kingdom as the spouse (husband or wife) or unmarried partner of a person present and settled here

Form FLR (O)

- Use this form to apply for an extension of stay in the United Kingdom if you are applying in any of the following categories:
  - Visitor
  - Visitor undergoing private medical treatment
  - Postgraduate doctor or dentist
  - Au Pair
  - Teacher or language assistant under an approved scheme
  - Representative of an overseas newspaper, news agency or broadcasting organisation
  - Private servant in a diplomatic household
  - Domestic worker in a private household
  - Overseas government employee
  - Minister of religion, missionary or member of a religious order
  - Member of the ground staff of an overseas-owned airline
  - Person with United Kingdom ancestry
  - Writer, composer or artist
  - Member of the crew of a ship, aircraft, hovercraft, hydrofoil or train
  - Other purposes/reasons not covered by other application forms, including prospective student

Form FLR (S)

- Use this form to apply for an extension of stay in the United Kingdom as a student or student nurse, to re-sit an examination, or to write up a thesis.

Form SET (M)

- Use this form to apply for indefinite leave to remain in the United Kingdom as the spouse (husband or wife) or unmarried partner of a person who is present and settled

Form SET (O)

- Use this form to apply for indefinite leave to remain in the United Kingdom when approaching five years of continuous leave to remain in the United Kingdom in one of the following categories:
  - Work permit holder
  - Highly skilled migrant
  - Representative of an overseas newspaper, news agency or broadcasting organisation
  - Private servant in a diplomatic household
  - Domestic worker in a private household
  - Overseas government employee
  - Minister of religion, missionary or member of a religious order
  - Member of the operational ground staff of an overseas-owned airline
  - Person with United Kingdom ancestry
  - Writer, composer or artist
- Or to apply for indefinite leave to remain in one of the following categories:
  - Long residence in the United Kingdom
  - Other purposes/reasons not covered by other application forms

Form SET (DV)

- This form is used specifically for applying for settlement under the rules for victims of domestic violence whose relationships have broken down during the probationary period because of that domestic violence

Form SET (F)

- Use this form to apply for indefinite leave to remain in the United Kingdom as a family member (other than husband or wife or unmarried partner) of a person present and settled in the United Kingdom, that is:
  - A child under 18 of a parent, parents or relative present and settled in the UK
  - The adopted child under 18 of a parents or parents present and settled in the UK
  - The parent, grandparent or other dependent relative of a person present and settled in the UK

All of the above forms are available for free to download from the UK Border Agency website: www.ukba.homeoffice.gov.uk.

Prescribed form of applications

The Immigration Rules allow for a particular application form to be mandatory and for certain information to be provided. The requirements are set out at rules

34 to 34D. These are the mandatory requirements and must be complied with for the application to be valid.

Examples of mandatory requirements

- The payment of a specified fee
- Inclusion of specified biographical information
- Attendance at a UKBA appointment
- Photographs as described on the form and in guidance
- Completion of the 'confirmation box' and other sections of the form said on the form to be mandatory

It may in some circumstances be possible to draw a distinction between mandatory and directory requirements on a given form if there is a dispute about whether a valid application has been made.

Application fees

Fees now apply to applications for variation, leave to remain and for the embossing of an indefinite leave to remain stamp. Fees are not applied to or are reduced for EEA applications or asylum or certain human rights applications or applications from citizens of countries that are signatory to the European Social Charter. The most commonly encountered fees, as of 1 October 2010 (some in fact come into effect November 2010) are as follows:

Application	Principal fee	Dependant fee
ILR postal	£900	£250
ILR PEO	£1250	£350
ILR dependant relative postal	£1680	-
ILR dependent relative PEO	£2050	-
LTR non student postal	£500	£150
LTR non student PEO	£800	£200
Tier 1 postal	£850	£250
Tier 1 PEO	£1150	£300
Tier 1 (PSW) postal	£550	£150
Tier 1 (PWS) PEO	£850	£250
Tier 2 postal	£500	£150
Tier 2 PEO	£800	£200
Tier 4 postal	£357	£100
Tier 4 PEO	£650	£150
Tier 5 postal	£130	£30
Tier 5 PEO	£600	£150

Some individuals are exempt:

- people applying for Indefinite Leave to Remain on the grounds of domestic violence where, at the time of making the application, the applicant appears to be destitute;

- children under 18 and receiving local authority support;

- persons granted limited leave to remain whilst they were under 18 on the rejection of their claim for asylum is now applying for further leave to remain outside the immigration rules;

- nationals of Bulgaria, Romania and Turkey and their dependants who are applying for leave to remain under the terms of a European Community Association Agreement;

- rejected asylum seekers who are seeking extensions of leave to remain in the United Kingdom outside the immigration rules;

- those applying for leave to remain where the basis of their claim is asylum or Article 3 ECHR.

- EEA nationals seeking residence permits or permanent residence, and their family members applying under EC law.

Role of further representations

There are many circumstances in which it will be appropriate to make further representations, either in the form of a 'covering letter' at the time of the application or after the application has been made. This is true in asylum and in and out of country immigration cases.

In late 2009 UKBA surprised immigration lawyers by introducing a new requirement for an asylum claimant to make any further representations in an asylum case in person at what was formerly the Liverpool Asylum Screening Unit. At the time of writing this requirement was under challenge because of the difficulties it causes many asylum applicants, who are simply unable in practical terms to make the expensive, long and unfunded journey to Liverpool.

Further representations should generally be as short and to the point as possible, as ECOs and Home Office caseworkers are unlikely to read or be persuaded by long-winded representations. The representations should draw out the key points, explain any unusual circumstances and explain the relevance of any non-standard documentation enclosed with the application. Direct references to or citation of case law should generally be kept to a minimum but references to the APIs, IDIs or other UKBA policy documents are likely to be highly persuasive – and also lay the foundations for a later judicial review should this become necessary.

Chapter 2: Immigration categories and policies

POINTS BASED SYSTEM 34

NAVIGATING THE RULES 34

COMMON REQUIREMENTS OF THE RULES 36

   MAINTENANCE WITHOUT RECOURSE TO PUBLIC FUNDS 36
      Meaning of public funds 37
      Required level of income 38
      Reliance on pre-existing benefits 39
      Third party support 40
      Sponsors and undertakings 40
   ADEQUATE ACCOMMODATION 41
   INTENTION TO LEAVE 43
   REPORTING CONDITIONS 44
   KNOWLEDGE OF LANGUAGE AND LIFE IN THE UK 45

VISITORS: R.40 TO 56 47

   TYPES OF VISITOR 47
   SPECIAL VISITORS 48
      Child visitor 48
      Private medical treatment visitors 48
      Parent of a child at school 49
      Visitors seeking to enter for the purposes of marriage 49
      Student visitors 49
   BUSINESS VISITOR 49
   SPORTS VISITOR 51
   ENTERTAINER VISITORS 52
   SWITCHING AND EXTENSIONS 53
   APPEALS FOR VISITORS 53

STUDENTS AND THEIR FAMILIES: R.57 TO 87 54

SHORT-TERM EMPLOYMENT CATEGORIES: R.88 TO 127 55

   SEASONAL WORKERS 55
   SECTOR-BASED WORKERS 55
   UK ANCESTRY VISAS 55

LONG RESIDENCE: R.276A TO 276D 56

   PERIOD OF RESIDENCE 56
   REQUIREMENT FOR RESIDENCE TO BE CONTINUOUS 57
   OTHER CONSIDERATIONS 58

SPOUSES AND CIVIL PARTNERS: R.277 TO 289C 59

   POLYGAMY 60
   AGE 60
      Concessions 60

Challenges	61
ENGLISH LANGUAGE	61
QUALIFYING RELATIONSHIPS	61
SWITCHING	64
GRANT OF LEAVE TO ENTER/REMAIN	65
MARRIAGES THAT HAVE ENDED DURING THE PROBATIONARY PERIOD	66
Bereaved spouses or partners	66
Victims of domestic violence	66
HOME OFFICE CERTIFICATE OF APPROVAL	67
FIANCÉ(E)S AND PROPOSED CIVIL PARTNERS: R.289AA TO 295	**69**
UNMARRIED PARTNERS: R.295AA TO 295O	**69**
CHILDREN: R.296 TO 316	**70**
SOLE RESPONSIBILITY	71
SERIOUS AND COMPELLING CIRCUMSTANCES MAKING EXCLUSION UNDESIRABLE	72
OTHER DEFINITIONS	73
CHILDREN OF FIANCÉ(E)S	74
ADOPTED CHILDREN	74
OTHER FAMILY MEMBERS: R.317 TO 319	**74**
PARENTS AND GRANDPARENTS	75
OTHER RELATIVES	76
EXERCISING RIGHTS OF ACCESS TO A CHILD RESIDENT IN THE UK	76
RETURNING RESIDENTS: R.18 TO 20	**77**
GENERAL GROUNDS FOR REFUSAL	**79**
REFUSAL OF LEAVE TO ENTER	79
REFUSAL OF LEAVE TO REMAIN	85
CURTAILMENT	85
POLICIES AND CONCESSIONS	**85**
FINDING POLICIES AND CONCESSIONS	85
ILR FAMILIES EXERCISE	87
LEGACY CASES	88
DELAYED CONSIDERATION POLICY	89
SEVEN-YEAR CHILDREN CONCESSION	90
DUTY TO SAFEGUARD CHILDREN	91
IN-COUNTRY MARRIAGE CASES OUTSIDE THE RULES: DP3/96	92
DELAY IN ASYLUM CASES	93
AGE AND ENFORCEMENT ACTION	93
ELDERLY DEPENDENT RELATIVES	94
CARERS POLICY	94
FAMILY PROCEEDINGS	95
CHILDREN IN THE CARE OF A LOCAL AUTHORITY	95
IRAQI RASHID TYPE CASES	95
LEGITIMATE EXPECTATION	97
POLICIES, CONCESSIONS AND THE LAW	97

Judicial review	98
The immigration tribunal	98
Not in accordance with the law	98
Article 8 ECHR	99

Points Based System

The immigration rules on students, employment and self employment are in a state of considerable flux at the time of writing. The Points Based System ('PBS') was incrementally introduced in 2008 and 2009, gradually replacing some of the key immigration categories. Even after the introduction of the PBS, however, there will be a need to be familiar with the old rules for some time, in order to properly understand a client's existing immigration status and also the 'switching' provisions of the new scheme.

Navigating the rules

The Immigration Rules provide the primary criteria on which people can seek to enter or remain in the UK. It must not be forgotten that there are also some Home Office policies outside the rules. The rules are contained in a House of Commons Paper – currently HC395 – which is drafted and then laid before Parliament under what is called a 'negative resolution' procedure. If no objections are made to the rules within 40 days they are considered to have been passed by Parliament. They are not debated in any way and so suffer from a deficit of proper scrutiny.

The rules are, simply, a list of the purposes or categories under which people can enter the UK – such as student, adopted child, parent with access to a child, artist or writer. Under each category the rules contain the criteria or requirements which must be met in order to be allowed to enter or remain.

Each category follows a broadly similar pattern, although there are some exceptions. The spouse rule can be used to illustrate this pattern:

Definition clauses

- For example, the spouse rules begin with some material addressing polygamy and age requirements: see r.277 to 280

Leave to Enter

- Criteria for qualification: r.281
- Period of leave that can be granted: r.282
- Circumstances where application will be refused: r.283

Leave to Remain

- Criteria for qualification (including switching rule if any): r.284
- Period of leave that can be granted: r.285
- Circumstances where application will be refused: r.286

Indefinite Leave to Remain

- Criteria for qualification: r.287
- Period of leave that can be granted: r.288
- Circumstances where application will be refused: r.289

Further rules

- The spouse rules include some supplementary provisions at rule 289A, 289B and 289C that provide for ILR as a victim of domestic violence. It is important to be aware of this type of exception and additional rules that break the pattern.

There are exceptions and variations. For example, the dependent relative provisions starting at r.317 are all wrapped up into one rule. As ILR will be granted outright in the event of a successful application, there is no need for separate leave to enter, leave to remain and indefinite leave to remain rules. The child settlement rules, however, follow a slightly different pattern and only make provision for indefinite leave to enter and indefinite leave to remain. Where a category of entry cannot lead to settlement (for example, visitors or students), there will be rules relating to leave to enter and leave to remain but not to indefinite leave to remain.

> **Top tip**
>
> It is important to read rules carefully and look for what is NOT in the rules as much as what IS in the rules.
>
> For example, rule 317 covers both leave to enter and leave to remain, but is silent on any current leave or entry clearance requirement for applications for leave to remain. Other examples of what might be regarded as quirks in the rules include 295D, which is mildly more generous towards switching into the unmarried partner category than spouses or civil partners, as there is no requirement to have held leave for six months or more, or the new PBS rules, which are silent on possession of current leave at the time of application.
>
> Do not make it even harder than it already is for immigrants by creating requirements that do not in fact exist!

Common requirements of the rules

Many immigration rules include similar provisions, and rather than repeat the information about matters such as maintenance and accommodation it is more convenient to deal with them in one place. However, there are slight variations in the wording of the maintenance and accommodation requirements for some of the rules, some of which have significance and which are addressed in the section on that particular immigration category. For example, the maintenance and accommodation requirements for children are a little different to those for other categories.

Maintenance without recourse to public funds

There are some requirements which are common to some or all of the rules. For example, immigration to the UK is almost always contingent on a person not relying on public funds, the only exemption being for the pre-existing families of recognised refugees. Generally the rules require a person to be able to maintain and accommodate themselves without recourse to public funds.

Key principles on maintenance

- 'Public funds' are exhaustively defined
- There must be no additional recourse; existing recourse by sponsor is permitted
- Income support and associated benefits provide an objective measure
- Adequacy requirement is not an excuse for inquiry into lifestyle
- Third party support is permitted in law but may be an evidential issue
- Multiple sponsors are permissible

Meaning of public funds

Public funds are exhaustively listed in r.6 of HC395. The list is exhaustive in the sense that any benefit not included in the rule is not considered to be public funds for the purposes of the immigration rules. As can be seen, there are some benefits, such as Incapacity Benefit, Employment and Support Allowance, education and health care that are not included in the definition:

> "public funds" means
> (a) housing under Part VI or VII of the Housing Act 1996 and under Part II of the Housing Act 1985, Part I or II of the Housing (Scotland) Act 1987, Part II of the Housing (Northern Ireland) Order 1981 or Part II of the Housing (Northern Ireland) Order 1988;
> (b) attendance allowance, severe disablement allowance, carer's allowance and disability living allowance under Part III of the Social Security Contribution and Benefits Act 1992;, income support, council tax benefit and housing benefit under Part VII of that Act; a social fund payment under Part VIII of that Act; child benefit under Part IX of that Act; income based jobseeker's allowance under the Jobseekers Act 1995, state pension credit under the State Pension Credit Act 2002; or child tax credit and working tax credit under Part 1 of the Tax Credits Act 2002.
> (c) attendance allowance, severe disablement allowance, carer's allowance and disability living allowance under Part III of the Social Security Contribution and Benefits (Northern Ireland) Act 1992;, income support, council tax benefit, housing benefit under Part VII of that Act; a social fund payment under Part VIII of that Act; child benefit under Part IX of that Act; or income based jobseeker's allowance under the Jobseekers (Northern Ireland) Order 1995.

The Government has made changes to the nature and title of several benefits and tax credits in recent years. These changes have not always been reflected in the immigration rules, meaning that rule 6 refers to several defunct benefits and tax credits. It has not yet been successfully argued that a strict approach should be followed to this issue and therefore that a person with a 'without recourse to public funds' condition may in fact have recourse to differently titled benefits and tax credits.

The equivalent housing and benefits provisions in Northern Ireland are also included in the immigration rules. Where a type of benefit is not listed, it is not considered to be a public fund for the purposes of the Immigration Rules. Education, health care and benefits such as incapacity benefit or contributory job seekers' allowance are not listed and therefore do not count.

Although child benefit is defined as a prohibited public fund in the Immigration Rules, the Home Office IDIs state that, where a spouse is seeking entry to the UK, the settled partner may claim working families' tax credit and child benefit to which they are entitled in respect of the spouse/partner and children without this acting to the detriment of the spouse seeking entry.

The expression 'without recourse to public funds' is further defined in r.6A of HC395, which states:

> 'For the purpose of these Rules, a person (P) is not to be regarded as having (or potentially having) recourse to public funds merely because P is (or will be) reliant in whole or in part on public funds provided to P's sponsor unless, as a result of P's presence in the United Kingdom, the sponsor is (or would be) entitled to increased or additional public funds (save where such entitlement to increased or additional public funds is by virtue of P and the sponsor's joint entitlement to benefits under the regulations referred to in paragraph 6B)'

In 2009, immigration rule 6A was amended as above and was supplemented by rules 6B and 6C. Rule 6B explicitly excludes from the definition of public funds benefits specified under section 115 of the Immigration and Asylum Act 1999 by virtue of regulations made under sub-sections (3) and (4) of that section or section 42 of the Tax Credits Act 2002.

Rule 6C provides as follows:

> 'A person (P) making an application from outside the United Kingdom will be regarded as having recourse to public funds where P relies upon the future entitlement to any public funds that would be payable to P or to P's sponsor as a result of P's presence in the United Kingdom, (including those benefits to which P or the sponsor would be entitled as a result of P's presence in the United Kingdom under the regulations referred to in to paragraph 6B).'

Essentially, this prevents reliance on future entitlement to child benefit or tax credit in an entry clearance application, but permits it in extension or settlement applications.

Required level of income

The level of maintenance required is simply stated in the rules as 'adequate'. The courts have considered whether this is an objective or a subjective level and reached the conclusion that generally speaking it is an objective one. Providing the level of maintenance is broadly equivalent to that of a person receiving income support and the associated benefits that normally accompany it (e.g. housing benefit, council tax relief, free school meals) then that will be considered to be adequate for the purposes of the immigration rules.

These principles are set out in the case of *Uvovo* (00/TH/01450) 15 June 2000. The rationale is worth quoting at length:

> '[3.] ...It appears to us that, generally speaking, it can be shown that the family will be no worse off than a family drawing Income Support, the Respondent cannot properly argue that they will not be adequately maintained. Income Support is what would be provided for the family if they were British residents of the United Kingdom with no other resources: it is not suggested in the rules that family members seeking immigration should be better maintained than those who are already here; and the government can hardly say that the level of support it provides for its destitute citizens is not 'adequate'. What the recipient or holder of the funds spends money on is his own business. We should in general take the view therefore that if the Appellants can show a level of income at the Income Support level or higher, that will be enough. It may not be an absolutely rigorous test, but it is a very good guide to what is 'adequate'.
>
> 4. It is, however, essential to maintain comparability. Income Support carries entitlement to a number of other benefits and, in particular, a family on Income Support will be able to obtain 'Housing Benefit'. The appropriate comparison is therefore between the Income Support level on the one hand and the family income net of accommodation costs on the other. (There are other Benefits to which Income Support is a 'gateway', such as free school meals and free prescriptions. These not always to be ignored, particularly where those seeking entry are of school age or have some medical condition.) It follows that, although we should be slow to enquire into the Sponsor' spending habits, we need to be satisfied that, at the date of decision, his income after paying his rent was sufficient to maintain himself and his wife. As a guide, we would require his income, net of rent, to reach a level of about £70.00 per week - the approximate Income Support level for a married couple.'

The reader should be aware that the current level of income support for a couple both aged 18 or over, at the time of writing, is £102.75 per week.

This approach was reaffirmed in the case of *KA and Others (Adequacy of maintenance) Pakistan* [2006] UKAIT 00065.

Reliance on pre-existing benefits

One legal battleground in recent years has been over the allocation of Disability Living Allowance and whether that can contribute towards 'adequate' maintenance of a spouse, even though the DLA is awarded to the sponsor. The tribunal decided that DLA is awarded to a disabled sponsor on the basis of need and is therefore to be taken as being needed for his or her own maintenance, meaning that there is not any 'spare' that might be used to support the spouse. In fact, practitioners have encountered many cases where a sponsor is entitled as of right to DLA and can and does live frugally, and can afford to maintain both him or herself and a spouse at an income equivalent to normal income support. DLA can be spent as the recipient chooses.

In cases such as *KA and Others (Adequacy of maintenance) Pakistan* [2006] UKAIT 00065 and *MK (Adequacy of maintenance – disabled sponsor) Somalia* [2007] UKAIT 00028 the tribunal held that DLA cannot be used to constitute 'adequate' maintenance for a spouse. The Court of Appeal disagreed on appeal in *MK (Somalia) v Entry Clearance Officer* [2007] EWCA Civ 1521.

Third party support

Although not specifically mentioned in the Immigration Rules, it was thought that maintenance could usually be provided by a third party sponsor such as a kindly relative and the rules would be considered to be met. This approach was suggested by the High Court in the case of *Arman Ali* [2000] INLR 89. There followed a string of litigation in recent years on whether the approach in *Arman Ali* is the correct one. The Immigration tribunal and the Court of Appeal took the view that third party support is not permissible in cases such as *AM (3rd party support not permitted R281(v)) Ethiopia* [2007] UKAIT 00058, *TS (Working Holidaymaker: no third party support) India* [2008] UKAIT 00024 and *AM (Ethiopia) & Ors v Entry Clearance Officer* [2008] EWCA Civ 1082.

Eventually, in *Mahad and Others* [2009] UKSC 16, the Supreme Court allowed the appeals of the various appellants and the position is restored to that many thought prevailed following *Arman Ali*: third party support is permissible as a matter of law, but it is a matter of evidence whether such support is considered sufficiently reliable to meet the requirements of the Immigration Rules.

Sponsors and undertakings

There is provision in the Immigration Rules at r.35 for the giving of undertakings relating to both maintenance and accommodation by sponsors. The IDIs elaborate on this as follows:

> 'Applications for leave to enter are sometimes supported by undertakings or guarantees from sponsors, Members of Parliament, community leaders or other persons of standing. It may be appropriate and acceptable to take into account promises of maintenance and accommodation made by a sponsor. There is a provision under the Rules [Paragraph 35] for a sponsor to be asked to sign an undertaking in writing that he will be responsible for the passenger's maintenance and accommodation for the duration of his stay. There is also provision [Paragraph 320(14)] for a person to be refused entry on the grounds that his sponsor has refused to give such an undertaking when requested to do so. It is not possible, however, to enforce guarantees by third parties that a passenger will abide by his conditions of stay or leave the United Kingdom at the end of a specific period. No such written guarantee or undertaking should therefore be either sought or accepted.'

In *AM (Ethiopia) & Ors v Entry Clearance Officer* [2008] EWCA Civ 1082 the Court of Appeal found that under immigration rule 317 it is possible to have joint sponsors available to give undertakings. This principle was upheld by the Supreme Court in *Mahad and Others* [2009] UKSC 16.

Adequate accommodation

> **Key principles on accommodation**
> - Third party provision is permitted
> - A room in a house is sufficient
> - Statutory overcrowding renders accommodation inadequate
> - Adequacy can have a wider meaning

Unlike with maintenance, there has never been a problem with accommodation being provided by a third party: *AB (Third-party provision of accommodation)* [2008] UKAIT 00018 and *Mahad and Others* [2009] UKSC 16.

Accommodation must be adequate for the person coming to the UK other than in the student category. For people seeking entry on a long-term basis there are two main considerations to the question of whether accommodation is adequate.

However, these are not necessarily the only considerations and the word 'adequate' must to an extent be given its ordinary meaning.

Firstly, the sponsor/applicant must 'own or exclusively occupy' the proposed accommodation in family cases. This is not quite as onerous as it sounds as the IDIs state that:

> 'Accommodation can be shared with other members of a family provided that at least part of the accommodation is for the exclusive use of the sponsor and his dependants. The unit of accommodation may be as small as a separate bedroom but must be owned or legally occupied by the sponsor and its occupation must not contravene public health regulations and must not cause overcrowding as defined in the Housing Act 1985'

The Immigration tribunal analysed this requirement in the case of *KJ ("Own or occupy exclusively") Jamaica* [2008] UKAIT 00006 and concluded that the approach in the IDIs is the correct one.

Secondly, the proposed accommodation must not be overcrowded once the applicant arrives. In the IDIs the test for whether a property will be overcrowded is based on the permitted number of persons in a room. There are two tests set out in the Housing Act 1985 for determining overcrowding. The Home Office in their instructions refer to the 'space standard' where the number of people that can stay in accommodation depends on the number of rooms available. A room must have a floor area larger than 50 Sq. ft. and normally used as a bedroom or living room. It relates number of rooms to number of persons, allowing for the fact that children aged between 1 and 10 years only count as half a person:

Rooms	Persons permitted
1	2
2	3
3	5
4	7.5
5	10
*	with an additional 2 persons for each room in excess of 5

Example

John is disabled. He recently married his girlfriend, Sarah, who is Australian. They met when she was in the UK on a visit visa and theirs was a whirlwind romance. She was advised to return to Australia and make a spouse application for entry clearance. She worked as a teacher in Australia. John receives disability living allowance and lives with his parents. He and Sarah plan to get a place of their own as soon as she gets a job in the UK. His parents are willing to keep them going to let them establish themselves.

John's reliance on benefits is not a problem of itself for the purposes of the Immigration Rules ans Sarah's application: rule 6A.

It is possible, folliowing *MK* (above) to argue that they can both live on John's benefits if his income is equivalent to income support levels for a couple. However, this would preferably be a fall-back position as an Entry Clearance Officer would very likely ignore the law and find that this did not amount to being 'adequately' maintained as John needs the benefits he receives to support himself. Winning the appeal months later is scant consolation.

Sarah would therefore be well advised to research her employment prospects and show she will be able to obtain a job. The offer from John's parents is helpful because it effectively gives Sarah a 'grace' period to find a job (subject to the offer being adequately evidenced and accepted by UKBA or an immigration judge). As will be seen below, accommodation at John's parent's house would actually be adequate for the purposes of the rules, as long as they have their own room.

Following *Mahad*, they could also seek to rely on third party support, for example from John's parents.

One further aspect of defining the adequacy of accommodation has been raised by the Court of Appeal who in one judgement (*M and A v SSHD* [2003] EWCA Civ 263) found that accommodation is not adequate if there is a risk from the parents who are to accommodate the child. In the particular case there was a risk of abuse from the parents which was held to warrant a refusal under the accommodation rules which was considered to be unsafe and therefore inadequate.

Intention to leave

> **Key principles on intention to leave**
> - Should not be based purely on suspicion but once raised, it is hard to dislodge suspicion
> - Being poor is not a proper reason to refuse
> - People are willing to spend a lot on family visits
> - Objective factors provide the best guide

Intention to leave the UK is a pre-requisite for all non Points based System categories which do not lead to settlement. In considering an intention to leave the United Kingdom the decision maker can look at all the circumstances of the applicant but must not make decisions based purely on suspicion.

Case law has consistently stated that, although an incentive to return can be evidence of an intention to return, financial incentives (or lack of financial incentives) cannot legitimately be used to raise a presumption that an applicant will remain in the UK. If such a presumption was good law it would preclude any person from a country less rich than the UK from being able to visit.

Relevant factors for the ECO and on appeal will include:

- Immigration history (previous compliance with immigration laws is an excellent indicator of intention to leave)

- Family links with own country, such as wife and children or elderly parents

- Other links, such as a job to return to or studies to complete

- Levels of income (not decisive taken alone, but it is not possible to argue this is not a relevant consideration)

- Absence or otherwise of links in the UK – this could cut both ways, as having a sponsor is helpful, especially if he or she can give evidence at an appeal hearing, and having someone to visit provides a visit-like purpose, but if the family has shown a 'history of immigration' this may cause some ECOs to refuse the application

Some entry clearance posts routinely assess intention to leave in a manner that is almost certainly racially discriminatory by applying additional unwritten requirements that are not applied elsewhere and by making generalisations about a given country and its economic circumstances. Race discrimination is discussed in a later section.

> **Examples**
>
> Saleem is from Bangladesh. He is applying for a student visa. He is 19 years old and has never left Bangladesh before, and he wants to study a foundation degree with a view to going on to undertake full degree level studies. He has a strong academic background and wants to go into business when he returns.
>
> Yolande is from Uganda. She is also applying for a student visa. She is 22 and also wants to study a foundation degree with a view, if successful, of going on to further studies. She has a sister in the UK who is a nurse on a work permit and Yolande previously visited her sister and returned to Uganda in accordance with the rules.
>
> Their situations differ little, but Yolande is in a stronger position to argue that she possesses the requisite intention to return as she has already proven that she abides by the rules. There is no real reason to suspect that Saleem will break the rules, but sadly this is the assumption that will be made by many ECOs examining his case, and it might prove difficult to get this decision overturned on appeal.

Reporting conditions

Under immigration rules 325-326, any foreign nationals from countries or territories listed in Appendix 2 to the Immigration Rules need to report, as do the stateless and those holding non-national travel documents, where they are given limited leave to enter the United Kingdom for longer than six months or given limited leave which takes them over 6 months from arrival.

Exempt from this requirement are seasonal agricultural workers, private servants in diplomatic households, ministers of religion, missionary or member of a religious order, persons whose leave flows from marriage to a person settled in the United Kingdom or unmarried partnership with a person settled here, persons exercising access rights to a child resident in the United Kingdom, parents of children at school, and those given leave following the grant of asylum.

Conditional leave was introduced under s.16 of the UK Borders Act 2007, which allows the Home Office to impose reporting, residence and other conditions on foreign nationals who are granted limited leave to enter or remain in the UK. Previously, such conditions could not be attached to grants of leave, in contrast to temporary admission.

Section 50 of the Borders, Immigration and Citizenship Act 2009 came into force on 21 July 2009. It amends the Immigration Act 1971, s 3(1)(c), by adding a new condition:

> (ia) a condition restricting his studies in the United Kingdom; ...

Section 3(1)(c)(ia) as amended permits *any* restriction on a person's studies in the United Kingdom to be attached to a grant of limited leave to enter or remain under *any* provision of the Immigration Rules or *any* grant of leave to enter or remain outside the rules (LOTR).

Under BCIA 2009, s 50(2), such a condition may be added on limited leave granted *before*, on, and after the passing of the BCIA 2009.

Lord West of Spithead, Parliamentary Under-Secretary of State at the Home Office at the time of the passage of the Act, set out how he envisaged the powers would be employed, by reference to Tier 4 (Students) of the PBS and the specified institutions:

> 'It is the Government's intention that the restriction on studies would be placed on those migrants granted leave to enter or remain as tier 4 migrants; that is, students. Furthermore, such a restriction will restrict a migrant to studying at a specified institution, rather than restricting their chosen course of study. I say to the noble Baroness, Lady Hanham, that I can provide an absolutely clear and unequivocal reassurance to the Committee that the Government do not intend to use this provision to prevent students from moving courses within the same sponsoring institution. By imposing a restriction on a migrant, so that he can study only at a specified institution, he would have to apply to the UK Border Agency to vary the conditions of his leave should he wish to change institution. This will allow the UK Border Agency to check that the institution to which the migrant wishes to move is a bona fide education provider, with a sponsor licence. Having the ability to link a student to a particular licensed institution is integral to the successful operation of tier 4, the student tier of the points-based system.'

This power does not appear to be in use although it is in force at the time of writing.

Knowledge of language and life in the UK

In order to obtain settlement (ILR) all applicants must demonstrate knowledge of language and life in the UK or that they meet the very narrow criteria for exemption.

The rules on showing sufficient knowledge of language and life in the UK are satisfied either by sitting an examination based on the book *Citizenship Materials for ESOL Learners* (ISBN 1-84478-5424) or by partaking a course. To satisfy the latter route the rules require at rule 33B(a) that an applicant:

> (a) has attended an ESOL course at an accredited college;

> (b) the course used teaching materials derived from the document entitled "Citizenship Materials for ESOL learners" (ISBN 1-84478-5424);
>
> (c) has demonstrated relevant progress in accordance with paragraph 33f; and
>
> (d) has attained a relevant qualification.

Rule 33C sets out the definition for an 'accredited college', which must be:

> (a) a publicly funded college that is subject to inspection by the office for standards in education, Children's services and skills (if situated in England), the Education and Training Inspectorate (if situated in Northern Ireland), Her Majesty's Inspectorate of Education (if situated in Scotland), Estyn (if situated in Wales); or an inspection programme that has been approved by the Island's Government (if situated in the Channel Islands or Isle of Man); or
>
> (b) a private college that has been accredited by Accreditation UK, The British Accreditation Council (BAC), the Accreditation Body for Language Services (ABLS), the Accreditation Service for International Colleges (ASIC).

Rule 33D defines 'relevant qualification' as follows:

> (a) an ESOL qualification in speaking and listening which is awarded or authenticated by a body which is recognised by the Office of Qualifications and Examinations Regulation (Ofqual) under section 132 of the Apprenticeships, Skills, Children and Learning Act 2009 and is determined by Ofqual as being at entry level; or
>
> (b) one National Qualifications Unit in ESOL at Access 2, Access 3 or Intermediate 1 Level approved by the Scottish Qualifications Authority.

Rule 33F defines 'demonstrated relevant progress' as follows:

> 33F An applicant has "demonstrated relevant progress" if he meets the requirements of paragraphs 33F (a) or (b).
>
> (a) The requirements in respect of a relevant qualification awarded or authenticated by a body which is recognised by Ofqual under section 132 of the Apprenticeships, Skills, Children and Learning Act 2009, are that the applicant provides evidence to the Secretary of State that –
> (i) prior to his commencing a course of study leading to a relevant qualification an ESOL assessment was undertaken by a suitably qualified person to assess his level of English language ability; and
> (ii) he has successfully completed a course of study leading to a relevant qualification; and
> (iii) having been assessed in accordance with paragraph (i) as being below Entry 1, he has attained a relevant qualification at Entry 1, 2 or 3; or
> (iv) having been assessed in accordance with paragraph (i) as being at Entry 1, he has attained a relevant qualification at Entry 2 or 3; or
> (v) having been assessed in accordance with paragraph (i) as being at Entry 2, he has attained a relevant qualification at Entry 3.

> (b) The requirements in respect of a relevant qualification approved by the Scottish Qualifications Authority are that the applicant provides evidence to the Secretary of State that —
> (i) prior to his commencing a course of study leading to a relevant qualification an ESOL assessment was undertaken by a suitably qualified person to assess his level of English language ability; and
> (ii) he has successfully completed a course of study leading to a relevant qualification; and
> (iii) having been assessed in accordance with paragraph (i) as being below Access 2, he has attained a relevant qualification at Access 2 or 3 or at Intermediate 1 Level; or
> (iv) having been assessed in accordance with paragraph (i) at Access 2, he has attained a relevant qualification at Access 3 or Intermediate 1 Level; or
> (v) having been assessed in accordance with paragraph (i) at Access 3, he has attained a relevant qualification at Intermediate 1 Level.

For the purposes of rule 33F (and generally, if the term is used anywhere else in the rules) a 'suitably qualified person' is defined at rule 33E as 'a person who is deemed suitably qualified by the institution in which the assessment is undertaken'.

Finally, rule 33G provides that the Secretary of State can waive the requirements if because of the applicant's physical or mental condition there are special circumstances that mean it would be unreasonable to expect that person to meet the requirements.

Visitors: r.40 to 56

Different types
- 'Normal', special, business, sports, entertainer

Intention to leave normally required
- Other than for private medical treatment visits

Main conditions
- 6 months leave normal maximum stay
- Switching not normally possible
- No working

No appeals other than for family visits

Types of visitor

The visitor rules underwent considerable change in late 2008 and a number of different categories of visitor have been created.

Special visitors

This is a term defined at rule 6 of the Immigration Rules that is applied to a group of different types of visitor, some of which are addressed in more detail in following sections:

- A person granted leave to enter or remain in the UK as a Child Visitor under paragraphs 46A - 46F of these Rules

- A person granted leave to enter or remain in the UK as a visitor for private medical treatment under paragraphs 51 - 56 of these Rules

- A person granted leave to enter or remain in the UK as a Parent of a child at school under paragraphs 56A - 56C of these Rules

- A person granted leave to enter or remain in the UK for the purpose of marriage under paragraphs 56D - 56F of these Rules

- A person granted leave to enter or remain in the UK as a Student Visitor under paragraphs 56K - 56M of these Rules

- A person granted leave to enter or remain in the UK as a Prospective Student under paragraphs 82-87 of these Rules

- A person granted leave to enter the UK as a Visitor in transit under paragraphs 47 - 50 of these Rules.

Child visitor

This category is for those below the age of 18 and includes some additional requirements. It is set out at 46A-46F of the rules. The applicant must demonstrate that suitable arrangements have been made for his travel to, and reception and care in the United Kingdom and that he has a parent or guardian in his home country or country of habitual residence who is responsible for his care. There is considerable additional detail in the IDIs about the mechanisms for ensuring these requirements are met and recorded. The principle behind these changes is to recognize the duty upon the UK Border Agency to protect children's interests, who cross international borders. This manual cannot address this issue in detail by the reader may want to source "Safeguarding children", a Government policy document designed to address the growing problem of child trafficking.

Private medical treatment visitors

This category has existed for some time and enables those who can afford it to travel to the UK for the specific purpose of receiving medical treatment in the UK. They must, as ever, show that adequate maintenance and accommodation is available without recourse to public funds but must also show that the cost of the medical treatment can be met and that the medical treatment is of 'finite duration'.

In the IDIs and in the case of *LB (Medical treatment of "finite" duration) Bangladesh* [2005] UKAIT 00175 it states that 'finite' might well be a substantial period of time, even years, but the proposed treatment must have a proposed end point.

There is no bar on the length of time a person may remain in the UK as a private medical treatment visitor. Evidence from an appropriately qualified NHS consultant or doctor on the Specialist Register of the General Medical Council is needed for an extension application.

Parent of a child at school

This specific category, set out at 56A to 56C is self explanatory.

Visitors seeking to enter for the purposes of marriage

This category of visitor is exempt from obtaining a Certificate of Approval in the UK in order to get married. The category is for those who wish to travel to the UK to get married and then return home afterwards. It is not suitable for those wanting to remain in the UK after marriage.

Entry clearance is mandatory.

The couple will need to produce satisfactory evidence, if required to do so, of the arrangements for giving notice of marriage or civil partnership, or for his wedding or civil partnership ceremony to take place. The marriage needs to be planned for the period of the visit.

Student visitors

For those seeking entry for a short course of study, this is probably the appropriate visa. Extensions and variations are not possible so it is for those planning to study a short course then leave the UK afterwards.

The Prospective Student category is for those wishing to travel to the UK to investigate studying, attend interviews and so forth. The category allows the person then to extend their stay as a full student under Tier 4.

Business visitor

This is a specific category, set out at rules 46G-46L, 75A-F or 75G-M. Confusingly, the latter two sets of rules in fact fall within the student section of the immigration rules. The following kinds of person fall within the business visitor category:

- Academic visitors

- Doctors taking the Professional and Linguistic Assessment Board (PLAB)

- Those seeking entry for Clinical Attachment/Dental Observation

- Visiting professors accompanying students undertaking study abroad programmes

- Film crews on location shoots only, provided they are employed or paid by an overseas company

- Representatives of overseas news media provided they are employed or paid by an overseas company and are gathering information for an overseas publication or programme

- Secondees from overseas companies

- Religious workers undertaking some preaching or pastoral work during a business visit (e.g. to attend a conference), provided their base is abroad and they are not taking up an office, post or appointment

- Advisers, consultants, trainers or trouble shooters employed abroad by the same company to which the client firm in the UK belongs, provided this does not amount to employment and/or productive work paid or unpaid for the UK branch

- Persons undertaking specific, one-off training in techniques and work practices used in the UK provided this is not on-the-job training. This training would typically be classroom based

- Those who intend to carry out one or more of the following `Permissible Activities' (defined in the IDIs):

    o Attending meetings, including interviews that have been arranged before coming to the UK or conferences.

    o Arranging deals or negotiating or signing trade agreements or contracts, undertaking fact finding missions

    o Conducting site visits

    o Those delivering goods and passengers from abroad such as lorry drivers and coach drivers provided they are genuinely working an international route;

    o Tour group couriers who are contracted to a firm outside the United Kingdom, who are seeking entry to accompany a tour group and who intend to leave with that tour group;

- Speaking at a conference where this is not run as a commercial concern (organisers not making a profit) and the conference is a "one off".

- Representing computer software companies by coming to install, debug or enhance their products. Representatives of such companies may also be admitted as business visitors in order to be briefed as to the requirements of a United Kingdom customer but if they are to provide a service involving the use of their expertise to make a detailed assessment of a potential customer's requirements this should be regarded as consultancy work for which entry under the Points Based System would be required; Representing foreign manufacturers by coming to service or repair their company's products within their initial period of guarantee;

- Representing foreign machine manufacturers by coming to erect and install machinery too heavy to be delivered in one piece, as part of the contract of purchase and supply. Interpreting or translating for visiting business persons, provided the interpreter/translator is employed by the overseas company and is coming solely to provide this service for the visiting company member.

- Monteurs (e.g. mechanic or serviceperson) - workers coming for up to six months to erect, dismantle, install, service, repair or advise on the development of foreign-made machinery.

- Board-level Directors attending board meetings in the United Kingdom provided they are not employed by a UK company, although they may be paid a fee for attending the meeting.

Sports visitor

There is specific category, at rules 46M-46R, for sports visitors intending to do one or more of the following:

- To take part in a particular sporting event as defined in guidance published by the United Kingdom Border Agency, tournament or series of events

- To take part in a specific one off charity sporting event, provided no payment is received other than for travelling and other expenses

- To join, as an Amateur, a wholly or predominantly amateur team provided no payment is received other than for board and lodging and reasonable expenses

- To serve as a member of the technical or personal staff, or as an official, attending the same event as a visiting sportsperson coming for one or more of the purposes listed in (a), (b) or (c).

Laborious guidance follows in the IDIs giving examples of the type of person who might seek entry as a sportsperson and defining such difficult terms as 'series of events' and 'amateur'.

Entertainer visitors

Entertainers also have their own little set of immigration rules, at 46S-46X. An applicant must intend to do one or more of the following:

- To take part as a professional entertainer in one or more music competitions; and/or

- To fulfil one or more specific engagements as either an individual Amateur entertainer or as an Amateur group; and/or

- To take part, as an Amateur or professional entertainer, in a cultural event (or one or more of such events) that appears in the list of events to which this provision applies that is published in guidance issued by the United Kingdom Border Agency; and/or

- Serve as a member of the technical or personal staff, or of the production team, of an entertainer coming for one or more of the purposes listed in (a), (b), or (c).

The IDIs go on to set out the following additional guidance illuminating the meaning of 'entertainer':

- Professional entertainers coming to take part in music competitions

- Internationally famous people coming to the UK to take part in broadcasts or public appearances provided they are not performing or not being paid

- Those undertaking an audition provided this is not performed in front of an audience (either paying or non-paying)

- Amateur entertainers seeking entry as an individual performer for a specific engagement

- Amateur entertainers seeking entry as part of a group, such as a choir or youth orchestra coming for a specific engagement; this may include conductors, choreographers, stage managers and other non-performing staff supporting the group

- Professional entertainers taking part in a charity concert or show where the organisers are not making a profit and no fee is to be paid to the entertainer

- Amateur or professional entertainer taking part in a cultural event sponsored by a government or recognised international organisation or a major arts festival included in the Permit Free Festival list.

- Members of the technical or support staff of amateurs or professionals who are attending the same event. Examples of such staff include make-up artists, personal bodyguards and press officers

- Officials attending the same event as the entertainer. Examples include choreographers and stage managers.

An "Amateur" is defined at rule 6 of the immigration rules as a person who engages in a sport or creative activity solely for personal enjoyment and who is not seeking to derive a living from the activity.

Switching and extensions

As six months is generally the maximum period a person can stay on any single visit (there are exceptions in some of the categories above, as for private medical treatment) an extension will not be granted if the period sought will result in a stay of longer than six months. Applications are sometimes exceptionally granted outside the Rules, however – see the discussion of the policy on carers.

The IDIs state that where an applicant seeks to remain for no more than a few weeks because he was unable to obtain an earlier flight, leave may be granted provided the application was "in time" (within the original period of leave) and the ticket with a confirmed flight is produced.

Appeals for visitors

Amongst visitors, only those visiting their family benefit from an appeal against a refusal of entry clearance (s.90 of 2002 Act). Family is defined for this purpose in the Immigration Appeals (Family Visitor) Regulations 2003 SI 2003/518 as:

> (a) the applicant's spouse, father, mother, son, daughter, grandfather, grandmother, grandson, granddaughter, brother, sister, uncle, aunt, nephew, niece or first cousin;
>
> (b) the father, mother, brother or sister of the applicant's spouse;
>
> (c) the spouse of the applicant's son or daughter;
>
> (d) the applicant's stepfather, stepmother, stepson, stepdaughter, stepbrother or stepsister; or
>
> (e) a person with whom the applicant has lived as a member of an unmarried couple for at least two of the three years before the day on which his application for entry clearance was made.

It should be noted that s.90 of the 2002 Act is in fact still in force in some respects. This is an unnecessarily complicated area of law as the Government passed two sections 88A and by virtue of regulation 4 of the commencement order for the second s.88A (SI 2008/310), the new s.88A only applies in respect of points based system applications, leaving the old s.88A, s.90 and s.91 in force in respect of all other cases. There are therefore two sections 88A to the 2002 Act, both in force in respect of different types of case.

Students and their families: r.57 to 87

The Points Based System replaced the old student rules in April 2009. Tier 4 of the PBS is dealt with in a later chapter. However, there are some residual immigration rules relating to certain types of student and to the family members of students.

The residual student categories are quite unusual and unlikely to be encountered in general practice as an immigration lawyer. The categories remaining outside the PBS are:

- Overseas qualified nurse or midwife
- Those taking the PLAB test
- Those undertaking a clinical attachment or dental observer post

The immigration rules also provide for the spouse and children of these non PBS students to join the student or prospective student in the UK. They must show that:

- the couple are married
- the marriage is subsisting
- there will be maintenance and accommodation without the need for public funds
- they only intend to take employment as permitted under the rules
- any children are under the age of 18 and have not formed an independent family unit

Evidence of a subsisting marriage is usually easier to show than where a person is seeking to join their spouse for settlement as there is often prior cohabitation to prove that part of the rule. For the tribunal's definition of subsisting marriage, see the starred decision of GA ("Subsisting" marriage) Ghana* [2006] UKAIT 00046.

Employment is usually permitted where the student whom the spouse is joining has or is given leave to remain for twelve months or more.

Short-term employment categories: r.88 to 127

Most of the short term employment categories (e.g. working holiday makers, au pairs) have been replaced or subsumed within the Points Based System. There are therefore only some residual parts to this once significant section of the immigration rules.

Seasonal workers

Rules 104-109 – this covers overseas students aged 18-25 coming to the UK for a brief period of employment at an agricultural camp. They require a Home Office work card and will only be allowed to remain in the UK for a maximum of 6 months in any one year under the scheme.

Sector-based workers

Rules 135I-135K – this quota based scheme is for people with employment in particular sectors of the economy (currently only food processing) for low-skilled workers. It is a requirement of the rule that the sector-based worker must show an intention to return. The rule allowing sector-based workers to switch into full work permit status was scrapped in 2004.

UK Ancestry Visas

A visa allowing free employment or self employment and leading to settlement is (or was) available to those who can show adequate maintenance and accommodation and:

- is a Commonwealth citizen; and

- is aged 17 or over; and

- can prove a relationship by blood or recognised adoption with a grandparent born in the United Kingdom and Islands; and

- is able to work and intends to take or seek employment in the United Kingdom.

It is no longer possible to switch to an ancestral visa from within the UK. It is mandatory to obtain entry clearance from the British Embassy or High Commission in the home country of the applicant.

One of the main attractions of the ancestral visa is that is leads to settlement after five years. In addition, there are no restrictions on employment and the IDIs suggest that examination of the applicant's ability to maintain him or herself is relatively limited, providing they can do so by some means that includes some sort of employment. It is not strictly necessary to show employment when applying for extensions, although it would certainly be helpful to be able to do so.

Long residence: r.276A to 276D

The idea of granting permanent settlement to a person who had been in the UK for many years was enshrined in Home Office policy for a long time and was partially incorporated into the rules from April 2003. Confusingly, the Home Office retained the pre-existing policy alongside the new immigration rules for many years, even though the terms of the policy were more generous than the terms of the rules.

There was then a short period where there was no distinct policy in existence, and the stringent terms of the rules caused many long residence applications to fail. This ended in 2009, when a new policy was introduced to mitigate the terms of the rules.

Period of residence

There are two routes to settlement on the grounds of long residence:

1. After ten continuous and lawful years of residence a person can potentially qualify, or

2. After 14 years of continuous residence (whether lawful, unlawful or some sort of combination of the two) a person can potentially qualify.

Lawful residence can include a period of time where a person had Temporary Admission, but only if they were subsequently granted leave to enter or remain or where they were exempt from immigration control.

In either case, being served with either a notice that the person is to be removed from the UK or a notice of intention to deport them from the UK precludes a successful application. The issuance of the notice is known commonly as "stopping the clock".

Clearly if a person is applying for leave to remain on the basis of unlawful residence they will have to provide evidence to prove the actual residence as unlawful residence will usually not be know to the Home Office who will not have a record of any period when a person did not have leave to enter or remain.

10 year rule

- Must be 10 years residence
- Must be continuous and lawful
- Very limited discretion to waive only short gaps in lawful leave
- Discretionary compassionate and desirability factors must be considered

14 year rule

- Must be 14 years residence: proof can be problematic
- Can be lawful, unlawful or mixed
- Discretionary compassionate and desirability factors must be considered

Requirement for residence to be continuous

The residence, whether lawful or otherwise, must be continuous residence. Continuous residence is not broken by an absence of six months or less, as long as the person had leave to remain at the time of their departure from and return to the UK. However, the period of continuous residence is considered to have been broken if the applicant:

- has been removed or deported from the UK having been refused leave to enter or remain

- has left the UK with an clear intention not to return

- has left the UK in circumstances where he would have no expectation that he could lawfully return

- has been convicted of an offence and sentenced to a term of imprisonment

- has spent a total of more than 18 months outside the UK during the total period of residence

The Home Office also apply a policy whereby a break in a person's leave while outside the UK will not count against them; where a person leaves the UK with leave in one category, that leave lapses, then the person re-enters the UK with leave in a different category, that will not be considered to be a break in 'continuous leave'. A break in leave of more than six months will be a break in continuous residence, however.

At the time of writing the IDIs include a policy on exercising discretion in lawful residence cases where there are short gaps in a person's leave. The policy is set out at section 2.3.3 of Chapter 18 of the IDIs:

2.3.3 Breaks in lawful residence and the use of discretion

> Caseworkers should be satisfied that the applicant has acted lawfully throughout the entire period and has made every attempt to comply with the immigration rules.
>
> If an applicant has a <u>single</u> short gap in lawful residence through making one <u>single</u> previous application out of time by a few days (not usually more than 10 calendar days out of time), caseworkers should use discretion granting ILR, so long as the application meets all the other requirements.
>
> It would <u>not usually</u> be appropriate to exercise discretion when an applicant has <u>more than one</u> gap in their lawful residence due to submitting more than one of their previous applications out of time, as they would not have shown the necessary commitment to ensuring they have maintained lawful leave throughout their time in the UK.
>
> It may be appropriate to use your judgement in cases where an applicant has submitted a single application more than 10 days out of time if there are extenuating reasons for this (e.g. postal strike, hospitalisation, administrative error on our part etc). This must be discussed with a Senior Caseworker.
>
> [original emphasis]

The IDIs go on to give examples of where it may be appropriate to exercise discretion. See also *SA (long residence concession) Bangladesh* [2009] UKAIT 00051 for a discussion of the policy and see also *MD (Jamaica) & Anor v Secretary of State for the Home Department* [2010] EWCA Civ 213, where the Court of Appeal adopts a strict approach to the construction of the long residence rules.

Other considerations

Given all the above requirements, an application will then be considered taking into consideration various factors, which are the person's:

- age

- strength of connections in the UK

- personal history: character, conduct, associations and employment record

- domestic circumstances

- previous criminal record

- compassionate circumstances

- any representations received on the person's behalf.

These factors were taken from the old r.364 deportation rule and enable the UK Border Agency to exercise discretion not to grant residence if, for example, the applicant has been convicted of a criminal offence.

The Court of Appeal has in at least two cases been critical of the UK Border Agency and immigration tribunal tendency to undermine the purpose of the long residence rule by taking too restrictive an approach to the latter set of considerations. In *ZH (Bangladesh) v SSHD* [2009] EWCA Civ 8 the Court of Appeal held that illegal working is not sufficient to exclude a person from the benefits of the long residence rule.

> ### Example
>
> Maria has been in the UK for just over 14 years. She entered as a visitor and overstayed, working for various individuals over the years as a cleaner. However, with the moving around she lost her original passport.
>
> Her first problem is proving when she entered the UK. Sometimes employers past or present are willing to give evidence, which would be very helpful. Friends and family will usually be willing to give evidence.
>
> Sometimes it is possible to obtain official or semi-official records. An attempt to contact the Home Office to obtain evidence of Maria's application for entry clearance (if she made one) or leave to enter could be made, although the chances of success are limited. Doctor or hospital or library records (or school records in a case involving a person who entered the UK when a child) would be of considerable assistance, as would bank or utility bills. An unlawful immigration may well not have generated such records, however. Photographs could help, whether date stamped or not, accompanied by an explanation of where and when they were taken.

Spouses and civil partners: r.277 to 289C

This section of the notes addresses the rules on the spouse or civil partner of a person present and settled in the UK. The rules for spouses and civil partners are essentially identical.

Restrictions
- Polygamy
- Age
- English language

Qualifying relationships
- Legality
- 'Genuineness'

Immigration status
- Switching
- Settlement
- Relationships that end

Polygamy

It is important to remember that under the immigration rules the spouse in a polygamous marriage is not permitted to enter or remain in the UK on the basis of the marriage if there is another person living who is the spouse of the sponsor and who *at any time* since their marriage has been in the UK or has been granted a certificate of entitlement.

See Immigration Rule 278. This does not mean that polygamous marriages are not recognised or lawful in the UK, but rather that only one wife or husband from such a marriage may enter the UK.

Age

As of 27 November 2008, the minimum age for both the person seeking a visa and the UK-based sponsor in spouse and partner rule applications has been raised from 18 to 21.

The justification put forward by the Home Office at the time of the change was that it would help to prevent forced marriages. Many suspect that the real objective was to reduce the number of young British Asians and young members of other minorities marrying foreigners and to encourage them to marry within the United Kingdom.

At the time of writing a challenge to the new age rules in the case of *Quila v SSHD* [2009] EWHC 3189 (Admin) had failed and news was awaited on further appeals in that and other cases.

Concessions

A limited concession was announced on 10 December 2008 whereby the increase in the spouse visa age applies only where the sponsor is present and settled in the UK or is being admitted for settlement on the same occasion as the applicant.

A further concession was announced on 18 March 2010, which came into effect in early April 2010 whereby members of the armed forces and their spouses and partners are exempted from the 21 and over requirement and need only be 18 or over.

Challenges

Any challenge on public law grounds will need to await the outcome of the *Quila* case if it proceeds, or one or more of the other cases stacked behind it. However, challenges based on individual circumstances might in the meantime succeed before the tribunal.

Clearly, marriage and country of residence raise Article 8 issues. Proportionality is therefore important, and the facts of individual cases may reveal potential challenges, particularly where there are very strong reasons why the UK-based spouse cannot relocate abroad. The test is expressed as the dilemma test in *VW (Uganda)* [2009] EWCA Civ 5. The reason for this is that it is not the ultimate decision reached but the dilemma faced by the migrant's family member in arriving at that decision that must be assessed.

English language

In June 2010 the Government announced plans to require those applying to enter the UK as spouses and partners would have to demonstrate a minimum level of competence in the English language. The plans are scheduled to commence from 29 November 2010.

The level of English required will be A1 on the Common European Framework of Reference, which is the same as that required for Tier 2 of the Points Based System. Applicants from majority English speaking countries will be exempted. The test will apply at the initial application stage (whether from inside or outside the UK) and also at the settlement stage. Tests will need to be carried out with an approved provider.

Further details were to be published closer to commencement date.

Qualifying relationships

Civil partnerships and marriages are dealt with identically under the Immigration Rules and the terms are effectively interchangeable. To succeed on a spouse visa application, the parties to the marriage or civil partnership need to show either that:

(a) the applicant is married to or the civil partner of a person present and settled in the UK or who is being admitted for settlement at the same time as the applicant, or

(b) the applicant is married to or the civil partner of a person with a right of abode or indefinite leave to remain who is seeking admission for settlement at the same time as the spouse where the parties were married at least four years ago and have been living together outside the UK since that time

The meaning of 'present and settled' is set out in r.6 of the Immigration Rules and in essence means possession of ILR or the right of abode combined with physical presence in the UK.

With the above requirements, group (b) would fall within group (a) anyway, so what is the purpose of the distinction? The answer lies at r.282 of the rules, which specifies that in situation (a), 27 months of leave to enter will be granted (the probationary period) whereas in situation (b), ILR will be granted outright.

The parties will need to show that they are legally married according to the laws of the country in which the marriage took place (although see above for polygamous marriages) or that they have contracted a legal civil partnership in a country in which such partnerships are recognised. These countries are listed at Schedule 20 of the Civil Partnership Act 2004. At the time of writing this included Andorra, Australia, Belgium, Canada, Denmark, Finland, France, Germany, Iceland, Luxembourg, Netherlands, New Zealand, Norway, Spain, Sweden and certain States of the USA (California, Connecticut, Maine, Massachusetts, New Jersey, Vermont).

The rule that marriages will be recognised if legal in the country in which they take place is a long standing rule of international private law. For authority see *Berthiaume v. Dastous* [1930] AC 79 and Rule 67 of Dicey 14th edition. This means that even quite unusual marriage arrangements, such as marriages by proxy, must be recognised (*CB (Validity of marriage: proxy marriage) Brazil* [2008] UKAIT 00080).

The requirement that the marriage is legal will in some cases mean that relevant formal divorce papers or other evidence of a divorce that was effective in the country in which it took place will need to be produced. The complex issue of domicile may also arise in some spouse cases.

> **Examples**
>
> Salim is a British citizen and has just married Kirsty, who is Canadian. They were married in Canada. Kirsty will now need to apply to enter the UK as a spouse and, if successful, she will be granted two years leave to enter, the probationary period. This is because she falls within group (a) above but not group (b).
>
> Leah is a British citizen and she has been married to Barry for six years. They met and married in Australia when Leah was travelling and they have lived there together ever since. However, they now want to relocate to the UK. Barry falls within group (b) above as they have been living together for four years or more and Leah possesses the right of abode. Barry therefore needs to apply for entry as a spouse and, if successful, he will be granted indefinite leave to enter. The couple will need to be careful that they satisfy the ECO that Barry meets the maintenance and accommodation requirements as neither of them is established in the UK at present.

In addition, the applicant in a spouse case must demonstrate that he or she has an intention to live permanently with the other and that the marriage is subsisting. The former phrase is defined in r.6 of HC395:

> '"intention to live permanently with the other" means an intention to live together, evidenced by a clear commitment from both parties that they will live together permanently in the United Kingdom immediately following the outcome of the application in question or as soon as circumstances permit thereafter'.

The words 'subsisting marriage' have no precise definition. In the starred determination of *GA ("Subsisting" marriage) Ghana* [2006] UKAIT 00046 the tribunal held that this sub-rule requires more than formal legal validity, but did not explore any further what it does mean, other than to say that it is an examination of the present state of the relationship rather than looking backwards or looking forwards in time, and that the past conduct of the parties can provide an indication of future intention.

If an ECO believes that the marriage is a sham marriage entered into for the purpose of simply gaining entry to the UK and that the spouses actually have no intention of living permanently with each other, then these two sub-rules will form the basis of refusal. However, they are not equivalent to the old 'primary purpose' rule, which used to require applicants to demonstrate that the application was not being made for the primary purpose of gaining entry to the UK, irrespective of whether the couple actually did intend to live together afterwards.

Lastly, the couple must have met at the time of the application. This allows arranged marriages where the couple do not meet until the day of the wedding, but it may exclude some marriages that would be legal in the country in which they take place, such as marriages *in absentia*, by telephone or by proxy – unless the couple has met by the time of the application, in which case such marriages will be acceptable.

Switching

It is only possible to switch to become a spouse or civil partner (i.e. apply for leave to remain under r.284) if the applicant is in possession of leave that was granted for a period of more than six months. This means that visitors cannot switch, given that they may not be granted more than six months leave. The requirement in this provision, at r.284(i), that the leave 'was given in accordance with any of the provisions of these Rules' means that those with leave to remain given outside the rules, such as holders of discretionary leave to remain, cannot switch into this category.

There are benefits to possession of leave granted in accordance with the immigration rules, so clients may want to consider applying for spouse status in the normal way if granted Discretionary Leave.

Examples

Duncan was a failed asylum seeker but was granted 3 years of Discretionary Leave on the basis of his marriage to a British citizen. After 3 years, he undergoes an active review and is granted a further 3 years of DL. At the end of 6 years in total, there is another active review, and he is finally granted ILR. If he is a victim of domestic violence or is bereaved during the six years, there is no way for him to apply for ILR (see below).

Mabel was in the same position as Duncan, but she chose to return to her country to make an entry clearance application as a spouse. She had help preparing the application from a good UK immigration lawyer and included all of the evidence and proof required. The application was granted and she returned to the UK after two weeks. After two years, she can apply for ILR and in the meantime she can also benefit from the domestic violence and bereavement rules, if necessary.

An alternative is to apply for and get Discretionary Leave and then voluntarily return home and apply for entry clearance. The Discretionary Leave does not lapse on leaving the UK. This approach has been successful in some cases.

Grant of leave to enter/remain

Spouses or civil partners will be granted 27 months of leave to enter or remain unless they fall within r.281(i)(b) as described above (in which case they are granted indefinite leave to enter immediately) and must apply on completion of that 'probationary period' apply for indefinite leave to remain. Indefinite leave to remain will be granted if:

- the couple are still married or living together in a subsisting relationship and have completed two years in that capacity

- the couple intend to live permanently together

- there will be adequate maintenance and accommodation for the couple without recourse to public funds

During this period the spouse/partner will have no restriction on employment (or on starting a business).

Marriages that have ended during the probationary period

Normally if a marriage or partnership has ended during the probationary period the foreign national is expected to leave the UK as he or she will have no right to remain unless he or she could qualify under another category in the rules. However, in two instances there are immigration rules accounting for particular compassionate circumstances leading to the end of a marriage which are outside the spouse's control.

Bereaved spouses or partners

Bereaved spouses or partners will be granted indefinite leave to remain if the spouse or partner they joined died during the two year probationary period and if they can show that they were still living together and intended to do so permanently at the time of the bereavement (rule 287(b) for spouses or civil partners or 295M for unmarried partners).

Victims of domestic violence

Victims of domestic violence may be granted indefinite leave to remain where the marriage or relationship breaks down during the initial two-year period provided they can produce evidence that the relationship was caused to permanently break down before the end of the two years as a result of domestic violence (r.289A). No fee is paid where the applicant can show they are destitute.

The Home Office specifies in the IDIs (chapter 8, section 4) certain types of evidence that have to be submitted, but on appeal the Immigration tribunal is not similarly restricted and can consider any relevant evidence including personal testimony (see *Ishtiaq v SSHD* [2007] EWCA Civ 386).

The Home Office evidence requirements are one of the following forms of evidence:

- an injunction, non-molestation order or other protection order made against the sponsor (other than an ex-parte or interim order); or

- a relevant court conviction against the sponsor; or

- full details of a relevant police caution issued against the sponsor.

Or more than one of the following forms of evidence:

- a medical report from a hospital doctor confirming that the applicant has injuries consistent with being a victim of domestic violence; OR, a letter from a GMC registered family practitioner who has examined the applicant and is satisfied that the applicant has injuries consistent with being a victim of domestic violence;

- an undertaking given to a court that the perpetrator of the violence will not approach the applicant who is the victim of the violence;

- a police report confirming attendance at the home of the applicant as a result of a domestic violence incident;

- a letter from a social services department confirming its involvement in connection with domestic violence;

- a letter of support or a report from a domestic violence support organisation which is identified at Annex AB of the IDIs

These forms of evidence are not simple to obtain, so the more relaxed approach to evidence laid down in *Ishtiaq* is very helpful. Nevertheless, every attempt should be made to obtain the Home Office specified evidence as it is far better to succeed at the initial application than much later on appeal.

> **Top tip**
>
> The domestic violence rule does not require the applicant to possess leave at the time of application. However, the relationship must have been caused permanently to break down during the two year probationary period, which can be a problem where there has not been a clean separation between the couple.

Home Office Certificate of Approval

The Home Office introduced a scheme commencing in 2005 which required all those subject to immigration control and not in possession of indefinite leave to remain to apply for permission to get married (or entering a civil partnership) and permitting them to get married only at certain designated registry offices. Unless the applicant had been granted six months leave to enter and still had three months left to run or could show exceptional circumstances, the application would be rejected.

The scheme has proven to be highly controversial and generated considerable litigation. On 26 July 2010 the Government announced that Certificates of Approval will be scrapped in late 2010 or early 2011. In the meantime, the requirement will continue to exist.

The legal challenges to the scheme began in the High Court and generated three complex linked judgments, then progressed to the Court of Appeal and then the House of Lords. The House of Lords held that the scheme was disproportionate and discriminatory under Articles 12 and 14 of the European Convention of Human Rights. The reasoning was, in summary, that the scheme, which affected an enormous number of genuine couples and prevented them from getting married, was disproportionate to the intended purpose. This purpose was to prevent abuse of immigration control through sham marriages, but the purpose could be fulfilled by far less intrusive means that did not effectively presume that anyone not settled in the UK and wanting to get married must be doing so for immigration purposes.

The scheme was amended following the Court of Appeal judgment to allow couples to establish that theirs is a genuine relationship even if they do not meet the original requirements for a certificate. Home Office guidance on proving the relationship requires of applicants the following information:

- when, where and how you and your fiancée(e)/proposed civil partner met
- when you decided to marry or enter into a civil partnership
- where you intend to live if permitted to marry or to enter into a civil arrangements for any religious ceremony, including the nature of the ceremony, the person conducting it and relevant contact details
- arrangements for any reception or celebration, including details of the location, proof of booking and relevant contact
- your relationship with your fiancé(e)/proposed civil partner if you are not living together (e.g. letters and photographs as evidence of the relationship)
- your life with your fiancé(e)/proposed civil partner if you are living together, including the address(es), how long you have lived together and documentary evidence in the form of correspondence addressed to both of you at the same address from utilities, government bodies, local authorities, financial institutions etc
- any children from your and your fiancé(e)/proposed civil partner's present or previous relationships, including where they now live, the length of time any of them have lived with you, the names of their natural parents and who supports them
- contact telephone numbers for yourself and your fiancé(e)/proposed civil partner in case an officer wishes to contact either of you
- any additional information about yourself and your fiancé(e)/proposed civil partner which you would like us to know about, and/or any additional supporting evidence or documentation which might help your application.

The information has to be presented in affidavit form (a type of witness statement), which means lawyers need to be involved.

The certificate of approval is not a grant of further leave to remain in the UK. The certificate only allows an individual to give notice to marry to a registrar at a designated register office.

Following the House of Lords judgment the Home Office retained the above affadavit requirements but eventually abolished the application fee for Certificates of Approval and made arrangements to refund fees in past cases (although this scheme closed on 31 July 2010).

Fiancé(e)s and proposed civil partners: r.289AA to 295

The purpose of the fiancé(e) or proposed civil partner visa is to allow a couple to come to the UK to get married or enter a civil partnership in the UK rather than abroad. After the marriage, the spouse can apply for an extension as a spouse and will commence the two-year probationary period. Entry clearance is mandatory – it is not possible to switch into this category as a prelude to a full spouse application.

Fiancé(e)s or proposed civil partners are granted six months' leave to enter during which time they are expected to marry. Employment is prohibited during these six months. At the end of the six months' they will be expected to be applying for the spouse to be granted leave to remain on the basis of their marriage (they are excluded from the six-month restriction on those seeking to switch to be granted leave to remain on the basis of a marriage).

If the couple have not married or entered a civil partnership during that period they must show 'good cause' why the marriage or civil partnership has not taken place and that it will take place at an early date and can then apply for a further six months' leave to remain as a fiancé/e or proposed civil partner.

The requirements are as follows:

- the parties to the proposed marriage or civil partnership have met

- they intend to live together permanently as man and wife or civil partners after the marriage or civil partnership

- they can maintain and accommodate themselves adequately without recourse to public funds (in accommodation which they own or occupy exclusively)

- they have valid prior entry clearance

Unmarried partners: r.295AA to 295O

The term 'unmarried partners' is used here distinctly from 'civil partners'. The rules for civil partners and spouses are essentially identical. Unmarried partners, meaning either same or different sex partners who have lived together for at least two years, are treated similarly to spouses but not identically. For example, there is no provision for an unmarried partner to enter in an equivalent capacity to a fiancé(e) or proposed civil partner. However, there are equivalent provisions for the grant of settlement in the event of the breakdown of the relationship due to domestic violence or bereavement.

The requirements are the same as for spouses in respect of intention to live permanently with the other, maintenance and accommodation and prior entry clearance but the following requirements for an unmarried partner applicant differ slightly from the spouse and civil partner requirements:

- he/she is the unmarried partner of a person present and settled in the UK or who is being admitted for settlement at the same time; and

- the couple have been living together in a subsisting relationship for two years or more; or

- the person seeking entry is the partner of a person with a right of abode or indefinite leave to remain who is seeking admission for settlement and the couple have lived together outside the UK for four years or more (in which case indefinite leave will be granted, as for spouses); and

- any previous marriage or similar relationship has permanently broken down; and that

- the couple are not in a consanguineous relationship

Rule 295D on switching into the unmarried partner category states that the applicant must have limited leave that was granted in accordance with the Immigration Rules. It is therefore possible to switch into the unmarried partner category from the visitor category. However, holders of Discretionary Leave or other types of leave granted outside the rules will not be able to switch.

Children: r.296 to 316

Position of the parents
- All remaining parents in or coming to UK
- OR sole responsibility
- OR exclusion undesirable

Position of the child
- Under 18
- Not living independent life

Maintenance and accommodation

A child seeking to join or accompany a parent *present and settled* in the UK must be joining either:

- both parents already present and settled or being admitted for settlement **or**

- one parent present and settled and the other being admitted for settlement **or**

- one parent present and settled or being admitted for settlement who can show that they have had sole responsibility for the child's upbringing *or*

- a parent or another relative present and settled or being admitted for settlement where there are serious and compelling family or other considerations which made the exclusion of the child undesirable and where there are suitable arrangements made for the child's care

It can be seen that there are additional requirements that apply where one of the parents is still alive and resides outside the UK. In such cases the UK-based parent will have to show a good reason why the child should be allowed to settle in the UK rather than stay with the other parent abroad. These reasons are examined in more detail below. Where all surviving parents are in the UK or coming to the UK, the application is relatively straightforward

In addition to the above requirements it must be shown in all cases that the child:

- is under 18, unmarried and must not be leading an independent life or have an independent family unit *and*

- can and will be maintained and accommodated adequately without recourse to public funds

Prior entry clearance is required where the child is seeking indefinite leave to enter will be granted to the child. However a child may switch into ILR. Under r.298(d)(ii) a child only has to have limited leave *and* be under 18, in whatever category they originally came *or* came with a view to settlement. It does not say that limited leave has to be in *that capacity* if under 18. A child who is here as a visitor, and then decides to settle because their parents are settled in the UK, is therefore allowed to do so.

Sole responsibility

In order to show that the sponsoring parent in the UK has sole responsibility for the child he or she will need to show not only financial responsibility for the child but also normal parental responsibility in respect of all other aspects of the child's life. It is acceptable that the child's day to day care is delegated to another person in their own country but evidence that ultimate control rests with the sponsoring parent is required. It is not necessary to show that the sponsoring parent has had sole responsibility for the whole of the child's life.

The IDIs elaborate on the meaning of sole responsibility and state that the following factors are to be used as guidance on how to assess it:

- the period for which the parent in the United Kingdom has been separated from the child;

- what the arrangements were for the care of the child before that parent migrated to this country;

- who has been entrusted with day to day care and control of the child since the sponsoring parent migrated here;

- who provides, and in what proportion, the financial support for the child's care and upbringing;

- who takes the important decisions about the child's upbringing, such as where and with whom the child lives, the choice of school, religious practice etc;

- the degree of contact that has been maintained between the child and the parent claiming "sole responsibility";

- what part in the child's care and upbringing is played by the parent not in the United Kingdom and his relatives.

The IDIs also say that sole responsibility should have been exercised for a substantial period of time. The Court of Appeal case of *Nmaju v ECO* [2000] EWCA Civ 505 (C/2000/6263) 31 July 2000, however, states that this is not the case, sole responsibility could be exercised for a short period of time and that the two key factors are:

1. What quality of control is involved?

2. For what period of time must this quality of control be exercised?

The tribunal case of *TD (Paragraph 297(i)(e): "sole responsibility") Yemen* [2006] UKAIT 00049 includes a useful summary of the relevant case law on this issue and holds that the test is whether the parent has continuing control and direction over the child's upbringing, including making all the important decisions in the child's life.

Serious and compelling circumstances making exclusion undesirable

There is no particular definition of what may constitute serious and compelling circumstances but the phrase 'family or other circumstances' suggests that the benefit of the child and the sponsoring parent/s or other relative could be a valid consideration in interpreting this part of the rule.

However, in *Hardward v SSHD* (00/TH/01522) 12 July 2000, the Tribunal suggested, after reviewing the case law that the key factors are:

- willingness and ability of the overseas adult to care for the child

- poor living conditions – but not necessarily intolerable

- greater vulnerability of small children.

> ### Example
>
> Fatima, from Egypt, entered the UK as a work permit holder and has worked as a nurse for over 5 years. She now has ILR. She is sponsoring her husband and child to come to the UK. This will be a straightforward application on both counts.
>
> However, if Fatima was applying for only the child to come to the UK to join her, it would be a far more problematic application. She would have to demonstrate sole responsibility or that the exclusion of the child would be undesirable.
>
> The evidence Fatima might consider seeking to obtain would include:
> - Evidence of contact with the child, including the frequency, quality and type of contact
> - Evidence of contact with the carer, including as to Fatima's exercise of control and direction over the child's upbringing through the carer
> - Letters from teachers and other figures in the child's life such as doctors or priests which shows interest and involvement by Fatima
> - If seeking to rely on sole responsibility, an explanation and any available evidence of lack of interest in the child's upbringing by the father. If the care or interest of the father was considered harmful to the child (for example, if there were allegations of neglect or abuse) then evidence would be needed and the case could perhaps be argued under the exclusion undesirable part of the rule.

Other definitions

Under r.6 of HC395 the definition of a 'parent' is deemed to include:

- stepfather of a child whose father is dead

- stepmother of a child whose mother is dead

- father or mother of an illegitimate child (providing he can prove paternity)

- an adoptive parent where the child was adopted in accordance with a decision taken by the competent court or administrative authority in a country whose adoption orders are recognised in the UK

Children of fiancé(e)s

The child of a fiancé(e) may join his or her parent if the child is under 18, unmarried, not leading an independent life and can be maintained and accommodated without recourse to public funds.

Adopted children

The admission of adopted children is provided for in r.309A of HC395. This rule also applies where there has been a *de facto* adoption - not a formal one - or one that is formal but not recognised in the UK. It must be shown that:

- immediately preceding the application the adoptive parent/parents have been living abroad (if two parents, living together) for at least eighteen months of which the twelve months preceding the application must have been spent living with the child

- the adoptive parents must have assumed the role of the child's parents since the beginning of the eighteen month period so that there has been a genuine transfer of parental responsibility

If the above requirements are met then the child must also show that they meet a further set of requirements, the same as those for natural children in order to be granted entry. If the requirements are met the child will be granted indefinite leave to enter the UK.

Alternatively, adoption cases can potentially be argued under Article 8 ECHR. See the case of *Singh v Entry Clearance Officer New Delhi* [2004] EWCA Civ 1075.

Other family members: r.317 to 319

These few paragraphs deal with the potential admission of dependant relatives other than children under the age of 18, spouses or partners. It is largely relevant to dependant parents and grandparents but there is also some provision for other dependant relatives to obtain entry.

Qualifying relationship
- Over 65: no extra test
- Under 65: most exceptional compassionate circumstances

Financial dependency

Maintenance and accommodation

No other close relatives to turn to

Parents and grandparents

The key to the entry of parents and grandparents is being able to show the requisite measure of dependency on relatives present and settled or being admitted for settlement in the UK. The rules specifically require that the relative must be either:

- widowed mother or grandmother over the age of 65

- widowed father or grandfather over the age of 65

- parent or grandparents travelling together of whom one is aged 65 or over

- a parent or grandparent over the age of 65 who has remarried but cannot look to the spouse or children of the second marriage for financial support

- parent or grandparent under the age of 65 if living alone outside the UK in the most exceptional compassionate circumstances and mainly dependent financially on relatives settled in the UK

In addition it must be shown that the dependent parent/grandparent is:

- financially wholly or mainly dependant on the relative present in the UK

- can be maintained and accommodated adequately without recourse to public funds (in accommodation owned or occupied exclusively by the sponsor)

- without other close relatives in his country to whom he could turn for financial support

Prior entry clearance is required and the applicant will be granted indefinite leave to enter the UK.

> **Example**
>
> Abdul is sponsoring his father to come to the UK as a dependent relative. His father is 71. The only criteria the father's application needs to satisfy are maintenance, accommodation, being 'mainly or wholly dependent' on Abdul and having no other close relatives to turn to in the country of origin.
>
> If Abdul's father was 64, however, the application criteria are far more onerous. The application could only succeed if it could be demonstrated that Abdul's father was living alone in the most exceptional compassionate circumstances, a very high test indeed.
>
> This more onerous criterion will also apply to applications of over-18 children of UK sponsors.

Other relatives

The only other relatives who can apply to enter or remain as dependant relatives are the son, daughter, sister, brother, uncle or aunt of a sponsor if they are:

- over the age of 18

- living alone outside the UK in the most exceptional compassionate circumstances *and*

- mainly dependent financially on relatives settled in the UK

It is important to remember that the list of relatives is exhaustive. All other family members are excluded unless permitted to enter or remain outside the immigration rules

Any of the above family members can switch into this immigration status once in the UK (although care must be taken that it does not appear that they are using an easier entry category in order to gain entry and then switch) as long as they meet the requirements of the rules.

Exercising rights of access to a child resident in the UK

Rules 246 to 248F make provision for parents to exercise rights of access to a child in the UK. The parent must prove their parentage of the child and that:

- the parent or carer with whom the child resides is resident in the UK

- the applicant has access rights through the courts in the form of a residence order or contact order (or a certificate from a district judge confirming the applicant's intention to maintain contact with the child)

- the applicant intends to take an active role in the child's upbringing

- the child is under 18 and that there will be adequate maintenance and accommodation for the applicant

The requirement of a certificate from a district judge is ill conceived and district judges (a) have never heard of any such certificate and (b) are unwilling to issue one. At the time of writing the IDIs acknowledged this (chapter 7, section 1) and stated that instead an affidavit from the UK-resident parent was necessary, confirming that the applicant parent can have access to the child, and describing in detail the arrangements made to allow for this, or if contact is supervised, then the statement must be sworn by the supervisor. This is similarly ill conceived, as the fact that the proceedings are necessary strongly suggests that the relationship between the parents has broken down very badly and the other parent is very unlikely to co-operate.

Prior entry clearance is required and the applicant will initially be granted 12 months leave to enter. On completion of the 12 months indefinite leave to remain will be granted if the applicant continues to play an active role in the child's upbringing and the child visits or stays with the applicant and the applicant can continue to maintain and accommodate himself without public funds. Employment is not prohibited.

An applicant can switch from another category provided that the general requirements above are met and that:

- the applicant has limited leave to remain as the spouse/partner of the person who the other parent of the child

- the applicant has not remained in breach of the immigration laws

The UK Border Agency will not usually seek to remove a person who is currently pursuing a contact or residence order through the family courts. See *MS (Ivory Coast) v SSHD* [2007] EWCA Civ 133 and CCD policy *Children and Family Process Instruction*.[1]

Returning residents: r.18 to 20

A person will automatically be re-admitted for settlement if he/she:

- had indefinite leave to enter/remain when he last left the UK

---

[1] tinyurl.com/37czrpc

- has not been away for more than 2 years

- did not receive assistance towards the cost of leaving

- now seeks admission for settlement

A person who has been away for more than two years may be admitted to the UK as a returning resident if, for example, he has lived here all his life and the only other bar to admission is that he has been away for more than two years (r.19). In fact, the IDIs, at Chapter 1, Section 3, Annexe K, are quite generous in their interpretation of this rule:

> '2. FACTORS TO BE CONSIDERED IN CASES WHERE PARAGRAPH 19 OF HC 395 MAY APPLY
>
> The factors that should be considered in assessing whether a person comes within Paragraph 19 are set out below:
> - the length of his original residence here;
> - the time the applicant has been outside the United Kingdom;
> - the reason for the delay beyond the 2 years - was it through his own wish or no fault of his own? Could he reasonably have been expected to return within 2 years?
> - why did he go abroad when he did and what were his intentions?
> - the nature of his family ties here - how close are they, and to what extent has he maintained them in his absence?
> - whether he has a home in the United Kingdom and, if admitted, would resume his residency.
>
> The longer a person has remained outside the United Kingdom over 2 years, the more difficult it will be for him to qualify for admission under the discretion contained in Paragraph 19.
>
> 2.1 Other circumstances to be considered
>
> Other more specific circumstances which might apply in favour of an individual are:
> - travel and service abroad with a particular employer prior to returning with him;
> - service abroad for the United Kingdom Government, as an employee of a quasi/government body, a British company or a United Nations organisation;
> - employment abroad in the public service of a friendly country by a person who could not reasonably be expected to settle in that country permanently;
> - a prolonged period of study abroad by a person who wished to rejoin his family here at the end of his studies;
> - prolonged medical treatment abroad of a kind not available here;
> - whether the person contacted a post abroad within 2 years to express his future intention to return to the United Kingdom.'

Nevertheless, the person's leave automatically lapses by operation of law if he or she has remained outside the UK for more than two years and he or she will be required to seek leave to enter, which will not be automatically granted. Where a person is refused leave to enter as a returning resident, the Immigration Officer will usually grant a period of six months leave to enter as a visitor. This enables the person to enter the UK and try to sort out their immigration status, including by appealing the decision of the Immigration Officer (although this is not legally straightforward given the constraints of s.82 of the 2002 Act).

> **Example**
>
> Alia is from Pakistan and she married a British citizen. She came to the UK several years ago and was granted limited leave then indefinite leave to remain.
>
> She had a child and her husband took her and the child to Pakistan, allegedly for a holiday. However, he abandoned them there, taking her passport. She stayed in Pakistan, not wanting to return to the UK as she had no alternative means of support there.
>
> Over two years passed, meaning that her ILR automatically lapsed. Her husband visited her and persuaded her to return to the UK. She did so, and the Immigration Officer appears not to have noticed that her leave had lapsed. It has been confirmed that she entered the UK, but there is no evidence of this in her passport.
>
> The husband then commenced Children Act proceedings to seek residence, which are ongoing. Alia needs to discover her immigration position and what options are available to her. Her immigration and family law positions are entwined and it is a complex case.

General grounds for refusal

The burden of proof to prove one of the general grounds for refusal always rests with the ECO: he who asserts must prove. The standard of proof for allegations is the normal civil standard. Any allegation of forgery must be backed by evidence.

Refusal of leave to enter

At rule 320 there are a number of grounds on which entry clearance or leave to enter can be refused. These were significantly amended in mid 2008 on a number of occasions, and several concessions were made to the original very harsh rules that were proposed and briefly implemented. The first grounds are mandatory bases for a refusal and they include:

(1) seeking entry for a purpose not covered by the rules

(2) seeking entry when the person is the subject of a deportation order

(3) failing to produce a passport or national ID document

(4) when entering or seeking entry through the Channel Tunnel with an intention of entering another part of the Common Travel Area (CTA), failing to show acceptability to the immigration authorities in that part of the CTA

(5) failing to produce an entry clearance where it is required

(6) where the Secretary of State personally directs that a person's exclusion from the UK is conducive to the public good

(7) medical grounds

(7A) where false representations have been made or false documents have been submitted (whether or not material to the application, and whether or not to the applicant's knowledge), or material facts have not been disclosed, in relation to the application.

(7B) subject to paragraph 320(7C), where the applicant has previously breached the UK's immigration laws by:

    (a) overstaying;
    (b) breaching a condition attached to his leave;
    (c) being an Illegal Entrant;
    (d) using Deception in an application for entry clearance, leave to enter or remain (whether successful or not);

unless the applicant:

    (i) Overstayed for 28 days or less and left the UK voluntarily, not at the expense (directly or indirectly) of the Secretary of State;
    (ii) used Deception in an application for entry clearance more than 10 years ago;
    (iii) left the UK voluntarily, not at the expense (directly or indirectly) of the Secretary of State, more than 12 months ago;
    (iv) left the UK voluntarily, at the expense (directly or indirectly) of the Secretary of State, more than 5 years ago, or
    (v) was removed or deported from the UK more than 10 years ago.

Where more than one breach of the UK's immigration laws has occurred, only the breach which leads to the longest period of absence from the UK will be relevant under this paragraph.

(7C) Paragraph 320(7B) shall not apply in the following circumstances:

    (a) where the applicant is applying as:
        (i) a spouse, civil partner or unmarried or same-sex partner under paragraphs 281 or 295A,

(ii) a fiancé(e) or proposed civil partner under paragraph 290,
(iii) a parent, grandparent or other dependent relative under paragraph 317,
(iv) a person exercising rights of access to a child under paragraph 246, or
(v) a spouse, civil partner, unmarried or same-sex partner of a refugee or a person with Humanitarian Protection under paragraphs 352A, 352AA, 352FA or 352FD; or

(b) where the individual was under the age of 18 at the time of his most recent breach of the UK's immigration laws.

In *AA (Nigeria) v SSHD* [2010] EWCA Civ 773 the Court of Appeal held that false representations must be deliberately false rather than accidentally incorrect in order to engage these general grounds. The Entry Clearance Guidance (ECG) was amended as of 4 August 2010 to reflect this change (see ECG RFL05).

Immigration Rule 320(7A) mandates automatic refusal of any entry clearance application where deception is used or there is material non-disclosure, whether knowingly or unknowingly. It operates as an absolute bar to the use of deception in a given application for entry clearance. However, as discussed in more detail further below, it only operates in respect of the instant application, it cannot lawfully be used to refuse on the basis of *previous* use of deception.

Immigration Rule 320(7B) is intended to prevent breaches of immigration law by immigrants currently in the UK by creating a serious immigration sanction against those who do breach immigration laws. It also appears to be intended to punish past breaches of immigration law and is of course retrospective in operation: with certain exceptions, discussed below, it operates even against those who committed the breaches before the rule was proposed or came into force and therefore had no knowledge that their actions might have the consequence of leading to future refusals on this basis.

Where an application for entry clearance has been refused on the basis of rule 320(7A) and use of deception, there will always be a serious risk that any future application will be refused under rule 320(7B) (unless the 320(7C) exemptions apply, of course).

Rule 320(7B) is broken into two parts. The first part lists the proscribed activities that might then engage the second part. The second consists of the various periods of exclusion, which are expressed as being conditional on factors such as voluntary removal at one's own expense.

Immigration Rule 320(7C) was later introduced belatedly to provide for exceptions to the harsh effects of rule 320(7B) primarily in cases of family members. Its scope is discussed further below.

There was also a concession announced in *Hansard* by Immigration Minister Liam Byrne MP and incorporated into the Entry Clearance Guidance that rule 320(7B) will not be applied to any persons present in the UK on 17 March 2008 when the concession was announced and depart from the UK voluntarily and at their own expense before 1 October 2008. Further concessions for those who were children at the time that immigration laws were breached and for trafficking victims were also announced and incorporated into the ECG.

A further set of reasons are given where entry should *normally* be refused but there is a discretion to allow entry:

(8) failure to furnish information/documents required to the Immigration Officer

(9) failure by a returning resident to show that he meets the requirements of the rules

(10) production of passport of a country not recognised by the UK

(11) where the applicant has previously contrived in a significant way to frustrate the intentions of these Rules. Guidance will be published giving examples of circumstances in which an applicant who has previously overstayed, breached a condition attached to his leave, been an Illegal Entrant or used Deception in an application for entry clearance, leave to enter or remain (whether successful or not) is likely to be considered as having contrived in a significant way to frustrate the intentions of these Rules.

(12) [deleted]

(13) failure, except by a person eligible for admission to the United Kingdom for settlement or a spouse or civil partner eligible for admission under paragraph 282, to satisfy the Immigration Officer that he will be admitted to another country after a stay in the United Kingdom

(14) refusal by a sponsor to give an undertaking in writing to be responsible for a person's maintenance and accommodation

(15) making false representations or failure to disclose material facts in the obtaining of a work permit

(16) failure, in the case of a child under the age of 18 years seeking leave to enter the United Kingdom otherwise than in conjunction with an application made by his parent(s) or legal guardian to provide the Immigration Officer, if required to do so, with written consent to the application from his parent(s) or legal guardian; save that the requirement as to written consent does not apply in the case of a child seeking admission to the United Kingdom as an asylum seeker

(17) refusal to undergo a medical examination

(18) other than where there are strong compassionate reasons, convictions of 12 months or more

(19) where exclusion is considered to be conducive to the public good

(20) failure by a person seeking entry into the United Kingdom to comply with a requirement relating to the provision of physical data to which he is subject by regulations made under section 126 of the Nationality, Immigration and Asylum Act 2002

'Contriving to frustrate' is given further definition in the Entry Clearance Guidance. The breach of immigration laws must include 'aggravating features, which are listed non-exhaustively as the following:

- absconding;
- not complying with temporary admission / temporary reporting conditions / bail conditions;
- not complying with reporting restrictions;
- failing to comply with removal directions (RDs) after port refusal of leave to enter (RLE);
- failing to comply with RDs after illegal entry;
- previous working in breach on visitor conditions within short time of arrive in the UK (ie pre-meditated intention to work);
- previous recourse to NHS treatment when not entitled;
- previous receipt of benefits (income, housing, child, incapacity or otherwise) or NASS benefits when not entitled;
- using an assumed identity or multiple identities;
- previous use of a different identity or multiple identities for deceptive reasons;
- vexatious attempts to prevent removal from the UK, eg feigning illness;
- active attempt to frustrate arrest or detention by UK Border Agency or police;
- a sham marriage / marriage of convenience / polygamous marriage in the UK;
- harbouring an immigration offender;
- facilitation / people smuggling;
- escaping from UK Border Agency detention;
- switching of nationality;
- vexatious or frivolous applications;
- not complying with re-documentation process.

It is strongly arguable that several of these factors cannot be reasonably said to be aggravating circumstances, not least because any person who overstays must almost necessarily have committed one of these acts.

Use of deception in current application

- Automatic refusal: Rule 320(7A) or 322(1A)

Past use of deception

- Automatic refusal and 10 year ban in entry clearance cases: Rule 320(7B)
- Rule 320(7C) exceptions apply
- Discretionary refusal in leave to remain cases: Rule 322(2)

Other breaches of immigration law

- Involuntary removal or deportation: 10 year ban
- Voluntary removal at SSHD expense: 5 year ban
- Voluntary departure at own expense: 1 year ban
- Overstaying but departing within 28 days: no ban
- Rule 320(7B) exeptions apply

Contriving to frustrate

- Should normally be refused: Rule 320(11)

> **Top tip**
>
> It is not unusual at the time of writing to see ECOs refuse applications on the basis of rule 320(7A) based on past deception in a previous application. This is based on a misreading of the rule, which clearly refers to the current application.
>
> The correct rule for refusal on the basis of past deception would be rule 320(11). However, the applicant has to have contrived to significantly frustrate the intention of the immigration rules. The burden rests with the ECO to prove this, and it seems clear from the wording of the rule and from the ECG that more than a past breach of immigration laws is required.

A person who holds prior entry clearance can also be refused on the basis that:

- whether or not to the holder's knowledge, false representations were employed or material facts not disclosed for the purpose of obtaining the entry clearance

- circumstances have changed since issue of the entry clearance which has removed the basis of the person's claim to admission

- restricted returnability

Similar provisions apply where a person has entry clearance that is deemed to be leave to enter but the result is that the leave to enter would be cancelled.

Refusal of leave to remain

An application for leave to remain must be refused where it is for a purpose not covered by the rules but may also be refused on the grounds of:

- false representations
- failure to observe a time limit or condition attached to a stay
- failure to maintain and accommodate without recourse to public funds
- undesirability on the grounds of a person's character, conduct or for national security reasons
- refusal by a sponsor to give an undertaking
- non-returnability, failure to produce documents, failure to attend an interview

Curtailment

Rule 323 provides that a person's leave may be curtailed for any one of the same reasons on which leave to remain can be refused and where a person ceases to meet the requirements of the rules on which leave to enter or remain was originally granted, or if a person is a dependant of a person so refused.

Policies and concessions

Finding policies and concessions

Knowledge of policies and concessions is a very important part of an immigration lawyer's arsenal. The immigration rules are a far from complete record of all of the groups of people who will be allowed to remain in the UK either temporarily or in the longer term, and awareness of the different policies and concessions is essential if a practitioner is to represent clients effectively.

There are some important concessions entirely outside the rules and there are also some very important policies that clarify how the rules are to be applied in certain circumstances. Several of these have been touched upon above – for example, the maintenance and accommodation requirements.

The majority of policies and concessions can be located in one or more of several key documents – the various instructions to Home Office caseworkers,

Immigration Officers and Entry Clearance Officers. These instructions are broken down as follows:

- **Asylum Policy Instructions (APIs)**: instructions to UK Border Agency caseworkers and Immigration Officers dealing with asylum cases. For example, includes the procedure to be followed in determining a disputed age assessment.

- **Asylum Process Guidance (APG)**: instructions on different stages of the asylum process, including a section on special cases, which covers children

- **Immigration Directorate Instructions (IDIs)**: includes many policies, sometimes in the annexes, on all matters immigration

- **Entry Clearance Guidance (ECG)**: formerly known as the Diplomatic Service Procedures (DSPs), these comprise instructions to ECOs on how to interpret the Immigration Rules and assess applications

- **Enforcement Guidance and Instructions (EGI)**: formerly known as the Operation Enforcement Manual (EIG), these are instructions to Immigration Officers carrying out removals and other enforcement action. The sections on bail and detention are useful. The chapters of the manual were re-numbered, rendering references to specific chapters in case law obsolete.

- **European Casework Instructions (ECI)**: guidance on assessing EC law applications

- **Nationality Instructions (NIs)**: for nationality applications

All of these documents are available on the internet. The ECG is available via www.ukvisas.gov.uk and the others are available via www.ukba.homeoffice.gov.uk under '*Policy and law*' then '*Guidance and instructions*'. They are very large documents and are frequently altered, so keeping a hard copy is a pointless exercise.

Other policies and concessions are not always published as such and at the time of writing the only way to evidence them is through photocopied pieces of Home Office correspondence with various practitioners. The only effective way to locate these is through back copies of the ILPA mailing, though the ILPA training pack on policies and concessions or in the HJT/ILPA policies and concessions publication.

> **Top tip**
>
> HJT Training has in conjunction with ILPA published a compilation of all Home Office policies stretching back several years, including information on when those policies were current. This policy manual is of considerable assistance to practitioners and their clients, particularly given the line of case law on failure to follow policies.
>
> Contact HJT Training or ILPA to purchase a copy.

ILR families exercise

Announced on 24 October 2003, this one-off exercise was intended to clear a backlog of family cases where the family:

- applied for asylum before 2 October 2000

- includes at least one dependent aged under 18 (other than a spouse) in the UK on 2 October 2000 **OR** 24 October 2003.

The deadline for making oneself known to the Home Office and benefiting from the concession was announced as 31 December 2004 but the UK Border Agency has continued to accept applications after this date.

The following people are disqualified from the concession:

- those with a criminal conviction for a recordable offence

- those who have or have had an anti-social behaviour order or sex offender order against them

- those who have made (or attempted to make) an application for asylum in the UK in more than one identity,

- those who should have their asylum claim considered by another country (i.e. they are the subject of a possible third country removal, but see also section on third country cases below);

- those who present a risk to security;

- those who fall within the scope of Article 1F of the Refugee Convention; or

- those whose presence in the UK is otherwise not conducive to the public good.

Legacy cases

On 25 July 2006, the then Home Secretary John Reid announced that his officials had found around 400,000 to 450,000 unclosed asylum files. These 'unresolved cases' soon came to be known as Legacy Cases to most in the sector, and the Home Office committed itself to 'resolving' these cases by 2011. The exercise is officially referred to as a 'case resolution exercise'.

The UK Border Agency approach has been to determine whether the subject of a case file is still contactable and then seek up to date information about the person using a questionnaire. Failed asylum seekers and others have been discouraged from contacting the UK Border Agency, but it has proven possible to request that a questionnaire is sent to a client.

There have been press reports that the exercise amounts to an amnesty. This is certainly not the case as some clients have been removed from the UK following consideration of their cases. However, there has been a high grant rate, estimated to be around 80%.

Home Office policy is that the following types of case are prioritised:

i. Cases in which the individuals concerned may pose a risk to the public. These will be a top priority.

ii. Cases relating to individuals who are in receipt of public support (formerly through the National Asylum Support Service).

iii. Cases in which it is likely that a decision will be made to grant leave to enter or remain in the UK.

iv. Cases where the individuals can more easily be removed.

Suicide risk cases, cases where an undertaking has been given by UKBA to an MP or in a JR case, cases where the person or a close member of their family requires medical treatment, where the Home Office accept that an error was made, where an initial asylum decision has not been taken, the case is out of line with linked cases (e.g. family members) or an appeal outcome has not been implemented, where the person is vulnerable (e.g. is a minor) or where the person has a seriously ill close relative abroad or wishes to attend a funeral are also given priority .

The UK Border Agency has also stated that exceptional or compassionate circumstances could be cited to seek to secure an early outcome, but there is no clear mechanism for this at present other than simply to write to the UK Border Agency.

Delayed consideration policy

In the case of *R (on the application of S) v SSHD* [2007] EWCA Civ 546 the Court of Appeal held that it was unlawful for the Home Office to have delayed consideration of a person's case in order to meet Public Sector Agreement (PSA) targets for consideration of new cases, thereby depriving that person of a benefit to which he would otherwise have been entitled.

The case was brought be an Afghan who had entered the UK at the same time as his cousin in 1999. His cousin had been granted four years of Exceptional Leave to Remain (ELR), in line with the policy then in existence not to return anyone to Afghanistan. The cousin was then, as was normal, granted ILR after four years.

S himself was not so fortunate. His claim was deliberately delayed by the Home Office as a matter of policy in order to meet PSA targets. By the time a decision was reached on S's case, it was 2004 and there was no longer a policy to grant ELR to Afghans. His application was turned down and he then lost his appeal.

The Court of Appeal decided this was a 'textbook' example of unlawful fettering of discretion. The Home Office had delayed S's case purely to meet Treasury-imposed Public Sector Agreement targets and thereby deprived him of the benefit of a policy to which he would otherwise have been entitled.

In September 2008 the Home Office responded to the judgment by publishing a new policy applying to those who should have qualified for ELR at the time they applied for asylum.

The policy applies to:

i. Anyone from a country which on 1 January 2001 had an ELR policy attached to it (see the policy itself, but that includes Angola, Afghanistan, Burundi, Iraq (not the Kurdish north), Liberia, Rwanda, Sierra Leone and Somalia; and

ii. Who made an asylum claim before the policy was cancelled (different dates for different countries between late 2001 to early 2003); and

iii. Who was refused asylum before the expiry of the ELR policy in question or is now to be refused asylum; and

iv. Who is not to be turned down for committing crimes in the UK or similar.

Any person who was later granted ELR of less than four years and was therefore not eligible for ILR can also apply under the policy.

> **Example**
>
> Justin from Sierra Leone entered the UK in July 2001 and claimed asylum on arrival. At that time there was a policy to grant ELR to people from Sierra Leone. However, the Home Office did not make a decision on Justin's case until 2002, by which time the policy had been withdrawn. He was refused asylum at this time.
>
> On appeal, the adjudicator dismissed Justin's asylum appeal. Justin became 'appeal rights exhausted', in Home Office speak, but remained in the UK.
>
> Justin qualifies under the Home Office policy for implementing *R (S)*.

The list of old ELR policies to which the Home Office policy applies is as follows (in force at 1 January 2001 with end dates):

Angola (non-Luandan claimants only):	31 October 2002
Afghanistan 18th April 2002 Burundi:	7 October 2002
Iraq (Government Controlled Iraq (GCI) claimants only):	20 February 2003
Liberia:	7 October 2002
Rwanda:	27 August 2002
Sierra Leone:	6 September 2001
Somalia:	10 September 2001

Seven-year children concession

This concession used to apply to children with long residence of 7 years or over in the UK. However, it was abolished as of 9 December 2008. The new policy is that human rights will be the determining factor in all cases involving children. Cases already under consideration at the time the policy was scrapped will still be considered under its terms.

For this reason it is useful to set out the terms of the policy, which were follows when announced by Under-Secretary of State for the Home Department Mr O'Brien on 24 February 1999:

> 'Whilst it is important that each individual case must be considered on its merits, there are specific factors which are likely to be of particular relevance when considering whether enforcement action should proceed or be initiated against parents who have children who have lengthy residence in the United Kingdom. For the purposes of proceeding with enforcement action in a case involving a child, the general presumption is that we would not usually proceed with enforcement action in cases where a child was born here and has lived here continuously to the age of seven or over, or where, having come to the United Kingdom at an early age, they have accumulated seven years or more continuous residence. However, there may

> be circumstances in which it is considered that enforcement action is still appropriate despite the lengthy residence of the child, for example in cases where the parents have a particularly poor immigration history and have deliberately seriously delayed consideration of their case. In all cases the following factors are relevant in reaching a judgement on whether enforcement action should proceed:
>
> - the length of the parents' residence without leave; whether removal has been delayed through protracted (and often repetitive) representations or by the parents going to ground;
>
> - the age of the children;
>
> - whether the children were conceived at a time when either of the parents had leave to remain;
>
> - whether return to the parents' country of origin would cause extreme hardship for the children or put their health seriously at risk;
>
> - whether either of the parents has a history of criminal behaviour or deception.
>
> It is important that full reasons are given making clear that each case is considered on its individual merits.'

The policy applied to administrative removals as well as deportations (letter to Afrifa and Partners, 19 April 1999). It was not possible to make a formal application under the concession, however, the 'applicant' had to just wait for consideration. Representations could be made to bring a case to the attention of the immigration authorities, and some practitioners found that making a formal application on a SET(O) will at least trigger a response and lead to a grant of leave.

The scrapping of the policy was the subject of comment by the President in *LD (Article 8 best interests of child) Zimbabwe* [2010] UKUT 278 (IAC):

> 'The policy may have been withdrawn but substantial residence as a child is a strong indication the judicial assessment of what the best interests of the child requires. The UN Convention on the Rights of the Child 1989 Art 3 makes such interests a primary consideration.'

The President goes on in that case to hold that the best interests of a child are a primary consideration in immigration cases.

Duty to safeguard children

Section 55 of the Borders, Citizenship and Immigration Act 2009 introduced a new and more demanding obligation on the Secretary of State, in place of that found in s.21 of the UK Borders Act 2007 (to keep children safe from harm), namely an obligation to make arrangements to ensure that specified functions are discharged having regard to *the need to safeguard and promote the welfare of children* who are in the United Kingdom. In so doing it aligns the duty imposed with that imposed on public authorities under the Children Act 2004, s.11(2).

The duty applies to UKBA and also to those performing immigration functions, broadly defined. It only applies to children present in the UK, although the guidance (see below) encourages officials abroad to act compatibly.

By section 55(3), a person exercising any of the specified functions must, in so exercising them, have regard to any guidance given to the person by the Secretary of State for the purpose specified in BCIA 2009, s 55(1). The statutory guidance *Every Child Matters: Change for Children* was issued in November 2009.

Section 55 is a binding legal obligation rather than a policy, but it is convenient to remind readers of the existence of this duty in this section of the manual, particularly as the duty is enforced primarily by means of various policies. One of these policies, the *Children and Family Process Instruction* for the Criminal Casework Directorate, includes specific procedural safeguards that UKBA caseworkers are supposed to apply in order to ensure that the duty is complied with. For example, section 3.1.2 requires as follows:

> 'In those cases where we do not propose to deport or otherwise remove some family members in the UK (and their nationality is immaterial) the appropriate parties (see section 1.1 [i.e. CAFCASS and social services]) must be consulted for advice on the effect of the split on the child. It is essential that enquiries are made, prior to referral if possible, to ensure that as much background information can be provided with respect to the potential effect of our actions on any children. It is important that staff also consider (and consult) whether there is any effective legal or welfare barrier to the family member(s) accompanying or joining the deportee on a voluntary basis. This will also have the effect of allowing these issues to be considered at any appeal against the deportation decision.'

Other parts of the policy deal with the detention of children and not normally pursuing removal or deportation in cases where there are ongoing family proceedings.

In-country marriage cases outside the Rules: DP3/96

Until its abolition on 24 April 2008, policy DP3/96 governed the Home Office approach to cases where enforcement action (deportation or administrative removal) was being taken against a person who was married to a person settled in the UK. The policy was that removals would not usually be enforced where:

- The person had a genuine and subsisting marriage with someone settled in the UK and the couple had lived together in the UK continuously since their marriage for at least two years before commencement of enforcement action; AND

- It was unreasonable to expect the settled spouse to accompany his/her spouse on removal.

Further clarification is available in the EGI at chapter 53, section 3 and various letters since the introduction of the policy, available in the ILPA mailings. See also the case of *BP (DP3/96 – Unmarried Partners) Macedonia* [2008] UKAIT 00045.

Chapter 53 of the EIG also make provision for similar treatment of unmarried partners. In the case of *BP*, above, the tribunal held that this policy was essentially identical to DP3/96 even though it was less well known. Shortly after that determination was publicised, both policies were abolished.

However, the transitional arrangements are important as many cases were already being considered under DP3/96 at the time of abolition. The EIG state that where a case was already being considered under the relationship policies, those policies would still be applied.

Delay in asylum cases

In the summer of 2009 the Home Office amended Chapter 53 of the Enforcement Guidance and Instructions in order to attach more weight to length of residence in the UK and delay by the Home Office when considering whether to enforce removal of failed asylum seekers.

The relevant passages are at 53.1.2 in the section dealing with Immigration Rule 395C. The most pertinent parts suggest caseworkers place weight on significant delay in cases including:

> - 'Family' cases where delay by UKBA has contributed to a significant period of residence (for the purposes of this guidance, 'family' cases means parent as defined in the Immigration Rules and children who are emotionally and financially dependent on the parent, and under the age of 18 at the date of the decision). Following an individual assessment of the prospect of enforcing removal, and where other relevant factors apply, a 3 year period of residence may be considered significant, but a more usual example would be 4-6 years. Family units may be also be exceptionally considered where the dependent child has experienced a delay of 4-6 years whilst under the age of 18.
>
> - Any other case where delay by UKBA has contributed to a significant period of residence, Following an individual assessment of the prospect of enforcing removal, and where other relevant factors apply, 4-6 years may be considered significant, but a more usual example would be a period of residence of 6-8 years.

Many practitioners have found that the Home Office has been acting more generously since the policy was amended.

Age and enforcement action

It was previously the case that enforcement action (i.e. removal or deportation) would not be pursued against the over-65s. That policy was changed in late 2004 and replaced with EPU10/04, which includes the following explanation of the new approach:

> 'Ministers have agreed that a persons age is not by itself, a realistic or reliable indicator of a person's health, mobility or ability to care for themselves. Many older people are able to enjoy active and independent lives. Cases must be assessed on their individual merits.
>
> Age is just one of several factors to be taken into account when considering a person's enforced removal from the United Kingdom. Other factors include length of residence in the UK strength of connections, domestic and other compassionate circumstances.
>
> The onus is on the applicant to show that there are extenuating circumstances, such as particularly poor health, close dependency on family members in the UK coupled with a lack of family and care facilities in the country of origin, which might warrant a grant of leave.'

This text is available on the UKBA website.

Elderly dependent relatives

The IDIs state at c.8, s.6, para. 3 that in in-country cases, 'where the applicant is over the age of 65 detailed enquiries will not be necessary.' The exact meaning of this passage is unclear, but it appears to confirm the earlier policy that any elderly dependent relative in the UK who is over the age of 65 (not just those referred to at r.317 of the Rules) should normally be granted settlement, providing the sponsor is settled and the sponsor signs a sponsorship undertaking. See Home Office policy letter dated January 1994 and letter to Bindmans dated 12 August 1997 (ILPA mailing).

Carers policy

There is a policy which is published at Chapter 17, section 2 of the IDIs relating to carers and this states, *inter alia*, that:

> 'Applications from persons here in a temporary capacity seeking leave to remain to care for a sick relative or friend who is suffering from a terminal illness, such as cancer or AIDS, or who is mentally or physically disabled fall to be treated under the Secretary of State's discretion outside the Immigration Rules. All such applications should be considered on the individual merits of the case. Where there are sufficient compassionate circumstances to warrant the grant of leave to remain it should be made clear to the applicant that it is only a temporary capacity and that once alternative arrangements have been made or if the patient should die then the 'carer' will be expected to return home.
>
> An extension of stay on this basis will not normally lead to settlement.'

The policy on carers suggests that 3 months leave to remain will be granted initially, with further periods of 12 months to follow in exceptional cases subject to favourable medical and welfare reports. There is also a duty on the Home Office to make enquiries as to the provision of satisfactory care for the person receiving care in the event of removal of the carer.

Family proceedings

In the case of *MS (Ivory Coast) v SSHD* [2007] EWCA Civ 133 it emerged that the Home Office has a policy whereby removal or deportation action will not pursued where family proceedings are pending. The facts of that case were somewhat unsympathetic: a mother had commenced family proceedings and it was very far from clear that she would succeed in her application for contact given her conviction for abuse of her own children, her mental health difficulties and the time that had elapsed since her last contact.

This policy is reflected in an internal Criminal Casework Directorate document entitled Children and Family Process Instruction. The policy is of assistance in children cases and also states at section 7 that removal or deportation will not normally be pursued where there are ongoing family proceedings.

Children in the care of a Local Authority

Part 8 of Annex M to Chapter 8 of the Home Office's Immigration Directorate Instructions:

> **Children in care**
>
> Decisions about the future of children in the care of the local authority should be left primarily in the hands of their social services department as they will be best placed to act in the child's best interests.
>
> While the local authority may look into the possibility of arranging the repatriation of a child in their care, such action will only be taken if it is in the child's best interests. Where they consider it may be in the child's best interests to be repatriated, they will normally make full enquiries to ensure that suitable arrangements are made for the child's care and to satisfy themselves that repatriation is indeed in the child's best interests. We should ask to be kept informed of developments.
>
> If the social services advise that it would be appropriate for the child to remain in the United Kingdom, consideration should be given to granting the child leave to remain.
>
> If there is a realistic possibility of the child returning to his parent(s) and/or country of origin in the future, the child may be granted limited leave for periods of 12 months on Code 1. Where there is no prospect of the child leaving, the child may be granted leave to remain for 4 years on Code 1. In both cases, after 4 years of limited leave to remain, if there is no prospect of removal, indefinite leave to remain may be granted.

Iraqi *Rashid* type cases

In the related cases of *SSHD v R (on the app. of Rashid)* [2005] EWCA Civ 744 and *R (on the app. of A, H and AH) v SSHD* [2006] EWHC 526 (Admin) the Home Office was found to have committed an abuse of process by failing to apply its own policy of recognising as refugees Iraqi Kurds from the non-Kurdish area of Iraq, i.e. the bulk of the country controlled by the Iraqi government of President Saddam Hussein prior to March 2003. The courts held that it was appropriate in the circumstances that the victims of this abuse of process be compensated by being granted ILR, even though there was now no direct threat of persecution in Iraq and no need for international protection.

On 1 August 2006, belatedly responding to the judgments in *Rashid* and *A, H and AH,* the Home Office issued a policy bulletin governing the circumstances where an Iraqi applicant for asylum meeting the following sets of criteria will be granted ILR.

In situation 1, a 'pure' *Rashid* case, the case would need to:

(a) have been decided by the Secretary of State, or held on appeal (at the date of appeal hearing), between April 1991 and 20 March 2003 (when the policy of not advancing internal relocation to the former Kurdish Autonomous Zone (KAZ) as a reason for refusing asylum was in operation), and

(b) involve a claimant from the part of Iraq formerly controlled by Saddam Hussein who was accepted by the Secretary of State, or on appeal, to have a well founded fear of persecution in that area at the date of decision, and

(c) have been refused asylum and/or ELR, by UKBA or dismissed on appeal, on the basis that the appellant could internally relocate to the KAZ.

Situation 2, because of a related case called *Magdeed* [2002] UKIAT 03631, would be where:

(a) a first decision had been made, or held on appeal (at the date of appeal hearing), between 23 October 2002 and 20 February 2003, and

(b) it was accepted that the claimant had a well founded fear of persecution, but was refused asylum and/or ELR, by UKBA or dismissed on appeal, on the basis of internal flight from a PUK territory to a KDP territory (or vice versa) within the KAZ.

In situation 3, because of the *A, H and AH* case, the case would need to:

(a) have been an Iraqi asylum claim, from any area of Iraq, refused by the Secretary of State between April 1991 and 20 October 2000 (when the practice was to grant 4 years' ELR to all Iraqis who had been unable to establish a valid claim under the refugee convention), and

(b) have not been granted 4 years' ELR

Situation 4 is an alternative to situation 3 and is also an *A, H and AH* case, where the case would need to:

(a) have been from the government controlled area of Iraq (GCI) and refused by the Secretary of State between April 1991 and 20 February 2003 (when the practice was to grant 4 years' ELR to claimants from GCI), and

(b) have not been granted 4 years' ELR

The policy bulletin is not necessarily a definitive exposition of all the circumstances in which an Iraqi asylum claimant might benefit retrospectively from the abuse of process that was revealed in *Rashid*.

Legitimate expectation

There have been a number of cases involving a claim of legitimate expectation by an immigrant. Typically, the Home Office has changed the law or rules in a way that is disadvantageous to the immigrant even though the immigrant had reasons to believe such a change would not take place and suffered real prejudice as a result.

One such case, *R (on the application of Bapio Action Ltd) v SSHD* [2008] UKHL 27, reached the House of Lords. The case was brought by Bapio Action Ltd, a company formed by the British Association of Physicians of Indian Origin to represent the interests of junior overseas doctors who had been lured to the UK by promises of a career here but after arrival were being deprived of an opportunity to apply for jobs.

The judgments differ considerably in their reasoning. Lord Bingham held that the email that effectively made the change sent out by a Home Office official was an unlawful exercise of the power to regulate immigration status that can only be exercised by the Secretary of State (and is rather critical of the attempt to affect so many lives by such informal, ill-considered means). Lord Carswell agreed with him, more or less. Lord Mance disagrees and decides that the email did not directly affect immigration status, but that the email was a breach of legitimate expectation. Lord Rodger agrees with Lord Mance. Lord Scott disagrees with all of them and allows the Home Office appeal. The result is therefore clear in that the application was allowed, but there is no majority reasoning as such.

Similarly, in *R (on the application of HSMP Forum Ltd) v SSHD* [2008] EWHC 664 (Admin) Mr Justice Bean held that a promise was made to those that were enticed to enter the UK under the HSMP scheme and leave behind them their jobs in order to make new lives for themselves and their families in the UK. The promise was that the rules under which they entered the UK would be the rules under which their settlement applications would be decided in four years' time. In fact, the Home Office tightened up the rules considerably, preventing many from qualifying for settlement. The court held that there was a legitimate expectation on the part of the migrants.

Policies, concessions and the law

The Home Office cannot operate a policy that is stricter than the Immigration Rules. They can however operate policies that are more generous than the

Rules or to cover situations not dealt with under the Rules. Where an ECO or the Home Office fail to act on a policy, there may be remedies available, even though the policy or concession is not the law as such, as it neither primary nor secondary legislation.

Judicial review

Where it can be established that the Home Office has acted contrary to a policy, the decision may be amenable to judicial review on the basis of breach of legitimate expectation or even abuse of process by the Home Office. Judicial review applications are made to a High Court judge in the Administrative Court, and the judge has the power to quash a decision of the Home Office.

Usually, this remedy will only be able to achieve proper consideration by the Secretary of State under a policy – the nature of policies and concessions are that they are discretionary, and unless they are expressed in absolute terms the courts will not force the Secretary of State to make a particular discretionary choice.

Judicial review cannot be pursued where there is an alternative remedy, such as an appeal to the immigration tribunal. However, appeal rights are limited, particularly by s.82 of the 2002 Act and the restricted definition of an 'immigration decision', so it may be the case that JR is the only available remedy.

The immigration tribunal

There are two ways in which enforcement of a policy or concession might be pursued within an immigration tribunal appeal. The tribunal case of *AG and others (Policies; executive discretions; Tribunal's powers) Kosovo* [2007] UKAIT 00082 examines both of these options.

Not in accordance with the law

Where a client has a right to an appeal to the immigration tribunal, it can be argued that a decision is *"not in accordance with the law"* where it can be shown that an appellant has been wrongly denied the benefit of a Home Office policy due to, for example, a misapprehension of the facts of the case (e.g. *Abdi v SSHD* [1996] Imm AR 148) or abuse of process (e.g. in *Rashid* and *A, H and AH*, above). It was thought that the immigration tribunal could not force the Secretary of State to make a particular choice but could intervene to force him to consider the case within the terms of the policy in question – and also make factual finding that would in effect bind the hands of the Secretary of State and force him to act in a certain way. However, the case of *Fouzia Baig v SSHD* [2005] EWCA Civ 1246 suggests that the immigration tribunal can go beyond this constraint and actually allow an appeal outright on the basis of failure to follow a policy. *AG* (above) agrees that this is the case, but only where the policy in question does not involve the exercise of discretion on the part of the SSHD; where the claimant clearly falls under a policy and that policy is quite clear in demanding that leave be granted, the immigration tribunal may follow this course.

The Nationality, Immigration and Asylum Act 2002 made it difficult to appeal against decisions on applications made *outside the Rules* (see s.88). The 2002 Act means that it should not be possible to appeal an application made for a purpose outside the Rules, but there may still be scope in appeals against applications that would have to be refused on the basis of the Immigration Rules but which were nevertheless for a purpose covered by the Rules to ask adjudicators to make factual findings and allow the appeal on the basis that the decision was not in accordance with the law.

Article 8 ECHR

As discussed in the Chapter on human rights, where an immigrant falls within the scope of a policy, a decision to expel them from, or refuse to admit them to, the United Kingdom, is likely to be disproportionate.

Chapter 3: International Protection

REFUGEE LAW AND HUMANITARIAN PROTECTION 103

THE REFUGEE CONVENTION 103

WELL FOUNDED FEAR 105

    STANDARD OF PROOF 105
    CREDIBILITY 106
        Qualification Directive 106
        Asylum and Immigration (Treatment of Claimants etc) Act 2004 107
        Inconsistencies 109
        Plausibility 111
        Dishonesty 113
        Demeanour 113
    FUTURE RISK 113
        Country information 114
        Relevance of past experiences to future risk 116
        Specific individual risk 116
        Generic risk cases 117
        Activities in the United Kingdom and claims made in bad faith 118
        Future activities 119

BEING PERSECUTED 121

    ACTORS OF PERSECUTION 121
    ACTS OF PERSECUTION 122
    HUMAN RIGHTS ANALYSIS 123
    SUBJECTIVE NATURE OF BEING PERSECUTED 124
    ROLE OF CONVENTION REASONS 125
        Prosecution and persecution 126
        Military service 127
        Civil war 128

THE CONVENTION REASONS 129

    RACE 130
    RELIGION 130
    NATIONALITY 130
    MEMBERSHIP OF A PARTICULAR SOCIAL GROUP 130
    POLITICAL OPINION 132
    ATTRIBUTED CONVENTION REASONS 132

PROTECTION AND RELOCATION 133

    PROTECTION FROM NON-STATE PERSECUTION 133
    INTERNAL RELOCATION 135

NON REFOULEMENT 138

CESSATION CLAUSES 138

EXCLUSION CLAUSES ... 140
ARTICLE 1(D) ... 140
ARTICLE 1(F) ... 140
Nexus to acts falling within Article 1F ... 141
Evidence ... 143
Relevance and definition of terrorist acts ... 143
ARTICLE 33(2) ... 144

HUMANITARIAN PROTECTION ... 145
SERIOUS HARM ... 146
ARTICLE 15(C) ... 147
"Conflict" ... 148
Standard of Proof ... 148
"Indiscriminate violence" ... 148
"Life or Person" ... 149
The critical question ... 149

Refugee Law and Humanitarian Protection

Because both refugee status and Humanitarian Protection now have their foundation in European Community law, and give rights of family reunion and travel document to asylum seekers beyond the simple entitlement not to be removed, we address them both in this chapter.

The Refugee Convention

The fundamental provision of the UN Convention on the Status of Refugees (read with the 1967 New York Protocol to which most states sign up), usually referred to as the Refugee Convention, is Article 1(A)(2). A refugee is defined as a person who:

> "Owing to well-founded fear of being persecuted for reasons of race, religion, nationality, membership of a particular social group or political opinion is outside the country of his nationality and is unable or owing to such fear, is unwilling to avail himself of the protection of that country; or who, not having a nationality and being outside the country of his former habitual residence is unable or, owing to such fear, unwilling to return to it."

This paragraph deals with the situation of the persons with a nationality in its first sentence, then, after the semi-colon, with the situation of people without a nationality (the "stateless"). The courts have interpreted the requirements of the definition to be the same in both categories of case.

The definition can be broken into its constituent parts:

1. Possession of a well-founded fear
2. Of treatment that amounts to being persecuted
3. For one of five reasons, referred to as the Convention reasons
4. Being outside one's country
5. Being unable or unwilling to obtain protection

The Refugee Convention has existed for over fifty years and inevitably there are various authorities that provide guides to the meaning and construction of the Convention.

EC Council Directive 2004/83/EC of 29 April 2004 on minimum standards for the qualification and status of third country nationals or stateless persons as refugees or as persons who otherwise need international protection and the content of the protection granted is one of the most important of these guides to Refugee Convention construction. This is usually referred to for reasons of convenience as the Qualification Directive as it sets out definitions for who qualifies for protection. It has been transposed into UK law through The Refugee or Person in Need of International Protection (Qualification) Regulations 2006 and modifications to the asylum section of the immigration rules at part 11.

The *Handbook on Procedures and Criteria for Determining Refugee Status*, published by UNHCR in 1978 in Geneva, is a fundamental text for any practitioner, particularly in the paragraphs (193 onwards) where it concentrates on the processes for determination of the facts of the case.

UNHCR also give other guidance beyond the UNHCR Handbook, in terms of occasional statements on best practice (there has been an influential one on detention, for example); they also intervene in cases occasionally, although these days they are increasingly doing so via legal interventions in test cases rather than assisting with country information. Their online facility Refworld is a very impressive and useful database of national and international legal authority relevant to refugee law.

The Preamble to the Convention is a useful reminder that the Convention is related to other international legal materials such as other human rights instruments (e.g. the Universal Declaration of Human Rights, the International Covenant of Civil and Political Rights).

Judicial decisions from the Immigration and Asylum Chamber of the Upper Tribunal (and its predecessors), the Court of Appeal and the House of Lords provide additional guidance. Because the Convention is international in nature, it is also possible to look further afield. The highest courts of Canada, America, New Zealand and Australia, and the works of legal scholars, have often cast light upon the proper approach to the Convention. In the future the inspiration may come from European Community law principles, and from academic writers who address the law of international protection of that legal area.

Top tip

HJT strongly recommends reading the following ILPA best practice guides, which are essentially asylum skills guides. They are written by skilled, experienced practitioners who have distilled their learning into readable and accessible form. Aspiring practitioners would be mugs to pass by the opportunity to learn from them! Contact ILPA for details.

Best practice guide to asylum and human rights appeals, Mark Henderson (2003). The second edition was published in 2003 but an updated version has been made available electronically via the Electronic Immigration Network

Making an asylum application: a best practice guide, Jane Coker, Garry Kelly, Martin Soorjoo (2002)

Well founded fear

There are two key aspects to the possession of a well founded fear. The first is truthfulness or credibility: is an asylum claimant telling the truth about what happened to him or her in the past? If not, it is unlikely that the claimant really has a well founded fear, unless they are a member of a class of persons who are all at risk (as has been accepted in the past regarding members of Somali minority clans, who might succeed in showing an entitlement to refugee status because of discrimination and human rights abuses visited on their clan as a whole, notwithstanding the rejection of their own account of the problems that happened to them in particular; or regarding returns to a particular country of origin, because of the view taken by the authorities there of asylum seekers regarding from abroad in general or the UK in particular, as has been found, temporarily at least, regarding countries such as Sudan and Zimbabwe in the past).

The second aspect is future risk. The claimant might fear return, but is that fear well founded in the sense of there being a sufficient likelihood of those fears being realised?

So these are the two key questions in status determination, although they can be broken down further:

Historic fact

- Standard of proof
- Credibility
- Plausibility

Future risk

- Country information
- Past persecution
- Specific or general risk
- Activities in the United Kingdom
- Future behaviour

Standard of proof

The standard of proof for both aspects of well founded fear is that of 'a reasonable degree of likelihood', which is lower than the civil standard of the balance of probabilities and is sometimes expressed as 'substantial grounds for believing' or 'real risk'. The leading case is *Ravichandran* [1996] Imm AR 97.

This was further elaborated on by the Court of Appeal in an important and often misunderstood case, *Karanakaran* [2000] Imm AR 271. Effectively, the Court of

Appeal found that the concept of a legal standard of proof akin to the balance of probabilities, where probabilities are artificially elevated to certainties once a threshold is crossed, is redundant in asylum cases. Instead, a decision-maker should simply evaluate the risk on the basis of relevant evidence. The Court held that the first three of the following four categories of evidence identified by a decision maker are relevant for this purpose:

(i) evidence they are certain about

(ii) evidence they think is probably true

(iii) evidence to which they are willing to attach some credence, even if they could not go so far as to say it is probably true

(iv) evidence to which they are not willing to attach any credence at all.

See also the comments of Brooke LJ in *Karanakaran*:

> "... when considering whether there is a serious possibility of persecution for a Convention reason if an asylum seeker is returned, it would be quite wrong to exclude matters totally from consideration in the balancing process simply because the decision-maker believes, on what may sometimes be somewhat fragile evidence, that they probably did not occur."

The requirement to give the benefit of the doubt applies only where the account is generally credible (UNHCR Handbook paras 196, 204 and the Qualification Directive at Art.4(5)). The low standard of proof operates for the benefit of asylum seekers, and should never be employed to their detriment. Thus it is unacceptable to make a finding based on the chance that an alternative explanation for certain matters to that put forward by the applicant is 'reasonably likely'.

Credibility

The assessment of past facts in asylum cases is a complex process. There are several statutory provisions that have an impact on the assessment of credibility and there are also many cases and other forms of guidance.

Qualification Directive

Due to the Qualification Directive, the immigration rules now include at paragraph 339L the following guidance for decision-makers in assessing credibility:

> 339L. It is the duty of the person to substantiate the asylum claim or establish that he is a person eligible humanitarian protection or substantiate his human rights claim. Where aspects of the person's statements are not supported by documentary or other evidence, those aspects will not need confirmation when all of the following conditions are met:

> (i) the person has made a genuine effort to substantiate his asylum claim or establish that he is a person eligible humanitarian protection or substantiate his human rights claim;
> (ii) all material factors at the person's disposal have been submitted, and a satisfactory explanation regarding any lack of other relevant material has been given;
> (iii) the person's statements are found to be coherent and plausible and do not run counter to available specific and general information relevant to the person's case;
> (iv) the person has made an asylum claim or sought to establish that he is a person eligible for humanitarian protection or made a human rights claim at the earliest possible time, unless the person can demonstrate good reason for not having done so; and
> (v) the general credibility of the person has been established.

This should be the starting point for the assessment of credibility. The rider that the applicant must be generally credible enables decision makers to attach appropriate weight to inconsistencies and other credibility issues, but this paragraph provides a useful reminder that corroborating evidence is not required and that the benefit of the doubt should be given. It also strongly suggests that where attempts have been made to substantiate a claim these should be explained to the decision maker.

Example

Irene was a journalist in Zimbabwe writing under a pseudonym. She cannot easily prove that it was she who wrote the articles in question, nor is it easy for her to obtain copies of the articles from Zimbabwe.

To an extent, she can address this is a witness statement and explain everything she remembers about the articles she wrote and the process of getting them published. However, her case would be much stronger if she could obtain copies of the articles or something that links her to the pseudonym she used, such as a letter from the publisher.

Failing that, most immigration judges would view her case more sympathetically if she could at least demonstrate that she has tried very hard to obtain the relevant evidence and show copies of letters written, calls made and so on, and explain in her statement what steps she has taken to try to obtain the evidence. This would distinguish her case from someone who makes a claim but makes no attempt to substantiate it, at least as far as the judge can see. Rules 339L(i) and (ii) lend support to this approach.

Asylum and Immigration (Treatment of Claimants etc) Act 2004

Section 8 of the 2004 Act introduces a mandatory requirement that forms of 'behaviour' be considered as damaging credibility by decision makers, including the immigration tribunal: various forms of overt dishonesty, reliance on false documents, destruction of documents, claiming asylum after receiving an immigration decision or after arrest, and not claiming asylum despite having had a reasonable opportunity to do so in a "safe" third country (although safe third country is given a specific meaning later in the section).

A number of criticisms have been made of what many consider to be a crass attempt to impose un-evidenced assumptions about the norms of refugee behaviour. The judiciary has proven jealous of its role in assessing credibility and in *SM (Section 8: Judge's process) Iran* [2005] UKAIT 00116 the Asylum and Immigration Tribunal found that even where section 8 applies, the tribunal should look at the evidence as a whole and decide which parts are more important and which less and that section 8 does not require the behaviour to which it applies to be treated as the starting-point of the assessment of credibility.

The legally controversial principle has been the subject of significant criticism by some Court of Appeal judges granting permission to appeal. Thus in *ST (Libya) v Secretary of State for the Home Department* [2007] EWCA Civ 24 (12 January 2007) Sedley LJ thought there should at least be some link between, for example, a failure to claim asylum in a safe third country and the substantive case for asylum before an adverse inference could be drawn. And it probably runs foul of the seventh tenet of the rule of law as set out in the lecture by The Rt. Hon Lord Bingham of Cornhill KG (16th November 2006; the Centre for Public Law), *The Rule of Law*: "First and foremost, I suggest, that decisions are made by adjudicators who, however described, are independent and impartial: independent in the sense that they are free to decide on the legal and factual merits of a case as they see it, free of any extraneous influence or pressure, and impartial in the sense that they are, so far as humanly possible, open-minded, unbiased by any personal interest or partisan allegiance of any kind."

Nevertheless, the types of behaviour falling within section 8 should as far as possible be addressed in individual claims.

Failure to Claim Asylum in a Safe Third Country

Regarding the safe country assumption, first of all check that the any countries through which the claimant has passed are actually defined as safe in section 8(7) itself, i.e. whether they are countries listed at Part 2 of Schedule 3 of the 2004 Act. Even if the country concerned is on this list, there is no principle in international law to the effect that an asylum seeker should seek asylum in the first available country they pass through, though the authors of Home Office decision letters often speak as if there was one. That they are incorrect is shown by the decision of the Divisional Court in *R v Uxbridge Magistrates Court ex parte Adimi, & Ors* [1999] Imm AR 560:

> "... I am persuaded by the applicants' contrary submission, drawing as it does on the travaux préparatoires, various Conclusions adopted by UNHCR's Executive Committee ('ExCom'), and the writings of well-respected academics and commentators (most notably Professor Guy Goodwin-Gill, Atle Grahl-Madsen, Professor James Hathaway, & Dr Paul Weis), that some element of choice is indeed open to refugees as to where they may properly claim asylum."

However, an explanation should always be sought as to a failure to claim asylum abroad, particularly if there has been a lengthy stay in a country. A desire to join relatives in the UK, or a pre-arranged journey with only transit stops abroad, might be possible explanations; as might an ability to speak English, so might conditions in the third country (e.g. colonial or diplomatic relationships with the asylum seeker's country of origin might encourage or discourage an asylum claim).

Regarding delays in claiming asylum, much depends on the individual circumstances. Many asylum seekers who attempt to enter the country before making their claims will do so for the good reasons laid out by agencies such as the UNHCR, e.g. the effects of trauma, language problems, lack of information, previous experiences with authority and feelings of insecurity, rather than with a view to falsifying their claims with the assistance of contacts in this country – see Simon Brown LJ in *R v Uxbridge Magistrates Court, ex p Adimi* [1999] Imm AR 560.

Entering the Country

The capacity in which a person enters the country ought not to carry decisive weight in the analysis of their claim to need international protection. Someone might claim asylum having entered as a visitor: the UNHCR has warned that this will often arise out of an understandable desire to secure some form of temporary stay in a country, to avoid simply being returned home from the border.

Simon Brown stated in *Adimi* "Most asylum seekers who attempt to enter the country before making their claims will do so for the reasons suggested by UNHCR rather than with a view to falsifying their claims with the assistance of friends and contacts here."

Inconsistencies

Although there are lots of possible explanations for discrepancies, inconsistencies can properly found a finding of a lack of credibility. For this reason one of the practitioner's most important functions is taking full and accurate instructions, in order to avoid matters which seem like discrepancies appearing in the account.

Best practice, if not necessarily the settled law, would have it that the tribunal should put discrepancies to an applicant. Equally they should indicate any other element of the account with which they are dissatisfied, to give an opportunity in natural justice for an explanation to be given.

One area in which reliance upon inconsistencies to found a finding that an asylum seeker's account lacks credibility will be particularly objectionable will be where the individual is giving an account of traumatic past events: *Jakitay* (12658; 15 November 1995). On an appeal in a case where a lack of self-confidence in relating traumatic factors is present, you might wish to advise your client to give evidence in private. The specialist international Tribunal regarding torture, the United Nations Committee against Torture (UNCAT), has warned that complete accuracy is seldom to be expected from victims of torture: *Alan v Switzerland* (UNCAT) [1997] INLR 29.

> **Top tip**
>
> There is no such thing as perfect recall and no human being is capable of giving a completely consistent account of the same events on different occasions. The reasons for this lie in the way that memories are made.
>
> Firstly memories must be **recorded**. Bystanders to the same events always perceive the same events differently and attach significance to different aspects of those events. The human brain searches for patterns and where information is absent (or even where it is present sometimes) the brain completes the 'picture' by filling in blanks.
>
> Secondly, memories must be **stored**. Sometimes memories are simply lost or partially lost and blanks filled in. Minor aspects of events, such as sensations, may be recalled long after the event even though major events are forgotten. The passage of time generally degrades memories.
>
> Thirdly, memories must then be **recalled and recounted**. There is ample opportunity for memories to be recalled differently on different occasions. For example, the use of leading questions will often change the way that memories are recalled, particularly in children.
>
> Despite this, the fact is that in many asylum cases the only evidence is the witness' own testimony. If it is perceived as flawed, it will be rejected.

Due allowance must be made for the different stages of the asylum process, and the various ways in which information is elicited - the nature of the process is such that a single perfectly consistent telling of the story is unlikely. Whilst the Tribunal has agreed that inconsistencies between accounts given at different times can properly be referred to for the purpose of assessing credibility, 'adjudicators should always bear in mind the circumstances in which these interviews take place and the, often, somewhat amateurish nature of the questioning techniques'.

> **Top tip**
>
> Not all additional information is necessarily inconsistent with an earlier account. It is the very nature of the process that further questions are asked later on about an account that has already been given. Indeed, this is the whole purpose of a Home Office asylum interview. It would be truly absurd, then, to say that the provision of additional information is an elaboration of an account that is in some way not credible.
>
> However, providing additional information is not the same as making changes to an account or adding new events, which are likely to cause significant credibility issues.

Failure to read back the contents of the interview to its subject may make it a very unreliable basis for criticising an account, though see *DA (Unsigned interview notes) Turkey* [2004] UKIAT 00104 (14 May 2004) for the fact that an objection to an interview's conduct plus a mere failure to sign does not of itself mean an interview should be disregarded without analysing the circumstances of that interview. Contemporaneous complaints about unsatisfactory interviews will be more telling than late challenges at appeal. The screening interview is not intended to be a vehicle for exploring the substance of the asylum claim.

Some claimants fail to satisfy the Secretary of State or an immigration judge of the truth of their account because they cannot provide adequate detail to the decision maker. Others may be unable to meet the burden not because their accounts are false, but because they simply do not possess the relevant detail, or because their level of their education deprives them of the opportunity to convey the story in the requisite structured and measured fashion. Vagueness should always be identified, though, see *B (DR Congo)* [2003] UKIAT 00012 (12 June 2003).

Plausibility

A person who advances an account which falls outside the realms of possibility is unlikely to be able to establish themselves as a refugee. However, when judging questions of plausibility, the particular nature of the asylum seeker's evidence must be taken into account, and it must be adjudicated upon by the standards of the country of origin. As the Tribunal wrote in *Suleyman* (16242; 11 February 1998):

> 'It is clear to us that a repressive regime ... may well act in ways which defy logical analysis. A person who is genuinely a victim of such a regime may well find that the partial account he is able to give of its activities as they have affected him is not something which will stand up to a strictly logical analysis. The regime may seem to govern by confusion; it may engage in other activities, of which the Appellant knows

> nothing; it may simply behave in a way which a person sitting in safety in the United Kingdom might regard as almost beyond belief'.

Country information and understanding of the conditions and culture in a given country is absolutely crucial when assessing plausibility. There are many quotations from case law to this effect, but one of the most frequently cited is from *Horvath* [1999] INLR 7:

> 'One cannot assess a claim without placing that claim into the context of the background information of the country of origin. In other words, the probative value of the evidence must be evaluated in the light of what is known about the conditions in the claimant's country of origin.'

Unfortunately the message that plausibility must be assessed through the prism of country information (and expert evidence) and not based on the life experiences of the immigration judge has not been taken on board by all immigration judges. In the case of *HK v SSHD* [2006] EWCA Civ 1037 the Court of Appeal was critical of the tribunal's approach to expert evidence and to the issue of plausibility and Neuberger LJ held as follows at paragraph 29:

> 'Inherent probability, which may be helpful in many domestic cases, can be a dangerous, even a wholly inappropriate, factor to rely on in some asylum cases. Much of the evidence will be referable to societies with customs and circumstances which are very different from those of which the members of the fact-finding tribunal have any (even second-hand) experience. Indeed, it is likely that the country which an asylum-seeker has left will be suffering from the sort of problems and dislocations with which the overwhelming majority of residents of this country will be wholly unfamiliar.'

Chadwick LJ agreed:

> 'On analysis of the tribunal's reasoning, I am unable to avoid the conclusion that the applicant's account has been rejected simply because the facts that he describes are so unusual as to be thought unbelievable. But, as Lord Justice Neuberger has pointed out, that is not a safe basis upon which to reject the existence of facts which are said to have occurred within an environment and culture which is so wholly outside the experience of the decision maker as that in the present case. There is simply no yardstick against which the decision maker can test whether the facts are inherently incredible or not. The tribunal's failure to confront that problem must lead to the conclusion that they erred in law.'

The application of tests of likelihood based upon any form of presumption as to how a "reasonable man" would act is particularly unreliable in the refugee context. See Bingham MR in (1985) 38 Current Legal Problems 14 cited as relevant in this area of law in *Kasolo* (13190; 1 April 1996):

> 'No judge worth his salt could possibly assume that men of different nationalities, educations, trades, experience, creeds and temperaments would act how he might think he would have done or even – which may be quite different – in accordance with his concept of what a reasonable man would have done.'

As has been pointed out by both the Court of Appeal subsequently (*Y v SSHD* [2006] EWCA Civ 1223) and the tribunal, this does not mean that an account must be accepted at face value nor that the decision maker must suspect their own judgment entirely.

Dishonesty

Proven, or admitted, dishonesty counts against any person who seeks to demonstrate their story's truthfulness, but a lack of veracity on one issue does not necessarily disprove the remainder of the account. Any acts of dishonesty must be specifically explained (for example entering the country on false documents). The core of an account may be credible even though some elements are not made out - *Chiver* (10758; 24 March 1994). Though see *K (DR Congo)* [2003] UKIAT 00014 (23 June 2003) for the fact that an account may be found lacking in credibility notwithstanding discrepancies only being found in peripheral details.

Demeanour

An immigration judge who hears oral evidence from an asylum seeker will have the opportunity to assess their demeanour. If such is to be relied upon, then caution should be exercised, for cultural reasons: *Kasolo* (13190); *B (DR Congo)* [2003] UKIAT 00012 (12 June 2003). Whatever the role given to demeanour, it would be wrong to presume that a witness would necessarily give evidence in a particular emotional state: see the Tribunal in *M (Yugoslavia)* [2003] UKIAT 00004 (29 May 2003):

> 'Given the adjudicator's apparent awareness of the medical evidence that the appellant suffered from Post Traumatic Stress Disorder one of whose symptoms is emotional numbness, we do not think the adjudicator was justified in counting against the appellant at paragraph 26 his failure at the hearing to "show emotional distress when the traumatic events were raised...'

Future risk

The asylum applicant must demonstrate that there is a serious possibility of the events which he fears actually occurring. Thus Lord Keith in *Sivakumaran* [1988] 1 AC 958 stated:

> "...protection ... does not extend to the allaying of fears not objectively justified, however reasonable these fears may appear from the point of view of the individual in question..."

Future risk is sometimes referred to as objective risk. The applicant must demonstrate that something bad will happen to them if they are sent to their country of origin. The question of how bad these future experiences must be before the protection of the Refugee Convention is engaged is addressed below in the section on persecution.

Since the advent of the Country Guideline system in the immigration tribunal, it has become essential to check whether an applicant falls within guidance previously given by the tribunal. A list of Country Guideline ('CG') cases is kept on the immigration tribunal website and is regularly updated. Cases are both added and removed from this list.

Most CG cases include clear pointers as to future risk for various categories of asylum claimants.

Criticisms have been made of the CG system (see IAS report *Country Guideline cases: benign and practical?* available for download from www.iasuk.org under 'publications') and if an applicant does seem to fall within facts dealt with in a previous CG case it will prove very difficult to persuade an immigration judge to depart from the previous guidance (see the immigration tribunal Practice Direction, suggesting failure to follow CG cases is an error of law) unless the case can somehow be distinguished. The production of recent evidence not previously considered in the CG case may assist (for example an expert report), although the starting point is likely to be whether this is sufficient to displace previous guidance, as opposed to re-assessing all of the evidence in the round.

Country information

Country information, sometimes (arguably inaccurately) referred to as objective evidence, is the main tool for demonstrating future risk, assuming that credibility is established in full or in part.

There are many different sources of country information, and each source has its advantages and disadvantages. A high quality source to which weight is likely to be attached would possess the following qualities:

- **Up to date**: the source would be a recent one, or failing that there would be information that suggested the situation or subject matter of the report was unlikely to have changed.

- **Objective**: there is no such thing as an entirely objective source, but clearly biased sources or sources more likely to have an agenda of some kind may be considered less reputable. However, even a biased source might include useful factual information: much depends on how the information is used and presented.

- **Origins**: the sources used by a report would be as well-informed as possible and their research methodology would be clear.

Common types of information source include:

- **Government reports**. E.g. Country of Origin Information Service (COIS) reports, US Department of State reports may reflect the agenda of the government or government department concerned but subject to public review. Tend to be infrequently updated.

- **Inter-governmental reports**. E.g. UNHCR, African Union. May be compromised by the agendas of different constituent governments or by the organisation's own agenda or remit. Tend to be infrequently updated.

- **Non-governmental reports**. E.g. Amnesty International, Human Rights Watch. May reflect campaigning agenda of the organisation concerned, but research methodology may be clear and the organisations have their reputations to protect. Annual reports are infrequent but updates are sometimes published.

- **Press**. E.g. national or international newspapers and websites. Some articles may be the product of good quality journalism, others less so. Tends to be very recent.

> ## Example
>
> The suitability of a source depends on the context in which it is used. Normally, a blog post from an anonymous blogger in the country of origin would be given little weight. However, if the blog is long standing and appears unconnected personally to the asylum seeker, it might be useful corroboration of a claimed fact of some sort, particularly if backed up directly or indirectly by other sources.
>
> An opposition newspaper might be expected by the reader to be highly critical of the government it opposes and to contain 'biased' information that suggests the opposition is badly treated. However, it may be corroborated by other sources and may contain specific facts or details that have a direct bearing on the account of a given asylum seeker.
>
> Unusual sources should not lightly be discarded merely because they can be said to be biased, but they should be used with care and further corroboration should always be sought.

The Home Office COIS produces information about conditions in asylum seekers' countries of origin for caseworkers and others involved in processing asylum applications, and their researches are crystallised into reports that publish in October and April each year. These reports often provide a useful starting point to research issues.

The COIS reports are considerably improved on those of its predecessor, the now defunct Country Information and Policy Unit (CIPU), whose reports were the subject of criticism by agencies such as the Immigration Advisory Service. The Advisory Panel on Country Information (APCI) is an independent body established under the Nationality Asylum and Immigration Act 2002, "to consider and make recommendations to the Secretary of State about the content of country information", and has its own website at http://www.apci.org.uk. It meets twice a year and the research and reports produced are sometimes of use to asylum practitioners.

The Home Office continues to publish Operational Guidance Notes (OGNs). These are not held out as being and should not be regarded as country information. They set out the policy position of the senior echelons of the Home Office. They often very selectively draw on COIS reports and identify what the Home Office consider to be risk categories.

For the view of some senior members of the tribunal on the use of country information and expert evidence see, for example, the case of TK *(Tamils, LP updated) Sri Lanka (Rev 1) CG* [2009] UKAIT 00049.

Relevance of past experiences to future risk

The fact of past ill-treatment, be it severe enough to be deemed persecution or not (although the more severe the better from the viewpoint of making a good case), is a matter to be strongly taken into account when assessing the risk of any recurrence. Professor Hathaway's test was approved by Stuart Smith LJ in the Court of Appeal in *Demirkaya v Secretary of State for the Home Department* [1999] Imm AR 498:

> 'Where evidence of past maltreatment exists, however, it is unquestionably an excellent indicator of the fate that may await an applicant on return to her home. Unless there has been a major change of circumstances within that country that makes prospective persecution unlikely, past experience under a particular regime should be considered probative of future risk ... In sum, evidence of individualised past persecution is generally a sufficient, though not a mandatory, means of establishing prospective risks.'

However, it is not the only relevant consideration, as there may have been a change in circumstances in the country in question. Past persecution is therefore useful as an indicator of future risk, but it would be wise to seek to demonstrate that the causes of that past persecution continue to be active now.

This principle is now embedded in the immigration rules, thanks to the Qualification Directive. See rule 339K:

> 'The fact that a person has already been subject to persecution or serious harm, or to direct threats of such persecution or such harm, will be regarded as a serious indication of the person's well-founded fear of persecution or real risk of suffering serious harm, unless there are good reasons to consider that such persecution or serious harm will not be repeated.'

Specific individual risk

It is always important in an asylum case to look at individual risk factors thrown up in the individual case.

For example, if the claimant possesses a passport, this will be noted by the authorities in the UK, and an explanation needs to be sought as to why an individual travelled on their own documentation as this might suggest that the authorities of his or her home country allowed him or her to leave. An asylum seeker may be a person of whom the authorities are pleased to be rid, or one who is a member of a class of persons at risk albeit that as an individual he is not being actively sought at the time of departure, or one coming from a country where inefficient or corrupt security services cannot be relied upon to routinely enforce the will of their superiors.

'The *UNHCR Handbook* makes it clear that 'possession of a passport cannot … always be considered as evidence of loyalty on the part of the holder, or … of the absence of fear' and that passports are often 'issued to a person who is undesired in his country of origin [for] the sole purpose of securing his departure': para 48. (Collins J in the Administrative Court in *R v Secretary of State for the Home Department, ex p Q* [2003] EWHC 195 Admin spoke of the ease with which false passports could be obtained abroad and then used to pass through UK immigration control.)

Generic risk cases

Where an individual is relying for their claim of persecution not on a desire by officials or non-state actors to target them as an individual, but rather from general problems (e.g. poor prison conditions: see *Batayav v SSHD* [2003] EWCA Civ 1489 and again at [2005] EWCA Civ 366), then it will be necessary to show that the matters complained of are truly endemic. See the Court of Appeal in *Hariri v SSHD* [2003] EWCA Civ 807:

> 'The point is one of logic. Absent evidence to show that the appellant was at risk because of his specific circumstances, there could be no real risk of relevant ill-treatment unless the situation to which the appellant would be returning was one in which such violence was generally or consistently happening. There is nothing else in the case that could generate a real risk. In this situation, then, a "consistent pattern of gross and systematic violation of fundamental human rights", far from being at variance with the real risk test is, in my judgment, a function or application of it.'

This test, requiring gross and systematic violation of fundamental human rights before a case based on generic risk can succeed, has itself been criticised, and the Tribunal has increasingly referred to the test being whether there is "a consistent pattern of such mistreatment". Thus in *AA (Risk for involuntary returnees) Zimbabwe CG Rev 1* [2006] UKAIT 00061 the Tribunal stated:

> "The appellant does not need to show a certainty or a probability that all failed asylum seekers returned involuntarily will face serious ill-treatment upon return. He needs to show only that there is a consistent pattern of such mistreatment such that anyone returning in those circumstances faces a real risk of coming to harm even though not everyone does."

Generic risk arguments have been attempted for Iraq, Somalia and Zimbabwe and have succeeded in the case of the latter two countries. There is interesting overlap here with Article 15(c) of the Qualification Directive, which is dealt with in the section on humanitarian protection.

Activities in the United Kingdom and claims made in bad faith

Activities in the United Kingdom

Refugees can base their claim for asylum on activities that post-date their departure from their country of origin, or in changes in the situation there (eg a coup that places all those holding their political affiliation at risk; or it may be that whereas they might not have been at risk had they never left the country, the increased attention they will attract on a return at the border will itself create a risk of persecution). These are known as "sur place" claims.

Immediate risk on return at an airport has been explored in considerable detail for some countries, such as Zimbabwe and Turkey, and is also argued for other countries, such as Eritrea and Sri Lanka. Compelling evidence is usually needed to succeed with such arguments as they affect a large number of asylum applicants. The latest Country Guideline cases should always be checked.

Returnees cannot be expected to lie about their beliefs or how they have spent their time in the UK – see *IK (Returnees - Records – IFA) Turkey CG* [2004] UKIAT 00312 – re Turkey, but of interest in any "questioning on return" case: "It will be for an Adjudicator in each case to assess what questions are likely to be asked during such investigation and how a returnee would respond without being required to lie. The ambit of the likely questioning depends upon the circumstances of each case."

If a claimant has engaged in activities directed against his or her own government while in the UK, it will usually be impossible to obtain evidence that the government in question (a) monitors UK based opposition activities, (b) communicates that information to the domestic authorities and (c) that those authorities make use of that information to target the individuals concerned.

In *YB (Eritrea) v SSHD* [2008] EWCA Civ 360 the Court of Appeal dealt with this question in the context of Eritrea and concluded that a commonsense approach should be followed where the emphasis was on consequences rather than solidity of evidence:

> '17. As has been seen (§7 above), the tribunal, while accepting that the appellant's political activity in this country was genuine, were not prepared to accept in the absence of positive evidence that the Eritrean authorities had "the means and the inclination" to monitor such activities as a demonstration outside their embassy, or that they would be able to identify the appellant from photographs of the demonstration. In my judgment, and without disrespect to what is a specialist tribunal, this is a finding which risks losing contact with reality. Where, as here, the tribunal has objective evidence which "paints a bleak picture of the suppression of political opponents" by a named government, it requires little or no evidence or speculation to arrive at a strong possibility – and perhaps more – that its foreign legations not only film or photograph their nationals who demonstrate in public against the regime but have informers among expatriate oppositionist organisations who can name the people who are filmed or photographed. Similarly it does not require affirmative evidence to establish a probability that the intelligence services

> of such states monitor the internet for information about oppositionist groups. The real question in most cases will be what follows for the individual claimant.'

Bad faith activities

The issue of the wilful creation of an asylum claim through activities found to be conducted in "bad faith" outside the country of origin (for example, cynical attendance at demonstrations outside an embassy) has occasionally arisen. In *Danian v SSHD* [2000] Imm AR 96 the Court of Appeal held that the motive behind activities is irrelevant, the only questions is whether there is a well founded fear of being persecuted for a Convention reason.

The question of an asylum claim made in "bad faith" was canvassed in the Zimbabwe litigation, in the case of *AA and LK v SSHD* [2006] EWCA Civ 401. There the argument for the asylum seekers was that the security forces in Zimbabwe would persecute returnees because of the political opinion they would attribute to them for having claimed asylum in the UK, regardless of how opportunistic their motivation. The Court of Appeal did not overturn the reasoning in *Danian*, but did find that a person who could safely make a voluntary return to their country of origin even though a forced return would put them at risk is not a refugee because that person is not outside his or her country of origin for reason of a well founded fear of being persecuted.

Under rule 339J(iv) the immigration rules now state that the Secretary of State must take into account in making an asylum decision 'whether the person's activities since leaving the country of origin or country of return were engaged in for the sole or main purpose of creating the necessary conditions for making an asylum claim or establishing that he is a person eligible for humanitarian protection or a human rights claim, so as to assess whether these activities will expose the person to persecution or serious harm if he returned to that country'. This rule reflects the Refugee Qualification Directive. So consistency of present activities with past beliefs and behaviour will be of critical significance.

So, critical issues in a "sur place" claim based on UK activities will be

- What activities were carried out?

- If so, it can be assumed they have come to the attention of a country of which the human rights reports depict a "bleak picture" regarding suppression of political opponents

- In any event, an asylum seeker cannot be expected to lie on a return to their country of origin, and so if there is evidence regarding interrogation at the border, this must be taken into account

Future activities

In the case of *HJ (Iran) and HT (Cameroon) v Secretary of State for the Home Department* [2010] UKSC 31 the Supreme Court fundamentally changed the approach of the UK courts to the issue of how future behaviour will be considered relevant to the assessmernt of entitlement to refugee status. The previous settlement, established by the case of Iftikar Ahmed [2000] INLR 1, was a very British and pragmatic one. Essentially, the question of whether future behaviour could make a person a refugee became a simple question of fact: would the person in question in fact, despite the dangers, behave in a way that would expose him or her to risk of persecution?

HJ (Iran) establishes that where a person would in future refrain from behaving in a way that would expose them to danger *because of the risk of persecution that behaviour brings*, that person is a refugee.

The context in HJ (Iran) is famously homosexuality — would a gay man or lesbian woman have to conceal aspects of their sexuality in order to avoid persecution — but the legal principle is a wider one of profound significance.

The leading judgment is that of Lord Rodgers, who gives guidance on the proper approach as follows:

> When an applicant applies for asylum on the ground of a well-founded fear of persecution because he is gay, the tribunal must first ask itself whether it is satisfied on the evidence that he is gay, or that he would be treated as gay by potential persecutors in his country of nationality.
>
> If so, the tribunal must then ask itself whether it is satisfied on the available evidence that gay people who lived openly would be liable to persecution in the applicant's country of nationality.
>
> If so, the tribunal must go on to consider what the individual applicant would do if he were returned to that country.
>
> If the applicant would in fact live openly and thereby be exposed to a real risk of persecution, then he has a well-founded fear of persecution – even if he could avoid the risk by living "discreetly".
>
> If, on the other hand, the tribunal concludes that the applicant would in fact live discreetly and so avoid persecution, it must go on to ask itself why he would do so.
>
> If the tribunal concludes that the applicant would choose to live discreetly simply because that was how he himself would wish to live, or because of social pressures, e g, not wanting to distress his parents or embarrass his friends, then his application should be rejected. Social pressures of that kind do not amount to persecution and the Convention does not offer protection against them. Such a person has no well-founded fear of persecution because, for reasons that have nothing to do with any fear of persecution, he himself chooses to adopt a way of life which means that he is not in fact liable to be persecuted because he is gay.
>
> If, on the other hand, the tribunal concludes that a material reason for the applicant living discreetly on his return would be a fear of the persecution which would follow if he were to live openly as a gay man, then, other things being equal, his application should be accepted. Such a person has a well-founded fear of persecution. To reject his application on the ground that he could avoid

> the persecution by living discreetly would be to defeat the very right which the Convention exists to protect – his right to live freely and openly as a gay man without fear of persecution. By admitting him to asylum and allowing him to live freely and openly as a gay man without fear of persecution, the receiving state gives effect to that right by affording the applicant a surrogate for the protection from persecution which his country of nationality should have afforded him.

The judgment is also significant for what it says about internal relocation in these cases. At paragraph 84 Lord Rodgers goes on:

> I add a comment on the case of HT. The tribunal rejected his application on the ground that, on his return to Cameroon, he could go to live in another part of the country and live discreetly there. In that event he would have no real fear of persecution. But there appears to have been nothing in the evidence to suggest that there was any area of Cameroon where gay men could live openly without any fear of persecution. So in no sense would the applicant be returning to a part of the country where the state would protect him from persecution. In effect, therefore, the tribunal was simply saying that his application should be rejected because, on return, he could take steps to avoid persecution by conducting himself discreetly. For the reasons which I have given, that approach is inconsistent with the very aims of the Convention.

This also applies more widely than just in gay cases. If a political or religious activist would want to continue his or her activities in future but would not be able to because of the fear of persecution, it is no answer to say that person can move to another part of the country and remain effectively gagged and bound there as well.

Being persecuted

There are two main elements to examine in the context of the requirement to show a risk of being persecuted:

Actors
- State
- Non-state

Acts
- Human rights analysis
- Subjective element
- Role of Convention reasons

Actors of persecution

The Refugee or Person in Need of International Protection (Qualification) Regulations 2006 which transpose the Qualification Directive specify at regulation 3 that the following actors can act as persecutors for the purposes of assessing cases under the Refugee Convention:

(a) the State;

(b) any party or organisation controlling the State or a substantial part of the territory of the State;

(c) any non-State actor if it can be demonstrated that the actors mentioned in paragraphs (a) and (b), including any international organisation, are unable or unwilling to provide protection against persecution or serious harm.

This broadly reflects the position under UK law.

Acts of persecution

The Qualification Directive sets out a minimum definition of what might constitute acts of persecution at Art.9, which has been transposed into the Refugee or Person in Need of International Protection (Qualification) Regulations 2006 as follows:

> 5. —(1) In deciding whether a person is a refugee an act of persecution must be:
> (a) sufficiently serious by its nature or repetition as to constitute a severe violation of a basic human right, in particular a right from which derogation cannot be made under Article 15 of the Convention for the Protection of Human Rights and Fundamental Freedoms; or
> (b) an accumulation of various measures, including a violation of a human right which is sufficiently severe as to affect an individual in a similar manner as specified in (a).
>
> (2) An act of persecution may, for example, take the form of:
> (a) an act of physical or mental violence, including an act of sexual violence;
> (b) a legal, administrative, police, or judicial measure which in itself is discriminatory or which is implemented in a discriminatory manner;
> (c) prosecution or punishment, which is disproportionate or discriminatory;
> (d) denial of judicial redress resulting in a disproportionate or discriminatory punishment;
> (e) prosecution or punishment for refusal to perform military service in a conflict, where performing military service would include crimes or acts falling under regulation 7 [i.e. exclusion clauses].
>
> (3) An act of persecution must be committed for at least one of the reasons in Article 1(A) of the Geneva Convention.

The definition impinges on several existing aspects of UK case law on persecution. It appears to take a restrictive approach to the definition of persecution in sub clause (1). However, some of the specific examples in sub clause (2) appear to be very generous. Parts (2)(b) and (d), for example, both appear to go beyond a severe violation of the human rights from which derogation cannot be made.

Sub clause (1) is quite explicit in stating that acts of persecution can be rendered serious by their nature or their repetition, meaning a sufficiently serious one-off act is capable of amounting to persecution. This construction was endorsed by Keene LJ in the Court of Appeal in *BA (Pakistan) v Secretary of State for the Home Department* [2009] EWCA Civ 1072: '[21] That phrase "by their nature or repetition" is disjunctive. It emphasises that there need not be repeated acts if an act is sufficiently serious.'

In the Court of Appeal case of *MA (Ethiopia) v Secretary of State for the Home Department* [2009] EWCA Civ 289 (02 April 2009) Elias LJ commented as follows regarding deprivation of nationality and persecution:

> '60 ... if the appellant were able to establish that she has been arbitrarily refused the right to return to Ethiopia for a Convention reason, that would in my view amount to persecution. It would negate one of the most fundamental rights attached to nationality, namely the right to live in the home country and all that goes with that. Denial of that right of abode would necessarily prevent the applicant from exercising a wide range of other rights - if not all - typically attached to nationality, as well as almost inevitably involving an interference with private and/or family life in breach of Article 8 of the ECHR.'

The case is an illustration of the cross over between the refugee and human rights conventions.

Human rights analysis

The Qualification Directive clearly links the concept of persecution to human rights law principles. This is not an entirely new approach in UK case law. In the case of *Gashi* [1997] INLR 97, as approved by the House of Lords in *Ullah* [2004] UKHL 26, the Tribunal adopted the following approach:

> In aid of this sometimes difficult assessment, UNHCR generally agrees with Professor Hathaway's formulation that persecution is usually the "sustained and systemic denial of core human rights" (J Hathaway at p.112). Clearly, some human rights have greater pre-eminence than others and it may be necessary to identify them through a hierarchy of relative importance. This can be achieved by reference to the International Bill of Rights as the universal measure of appropriate standards.
>
> (a) The first category includes inviolable human rights such as the right of life and the prohibition against torture, cruel, inhuman or degrading punishment or treatment. A threat to these rights would always be a serious violation amounting to persecution, as referred to in paragraph 51 of the Handbook.'
>
> (b) The second category includes rights where limited derogation or curtailment by the state in times of public emergency can be justified. They would include, inter alia, the rights to be free from arbitrary arrest and detention, and the right to freedom of expression. A threat to these rights may amount to persecution if the state cannot demonstrate any valid justification for their temporary curtailment. In any event, the measures will usually be accompanied by other forms of discrimination treatment which if assessed cumulatively, could amount to persecution.'

> (c) The third category are rights which although binding upon states, reflect goals for social, economic or cultural development. Their realisation may be contingent upon the reasonable availability of adequate state resources. But the state must nonetheless act in good faith in the pursuit of these goals and otherwise in a manner which does not violate customary norms of non-discrimination. This category would include, inter alia, the right to basic education and the right to earn a livelihood. In appropriate circumstances, a systemic and systematic denial of these rights may lead to cumulative 'consequences of a substantially prejudicial nature for the person concerned' of such severity as would amount to persecution within the meaning and spirit of the Convention. This would be particularly so where the state has adequate means to implement the rights but applies them in a selective and discriminatory manner.

The Qualification Directive and implementing regulations certainly affirm this approach to the interpretation of persecution regarding first and second category rights, as can be seen from Article 5 of the regulations quoted above. Whether the Directive embraces third category rights is less clear, but the Preamble, Recital (11), holds "With respect to the treatment of persons falling within the scope of this Directive, Member States are bound by obligations under instruments of international law to which they are party and which prohibit discrimination."

Subjective nature of being persecuted

The threshold at which ill-treatment becomes persecution is undoubtedly a high one. However, the threshold is not identical in all cases, as being persecuted is in part a subjective concept: what amounts to persecution for one person does not necessarily for another. The UNHCR Handbook states as follows at paragraph 55:

> 'Whether other prejudicial actions or threats would amount to persecution will depend on the circumstances of each case, including the subjective element to which reference has been made in the preceding paragraphs. The subjective character of fear of persecution requires an evaluation of the opinions and feelings of the person concerned. It is also in the light of such opinions and feelings that any actual or anticipated measures against him must necessarily be viewed. Due to variations in the psychological make-up of individuals and in the circumstances of each case, interpretations of what amounts to persecution are bound to vary.'

In *Katrinak v SSHD* [2001] EWCA Civ 832 the Court of Appeal endorsed this approach:

> '[21] ...the attacks also potentially evidence the appellants' vulnerability in the future. An activity which would not amount to persecution if done to some people may amount to persecution if done to others. It is easier to persecute a husband whose wife has been kicked in a racial attack whilst visibly pregnant than one whose family has not had this experience. What to others may be an unbelievable threat may induce terror in such a man.'

The Qualification Directive reiterates this approach at Article 9 (regulation 5 of the UK regulations). Acts of a gender specific or child specific nature are specifically mentioned in the Directive as examples of acts that might constitute persecution (although these references are not transposed into national law and are omitted from the Refugee or Person in Need of International Protection (Qualification) Regulations 2006), as is mental as well as physical violence. The reference at Article 9(1)(b) of the Directive to the effect *on an individual* suggests a proper focus on the subjective aspect of persecution.

Role of Convention reasons

In the course of his judgment in the case of *Sepet and Bulbul v SSHD* [2001] EWCA Civ 681, Lord Justice Laws provided a very useful exposition of the role of a Convention reason in defining persecution:

> 63. There are some classes of case in which the threatened conduct is of such a kind that it is universally condemned, by national and international law, and always constitutes persecution: torture, rape (though of course it is not necessarily persecution for a Convention reason). In those instances, the question whether or not there is persecution is straightforwardly a matter of fact. But it is not always so; and Kagema [1997] IAR 137 (relied on by Mr Macdonald in reply) is no authority that it is. There are other classes of case in which the threatened conduct is by no means necessarily unjustified at the bar of law or opinion: imprisonment is a plain instance (where its length is not disproportionate and its conditions are not barbarous). In such a case some further factor is required to turn the treatment in question into persecution. Torture is absolutely persecutory; imprisonment only conditionally so.
>
> 64. What is the further factor that may turn imprisonment into persecution? It can only be that the claimant is liable to be imprisoned for a Convention reason. There can be no other way in to the regime of Convention protection. In this case, then, the existence of a Convention reason is what defines the treatment as persecutory.
>
> 65. See where this leads. The putative act of persecution - imprisonment - is only such if it is inflicted for a Convention reason. (I leave aside all the uncontentious possibilities: that the military service involves acts or conditions which are barbarous, or that the punishment for draft evasion is barbarous or disproportionate). It is the why and wherefore of the punishment's infliction that alone can transform the imprisonment suffered into persecution. But then it must constitute persecution according to the Convention's common standard, within and according to the autonomous international meaning of the Convention.

The House of Lords later gave judgment in the same case (neutral citation [2003] UKHL 15), but this passage from the Court of Appeal judgment stands as both a masterful exposition and a useful starting point for further exploration of the role of Convention reasons in determining what is and is not an act of persecution. In making apparently difficult judgments about whether a criminal offence (e.g. homosexual acts or exercise of the right to protest) are 'reasonably' defined as crimes in a given country, the starting point is international human rights law. If international standards as defined in the UN Conventions prohibit certain laws or State actions then that will be a useful guide to whether a punishment is capable of being an act of persecution.

Prosecution and persecution

Simple fugitives from justice are not refugees. However to suggest that anyone who flees forms of harm that arise via prosecution is a criminal rather than a refugee is to over-simplify the question and it is clear from the Qualification Directive that there are circumstances where prosecution will amount to persecution: where it is disproportionate or discriminatory.

The UNHCR Handbook similarly suggests, at paragraph 57, that excessive punishment upon conviction imposed for a Convention reason would be persecutory:

> 'A person guilty of a common law offence may be liable to excessive punishment, which may amount to persecution within the meaning of the definition.'

The question of proportionality must be determined according to international human rights and criminal law standards, as set out in the various international treaties.

That which is apparently prosecution may be rendered persecutory by a discriminatory manner of application: e.g. directing prosecution for public order offences only against supporters of the political opposition. See the UNHCR Handbook, paragraph 59 showing that it will be necessary to examine whether there is discriminatory application of the law for political offences:

> "More often, however, it may not be the law but its application that is discriminatory. Prosecution for an offence against 'public order', e.g. for distribution of pamphlets, could for example be a vehicle for the persecution of the individual on the grounds of the political content of the publication."

Prosecution may also be heightened to persecution by the absence of due process within the justice system, so long as the procedural deficiencies are directed on Convention grounds (e.g. convicting opposition political supporters without a fair trial).

States which punish people for the exercise of fundamental human rights may be persecuting individuals rather than simply prosecuting them, see the Court of Appeal in *Tientchu v Immigration Appeal Tribunal* (C/2000/6288; 18 October 2000):

> '...having accepted ... certain parts of her evidence ... in my judgment he could only properly have refused her claim for asylum, given the wealth of evidence before him of the gravest human rights abuses in Cameroon, had there been some evidence truly pointing towards this applicant having committed a non-political offence, rather than having acted in a way which the international community would surely regard as involving the legitimate expression and advancement of a political view.'

In fact this principle extends beyond narrow political opinion cases into those cases where it is the loss of the ability to give expression to one's sexual identity (because doing so would expose the individual to prosecution) that forms the basis of the persecution, see *Jain v Secretary of State for the Home Department*

[2000] Imm AR 76 (as where a homosexual faces prosecution simply for consensual actions committed in private).

Military service

It has been found that there is no international human right to conscientious objection. See *Sepet and Bulbul* [2001] EWCA Civ 681:

> '[T]here is no material to establish a presently extant legal rule or principle which vouchsafes a right of absolute conscientious objection, such that where it is not respected, a good case to refugee status under the Convention may arise. No such putative rule or principle is to be found in the Convention's international autonomous meaning or common standard'.

The necessary implication is that prosecution for refusal to perform military service is therefore, at least potentially, legitimate prosecution for breach of a state's criminal law. The act of imprisonment would not therefore amount to being persecuted as there is no Convention reason behind the punishment in question.

This approach was upheld by the House of Lords on appeal ([2003] UKHL 15). Lord Bingham commented that there are, though, circumstances where a conscientious objector might succeed in a claim for refugee status:

> 'There is compelling support for the view that refugee status should be accorded to one who has refused to undertake compulsory military service on the grounds that such service would or might require him to commit atrocities or gross human rights abuses or participate in a conflict condemned by the international community, or where refusal to serve would earn grossly excessive or disproportionate punishment...'

In *Krotov v SSHD* [2004] EWCA Civ 69 the Court of Appeal held that "a genuine conscientious refusal to participate in a conflict in order to avoid participating in inhumane acts required as a matter of state policy or systemic practice [amounts] to an (implied or imputed) political opinion as to the limits of governmental authority". However, the asylum seeker will have to show that they would personally be associated with actions whose "defining characteristic and hallmark is service in a military which breaches international standards."

This approach was effectively transposed to peace-time atrocities as well, in the case of *BE (Iran) v SSHD* [2008] EWCA Civ 540. Sedley LJ gave the judgment of the court and concluded as follows:

> '40. In our judgment, on the limited facts before the tribunal, this appellant was entitled to succeed in his claim for international protection. It is common ground that, once it is established that the individual concerned has deserted rather than commit a sufficiently grave abuse of human rights, whatever punishment or reprisal consequently faces him will establish a well-founded fear of persecution for reasons of political opinion.
>
> 41. For the reasons we have given, we hold that what this appellant was seeking to avoid by deserting was the commission of what this country and civilised opinion

> worldwide recognise as an atrocity and a gross violation of human rights – the unmarked planting of anti-personnel mines in roads used by innocent civilians. He is consequently entitled to asylum, and his appeal accordingly succeeds.'

The Qualification Directive and regulations specifically refer in the examples of possible acts of persecution (Article 9 or regulation 5) to "prosecution or punishment for refusal to perform military service in a conflict, where performing military service would include crimes or acts falling under [the exclusion provisions". There is no reference here to disproportionate acts of punishment, but this need not prevent such cases being argued as (a) the directive imposes minimum requirements and that level of protection can be exceeded and (b) a disproportionate punishment case can be pursued under a more conventional analysis, where there must be a Convention reason (e.g. race or religion) behind the disproportionate punishment and that punishment must amount to being persecuted.

Civil war

In relation to civil war victims, see also the later section on Humanitarian Protection. As can be seen below, the Refugee Convention has not proven helpful to many victims of civil war, and the Qualification Directive fills some of the resulting protection gap (see further below).

In order to secure refugee status, persons fleeing civil war must demonstrate that they face a differential impact over and above the general risks of a civil war in which law and order has broken down completely: the House of Lords in *R v Secretary of State for the Home Department ex parte Adan* [1998] Imm AR 338. The reasoning is essentially that of 'collateral damage': the ordinary victims of civil war are not being specifically targeted, rather they are simply in the way of the opposing factions and are accidentally caught in the crossfire. Civilians who can show that they are specifically targeted for a Convention reason or who suffer a differential impact in related activities such as looting and robbery following the breakdown of law and order can potentially make out a claim for refugee status.

However, egregious breaches of international humanitarian law are not part of the ordinary risks of civil war: the Tribunal in *Rudralingam* (00/TH/02264; 24 November 2000). So if people suffer torture, or civilians are killed, or hospitals attacked, on "Convention" grounds, then persecution may still be found, even in a civil war.

> **Example**
>
> In the case of Somalia, it was found that there was a general state of civil war and lack of law and order. All or many citizens of Somalia could be said to be victims of the civil war in a wide sense. In the leading judgment in Adan, Lord Lloyd cited a number of authorities, including Hathaway: "victims of war and conflict are not refugees *unless* they are subject to differential victimisation based on civil or political status."
>
> The same reasoning would not necessarily apply in a country such as 1994 Rwanda, where victims of genocide were being targeted for the very specific Convention reason of race. This went far beyond the normal threat from a general civil war.

The Convention reasons

The Convention reasons are central to the Refugee Convention. A refugee is a person with a 'well founded fear of being persecuted for reasons of…'. There must therefore be a causal link between the harm suffered and one of the five Convention reasons.

In addition, as described above, the Convention reasons can have a transformative effect on certain types of harm. For example, imprisonment as a result of criminal behaviour does not amount to persecution, whereas imprisonment for reasons of a Convention reason would amount to persecution.

The Convention reasons are as follows:

- Race
- Religion
- Nationality
- Membership of a particular social group
- Political opinion

Race

"Race" is interpreted to include "...all persons of identifiable ethnicity" (quote from Professor Hathaway's *The Law of Refugee Status*). The Qualification Directive states that 'the concept of race shall in particular include considerations of colour, descent or membership of a particular ethnic group'.

Religion

The Qualification Directive offers a very inclusive definition of religion:

> "the concept of religion shall in particular include the holding of theistic, non-theistic and atheistic beliefs, the participation in, or abstention from, formal worship in private or in public, either alone or in community with others, other religious acts or expressions of view, or forms of personal or communal conduct based on or mandated by any religious belief"

Cases of religious conversion can be controversial, and are best prepared by anticipating possible Home Office objections to the credibility of any conversion. However, the depth of religious conviction of the apostate should not be permitted to obscure the fact that the agents of persecution may not be overly concerned about the theological commitment of the convert.

Whether or not one has a well-founded fear of persecution on the basis of future activities will be governed by the principle in *Iftikar Ahmed* (discussed above): will the appellant in reality carry out the threatened activities, and will those actions lead to a well-founded fear of persecution?

Nationality

The Qualification Directive definition of nationality is an interesting one that extends conventional understanding of the concept:

> "the concept of nationality shall not be confined to citizenship or lack thereof but shall in particular include membership of a group determined by its cultural, ethnic, or linguistic identity, common geographical or political origins or its relationship with the population of another State".

Membership of a particular social group

Discrimination is the focal point of determining whether a person is a member of a particular social group. Other relevant criteria are whether the discrimination is on the basis of an immutable characteristic of the individual: i.e. one that is either beyond the power of an individual to change (i.e. is innate) or one that it would be contrary to their fundamental human rights for them to forgo (i.e. is non-innate).

Innate characteristic
- e.g. gender, sexuality

Common background that cannot be changed
- e.g. being a former teacher or policeman

Fundamental belief or characteristic
- e.g. home schooling

The House of Lords held in *Shah and Islam* that women in Pakistan constituted a particular social group. This was because they share the common immutable characteristic of gender, they were discriminated against as a group in matters of fundamental human rights and the State gave them no adequate protection because they were perceived as not being entitled to the same human rights as men.

The Qualification Directive adopts the *Shah and Islam* approach but also elevates societal attitude to a strict requirement; both have to be shown to establish that there is a social group. This is also reflected in the Refugee or Person in Need of International Protection (Qualification) Regulations 2006 at regulation 6(d) and (e):

> (d) a group shall be considered to form a particular social group where, for example:
>
> (i) members of that group share an innate characteristic, or a common background that cannot be changed, or share a characteristic or belief that is so fundamental to identity or conscience that a person should not be forced to renounce it, and
>
> (ii) that group has a distinct identity in the relevant country, because it is perceived as being different by the surrounding society;
>
> (e) a particular social group might include a group based on a common characteristic of sexual orientation but sexual orientation cannot be understood to include acts considered to be criminal in accordance with national law of the United Kingdom

The Qualification Directive is therefore be more restrictive than the current UK case law position, as societal identification of the group is not a requirement in *Shah and Islam*. Indeed, it would be difficult to argue that Pakistani society regarded women as a distinct social group. In *SSHD v K; Fornah v SSHD* [2006] UKHL 46 the House of Lords ruled that it is the more generous UK approach that should prevail.

A social group cannot be defined by the persecution which a potential member is experiencing. It has to exist independently of the persecution, although the persecution may play a role in the group becoming identifiable. This does not prevent future victims of Female Genital Mutilation constituting a particular social group: *SSHD v K; Fornah v SSHD* [2006] UKHL 46.

In *SB (PSG, Protection Regulations, Reg 6) Moldova CG* [2008] UKAIT 00002 the Tribunal found that "Former victims of trafficking" and "former victims of trafficking for sexual exploitation" are capable of being members of a particular social group within regulation 6(1)(d) because of their shared common background or past experience of having been trafficked. This recognition that historical experience can give rise to membership of a particular social group is important: hitherto cases had succeeded only on the basis of some characteristic that the individual was born with, or was fundamental to their identity.

In *K and Fornah* (above) the Law Lords accepted that the family was a particular social group, opening up the claims, for example, of individuals whose fears arose from a family involvement in blood feuds, as being able to make good their claims.

Political opinion

Express political opinion is perhaps the most often cited Convention reason. Most obviously it will reflect a political opinion against the interests of the state itself, but the Qualification Directive (as transposed) does not limit the definition

> 'the concept of political opinion shall include the holding of an opinion, thought or belief on a matter related to the potential actors of persecution mentioned in regulation 3 [see actors of persecution, above] and to their policies or methods, whether or not that opinion, thought or belief has been acted upon by the person'

The definition appears wider than that offered in the previous leading case on political opinion, *Guteirrez Gomez* (00/TH/02257; 20 November 2000; Starred:

> 'To qualify as political the opinion in question must relate to the major power transactions taking place in that particular society. It is difficult to see how a political opinion can be imputed by a non state actor who (or which) is not itself a political entity.'

The Qualification Directive definition would encompass groups such as feminists and single issue campaigners, which were arguably excluded from Refugee Convention protection by the *Gomez* approach.

Many claimants will be able to demonstrate a fear of persecution based on what they have already done, or are thought to have done. Whether or not one has a well-founded fear of persecution on the basis of activities that are intended in the future will be governed by the principle in *Iftikar Ahmed* (discussed above): will the appellant in reality carry out the threatened activities, and will those actions lead to a well-founded fear of persecution?

Attributed Convention reasons

Paragraph 81 of the UNHCR Handbook demonstrates that an opinion need not in fact be held, but may be externally ascribed to an individual. In the context of political opinion, this has long been referred to as 'imputed' political opinion in the UK.

It is re-titled 'attributed' political opinion in the Qualification Directive and features explicitly in the implementing domestic regulations at regulation 6(2):

> 'In deciding whether a person has a well-founded fear of being persecuted, it is immaterial whether he actually possesses the racial, religious, national, social or political characteristic which attracts the persecution, provided that such a characteristic is attributed to him by the actor of persecution.'

As can be seen, the Qualification Directive extends the concept of an attributed reason to the other Convention reasons beyond political opinion.

Protection and relocation

Protection from non-state persecution

The issue of the availability of protection arises most acutely in non-state persecution cases. In *Horvath*, the House of Lords held that persecution by non-state actors is only persecution within the meaning of the Refugee Convention if the state is unable to provide a system of protection.

This approach is also followed in the Qualification Directive, as transposed in the Refugee or Person in Need of International Protection (Qualification) Regulations 2006 at regulations 3 and 4 read together:

> 3. In deciding whether a person is a refugee or a person eligible for humanitarian protection, persecution or serious harm can be committed by:
>
> (a) the State;
>
> (b) any party or organisation controlling the State or a substantial part of the territory of the State;
>
> (c) any non-State actor if it can be demonstrated that the actors mentioned in paragraphs (a) and (b), including any international organisation, are unable or unwilling to provide protection against persecution or serious harm.
>
> 4. —(1) In deciding whether a person is a refugee or a person eligible for humanitarian protection, protection from persecution or serious harm can be provided by:
>
> (a) the State; or
>
> (b) any party or organisation, including any international organisation, controlling the State or a substantial part of the territory of the State.
>
> (2) Protection shall be regarded as generally provided when the actors mentioned in paragraph (1)(a) and (b) take reasonable steps to prevent the persecution or suffering of serious harm by operating an effective legal system for the detection,

> prosecution and punishment of acts constituting persecution or serious harm, and the person mentioned in paragraph (1) has access to such protection.
>
> (3) In deciding whether a person is a refugee or a person eligible for humanitarian protection the Secretary of State may assess whether an international organisation controls a State or a substantial part of its territory and provides protection as described in paragraph (2).'

Horvath is a difficult judgment to read as none of their Lordships offer a clear definition of what is meant by a system of protection. The consensus among asylum lawyers and judges is that the *Horvath* test is:

(i) whether or not there is a system in place to offer protection and

(ii) whether there is a reasonable willingness in the country to operate such a system.

All of the judgments differ in emphasis but perhaps the most practical test is that adopted by Lord Lloyd, actually that of Stuart-Smith LJ in the Court of Appeal below (paragraphs 20, 22, & 44 of Stuart-Smith's judgment):

> "... the state may be unwilling to afford protection to a certain class of its citizens if there is widespread and systemic indifference to their plight on the part of the law enforcement agencies such as the police and the courts
>
> ...No state can guarantee the safety of its citizens. And to say that the protection must be effective suggests it must succeed in preventing attacks, which is something that cannot be achieved. Equally to say that the protection must be sufficient, begs the question, sufficient for what? In my judgment there must be in force in the country in question a criminal law which makes the violent attacks by the persecutors punishable by sentences commensurate with the gravity of the crimes. The victims as a class must not be exempt from the protection of the law. There must be a reasonable willingness by the law enforcement agencies, that is to say the police and courts to detect, prosecute and punish offenders. It must be remembered that inefficiency and incompetence is not the same as unwillingness, unless it is extreme and widespread. There may be many reasons why criminals are not brought to justice including lack of admissible evidence even where the best endeavours are made; they are not always convicted because of the high standard of proof required, and the desire to protect the rights of accused persons. Moreover, the existence of some policemen who are corrupt or sympathetic to the criminals, or some judges who are weak in the control of the court or in sentencing, does not mean that the state is unwilling to afford protection. It will require cogent evidence that the state which is able to afford protection is unwilling to do so, especially in the case of a democracy...
>
> ...In some cases where individuals are targeted by terrorists or dissidents it may be possible for the state to provide special police protection, for example by an armed guard or the provision of a new identity in a different part of the territory. But these attacks are unpredictable as to victims, time and location, and it is clear that the only form of protection which can be provided is in the form of deterrence through detection, prosecution, convictions and sentencing of criminals."

As can be seen, the Qualification Directive test is simpler, and it refers explicitly to the protection being both available to the person concerned and the system of protection including an 'effective legal system for the detection, prosecution and punishment of acts constituting persecution'. At the time of writing there is no case law on whether there is any difference between the two tests.

In both tests, the focus should be on the plight of the individual, and whether they can avail themselves of the protection of their country. Past failures of protection may assist an applicant in establishing that the protection supposedly available in the future would not be adequate (*Haddadi* (00/TH/02141)).

The greater the link between the authors of harm and the state itself, then the more attention must be paid to the efforts made by the state to provide protection – the steps that can be taken to rein in "uniformed persecutors" may be more extensive than those possible for individuals with no association with the state, see *Svazas v Secretary of State for the Home Department* [2002] EWCA Civ 74.

Example

Leroy is from Jamaica. He witnessed a murder and has been targeted by the criminal gang responsible.

Jamaica is a democracy and although there are serious problems with crime and organised crime, the criminal justice system does broadly function, albeit not very well. The case of *AB (Protection - criminal gangs - internal relocation) Jamaica CG* [2007] UKAIT 00018 deals with this subject and states that cases have to be decided on their own facts; some asylum claimants will be able to show inadequate protection is available given their particular circumstances. Depending on what has already happened to Leroy, he might well have a strong claim for protection.

Internal relocation

Situations arise where an individual may face persecution in a particular part of their country of origin but will be expected to relocate to a different part of their country where they can live in safety. This usually arises in non-state persecution cases, as it is difficult to imagine where a person might be able to relocate within the territory of a state while fearing persecution by that state. In *Januzi v SSHD* [2006] UKHL 5, the House of Lords held that there is, however, no legal presumption that internal relocation is not viable in state persecution cases.

The immigration rules refer to the concept of internal relocation and transpose the requirements of the Qualification Directive at rule 339O:

> (i) The Secretary of State will not make:

> (a) a grant of asylum if in part of the country of origin a person would not have a well founded fear of being persecuted, and the person can reasonably be expected to stay in that part of the country;
>
> or
>
> (b) a grant of humanitarian protection if in part of the country of return a person would not face a real risk of suffering serious harm, and the person can reasonably be expected to stay in that part of the country.
>
> (ii) In examining whether a part of the country of origin or country of return meets the requirements in (i) the Secretary of State, when making his decision on whether to grant asylum or humanitarian protection, will have regard to the general circumstances prevailing in that part of the country and to the personal circumstances of the person.
>
> (iii) (i) applies notwithstanding technical obstacles to return to the country of origin or country of return

The rule (and the Directive) does not provide much practical guidance on approaching the question of whether internal relocation is applicable in a given case. Logically, there should be three stages of reasoning:

(i)   Is there persecution in the 'home area'?

If there is no persecution in the home area then the question of internal relocation does not arise. However, in other cases it is still important to start with this question because you cannot properly assess whether an applicant will be safe after return in another area if you have not examined the nature and severity of the threat they face in their home area.

(ii)   Is there a 'safe place' to which the person can relocate?

In cases of state persecution the answer to this question will often be 'no' but cases might arise where a person has been targeted by local government and could relocate to another area. In cases of non-state persecution, the influence and reach of the non-state actors will need to be assessed, particularly though country information.

(iii)   Would it be reasonable to require the person to relocate there?

If there is a safe place, the last and most difficult question is whether it is reasonable to expect a person to relocate there. There may be inhospitable jungle or desert in a given country where a person would be free from persecution, but it would be unduly harsh to expect the person to live there.

This last question was the main subject of the major House of Lords decision in *Januzi v SSHD* [2006] UKHL 5, which effectively replaces *R v Secretary of State for the Home Department & Immigration Appeal Tribunal ex parte Robinson* [1997] Imm AR 568 as the principal authority on internal relocation. *Januzi* itself was then the subject of further explanatory litigation in *AH Sudan* in the Court of

Appeal ([2007] EWCA Civ 297) and again in the House of Lords ([2007] UKHL 49).

In this last case, the House of Lords upheld an immigration tribunal decision finding that relocation to refugee camps around Khartoum by Darfuri refugees was reasonable. The House of Lords did however stress that it would be an error of law to impose the standard of breaches of Article 3 ECHR for the reasonableness threshold and that both the conditions in the home area and in the proposed area of relocation were relevant to the question of whether relocation was reasonable. The approach was summarised thus, by Lord Bingham, citing himself in *Januzi*:

> 'The decision-maker, taking account of all relevant circumstances pertaining to the claimant and his country of origin, must decide whether it is reasonable to expect the claimant to relocate or whether it would be unduly harsh to expect him to do so... The decision-maker must do his best to decide, on such material as is available, where on the spectrum the particular case falls... All must depend on a fair assessment of the relevant facts.'

He then went on:

> 'Although specifically directed to a secondary issue in the case, these observations are plainly of general application. It is not easy to see how the rule could be more simply or clearly expressed. It is, or should be, evident that the enquiry must be directed to the situation of the particular applicant, whose age, gender, experience, health, skills and family ties may all be very relevant. There is no warrant for excluding, or giving priority to, consideration of the applicant's way of life in the place of persecution. There is no warrant for excluding, or giving priority to, consideration of conditions generally prevailing in the home country.'

Baroness Hale alongside him:

> 'As the UNHCR put it in their very helpful intervention in this case,
>
> > "...the correct approach when considering the reasonableness of IRA [internal relocation alternative] is to assess all the circumstances of the individual's case holistically and with specific reference to the individual's personal circumstances (including past persecution or fear thereof, psychological and health condition, family and social situation, and survival capacities). This assessment is to be made in the context of the conditions in the place of relocation (including basic human rights, security conditions, socio-economic conditions, accommodation, access to health care facilities), in order to determine the impact on that individual of settling in the proposed place of relocation and whether the individual could live a relatively normal life without undue hardship."'

Note that the position in Sudan has changed since this judgment and the Home Office's current position at the time of writing was that it was not reasonable to expect a Darfuri refugee to relocate to the refugee camps around Khartoum.

> **Example**
>
> In the case of *AA (Uganda) v SSHD* [2008] EWCA Civ 579 the Court of Appeal held that it was not reasonable to expect a particularly vulnerable single young woman to relocate from her home area to the capital, where she had no connections and an expert had concluded she would be forced to make a living as a prostitute. There is therefore scope to argue internal relocation is unreasonable, but evidence rather than generalised assertions is necessary.

Non Refoulement

The previous sections have all dealt with Article 1A of the Refugee Convention, which sets out the definition of a refugee. Other clauses set out the rights that a refugee should enjoy. Article 33 sets out the most important right for refugees, the right not to be returned to the frontiers of territories where they fear persecution (note there is no absolute right to non-return to other territories).

> "1. No Contracting State shall expel or return ("refouler") a refugee in any manner whatsoever to the frontiers of territories where his life or freedom would be threatened on account of his race, religion, nationality, membership of a particular social group or political opinion."

Even this fundamental right has limitations however, see below. The word 'refouler' is used because it implies return to the frontier of a territory where life or freedom would be threatened – this means that returns to third countries where there would be no persecution are not necessarily prohibited.

Cessation Clauses

Refugee status is not necessarily permanent as the Refugee Convention includes several cessation clauses governing the circumstances in which a recognised refugee's status as a refugee ceases. A person under this Article will cease to be a refugee if they have:

(i) • Voluntarily availed themselves of the protection of the country of their nationality

(ii) • Voluntarily re-acquired a lost nationality

(iii) • Acquired the nationality of a country (including the UK) and availed themselves of the protection of that country

(iv) • Voluntarily established themselves in a country in respect of which they were a refugee

(v) • If the circumstances in their country of origin have changed such that the person no longer has a well-founded fear of persecution there.

It can be seen that the Refugee Convention does not oblige States to offer settlement to refugees. Indeed, refugee status appears as a temporary form of protection in the Convention itself.

In the United Kingdom, a successful asylum claimant will be recognised as a refugee and five years leave to remain will be granted. In the past ILR was granted but this policy was altered in August 2005.

If the refugee reaches the end of the five year period without his or her case having been reviewed, ILR will normally be granted, subject to a citizenship test and the absence of criminal convictions. If, during the five year period, a Minister has issued a ministerial declaration that a particular country is now considered to be generally safe, all refugees of that nationality will have their cases individually reviewed, with a right of appeal against any decision to revoke refugee status. The burden will rest with the Home Office to establish that the individual is no longer a refugee. Assurances have been given that there will be few declarations, but this remains to be seen in practice.

Detailed guidance is provided to Home Office caseworkers in the API on Cessation, Cancellation and Withdrawal of Refugee Status.

Where there has been a grant of refugee status abroad, the asylum seeker should not have their claim addressed in the UK without regard to the fact. Thus the Tribunal's consideration is only on the basis that they have (as *LW (Cancellation refugee status: UNHCR Note) Ethiopia* [2005] UKIAT 00042)

> "Refugee status, once granted, should not be reviewed or annulled except on the most substantial and clear grounds."

This is very important – it effectively puts the burden of proof on the Home Office to show a change of circumstances, which is very important, given the tendency to inertia in Home Office advocacy and case preparation.

Exclusion clauses

It will be noted that the Convention has several forms of exclusion clause within it, for example Article 1E for possession of rights akin to nationality, the second limb of Article 1A(2) for dual nationals, the better known Article 1F exclusions for crimes against international law and serious criminal activity of a non political nature. But even those accepted to be refugees may face limitations of the rights they enjoy, including even Article 33.

> "33(2). The benefit of the present provision may not, however, be claimed by a refugee whom there are reasonable grounds for regarding as a danger to the security of the country in which he is, or who, having been convicted by a final judgment of a particularly serious crime, constitutes a danger to the community of that country."

The UK has chosen to automatically declare offences of certain kinds as meeting these criteria under the 2002 Act; this is dealt with below.

Article 1(D)

Applicable to a very small proportion of people, namely those who were receiving protection from the UN in 1951, at the time the Refugee Convention was signed - in practice, only Palestinian refugees receiving UNWRA assistance at that time.

Article 1(F)

The following forms of behaviour lead to a person who would otherwise be a refugee being excluded from the Convention by virtue of Article 1F:

(a) Has committed a crime against peace, a war crime, or a crime against humanity, as defined in the international instruments drawn up to make provision in respect of such crimes

(b) Has committed a serious non-political crime outside the country of refuge prior to his admission to that country as a refugee

(c) Has been guilty of acts contrary to the purposes and principles of the United Nations.

The exclusion clauses are part of the Refugee Convention (and similar ones appear in the Refugee Qualification Directive) and so can be considered by the immigration tribunal even where the Secretary of State has not raised them, subject to giving an opportunity to an Appellant to deal with such issues – the foreseeability of the issue arising will be relevant to the need for an adjournment.

The Refugee Qualification Directive has added words to its interpretation of the Refugee Convention, so that regarding Art 1F(b) cases, "prior to his admission" means prior to "the time of issuing a residence permit based on the granting of refugee status" (Art 12(2)(b) of Directive).

Discussion of Art 1F cases has often concentrated on whether a crime is political or non-political in nature. The House of Lords in *'T' (T v Secretary of State for the Home Department* [1996] Imm AR 443) rejected the idea that any crime that was incidental to a political cause could be insulated from categorisation as 'non-political'. Acts of terrorism, being incidents of depersonalised and abstract violence coldly indifferent to the human rights of the victims, are sufficiently divorced from the objectives they are thought to serve to sever them of true political content.

Nexus to acts falling within Article 1F

The question of guilt by association has recurred in case law over the exclusion clauses. In the starred case of *Gurung* [2002] UKIAT 04870, the Tribunal suggested that membership of an organisation that committed terrorist acts might well lead to one's exclusion from the Refugee Convention. It also suggested locating the organisation in question on a continuum, where some organisations carry out both legitimate and terrorist activities and that some members of terrorist organisations would not be excluded from refugee status. The implication was that the nature of an organisation was an important indicator of whether a member should be excluded from refugee status for commission of war crimes.

The Court of Appeal revisited this issue in two cases in 2009 and the Supreme Court gave judgment again on the issue in 2010.

In *KJ (Sri Lanka) v SSHD* [2009] EWCA Civ 292 the Court of Appeal held that acts of a military nature committed by an independence movement (such as the LTTE) against the military forces of the government are not themselves acts contrary to the purposes and principles of the United Nations and suggested that an armed campaign against a government would not necessarily constitute acts contrary to the purposes and principles of the United Nations.

The Court went on to find that that mere membership of an organisation that, among other activities, commits acts of terrorism does not suffice to bring the exclusion into play. In contrast, where an organisation's activities are *only* acts of terrorism and a claimant is an active member, Article 1F is likely to apply. The Court then goes on to hold as follows:

> '38. However, the LTTE, during the period when KJ was a member, was not such an organisation. It pursued its political ends in part by acts of terrorism and in part by military action directed against the armed forces of the government of Sri Lanka. The application of Article 1F(c) is less straightforward in such a case. A person may join such an organisation, because he agrees with its political objectives, and be willing to participate in its military actions, but may not agree with and may not be willing to participate in its terrorist activities. Of course, the higher up in the organisation a person is the more likely will be the inference that he agrees with and promotes all of its activities, including its terrorism. But it seems to me that a foot soldier in such an organisation, who has not participated in acts of terrorism, and in particular has not participated in the murder or attempted murder of civilians, has not been guilty of acts contrary to the purposes and principles of the United Nations.'

In the case of *R (on the application of JS (Sri Lanka)) v SSHD* [2010] UKSC 15 the Supreme Court explicitly rejected the approach of the tribunal in *Gurung*:

> '29... In the first place, it is unhelpful to attempt to carve out from amongst organisations engaging in terrorism a sub-category consisting of those "whose aims, methods and activities are predominantly terrorist in character", and to suggest that membership of one of these gives rise to a presumption of criminal complicity: "very little more will be necessary" (Gurung para 105).'

The Supreme Court suggests a different approach:

> '30. Rather, however, than be deflected into first attempting some such sub-categorisation of the organisation, it is surely preferable to focus from the outset on what ultimately must prove to be the determining factors in any case, principally (in no particular order) (i) the nature and (potentially of some importance) the size of the organisation and particularly that part of it with which the asylum-seeker was himself most directly concerned, (ii) whether and, if so, by whom the organisation was proscribed, (iii) how the asylum-seeker came to be recruited, (iv) the length of time he remained in the organisation and what, if any, opportunities he had to leave it, (v) his position, rank, standing and influence in the organisation, (vi) his knowledge of the organisation's war crimes activities, and (vii) his own personal involvement and role in the organisation including particularly whatever contribution he made towards the commission of war crimes.'

There should be no presumption, rebuttable or not, of individual liability, and the nature of an organisation and its aims and objectives are irrelevant to the question of whether a particular individual is guilty of war crimes.

In the Court of Appeal judgment under appeal in JS, the ambit of the exclusion clauses was very narrowly drawn with reference to the concept of criminal liability. The Supreme Court considered that this was too narrow an approach and lay down a different, rather wider analysis:

> '38... Put simply, I would hold an accused disqualified under article 1F if there are serious reasons for considering him voluntarily to have contributed in a significant way to the organisation's ability to pursue its purpose of committing war crimes, aware that his assistance will in fact further that purpose.'

Evidence

In *Al-Sirri v SSHD & Anor* [2009] EWCA Civ 222 the Court of Appeal finds unequivocally that in assessing whether there are 'serious reasons for considering' that a claimant has committed acts covered by the exclusion clauses, no weight whatsoever should be attached to a criminal conviction in another country based on evidence obtained by torture.

Relevance and definition of terrorist acts

Two Court of Appeal cases deal with this question: *KJ (Sri Lanka) v SSHD* [2009] EWCA Civ 292 and *Al-Sirri v SSHD & Anor* [2009] EWCA Civ 222. Both allow for a distinction between military activities against a government and terrorist activities against civilians. Insofar as there is a conflict, *Al-Sirri* is probably to be preferred as the argument on this question was far fuller than in *KJ (Sri Lanka)*.

Section 54 of the Immigration, Asylum and Nationality Act 2006 seeks to add domestic definition to the exclusion clauses and provides as follows:

> Refugee Convention: construction
>
> (1) In the construction and application of Article 1(F)(c) of the Refugee Convention the reference to acts contrary to the purposes and principles of the United Nations shall be taken as including, in particular—
> (a) acts of committing, preparing or instigating terrorism (whether or not the acts amount to an actual or inchoate offence), and
> (b) acts of encouraging or inducing others to commit, prepare or instigate terrorism (whether or not the acts amount to an actual or inchoate offence).
>
> (2) In this section—
> "the Refugee Convention" means the Convention relating to the Status of Refugees done at Geneva on 28th July 1951, and
> "terrorism" has the meaning given by section 1 of the Terrorism Act 2000 (c. 11).

Section 1 of the Terrorism Act 2000 as amended then provides as follows:

> Terrorism: interpretation

> (1) In this Act "terrorism" means the use or threat of action where—
> (a) the action falls within subsection (2),
> (b) the use or threat is designed to influence the government [or an international governmental organisation] or to intimidate the public or a section of the public, and
> (c) the use or threat is made for the purpose of advancing a political, religious, [racial] or ideological cause.
>
> (2) Action falls within this subsection if it—
> (a) involves serious violence against a person,
> (b) involves serious damage to property,
> (c) endangers a person's life, other than that of the person committing the action,
> (d) creates a serious risk to the health or safety of the public or a section of the public, or
> (e) is designed seriously to interfere with or seriously to disrupt an electronic system.
>
> (3) The use or threat of action falling within subsection (2) which involves the use of firearms or explosives is terrorism whether or not subsection (1)(b) is satisfied.
>
> (4) In this section—
> (a) "action" includes action outside the United Kingdom,
> (b) a reference to any person or to property is a reference to any person, or to property, wherever situated,
> (c) a reference to the public includes a reference to the public of a country other than the United Kingdom, and
> (d) "the government" means the government of the United Kingdom, of a Part of the United Kingdom or of a country other than the United Kingdom.
>
> (5) In this Act a reference to action taken for the purposes of terrorism includes a reference to action taken for the benefit of a proscribed organisation.

However, the Qualification Directive gives effect to the Refugee Convention in UK law and in setting out the exclusion clauses it specifically refers to 'acts contrary to the purpose and principles of the United Nations as set out in the Preamble and Articles 1 and 2 of the Charter of the United Nations'. Articles 1 and 2 cannot be construed as being as wide as the definition of terrorism in the Terrorism Act 2000. In the case of *Al-Sirri v SSHD & Anor* [2009] EWCA Civ 222 the Court of Appeal held that the Terrorism Act 2000 therefore had to be 'read down' to be compatible with the Qualification Directive. The Court goes on to define terrorism as 'the use for political ends of fear induced by violence' and also finds that there must be an international element to the terrorism in order to bring it within the scope of the exclusion clauses.

Article 33(2)

Article 33(2) of the Refugee Convention lifts the ban on return to the frontiers of territories where they fear persecution ("non-refoulement") for refugees for whom there are reasonable grounds for regarding as a danger to the security of the country in which he is, or who have been convicted of a particularly serious crime. It is not limited to crimes committed outside the country of asylum, which is a difference between it and Art 1(F)(b).

It had long been thought that this provision would only operate with respect to individuals who committed serious crimes either after obtaining asylum, or in the course of their asylum claim being considered.

However, NIAA 2002, section 72, which brings Article 33(2) into domestic law, in effect excludes from refugee status those deemed to fall within the terms of that Article in advance of an immigration judge considering their asylum claim.

Section 72 has the effect of creating a presumption that a person convicted of certain criminal offences for which he was sentenced to a period of imprisonment of 2 years either in or outside the UK is a danger to the community. The presumption also arises if he was convicted of a certain crime in the UK, specified by an order, or if the SSHD certifies that a conviction abroad is of a crime similar to one specified in the order. If the SSHD issues a certificate asserting that the presumption is engaged, unless that appellant persuades the immigration judge at the start of the hearing that the presumption should not apply to him, or is rebutted, the appellant's appeal on the grounds that his removal would breach the Refugee Convention must be dismissed.

The applicant retains the right to establish that his removal would be in breach of the ECHR, so this provision prevents people becoming refugees and (presently) obtaining indefinite leave to remain rather than condemning them to a return abroad to face torture or inhuman treatment, etc). So there would be no inhibition on their arguing their human rights grounds before an Immigration judge if the Secretary of State did not accept their 'well foundedness'.

The SSHD passed an order setting out certain offences, which, under section 72(4) and (5), gave rise to the presumption that the appellant is a danger to the community, regardless of the sentence. However, this order was declared unlawful by the Court of Appeal in the case of *EN (Serbia) v SSHD* [2009] EWCA Civ 630 and at the time of writing the position remains that the entire order is *ultra vires* and therefore ineffective.

It is moot as to whether section 72 should be considered notwithstanding the issue of a certificate by the Secretary of State.

Humanitarian Protection

Under the Refugee Convention, a person whose removal from the territory would threaten their life or freedom is entitled to remain in the country of asylum, and to various other rights to be enjoyed for the course of stay as a refugee (including non-discrimination). However, the European Convention on Human Rights, which has since 2 October 2000 been effective in domestic law to supplement the Refugee Convention as a way of receiving protection, did not give any rights to those who benefit from its provisions to the extent of removing return to their country of origin – in essence the only right is to be free from torture, etc, not to other rights regarding the form of leave to remain, family reunion or travel documents.

From 1 April 2003 it became Home Office policy to give some formal rights to asylum seekers who were staying for "human rights" reasons. These forms of leave were known either "Humanitarian Protection" or "Discretionary Leave". Formerly, with some variations in practice, general policy was to grant Exceptional Leave to Remain.

From 10 October 2006 the EC Qualification Directive entered force. It brings a new era of protection and includes both refugee status and Humanitarian Protection under its wing. It is important to realise that Humanitarian Protection prior to that date was no more than a form of leave to remain given by virtue of Home Office policy – ie an administrative discretion. Humanitarian Protection after that date is a form of international protection given under directly effective European Community law (in EC law it is known as Subsidiary Protection, but the UK has chosen to keep the name for the pre-existing form of leave). Whilst the name may be the same, the legal basis is quite different.

Serious harm

Humanitarian Protection is received by those who face a risk of 'serious harm'. The forms of serious harm are as follows, see Article 15(a) of the Directive:

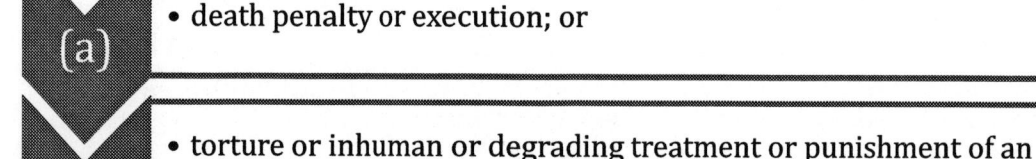

(a)
- death penalty or execution; or

(b)
- torture or inhuman or degrading treatment or punishment of an applicant in the country of origin; or

(c)
- serious and individual threat to a civilian's life or person by reason of indiscriminate violence in situations of international or internal armed conflict.

This has been incorporated into the immigration rules (Rule 339C) thus:

> Grant of humanitarian protection
>
> 339C. A person will be granted humanitarian protection in the United Kingdom if the Secretary of State is satisfied that:
>
> ...
>
> (iii) substantial grounds have been shown for believing that the person concerned, if he returned to the country of return, would face a real risk of suffering serious harm and is unable, or, owing to such risk, unwilling to avail himself of the protection of that country; and
>
> Serious harm consists of:

> (i) the death penalty or execution;
> (ii) unlawful killing;
> (iii) torture or inhuman or degrading treatment or punishment of a person in the country of return; or
> (iv) serious and individual threat to a civilian's life or person by reason of indiscriminate violence in situations of international or internal armed conflict."

Basically, then, the question is whether the individual faces a real risk of "serious harm" for one of this quartet of reasons.

It will be noted that the forms of harm are reminiscent of the some of the more basic protections afforded by the ECHR (rule 339C(ii) is like Article 2 ECHR; rule 339C(iii) resembles Article 3 ECHR), and indeed Immigration Judges and the Home Office's lawyers speak as if there was no difference between the era of the Refugee Qualification Directive and that of bare human rights protection.

However there are numerous differences. European Community law has its own maxims of interpretation that are different to international or domestic law: it is significantly more purposive.

In addition, it is accepted in Strasbourg and domestically that ECHR Art 6 (the right to fair trial) does not apply in immigration proceedings. However because there is now a right under European Community law to refugee status or Humanitarian Protection, this may well have to be revisited. The Court of Appeal have resisted the temptation to do in *R (on the application of MK (Iran)) v Secretary of State for the Home Department* [2010] EWCA Civ 115 finding that this was a matter for the Strasbourg Court alone.

The right to refugee status and Humanitarian Protection demands that the Secretary of State determine applications on those grounds (rather than leaving them to the immigration tribunal as has often been done in recent years regarding those earmarked for deportation on criminal grounds), and requires a fully effective right of appeal for those seeking Humanitarian Protection (section 83 of the Nationality Immigration and Asylum Act 2002 only gives an upgrading appeal on refugee grounds): the Court of Appeal found that in fact it was necessary to read words into the Nationality Immigration and Asylum Act 2002 such that the appeal provisions addressing refugee law rights of appeal extended to Humanitarian Protection ones too: *FA (Iraq) v Secretary of State for the Home Department* [2010] EWCA Civ 696 (18 June 2010).

Article 15(c)

These differences aside, it will be seen that Article 15(c) (immigration rule 339C(iv)) finds no obvious reflection in human rights law. The issue has been investigated by the Tribunal and Courts in a string of cases now, starting from the ill-fated first foray by the Tribunal in *KH (Article 15(c) Qualification Directive) Iraq CG* [2008] UKAIT 00023. Whilst many of the decisions recognise that this is a new form of international protection, collectively they severely limit the extra scope the provision offers beyond that of the Refugee and European Conventions.

"Conflict"

In *KH Iraq* the Tribunal find that the matters to be investigated in determining whether there is an "internal armed conflict" are

- firstly, whether there can be said to be "parties to the conflict";

- secondly, their "degree of organization";

- thirdly, the "level of intensity" of the conflict (which has to be higher than "situations of internal disturbances and tensions, such as riots, isolated and sporadic acts of violence, or other acts of a similar nature"); and

- fourthly, the "protraction" of the conflict.

However, it is doubtful whether this form of analysis remains necessary: because the Court of Appeal in *QD Iraq* find in the special sense of Article 15(c), "armed conflict" has "an autonomous meaning broad enough to capture any situation of indiscriminate violence, whether caused by one or more armed factions or by a state." The third and fourth factors will be relevant to the rest of the Article 15(c) enquiry though, because they are relevant to whether there are sufficient dangers as to amount to a "real risk" of "indiscriminate violence".

Standard of Proof

Some respectable commentators and judges have thought the critical issue that differentiates Article 15(c) from the other forms of international protection is that the provision was built around a form of harm other than that where a "real risk" was present, i.e. that the provision's aim was to address a bare *threat* of harm. Certainly this fits with the language of "real risk ... of a threat". This would have represented a broader form of protection than for the more familiar parts of human rights and refugee law, where there must actually be a "real chance" of ill-treatment or persecution.

However, this idea seems to have been rejected by the Court of Appeal in *QD Iraq v Secretary of State for the Home Department* [2009] EWCA Civ 620 which found that 15(c) "seeks to cover ... real risks and real threats presented by the kinds of endemic act of indiscriminate violence."

The big remaining question will be when it can be said that civilians face real risks: some authorities have spoken, in other contexts, of a "well founded fear" of persecution equating to a 10% chance of persecution, or that there might be a "real risk" of a human rights breach there was a one in ten chance of it happening (*Batayav v Secretary of State for the Home Department* [2003] EWCA Civ 1489). There can be few conflicts in history that have produced such casualty rates.

"Indiscriminate violence"

The European Court of Justice in *Elgafaji (Justice and Home Affairs)* [2009] EUECJ C-465/07 (17 February 2009) decided that "indiscriminate violence" refers to a high intensity of violence: so high, in fact, that the side effects of armed conflict "may extend to people irrespective of their personal circumstances." In addition:

- there might be classes of individual at enhanced risk due to personal factors (in UK case law, examples given in *GS Afghanistan* were the disabled person who cannot flee shellfire as swiftly as the able-bodied civilians around them, and members of groups who might be sought out by parties to the conflict, or taking advantage of the conflict, for special attention);

- past exposure to violence in a conflict might show a likelihood of a repetition of such experiences absent a change of circumstances (the sentiment here is probably better than the logic).

In *GS (Existence of internal armed conflict) Afghanistan CG* [2009] UKAIT 00010 the Tribunal found that "indiscriminate violence" would include that meted out by criminals taking advantage of the law and order vacuum created by the conflict.

"Life or Person"

However, the personal interests threatened, according to both the *KH* and *GS* Tribunals, must be of the most extreme variety: thus "life and person" might be murder, mutilation, cruel treatment and torture, but not "mere" inhuman or degrading treatment. The Court of Appeal seemed not to agree in *QD Iraq*, but they failed to develop this by offering any broader alternative.

So, Article 15(c) presently requires the following:

- a real risk of a threat

- perhaps, the threat being of dangers to life and person narrowly construed as death or serious physical injury

- in circumstances where there is a high intensity of violence such that civilians can be said to be at risk on an "indiscriminate basis" (subject to "enhanced risks")

The critical question

The conclusion of the Court of Appeal in *QD* was that "the critical question" was:

> "Is there in Iraq or a material part of it such a high level of indiscriminate violence that substantial grounds exist for believing that an applicant ... would, solely by being present there, face a real risk which threatens his life or person?"

At the time of writing internal armed conflicts had been found by the tribunal to exist in Iraq (as above), Somalia (*AM & AM (armed conflict: risk categories)*

Somalia CG [2008] UKAIT 00091) and Afghanistan (*GS Afghanistan*). However, civilians in Afghanistan and Iraq were not at sufficient risk to enliven Article 15(c); and in Somalia, the violence was so extensive that their cases would succeed on Refugee Convention grounds or human rights ones, making it unnecessary to make findings on their claims under Article 15(c).

Chapter 4: Asylum process and practice

CLAIMING ASYLUM 153
    DEFINITION OF 'ASYLUM CLAIM' 154
    SCREENING INTERVIEW 154
    ASYLUM INTERVIEW 155
    DECISION 155
    FURTHER GROUNDS: SECTION 120 STATEMENT 156
    LODGING THE APPEAL 156

AGE DISPUTES 156
    RELEVANCE OF AGE 156
    CHALLENGING AN AGE ASSESSMENT 157

FAST-TRACK APPEALS 159

THIRD COUNTRY CASES 161
    DUBLIN II 161
    HOME OFFICE POLICY ON THIRD COUNTRY CASES 163
    THIRD COUNTRY CERTIFICATES 163
        Returns to European Member States 164
        Removals to non-EU states: Refugee Convention and ECHR 165
        Removals to non-EU states: designated safe under RC51 165
        Removals to non-EU states: safe on facts under RC51 166
    SUBSTANCE OF THIRD COUNTRY CHALLENGES 166
        Refoulement challenges 166
        Article 3 and 8 challenges 167

'CLEARLY UNFOUNDED' CERTIFICATES 168

FRESH CLAIMS 169
    LEGAL TEST 169
    PROCESS 170
    RIGHTS OF APPEAL 171
        Prohibition on further appeals or raising grounds late 172
        Fresh claims and clearly unfounded certificates 173
        In country rights of appeal 174
    CASE LAW 175
    EVIDENCE 177
        Previously available evidence 177
        Sur place style arguments 179
        Article 8 private and family life 180
    RIGHT TO WORK 183

BENEFITS OF RECOGNITION AS A REFUGEE 183
    REFUGEES AND IMMIGRATION STATUS 183
    REFUGEE FAMILY REUNION 184

Under the rules 184
Outside the rules 185
Making an application 185
REFUGEES AND WORK, BENEFITS AND EDUCATION 185

BENEFITS OF HUMANITARIAN PROTECTION 187

IMMIGRATION STATUS 187
EXCLUSION 187
FAMILY REUNION AND TRAVEL DOCUMENTS 188

Claiming asylum

The procedure by which an asylum claim is made has tended to vary in recent years as the Home Office has introduced various expedited or abbreviated processes for particular classes of case. However, a certain amount of stability should be expected in future now that what has become known as the New Asylum Model (no longer officially referred to as such in the Home Office) is fully operational. All new asylum claims have been processed under the New Asylum Model as of May 2007.

The key feature of the new process is that a Home Office official called a Case Owner is allocated to a case after screening, who is then intended to be responsible for seeing that case through from start to finish and managing all aspects of the case, including welfare support and reporting conditions. This differs from the previous regime, where a different official would be responsible for every action taken on a file, meaning there was no sense of overall responsibility or accountability, and no feedback from later in the process could be taken into account earlier in the process.

The process is broadly as follows:

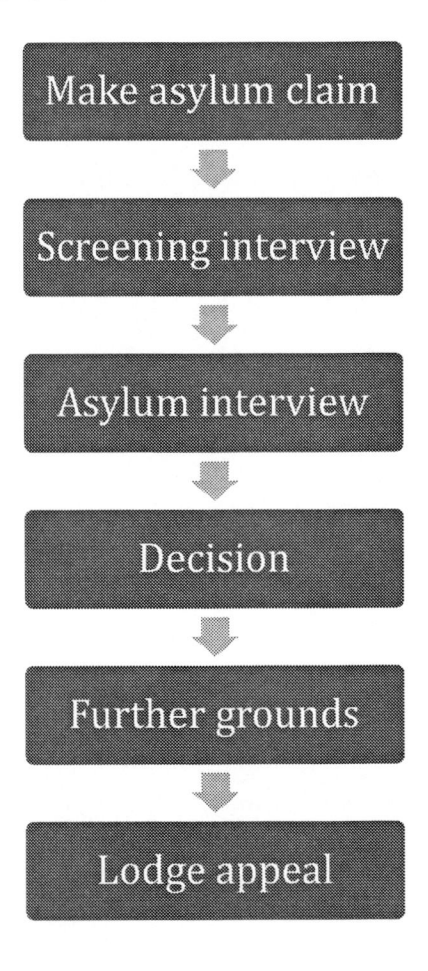

- Make asylum claim
- Screening interview
- Asylum interview
- Decision
- Further grounds
- Lodge appeal

Definition of 'asylum claim'

An 'asylum claim' is tightly legally defined at section 113 of the Nationality, Immigration and Asylum Act 2002. This definition has been changed by section 12 of the 2006 Act but at the time of writing this change had not been brought into effect by a commencement order. Both definitions are therefore set out here.

The old unamended definition (in force at time of writing) is as follows:

> "asylum claim" means a claim made by a person to the Secretary of State at a place designated by the Secretary of State that to remove the person from or require him to leave the United Kingdom would breach the United Kingdom's obligations under the Refugee Convention,

The new amended definition (possibly to be brought into force at an as yet unknown date) is as follows:

> "asylum claim"-
> (a) means a claim made by a person that to remove him from or require him to leave the United Kingdom would breach the United Kingdom's obligations under the Refugee Convention, but
> (b) does not include a claim which, having regard to a former claim, falls to be disregarded for the purposes of this Part in accordance with immigration rules"

The amended definition, if ever brought into force, will exclude claims not recognised as fresh claims under rule 353 of the immigration rules (see further below) from being considered as asylum claims for the purposes of, amongst other things, asylum support. The new definition does remove the requirement to make a claim at a designated place, however, which is a positive step.

Screening interview

Once a claim has been made, the next step is the screening process. This includes fingerprinting of the applicant and the entry of those fingerprints into the EURODAC database to detect any multiple applications (including made in other EC countries).

A screening interview takes place, which concentrates on personal details and mode of entry and travel to the United Kingdom, said by the Home Office to be intended to address identity and nationality. This questioning will also address whether the applicant has potentially committed a criminal offence under s.2 of the 2004 Act (see later chapter on criminal offences). If the answers given by the applicant suggest the offence may have been committed, a referral to the police and CPS will be considered by the Home Office.

If it transpires that the applicant has made a very late claim for asylum having been inside the UK for several weeks, months or years, section 55 of the 2002

Act may be applied, which deprives the applicant of asylum welfare support. This is, however, rare now.

Applicants are given a form of induction during which they receive an Application Registration Card (ARC) which contains their personal details and acts as a form of identity (now more popular than the Standard Acknowledgment Letter, the SAL). As of February 2005, the immigration rules (rule 359) require the Secretary of State to provide to an asylum seeker a document certifying their status as such, within 3 days of their arrival.

Under immigration rule 358, the Secretary of State must now inform asylum seekers, "within fifteen days after their claim for asylum has been recorded of the benefits and services that they may be eligible to receive and of the rules and procedures with which they must comply relating to them."

Asylum interview

Under previous asylum determination processes, a self-completion Statement of Evidence Form (SEF) would often be sent to an asylum applicant, who would then have the opportunity to set out his or her claim before being interviewed, so that in theory the interview could be focussed on important matters.

Under the new process, no self-completion SEF is sent to applicants, who are simply interviewed by a Case Owner from a standing start. These interviews often take several hours.

Representatives are not at present usually funded by the Legal Services Commission to attend interviews. As a consequence of this funding bar, the Home Office has been forced to offer that interviews are recorded: see the case of *R (Dirshe) v SSHD* [2005] EWCA Civ 421. It is strongly advisable that asylum applicants make use of this facility, which is available on demand but is not automatic.

Decision

Decisions follow quite quickly from asylum interviews, although the time taken by individual Case Owners varies, depending on their working speed and whether they agree to wait for additional evidence or submissions.

Asylum seekers are now permitted to apply for permission to take up employment, although not self employment or to engage in a business or professional activity, if a decision at first instance has not been taken on their asylum application within one year of the date on which it was recorded – so long as the delay is not attributable to them. The Secretary of State shall only consider such an application if, in his opinion, any delay in reaching a decision at first instance cannot be attributed to the applicant (rule 360).

Further grounds: Section 120 statement

When a person makes an application to enter or remain in the UK, the SSHD or an immigration officer may serve a notice on him asking for him to state in writing:

(a) his reasons for wishing to enter or remain in the United Kingdom,

(b) any grounds on which he should be permitted to enter or remain in the United Kingdom, and

(c) any grounds on which he should not be removed from or required to leave the United Kingdom.

Where a person has an immigration decision within the meaning of section 82 of the 2002 Act made in respect of them, the SSHD may serve a similar notice on the applicant asking for the same information.

There is no requirement for a repetition of reasons or grounds contained in the original application or that have already been considered in the immigration decision (2002 Act, s120).

Lodging the appeal

The deadline for the submission of an asylum appeal varies depending on the exact circumstances of the appellant:

- In-country, not detained: 10 working days
- In-country, detained: 5 working days
- Out of country: 28 working days

These time limits originate in the Asylum and Immigration Tribunal Appeal (Procedure) Rules 2005. Appeals law is covered in more detail in a later chapter, including business and calendar days, time for postage and submission of late appeals.

An asylum appeal will normally be lodged with the Immigration tribunal directly (until 2005 appeals were lodged with the Home Office) but detainees have the option of lodging an appeal with their custodian.

Age disputes

Relevance of age

There has been considerable litigation around disputed age assessments of young asylum seekers. If UKBA do not believe that an asylum claimant is really under the age of 18, as they claim, then that claimant will be treated as an adult. UKBA policy is that age will only be disputed where it appears very obvious that the claimant is over the age of 18, but the assessment process is carried out by untrained and inexpert staff simply on the basis of a visual assessment.

If children are wrongly assumed to be adults this will lead to their applications for asylum and other international protection being assessed by processes designed for adults rather than children.

This could lead to them being detained within the fast track system with adults. They may also be detained because the doubt about their age has damaged their overall credibility. If they are relying on having been subjected to child specific forms of persecution their applications may be fatally undermined. Age is also a central part of a child's identity and a failure to believe that they are children could lead to them losing all confidence in the decision making system and failing to disclose further and necessary details about their past persecution and future fears.

They will also be refused accommodation under Section 20 of the Children Act 1989 and will be dispersed to NASS accommodation as adults.

Because of the additional care and rights that a child in the asylum process has over an adult, it is therefore important to challenge an assessment that a claimant is over the age of 18.

Challenging an age assessment

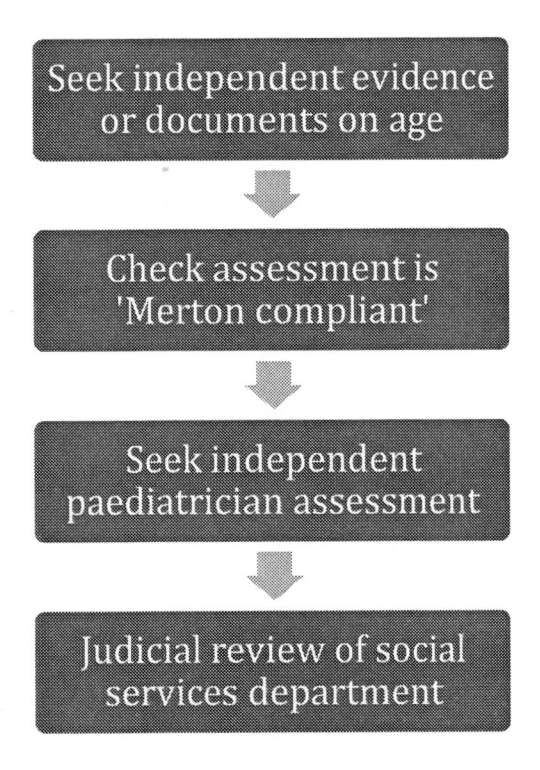

1. Seek independent evidence or documents on age
2. Check assessment is 'Merton compliant'
3. Seek independent paediatrician assessment
4. Judicial review of social services department

Before seeking to challenge a UKBA age assessment it is important to obtain any independent evidence available as to a person's age. Any such evidence will carry weight with whoever conducts an age assessment. Attempts should therefore be made to verify any documentation the child may have with them in the form of passports, national or school identity cards, family records or similar. Schools, doctors, hospitals, local officials, NGOs in the field and other objective sources of data about their age will need to be followed up. Statements and affidavits from family and community members should also be sought.

The first avenue for challenge is to approach the local social services department, which has a duty to conduct an age assessment in order to determine whether the person is a child and if so a child in need. This social services age assessment must be 'Merton compliant', i.e. comply with the standards set down in the case of *R (on the application of B) v London Borough of Merton Council* [2003] EWHC 1689 (Admin), in which it was held that:

> "...the decision maker cannot determine age solely on the basis of the appearance of the applicant. In general, the decision maker must seek to elicit the general background of the applicant, including his family circumstances and history, his educational background, and his activities during the previous few years. Ethnic and cultural information may also be important. If there is reason to doubt the applicant's statement as to his age, the decision maker will have to make an assessment of his credibility, and he will have to ask questions designed to test his credibility."

In *R (on the application of T) v London Borough of Enfield* [2004] EWHC 2297 (Admin), Jackson J held in addition that it was necessary to ask the individual why they believed that they were a minor and take into account any evidence which indicates that they are suffering from trauma and/or have any special educational needs.

If the social services age assessment is unfavourable, there are different courses of action that can be pursued, including:

1. Seeking alternative independent evidence of age as suggested above. Should new evidence become available social services will need to conduct a new age assessment.

2. Seeking a paediatrician age assessment. This is simply one form of independent evidence, but it is a controversial one because of the case of *A v London Borough of Croydon & SSHD (Interested Party), WK v SSHD and Kent County Council* [2009] EWHC 939 (Admin). In this case Collins J held that paediatrician age assessments are unreliable and do not have to be given any particular weight by social services. The judgment is under appeal but in the meantime, this case will be taken as good law by social services departments.

3. Judicial review of social services. In the case of *R (on the application of A) v London Borough of Croydon* [2009] UKSC 8 the Supreme Court held that an age assessment by social services is subject to a full appeal in the courts, rather than being a matter simply for the social services department. This is very helpful when it comes to challenging a social services department. The Supreme Court case came after the judgment of Mr Justice Collins (they are related but distinct cases) and undermines key parts of the reasoning of the

earlier case, so it may prove to be the case that paediatrician assessments will be considered more acceptable again in future.

The fact is that deciding someone's age is an extremely difficult exercise and it is not possible to be completely accurate. The most honest assessments include a margin of error of around two years either way. Any relevant evidence is therefore highly relevant to the assessment.

Fast-track appeals

The key features of fast track appeals are as follows:

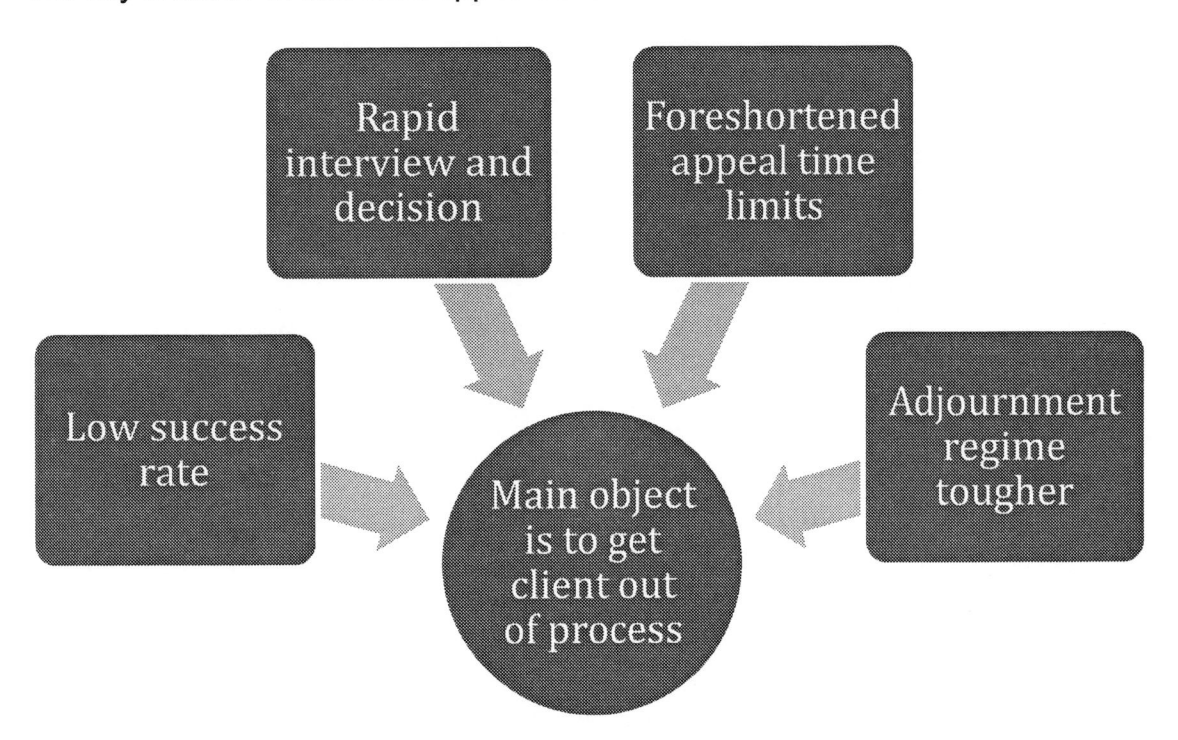

- Rapid interview and decision
- Foreshortened appeal time limits
- Low success rate
- Adjournment regime tougher

→ Main object is to get client out of process

The 'fast track' procedure is one whereby the asylum decision and appeal takes place in a short time frame. In order to ensure compliance with this process, the subject is detained throughout. The success rate of cases going through the fast track process is very low indeed, at around a 99% failure rate. Whether this is because UKBA is spectacularly successful at selecting low merit cases for the process or because any case that goes through the process thereby becomes low merit is a question many practitioners have posed.

Those who are allocated to the fast track processes at Harmondsworth and Yarl's Wood receive a decision on their claim within 3 days of arrival and are subjected to an expedited appeals procedure.

The Asylum and Immigration Tribunal (Fast Track Procedure) Rules 2005 govern appeals under the accelerated regime where the appellant was in immigration detention at a place specified in the Schedule to the Rules (presently Harmondsworth, Yarls Wood, Campsfield and Colnbrook).

The procedure under these Rules differs from that under the Principal Rules principally in the following ways -

(a) there are shorter time limits for the parties and the Tribunal to take certain steps (rules 7 to 12, 14, 19, 21, 23, 25 and 26);

(b) the procedures for deciding certain issues are simplified or modified to reflect the shorter timetable in fast track proceedings (rules 12, 13, 22 and 28);

(c) in all fast track cases, including cases where the appeal relates in whole or in part to an asylum claim, the Tribunal must serve its determinations and decisions on every party to the appeal (rules 14, 19 and 23); and

(d) in the fast track, an application under section 103A of the 2002 Act must be served on the party to the appeal other than the applicant, who may file submissions in response to the application, which the immigration judge must consider (rules 17 and 18).

An adjournment may be granted only where there is insufficient time to hear the appeal, where a party has not been served with the hearing notice in accordance with the rules 28(2)(a)(b)), where the matter is taken out of the process (rule 30) or where the interests of justice point towards dealing with the case later (rule 28(2)(c)) and if there is an identifiable future date, not more than ten days after the date on which the appeal is listed for hearing, by which the appeal can be justly determined (rule 28(2)(c)(ii)). It can be seen, therefore, that the scheme of the process is to the effect that only a very short adjournment should be granted unless the matter is being removed from the process.

There is a power in the immigration tribunal to order removal of the appeal from the fast track procedure:

(a) if all the parties consent (rule 30(1)(a));

(b) exceptionally, if evidence filed or given by or on behalf of a party that the appeal cannot otherwise be justly determined (rule 30(1)(b); or

(c) if the Respondent fails to comply with the 2005 rules (fast track or principal) or a direction of the immigration tribunal, where the appellant would be prejudiced by that failure if the appeal were determined in accordance with the fast track rules (rule 30(1)(c)).

When making an order for removal from the procedure, the immigration judge may adjourn the appeal, giving directions if thought fit; the closure date rule then applies (rule 30(3)).

A case turning on authenticity of documents would be one example unsuitable for treatment under this procedure, see Lord Phillips MR in the Court of Appeal in *ZL and VL v Secretary of State for the Home Department and Lord Chancellors*

Department [2003] EWCA Civ 25. Any case where complex evidence is available or sought (eg medical evidence or country expert evidence) may become unsuitable, as suggested by ILPA in their Response to Inquiry into Asylum and Immigration Appeals.

On a removal from the process, any time periods for acts to be done which are then running are to be replaced by their equivalent in the principal rules (rule 31).

Third Country Cases

An asylum applicant cannot normally be removed from the UK whilst their claim is pending a decision upon it (2002 Act, section 77). An exception to this is where UKBA intends to remove the asylum applicant to a third country. Thus asylum claims may be refused without substantive consideration of the claim if the applicant can be returned to a safe third country.

Dublin II

The old Dublin Convention has been replaced by a new instrument, which has changed the order of the hierarchy for consideration in order to place more weight on some family connections.

Council Regulation Number 343/2003 ("the Dublin II Regulation") applies to asylum applications lodged on or after 1 September 2003; and to those where a request to take back an asylum seeker is made after 1 September 2003, regardless of when the asylum claim was made. The hierarchy of criteria is as follows:

- Unaccompanied minors – where family member is present so long as in their best interests

- Asylum seeker with family members resident in a state – so long as they so desire, in the latter's host state

- Asylum seeker with family members with asylum claim pending first decision– so long as they so desire, in the host state

- Asylum seeker with valid residence document – in issuing state

- Asylum seeker with valid visa – in issuing state

- Asylum seeker with valid visas for different states – in state of longest visa validity period, or state of earlier grant if periods are the same

- Asylum seeker with residence documents that expired less than 2 years ago – in issuing state

- Asylum seeker with residence documents that expired more than 2 years ago – in state of asylum application

- Asylum seeker who entered European Union unlawfully – in state where entered Union

- Asylum seeker details of whose entry cannot be established – place of continuous residence for 5 months

- State which has waived visa requirements

- State where asylum application first lodged

- Where multiple asylum claims made by family members who would under the foregoing criteria be dispersed across Europe, the responsible state should be that where the greatest number is lodged or that where oldest claimant should be processed.

There are time limits within which responsibility of a third country should be dealt with by the country in which the asylum application has been lodged, see the Convention Article 11: "If the request that charge be taken is not made within the six-month time limit, responsibility for examining the application for asylum shall rest with the State in which the application was lodged."

There is one very important difference between the Dublin Convention and Dublin II, which is that the latter is directly effective, which means there may be circumstances under which someone might be able to challenge a decision to consider their case in a third country where they had family in the UK using Dublin II.

The meaning of "Family members" receives specific definition in Dublin II:

> (i) family members" means insofar as the family already existed in the country of origin, the following members of the applicant's family who are present in the territory of the Member States:
> (ii) the spouse of the asylum seeker or his or her unmarried partner in a stable relationship, where the legislation or practice of the Member State concerned treats unmarried couples in a way comparable to married couples under its law relating to aliens;
> (iii) the minor children of couples referred to in point (i) or of the applicant, on condition that they are unmarried and dependent and regardless of whether they were born in or out of wedlock or adopted as defined under the national law;
> (iv) the father, mother or guardian when the applicant or refugee is a minor and unmarried.

Where an applicant is dependent on the assistance of a relative on account of pregnancy or a new-born child, serious illness, severe handicap or old age, member states shall normally keep or bring together the asylum seeker with the relative, provided that family ties existed between them in the country of origin (Dublin II, 15(2)), which also gives protection to minors:

> "15(3). If the asylum seeker is an unaccompanied minor who has a relative or relatives in another Member State who can take care of him or her, Member States shall if possible unite the minor with his or her relative or relatives, unless this is not in the best interests of the minor."

Home Office policy on third country cases

In all third country cases the Home Office Third Country Unit must be satisfied that:

- the applicant is not a national or citizen of the country of destination;

- the applicant's life and liberty would not be threatened in that country by reason of race, religion, nationality, membership of a particular social group or political opinion; and

- the government of that country would not send the applicant to another country other than in accordance with the 1951 Convention (the concept of 'non-refoulement').

The Home Office APIs tell us that non-EU cases will be "third-countried" only if they are "port" cases, because of the speed of arrangements that must be achieved in order to get states with which the UK has less close relations to readmit the applicant.

They add that a return can be attempted only where either the applicant:

- had an opportunity at the border or within the territory of a safe third country to make contact with that country's authorities in order to seek protection; or

- that there is other clear evidence of the applicant's admissibility to a safe third country.

Third country certificates

The law in this area has been significantly altered by the Asylum and Immigration (Treatment of Claimants') Act 2004 ("2004 Act"), Section 33 of which, together with Schedule 4, now comprises the substantive law that deals with return to third countries. This replaces the earlier regime, which was based on a combination of the Immigration and Asylum Act 1999 and Nationality Immigration and Asylum Act 2002.

Many challenges have been brought to removals to so-called safe third countries in the last few years, often on the grounds that the third country will not consider their asylum or human rights claim properly. The Secretary of State has divided countries up into four lists, the first of which comprises the EU countries, the others of which are to comprise countries which are to be notified by designation by Order. The deeming provisions which insulate third country removals from challenge are being significantly extended, depending on the category of country in question – as the Explanatory Note to the Act puts it, "The provisions therefore take a graduated approach to the "safety" of third countries for Refugee Convention and ECHR purposes."

Returns to European Member States

Wherever there is a wish to return an individual to a third country, Schedule 3 to the 2004 Act comes into play. There are now deeming provisions regarding questions of safety of third countries which are EU members (to state the obvious, this applies as much to recent accession countries such as the Czech Republic as to France; in total, the countries are those which are subject to, or have agreed to be bound by the Dublin arrangements - currently the members of the enlarged European Union as from May 2004 together with Norway and Iceland) in so far as the matter is for "the determination by any person, tribunal or court" (Sch 3, paragraph 3) – with the intended consequence that the Administrative Court on judicial review is no more able to disagree with the view of the Secretary of State than anyone else. The consequence of the provision is that such territories are deemed safe for three purposes – (1) as to their safety as places where persecution might occur themselves, (2) as to the manner in which they deal with asylum claims, and (3) as to the manner in which they deal with human rights claims (Sch 3, paragraph 3(2)). So in theory there can be no tenable claim that an EU country will either ill-treat an individual themselves, or that they will send a person onwards to face Article 3 mistreatment or persecution elsewhere.

So long as the Secretary of State certifies that the individual is not a national or citizen of the third country, then there is no suspension on removal there as would normally be the case once an asylum claim is made (this being an exception to section 77 of the 2002 Act, which in general protects those with undetermined claims from being sent abroad).

The "in-country" right of appeal against the decision is not available on asylum or human rights grounds where the allegation is to the effect that the third country would send the person onwards incompatibly with either of the Conventions (Sch 3, paragraph 5(3)). It is available regarding other allegations of human rights incompatibility (e.g. where it is not the behaviour of the third country so much as the removal itself which is said to infringe human rights, as in *Razgar*) – but only if the Secretary of State does not issue a certificate stating it to be clearly unfounded, and if there is a presumption either way, it is in favour of issuing a certificate, because "the Secretary of State shall certify a human rights claim to which this sub-paragraph applies unless satisfied that the claim is not clearly unfounded" (Sch 3, paragraph 5(4)(5)). Even the "out-of-country appeal" is now ousted in cases where the grounds within it run contrary to the presumptions of safety already discussed – ie in terms of Refugee Convention problems within the country itself, or sending the person onwards without considering either a human rights or Refugee Convention claim.

Removals to non-EU states: Refugee Convention and ECHR

There are separate regimes for non-EU countries (Sch 3 Part 3). The Secretary of State may designate certain countries by orders (historically the USA, Canada, Norway and Switzerland have been designated). Removals to designated countries will enjoy immunity from challenge (by appeal or judicial review) via similar presumptions to those addressed above. Specifically they will be deemed safe both as to the threat of persecution within their borders and in terms of their dealing with asylum claims (Sch 3 para 8(2)) – although there is no deeming provision regarding their safety as to how they would deal with human rights claims (perhaps because they will at least sometimes be countries that are not ECHR-signatories), so this facet of their safety could be challenged on a judicial review application.

So long as the Secretary of State certifies that the individual is not a national or citizen of the third country, then there is no suspension on removal there as would normally be the case once an asylum claim is made (this being an exception to section 77 of the 2002 Act, which in general protects those with undetermined claims from being sent abroad) (Sch 3 paragraph 9).

The "in-country" right of appeal against the decision is not available on Refugee Convention grounds where the allegation is to the effect that the third country would either be a place of persecution itself or might send the person onwards incompatibly with the Refugee Convention (Sch 3, paragraph 10(3)). It is available regarding all allegations of human rights incompatibility (both where it is the behaviour of the third country in terms of not properly considering human rights claims, and where the removal to the third country is in itself a direct human rights breach because it interferes with an individual's physical and moral integrity) – but only if the Secretary of State *does not* issue a certificate stating it to be clearly unfounded, and once again there is a pointer towards issuing a certificate, because "the Secretary of State shall certify a human rights claim to which this sub-paragraph applies unless satisfied that the claim is not clearly unfounded" (Sch 3, paragraph 10(4)). The "out-of-country appeal" is ousted in cases where the grounds within it run contrary to the presumptions of safety already discussed – ie in terms of Refugee Convention problems within the country itself, or sending the person onwards without considering a Refugee Convention claim.

Removals to non-EU states: designated safe under RC51

There is provision made for a further list of countries which may be designated dealt with by paragraphs 12-16 of the Third Schedule. It would seem that this list is intended to operate similarly to that just described: but there is to be no presumption that human rights claims are unfounded in those cases (contrast Sch 3 paras 10(4) and 15(4), the former of which contains the presumption, the latter of which does not).

Removals to non-EU states: safe on facts under RC51

Further to the ability to treat people differently depending on the category of third country by which they have travelled, there is also provision for returns to be made where on the facts of the particular case the country is said to be safe. So this could apply whatever the third country involved; whereas one at least hopes that the countries that reach the threshold of safety in dealing with asylum claims under the second and third designated categories will be fairly limited in number (if only because the legislation may be vulnerable to challenge otherwise as being itself incompatible with human rights).

Once again these destinations must be ones of which the individual is not a national or citizen. In these cases there are the now familiar ousters of appeals: no "in-country" challenge to the notion that the state is safe, both in terms of being a place of potential persecution and also so far as it treats refugee claims itself (Sch 3 paragraph 19(a)(b)). Again there is no prospect of bringing a human rights claim at all if a certificate is made stating it to be "clearly unfounded" (Sch 3 paragraph 19(c)); and the "out-of-country" appeal cannot challenge the Secretary of State's conclusions as to the destination's safety with regard to the Refugee Convention (Sch 3 paragraph 19(d)). However these presumptions are not expressed so as to bind reviewing courts, so there is no ouster of judicial review on this occasion.

Substance of third country challenges

Refoulement challenges

In the case of *TI v United Kingdom* [2000] INLR 211 the European Court of Human Rights held that Dublin II did not absolve the United Kingdom from responsibility to ensure that a decision to expel an asylum seeker to another Member State did not expose that asylum seeker, once removed, to treatment contrary to article 3 of the Convention.

The case of *Nasseri* [2009] UKHL 23 was brought by an Afghan national who was to be returned to Greece under Dublin II. Mr Nasseri claimed that if he was returned to Greece that would amount to a breach of Article 3 ECHR because it would be unlawful *refoulement* to Afghanistan, as the Greek authorities would not properly consider his claim and would return him to Afghanistan. There was considerable evidence to show that the Greek ability to assess asylum and human rights claims were very seriously deficient and that cases were automatically rejected after an absence from the country of three months, which would almost always be the case after a Dublin II return.

The claim succeeded in the High Court but failed in the Court of Appeal and also in the Lords. It was accepted that Greek asylum status determination was appalling but there was no evidence that Greece actually removed anyone anywhere, so there was no risk of *refoulement* in practice. However, it was explicitly left open for a future case to succeed on the basis that there was an actual risk of *refoulement*.

At the time of writing a further case on third country Dublin II removals to Greece, *R (on the application of Saeedi) v Secretary of State for the Home Department* [2010] EWHC 705 (Admin), had been dismissed in the High Court and was under appeal to the Court of Appeal. On 12 July 2010 the Court of Appeal gave an interim judgment in the appeal, in *R(NS) v Secretary of State for the Home Department* (C4/10/0943). The Court of Appeal made a Reference to the Court of Justice of the European Union. The Reference addresses issues such as whether the discretion at para 3(2) of the Dublin II Regulation falls within the scope of EU law, and the consequence of breaches of the Procedures and Reception Directives and of the Charter for Fundamental Rights in the country allocated responsibility under Dublin II on the operation of "third country" returns.

Article 3 and 8 challenges

An alternative challenge to one based on risk of *refoulement* has been attempted in respect of removals to Italy. The challenges have been based on a breach of human rights in Italy itself, founded on the principles in *Razgar*.

In *R (on the application of EW) v Secretary of State for the Home Department* [2009] EWHC 2957 (Admin) it was argued that the treatment of asylum seekers in Italy was so appalling that return under Dublin II to Italy would lead to a breach of Article 3 in Italy itself. The claim was comprehensively dismissed on the grounds that failure to provide reception facilities did not even engage Article 3 as it was not 'treatment' and even if it did the conditions did not pass the threshold for 'inhuman or degrading'. The High Court (and Court of Appeal in refusing permission to appeal) also held that that there is a presumption that states comply with their international obligations (para 111).

However, in another challenge also to removal to Italy, in the case of *T, R (on the application of) v Secretary of State for the Home Department* [2010] EWHC 435 (Admin), Mr Justice Collins held that the removal had been unlawful. The judgment focuses on the lawfulness of a same-day no-notice removal, however, and the facts were unusually strong. In one of the two linked cases a 15 year old was detained without warning at her foster carer's address in a dawn raid. She was handcuffed. Her removal was stopped as she managed to get in touch with her lawyers. In the other case a 16 year old also in the care of social services and placed with a foster carer was also detained in another dawn raid, but this time she was unable to contact her lawyers and was removed. She had disclosed to social services that she had experienced sexual assault previously in Italy and been forced to work as a prostitute, and the Third Country Unit knew this. On return to Italy she was held in a cell then released onto the streets with no accommodation or money.

The current legal position is therefore that if there is very good evidence that a Dublin II destination state is failing to assess protection needs and then is actually removing people to their home countries, a successful challenge could be mounted to a Dublin II removal notwithstanding the statutory presumptions.

Similarly, if there was extremely good evidence that there was active 'treatment' of Dublin removees in Italy or elsewhere that crossed the inhuman and degrading threshold (widespread police beatings or similar) then an Article 3 claim could succeed.

The 2004 Act is therefore potentially but not actually at the current time incompatible with Article 3 ECHR. As Lord Justice Laws commented in *Nasseri* in the Court of Appeal, that makes the UK's compliance with its human rights obligations very fragile.

'Clearly unfounded' certificates

Key points:

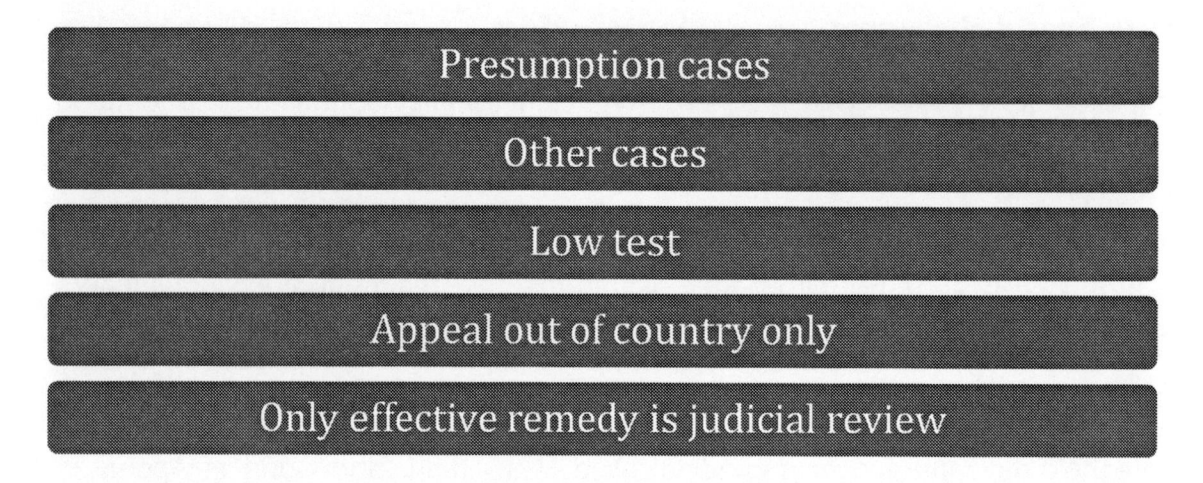

- Presumption cases
- Other cases
- Low test
- Appeal out of country only
- Only effective remedy is judicial review

An appellant cannot normally be removed from the UK whilst an asylum application or appeal is pending (2002 Act, s.78 and 79). However, the SSHD has the power to certify asylum or human rights claims as clearly unfounded. If the SSHD issues such a certificate the applicant cannot appeal under s.82 of the 2002 Act whilst he is in the UK.

Section 94 of the 2002 Act creates a presumption that all claims where the applicant is entitled to reside in listed countries are "clearly unfounded". The Home Office must certify such claims as clearly unfounded unless satisfied that they are not so. The list in the statute is frequently changed but at the time of writing includes Albania, Bolivia, Brazil, Bulgaria, Ecuador, Serbia and Montenegro, Kosovo, India, Jamaica, Macedonia, Moldova, Mongolia, Romania, South Africa, Ukraine, Ghana (for men) and Nigeria (for men).

Bangladesh was added to the list but has been removed, as was Sri Lanka. In *R v Secretary of State for the Home Department ex parte Husan* [2005] EWHC 189 (Admin), Wilson J concluded that the inclusion of Bangladesh on the list was unlawful:

> "...whether in July 2003, when it was added to the list, or at any time since then, no rational decision-maker could have been satisfied that there was in general in Bangladesh no serious risk of persecution of persons entitled to reside there or that removal of such persons thither would not in general contravene the UK's obligations under the Human Rights Convention. The objective material drove and drives only one rational conclusion; and it is to the contrary."

There are therefore two kinds of "clearly unfounded" case. There are those where the country is designated by inclusion on a list, which creates a presumption of certification; and there are those where the claim is viewed by the SSHD as so hopeless as to merit certification even without the general presumption, i.e. cases that are weak on their own facts, so it is not the designation of the country which is determinative. For example, Mr Husan, the claimant whose judicial review succeeded in establishing that Bangladesh should not have appeared on the list, still lost his case on its being clearly unfounded in its own terms.

Decision makers should be slow to find a claim to be clearly unfounded, especially on grounds of credibility – in fact some judges have recommended that the case be taken at its highest for the purposes of considering whether it is unfounded. As the test was put in *R v SSHD ex parte Thangarasa; Yogathas* [2002] UKHL 36:

> "The question to which the Secretary of State had to address his mind....is whether the allegation is so clearly without substance that the appeal would be bound to fail."

On judicial review, the judge will look to see whether the SSHD correctly applied the tests set out above. In *ZT (Kosovo) v SSHD* [2009] UKHL 6 the House of Lords held that a Administrative Court Judge reviewing a clearly unfounded certificate must (i) ask the questions which an immigration judge would ask about the claim and (ii) ask itself whether on any legitimate view of the law and the facts any of those questions might be answered in the claimant's favour.

Fresh claims

Making a fresh asylum or human rights claim if a previous asylum or human rights claim has failed may sometimes be possible. A fresh claim is essentially a new claim for protection that differs substantially from the previous claim because either:

1. there is new evidence relating to a claim, such as evidence of a new threat to safety, or

2. there is new evidence that suggests that the previous decision or appeal was incorrectly decided

Legal test

In order to prevent repeat claims and appeals, however, the Immigration Rules set out circumstances where fresh claims will be accepted as constituting a fresh claim for asylum or human rights protection:

> '353. When a human rights or asylum claim has been refused and any appeal relating to that claim is no longer pending, the decision maker will consider any

> further submissions and, if rejected, will then determine whether they amount to a fresh claim. The submissions will amount to a fresh claim if they are significantly different from the material that has previously been considered. The submissions will only be significantly different if the content:
>
> (i) had not already been considered; and
>
> (ii) taken together with the previously considered material, created a realistic prospect of success, notwithstanding its rejection.
>
> This paragraph does not apply to claims made overseas.'

The key elements are that:

- The material has not been considered
- It should be considered in the context of the previous material
- It must create a realistic prospect of success

Process

In the past, fresh claims were usually made by post. However, in late 2009 UKBA began only to accept fresh claims (and further representations) from the applicant in person at what was formerly the Liverpool Public Enquiry Office. This is a serious disincentive to making a fresh claim as transport and accommodation costs to and in Liverpool are not provided by UKBA. The policy was under challenge at the time of writing.

The fresh claims process is a three stage one in most cases:

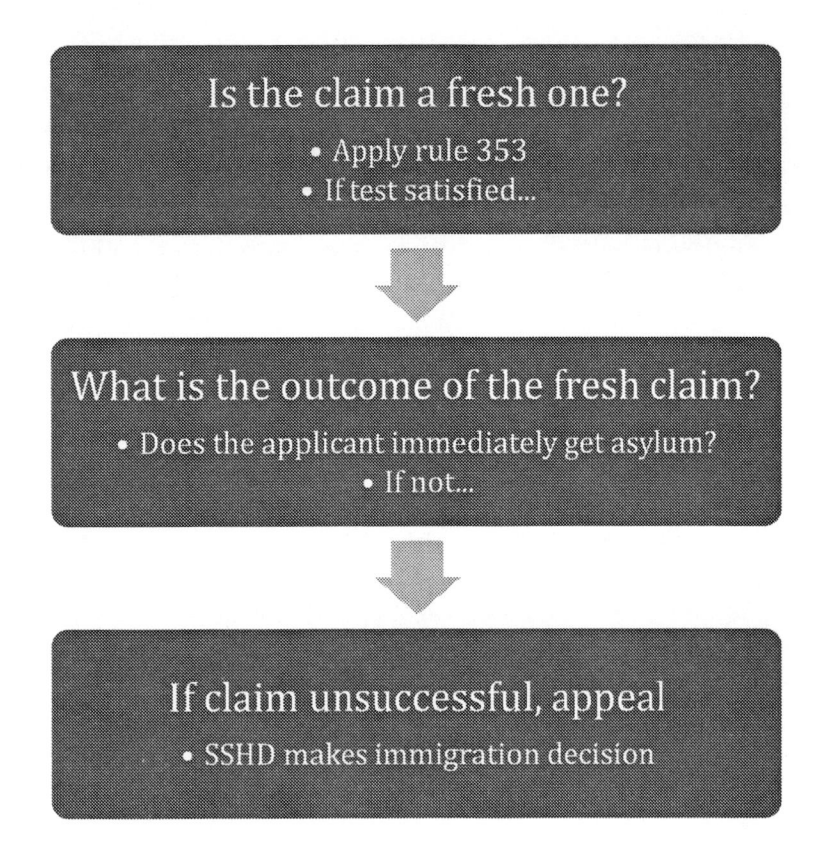

```
┌─────────────────────────────────────┐
│      Is the claim a fresh one?      │
│         • Apply rule 353            │
│         • If test satisfied...      │
└─────────────────────────────────────┘
                  ▼
┌─────────────────────────────────────┐
│  What is the outcome of the fresh claim?  │
│   • Does the applicant immediately get asylum?  │
│                • If not...          │
└─────────────────────────────────────┘
                  ▼
┌─────────────────────────────────────┐
│      If claim unsuccessful, appeal  │
│      • SSHD makes immigration decision │
└─────────────────────────────────────┘
```

The test under Immigration Rule 353 is therefore merely the trigger for the assessment of a fresh claim, or rather just a decision on whether the fresh claim will even be looked at. The decision under r.353 is not a substantive decision on whether asylum is to be granted or not. This substantive decision only takes place if the r.353 test is satisfied.

If the r.353 test is satisfied, it is Home Office policy to make a fresh immigration decision. The APIs state that, for example, in a Port applicant case a fresh decision on leave to enter will be made and in illegal entrant cases a fresh decision to remove will be made. See section 5 of the 'Further representations and fresh claims' API. The immigration decision will trigger a right of appeal to the immigration tribunal in accordance with s.82 and s.83 of the 2002 Act.

It is the experience of many practitioners that very few fresh claims are accepted by the Home Office, in the sense that the Home Office takes the view that few fresh claims satisfy the r.353 test.

The only remedy in these circumstances is judicial review as where the r.353 test is not satisfied the Home Office will not make a fresh immigration decision and there will therefore be no right of appeal to the immigration tribunal: the applicant will not cross the first hurdle in the above diagram.

Rights of appeal

There is no right of appeal to the immigration tribunal against a decision that a fresh claim for asylum does not meet the criteria for r.353. The only remedy for such a decision is judicial review.

However, as discussed earlier, if the r.353 test is met then it is Home Office policy (section 5 of the relevant API) to issue a new immigration decision which will trigger a right of appeal to the immigration tribunal. Normally section 96 of the 2002 Act limits rights of appeals where there has been an earlier immigration decision and/or appeal. However, the API states at section 1.1 that where a fresh claim is accepted, no certificate under s.96 should be imposed (see below).

Prohibition on further appeals or raising grounds late

If a matter is not raised in the "One Stop" Notice, then, if an attempt is made to raise it later after the appeal against a refusal of the original application has been dealt with, then the decision maker may issue a certificate that prevents any appeal. Although this power still arise under NIA 2002 section 96, as of 1 October 2004, that provision has been amended by section 30 of the Immigration and Asylum (Treatment of Claimants) Act 2004.

Now, certification is likely to follow

> where the claim or application to which the new decision relates relies on a matter that could have been raised in an appeal against the old decision, and

> where, in the opinion of the Secretary of State or the immigration officer, there is no satisfactory reason for that matter not having been raised in an appeal against the old decision.

Example

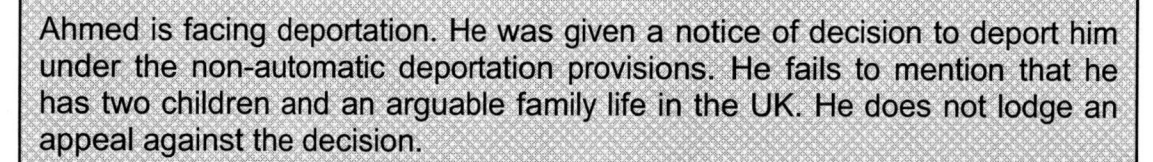

Ahmed is facing deportation. He was given a notice of decision to deport him under the non-automatic deportation provisions. He fails to mention that he has two children and an arguable family life in the UK. He does not lodge an appeal against the decision.

Ahmed is in a difficult situation. If he puts forward his family life arguments now in representations, he risks certification. He would need to show that he meets the test for a fresh claim. It might also be worth investigating whether to make a late appeal to the AIT, if Ahmed had difficulty obtaining legal representation in detention, was not given appeal forms at the time of the immigration decision or something similar.

"One stop" notices and rights of appeal accruing under the 1999 Act count as if they were given or arose under the 2002 Act, so the effect is that anyone who has been served with an immigration decision and been through the appeals system since either statute was in force (i.e. since 2 October 2000) is liable to certification.

The only remedy against these decisions to certify will be judicial review, i.e. an application to the Administrative Court showing that the certificate is wrongly made on grounds such as an error of law within it, or because of a failure to take account of all relevant evidence.

The provisions are designed to catch all circumstances, whether or not an appeal was brought, or if one was brought, whether or not it has been determined. Once an appeal has been instituted, however, there can be no certification (section 96(7) as amended by the 2004 Act, which suggests that if there is no certification in the fresh refusal letter, an appeal cannot be cut off by a subsequent certificate).

These provisions apply whether or not the appellant has been outside the UK since the requirement to state additional grounds arose or since the right of appeal arose (2002 Act, s96(5)).

Fresh claims and clearly unfounded certificates

In *ZT (Kosovo) v SSHD* [2009] UKHL 6, the House of Lords considered the interaction of the test for a fresh human rights claim and a clearly unfounded certificate imposed under s.94 of the 2002 Act.

Firstly, the majority in the Lords held that rule 353 does potentially apply where a person in receipt of a s.94 certificate but who has not yet left the UK and therefore still has a future right of appeal (albeit one that can only be exercised after departure) makes new representations to the Home Office. Those in favour are Lords Phillips, Carswell, Brown and Neuberger. Lord Hope dissents on this point.

A differently comprised majority then hold that there is a potential difference between the outcomes of considering a case under s.94 and rule 353. Lords Phillips and Brown dissent and hold that there is no difference, but Lords Hope, Carswell and Neuberger form the majority on this issue.

The two tests are similar sounding to the layman:

Section 94
- Does the claim exceed the relatively modest 'clearly unfounded' threshold?

Rule 353
- Does the claim have a realistic prospect of success?

Indeed, in *R (on the application of YH) v Secretary of State for the Home Department* [2010] EWCA Civ 116 the Court of Appeal held that for all intents and purposes the tests are indistinguishable.

Nevertheless, an asylum seeker who is certified under s.94 can put forward a fresh claim which must be considered by the Home Office under the rule 353 criteria.

> **Example**
>
> Mirza claims asylum and his claim is certified as 'clearly unfounded' under section 94 of the 2002 Act. However, he is not immediately removed from the UK. In the meantime, he manages to acquire documentary evidence that assists his case.
>
> The new evidence is put forward as a fresh human rights claim.
>
> The fresh claim must be assessed by the Home Office under rule 353 and the 'realistic prospect of success' test applied. Assuming the Home Office decide that the test was not passed, no immigration decision (under s.82(2)) will be made and there is no right of appeal to the tribunal. The only remedy would be an application for judicial review.

In country rights of appeal

In *R (on the app of BA (Nigeria)) v SSHD* [2009] UKSC 7 the Supreme Court held that it is not necessary to qualify under rule 353 in order to obtain an in-country right of appeal under section 92(4)(a) of the 2002 Act if putting forward a human rights claim. However, importantly, it is seldom the case that any right of appeal whether in or out of country will be generated by a fresh human rights claim unless the rule 353 test is actually satisfied and the Secretary of State therefore makes an immigration decision that can be appealed.

The only reason that the issue arose in *BA (Nigeria)* was that the putative appellant had applied to revoke a deportation order, and a refusal to revoke a deportation order is always an immigration decision under s.82(2)(k).

> **Example**
>
> In the example above, the case of Mirza, there was no right of appeal unless the rule 353 test was satisfied. An immigration decision is always required in order for a right of appeal to arise and refusal of a human rights claim is not by itself one of the immigration decisions listed in s.82(2).
>
> If Mirza had already been served with a deportation order but had not been removed and had now put forward a fresh human rights claim and on that basis applied for his deportation order to be revoked, refusal of the human rights claim *would* attract a right of appeal under s.82(2)(k). Because of *BA (Nigeria)* that appeal would be an in-country one, by virtue of s.92(4)(a).
>
> Although there has been some uncertainty in some quarters about the effect of *BA (Nigeria)* and whether it magically generates a right of appeal out of no immigration decision in case where a human rights claim is refused, the correct interpretation is confirmed by *R (on the application of ZA (Nigeria)) v Secretary of State for the Home Department* [2010] EWHC 718 (Admin).

The remedy to the *BA (Nigeria)* judgment from the perspective of the Home Office is to certify more attempted fresh claims under s.94 and to bring into force s.12 of the Immigration, Asylum and Nationality Act 2006, which amends the definitions of asylum claim and human rights claim in s.113 of the 2002 Act so as to exclude fresh claims not recognised under rule 353 of the rules.

The practical effect of *BA Nigeria* is enhanced in some circumstances by *R (on the app of AM (Ethiopia)) v SSHD* [2009] EWCA Civ 114, in which it is held that a section 94 certificate cannot 'kill' an appeal that is already in existence, it can only prevent an appeal being instituted if it has not already begun.

Case law

The case law on fresh claims needs to be read with a certain amount of caution as the immigration rules now set out a test for the acceptance of a claim as fresh and this test has subsequently been amended.

The original case on the circumstances where a fresh claim must be accepted is *ex p. Onibiyo* [1996] Imm AR 370 in the Court of Appeal. Sir Thomas Bingham held as follows in relation to the question 'what constitutes a fresh claim?':

> "The acid test must always be whether, comparing the new claim with that earlier rejected, and excluding material on which the claimant could reasonably have been expected to rely in the earlier claim, the new claim is sufficiently different from the earlier claim to admit of a realistic prospect that a favourable view could be taken of the new claim despite the unfavourable conclusion reached on the earlier claim."

In the case of *WM (DRC) v SSHD* [2006] EWCA Civ 1495 the Court of Appeal gave guidance on the task of the Secretary of State under the modern rule and held that the Secretary of State should consider whether an immigration judge on a future appeal would consider that the test was satisfied, bearing in mind that the test was a 'somewhat modest' one. The reliability of any new material is an important consideration, as are any findings by a previous judge as to the claimant's honesty and reliability as a witness. The Court went on to suggest that the role of the court in judicially reviewing such a decision is confined to the principles of judicial review, i.e. a Wednesbury unreasonable test applies, although the principle of anxious scrutiny means that the decision will be unreasonable if not reached with most anxious scrutiny.

Since then in *(R on the application of TR (Sri Lanka)) v Secretary of State for the Home Department* [2008] EWCA Civ 1549 and *R (on the application of YH) v Secretary of State for the Home Department* [2010] EWCA Civ 116 the Court of Appeal has held that on an application for judicial review it was for the court to decide for itself whether the relevant threshold is met rather than to apply *Wednesbury* principles in conducting the review.

Although the test is in law a 'relatively modest' one and little or no deference is due to the Home Office view, it can nevertheless be an uphill struggle to engage the interest of a High Court judge in a fresh claim application for judicial review. This is particularly the case where the claimant was previously found to be dishonest. The challenge is therefore obtaining good quality evidence on which to base the claim.

Example

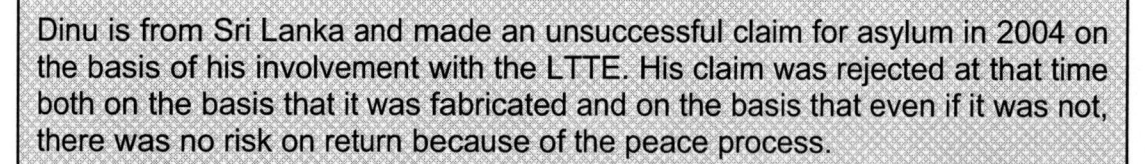

Dinu is from Sri Lanka and made an unsuccessful claim for asylum in 2004 on the basis of his involvement with the LTTE. His claim was rejected at that time both on the basis that it was fabricated and on the basis that even if it was not, there was no risk on return because of the peace process.

Even at the height of the conflict between the Sri Lankan government and the LTTE it would have been very hard for Dinu to make out a successful fresh claim on the basis of his own evidence or deterioration in the country situation because of the earlier adverse credibility findings. He would have needed independent evidence to suggest that the credibility findings were in fact wrong, such as compelling documentary evidence.

Evidence

Previously available evidence

There is no legal bar to reserving or failing or omitting to put forward evidence or submissions as part of a previous application and appeal and then seeking to institute a later fresh claim on the basis of such evidence or submissions (although as discussed earlier this may lead to certification under s.96 of the 2002 Act, meaning no right of appeal).

This, after all, is what happens where a person is very poorly represented by a previous lawyer or simple but highly prejudicial mistakes are made by that representative and the case is then put forward afresh. In *FP (Iran) v SSHD* [2007] EWCA Civ 13 the Court of Appeal held that "there is no general principle of law which fixes a party with the procedural errors of his or her representative", particularly in asylum cases.

However, there being no legal bar does not mean that relying on old and available evidence is straightforward. Part of the context to any discussion of this subject has to be the old case of *Ladd v. Marshall* [1954] 1 WLR 1489. There the principles governing admission of new evidence into appeal proceedings were said to be previous unavailability, significance and apparent credibility, or, more fully:

(1) the fresh evidence could not have been obtained with reasonable diligence for use at the trial

(2) if given, it probably would have had an important influence on the result

(3) it is apparently credible although not necessarily incontrovertible.

The *Ladd v Marshall* test does not strictly apply in a fresh claim situation, but it is very likely to be in the mind of any judge and commonsense dictates that due heed is given. Very good reasons will need to be given as to why the material was not previously submitted.

The way in which the Home Office and perhaps the court will reject newly submitted evidence that was previously available is by suggesting that it is not credible that such evidence would not have been forward sooner if it was available. Essentially, it is to allege that the evidence is forged or at least that even the claimant sets little store by it.

Chapter 4 – Asylum process and practice

> **Example**
>
> Takunda made a claim for asylum in 2008 and it was dismissed. He was found to have fabricated his account. At that time, he had no documentary evidence to support his claim.
>
> He later makes a fresh claim, having in the meantime acquired some documentary evidence that supports important parts of his case, including his claimed identity. He did not seek to acquire this earlier because his representative did not suggest it and he had not realised it could be important.
>
> If this evidence is from an independent source and cannot be easily dismissed as itself being fabricated then he may well have a good case for why the evidence should be considered and a good fresh claim.

Good reasons for departing from the general principles could, as discussed above, include negligence or omission by a previous representative. In *R (Gungar) v Secretary of State* [2004] EWHC 2117 (Admin) 7 September 2004 Collins J stated in respect of Rule 346 (which still applied at that time and is differently worded to rule 353 in respect of old evidence):

> 'The effect of all that, as I see it, is that, as the court said in E, Ladd v Marshall is the starting point and availability is a factor to be taken into account and certainly will be given considerable weight because it is important that there should be finality. It seems to me that in cases of availability the court should look with care to see whether in reality the evidence could have affected the result and if ignored would mean that there was a risk that human rights would be breached. I also bear in mind that it is said forcibly in this case, and I have no reason to doubt it since complaints have been made to the OSS about the conduct of the previous solicitors, that they did not prepare and so present the claimant's case as competently as they ought to have done and in particular they did not obtain, as they should, some material which would have assisted his claim.' (para 19)

As should be clear from this quote, care needs to be taken in making such allegations against a representative. Unless a complaint is made to the relevant regulator (the Solicitor Regulation Authority or the OISC, depending on the firm or organisation) then the courts are not likely to be interested in intervening. Without such a formal complaint the allegation will look like hot air. See *BT (Former Solicitors' alleged misconduct) Nepal* [2004] UKIAT 00311 for further guidance on how to address this issue. The Home Office may prove to be more flexible, however, as proved to be the case with one of the above scenario examples.

Another good reason might be that the issue was never raised or the claimant thought that sufficient evidence had already been submitted. For example, if an IJ finds against a claimant on credibility and truthfulness grounds – particularly where the RFRL did not raise the issue in question – that claimant might well be able to obtain more evidence substantiating that, for example, he was a lawyer, teacher or political activist.

Sur place style arguments

Many fresh claims rely on new evidence that has been obtained regarding risk on return. Examples might include:

- New documents that post-date the previous case that have been obtained from the home country, such as an arrest warrant, a witness statement or a newspaper article

- New witness evidence from within the UK, such as from representatives of the claimant's political party or family members who have recently arrived

- New expert evidence of some kind

The problem with any new evidence is that if the claimant has already been found to be untruthful and capable of deceit, any new evidence put forward will probably need to come from an independent source to stand much chance of being accepted by the Home Office or a judge.

It is also worth taking note of Mr Justice Collins' comments in the case of *R (on the app. of Rahimi) v SSHD* [2005] EWHC 2838 (Admin). Collins J outlined the test to be applied by the Secretary of State in deciding whether any new material is credible and therefore sufficient to found a fresh asylum claim and found that it is a low test of whether the evidence is capable of belief.

In practical terms, it is important to be careful about how any new evidence is presented. For example, an original document with good, certified translation and an authentication report by an expert is more likely to work than a badly faxed and poorly translated document.

As well as new evidence, there may well be new developments in the country of proposed removal that mean the case must be looked at afresh. The obvious example at the time of writing is Zimbabwe. The case of *RN (Returnees) Zimbabwe CG* [2008] UKAIT 00083 states, in essence, that anyone who is unable positively to demonstrate loyalty to ZANU-PF is at risk to return. This case marked a significant change in position, and it meant that many failed asylum seekers (and others) might now qualify for asylum. Many Zimbabweans living in the UK, particularly failed asylum seekers, did then put forward asylum claims.

Another contemporary example is to be found with Sri Lanka. During the peace process many claims for asylum failed, but when that broke down and then ended, many Sri Lankans have put forward fresh claims. The situation changed again with the military defeat of the LTTE, potentially undermining those fresh claims.

These Sri Lankan claims often illustrate the potential problem with putting forward a new claim based on a change of circumstances (or on new evidence for that matter). If the claimant was previously found to be dishonest and, for example, was found not really to have been a member of the LTTE or not really to have been harassed and detained by the authorities, then a fresh claim is unlikely to get far. The Home Office and then a High Court judge will find that there is still no risk as there is no reason for the authorities to be interested in the claimant.

However, where there have been positive findings of fact, for example in a case where it was found that the claimant was detained and that there might be a record of that detention, but that there was no risk because of the peace process, then the claimant might have a sound fresh claim.

Example

In the earlier example of Dinu from Sri Lanka, his first asylum claim had been dismissed on both credibility and future risk grounds.

If it has been accepted that he had been telling the truth about several detentions he had suffered then his claim might still have been rejected at the time that the peace process was going on.

Assuming he was not removed in the meantime, the breakdown of the peace process might well have been sufficient change of circumstances that a fresh claim could have succeeded.

Article 8 private and family life

Many fresh claims rely on Article 8, either or both in respect of family and private life. The fact is that many asylum seekers and other illegal immigrants or overstayers are not removed and do not voluntarily depart when their cases are concluded, remain in the UK for sometimes many years and then either step forward voluntarily to put forward a new case or come to the attention of the immigration authorities in some way.

With claims based on family life relationships, it is crucial to put forward good evidence of the relationship by the parties but also from other sources. As well as the parties to the relationship, friends and family can give witness statements and utility bills or correspondence placing the parties at the same address are very helpful as a form of objective proof.

> **Example**
>
> Victor entered the UK many years ago and claimed asylum. He failed to attend his hearing and his case was dismissed. The Home Office made no attempt to remove him.
>
> He comes to the attention of the police and is detained for removal as an illegal entrant.
>
> His solicitors assert in representations that Victor has a long term relationship with a British lady and is joint carer for a stepson and a child of the relationship. However, Victor is removed because the solicitors failed to include any evidence of family life.

Evidence to consider putting forward includes:

- Witness statement from claimant including history of relationship, meaning of relationship to him/her, why he/she likes the partner, activities together,

- Witness statement from partner as above and, if possible, including plans for the future should the claimant be removed

- Witness statement from family members of the partner

- Witness statements from mutual friends or others who have seen the parties together and can confirm and describe the relationship

- Correspondence placing the parties at the same address

- Photographs of the parties together

- Receipts, tickets, bank statements or other evidence of expenditure on activities together (ask the parties to empty their handbags, coat pockets, wallets and drawers to search for any such material)

- Telephone bills showing calls to each other (with proof of the owner of the respective telephone numbers)

- Correspondence between the parties such as letters, emails, texts, cards

- Any local press coverage of the case. Local newspapers can be sympathetic in these cases, particularly where the claimant has been detained.

Where there are children affected by a decision (whether the biological children or step children of the claimant), the House of Lords cases of *Beoku-Betts* and *EM (Lebanon)* require that the immigration authorities consider the rights of those affected by an immigration decision but also give careful separate consideration to the rights of affected children. Evidencing the effect on children is not straightforward but the following may help:

- Witness statement from the UK-based parent (and others, potentially) describing the relationship between the claimant and affected children, including how the child regards the claimant, describing activities together and claimant's role in upbringing and day to day care

- Photographs of the claimant and child together

- Report of an Independent Social Worker

The latter can be expensive but can also be invaluable in providing qualitative evidence of the nature of the relationship.

Where the relationship between the adults has broken down, obtaining evidence on the relationship with the children can be highly problematic. Some partners are willing to put aside their differences for the sake of the children and co-operate with obtaining evidence for an immigration case. In other cases, the breakdown is too acrimonious and there may even be serious allegations made against the claimant.

In such cases the following evidence should be considered:

- Witness summons of the partner under procedure rule 50 – this may well not be a sensible move for obvious reasons, but an application to treat the witness as hostile is possible

- Disclosure of family proceedings papers into the immigration proceedings, *with the permission of the relevant judge*. Children proceedings are strictly confidential and reading papers from a children case can be a serious contempt of court, so caution is needed, as well as attempted co-operation with the family solicitors (some are unwilling to assist without being paid) and with the partner's solicitors. If agreement from the other side can be obtained, a judge will usually endorse this. The relevant papers will include but not be limited to any s.7 Children Act 1989 report by a local authority, any CAFCASS and/or Guardian reports on contact or residence and, if care proceedings have been instituted, any social services reports.

- Witnesses from the family proceedings could potentially be called, using a summons if necessary, for example, the CAFCASS officer or social worker.

- Failing this, an Independent Social Worker will need to be instructed, although access to the children may prove to be very difficult if the mother is not co-operating.

A record should be kept of any steps taken to obtain evidence, which can then be shown to the Home Office or High Court judge.

Right to work

In the case of *ZO (Somalia) v SSHD* [2010] UKSC 36 the Supreme Court held that asylum seekers pursuing fresh claims have the right to work after a year awaiting the outcome of their claim. The judgment is a short and simple one based on the EC Reception Directive. At the time of writing the Home Office response had been, through Statement of Changes CM 7929, to allow work only in a shortage occupation as defined in the documentation relating to Tier 2 of the Points Based System.

Benefits of recognition as a refugee

Refugees and immigration status

If it is an asylum case allowed under the Refugee Convention, then the applicant will be recognised as a refugee and (since 30 August 2005) five years leave to remain will be granted. In the past ILR was granted.

If the refugee reaches the end of the five year period without his or her case having been reviewed, ILR will normally be granted, subject to a life in the UK test and the absence of criminal convictions. If, during the five year period, a Minister has issued a ministerial declaration that a particular country is now considered to be generally safe, all refugees of that nationality will have their cases individually reviewed, with a right of appeal against any decision to revoke refugee status. The burden will rest with the Home Office to establish that the individual is no longer a refugee. Assurances have been given that there will be few declarations.

No declarations had been made at the time of writing and given existing Home Office workloads, it seems unlikely that any such declarations will be made in the near future. It is likely that the real reason for the change in policy was to exclude what the Home Office terms 'chain migration'. Refugees are no longer able to sponsor immigration applications from abroad (aside from under the rule for refugee spouses etc, discussed below) as they are no longer 'present and settled' under the immigration rules, at least until they have acquired ILR.

It is worth noting that switching into another immigration category will protect the applicant from ministerial declarations. For example, getting married to a settled person would avoid removal as a consequence of any review of status later on.

Refugee family reunion

The origin of the Home Office policy on family reunion lies in the Final Act of the United Nations Conference on the Status of Refugees and Stateless Persons. As set out at Annex I of the UNHCR Handbook, the Conference, considering that the family was "the natural and fundamental group of society" and that unity of the family was "an essential right of the refugee" recommended that Governments... take the necessary measures for the protection of a refugee's family, especially with a view to ... ensuring that the unity of the refugee's family is maintained particularly in cases where the head of the family has fulfilled the necessary conditions for admission to a particular country".

Under the rules

The accommodation and maintenance requirements which ordinarily apply to dependants seeking admission for settlement under the immigration rules are waived for family members of those with refugee status. The present immigration rules read:

> 352A. The requirements to be met by a person seeking leave to enter or remain in the United Kingdom as the spouse [or] civil partner of a refugee are that:
> (i) the applicant is married to or the civil partner of a person granted asylum in the United Kingdom ; and
> (ii) the marriage or civil partnership did not take place after the person granted asylum left the country of his former habitual residence in order to seek asylum; an
> (iii) the applicant would not be excluded from protection by virtue of article 1F of the United Nations Convention and Protocol relating to the Status of Refugees if he were to seek asylum in his own right; and
> (iv) each of the parties intends to live permanently with the other as his or her spouse civil partner and the marriage is subsisting; and
> (v) if seeking leave to enter, the applicant holds a valid United Kingdom entry clearance for entry in this capacity.

Where members of the family eligible under this rule are not of the same nationality as the principal, or do not wish for refugee status, the Home Office will still consider them under the generous provisions of rule 352A.

There is also a rule for unmarried and/or same sex partners (352AA) and for the pre-departure children of the refugee (352D).

The Court of Appeal held in the case of *DL (DRC) & the Entry Clearance Officer, Pretoria v The Entry Clearance Officer, Karachi* [2008] EWCA Civ 1420 that the sponsor must possess current refugee status in order to qualify. This judgment was successfully appealed to the Supreme Court but at the time of writing judgment was not available. In the case of *MS and others (family reunion: "in order to seek asylum") Somalia* [2009] UKAIT 00041 the tribunal held that a sponsor under the refugee family reunion rules had to have left their country of origin or habitual residence in order to seek asylum, meaning in order to claim asylum in their own right. This prevents *sur place* and those who themselves entered the UK as family members from sponsoring their own family members under these rules. The determination was under appeal to the Court of Appeal at the time of writing.

Outside the rules

The Home Office Policy on family reunion requires that *compelling compassionate circumstances* be shown for other members of the family, whose cases will be referred to the Home Office by ECOs, including:

- Spouse and minor children who were not part of the family unit prior to the sponsor's flight (though they will qualify if the marriage took place in a country other than the country of nationality where one was habitually resident - *A (Somalia* [2004] UKIAT 00031*)* (24 February 2004);

- Elderly parents;

- The parents and siblings of a minor who has been recognised as a refugee.

If discretion is not exercised outside the rules, these family members can only be considered under Article 8 ECHR or paragraph 317 of the Immigration Rules, which has a very high threshold for qualification and requires the sponsor to be present and settled in the UK, which refugees are not for at least five years. The usual settlement fees would be payable.

Making an application

Family reunion applications must be made at entry clearance posts overseas.

Where the principal has been recognised as a refugee in the UK the Home Office will normally recognise family members in line with them.

Note that under Article 1(C)(3), a refugee ceases to be a refugee once they have acquired a new nationality; in other words, once a refugee obtains British citizenship they are no longer a refugee, and therefore no longer entitled to the benefits afforded to refugees such as family reunion. See *DL (DRC) v ECO, Pretoria* [2008] EWCA Civ 1420. Any application for family members to join the principal would have to be made through the immigration rules excluding those relating to family unity for refugees.

Refugees and work, benefits and education

Any person with refugee status, indefinite leave to remain (ILR), exceptional leave to remain (ELR), humanitarian protection, or discretionary leave has the right to work in the UK and does not need to ask permission from, or inform the Home Office, before taking up employment or setting up a business. This will be shown in the letters granting them leave to enter or remain.

Section 12 of the 2004 Act has abolished the entitlement to backpayments of income support, housing benefit and council tax benefit for those who are recorded as refugees. Section 13 of the Act permits the Secretary of State to make regulations enabling him to make loans to refugees to assist with their integration into the community.

The following information comes from the website of Education Action International. Note that their use of language tends to equate refugees and asylum seekers.

> [T]here are no legal restrictions to refugees' access to education in the UK. Refugees are free to study any course at any level or in any mode (part-time/full-time), as long as they meet the following conditions:
> They must be able to satisfy the entry requirements of the course in terms of their language skills and their academic/ vocational/ experiential background.
> They must have the financial ability to pay the course fees and maintain themselves while studying. This is especially important if they are ineligible for statutory financial support, ie. Student Loans, Access Funds, Hardship Funds and Learner Support Funds.
>
> 1.1. Eligibility for remission of fees:
>
> All categories of refugees, including asylum seekers, who are in receipt of state benefits are eligible for the Learning and Skills Council funding, therefore they do not need to pay tuition fees. This policy is referred to as "remission of fees" or "nil fees" policy, according to which refugees should be receiving either:
>
> - a means tested state benefit, ie. Income Support, Job Seekers Allowance, Housing Benefit etc. or
> - assistance from the National Asylum Support Service (NASS), or
> - assistance from the Social Services.
>
> Dependants of the above mentioned refugees are also entitled to free education.
>
> During enrolments colleges may charge a College Registration Fee.
>
> It should be noted that refugees who are in receipt of Job Seekers Allowance should not be studying for more than 16 hours per week, as this affects their eligibility to this benefit.
>
> It should also be remembered that the "remission of fees policy " of the Learning and Skills Council does not apply to those courses classified as "self-financing" or "full-cost" courses.
>
> 2.1. Refugees and rates of tuition fees:
>
> There are two rates for tuition fees: The Overseas student rate and the Home student rate. The latter is much cheaper that the former. Refugees' eligibility for the Home Student or Overseas Student rate of fees is determined by the Education (Fees and Awards) Regulations 1997. According to these regulations refugees with full Refugee Status (currently given together with Indefinite Leave to Remain) and Exceptional Leave to Remain or Enter are entitled to pay fees at the Home Student rate. In other words, charging these categories of refugees Overseas Student fees is an illegal action, and it can be challenged. Refugees who have been given Indefinite Leave to Remain under the Home Office's "Backlog Clearing Scheme" are also eligible for Home Student fees after fulfilling the "three year ordinary residence"

> requirement before the start of the course. Asylum seekers, however, can legally be charged at the Overseas Student rate, but the Regulations left this to the discretion of the educational institutions. This means it is up to the educational institutions to charge asylum seekers Home Student fees or Overseas Student fees. Many universities have a policy of charging asylum seekers Home Student fees. Some universities may consider individual cases for Home Fees, but as a rule they charge asylum seekers Overseas Student rate of fees.
>
> ...
>
> Refugees' eligibility for statutory student support:
>
> Refugees' eligibility for statutory student support, including fee waivers, depends on their immigration status: According to the Education (Student Support) Regulations 2002, refugees with full refugee status (recently given together with indefinite leave to remain) are eligible immediately for such support, but refugees with Exceptional Leave to Remain need to fulfil the " three year ordinary residence requirement before the start of their course. Asylum seekers are ineligible, regardless the length of their stay in the UK."

Benefits of Humanitarian Protection

Immigration status

'Subsidiary protection' status is in many ways equivalent to refugee status as it exists under the Directive. A person who qualifies for Humanitarian Protection should be granted leave for 5 years.

If the circumstances which gave rise to the need for protection continue to exist, holders of Humanitarian Protection who have completed 5 years of leave will be eligible to apply for Indefinite Leave to Remain (ILR), also known as settlement. The individual should apply for settlement shortly before the expiry of their Humanitarian Protection leave. The application for settlement should be considered in the light of the circumstances prevailing at that time.

In order to assess properly whether circumstances continue to exist, there will be an active review of any application for further leave, normally just on the papers.

Exclusion

Persons who face a real risk of treatment which meets the criteria for Humanitarian Protection will not be granted leave on that basis where they fall into the exclusion criteria set out the Home Office instruction and the EC Qualification Directive. These criteria include:

- Those whose presence in the UK is not conducive to the public good, for example because of their criminal behaviour and/or their threat to security of the United Kingdom.

- Those falling under the exclusion criteria for the Refugee Convention in Articles 1F and 33(2) (ie those of whom there are serious reasons for considering them to have committed war crimes etc, serious non-political crimes, crimes against purposes of United Nations; and those convicted of serious crimes in the UK or abroad, regardless of motive, one for which a custodial sentence of at least 12 months has been imposed in the United Kingdom).

- Those considered to be a threat to national security.

- Those whose character, conduct or associations counts against them. For example, where deportation action has been considered and has only not been pursued or has been abandoned because Article 2 or Article 3 considerations render removal impossible for the time being.

A "serious crime" for these purposes is or a crime considered serious enough to exclude the person from being a refugee in accordance with Article 1F(b) of the Convention. For the purposes of Humanitarian Protection, those who commit serious crimes are excluded whether or not they have a political motive. The ability of the state to exclude an asylum seeker for a "serious crime" for Humanitarian Protection is much more extensive than their ability to do so for Refugee Convention purposes.

There are provisions for the ending of Humanitarian Protection if an individual takes actions such as re-availing themselves of their country's protection that mirror the Cessation Clauses within the Refugee Convention. There is also provision for revocation where it comes to light that the exclusion criteria are satisfied, or where dishonesty is discovered to have founded the grant of HP.

Family reunion and travel documents

Under the EC Qualification Directive, those with subsidiary protection are entitled to family reunion, on the same terms as refugees (the Secretary of State has made this effective from earlier than the date of the Directive's own directive effect, namely where the grant of Humanitarian Protection took place after 30 August 2005): ie those eligible are pre-flight spouses and civil partners where there is an intention to live together permanently who would not be excluded from refugee status in their own right; and pre-flight children under the age of 18, not leading an independent life, unmarried or civilly partnered, who have not formed an independent family unit (339FG). From 9 October 2006 unmarried and same-sex partners similarly qualify (339FD).

A person with Humanitarian Protection can obtain travel documents "where that person is unable to obtain a national passport or other identity documents which enable him to travel, unless compelling reasons of national security or public order otherwise require": rule 334A(ii). If such a person can theoretically obtain such documents but has not done so, then a travel document may be issued if "he can show that he has made reasonable attempts to obtain a national passport or identity document and there are serious humanitarian reasons for travel": rule 334A(iii).

Chapter 5: Human rights law

HUMAN RIGHTS ACT 1998 191
INTERPRETATION OF STATUTE 191
EFFECT ON PUBLIC AUTHORITIES 192
DAMAGES AND COMPENSATION 192
HUMAN RIGHTS AS A GROUND OF APPEAL 193

EUROPEAN CONVENTION ON HUMAN RIGHTS 193
ARTICLES OF THE ECHR 193
CATEGORIES OF RIGHTS 195
STANDARD OF PROOF 195

ECHR AND IMMIGRATION LAW 196
APPLICABILITY OF ECHR IN IMMIGRATION CASES 196

ARTICLE 2 196

ARTICLE 3 197
ABSOLUTE NATURE OF ARTICLE 3 198
TORTURE 199
INHUMAN TREATMENT OR PUNISHMENT 199
DEGRADING TREATMENT OR PUNISHMENT 200
SPECIFIC TYPES OF CASE 202
Absence of exclusion clauses 203
Absence of Convention reasons 203
Sufficiency of protection test 203
Destitution in the UK 204
Unavailability of medical treatment abroad 204
Effect of the act of removal 207

ARTICLE 4 207

ARTICLE 5 207

ARTICLE 6 209

ARTICLE 8 210
INTERFERENCE WITH ARTICLE 8 RIGHTS 211
Family relationships 211
Private life 213
Threshold for interference in foreign cases 215
Relocating the family 215
Applying for entry clearance from abroad 217
ENGAGING ARTICLE 8 218
IN ACCORDANCE WITH THE LAW 218
FOR A LEGITIMATE AIM 218
NECESSARY IN A DEMOCRATIC SOCIETY 219

PROPORTIONALITY	220
General factors	221
Home Office delay	223
Failure to apply a policy	225
THIRD PARTY RIGHTS	225
ARTICLE 14	**226**
DISCRETIONARY LEAVE	**226**
TRAVEL DOCUMENTS	**228**

Human Rights Act 1998

The Human Rights Act 1998 came into force in the United Kingdom on 2 October 2000. It brought the European Convention of Human Rights and Fundamental Freedoms (ECHR) into domestic law and made the rights protected by the ECHR directly enforceable in the British courts.

The Act has had a very important impact on immigration and asylum law.

Mechanisms for protection of human rights

- Interpretation of statute and rules
- Binding on public authorities
- Damages and compensation for breaches
- Ground on which immigration appeals can be allowed

Interpretation of statute

Decisions and other material emanating from the European Court of Human Rights (ECtHR, often referred to by the shorthand 'Strasbourg' as this is where the court sits) must be taken into account by judges here (section 2(1) HRA). The English judiciary has indicated that they will not deviate from the Strasbourg approach. Lord Slynn of Hadley in *R (Alconbury Developments Ltd) v Secretary of State for the Environment* [2001] 2 WLR 1389 at paragraph 26:

> "In the absence of some special circumstances it seems to me that the court should follow any clear and constant jurisprudence of the European Court of Human Rights."

Section 3(1) of the HRA is the key to the interpretation of English statute that must be taken in future by the judiciary:

> "So far as it is possible to do so, primary legislation and subordinate legislation must be read and given effect in a way which is compatible with the Convention rights."

The Immigration Rules must, in line with section 3(1), be read to conform with human rights obligations. See Mr Justice Collins in *Arman Ali* [2000] INLR 89, finding that the (then) interpretation of the immigration rules did not seem to be so compatible (because it potentially forbade reliance on third party support):

> "The interference may be justified under Article 8(2), but it must be proportionate to the legitimate aim concerned, which in this case is the maintenance of the economic well-being of the state: see *Beldjoudi v France* (1992) 14 EHRR 801. Thus it is, as it seems to me, justifiable to avoid any recourse to public funds. But the barrier must not be greater than necessary. Accordingly, the Rules would not in my view be in accordance with Article 8 if they were construed so as to exclude a spouse when his or her admission would not affect the economic well-being of the country

> because there would be no recourse to public funds or any other detriment caused by it."

This approach was endorsed by the Supreme Court in the case of *Mahad* [2009] UKSC 16.

Effect on public authorities

Section 6(1) of the HRA demonstrates that the ambit of the Act is in no way limited to the review of statutory material - rather, any acts of a public authority may be challenged if they conflict with the fundamental rights and freedoms recognised in the ECHR:

> "It is unlawful for a public authority to act in a way which is incompatible with a Convention right."

This includes the Home Office and UKBA and also the courts and tribunals, including the Immigration tribunal.

Under the HRA 1998 itself, section 7(1), a person who claims that a public authority has acted (or proposes to act) incompatibly with the European Convention on Human Rights brings proceedings against the authority under the HRA 1998 in the appropriate court or tribunal, or may rely on the Convention right or rights concerned in any legal proceedings (that is to say, the immigration tribunal will normally be the appropriate venue; otherwise the ECHR may be relied on in any judicial review proceedings). Such an individual has to demonstrate that they would be a victim of the act to have standing (section 7(3) HRA 1998). As will be explored below, this provides a free standing right of judicial review of an act that will breach human rights, but this represents a fall-back level of protection in many immigration and asylum situations. The first port of call will be an appeal to the immigration tribunal, where a right of appeal exists (see further below).

Damages and compensation

Under section 8(2) HRA 1998 damages may be awarded only by a court which has power to award damages, or to order the payment of compensation, in civil proceedings. The immigration tribunal lacks powers of this kind: however, the High Court and the Court of Appeal do possess them.

Section 9(3) HRA indicates that the opportunity to obtain damages for judicial errors regarding human rights will be limited, except, perhaps, in bail cases:

> "In proceedings under this Act in respect of a judicial act done in good faith, damages may not be awarded otherwise than to compensate a person to the extent required by Article 5(5) of the Convention."

Under section 9(1) HRA 1998, proceedings under section 7(1)(a) in respect of a judicial act may be brought only by exercising a right of appeal, on an application for judicial review, or in such other forum as may be prescribed by rules.

Whereas challenges to removal will be brought via the immigration tribunal (i.e. the "right of appeal" route), challenges to breaches of human rights in the UK (e.g. regarding conditions of detention in reception centres, NASS withdrawal leading to destitution sufficiently severe to raise Article 3 issues, etc) will go via the judicial review route. Occasionally there may be two avenues for challenge for the same kind of decision (as where some human rights affected by an immigration decision belong to individuals not subject to immigration control: see *Kehinde* below).

Section 9(5) defines a "judicial act" as including an act done by a "judge". A "judge" includes a member of a tribunal "or other officer entitled to exercise the jurisdiction of a 'court'" which includes a tribunal. So the members of the immigration tribunal are potentially caught by this provision. In general, complaints about human rights that relate to removal, or possibly the manner in which a decision has been taken, will be challenged via the statutory appeal in the immigration tribunal (see generally section 7 below). But complaints about other treatment by public authorities, relating to detention, welfare, and human rights interferences suffered by individuals outside the appeals process, will be brought by way of judicial review.

Human rights as a ground of appeal

The above passages relate to the Human Rights Act itself. Where a right of appeal to the immigration tribunal exists, though, the main mechanism for preventing breaches of human rights is to appeal the immigration decision relying on the ground that the decision will breach human rights. This ground of appeal is specified at section 84(c) and also (g).

European Convention on Human Rights

Articles of the ECHR

The ECHR has a very useful website with the full texts of the Convention and Protocols and the Rules of Court along with all of the judgments and admissibility decisions of the Court and the old Commission. It is found at http://www.echr.coe.int. It includes a search engine, known as HUDOC.

Section 1 of the Human Rights Act explains which Convention rights are incorporated. The rights and fundamental freedoms protected are, in summary:

Article 2	• Right to life
Article 3	• Prohibition of torture or inhuman or degrading treatment of punishment
Article 4	• Prohibition of slavery and forced labour
Article 5	• Right to liberty and security of the person
Article 6	• Right to a fair trial
Article 7	• Freedom from retrospective criminal offences and punishment - "no punishment without law"
Article 8	• Right to respect for private and family life
Article 9	• Freedom of thought, conscience and religion
Article 10	• Freedom of expression
Article 11	• Freedom of assembly and association
Article 12	• Right to marry and found a family
Article 14	• Prohibition of discrimination in the enjoyment of Convention Rights
1st Protocol	• Art 1: Protection of property; Art 2: Right to education; Art 3: Right to free elections
13th Protocol	• Art 1: Prohibition on death penalty

Article 1 of the European Convention on Human Rights requires the contracting states to secure to everyone *'within their jurisdiction'* the Convention rights and freedoms. This was not actually incorporated into domestic law by the Human Rights Act 1998.

Top tip

Although it is important to know about all the rights enshrined in the ECHR, the most useful and frequently relied on by immigration lawyers are Articles 3 and 8.

The other rights are frequently relied on but very rarely successfully so.

Categories of rights

The rights and freedoms dealt with by the European Convention on Human Rights can be categorised in three ways:

Unqualified rights

- Those rights which apply absolutely without qualification and from which there can be no derogation by the state party even in time of war or public emergency threatening the life of the nation.
- e.g. the right to life, the right not to be condemned to the death penalty or executed except in time of war, the right not to be subjected to torture or to inhuman or degrading treatment or punishment, the right not to be held in slavery or servitude and the right not to be punished by retrospective laws.

Limited rights

- Those rights which display some limitation on their face (and which when read in context with the whole of the European Convention on Human Rights are subject to exceptions and which in time of war or public emergency threatening the life of the nation may be the subject of derogations).
- e.g. the right to liberty and security, the right to fair trial, the right to freedom of thought, conscience and religion, the right to education and the right to enjoy Convention rights and freedoms without discrimination.

Qualified rights

- Rights which are expressly qualified on their face and which must be balanced against, and may have to give way to, other competing public interests.
- e.g. the rights to respect for private and family life, home and correspondence, freedom to manifest one's religion and beliefs, freedom of expression and to hold opinions, freedom of peaceful assembly and association, and freedom of movement.

Standard of Proof

The standard of proof for assessing whether the likelihood of a human rights breach is sufficient for the ECHR to be engaged is whether there is a 'real risk' of the claimed problem actually happening, or 'substantial grounds for believing' a breach will occur. The test is essentially the same as the 'reasonable degree of likelihood' test in refugee cases.

However, in some cases, the claimant may assert that she will be subject to a generalised risk of a breach of her rights, for example by being exposed to poor environmental conditions in a country's prisons system or generalised problems in military service in a given country. In such cases the Tribunal is of the view that it is necessary to show gross, flagrant and systematic breaches of human rights before all members of the category can be accepted as being at risk. The leading case on this subject is generally acknowledged to be *Hariri v SSHD* [2003] EWCA Civ 807.

ECHR and immigration law

Applicability of ECHR in immigration cases

The protected Convention rights are universal and intended to apply to everyone within the United Kingdom's jurisdiction, not just to British nationals. Furthermore, the preamble of the ECHR describes the rights as having a *universal* quality - they apply to all persons regardless of nationality, race, sex or other "status".

There are two broad categories of case where the ECHR has an impact in the field of immigration and asylum law, identified by the House of Lords in *Ullah and Do*:

Domestic cases
- Acts or omissions by the UK authorities
- e.g. breach of private and family life established in the UK
- e.g. catastrophic deterioration of medical condition owing to absence of treatment after removal

Foreign cases
- Acts or omissions by a foreign state after removal
- e.g. detention in breach of Article 5
- e.g. total deprivation of contact with child

It was the House of Lords case of *Ullah and Do* that established definitely in UK law that all of the articles of the ECHR can potentially be relied on in foreign cases. The Strasbourg cases of *Soering v UK* (1989) 11 EHRR 439 and *Chahal v UK* (1996) 23 EHRR 413 had already established that Article 3 could operate to prevent removal where there was a real risk of a future breach of human rights. However, for articles other than article 3, it is necessary to show that there would be a 'flagrant breach' of the right or rights in question, or that the right or rights would be completely nullified. This is sometimes referred to as the *Devaseelan* test after the starred determination that first set out this test, later approved by the House of Lords in *EM (Lebanon) v SSHD* [2008] UKHL 64.

Article 2

Article 2 of the ECHR is as follows:

> "1. Everyone's right to life shall be protected by law. No one shall be deprived of his life intentionally save in the execution of a sentence of a court following his conviction of a crime for which this penalty is provided by law.

> 2. Deprivation of life shall not be regarded as inflicted in contravention of this article when it results from the use of force which is no more than absolutely necessary:
> (a) in defence of any person from unlawful violence;
> (b) in order to effect a lawful arrest or to prevent the escape of a person lawfully detained;
> (c) in action lawfully taken for the purpose of quelling a riot or insurrection."

So far, in immigration cases, the article tends to be argued in addition to Article 3, for the simple reason that death or execution would be rather likely to be considered in the modern world to cross the threshold for Article 3 ill treatment in any event. There has not yet been a removal case in the UK or at Strasbourg that has succeeded on Article 2 but not on Article 3. It is worth remembering that in *Soering* the claimant feared execution and the experience of 'death row', and his case succeeded on the latter ground only.

Protocol 13, Article 1 contains an absolute prohibition on the death penalty. Following UK ratification of the 13th Protocol reference to Article 13 has now been inserted into the HRA 1998, see SI 2004/1574, in force from 22 June 2004). Thus, where there are "substantial grounds for believing" that following a removal from this country a person will be condemned to death or executed, even if for murder, such removal would be to breach their human rights. The Article reads:

> 'The death penalty shall be abolished. No-one shall be condemned to such penalty or executed.'

Article 3

The right is expressed in these terms, and is notably unqualified:

> 'No one shall be subjected to torture or to inhuman or degrading treatment or punishment.'

There are therefore three forms of ill treatment, but each is afforded the same level of protection in immigration proceedings:

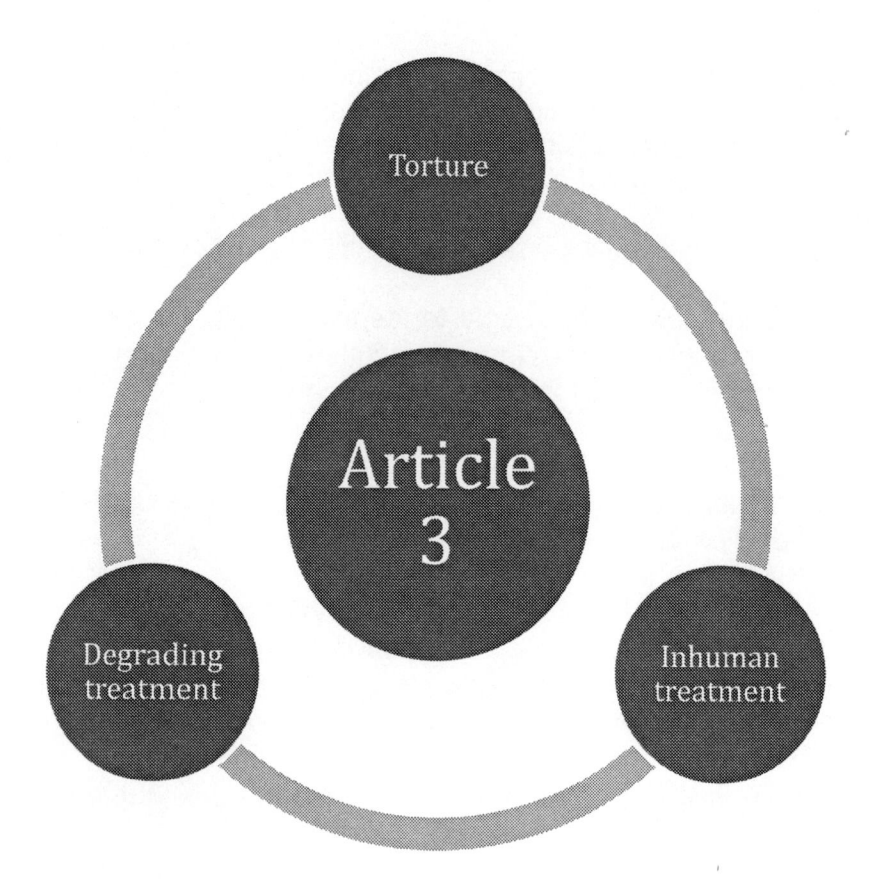

Outside an immigration context, these three forms of ill treatment can be seen as a spectrum, with torture at the most serious end, going through inhuman treatment and then degrading treatment. However, for ill treatment to amount to torture it would probably always have to be deliberately inflicted and intentional, whereas, as is discussed below, inhuman and degrading treatment can potentially be passive in nature.

Absolute nature of Article 3

Article 3 is absolute in nature, meaning that there are no circumstances in which it can be derogated from, nor can there be any justification for failure to observe it. This means that even very unpleasant individuals who have committed very serious crimes can benefit from its protection.

In *Soering*, the claimant was mentally ill and had horribly murdered two people in the United States. His extradition to stand trial there was being sought. Strasbourg held that he could not be extradited because of the real risk of exposure to the death row experience, which would breach Article 3.

In *Chahal*, the claimant was accused of being a terrorist extremist and a danger to the national security of the United Kingdom, but the ECtHR in *Chahal v United Kingdom* (1997) 23 EHRR 413 found that because right is absolute his removal to India was not permitted because 'the activities of the individual in question, however undesirable or dangerous, cannot be a material consideration' (para 80).

Whether Article 3 is breached or not in an individual case is a question of fact, based on measuring up all the relevant considerations – so it is always necessary to examine the impact of the feared future treatment on *this* individual. The courts say that (e.g. *Ireland v United Kingdom* (1978) 2 EHRR 25 at para 162):

> '...ill-treatment must attain a minimum level of severity if it is to fall within the scope of Article 3. The assessment of this minimum is, in the nature of things, relative; it depends on all the circumstances of the case, such as the nature and context of the treatment or punishment, the manner and method of its execution, its duration and its physical or mental effects.'

The right operates so as to prevent removal of a person within a country's territory to another territory in which there would be a breach of Article 3 of the ECHR. It is, therefore, irrelevant from an immigration perspective whether the breach of which the claimant complains will be one that amounts to torture, inhuman treatment or degrading treatment. For the purposes of understanding Article 3 is it is nevertheless important to explore the nature of each type of ill treatment.

Torture

In *Ireland v UK* (1978) 2 EHRR 167 torture was defined as "deliberate inhuman treatment causing very serious and cruel suffering". This was a thought to be a very high threshold, and very few cases were found to reach this high level.

In *Selmouni v France* (1999), the ECtHR revised this approach and derived assistance from the UN Convention against Torture, and ultimately adopted a definition which could be summarised as the situation where "physical and mental violence, considered as a whole, committed against the applicant's person caused 'severe' pain and suffering and was particularly serious and cruel". Although still high, the threshold at which torture is set is now lower than before the *Selmouni* case.

In the case of *Aydin v Turkey* (1998) 25 EHRR 251 the ECtHR found that rape amounted to torture.

Inhuman treatment or punishment

Ireland v UK (1978) 2 EHRR 167 saw the European Court finding that a combination of forms of ill-treatment of detainees (deprivation of food, drink and sleep, hooding, subjection to noise and being stood up against a wall) amounted to inhuman and degrading treatment.

> '167. The five techniques were applied in combination, with premeditation and for hours at a stretch; they caused, if not actual bodily injury, at least intense physical and mental suffering to the persons subjected thereto and also led to acute psychiatric disturbances during interrogation. They accordingly fell into the category of inhuman treatment within the meaning of Article 3 (art. 3).'

Pretty v United Kingdom (2002) 35 EHRR 1 at para 52 shows that natural illness, if made worse by certain conditions, may cross the threshold:

> 'As regards the types of 'treatment' which fall within the scope of Article 3 of the Convention, the Court's case law refers to 'ill-treatment' that attains a minimum level of severity and involves actual bodily injury or intense physical or mental suffering... Where treatment humiliates or debases an individual showing a lack or respect for, or diminishing, his or her human dignity or arouses feelings of fear, anguish or inferiority capable of breaking an individual's moral and physical resistance, it may be characterised as degrading and also fall within the prohibition of Article 3.... The suffering which flows from naturally occurring illness, physical or mental, may be covered by Article 3, where it is, or risks being, exacerbated by the treatment, whether flowing from conditions of detention, expulsion or other measures, for which the authorities can be held responsible...'

The death row phenomenon can constitute inhuman punishment, see *Soering v United Kingdom* (1989) 11 EHRR 439.

Degrading treatment or punishment

In *Ireland v UK* the court said the following about the nature of degrading treatment:

> 'The techniques were also degrading since they were such as to arouse in their victims feelings of fear, anguish and inferiority capable of humiliating and debasing them and possibly breaking their physical or moral resistance.'

The ECHR has held that prison conditions can amount to degrading treatment, and even inhuman treatment. See for example *Kalashnikov v Russia* (2002) 36 EHRR 587:

> '...The suffering and humiliation involved must in any event go beyond that inevitable element of suffering or humiliation connected with a given form of legitimate treatment or punishment.
>
> Measures depriving a person of his liberty may often involve such an element. Yet it cannot be said that detention on remand in itself raises an issue under Article 3 of the Convention...
>
> Nevertheless, under this provision the State must ensure that a person is detained in conditions which are compatible with respect for his human dignity, that the manner and method of the execution of the measure do not subject him to distress or hardship of an intensity exceeding the unavoidable level of suffering inherent in detention and that, given the practical demands of imprisonment, his health and well-being are adequately secured.
>
> When assessing conditions of detention, account has to be taken of the cumulative effects of those conditions, as well as the specific allegations made by the applicant.'

Munby J, in the Court of Appeal in *Batayav v Secretary of State for the Home Department* [2003] EWCA Civ 1489, found that it was dangerous for the Tribunal to find that Article 3 was not engaged by Russian prisons when the European

Court had disagreed so recently. However, on the presumption that this complaint is raised on the basis of general prison conditions in a country rather than any particular feature of the applicant's account, when considering this kind of case it is necessary for the individual to show a generic risk (in the sense of showing that all individuals in prisons face a real risk of human rights abuses). The Tribunal accordingly says that it is necessary to demonstrate a consistent pattern of gross and systematic violations of the human rights of those detained before it will be satisfied of the extent of the risk. Nevertheless, cases have been successful on this basis. See, for example, *PS (prison conditions; military service) Ukraine CG* [2006] UKAIT 00016.

> **Top tip**
>
> While the law says that a person cannot be removed if he or she is going to be detained in conditions that would be contrary to Article 3 ECHR, it is not at all easy to prove that the conditions will in fact be so bad as to meet this threshold. A line from a US Department of State report will not be sufficient.
>
> Expert evidence will be needed, and/or specific reports on detention conditions in that country by a relevant international NGO or monitoring organisation of some sort, such as Penal Reform. ECHR signatories are monitored by the Committee for the Prevention of Torture, an official organ of the Council of Europe. The reports of the CPT were instrumental in the Ukrainian case. Unfortunately, such detailed and influential reports do not generally exist outside Council of Europe countries, so other forms of evidence must be sought.

In *Tyrer v United Kingdom* (1978) EHRR 1 the ECtHR held that corporal punishment of a minor amounted to degrading treatment or punishment, but said that the punishment must exceed the usual element of humiliation involved in the criminal justice system, and that "a punishment does not lose its degrading character just because it is believed to be, or actually is, an effective deterrent or aid to crime control":

> '30. In the Court's view, in order for a punishment to be "degrading" and in breach of Article 3 (art. 3), the humiliation or debasement involved must attain a particular level and must in any event be other than that usual element of humiliation referred to in the preceding subparagraph. The assessment is, in the nature of things, relative: it depends on all the circumstances of the case and, in particular, on the nature and context of the punishment itself and the manner and method of its execution.
>
> ...As regards their belief that judicial corporal punishment deters criminals, it must be pointed out that a punishment does not lose its degrading character just because it is believed to be, or actually is, an effective deterrent or aid to crime control. Above all, as the Court must emphasise, it is never permissible to have recourse to

> punishments which are contrary to Article 3 (art. 3), whatever their deterrent effect may be.'

In *Ocalan v Turkey* (2003) 37 EHRR 10 at para 220 the Court took the object of the punishment or treatment into account, so that if the object of the ill-treatment is humiliation or debasement, it will be easier to find that the threshold has been crossed into Article 3 territory:

> 'Furthermore, in considering whether a punishment or treatment is "degrading" within the meaning of Art. 3, the Court will have regard to whether its object is to humiliate and debase the person concerned and whether, as far as the consequences are concerned, it adversely affected his or her personality in a manner incompatible with Art. 3.'

In *East African Asians v UK* (1981) 3 EHRR 76 the court concluded that discrimination based on race could, in certain circumstances, of itself amount to degrading treatment

> '[207] ... that discrimination based on race could, in certain circumstances, of itself amount to degrading treatment within the meaning of Article 3 ... The Commission recalls in this connection that, as generally recognised, a special importance should be attached to discrimination based on race; that publicity [sic] to single out a group of persons for differential treatment on the basis of race might, in certain circumstances, constitute a special form of affront to human dignity; and that differential treatment of a group of persons on the basis of race might therefore be capable of constituting degrading treatment when differential treatment on some other ground would raise no such question.'

The Tribunal in *S&K* [2002] UKIAT 05613 (3 December 2002) (starred) found that racial motivation could cause the threshold to be crossed, for example where ill-treatment is motivated by racial grounds.

> 'We do not doubt that discrimination on the ground of race is a factor that should be taken into account in deciding whether a breach of Article 3 has been established. It may in some circumstances tip the balance.'

Specific types of case

- No exclusion clauses
- No Convention reasons
- Sufficiency of protection
- Destitution in UK
- Medical treatment cases
- Effect of act of removal

Absence of exclusion clauses

Article 3 is subject to no limitation, and unlike the Refugee Convention, there are no exclusion clauses to deprive an individual of the rights which it recognises, see *Chahal v UK* (1996) 23 EHRR 413. Nevertheless whilst the Secretary of State cannot remove some individuals, he can treat them differently vis-à-vis the form of leave to remain he gives them – so an individual who can establish a risk of a human rights breach on removal but who has committed serious criminal offences may well find that they receive Discretionary Leave to Remain rather than Humanitarian Protection. Even a person who can establish the inclusion requirements for refugee status may suffer the same fate if they are excluded under the Refugee Convention.

In the most serious cases UKBA policy is to grant six months Discretionary Leave at a time, which a review on each occasion until the individual has attained 10 years of residence.

Absence of Convention reasons

It will be obvious that, unlike the Refugee Convention, there is no requirement under the ECHR that the harm feared be linked to the individual's race, religion, nationality, membership of a particular social group or political opinion. In cases where the individual faces serious ill treatment or harm on return but behind which there is no Convention reason, the individual may not be entitled to refugee status but may not nevertheless be removed.

Sufficiency of protection test

In the case of *Bagdanavicius* [2005] UKHL 38 the House of Lords held that although there was some difference in wording between *Horvath* formulation of the standard of protection required by the Refugee Convention and the Strasbourg forumulation in *HLR v France* (1998) 26 EHRR 29, the tests were to all intents and purposes the same.

It is therefore not possible to argue that the 'sufficiency of protection' test does not apply in human rights cases or that it is a different test to that which applies under the Refugee Convention.

Destitution in the UK

A number of cases explored the circumstances in which the problems that ensue from blocking support might engage Article 3 of the ECHR, which are discussed in the chapter on benefits.

Unavailability of medical treatment abroad

It is argued in some cases that a difference in medical treatment between the UK and the country to which a person is to be removed will cause suffering or death and that removal would therefore breach the person's human rights and engage the UK's responsibilities.

Such arguments can be pursued in two ways, although these are not mutually exclusive. One is to argue the suffering will be so serious as to amount to a breach of Article 3, relying on a principle established in the case of *D v UK* (1997) 24 EHHR 423. The other is to argue that although the suffering would not be so serious as to engage Article 3, a lower threshold applies to breaches of Article 8 and this article would instead be breached, relying on the case of *Bensaid v UK* (2001) 33 EHRR 205.

In *N v UK* (Application no. 26565/05) [2008] ECHR 453 Strasbourg examined the case of a Ugandan woman known as N who had contracted HIV/AIDS and was receiving treatment in the UK. The case was an appeal from the House of Lords, who had earlier ([2005] UKHL 31) examined N's case and rejected it.

Strasbourg upheld the House of Lords reasoning, and it is worth quoting extensively from the judgment to illustrate how unwavering it is. For example, it was accepted that the claimant would die in unpleasant circumstances within approximately one year if removed, as Lord Hope made abundantly clear at paragraph 20 of the judgment:

> 'The decision which your Lordships have been asked to take in this case will have profound consequences for the appellant. The prospects of her surviving for more than a year or two if she is returned to Uganda are bleak. It is highly likely that the advanced medical care which has stabilised her condition by suppressing the HIV virus and would sustain her in good health were she to remain in this country for decades will no longer be available to her. If it is not, her condition is likely to reactivate and to deteriorate rapidly. There is no doubt that if that happens she will face an early death after a period of acute physical and mental suffering. It is easy to sympathise with her in this predicament.'

At paragraph 50 Lord Hope outlines the circumstances that would have to be satisfied of a case were to be successful:

> 'For the circumstances to be, as it was put in *Amegnigan v The Netherlands*, "very exceptional" it would need to be shown that the applicant's medical condition had

> reached such a critical stage that there were compelling humanitarian grounds for not removing him to a place which lacked the medical and social services which he would need to prevent acute suffering while he is dying.'

The Strasbourg judges ruled against N because:

(a) she was "not ... at the present time critically ill";

(b) the rapidity of the deterioration which she would suffer and the extent to which she would be able to obtain access to medical treatment, support and care, including help from relatives, involved a certain degree of speculation; and

(c) this speculation was "particularly [due to] ... the constantly evolving situation as regards the treatment of HIV and AIDS worldwide."

Conceivably the Strasbourg decision in N is moderately better for claimants than was that of the House of Lords, which effectively limited success to deathbed cases: the European Court sets the benchmark at their being "critically ill"; and in refusing the case, they place significant weight on the element of speculation that attended the predictions for the future of Ms N, whereas some immigrants might be able to put forward more concrete materials. Strasbourg also seems to have based its findings on the premise that the necessary treatment is widely available in Uganda (paragraph 48). This is absolutely not the case in many countries.

Strasbourg declined to examine the case under Article 8. However, in the case of KH (Afghanistan) v SSHD [2009] EWCA Civ 1354 the Court of Appeal held that the high threshold in N is also to be applied in cases of mental illness considered under Article 3. The Court went on to dismiss the Article 8 case as well, suggesting it would be very rare for a medical case of this nature to succeed under Article 8 if it failed under Article 3.

Given the high standards of medical care a person will normally receive once inside the UK and the traditional duration of the asylum process, very few claimants will still be seriously ill by the time they are eligible for removal even if they were very ill on arrival. With increasing fast-tracking and a shorter appeals process, this may start to change in future.

There has been discussion around the continued applicability of the approach taken by the Court of Appeal in the case of CA v SSHD [2004] EWCA Civ 1165. In CA the Court of Appeal found that return of a mother and child to a country where there would be inadequate medical treatment would breach Article 3 because of the effect on the mother of watching her child suffer and die: "It seems to me obvious simply as a matter of humanity that for a mother to witness the collapse of her newborn child's health and perhaps its death may be a kind of suffering far greater than might arise by the mother's confronting the self-same fate herself" (Laws LJ). It has been suggested that this reasoning, which has been applied in a number of other cases, cannot survive N in Strasbourg.

There is some Strasbourg authority behind the argument that a parent can be the victim of a breach of the human rights of the child. Although the case is a detention case, see *Mubilanzila Mayeka and Kaniki Mitunga v. Belgium*, no. 13178/03, ECHR 2006:

> The Court reiterates, secondly, that the issue whether a parent qualifies as a "victim" of the ill-treatment of his or her child will depend on the existence of special factors which gives the applicant's suffering a dimension and character distinct from the emotional distress which may be regarded as inevitably caused to relatives of a victim of a serious human rights violation. Relevant elements will include the proximity of the family tie – in that context, a certain weight will attach to the parent-child bond –, the particular circumstances of the relationship and the way in which the authorities responded to the parent's enquiries. The essence of such a violation lies in the authorities' reactions and attitudes to the situation when it is brought to their attention. It is especially in respect of this latter factor that a parent may claim directly to be a victim of the authorities' conduct (see, mutatis mutandis, Çakıcı v. Turkey [GC], no. 23657/94, ECHR 1999-IV, § 98; and Hamiyet Kaplan and Others v. Turkey, no. 36749/97, § 67, 13 September 2005).

It has also been successfully argued that a lower threshold of suffering should apply to children than adults as they are less able to bear it than adults. There is considerable authority behind the proposition that treatment or punishment that would not breach the rights of an adult may nevertheless breach the rights of a child.

Following the Court of Appeal case of *JA (Ivory Coast) v SSHD* [2009] EWCA Civ 1353 there is hope for some in the UK who were previously granted leave on the basis of their medical condition. Although this relates to Article 8, it is convenient to deal with it here. The Court allowed the appeal (albeit only to the extent of remitting it to the tribunal) of a woman with HIV/AIDS on the basis that she was a lawful entrant, had previously been granted leave on the basis of her medical condition and had been lawfully resident in the UK for quite some time on that basis. These features were found to distinguish the case from Article 3 cases like *D v UK* and *N v UK* and placed the woman in a different legal context.

The co-appellant was unsuccessful on the basis that the immigration judge had found that she could find work in her home country and support her treatment costs. Giving the leading judgment, Sedley LJ went on:

> JA's is a markedly different case. Her position as a continuously lawful entrant places her in a different legal class from N, so that she is not called upon to demonstrate exceptional circumstances as compelling as those in D v United Kingdom. There is no finding by the AIT that she has much if any hope of securing treatment if returned to Ivory Coast, or therefore as to the severity and consequences of removal (see Razgar [2004] UKHL 27). Depending on these, the potential discontinuance of years of life-saving NHS treatment, albeit made available out of compassion and not out of obligation, is in our judgment capable of tipping the balance of proportionality in her favour.

The Court found that it was *possible* for JA to succeed on the basis of Article 8. Whether on the facts of an individual case a particular appellant does so succeed will be at the discretion of the individual immigration judge.

Effect of the act of removal

Circumstances might be different where medical problems ensue other than from a want of resources, however, where the human rights interference is caused not by the difference in treatment between here and abroad and the medium term repercussions of that difference, but where the act of removal actually causes a deterioration in physical or mental health. See *J v SSHD* [2005] EWCA Civ 629 where it was the trauma of removal bringing with it an enhanced risk of suicide rather than any "want of resources" that led to the human rights interference.

Article 4

Article 4(1) is the only absolute right amongst the parts of this Article, which could capture cases involving the future threat of trafficking, forced prostitution, or bonded labour:

> 1. No one shall be held in slavery or servitude.
>
> 2. No one shall be required to perform forced or compulsory labour.
>
> 3. For the purpose of this article the term "forced or compulsory labour" shall not include:
> (a) any work required to be done in the ordinary course of detention imposed according to the provisions of Article 5 of this Convention or during conditional release from such detention;
> (b) any service of a military character or, in case of conscientious objectors in countries where they are recognised, service exacted instead of compulsory military service;
> (c) any service exacted in case of an emergency or calamity threatening the life or well-being of the community;
> (d) any work or service which forms part of normal civic obligations.

It seems highly unlikely that a situation involving a risk of Article 4 ill treatment could arise that would not also breach Article 3. However, in removal cases the existence of Article 4 can perhaps serve as a reminder of a species of Article 3 ill treatment.

Article 5

Article 5 ECHR is as follows:

> 1. Everyone has the right to liberty and security of person. No one shall be deprived of his liberty save in the following cases and in accordance with a procedure prescribed by law:
> (a) the lawful detention of a person after conviction by a competent court;
> (b) the lawful arrest or detention of a person for non-compliance with the lawful order of a court or in order to secure the fulfilment of any obligation prescribed by law;

> (c) the lawful arrest or detention of a person effected for the purpose of bringing him before the competent legal authority on reasonable suspicion of having committed an offence or when it is reasonably considered necessary to prevent his committing an offence or fleeing after having done so;
> (d) the detention of a minor by lawful order for the purpose of educational supervision or his lawful detention for the purpose of bringing him before the competent legal authority;
> (e) the lawful detention of persons for the prevention of the spreading of infectious diseases, of persons of unsound mind, alcoholics or drug addicts or vagrants;
> (f) the lawful arrest or detention of a person to prevent his effecting an unauthorised entry into the country or of a person against whom action is being taken with a view to deportation or extradition.
>
> 2. Everyone who is arrested shall be informed promptly, in a language which he understands, of the reasons for his arrest and of any charge against him.
>
> 3. Everyone arrested or detained in accordance with the provisions of paragraph 1.c of this article shall be brought promptly before a judge or other officer authorised by law to exercise judicial power and shall be entitled to trial within a reasonable time or to release pending trial. Release may be conditioned by guarantees to appear for trial.
>
> 4. Everyone who is deprived of his liberty by arrest or detention shall be entitled to take proceedings by which the lawfulness of his detention shall be decided speedily by a court and his release ordered if the detention is not lawful.
>
> 5. Everyone who has been the victim of arrest or detention in contravention of the provisions of this article shall have an enforceable right to compensation.

Article 5 applies in the UK scheme of detention for the purposes of immigration control.

However, *R v Secretary of State for the Home Department ex parte Saadi & Ors* [2001] EWCA Civ 1512 (and the House of Lords then Strasbourg case that followed) shows that short-term detention of asylum seekers is permissible, even absent any risk of their absconding.

As mentioned above, damages are available under section 9(3) of the HRA, even for judicial acts carried out in good faith. There have been a number of successful claims for damages in immigration detention cases.

The requirements that liberty be lost only pursuant to "a procedure prescribed by law" has the consequence that the Secretary of State must reveal any policies which underlie detention decisions. For example, in *Nadarajah v Secretary of State for the Home Department* [2003] EWCA Civ 1768 the Court of Appeal found that, given that the ECtHR had held that the phrase "prescribed by law" in Article 10(2) required that the law must be adequately accessible, those subject to the law must have an indication which is adequate in the legal circumstances of the legal rules which are applicable to the given case. This means that any Home Office policies that underlie detention should be accessible.

As discussed above, a flagrant breach of Article 5 can inhibit removal. Given that only the authorities of a country can presumably deprive of an individual of their liberty pursuant to law, there must be a strong argument that loss of liberty at the hands of non-state actors constitutes a fundamental breach of the Article.

Article 6

Article 6 ECHR reads as follows:

> 1. In the determination of his civil rights and obligations or of any criminal charge against him, everyone is entitled to a fair and public hearing within a reasonable time by an independent and impartial tribunal established by law. Judgment shall be pronounced publicly but the press and public may be excluded from all or part of the trial in the interests of morals, public order or national security in a democratic society, where the interests of juveniles or the protection of the private life of the parties so require, or to the extent strictly necessary in the opinion of the court in special circumstances where publicity would prejudice the interests of justice.
>
> 2. Everyone charged with a criminal offence shall be presumed innocent until proved guilty according to law.
>
> 3. Everyone charged with a criminal offence has the following minimum rights:
>   (a) to be informed promptly, in a language which he understands and in detail, of the nature and cause of the accusation against him;
>   (b) to have adequate time and facilities for the preparation of his defence;
>   (c) to defend himself in person or through legal assistance of his own choosing or, if he has not sufficient means to pay for legal assistance, to be given it free when the interests of justice so require;
>   (d) to examine or have examined witnesses against him and to obtain the attendance and examination of witnesses on his behalf under the same conditions as witnesses against him;
>   (e) to have the free assistance of an interpreter if he cannot understand or speak the language used in court.

The Tribunal in *MNM* (00/TH/02423; 1 November 2000) (starred) confirms that, consistently with the decision of the ECHR in *Maaroui v France*, Article 6 does not apply in immigration appeals in the UK because immigration rights are not "private" in nature and therefore do not amount to civil rights and obligations. However the Tribunal took the view that the common law would guarantee everything that Article 6 would provide, anyway, so this should not matter very much. Article 6 may also have some limited applicability in preventing removal if a lack of fair trial would be the gateway to article 3 breaches.

> "16...The fact is that the IAA provides an independent and impartial tribunal established by law. The hearing is in public and the procedures are designed to ensure that it is fair. If there is any unfairness, the tribunal or the Court of Appeal will correct it. Thus any complaints that the special adjudicator conducted an unfair hearing fall to be considered by us and we apply the same tests as would be applicable if Article 6(1) applied. The only advantage which Article 6(1) might confer is the requirement that the hearing be held within a reasonable time. That does not arise in this case and should not, unless some disaster occurs, arise in any case

> having regard to the timetables and procedures laid down by the adjudicators and the tribunal."

Their Lordships confirmed in *Ullah* that "It can be regarded as settled law that where there is a real risk of a flagrant denial of justice in the country to which an individual is to be deported article 6 may be engaged."

The issue was revisited in practice in *RB (Algeria) v SSHD* [2009] UKHL 10. Lord Phillips in the House of Lords held that the Court of Appeal's statement of the test for a flagrant breach of Article 6 was the correct one – a real risk of a total denial of the right to a fair trial -- but went on:

> 136. This is neither an easy nor an adequate test of whether article 6 should bar the deportation of an alien. In the first place it is not easy to postulate what amounts to "a complete denial or nullification of the right to a fair trial" That phrase cannot require that every aspect of the trial process should be unfair. A trial that is fair in part may be no more acceptable than the curate's egg. What is required is that the deficiency or deficiencies in the trial process should be such as fundamentally to destroy the fairness of the prospective trial.
>
> 137. In the second place, the fact that the deportee may find himself subject in the receiving country to a legal process that is blatantly unfair cannot, of itself, justify placing an embargo on his deportation. The focus must be not simply on the unfairness of the trial process but on its potential consequences. An unfair trial is likely to lead to the violation of substantive human rights and the extent of that prospective violation must plainly be an important factor in deciding whether deportation is precluded.

Because there is now a right under European Community law to refugee status or Humanitarian Protection, it may be that ECHR Art 6 applies to asylum appeals brought under the Refugee Qualification Directive – see the Court of Appeal recognising this as arguable in *HH (Iran) v Secretary of State for the Home Department* [2008] EWCA Civ 50.

Article 8

Article 8 provides as follows:

> (1) Everyone has the right to respect for his private and family life, his home and his correspondence.
> (2) There shall be no interference by a public authority with the exercise of this right except such as is in accordance with the law and is necessary in a democratic society in the interests of national security, public safety or the economic well-being of the country, for the prevention of disorder or crime, for the protection of health or morals, or for the protection of the rights and freedoms of others.

In paragraph 17 of *Razgar* [2004] 2 AC 368, Lord Bingham set out five questions that must be posed in assessing whether an act of removal from the UK would breach Article 8 in a given case:

(i) Is there an interference?

(ii) Is the interference sufficiently serious?

(iii) Is the interference lawful?

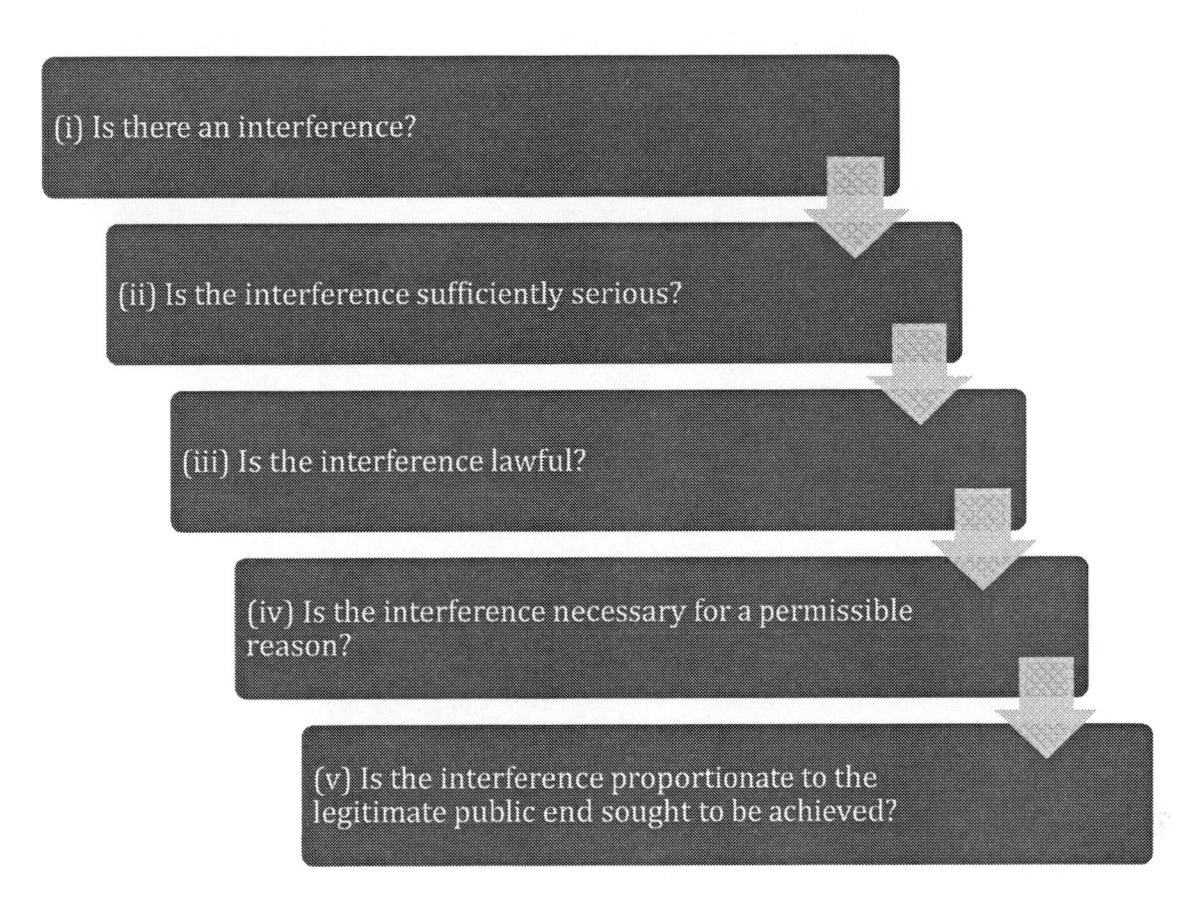

(iv) Is the interference necessary for a permissible reason?

(v) Is the interference proportionate to the legitimate public end sought to be achieved?

These five questions are critical. Firstly, the five step approach provides an essential tool for analysing any Article 8 factual scenario. Secondly, it has been recognised that it may well amount to an error of law for an immigration judge to fail to follow the five step approach.

Interference with Article 8 rights

In order to establish that that there will be an interference with an Article 8 right, it is first necessary to show that there is an Article 8 relationship (or relationships) in place.

Family relationships

Family life can include various relationships. *Marckx v Belgium* (1979) 2 EHRR 330:

> 'The Court concurs entirely with the Commission's established case-law on a crucial point, namely that Article 8 (art. 8) makes no distinction between the 'legitimate' and the 'illegitimate' family. Such a distinction would not be consonant with the word 'everyone', and this is confirmed by Article 14 (art. 14) with its prohibition, in the enjoyment of the rights and freedoms enshrined in the Convention, of discrimination grounded on 'birth.'
>
> ...'[F]amily life', within the meaning of Article 8 (art. 8), includes at least the ties between near relatives, for instance those between grandparents and grandchildren, since such relatives may play a considerable part in family life.'

In *Sen v Netherlands* (2003) 36 EHRR 81, the European Court of Human Rights made it very clear that a biological parent-child relationship will almost always give rise to family life:

> 'The respondent Government acknowledges that the existence of "family life" between the applicants has been established. The Court reiterates in this regard that a child born of a marital union is *ipso jure* part of that relationship; hence from the moment of the child's birth and by the very fact of it, there exists between him and his parents a bond amounting to family life (*Gul v. Switzerland* (1996) 22 EHRR 93, para 32; *Boughanemi v. France* (1996) 22 EHRR 228, para 35) which subsequent events cannot break save in exceptional circumstances (*Berrehab v. Netherlands* (1989) 11 EHRR 322, para 21; *Ahmut v. Netherlands* (1997) 24 EHRR 62, para 60).'

In *Singh v ECO New Delhi* [2004] EWCA (Civ) 1075 the Court of Appeal examined Strasbourg case law which shows that family and private life is a question of fact and can cover a range of diverse situations:

> '...the starting point of the law is a tolerant indulgence to cultural and religious diversity and an essentially agnostic view of religious beliefs ... such is the diversity of forms that the family takes in contemporary society that it is impossible to define, or even to describe at anything less than almost encyclopaedic length, what is meant by "family life" for the purposes of Article 8. The Strasbourg court, as I have said, has never sought to define what is meant by family life. More importantly for present purposes, and this is a point that requires emphasis, the Strasbourg court has never sought to identify any minimum requirements that must be shown if family life is to be held to exist. That is because there are none...
>
> The existence or non-existence of "family life" for the purposes of Article 8 is essentially a question of fact depending upon the real existence in practice of close personal ties'

The ECHR in *Berrehab v Netherlands* (1988) 11 EHRR 322 held that cohabitation, whilst strong evidence, is not an essential feature of family life:

> 'The Court likewise does not see cohabitation as a *sine qua non* of family life between parents and minor children. It has held that the relationship created between the spouses by a lawful and genuine marriage – such as that contracted by Mr. and Mrs. Berrehab – has to be regarded as 'family life' (see the *Abdulaziz, Cabales and Balkandali* judgment of 28 May 1985, Series A no. 94, p. 32, § 62). It follows from the concept of family on which Article 8 (art. 8) is based that a child born of such a union is ipso jure part of that relationship; hence, from the moment of the child's birth and by the very fact of it, there exists between him and his parents a bond amounting to 'family life', even if the parents are not then living together ... Subsequent events, of course, may break that tie ...'

But family life will not necessarily be accepted to be established between adults (e.g. adult children and their parents, adult siblings), see *Advic v United Kingdom* 00025525/94 (6 September 1995):

> 'Although this will depend on the circumstances of each particular case, the Commission has already considered that the protection of Article 8 (Art. 8) did not cover links between adult brothers who had been living apart for a long period of

> time and who were not dependent on each other (No. 8157/78, Dec. 5.12.79, unpublished). Moreover, the relationship between a parent and an adult child would not necessarily acquire the protection of Article 8 (Art. 8) of the Convention without evidence of further elements of dependency, involving more than the normal, emotional ties (No. 10375/83, Dec. 10.12.84, D.R. 40 p. 196).'

However, in *ZB (Pakistan) v SSHD* [2009] EWCA Civ 834 the Court of Appeal held that *Advic* and other cases should not be seen as precluding the existence of family life between adults in cases involving extended families. The Court was highly critical of the tribunal's determination in the case, finding that it did not show a proper appreciation for the need to respect family life or the importance of family life to those who have one and then that the tribunal had artificially compartmentalised individual relationships within the family group rather than looking at the family as a whole. In deciding whether there is a family life between adults, the Court held that the relevant question is how dependent is the older relative on the younger ones in the UK and does that dependency create something more than the normal emotional ties?

Private life

The concept of private life as protected by Article 8, has repeatedly been held to be a very broad one. In *Niemietz v Germany* (1992) 16 EHRR 97 the EctHR said as follows at para 29:

> 'The Court does not consider it possible or necessary to attempt an exhaustive definition of the notion of "private life". However, it would be too restrictive to limit the notion to an "inner circle" in which the individual may live his own personal life as he chooses and to exclude therefrom entirely the outside world not encompassed within that circle. Respect for private life must also comprise to a certain degree the right to establish and develop relationships with other human beings.'

In the House of Lords case of *Razgar*, Lord Bingham said the following about the nature of private life (paragraph 9):

> 'This judgment establishes, in my opinion quite clearly, that reliance may in principle be placed on article 8 to resist an expulsion decision, even where the main emphasis is not on the severance of family and social ties which the applicant has enjoyed in the expelling country but on the consequences for his mental health of removal to the receiving country. The threshold of successful reliance is high, but if the facts are strong enough article 8 may in principle be invoked. It is plain that "private life" is a broad term, and the Court has wisely eschewed any attempt to define it comprehensively. It is relevant for present purposes that the Court saw mental stability as an indispensable precondition to effective enjoyment of the right to respect for private life. In *Pretty v United Kingdom* (2002) 35 EHRR 1, paragraph 61, the Court held the expression to cover "the physical and psychological integrity of a person" and went on to observe that
>
>> "Article 8 also protects a right to personal development, and the right to establish and develop relationships with other human beings and the outside world."

> Elusive though the concept is, I think one must understand "private life" in article 8 as extending to those features which are integral to a person's identity or ability to function socially as a person. Professor Feldman, writing in 1997 before the most recent decisions, helpfully observed ("The Developing Scope of Article 8 of the European Convention on Human Rights", [1997] EHRLR 265, 270):
>
>> "Moral integrity in this sense demands that we treat the person holistically as morally worthy of respect, organising the state and society in ways which respect people's moral worth by taking account of their need for security."'

The concept is clearly an exceedingly broad one. In *Janjanin v Secretary of State for the Home Department* [2004] EWCA Civ 448 the Court of Appeal did not refuse to recognise that valuable and responsible work in the National Health Service could constitute private life. Equally someone who made a great contribution to the community outside work, or who has close relationships in the UK such as being someone's carer, might be able to build a case.

Article 8 does not only deal with strict family life scenarios. It may also prevent a person's removal where their private life in terms of their mental (or perhaps physical) health would be affected seriously whilst falling short of Article 3 ill-treatment, however such a breach would need to be flagrant - see *Ullah* (HL):

> 'Another possible field of application could be the expulsion of an alien homosexual to a country where, short of persecution, he might be subjected to a flagrant violation of his article 8 rights. In *Z v Secretary of State for the Home Department* [2002] Imm AR 560 this point came before the Court of Appeal. Schiemann LJ (with whom the other members of the court agreed) was not prepared to rule out such an argument. In my view he was right not to do so. Enough has been said to demonstrate that on principles repeatedly affirmed by the ECtHR article 8 may be engaged in cases of a real risk of a flagrant violation of an individual's article 8 rights.'

See also for example the Strasbourg court in *Bensaid v UK* (2001) 33 EHRR 10.

> 'Not every act or measure which adversely affects moral or physical integrity will interfere with the right to respect to private life guaranteed by Article 8. However, the Court's case-law does not exclude that treatment which does not reach the severity of Article 3 treatment may nonetheless breach Article 8 in its private life aspect where there are sufficiently adverse affects on physical and moral integrity. Private life is a broad term not susceptible to exhaustive definition. The Court has already held that elements such as gender identification, name and sexual orientation and sexual life are important elements of the personal sphere protected by Article 8. Mental health must also be regarded as a crucial part of private life associated with the aspect of moral integrity. Article 8 protects a right to identity and personal development, and the right to establish and develop relationships with other human beings and the outside world. The preservation of mental stability is in that context an indispensable precondition to effective enjoyment of the right to respect for private life...'

See the more abbreviated definition from the House of Lords in *Razgar* [2004] UKHL 27 quoted above: "those features which are integral to a person's identity or ability to function socially as a person."

One point to emerge from the House of Lords judgment in *EM (Lebanon) v SSHD* [2008] UKHL 64 is that it is the existing family and/or private life right that has to be considered, not some future alternative relationships that might or might not be developed in the future (paragraph 39 of judgment). This may go some way to defeating the standard Home Office submission in Article 8 cases that an alternative family life is available to the person in their country of origin, but as ever much depends on the facts of the case. *EM (Lebanon)* also corrected the position erroneously set by *Kehinde v SSHD*, a starred IAT case from 1999, which maintained that only the rights of the appellant could be considered in an Article 8 claim. Baroness Hale observed that the one stop principle was frustrated by such an interpretation.

Another long standing tribunal error was rectified in the case of *AG (Eritrea) v SSHD* [2007] EWCA Civ 801, whereby the impossibly high threshold test of 'truly exceptional' was found to be a misinterpretation of *dicta* issued in *Huang & Ors* [2007] UKHL 11. It was determined that 'truly exceptional' was not an additional element to the test set out in *Razgar*, above, as had been the practise of the tribunal. It was merely expected that 'only a small minority of exceptional cases' would be expected to succeed under Article 8, outside the immigration rules. At paragraphs 27 and 28 of the judgment in *AG (Eritrea)* the Court emphasises that the threshold for engaging Article 8 is 'not a specially high one', although it must be real.

In *CDS (PBS: "available": Article 8) Brazil* [2010] UKUT 00305 (IAC) the tribunal held that temporary migrants, for example under the Points Based System, do build up an Article 8 private life even before settlement. The extent of any failure to qualify under the Immigration Rules must therefore be considered.

Threshold for interference in foreign cases

In 'foreign cases' (a term used in *Ullah and Do*), i.e. cases where there is argued to be a breach of rights that will take place in the future, after removal from the UK rather than inside the UK itself by the action or inaction of the UK authorities, it has to be shown that there will be a 'flagrant denial' of the right in question if it is not an absolute right.

The leading case is *EM (Lebanon) v SSHD* [2008] UKHL 64, in which the House of Lords holds that the 'complete nullification' and 'flagrant denial' tests, which seemed in the lower courts to have been understood to represent different thresholds, are simply reflections of the same test. *EM (Lebanon)* is believed to have made European legal history by being the first significant decision in which this very high test was made out.

Relocating the family

The Home Office will routinely argue in Article 8 cases that turn on a relationship that was formed in the UK that it is not the decision of the Home Office to remove the illegal immigrant that would sunder the relationship, it is the refusal of the UK-based person to relocate to the foreign country in question. The right of a state to regulate immigration control is cited, and the fact that couples do not have an automatic right to choose their country of residence together.

One of the key cases on this issue, albeit one that is flawed and requires further analysis, is *R (Mahmood) v SSHD* [2001] 1 WLR 840, in which Phillips MR (as he then was) reviews a number of Strasbourg authorities and as one of six observations on Article 8 in immigration cases says:

> 'Article 8 is likely to be violated by the expulsion of a member of a family that has been long established in a State if the circumstances are such that it is not reasonable to expect the other members of the family to follow that member expelled.'

This was taken by some to impose a test of there having to exist 'insurmountable obstacles' to the UK-based family going abroad to live with the claimant migrant. This inaccurate interpretation of *Mahmood* has been laid to rest by Lord Bingham at paragraph 12 of his judgment in *EB (Kosovo) v SSHD* [2008] UKHL 41, in which there is no reference at all to an 'insurmountable obstacles' test:

> ...it will rarely be proportionate to uphold an order for removal of a spouse if there is a close and genuine bond with the other spouse and that spouse cannot reasonably be expected to follow the removed spouse to the country of removal...

The correctness of a simple reasonableness test is confirmed by the Court of Appeal in *VW (Uganda) v SSHD* [2009] EWCA Civ 5. However, it remains a difficult test to satisfy, even if not literally an insurmountable one. As an example, in *Amrollahi v Denmark* (Appl no 56811/00; 11 October 2002), where the applicant was a convicted drug trafficker, the Court did find that it was not reasonable to pursue family life abroad but on the following facts:

> '41. The applicant's wife, A, is a Danish national. She has never been to Iran, she does not know Farsi and she is not a Muslim. Besides being married to an Iranian man, she has no ties with the country. In these circumstances the Court accepts even if it is not impossible for the spouse and the applicant's children to live in Iran that it would, nevertheless, cause them obvious and serious difficulties. In addition, the Court recalls that A's daughter from a previous relationship, who has lived with A since her birth in 1989, refuses to move to Iran. Taking this fact into account as well, A cannot, in the Court's opinion, be expected to follow the applicant to Iran.'

Top tip

In reality it will often be necessary to show that there is an affected child who cannot reasonably be expected to live to a foreign country because of the disruption this would engender or that an affected adult is a carer and cannot be expected to abandon the caree. Failing this, some other similarly strong and compelling reason will be necessary.

In investigating whether the UK-based party to the relationship can move abroad, it may be the case that they have refugee status or humanitarian protection in the United Kingdom. Whilst this may be though by some to be sufficient to show that the person cannot be expected to relocate to their home country, the tribunal will often require proof that this remains the case, particularly if the status was granted some time previously. See, for example, *Kilala* [2002] UKIAT 05220 and *L (Afghanistan)* [2003] UKIAT 00092 for potential difficulties without evidence of current risk.

Provision of the determination of an immigration judge or adjudicator or other papers that go to explain the substance of their claim will therefore be necessary. Some members of the immigration judiciary have been known to state that the absence of reasons on a grant letter means that it is not adequate evidence of current well founded fear. A SEF, interview record or statement may be necessary.

Applying for entry clearance from abroad

Another Home Office argument on the question of whether there is a real interference with the Article 8 rights of a person facing removal is that the person can apply for entry clearance in the normal way. Where a person is unlawfully present in the UK, it is said that they have jumped the queue and evaded necessary immigration regulation and control systems. If they have a claim to be permitted to enter and remain in the UK, it should be processed in the proper way, and an Entry Clearance Officer, bound by the terms of the Human Rights Act, will take all relevant circumstances into account.

The argument is not that the person can quickly apply for entry clearance therefore meaning that the breach in Article 8 rights is only temporary; rather that an in-country Article 8 claim is not the proper way to litigate that person's rights, instead they should apply in the proper manner. The argument implicitly recognises that entry might not ultimately be granted.

However, the House of Lords effectively rejected this approach in the case of *Chikwamba v SSHD* [2008] UKHL 40, holding that it was more sensible to assess human rights at the point of application:

> 40. ... it seems to me that only comparatively rarely, certainly in family cases involving children, should an article 8 appeal be dismissed on the basis that it would be proportionate and more appropriate for the appellant to apply for leave from abroad. Besides the considerations already mentioned, it should be borne in mind that the 1999 Act introduced one-stop appeals. The article 8 policy instruction is not easily reconcilable with the new streamlined approach. Where a single appeal combines (as often it does) claims both for asylum and for leave to remain under article 3 or article 8, the appellate authorities would necessarily have to dispose substantively of the asylum and article 3 claims. Suppose that these fail. Should the article 8 claim then be dismissed so that it can be advanced abroad, with the prospect of a later, second section 65 appeal if the claim fails before the ECO (with the disadvantage of the appellant then being out of the country)? Better surely that in most cases the article 8 claim be decided once and for all at the initial stage. If it is well-founded, leave should be granted. If not, it should be refused.

UKBA have been slow to recognise the *ratio* of *Chikwamba* and it is standard for UKBA to argue that Chikwamba applies only in situations such as that pertaining in Zimbabwe at the time of the judgment. This confusion of fact with law should be resisted.

Engaging Article 8

For a time the immigration tribunal took the view that a strong Article 8 private and family life needed to be established in order to answer Lord Bingham's second question in the affirmative. However, since the case of *AG (Eritrea) v SSHD* [2007] EWCA Civ 801 the tribunal and courts have accepted that the threshold of engagement is not a particularly high one. See Lord Justice Sedley's comments at paragraph 28 of that judgment:

> '...while an interference with private or family life must be real if it is to engage art. 8(1), the threshold of engagement (the "minimum level") is not a specially high one. Once the article is engaged, the focus moves, as Lord Bingham's remaining questions indicate, to the process of justification under art. 8(2). It is this which, in all cases which engage article 8(1), will determine whether there has been a breach of the article.'

In accordance with the law

Immigration control is in accordance with the law for Article 8 purposes, in relation to interference with family and private life as well as in relation to moral and physical integrity cases. Strasbourg tends to construe "in accordance with the law" as meaning there is a power in law to make the decision in question: and most would-be immigrants are the subject of lawful decisions in this sense, e.g. a person who does not fit into the immigration rules and is rejected as a refugee will not be able to establish any basis to come enter the country, and hence there will be a power in law to refuse them leave to enter.

For a legitimate aim

The potential legitimate aims listed at Article 8(2) are as follows:

(i) • public safety

(ii) • the economic well-being of the country

(iii) • for the prevention of disorder or crime

(iv) • for the protection of health or morals

(v) • for the protection of the rights and freedoms of others

As indicated already, this tends to be automatically answered against the immigrant. Lord Bingham in *Razgar* in the House of Lords [2004] UKHL 27:

> "19. Where removal is proposed in pursuance of a lawful immigration policy, question (4) will almost always fall to be answered affirmatively. This is because the right of sovereign states, subject to treaty obligations, to regulate the entry and expulsion of aliens is recognised in the Strasbourg jurisprudence (see *Ullah and Do, para 6*) and implementation of a firm and orderly immigration policy is an important function of government in a modern democratic state. In the absence of bad faith, ulterior motive or deliberate abuse of power it is hard to imagine an adjudicator answering this question other than affirmatively."

The European Court in *Bensaid v United Kingdom* (E. Ct. H.R. 6 February 2001): speaking of interferences compelled by the consequences of immigration control:

> "... the Court considers that such interference may be regarded as complying with the requirements of the second paragraph of Article 8, namely as a measure 'in accordance with the law', pursuing the aims of the protection of the economic well-being of the country and the prevention of disorder and crime, as well as being 'necessary in a democratic society' for those aims."

Necessary in a democratic society

It is necessary for the Home Office to show that a removal or deportation is necessary in a democratic society in the interests of interests of national security, public safety or the economic well-being of the country, for the prevention of disorder or crime, for the protection of health or morals, or for the protection of the rights and freedoms of others. Where the Home Office cannot do so, the case must succeed. See, for example, *A (Afghanistan) v SSHD* [2009] EWCA Civ 825, which succeeded on this ground alone.

In cases involving a person unlawfully present in the UK, the justification is that a system of immigration control needs to be maintained, and if persons are permit to evade that system, the system is rendered meaningless and will fall apart.

Different considerations apply where a person is lawfully present in the UK, either with current limited leave or with indefinite leave. Curtailment is an option in the former case, for example where the person no longer meets the requirements of the system of immigration control. Deportation is necessary for holders of indefinite leave.

Deportation is dealt with in a separate section, but there is considerable overlap with human rights law and Article 8, not least as it is now all but impossible to succeed in an appeal against deportation unless a human rights case can be made out.

In *N (Kenya) v SSHD* [2004] EWCA Civ 1094 the Court of Appeal emphasised that the courts should give proper weight to the opinion of the Secretary of State regarding the public interest in removal of persons who have committed very serious offences. In dismissing the claimant's appeal May LJ (with whom Judge LJ agreed but Sedley LJ disagreed) commented as follows:

> 'The risk of re-offending is a factor in the balance, but, for very serious crimes, a low risk of re-offending is not the most important public interest factor. In my view, the adjudicator's decision was over-influenced in the present case by his assessment of the risk of re-offending to the exclusion, or near exclusion, of the other more weighty public interest considerations characterised by the seriousness of the appellant's offences.'

Proportionality

The concept of proportionality is central to the application of Article 8, although it is very important to follow the five-step approach and not jump straight to proportionality.

Proportionality in the context of the exercise of immigration control usually boils down to a question of identifying the few cases where the adverse effect on the individual is so disproportionate to the need to maintain an effective system of immigration control that removal from the UK is not permissible. A series of Court of Appeal and House of Lords decisions have examined the test for proportionality. For a time it was thought by the Immigration tribunal that a case had to be found to be 'truly exceptional', seizing on a phrase used by Lord Bingham in the case of *Razgar*, in order to succeed. However, the House of Lords held that this was incorrect in the later case of *Huang* and observed that Lord Bingham's earlier comments were merely predictive of the numbers of cases that might succeed, they did not amount to a legal test.

In the case of *AG (Eritrea) v SSHD* [2007] EWCA Civ 801 the Court of Appeal at paragraph 31 comments on this as follows:

> 'The fact that in the great majority of cases the demands of immigration control are likely to make removal proportionate and so compatible with art.8 is a consequence, not a precondition, of the statutory exercise. No doubt in this sense successful art.8 claims will be the exception rather than the rule; but to treat exceptionality as the yardstick of success is to confuse effect with cause.'

Assessing proportionality is sometimes compared to a balancing exercise. The scales and the weights on each side of the fulcrum can be represented thus:

Scales diagram

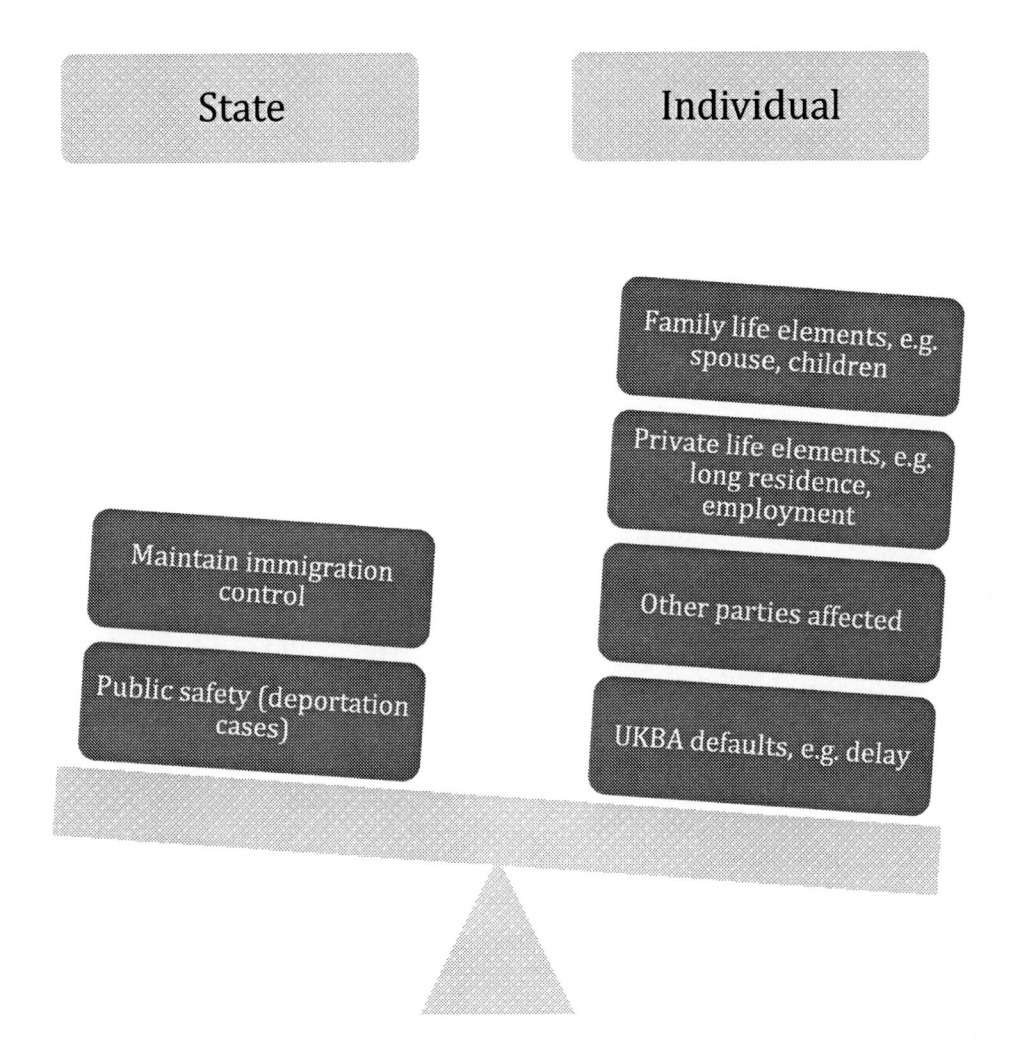

State side:
- Maintain immigration control
- Public safety (deportation cases)

Individual side:
- Family life elements, e.g. spouse, children
- Private life elements, e.g. long residence, employment
- Other parties affected
- UKBA defaults, e.g. delay

General factors

The leading case on Article 8 and proportionality is the Strasbourg case of *Uner v The Netherlands* [2006] ECHR 873. It is, however, a deportation case and therefore needs to be adapted in non-deportation cases. The claimant had been convicted of violent assaults on previous occasions and the incident that triggered his deportation involved him shooting one man in the leg and injuring him and another man in the head and killing him. The claimant was sentenced to seven years in jail. The Court ultimately concluded that in expelling the claimant, a correct balance had been struck in this case.

As the Court of Appeal has recognised in *KB (Trinidad and Tobago) v SSHD* [2010] EWCA Civ 11 and *JO (Uganda) v SSHD* [2010] EWCA Civ 10, the approach in deportation and ordinary immigration cases must be different, as there is a stronger interest in expulsion of the individual in a deportation case.

The key factors to be examined in *Uner*, the first eight of which are extracted from *Boultif v Switzerland* [2001] ECHR 497 and the final two added in *Uner*, are as follows:

(i) the nature and seriousness of the offence committed by the applicant;

(ii) the length of the applicant's stay in the country from which he or she is to be expelled;

(iii) the time elapsed since the offence was committed and the applicant's conduct during that period;

(iv) the nationalities of the various persons concerned;

(v) the applicant's family situation, such as the length of the marriage, and other factors expressing the effectiveness of a couple's family life;

(vi) whether the spouse knew about the offence at the time when he or she entered into a family relationship;

(vii) whether there are children of the marriage, and if so, their age; and

(viii) the seriousness of the difficulties which the spouse is likely to encounter in the country to which the applicant is to be expelled.

(ix) the best interests and well-being of the children, in particular the seriousness of the difficulties which any children of the applicant are likely to encounter in the country to which the applicant is to be expelled; and

(x) the solidity of social, cultural and family ties with the host country and with the country of destination.

Uner is itself then supplemented by another later case, *Maslov v Austria* 1638/03 [2008] ECHR 546:

> '74. Although Article 8 provides no absolute protection against expulsion for any category of aliens (see *Üner*, cited above, § 55), including those who were born in the host country or moved there in their early childhood, the Court has already found that regard is to be had to the special situation of aliens who have spent most, if not all, their childhood in the host country, were brought up there and received their education there (see *Üner*, § 58 *in fine*).
>
> 75. In short, the Court considers that for a settled migrant who has lawfully spent all or the major part of his or her childhood and youth in the host country very serious reasons are required to justify expulsion. This is all the more so where the person concerned committed the offences underlying the expulsion measure as a juvenile.'

Maslov emphasises that cases involving long-settled migrants, particularly who entered the UK as children, involve very substantial interferences with Article 8 which must be properly weighed in the balance. In *JO (Uganda) v SSHD* [2010] EWCA Civ 10 Lord Justice Richards emphasizes that long residence is an important factor and it need not be long *lawful* residence in order to carry weight.

In *LD (Article 8 best interests of child) Zimbabwe* [2010] UKUT 278 (IAC) the President of the Immigration and Asylum Chamber of the Upper Tribunal found that the UN Convention on the Rights of the Child is highly relevant to Article 8 ECHR:

> 27. The two younger children of the appellant have lived in the UK continuously for eleven years and for most of their lives. PreviouslyHome Office policy tended to identify seven years of residence of a child as one that would presumptively require regularisation of immigration status of child and parents in the absence of compelling countervailing factors. That was really an administrative way of giving effect to the principle of the welfare of the child as a primary consideration in such cases and when it was considered that those interests normally required regularisation of the immigration position of the family as a whole. The policy may have been withdrawn but substantial residence as a child is a strong indication the judicial assessment of what the best interests of the child requires. The UN Convention on the Rights of the Child 1989 Art 3 makes such interests a primary consideration.
>
> 28. Although questions exist about the status of the UN Convention on the Rights of the Child in domestic law, we take the view that there can be little reason to doubt that the interests of the child should be a primary consideration in immigration cases. A failure to treat them as such will violate Article 8(2) as incorporated directly into domestic law.

Home Office delay

The definitive case on delay by UKBA as a factor in assessing proportionality is that of the House of Lords in *EB (Kosovo) v Secretary of State for the Home Department* [2008] UKHL 41. In summary, the three ways in which Lord Bingham says that delay may affect an Article 8 claim are as follows:

(i) The Article 8 family and/or private life rights will develop and grow during a period of delay.

(ii) Delay reduced the weight to be attached to the consideration that a relationship was entered into in the knowledge of its precariousness owing to immigration control considerations. To put it another way, delay allows Article 8 rights to become established and entrenched, and the decision-maker must show appropriate recognition of this reality.

(iii) Delay reduces the significance of the Article 8(2) consideration of the need to maintain immigration control because delay gives rise to 'a dysfunctional system which yields unpredictable, inconsistent and unfair outcomes'.

Lord Bingham's warns at paragraph 12 that an overly prescriptive approach is incompatible with the Article 8 assessment exercise, and that Article 8 is an important and fundamental human right worthy of genuine respect:

> Thus the appellate immigration authority must make its own judgment and that judgment will be strongly influenced by the particular facts and circumstances of the particular case. The authority will, of course, take note of factors which have, or have not, weighed with the Strasbourg court. It will, for example, recognise that it

> will rarely be proportionate to uphold an order for removal of a spouse if there is a close and genuine bond with the other spouse and that spouse cannot reasonably be expected to follow the removed spouse to the country of removal, or if the effect of the order is to sever a genuine and subsisting relationship between parent and child. But cases will not ordinarily raise such stark choices, and there is in general no alternative to making a careful and informed evaluation of the facts of the particular case. The search for a hard-edged or bright-line rule to be applied to the generality of cases is incompatible with the difficult evaluative exercise which article 8 requires.

Encouragingly, the Home Office policy on delay set out in Chapter 53 of the Enforcement Instructions and Guidance is far more generous and suggests that delay should be given weight where there is a delay of four years or more. See earlier section on Home Office policies for details.

Example

Deidre has been waiting for five years for a decision on her application to remain in the UK as the spouse of Barry. She originally entered the UK several years before that as a visitor and she overstayed her visa. She met and married Barry and they have two children now. They made an application under DP3/96 after they had been married for two years.

Deidre has not suffered any procedural prejudice by the delay she has experienced, as she was unlawfully present when she made the application and had overstayed her original visa with no expectation of being allowed to remain. She would not therefore have benefited from *HB (Ethiopia)*, but *EB (Kosovo)* is more helpful to her.

She has a very strong case even aside from *EB (Kosovo)*. Although DP3/96 has been abolished (see section on immigration policies), consideration under the policy had begun and the Home Office say they will apply DP3/96 to any cases already under consideration.

If the application was ultimately rejected for some reason, Deidre would have a good case on appeal for the tribunal to apply the policy itself in accordance with *AG and others (Policies; executive discretions; Tribunal's powers) Kosovo* [2007] UKAIT 00082 (see further below). In addition, a delay of five years is a very long one and is a relevant factor, and the couple have established a very strong family life in the UK during that time.

Failure to apply a policy

If the facts of the case bring the claimant within a policy that has not been properly considered in their case, this is very likely to render disproportionate a failure to apply that policy. For example, in *AA (Afghanistan) v SSHD* [2007] EWCA Civ 12 Keene LJ said the following at paragraph 15:

> 'This court has held more than once that for the Secretary of State to fail to take account of or give effect to his own published policy renders his decision not "in accordance with the law": see, for example, *Secretary of State for the Home Department v. Abdi* [1996] Imm. AR 148 at 157. Likewise the AIT should have concluded that the adjudicator had made an error of law.'

Where an individual fits within a policy, that will suggest that a decision inconsistent with the policy will be disproportionate: for the existence of the policy will strongly suggest where the public interest lies.

However, the tribunal are reluctant to make decisions for itself under policies that retain a degree of Home Office discretion. Where a policy is found by the tribunal to apply to a person and the outcome is clear-cut, the appeal should be allowed. Where it is not clear-cut that the policy should be applied, the tribunal will allow an appeal as being not in accordance with the law (because the policy has not been considered), but expect the Home Office to make their own decision about whether the policy does in fact apply: *AG and others (Policies; executive discretions; Tribunal's powers) Kosovo* [2007] UKAIT 00082.

The fact that on arrival in the United Kingdom the applicant had a legitimate claim to enter can also be a determinative factor in assessing the proportionality of a decision to refuse status. In the related cases of *SSHD v R (on the app. of Rashid)* [2005] EWCA Civ 744 and *R (on the app. of A, H and AH) v SSHD* [2006] EWHC 526 (Admin), it was held that the Home Office had acted unlawfully in concealing a policy from the applicants and then denying status once that policy had been ended. The case clearly has wider ramifications for other nationalities.

Third party rights

In Strasbourg cases, such as *Berrehab v Netherlands* (1989) 11 EHRR 322, *Beldjoudi v France* (1992) 14 EHRR 801 and *Amrollahi v Denmark* [2002] ECHR 585 (arguably, at least), the European Court of Human Rights considers the rights of the family as a whole, including the rights of the family members with a right to reside in the country concerned. Whatever the final outcome of these cases, many of which are successful, it is clear from the judgments that the collective rights of the family as a whole have been considered.

For some years the Tribunal maintained a restrictive approach to third party rights. However in *Beoku-Betts v Secretary of State for the Home Department* [2008] UKHL 39 (25 June 2008) the House of Lords reversed this, in the context of the right of appeal set out in the Immigration and Asylum Act 1999 but which will demand the same approach in appeals brought under the Nationality Immigration and Asylum Act 2002.

> "Once it is recognised that ... "there is only one family life", and that, assuming the appellant's proposed removal would be disproportionate looking at the family unit as

> a whole, then each affected family member is to be regarded as a victim, section 65 seems comfortably to accommodate the wider construction."

The implications for practice and evidence are considerable. Evidence from family members may now prove crucial, particularly in relation to:

(i) Strength and depth of relationship and/or attachment, and what the applicant means to the family member concerned.

(ii) Reasons why the family member(s) cannot or should not be expected to relocate to the country concerned.

(iii) Information regarding the effect on any children affected, ideally from family court proceedings (permission will be needed), child psychologist or from an Independent Social Worker.

Beoku-Betts was followed by another landmark House of Lords case, *EM (Lebanon) v SSHD* [2008] UKHL 64. The Lords held that the rights of the child in this case had to be considered separately to the mother (both were facing removal) and also suggested that separate representation for a child might be appropriate in some cases.

Article 14

Article 14 prohibits discrimination only in when it can be linked with a lack of respect for one or more of the rights otherwise set out in the European Convention on Human Rights – it is the enjoyment of those rights which must be secured without discrimination. There is very little in the way of helpful case law on the issue so far.

Discretionary Leave

This is a residual form of leave to remain given to individuals who do not qualify for other forms of leave to remain.

The most common situation where you can expect to see a grant of discretionary leave to remain will be in Article 8 cases where removal is said to breach the right to a private and family life in the United Kingdom, or where a person's medical condition would breach Article 8.

Children who are not accompanied and there are not adequate reception arrangements available in their own country will obtain a certain minimal level of protection. If they qualify for discretionary leave on this basis, and under another basis too, they should receive the higher quality leave to remain.

The Home Office APIs state as follows:

> "There are likely to be very few other cases in which it would be appropriate to grant Discretionary Leave to an unsuccessful asylum seeker. However, it is not possible to anticipate every eventuality that may arise, so there remains scope to grant

> Discretionary Leave where individual circumstances, although not meeting the criteria of any of the other categories listed above, are so compelling that it is considered appropriate to grant some form of leave."

Individuals who would have qualified for HP but for committing activities that have caused their exclusion will receive Discretionary Leave – "a person whose removal, not withstanding their actions, would breach the ECHR and who does not qualify for any other form of leave should normally (unless the option of deferred removal is taken ..) be granted a limited period of Discretionary Leave even if they fall within the exclusion criteria."

The normal period of grant of Discretionary Leave is three years. The exceptions are for minors, who will be granted DL to the age of 17.5, and in exclusion cases where the person is excluded from other forms of protection but a grant of leave is nevertheless appropriate. In these cases, a grant of six months will be made.

Those who succeed in establishing an Article 8 interference in family life cases based on marriage will be treated in line with other Article 8 cases and therefore receive a period of 3 years, to be renewed for a further 3 years on active consideration. Claimants therefore may wish to consider the potential immigration status and settlement benefits of leaving the United Kingdom to apply for entry clearance as a spouse.

An application for extension can be made where there is a continued need for DL.

In all cases, the holder of DL must have completed six years of DL (10 years in exclusion cases) before being eligible to apply for settlement.

There are provisions for revocation of DL. However, given that discretionary leave to remain does not normally result from any "protection" need but rather is based on relationships or care in the UK, travel to the country of origin and use of their own national passport does not bring with it the same negative connotations as in asylum and humanitarian protection cases.

For those who hold Discretionary Leave, applications for family reunion may be considered before the sponsor has been granted ILR but the Home Office will only grant entry clearance in those cases where there are compelling, compassionate circumstances. In all cases the sponsor will be expected to satisfy the maintenance and accommodation requirements as set out in the Immigration Rules – ie they must show that there will be adequate accommodation for the family unit without recourse to public funds in accommodation which they own or occupy exclusively; and that they will be able to maintain themselves and any dependants adequately without recourse to public funds.

Family reunion applications must be made at entry clearance posts overseas.

The Home Office website states that all concessions to this practice have been withdrawn. Further enquiries should normally be made in writing via a senior caseworker to Group 6, Asylum Policy Unit at the Home Office.

Travel documents

There is a possibility to travel with these forms of leave. Applicants must show that they need to travel for one of four reasons by producing documentary evidence (explained in the guidance notes):

1. Essential employment/business related reasons
2. Exceptional compassionate grounds
3. Study reasons
4. Religious reasons and other important reasons of conscience.

The Home Office website recommends that applicants allow for up to 5-8 weeks for the application to be processed, warning that it would be helpful if no telephone calls were made to check on progress unless the applicant has been waiting for longer than that time. The UKBA deals with all applications in the order that they are received, unless a travel document is needed due to a medical emergency - evidence of the same (for example, a recent medical report or doctors report) should accompany one of these applications.

Applicants must specify the country or countries they wish to visit (including any countries they may need to pass through in transit). Their documents will not be valid for travel to any other country. Other than in very exceptional circumstances, travel documents may not be used to travel to the country of origin, or to the country that the client sought asylum from. The documents are valid for five years.

Children can be included on a travel document. The Home Office permit a maximum of two children to be included on a travel document. Any additional children will be included on another travel document that they will issue to an older brother or sister, although all children should be named on the same application form. Their travel document will be endorsed to show that they must travel with the applicant. It is possible to apply for children to have their own travel documents, though expensive – the applicant will need to pay the full fee for each application, completing separate application forms for each child. Then the children will be able to travel without the applicant.

The Home Office website sets out the requirements for amendments to applications and travel documents. In virtually all cases a full further application form (and full fee) needs to be sent together with extrinsic evidence (eg on a change of name, the relevant legal documentation must be produced; if documents are lost or stolen, a police report must be provided). Children can be added or removed to the documents on a full application (in the latter case the old document is cancelled and a new one issued). If details on the travel document that is issued are incorrect, and the UKBA are at fault, then there will be no further fee. The documents are not extendable, and if they expire whilst the holder is abroad, then it will be necessary to apply to the nearest British Embassy or High Commission for advice.

There will be an investigation into the loss and so the Home Office warns that applications to replace lost documents can take considerably longer than the usual 5-8 weeks period.

Do not forget the position of the Legal Services Commission re travel documents:

> "We will not pay for assistance with simple form filling in immigration or asylum matters, which does not require legal advice. This will include (but is not limited to) the filling in of travel document forms for persons accepted as refugees under the 1951 UN Convention, passport applications and citizenship applications. It may be reasonable for you to provide advice regarding the completion of these forms in limited circumstances where an issue of law arises. In these circumstances you must keep a specific attendance note on the file explaining what legal issues were raised and why Legal Help was required.
>
> For example: It may be reasonable to provide legal advice where an application is to be decided by the Home Office on a discretionary basis."

Chapter 6: European Community law

PRINCIPLE OF FREE MOVEMENT 233

COUNTRIES TO WHICH FREE MOVEMENT LAW APPLIES 233

    EUROPEAN UNION 233
    EUROPEAN ECONOMIC AREA 234
    ACCESSION STATES 235
    ASSOCIATION AGREEMENTS 235

INTERACTION OF UK AND EC LAW 236

    RIGHTS NOT PRIVILEGES 236
    IMPLEMENTATION OF EC LAW 237
    DUAL NATIONALITY 238
    CHOICE OF METHOD OF ENTRY 238
    EC LAW AND THE ECHR 239

WHO BENEFITS? 240

    EEA NATIONALS EXERCISING TREATY RIGHTS 240
        Workers and jobseekers 241
        Self employed persons 243
        Self sufficient persons 243
        Students 245
    UK NATIONALS EXERCISING TREATY RIGHTS 245
    FAMILY MEMBERS OF QUALIFIED PERSONS 246
        Immediate family members 247
        Extended family members 249
        Proving the relationship 251

BENEFITS OF THE EXERCISE OF TREATY RIGHTS 251

    ADMISSION AND ENTRY 251
    INITIAL RIGHT OF RESIDENCE 253
    RESIDENCE 253
    PERMANENT RESIDENCE 254
    RETAINED RIGHTS OF RESIDENCE 255

EXCLUDING AND REMOVING EEA NATIONALS FROM UK 257

    CEASING TO BE QUALIFIED 257
    PUBLIC POLICY REMOVALS AND EXCLUSIONS 258

RIGHTS OF APPEAL 260

ACCESSION STATES 261

    A8 NATIONALS 262
        Registration 262
        Rights and entitlements 263
        Family members of A8 workers 263

A2 NATIONALS	264
THE ANKARA AGREEMENT	**264**
WORKERS	264
Rights of residence	268
Expulsion	268
Family members	268
SELF-EMPLOYED	269
Rights of Establishment	269
Lawful entry	269
Applications	270
Appeals	271
ADDITIONAL AGREEMENTS	271

Principle of free movement

When discussing this area of law, the correct terminology is to refer to European Community ('EC') law as this is the relevant treaty framework. However, it is more convenient to refer to the area of law as European Economic Area or EEA law, as it is to the EEA that the relevant laws apply, as is explained below.

The object of EEA law is straightforward: EEA nationals and their family members are entitled to move freely among Member States to work, set up in self employment, retire and study. The rights are not wholly unrestricted, particularly regarding the ability to secure stay for family members, but they are powerful nonetheless.

The key to their enjoyment is that the individual (or their family member) wishing to assert them is exercising Treaty rights of free movement. Non-British EEA citizens may therefore make use of these rights when pursuing certain activities in the UK, but there are also circumstances, examined below, where a British citizen may make use of EEA freedom of movement law to benefit his or her family members rather than having to rely on UK immigration law. Immigration lawyers are likely to have clients who are "third country" nationals (ie not citizens from Member States of the EC) who want to use their relationship with EEA nationals to improve their immigration status, so it will often be of critical importance to identify a person exercising their Treaty rights and then to determine what benefits might flow for the third country national.

As will be seen below, the principal advantage of reliance on EEA law rather than UK immigration law is that EEA law is far simpler than UK immigration law and does not include, for example, restrictions relating to maintenance and accommodation.

Countries to which free movement law applies

European Union

The European (Economic) Community came into existence as a result of the Treaty of Rome of 1957, as amended. Its successor organisation, the European Union, now comprises 27 Member States. However, in free movement law there are some differences between the treatment of nationals of the new 'Accession States' as opposed to the pre-existing members:

The 15 pre-existing Member States were as follows:

Austria	Italy
Belgium	Luxembourg
Denmark	The Netherlands
Finland	Portugal
France	Spain
Germany	Sweden
Greece	The United Kingdom
Ireland	

The two Accession States which joined the EU on 1 May 2004 and immediately gained full free movement rights for their citizens were as follows:

Cyprus	Malta

The eight Accession States which joined the EU on 1 May 2004 and were not immediately granted full free movement rights, often referred to as the 'A8' countries, were as follows:

Czech Republic	Lithuania
Estonia	Poland
Hungary	Slovakia
Latvia	Slovenia

Two further countries then joined the EU on 1 January 2007 and, again, were not immediately granted full free movement rights for their citizens. As is discussed below, they were treated even less generously than the A8 countries. The countries concerned (sometimes called the 'A2' countries) are:

Bulgaria	Romania

European Economic Area

The European Economic Area (EEA) took effect from the 1 January 1994, and now comprises the existing EU Member States plus Iceland, Norway and Liechtenstein. For freedom of movement purposes, Switzerland is also treated by all EEA members as if it was a member of the EEA.

The following diagram may help with avoiding misunderstanding about different European bodies:

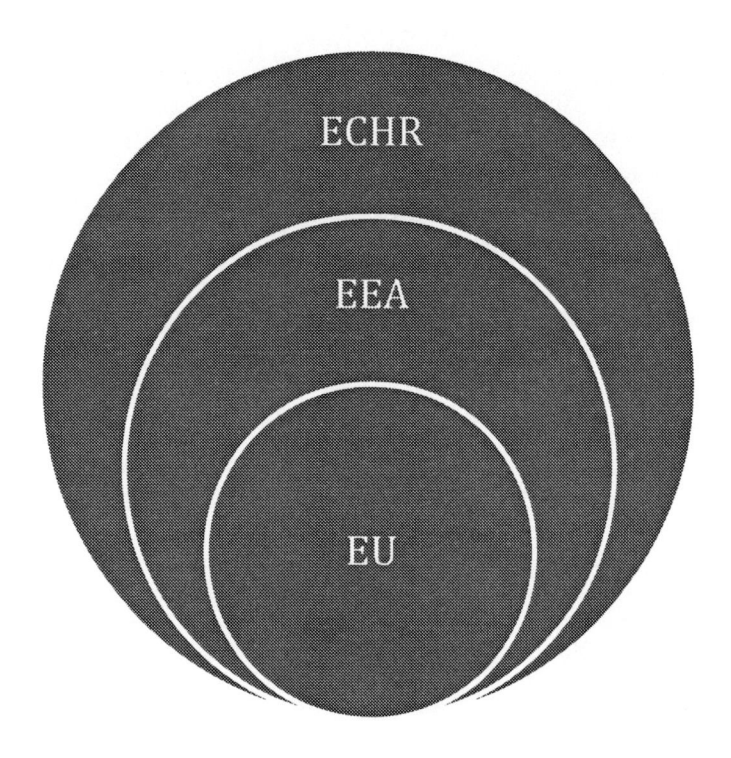

Accession States

Nationals of the Accession States, with the exception of Cyprus and Malta, did not obtain unfettered rights of free movement on the date of accession. Under the terms of accession existing Member States were entitled to impose restrictions on free movement rights for nationals of accession countries, and a panoply of severe restrictions - including either the suspension of rights for two years or the imposition of work permit requirement, or both – have been imposed by all existing members of the Union save the UK and Ireland.

The UK government has not sought to limit the rights of accession nationals beyond requiring registration on entry, and engagement in continuous work for one year before benefits such as jobseekers allowance and income support can be claimed (the benefits threshold is currently 6 months for nationals of existing Member States). Ireland has adopted a similar limitation on access to benefits.

The subject is addressed in more detail in a later section.

Association Agreements

Association Agreements are signed between the EU and third countries, usually states interested in becoming members. All of the Accession States had entered into EC Association Agreements before joining. The only current agreement with meaningful immigration consequences is now with Turkey, although agreements may be signed with other prospective members in future in the Balkans.

The agreements give self employed persons a right to establish themselves in business in the EEA. The idea is to promote integration of the economy prior to full membership. The agreement with Turkey extends some rights to workers who are in employment.

The Turkish agreement, often referred to as the Ankara Agreement, was signed between Turkey and the EEC before Britain joined in 1973. The effect of the agreement is that the UK cannot impose additional restrictions on workers or the self employed over and above those that were in place in 1973. This is by virtue of the 'standstill' clause of the agreement.

This subject is explored in more detail below in another section.

Interaction of UK and EC law

Key points:

- Rights not privileges
- Implementation issues
- Treatment of dual nationals
- Choice of laws
- EC law and the ECHR

Rights not privileges

There is a very important difference of principle between UK immigration law and EC freedom of movement rights. In UK law, if a foreign national wishes to come to the UK he or she must first make an application. There is no pre-existing 'right' to enter the UK. Stay in the UK is contingent on it being permitted by the Secretary of State: see section 1(2) of the Immigration Act 1971.

The position is very different in EC law. Certain individuals have a right to reside in the UK by virtue of their citizenship of another EEA country and their economic activities, or through their relationship with such a person. The UK is bound to recognise and promote this right.

A great deal flows from this distinction between inherent rights and discretionary privileges, and for those schooled in UK immigration law many aspects of EEA free movement law may seem counterintuitive. The facts that applications are free, that no particular application form (or indeed any form at all) is necessary, that leave of any kind literally cannot be given to EEA nationals, that EEA 'visas' (i.e. residence cards and similar) are unnecessary for the exercise of free movement rights are all natural consequences of the nature of pre-existing free movement rights in EC law.

Although there is no requirement for an application form to be used, UKBA has issued forms that can conveniently be used to make applications:

- Form EEA1 can be used by an EEA or Swiss national to apply for a registration certificate

- Form EEA2 can be used by a non-EEA or non-Swiss national family member of an EEA or Swiss national to apply for a residence card

- Form EEA3 can be used by an EEA or Swiss national to apply for permanent residence

- Form EEA4 can be used by a non-EEA or non-Swiss national family member of an EEA or Swiss national to apply for permanent residence.

In 2008, because of a serious and unlawful backlog on European casework that had been allowed to build up, UKBA introduced a screening process for EC applications. If an application does not include what appears to the UKBA caseworker to be the correct documentation, it will be returned. This approach is contrary to that required under EC law, which should be about swift action to realise and respect pre-existing rights rather than considering and granting new rights.

It is therefore advisable to use the provided forms and enclose the suggested paperwork, although the absence of the form or suggested documentation would not be fatal to an application in the long run.

Implementation of EC law

In UK law, EEA rights are expressed by the Immigration (European Economic Area) Regulations 2006. These are supposed to implement the changes to EC free movement law that were introduced by the Citizens' Directive. However, directly effective EC law will trump any provision contrary to its strictures – so if the Regulations are more restrictive than the principles they supposedly enshrine, then it is the EC law principles which will triumph.

The ultimate source of free movement law is not the Directive, though, but the very Treaty of Rome itself, which makes freedom of movement for workers and others, without discrimination, a core Treaty objective (Article 48 of the Treaty of Rome).

The other side of the coin to this is that the UK's implementation of the Citizens' Directive might be such as to include rights which go beyond those that the Directive strictly requires. This appears to be the view of the Tribunal regarding dependant family members in *AP and FP (Citizens Directive Article 3(2); discretion; dependence) India* [2007] UKAIT 00048 (13 June 2007) and the Court of Appeal in relation to spouses entering the UK from outside the EEA in *KG (Sri Lanka) v Secretary of State for the Home Department* [2008] EWCA Civ 13 (25 January 2008). So if a client fits into the terms of the UK Regulations, their application may be granted; but they cannot necessarily show that European law demands the grant of residence where the English courts do not accept that that law extends as far as the Regulations.

In cases of doubt over the proper interpretation of EEA provisions, then UK courts (including the immigration tribunal) can make a reference to the European Court of Justice to seek clarification.

The predecessor regulations to the current 2006 ones, introduced in 2000, were very heavily amended by the time they were superseded, as a number of successful challenges to them in the European Court of Justice had forced the UK government to make various changes. However, for most practical purposes, the current 2006 regulations provide a decent exposition of the way that the British government gives access to Treaty rights for the three categories of individual that benefits from Community law – (1) "qualified persons", usually being the EU nationals themselves, (2) their family members, and (3) those relatives who are dependant on them and were previously part of their households ("extended family members", as the 2006 Regulations call them).

Dual nationality

Dual nationals (e.g. those who hold dual British and Irish citizenship) exercising rights in the UK, can opt for the more convenient treatment under EC law or UK law, but can never lose their EC rights. This is because in EC law a person cannot lose rights to which they would otherwise be entitled as an EC national. A dual national need not have lived in both countries to be able to rely on EC rights.

However, a dual national might choose to take a particular route to secure stay for family members for the reasons set out below.

Choice of method of entry

An EEA citizen who is settled in the UK may have a choice as to whether to pursue an application under the rules or under EC law.

The choice of whether to seek admission of a dependant under the Immigration Rules or the under EC law should be carefully considered, as it can have longer term consequences.

For example whilst opting for the EC law route may ensure swifter entry than seeking to obtain entry clearance to the UK for the foreign spouse of a British national, the applicant may then find that choosing the European route has forestalled an application for ILR, because the immigration rules give speedier access to indefinite leave to remain for a spouse (under the immigration rules for normal spouses there is a two year "probation" period for spouses (rule 287(a)(i)(a)) whereas under the Immigration (EEA) Regulations 2006, access to settlement is available for qualified persons and their family members only after they have remained in the UK for five years.

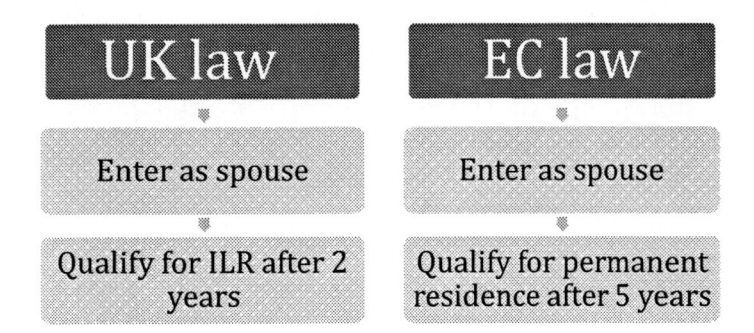

```
    UK law              EC law
       ↓                   ↓
 Enter as spouse      Enter as spouse
       ↓                   ↓
 Qualify for ILR    Qualify for permanent
    after 2 years   residence after 5 years
```

The benefits of relying on the EC law route will include the absence of any requirement for prior entry clearance, the absence of maintenance and accommodation requirements, the absence of any limitations on switching, the chance to be reunited with children and grandchildren at any age (subject to showing dependence if they are over 21), and with parents and grandparents and extended family, and that the right would run from the marriage rather than the Home Office acceptance of an application under the Rules.

The Home Office and others often talk about a need to "elect" the basis of entry, meaning that the person exercising Treaty rights should make a once-and-for-all choice in favour of the immigration rules or EEA rights. However Senior Treasury Counsel in *Zeghraba, R (on the application of) v Secretary Of State For Home Department* [1997] EWCA Civ 1486 (23rd April, 1997) agreed that they were not required to elect between the two schemes, national or Community. If one scheme failed to produce what they required they were entitled to follow up and adopt the alternative scheme.

EC law and the ECHR

Article 6(2) TEU provides:

> "The Union shall respect fundamental rights, as guaranteed by the European Convention for the Protection of Fundamental Freedoms signed in Rome …. And as they result from the constitutional traditions common to the Member States, as general principles of Community law".

From the case law of both the European Court of Human Rights and the European Court of Justice, as well as the Treaty on the European Union itself, it is possible to derive the proposition that European Community law must not contravene the European Convention on Human Rights (ECHR). However, the manner adopted by Member States in order to give effect to their obligations under the Convention is a matter for their discretion.

In *Kremzow v. Austrian State* the ECJ recognised the importance of the ECHR as the foundations of the fundamental rights which are the integral part of the general principles of Community law:

> "The [ECHR] has special significance… [I]t follows that measures are not acceptable in the Community which are incompatible with observance of the human rights thus recognised and guaranteed".

Case law has served to reinforce the relationship between EU free movement law and human rights, demonstrating the ECJ's determination to ensure the protection of the family life of Member State nationals in order to eliminate obstacles to the exercise of the fundamental freedoms guaranteed by the Treaty, even in the face of contrary domestic legislation:

Who benefits?

Below, we take the following approach to explaining the effect of the freedom of movement provisions:

(i) Who benefits from EC free movement rights?

(ii) What are those rights?

(iii) When can those rights be removed?

(iv) Accession State workers and the Association Agreements

EEA nationals exercising Treaty rights

The Citizens' Directive allows full free movement and residence privileges for certain categories of person, who are essentially economically active or self sufficient:

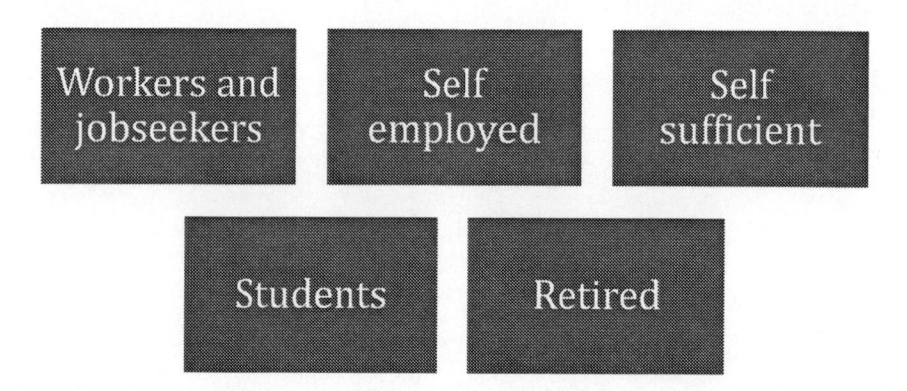

- Workers and jobseekers
- Self employed
- Self sufficient
- Students
- Retired

Such persons are referred to in the Immigration (European Economic Area) Regulations 2006 as 'qualified persons'. The definitions are set out at regulations 4, 5 and 6. Some of these definitions are quite helpful. For example, the definition of jobseeker at reg 6(4) as 'a person who enters the United Kingdom in order to seek employment and can provide evidence that he is seeking employment and has a genuine chance of being engaged' is fairly self explanatory. Other definitions refer back to the Treaty itself. The reason for this is to ensure that any case law of the ECJ is properly incorporated into the definition, as the ECJ is responsible for defining the terms of the Treaty and has had quite a lot to say about 'worker' and other key terms (see below).

Workers and jobseekers

The ECJ has defined a "worker" as (*Lawrie Blum* (1986) ECR 2121 – trainee teacher):

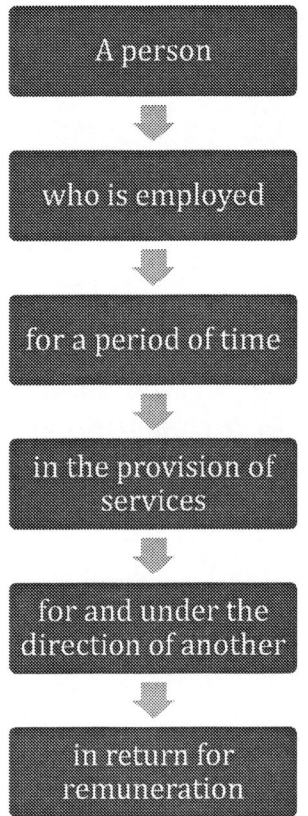

- A person
- who is employed
- for a period of time
- in the provision of services
- for and under the direction of another
- in return for remuneration

The definition is very broad indeed. The work need not be well paid nor full time so long as it is "effective and genuine" and not marginal or ancillary. If the work falls to be so defined it does not matter if the individual has to claim social assistance to top up their earnings, Article 7(2) of Regulation 1612/68 guarantees the right to do so on a non-discriminatory basis.

> "**Article 7**
>
> A worker who is a national of a Member State may not, in the territory of another Member State, be treated differently from national workers by reason of his nationality in respect of any conditions of employment and work, in particular as regards remuneration, dismissal, and should he become unemployed, reinstatement or re-employment.
>
> He shall enjoy the same social and tax advantages as national workers.
>
> He shall also, by virtue of the same right and under the same conditions as national workers, have access to training in vocational schools and retraining centres."

On this basis a part-time music teacher giving 12 lessons a week topped up with Dutch Social Security payments was a worker for Community purposes and entitled to a residence permit even if he was also receiving public funds (*Kempf v Staatsecretaris van justitie* 1987 1 C.M.L.R 764 ECJ).

There is no minimum period an EEA citizen must work in order to be a worker under Art 48 and so access social advantages, i.e. welfare benefits etc (Art 7 of Directive 68/360.

Temporary inability to work owing to illness or accident does not cause a worker to cease being considered a worker for the purposes of EC law.

Where a person has been unemployed for 6 months, however, the onus shifts to them to show that they remain active in the labour market (*Antonissen* (Case 292/89) 26 February 1991). In the case of *Akhtar*, however, the Tribunal was faced with a case where the SSHD had revoked the permit where the individual had been unemployed for 6 months and had just begun to receive benefits. They were unhappy with this approach, in the light of Regulation 19 of the old Immigration (EEA) Regulations 2000, which stated "On the occasion of the first renewal of a worker's residence permit the validity may be limited to one year if the worker has been involuntarily unemployed in the United Kingdom for more than one year"; by analogy, the Tribunal felt the Home Office had acted prematurely.

In determining whether an individual is a jobseeker or not, it is necessary to evaluate the merits of the case looking at the individual's intentions in entering the host Member State, his jobseeking history vis-à-vis the labour market and his chances of getting employment: *AG & Ors (EEA-jobseeker-self-sufficient person-proof) Germany* [2007] UKAIT 00075.

A worker (this also applies to self employed persons, below), continues to benefit from being a qualified person if he or she ceases activity in one of the following specified circumstances:

- Retirement, if resident in the UK for at least three years and working for at least a year prior to retirement and having reached state retirement age or having taken early retirement if a worker: reg 5(2)

- Permanent incapacity to work, if resident in the UK for at least two years prior to this incapacity and the incapacity is the result of an accident at work or an occupational disease that entitles him or her to a pension payable in full or in part by an institution in the United Kingdom: reg 5(3)

- Resident in the UK as a worker or self employed person for at least three years and has retained a place of residence, to which he or she returns as a rule at least once a week: reg 5(4), but also see reg 5(5) which states that prior residence in the UK is not necessary to benefit from this provision

In addition, reg 5(6) states that the above rules on periods of residence do not apply where the person is married to or the civil partner of a UK national.

> **Example**
>
> Jacques comes to the UK. He is a French national. He registers with a Job Centre and applies for jobs every week. After a year he has not found work here.
>
> The EEA regs at reg.5(7) make provision for involuntary periods of unemployment to count towards time qualifying the person as a 'worker who has ceased activity' but are silent on the same issue for actual workers. We must therefore turn to ECJ case law on the meaning of 'worker'. Jacques should be accepted as being a jobseeker so long as his expectations as to work are not unreasonable: the question is whether it is reasonable in all the circumstances to say that he is to be treated as a worker (*Antonissen*).

Self employed persons

Article 43 Treaty of the European Union (TEU) covers those who wish to set themselves up in business or become self-employed. Article 49 TEU covers those who wish to provide or receive services.

Differentiating between employed and self-employed status is relatively straightforward. An activity is regarded as self-employed where it is carried out under an agreement with other commercial operators or consumers, but there is absent the subordination of one party or another into a relationship of salaried employment, which is the key element in the *Lawrie Blum* test of who is a worker (see above).

Some third country workers may derive rights under the provision of services rubric, because the ECJ has taken the view that companies have their own legal personality which itself deserves free movement rights. The ECJ in *Van der Elst* determined that an employer based in one European Economic Area ("EEA") state providing services in another, may transfer third country nationals, i.e. non-EEA nationals who are lawfully in their employment to service such contracts on a "temporary basis".

Self employed persons who cease activity enjoy very similar protection as workers, as described above. See reg 5 of the Immigration (EEA) Regulations 2006.

Self sufficient persons

The self-sufficient enjoy unrestricted rights of residence, as long as they can show that they have sufficient funds not to become dependent on benefits and that they have health insurance (Citizens Directive Art 7(1)(b)). One judge has questioned whether this necessarily means private health insurance, although the general view has been that private care is required (see Sedley LJ in the Court of Appeal in *W (China) & Anor v Secretary of State for the Home Department* [2006] EWCA Civ 1494).

In *Chen v the United Kingdom* (C-200/02; 20 October 2004), the ECJ recognised the right of a particularly youthful EU citizen (a baby only a few months old) to reside in the host Member State and to be looked after by her mother, a third country national, her primary carer, the latter of whom accordingly acquired a right of residence in order to deliver the requisite care, so long as the parent had sufficient resources for that minor not to become a burden on the public finances of the host Member State, and provided that the minor was covered by appropriate sickness insurance. The fact that the family specifically went to the Member State where the child was born for the express purpose of the child's acquiring citizenship of the Union was irrelevant to the child's right to exercise her free movement and residence in the EU.

The ECJ went further in *Maria Teixeira v London Borough of Lambeth* (Case C-480/08) and expressly stated that in order to confer on a child a right of residence it is only required that he has lived with his parents or either one of them in a Member State while at least one of them resided there as a worker; a parent caring for the child of a migrant worker who is in education in the host Member State has a right of residence in that State and that right is not conditional on the parent having sufficient resources not to become a burden on the social assistance system.

The *Chen* judgment is incorporated into the Immigration Rules at 257C rather than the Immigration (EEA) Regulations 2006. Nevertheless, it gives rise to an EC law right of entry that cannot be restricted by the Immigration Rules: *M (Chen parents: source of rights) Ivory Coast* [2010] UKUT 277 (IAC).

The Tribunal does not accept that the self-sufficiency of an EEA national can be established by aggregating his resources and those of his family member(s), irrespective of whether the resources of the family member(s) have been lawfully acquired: *AG & Ors (EEA-jobseeker-self-sufficient person-proof) Germany* [2007] UKAIT 00075. The Court of Appeal agree, saying that the child's own right, which is the right given by Art. 18 EC to reside here and not any of the separate Treaty rights to work here, is itself qualified by a dual requirement: self-sufficiency and health insurance, and where neither the child nor the parents can lawfully work here, the child's status does not make it unlawful to deny the parents the right to work: *W (China) & Anor v Secretary of State for the Home Department* [2006] EWCA Civ 1494.

> **Example**
>
> Baby Jane is a British citizen with dual nationality of another EEA state.
>
> She and her carers will qualify under the *Chen* principle so long as both she and they have sufficient independent resources of their own in terms of health insurance and in terms of avoiding becoming a burden on the social assistance system of the United Kingdom, these resources being acquired without working here without permission.

Students

Those seeking to enter another Member State solely for the purposes of study must be enrolled at a recognised education establishment for the principal purpose of following a vocational training course, and must provide an assurance, in the form of a declaration or such like, that they are economically self sufficient. If such an assurance is provided admission is unrestricted and there is no requirement to demonstrate means through the production of objective evidence. Spouses and children of a student also enjoy a (derived) right of entry and/or residence.

The payment by a Member State of Students tuition fees falls within the scope of the EEC treaty for the purposes of Article 7 of Reg 1612/68, but the payment of grants for maintenance do not (*Brown* (Case 197/86, 1988 3 CMLR 403)).

A national of another Member State who enters into an employment relationship prior to the undertaking of university studies in the same field of activity who would not have been employed if he had not already been admitted to the university course is to be regarded as a worker (*Brown* (Case 197/86, 1988 3 CMLR 403)).

UK nationals exercising Treaty rights

There are clear benefits to a UK national being considered a qualified person, as it will be far easier, cheaper and more straightforward for such a person to bring a family member into the UK than the alternative, which is to rely on the UK Immigration Rules. As will be seen, EC freedom of movement law is far less restrictive than UK immigration law for family members. If a UK national is exercising Treaty rights of freedom of movement in the EEA, he or she should be able to benefit from the other Treaty law provisions and therefore make use of the more beneficial provisions on family members.

In the case of *Surinder Singh*, a UK national was living and working in Germany. She married a 3rd country foreign national (i.e. not a resident of the UK or the EEA) while there. They later decided to relocate to the UK. The UK authorities required them to apply under the Immigration Rules and the application was refused on maintenance and accommodation grounds.

They protested to the ECJ that the right to go and work in other EEA countries must necessarily include a corollary right to return to the UK afterwards, and therefore that EC freedom of movement law applied, not UK immigration law. The court accepted this argument.

The Immigration (EEA) Regulations 2006 incorporate the *Surinder Singh* (C-370/90, [1992] ECR I-4265) judgment at reg 9. However, the regulations arguably do not go far enough and do not incorporate the judgment in *Carpenter v United Kingdom*, which suggests that merely to have been providing and receiving services in another EEA Member State would have been sufficient.

Family members of qualified persons

This group of beneficiaries of the Citizens Directive includes both EEA nationals that are not themselves exercising Treaty rights and also non-EEA nationals, often referred to as third country nationals in this context. Both groups are entitled to accompany an EEA national who is exercising Treaty rights.

There are two tiers of family member. Confusingly, the Directive and the domestic regulations describe these two tiers differently.

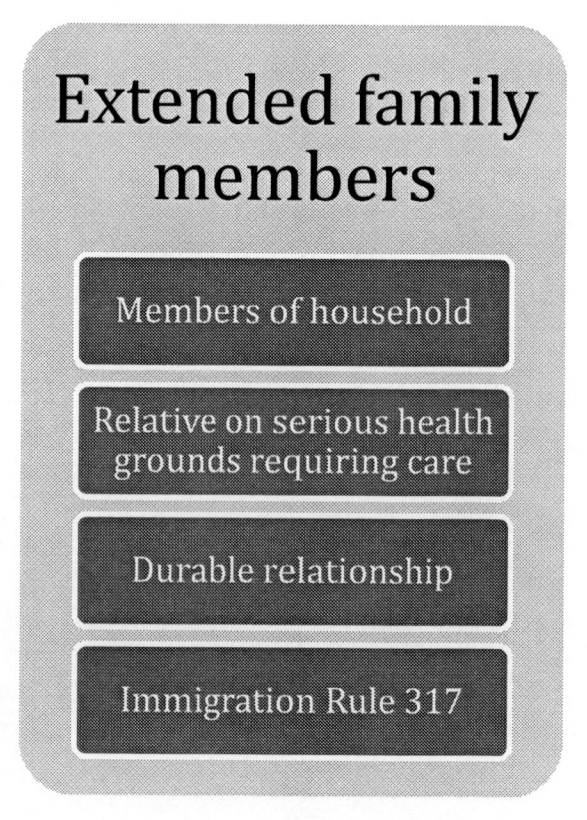

Immediate family members
- Spouses and civil partners
- Children
- Parents and grandparents

Extended family members
- Members of household
- Relative on serious health grounds requiring care
- Durable relationship
- Immigration Rule 317

The first tier comprises immediate family members, described fully below. This group is essentially the same as under the pre-Directive regime, but it now includes civil partners. The benefit of being an immediate family member is that free movement rights are innate and can be evidenced in any suitable way, they do not rely on the possession of a particular piece of paper.

The second tier is the "extended family member". This group benefit from the same rights of freedom of movement as immediate family members, but only if they have applied for and been granted the relevant piece of paper. Their rights are therefore subject to a successful application (and, according to the Tribunal in *AP and FP*, their substantive rights of entry are a matter of domestic legislation alone, their only European law rights being procedural ones of efficient examination).

Immediate family members

For most qualified persons the family members are defined at Article 2.2 of the Citizens' Directive:

> "Family member' means:
>
> (a) the spouse;
>
> (b) the partner with whom the Union citizen has contracted a registered partnership, on the basis of the legislation of a Member State, if the legislation of the host Member State treats registered partnerships as equivalent to marriage ... ;
>
> (c) the direct descendants who are under the age of 21 or are dependants and those of the spouse or partner as defined in point (b);
>
> (d) the dependant direct relatives in the ascending line and those of the spouse or partner as defined in point (b).'

These provisions are faithfully transposed into the domestic regulations at regulation 7(1).

For students, however,

- children must be dependent to be family members and

- there is no provision for dependent direct relatives in the ascending line.

In the case of *SM (India) v Entry Clearance Officer* [2009] EWCA Civ 1426 the Court of Appeal held that, contrary to some tribunal case law to the contrary, dependency is a simple question of fact in EC law, and it need not be dependency of necessity. This means that an enquiry is limited to whether a person is in fact dependent rather than why that person is dependent. Voluntary dependency is not therefore excluded, if for example a person chooses to give away or transfer their wealth.

These rights will not extend to a party to a marriage or civil partnership of convenience. In *IS (marriages of convenience) Serbia* [2008] UKAIT 00031 the Tribunal found that the appellant's general duty to prove his case includes a duty to prove that his marriage is not one of convenience.

> ### Case of Metock
>
> - Right of residence of family member not conditional on prior lawful residence in another Member State
> - Need not physically accompany EU citizen from one country to another
> - Does not matter if relationship post-dates entry of EU citizen

In the landmark case of *Metock and Ors v Ireland* (Case C-127/08) the European Court of Justice held that the right of a national of a non-member country who is a family member of a Union citizen to accompany or join that citizen cannot be made conditional on prior lawful residence in another Member State, nor can the right be said to be conditional on physically accompanying a Union citizen from one country to another. It is the exercise of the rights of free movement in the wider sense (rather than physically moving between countries) by the Union citizen that triggers the right to be accompanied by the spouse.

The Court goes on to hold specifically that a non-Community spouse of a Union citizen who accompanies or joins that citizen can benefit from the directive, irrespective of when and where their marriage took place and of how that spouse entered the host Member State. The Court states that the directive does not require that the Union citizen must already have founded a family at the time when he moves, in order for his family members who are nationals of non-member countries to be able to enjoy the rights established by the directive. The Court further considers that it makes no difference whether nationals of non-member countries who are family members of a Union citizen have entered the host Member State before or after becoming family members of that citizen; the host Member State is, however, entitled to impose penalties, in compliance with the directive, for entry into and residence in its territory in breach of the national rules on immigration.

Following *Metock*, the domestic Immigration (EEA) Regulations 2006 at regulation 12(1)(b) have been held to be unlawful (*Bigia & Ors v Entry Clearance Officer* [2009] EWCA Civ 79). This part of the regulations requires that, for the family member to be eligible for a family permit enabling entry to the UK, the family member must either meet the requirements of the normal UK immigration rules or be lawfully resident in an EEA state.

The UK has been very slow to respond to *Metock*. At the time of writing the Entry Clearance Guidance had been amended but the regulations continue to be unlawful.

Extended family members

The term 'extended family members' does not appear in the Directive. It is an invention of the domestic regulations. The Directive provides as follows at Article 3:

> '1. This Directive shall apply to all Union citizens who move to or reside in a Member State other than that of which they are a national, and to their family members as defined in point 2 of Article 2 who accompany or join them.
>
> 2. Without prejudice to any right to free movement and residence the persons concerned may have in their own right, the host Member State shall, in accordance with its national legislation, facilitate entry and residence for the following persons:
>
> (a) any other family members, irrespective of their nationality, not falling under the definition in point 2 of Article 2 who, in the country from which they have come, are dependants or members of the household of the Union citizen having the primary right of residence, or where serious health grounds strictly require the personal care of the family members by the Union citizen;
>
> (b) the partner with whom the Union citizen has a durable relationship, duly attested.
>
> The host Member State shall undertake an extensive examination of the personal circumstances and shall justify any denial of entry or residence to these people.'

To implement this part of the Directive, the Home Office included at regulation 7(3) a provision that a person falling under regulation 8 and who has been issued with an EEA family permit, a registration certificate or a residence card would be considered a full family member.

Regulation 8 is subtitled 'Extended family member' and defines the following as such:

- A relative of the EEA national, their spouse or civil partner who resides or resided in the same EEA state as the EEA national and is dependent on the EEA national or a member of his household (see reg 8(2) for full definition).

- A relative of the EEA national, their spouse or civil partner who on serious health grounds strictly requires the personal care of the EEA national, spouse or civil partner. The use of the word "serious" requires the "health grounds" to be well beyond ordinary ill health and as a matter of practice to require detailed medical evidence in support of any claim, importing a need for complete compliance or exact performance and reinforces the need for personal care (regarding the daily physical tasks and needs of the person cared for) to be provided on a day to day basis: *TR (reg 8(3) EEA Regs 2006)* [2008] UKAIT 00004.

- A partner of an EEA national in a durable relationship with the EEA national. The Home Office has taken the view that the same criteria as for the unmarried partner immigration rule must be satisfied, i.e. two years' residence together. However, this requirement does not feature in the Directive and an ECJ case will at some point define the extent of this category.

- A relative of the EEA national, their spouse or civil partner who would meet the requirements of r.317 of the Immigration Rules as a dependent relative.

It must be appreciated that the limitations regarding prior residence of dependant relatives under Regulation 8(2) are very restrictive: they require that the family member has previously lived in another EEA state, and that the dependency either existed in that state or the family member lived with the qualified person there (*RG (EEA Regulations, extended family members) Sri Lanka* [2007] UKAIT 00034). This removes the possibility of dependant family members coming directly from the country of origin. The Court of Appeal have agreed with this restrictive approach, in *KG (Sri Lanka) v Secretary of State for the Home Department* [2008] EWCA Civ 13, noting that the Directive seems to envisage dependency immediately before the exercise of Treaty rights.

Although parts of *KG (Sri Lanka)* cannot and have not survived *Metock* (see further below), in *Bigia & Ors v Entry Clearance Officer* [2009] EWCA Civ 79 the Court of Appeal upheld the earlier conclusion that 'extended family members' do not obtain freestanding rights from the Directive and other than the prior lawful residence requirement the domestic regulations are not unlawful. This is because Article 3 allows Member States to provide this group with rights of free movement and residence 'in accordance with national legislation', a phrase that has so far been interpreted by the UK courts to mean 'by legislating as they choose'.

In *AP and FP (Citizens Directive Article 3(2); discretion; dependence) India* [2007] UKAIT 00048 the Tribunal ruled that the grant of EEA family permits is subject to the provision in Reg 12(2)(c) – if "in all the circumstances, it appears to the entry clearance officer appropriate to issue the EEA family permit." This means that grant of the application is discretionary notwithstanding the fact that the criteria for entry are satisfied, which perhaps opens the door for the injection of criteria such as immigration history, maintenance and accommodation.

Nevertheless extended family members do enjoy some benefits. So long as national law grants them rights to come here in the first place, their entry and residence must be "facilitated", and there must be an "extensive examination" of their circumstances and a justification of refusal, which means that entry and residence must be made easy.

> **Example**
>
> Mr Srikanth's great aunt lived with him in Sri Lanka. He has sent her remittances since coming to Europe, where he obtained refugee status in Germany before entering the UK, where he now works.
>
> She will not qualify as an "extended family member" because of *AP and FP* and the cases that follow it, as she has not resided in an EEA state. On the analysis in those cases, Mr Srikanth's free movement within Europe will not be affected by preventing her joining him in the UK.

Proving the relationship

All the above, both immediate and extended family relationships, must of course be proven. An additional distinction emerges here between the first and second tier of relationship, as extended family members are subject to 'extensive examination' under the Citizens' Directive.

The level of evidence required for different purposes is addressed in the following section under 'documentation'.

Benefits of the exercise of Treaty rights

Key points:

- Admission and entry
- Initial right of residence
- Residence
- Permanent residence
- Retained rights of residence

Admission and entry

All EEA nationals (whether a 'qualified person' or not) and EEA family members have a right of admission without leave to enter or remain. The domestic regulations at first glance appear to require possession of a passport or valid national identity card for EEA nationals and a passport and EEA family permit, residence card or permanent residence card for family members (see reg 11(1) and (2)). However, as should be clear from the discussion early regarding rights not privileges, as there is an inherent right of entry, it would be surprising if any such documentary prerequisite could be imposed. Reading on in the regulations, one indeed finds that there are alternatives to possession of the above formal documents, and in essence any evidence of entitlement will be sufficient (reg 11(4).

There is no requirement for the family member to have lawfully resided in another EEA state prior to entry: *Metock* and *Bigia*. Further, the family relationship with the EEA citizen need not pre-date either party's entry to the UK.

Example

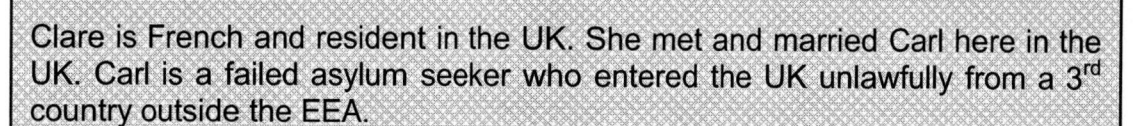

Clare is French and resident in the UK. She met and married Carl here in the UK. Carl is a failed asylum seeker who entered the UK unlawfully from a 3rd country outside the EEA.

Following *Metock*, Carl ought to obtain residence on the basis of his relationship with Clare. The only provisions that might stop him obtaining residence would be the public policy, public security or public health clauses, which are unlikely to apply in most cases.

A family member wishing to travel to the UK can apply to an Entry Clearance Officer for a family permit, which will considerably ease passage into the UK. The application is free and the permit must be issued as soon as possible if the person qualifies. As is discussed above in relation to the distinction between immediate and extended family members, an extended family member is subject to an extensive examination by the ECO, whereas an immediate family member need only furnish evidence of the qualifying relationship with the qualified person and of the fact that the qualified person is or will soon be entitled to reside in the UK under the terms of the Directive. See reg 12 for details. The Tribunal in *AP and FP* found "the procedure for application, reasoned refusal and right of appeal provided under our own legislation" was sufficient to count as "extensive examination".

In *CO (EEA Regulations: family permit) Nigeria* [2007] UKAIT 00070 the tribunal held that a family member who is unable to meet the requirements of regulation 12, or chooses not to obtain an EEA family permit, is at liberty to present himself to the Immigration Officer and prove his eligibility under regulation 11(4). The rights under the Directive transcend the controls imposed by the Immigration Rules, and besides EEA nationals and their family members do not require entry clearance.

Initial right of residence

In addition, all EEA citizens and their family members also now enjoy what is referred to in the Immigration (EEA) Regulations 2006 as an 'initial right of residence' (reg 13). This enables an EEA citizen to travel to the UK and reside here for three months as if he or she were a qualified person (which therefore includes being accompanied by family members) but without having to establish that he or she is yet a qualified person.

This provision enhances the possibilities of free movement around Europe by allowing for an unchallenged right to reside in order to become established.

Residence

Qualified persons have a right to reside in the UK as long as they remain qualified persons. In addition, in some circumstances, they are permitted to retain a right of residence even though their qualifying activity has ceased, as is discussed above (i.e. temporary incapacity, temporary unemployment, retirement, permanent incapacity or retention of a place of residence: reg 5).

During their period of 'extended residence', as it is referred to in the Immigration (EEA) Regulations 2006 at reg 14, qualified persons can apply for and must immediately be granted a registration certificate on production of a valid identity card or passport plus proof that the person is a qualified person (reg 16). This certificate is not necessary and it merely evidences the right, it does not create it. Nevertheless, such certificates can be useful, particularly for EEA citizens likely to be travelling in and out of the UK who might, because of an apprehension that they lack the right of abode, suffer the inconvenience of regular questioning by HM Immigration Officers.

Similarly, the right to extended residence for family members is set out at reg 14. However, the document to evidence their status and right of residence is referred to as a residence card, the details of which are set out at reg 17.

Qualified persons can carry out qualifying activities and must not be subject to any form of discrimination compared to the national workforce. This means that rights to benefits and other advantages enjoyed by the national workforce have to be enjoyed in equal measure. The main preoccupation of EC freedom of movement law, and this continues to be reflected in the Citizens' Directive, is with workers and the self employed, however.

The main right with which immigration lawyers are concerned, however, is that to bring one's family into the UK in accordance with EC law. This right can be very simply expressed, but it feels almost counterintuitive to a UK immigration practitioner accustomed to dealing with the UK immigration rules. As long as a family member falls within the definitions of family members set out in the Citizens' Directive and transposed into national law by the Immigration (EEA) Regulations 2006, that family member has a right to reside in the UK with the qualified person. There are no additional limitations relating to maintenance and accommodation, intention to live permanently with the other or subsisting marriage.

These rights have to be respected in an extremely proactive way by Member States. The rights are derived from the Treaty and are innate, meaning that it is for Member States to protect and promote these rights as far as possible. For example, when an EEA citizen enters a Member State, the authorities must merely check that documents are in order or every reasonable opportunity for them to establish their identity by other means. The authorities are not entitled to ask further questions about intention, availability of funds, sponsors or the like – although so long as they have a reasonable belief that there may be grounds for it, they may investigate exclusion on the grounds of public policy, public security or public health.

The family members of qualified persons enjoy the same rights to take up activities in Member States. The children of nationals of a Member State who are or who have been employed in the territory of another Member State are entitled to that State's general educational, apprenticeship and vocational training courses under the same conditions as a national. The child of a national of one Member State who resided in the territory of another Member State may not claim the benefit of that Regulation where a parent no longer residing in the host Member State, last resided there as a worker before the birth of the child.

It is worth noting that family members may be accompanied by their own children who are under 21 or are dependent or by their own direct dependent relatives in the ascending line. However, any of these family members do not have any right under EC law to be accompanied by other family members (e.g. a spouse or civil partner). They would need to rely on the UK immigration rules, which would be difficult as it cannot be said that a person reliant on EEA freedom of movement rights is present and settled in the UK (one of the requirements for most family applications) until that person has acquired the right of permanent residence, usually after five years.

Permanent residence

Under the Citizens' Directive, EEA citizens and family members have a right to settle permanently in the UK after five years residence under the Directive (reg 15). This might be five years as a qualified person or it might be five years consisting of a period as a qualified person followed by a period as a qualified person who has ceased activity in certain specified circumstances (retirement etc: reg 5).

The right of settlement brings with it enhanced protection from removal, as is discussed below.

An EEA citizen with the right of settlement must be issued with a certificate registering their right of permanent residence on proving that he or she qualifies (reg 18). As with the residence certificate, this is not necessary but may prove to be convenient.

Retained rights of residence

The rights of 3rd country national family members of EEA citizens were in the past entirely parasitic on the EEA citizen him or herself. If the EEA citizen moved away from the UK or died or ceased to be a qualified person, the family member would lose any right of residence in the UK. However, the European Court of Justice started to develop a body of case law which recognised that 3rd country national family members of EEA citizens might start to acquire independent rights of residence within the EEA in some circumstances.

In the case of *Baumbast* [2002] EUECJ C-413/99 (17 September 2002) an EEA citizen had been living and working in the UK, but returned to his own country. In the meantime, his wife and child had effectively settled in the UK and the child was attending an educational course. The mother did not want to leave the UK. The ECJ held that the child had acquired a right to reside in the UK to pursue this course and, in addition, that this right would be ineffective if the child's mother was not permitted to remain in the UK too care for the child.

The Citizens' Directive has formalised at least some of the rights that the ECJ had started to recognise, although the ECJ had in fact gone further than the Directive. Whether the ECJ maintains its more generous approach remains to be seen but appears likely.

First of all, it is important to note that the spouse (this will now also apply to civil partners) of an EEA citizen continues to be considered as a spouse and family member as long as the marriage formally persists. Separation does not dissolve this relationship for the purposes of EC law, nor does a *decree nisi*. It is only when a *decree absolute* has been issued that the relationship is considered no longer to qualify (*Diatta v Land Berlin* 1986 2 CMLR 164).

The Immigration (EEA) Regulations 2006 address the retention of rights at reg 10. In the following situations, the family member will be considered to retain rights of residence despite ceasing to be the family member of a qualified person:

- Where the qualified person dies but the family member has resided in the UK for at least one year and is either him or herself employed, self employed or self sufficient or is the family member of such a person (i.e. the child or dependent relative) (reg 10(2))

- Where the family member is the child of qualified person who has died or left the UK where the family member has been attending an educational course (or the child of the qualified person's spouse or civil partner in the same circumstances) (reg 10(3))

- Where the family member is a parent with actual custody of a child as described immediately above (reg 10(4))

- Where the family member ceased to be a family member of a qualified person on the termination of the marriage or civil partnership of the qualified person and was residing in the UK under the Directive at that time and is him or herself employed, self employed or self sufficient (or is the family member of such a person, i.e. the child or dependent relative) and either:

- prior to the initiation of the proceedings for the termination of the marriage or the civil partnership the marriage or civil partnership had lasted for at least three years and the parties to the marriage or civil partnership had resided in the United Kingdom for at least one year during its duration (reg 10(5)(d)(i))

- the former spouse or civil partner of the qualified person has custody of a child of the qualified person (reg 10(5)(d)(ii))

- the former spouse or civil partner of the qualified person has the right of access to a child of the qualified person under the age of 18 and a court has ordered that such access must take place in the United Kingdom (reg 10(5)(d)(iii)); or

- the continued right of residence in the United Kingdom of the person is warranted by particularly difficult circumstances, such as he or another family member having been a victim of domestic violence while the marriage or civil partnership was subsisting (reg 10(5)(d)(iv)).

The Tribunal has found that the burden of proof on establishing that the qualified person is no longer qualified lies upon the applicant, not the government: *MJ and others (Art.12 Reg.1612/68, self sufficiency?)* [2008] UKAIT 00034.

> ### Examples
>
> Robert and Steve became civil partners in the Netherlands six years ago. Robert is South African and Steve is Dutch. They lived in the Netherlands for two years and came to the UK four years ago when Steve was posted to the UK by the oil company he works for. The two of them have now separated and are going to dissolve their civil partnership. As long as Robert is employed, self employed or self sufficient, he can choose to remain in the UK after this occurs if he wants to, as the situation falls within reg 10(5)(d)(i). He will retain his right of residence.
>
> Marie and Peter were married four years ago. Marie is French and Peter is from Cameroon. Marie was already living and working in the UK when they got married and Peter came to the UK directly. They have one child, Cecile, who is four years old and has just started attending school. Marie now wants to return to France but Peter does not want to leave his part-time job in the UK and he wants Cecile to grow up in the UK. They decide to separate and Marie returns to France, leaving Peter to care for Cecile in the UK. Cecile will retain a right of residence under reg 10(3) and Peter will retain his right of residence under reg 10(4). In addition, it appears that both Cecile and Peter will soon qualify for a permanent right of residence in the UK.

Excluding and removing EEA nationals from UK

Ceasing to be qualified

A person who no longer satisfies the qualification requirements runs the risk of losing the benefits of Treaty rights. Thus under the Immigration (European Economic Area) Regulations 2006, reg 19(3), a person ceasing to be a qualified person faces revocation of their residence.

This means that where a relationship is terminated by divorce, the (former) family member no longer enjoys EEA rights; equally, once the qualified person leaves the UK, or stops working here, this too may remove the EEA status that permits the family member to reside here. The Tribunal has found that such individuals cannot try to switch into immigration stay under the rules: for the right of residence under EEA law is not the same as a limited leave to enter or remain (*TB (EEA national: leave to remain?) Nigeria* [2007] UKAIT 00020).

The ECJ has tempered this approach by requiring decisions on exclusion and removal be compatible with the provisions of the ECHR.

Public policy removals and exclusions

The Citizens' Directive enhanced the protection afforded to EEA citizens and their family members. The Secretary of State may refuse to issue, revoke or refuse to renew a registration certificate, a residence card, a document certifying permanent residence or a permanent residence card if the refusal or revocation is justified on grounds of public policy, public security or public health. Similarly, an Immigration Officer may revoke a family permit on a person's arrival in the UK on the same grounds. However, different periods of residence are rewarded with different levels of protection:

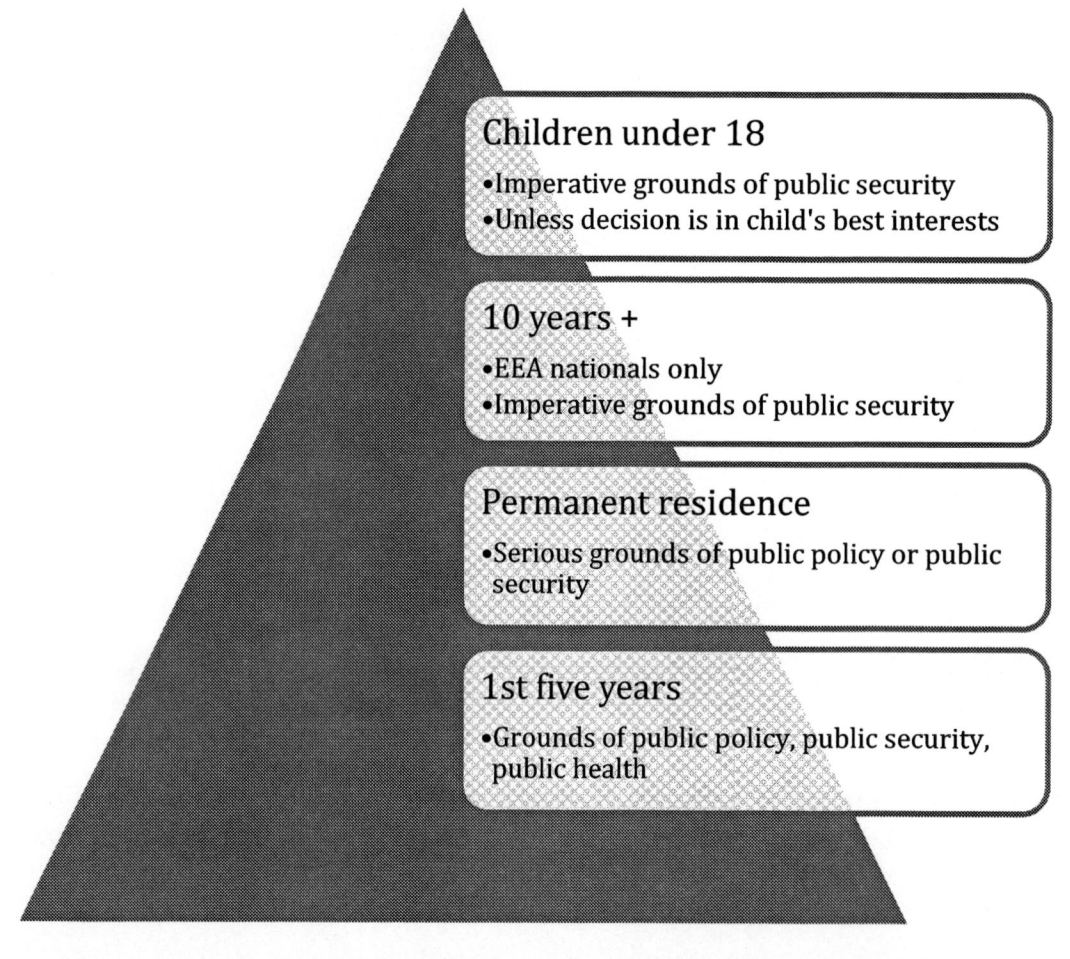

Children under 18
- Imperative grounds of public security
- Unless decision is in child's best interests

10 years +
- EEA nationals only
- Imperative grounds of public security

Permanent residence
- Serious grounds of public policy or public security

1st five years
- Grounds of public policy, public security, public health

In the case of *HR (Portugal) v SSHD* [2009] EWCA Civ 371 the Court of Appeal held that residence in prison does not count as residence for the purposes of regulation 21(4)(a):

> '23. In my judgment, recitals 23 and 24 make clear how Article 28.3 is to be applied in a case such as the present. "Residence" is presence in this country in the exercise of the rights and freedoms conferred by the Treaty. An EEA national who, having been convicted of a crime, is detained for a significant period in prison or other penal institution, is not resident in this country for the purposes of Article 28.3.'

HR (Portugal) should not be interpreted to require that any residence for the purposes of regulation 24(4)(a) must be residence while exercising treaty rights. The Court of Appeal specifically refers to recitals 23 and 24, which concern exclusions, and regulation 24(4)(a) itself is notably silent on any requirement for the residence to be in exercise of treaty rights.

Note that there are two ways in which the protection given by EEA law is enhanced with the length of stay in the UK: there is firstly a narrowing of the grounds, from "public policy, public security or public health", to "public policy and public security", to "public security" alone; secondly there is a raising of the threshold, from bare "grounds", to "serious grounds", to "imperative grounds".

The meaning of "imperative grounds of public security" awaits resolution. Although in *MG and VG Ireland* [2006] UKAIT 00053 it was said that the Secretary of State's considered view was that the phrase "public security" was directed to the risk of "terrorist offences", by the time of *LG (Italy) v Secretary of State for the Home Department* [2008] EWCA Civ 190 (18 March 2008)) it was noted that "Public security" was not to be equated with "national security", and that the words might equate to a "risk to the safety of the public or a section of the public". However in any event there was a need to show an actual risk to public security, so compelling that it justifies the exceptional course of removing someone who has become "integrated" by "many years" residence in the host state.

In addition, the following factors must be considered when reaching any decision based on public policy, public security or public health:

- the decision must comply with the principle of proportionality

- the decision must be based exclusively on the personal conduct of the person concerned

- the personal conduct of the person concerned must represent a genuine, present and sufficiently serious threat affecting one of the fundamental interests of society

- matters isolated from the particulars of the case or which relate to considerations of general prevention do not justify the decision

- a person's previous criminal convictions do not in themselves justify the decision

- in public policy and public security (not public health) cases, account must also be taken of considerations such as the age, state of health, family and economic situation of the person, the person's length of residence in the United Kingdom, the person's social and cultural integration into the United Kingdom and the extent of the person's links with his country of origin.

In *GW (EEA reg 21: "fundamental interests") Netherlands* [2009] UKAIT 00050 the tribunal held that the term 'fundamental interests' of a society is a question to be determined by reference to the legal rules governing the society in question, and that it is unlikely that conduct that is subject to no prohibition can be regarded as threatening those interests. The case concerned the attempt by the Secretary of State to exclude Geert Wilders from visiting the UK on the grounds of his unpleasant views about Islam. Mr Wilder's appeal was upheld.

A person who is subject to an attempted exclusion has the same legal remedies in respect of any decision concerning entry, or refusing the issue or renewal or a residence permit, or ordering expulsion from the territory, as are available to nationals of the State concerned in respect of acts of the administration. Additional procedural guarantees are provided for in specific cases (e.g. where there is no right of appeal to a court of law, or where the appeal cannot have a suspensive effect, etc.).

Any national of a Member State who wishes to seek employment in another Member State may re-apply for a residence permit, even after having previously been expelled or refused.

Rights of appeal

EEA decisions handed down after the 1st April 2003 are treated as immigration decisions and attract a right of appeal under section 82(1) of the 2002 Act against which a ground of appeal on EEA law grounds can be raised under section 84.

There is also a right of appeal under the 2006 Regulations against an EEA decision, which means that EEA rights can be vindicated even absent a relevant immigration decision (reg 26).

However the appeal under the Regulations requires that a person claiming to be an EEA national produces a valid national identity card or passport issued by an EEA State, and a person claiming to be the family member or relative of an EEA national produces an EEA family permit, or other proof that he is related as claimed to an EEA national (reg 26(2, 3)).

Appeals under the Regulations are from abroad where the decision is:

- to refuse to admit him to the United Kingdom;

- to refuse to revoke a deportation order made against him;

- to refuse to issue him with an EEA family permit; or

- to remove him from the United Kingdom after he has entered or sought to enter the United Kingdom in breach of a deportation order (unless asylum or human rights grounds are raised, and not certified: reg 27(3)).

However such appeals can still be brought "in country", despite being of the nature just described, where:

- the person held an EEA family permit, a registration certificate, a residence card, a document certifying permanent residence or a permanent residence card on his arrival in the United Kingdom or can otherwise prove that he is resident in the United Kingdom;

- the person is deemed not to have been admitted to the United Kingdom under regulation 22(3) but at the date on which notice of the decision to refuse to admit him is given he has been in the United Kingdom for at least 3 months;

- the person is in the United Kingdom and a ground of the appeal is that, in taking the decision, the decision maker acted in breach of his rights under the Human Rights Convention or the Refugee Convention, unless the Secretary of State certifies that that ground of appeal is clearly unfounded.

The procedures are broadly reminiscent of those applying to the immigration tribunal generally. However, where the SSHD certifies that the decision under challenge was taken 'wholly or partly' in the interests of national security or relations with a foreign State the right of appeal lies to the Special Immigration Appeals Commission (reg 28).

Additionally, the SSHD may bar reliance on particular grounds of appeal by certifying that the ground had been previously considered (reg 26(5)).

There is an upgrading appeal against refusal to recognise refugee status under section 83 of the 2002 Act available if the individual has a right to be admitted and reside under the Regulations.

Accession States

As Cyprus and Malta gained full free movement rights on entry, they do not need to be dealt with here. The provisions of the Citizens' Directive and EEA Regs 2006 apply to them in full.

The most straightforward way to understand the other Accession State nationals (A8 and A2 nationals, see further below) is to grasp that the UK's EEA regulations apply in full to them. The only difference – albeit a very important one – is that Accession State nationals do not enjoy an automatic right to work. They cannot therefore automatically qualify as a 'worker' for the purpose of the regulations and EEA free movement law, and following on from that cannot therefore automatically enjoy full free movement rights. They can nevertheless freely qualify as self employed, for example. It is only potential *workers* who face a potential obstacle to enjoyment of the benefits of being a qualified person.

If the Accession State national can somehow legally work, though, they are self evidently an EEA national and would qualify as a worker. It is the options for legal working that therefore become the gateway to full free movement rights for Accession State nationals.

A8 nationals

The eight Accession States which joined the EU on 1 May 2004 and were not immediately granted full free movement rights, often referred to as the 'A8' countries, were as follows:

Czech Republic	Lithuania
Estonia	Poland
Hungary	Slovakia
Latvia	Slovenia

However, the only restriction imposed on A8 nationals was the requirement to register on taking a job. This requirement is only 12 months in duration, and full free movement rights are enjoyed after 12 months of registration.

Registration

This scheme is that Workers Registration Scheme, instituted under the Accession (Immigration and Worker Registration) Regulations 2004 (SI 2004 No. 1219) and Immigration (European Economic Area) and Accession (Amendment) Regulations 2004.

A worker requiring registration may only work for an authorised employer. Workers must apply for a registration certificate within one month of starting work (the registration certificate will authorise work for a specified employer (rule 7-8)). To do so they should register under the Workers' Registration Scheme (application form WRS), for which purpose they require a letter from their employer confirming their employment, 2 passport photos, their passport or ID card, and a fee of £90 (the fee is not payable on applications to change employer during their registration period; nor need the passport or ID card be sent). See r.7 concerning authorised employers and r.8 on registration cards and certificates. The registration card is particular to the applicant, and the certificate is particular to the registered employment.

On a change of employment, it is necessary to apply for another certificate, but there is no need to pay a further fee. A change of employment, so long as a new job is found within 30 days, will not break continuity of working for the purposes of building up the year for entitlements to benefits and no longer having to register.

It is a criminal offence for an employer to employ a person who has not met the requirements of the scheme, unless the employer kept a copy of a document that looked like it met the requirements of the scheme (see rule 9).

An A8 national who already enjoys a right to work by other means, for example through pre-existing leave pre-dating 2004 or by newly obtained leave which includes permission to work, need not register under the scheme. This might apply to an A8 national with ILR or one who enters the UK as a spouse of a person present and settled in the UK.

Rights and entitlements

The Habitual Residence regulations added a condition to the "habitual residence" test in social security legislation that controls access to Council Tax Benefit, Housing Benefit, Income Support, Jobseeker's Allowance, and State Pension Credit. Henceforth only persons with the right to reside in the UK will be treated as habitually resident. This means that access to social security can be excluded for A8 nationals who have not registered, for such persons lack a right of residence.

Conditions of entitlement to benefits such as child benefit, tax credits, disability benefits and contributory benefits (those with low incomes may also be entitled to Housing Benefit and Council Tax benefit) are not varied, so these benefits can be accessed by EEA nationals notwithstanding the absence of any right to reside.

The following will not be eligible for those benefits which require habitual residence to be established:

a. A8 nationals who are seeking work
b. A8 nationals who cease to work during the first year of employment
c. Family members of the latter.

It is the status of the benefit claimant which is the focus for consideration, not that of the partner and any children.

This restriction applies to workers requiring registration and ceases to apply when the worker no longer requires registration, usually after 12 months of continuous employment. At this point there will be an entitlement to an EEA residence permit like other EU nationals.

Family members of A8 workers

Family members of EEA nationals (who are not themselves excluded accession workers) present in the UK as a worker, self-sufficient person, retired person or student are also exempt from registration (rule 2(6)(b)).

Registered workers are "qualified persons" and so can bring in the same family members as those dealt with in the 2006 Regulations.

Family members of A8 nationals may apply to reside and work in the UK. Family members will not be eligible for a residence document unless the principal is eligible for a residence permit. However, if the principal has registered under the Worker Registration Scheme, the family can obtain a family member residence stamp. Applications for family member residence stamps should be made on form EEC3 and sent to the address detailed on the form.

A2 nationals

Two further countries joined the EU on 1 January 2007:

| Bulgaria | Romania |

Unlike A8 nationals, Bulgarians and Romanians were not given all but unrestricted access to the labour market. Instead, no additional right to work was given, but the pre-existing routes to working were preserved. When the Points Based System was introduced for all other countries, the work permit scheme and High Skilled Migrant Programme were preserved for Bulgarians and Romanians.

The Ankara Agreement

The Ankara Agreement is the oldest Association Agreement, dating back to 1963, with an Additional Protocol of 1970. The rights granted to Turkish nationals are not reflected either in the Immigration Rules or in the Immigration (European Economic Area) Order and anybody seeking to benefit from them will therefore have to refer directly to EC law.

The Ankara Agreement and its associated decisions are entirely different in their structure and content from other Association Agreements.

However to the extent that the Ankara Agreement and its Protocol themselves refer to the free movement of workers provisions in the EC Treaty itself, interpretation of the Ankara is guided by the ECJ's extensive jurisprudence on free movement of EC workers. Article 12 of the Ankara Agreement states:-

> "The Contracting Parties agree to be guided by Articles 48, 49 and 50 of the Treaty establishing the Community for the purpose of abolishing restrictions on freedom of establishment between them."

The Additional Protocol includes a so-called "stand-still" provision which has the effect of requiring Member States, including the United Kingdom, not to introduce any new restrictions, after its entry into force in 1973, on the rights of Turkish nationals to set up in business as self-employed persons. Although it does not provide the Turkish national with a directly effective right of establishment (as is enjoyed by EEA nationals) it means that the Immigration Rules that should be applied to them are not those in force now but, in effect, the Immigration Rules in force in 1973, which imposed much less stringent requirements on being allowed to set up in business (see further: Self-Employed, below).

Workers

The rights of Turkish workers are laid down in a Decision of the Association Council, Decision 1/80 (unpublished). This provides Turkish workers who have been in 'legal employment' in a Member State for a certain period of time with a right to have their permission to work renewed and to have their right of residence renewed in line with the right to work.

The rights provided for in Article 6(1) only benefit those workers who fulfil the requirements in terms of legal employment, belonging to the labour force and time. These are the requirements:

a) He is a worker and legally employed
b) He is duly registered as belonging to the labour force
c) He has been legally employed for one of three possible time periods.

In *Payir and Ozturk v Secretary of State for the Home Department* (Case C-294/06; 24 January 2008) the European Court of Justice accepted that students and au pairs were workers and duly registered as part of the labour force, so that the benefits of this agreement were available to them.

a) He is a worker and legally employed

"Turkish worker" connotes the Community law definition. The requirement that the worker is legally employed within the territory of the Member State does not necessarily presuppose the possession of residence documents or even a work permit. The legality of employment is determined in the light of the legislation of the Member State governing the conditions under which the Turkish worker entered the national territory and is employed there. The worker cannot be working in breach of any legal conditions of stay or have entered on false documentation and thereby entered into employment as the result of fraudulent conduct.

The legality of employment "presupposes a stable and secure situation". There must be an undisputed right of residence, for any dispute as to that right leads to an instability in the worker's situation. Working pending an appeal against refusal of a residence permit is not sufficient, unless the appeal ultimately succeeds.

This means that a Turkish worker needs prior leave to remain (e.g. HP or DL) in order to set off their Ankara rights.

The reasons for a Member State allowing a Turkish national to work and reside in its territory are not relevant to the question of whether the employment was "legal". Even the fact that a Turkish worker expressly accepted restrictions on his length of stay does not deprive him of the rights acquired under Article 6(1) unless it was demonstrated that he had been deliberately deceiving the national authorities.

b) "He is duly registered as belonging to the labour force"

Relevant concerns are whether the worker:

- Is in an employment relationship or available for employment

    The question narrows down to whether or not the individual is in *"genuine and effective employment"*.

The mere fact that the employment in question was solely designed to qualify the worker for work elsewhere in the undertaking, did not deprive it of the character of "employment". Additionally the level of pay, and temporary nature of the employment are not determining factors.

- Is engaged in employment which can be located within the territory of the Member State or retains a sufficiently close link with that territory

    Breaks in employment. Temporary breaks in employment, annual holidays, absences for reason of maternity or an accident at work or short periods of sickness, will not disqualify an applicant. An "inactive" period cannot be treated as a period of legal employment, although the rights of the worker acquired as a result of previous employment cannot be affected.

    In the case of permanent incapacity, the worker can no longer be considered as available for work and there is no objective justification for guaranteeing him the right of access to the labour force and an ancillary right of residence.

    Retirement age will be that defined by the Member State's national legislation, regardless of capacity to work.

    Unemployment. In the case of involuntary unemployment, Article 6(2) provides that like in the case of long periods of absence due to sickness, the inactive period can not be treated as periods of legal employment for the purposes of Article 6(1) although they do not affect the rights which the worker acquired as the result of preceding employment.

    With regards voluntary unemployment applicants will be give a reasonable amount of time in which to find work. The ECJ has left it to the discretion of the Member States to determine how long a reasonable period for seeking employment would be but it may not deprive Article 6 of its substance by effectively jeopardising prospects of obtaining work.

    Links with the territory. The Court of Justice has held that factors such as place of hire, the location of paid employment, and national legislation re social security and employment law, should taken into account.

- Has completed the applicable formalities required by national law

    The requirement to fulfil formalities laid down in national law would include the payment of income tax, contributions for health, pension and unemployment insurance.

c) *"Legal employment" for one of three possible time periods*

In order to qualify under Article 6(1) of Decision 1/80 specifies time periods of legal employment which must have been fulfilled. See the Ankara Agreement:

> Article 6.1
> A worker shall, after one year's legal employment, be entitled to have his permit to work extended to continue to work for the same employer if a job is available.
> A worker shall be entitled to change employers within the same occupation after three years subject to EC nationals having priority.
> A worker shall be free to take any employment after 4 years.
>
> Article 6.2
> The rights at 6.1 are not affected by annual holidays, maternity leave, accidents at work or short periods of sick leave

One year's legal employment gives the Turkish worker a right to have his or her right to work renewed for the same employer and to have his or her leave to remain renewed in line. A Turkish national can only benefit from this right if he or she has been employed with the same employer for the whole year.

The Home Office website states "We would interpret this as the applicant remaining in the same job when a different employer takes over and keeps him on, since the spirit of the agreement is to benefit Turkish workers established in employment rather than United Kingdom firms."

Three years' legal employment with the same employer entitles a Turkish worker to a further renewal. At this stage the employer may be altered, however the occupation pursued must remain the same. Again, there is an entitlement to have the right of residence renewed in line with the right to work. In order to benefit from this right the Turkish national must have been employed with the same employer for three continuous years. If the Turkish worker has changed employment within the three years, she or he will either have to rely on the 'one year' rule, if one year has been achieved or, if not, will fall outside the benefit provided by Decision 1/80.

The Home Office website says "After 3 years with the same employer an applicant is entitled to change employers but only when the new employer cannot recruit from EC labour and if the new employment is in the same occupation. Caseworkers should therefore ask for evidence that the employer cannot fill the post from EC labour before granting leave to remain on Code 4 for 12 months at a time."

After four years' legal employment, a Turkish worker is entitled to free access to the labour market, which includes a right to give up his or her job and to be a job-seeker for a reasonable period of time, probably similar to that allowed for job seeking EEA nationals.

The Home Office website says "The Agreement does not provide for the removal of time limits, only for the freedom to take any employment after 4 years. Applications for indefinite leave to remain should be refused and further leave to remain granted on Code 1 for 12 months at a time."

Rights of residence

The rights that the Decisions give to Turkish workers re employment bring with them residence rights.

There is no requirement that lawfulness of employment be attested to by possession of any particular administrative document e.g. work permits – these would be "declaratory" of the existence of the worker's rights, they would not be the foundation of them.

Expulsion

Decision 1/80 makes the expulsion criteria of the Ankara arrangements reflective of those with which we are already familiar in EC law – i.e. public policy, public security or public health. The focus must be on the personal characteristics of the offender.

Family members

Ankara Agreement, Article 7

> "The members of the family of a Turkish worker who have been authorised to join him in a Member State may take jobs in that Member State after 3 years lawful residence subject to EC nationals having priority; and may freely take jobs in that Member State after 5 years lawful residence;
>
> The children of Turkish parents, one of whom has been legally employed in a Member State for 3 years, may, if they have completed a course of vocational training, take any job in that Member State, irrespective of how long they (the children) have resided there".

Thus there is no right of entry into the Member State for family members. However once they fulfil the conditions of Article 7 there is an implied recognition of a right of residence, given normal EC law principles that the right of residence for family members is essential to access to and the pursuit of any paid employment.

The Home Office website says "Applications for dependants to enter or remain should be considered under the Immigration Rules. The Agreement makes no provision for the *admission* of dependants to join Turkish workers in the United Kingdom. Applications from spouses and other dependants for entry clearance when the sponsor is in the United Kingdom *solely by virtue of the Agreement* should be refused."

There is no definition of the family member in the Agreement or any of the Council of Association decisions. However having regard to Community law provisions in the context of free movement of workers, family members arguably include:

- Spouses, their descendants under the age of 21 years or their dependants
- Dependant relatives in the ascending line of the worker and his spouse.

Self-employed

Rights of Establishment

The ECJ in Case C-37/98 *Savas* held that the 'standstill clause in Article 41(1) of the Additional Protocol of the Association Agreement was not in itself capable of conferring upon a Turkish national the benefit of the right of establishment and the right of residence which is its corollary. This means that a Turkish national's first admission to the territory of a Member State is governed exclusively by that State's own domestic law.

The standstill clause in Article 41(1) of the Additional Protocol precludes a Member State from adopting any new measure having the object or effect of making the establishment, and, as a corollary, the residence of a Turkish national in its territory subject to stricter conditions than those which applied at the time when the Additional Protocol entered into force with regard to the Member State concerned.

The UK became party to the European Community 1st January 1973 (and therefore party to the Agreement and the Additional Protocol). It is therefore the Immigration Rules HC 510 and 509 which were in force at the time that are applicable to Turkish nationals who wish to establish in business in the UK

In general HC510 and 509 are considerably more favourable than the current immigration rules pertaining to business people (HC395). The principal differences are:

- There was no minimum level of investment under HC510 or 509
- There was no requirement to offer employment to a minimum number of people under HC510 or 509
- There was no mandatory entry clearance requirement under HC510 and 509 and passengers arriving without entry clearance would be given a period of leave to enter to have their application examined by the Home Office

The main requirement under the 1973 Rules is for business people to demonstrate that they can maintain and accommodate themselves and any dependants from the profits of their business. If they are buying into an existing business they need to demonstrate that their investment is needed and they will have a controlling and active interest in the business.

Lawful entry

The Home Office had sought to distinguish between those lawfully and those illegally in the UK when applying *Savas*. The Home Office contended that where a person had committed a major illegality the current Immigration Rules HC 395 will be applied to them.

In *R (Veli Tum) v Secretary of State* the Secretary of State [2004] EWCA Civ 788, a case concerning Turkish asylum seekers who had sought to exercise his rights under the Ankara Agreement, the SSHD contended that if a person has lawfully entered this country, and, having done so, sought to establish himself here and to operate a business, he could rely on the law as it was in 1973. It was argued that this only applied to those who had so entered. In *Tum* it was contended that section 11 of the Immigration Act 1971, meant the Appellants were treated for legal purposes as having not entered the country, and therefore the position was that they are governed by the current domestic law.

The Administrative Court rejected this argument, stating that the "standstill" provisions are to apply to "a person whatever his status so far as his right to remain in this country or his right to enter this country is concerned". There was one caveat, regarding those obtaining entry via fraud:

> "23. The one exception that I would make to that clear position is with regard to a person who achieves entry to this country by the use of fraud. It has long been the situation that those who enter by fraud cannot benefit from the point of view of immigration status by so doing".

The European Court of Justice has upheld the approach of the English courts, in *Tum and Dari v Secretary of State for the Home Department* (C16-05; 20 September 2007). The mere fact of a prior unsuccessful asylum claim could not constitute abuse or fraud.

Thus only in instances of clear deception or fraud (this would include instances where an asylum claim was determined to be completely false or incredible) should a Turkish port of entry applicant for asylum be denied access to the Ankara Agreement. However, the Administrative Court in *Aldogan (R on the application of) v Secretary of State for the Home Department* [2007] EWHC 2586 (Admin) suggested that an application based on conduct whilst the individual was here unlawfully or while the business was carried on in breach of Immigration Rules was not to be encouraged.

Applications

The UKBA guidance found in the IDIs that implements the *Savas* decision basically follows the same requirements as are placed on nationals of Central and Eastern European Countries who are seeking to establish themselves under the terms of the Association Agreements with their countries. These are not particularly onerous requirements and are therefore in most cases non-objectionable.

Where all of the considerations are decided in favour of the applicant leave to enter/remain should be granted for two years in the first instance (immigration rule 215). It will then be for the applicant to apply for further leave to remain before the end of that two year period. If successful the next period of leave to be granted will be 3 years (r.220). There is provision for settlement after 4 years continuous leave in this category (r.222).

Appeals

The Home Office website acknowledges, with reference to the "not in accordance with the law" jurisdiction, that "an adjudicator would have jurisdiction to consider whether a person qualified by virtue of a directly enforceable right under the [Ankara] Agreement."

However appeals may be brought from within the UK only where there is a human rights claim or asylum claim made alongside them (as where there is an independent Article 8 claim regarding family or private life in the UK, possibly related to the importance of the business to the applicant's private life). The Tribunal in *SS & Ors (Ankara Agreement, no in-country right of appeal) Turkey* [2006] UKAIT 00074 (29 September 2006) found that an historic asylum or human rights claim would suffice, but in *Etame v Secretary of State for the Home Department & Anor* [2008] EWHC 1140 (Admin) (23 May 2008) the Administrative Court has said that in general, the suspension on removal brought by such claims is predicated on a link between the present application and human rights or asylum grounds. This is a complicated area that is not yet finally settled.

Additional agreements

In addition to the above Association Agreements, the EU has concluded a series of Association Agreements and Co-operation Agreements with countries such as Algeria, Tunisia and Morocco. The significance of these agreements in immigration terms is extremely limited in that they merely provide for non-discrimination clauses akin to those included for workers in the Europe Agreements. As was said there, the provisions do not create either a right of entry or residence nor do they create a right to have your leave to remain extended until the expiry of your employment contract.

Chapter 7: British Nationality Law

A BRIEF HISTORY OF NATIONALITY LAW 275
- PRE 1948 275
- 1948 TO 1983 275
- 1983 ONWARDS 276
- 2002 LEGISLATION 277
- 2006 LEGISLATION 278
- 2009 LEGISLATION 278

BIRTH OR ADOPTION IN THE UK 278
- PARENT IS BRITISH OR SETTLED 279
- CHILDREN BORN INSIDE UK TO MEMBERS OF THE ARMED FORCES 280
- ABANDONED MINORS 280
- REGISTRATION ON PARENTS BECOMING BRITISH OR SETTLED 281
- REGISTRATION DUE TO EARLY YEARS SPENT IN UK 281
- MINORS ADOPTED BY BRITISH CITIZENS 282

BIRTH OUTSIDE THE UK 282
- ACQUISITION BY DESCENT 283
- ACQUISITION BY REGISTRATION 283

ACQUISITION BY REGISTRATION AS AN ADULT 285

NATURALISATION 286
- PERIOD OF RESIDENCE 287
    - Non spouse cases 287
    - Spouse cases 287
    - In breach of the immigration laws 287
- THE GOOD CHARACTER REQUIREMENT 288
- SUFFICIENT KNOWLEDGE OF LIFE IN THE UK 288
- INTENTION TO LIVE IN THE UK 289
- CITIZENSHIP CEREMONIES 289

CHALLENGING NATIONALITY DECISIONS 290

STOPPING BEING BRITISH 291
- LOSS OF BRITISH NATIONALITY 291
- RENUNCIATION OF BRITISH NATIONALITY 291
- DEPRIVATION OF NATIONALITY 292

CHECKLIST FOR NATIONALITY 293

A brief history of nationality law

It is useful briefly to review the historical development of different forms of British nationality to ensure familiarity with the key terminology of nationality law. Also an old passport, or the passport of someone who has died, may be for a category of British nationality that is no longer current but may be useful to establish a person's current entitlements.

Pre 1948

Until 1948 the terminology used in law was "British Subject". The world was divided into British subjects, who were in the UK and overseas, and aliens, with the exception of British protected persons who were connected not to colonies but to British protectorates. They were not subject to immigration control.

1948 to 1983

The British Nationality Act 1948 created the status of a "Citizen of the UK and Colonies", often abbreviated to CUKC. All CUKCs had a right of abode in the UK. They were also, at the same time, British Subjects.

Citizens of colonies which had become independent were not CUKCs but they retained the status of British Subject and with it the right of abode. The term Commonwealth Citizen was also used for this group.

No change was made to British Protected Persons and the status of British Subject Without Citizenship was created for those for those who had not acquired the citizenship of the independent country, but were not CUKCs either.

As more colonies became independent after 1948 their citizens lost their CUKC status if they gained citizenship of the new country, and became British Subjects/Commonwealth citizens.

From the 1960s onwards, some CUKCs and some British subjects began to lose their right of abode. The IA 1971 introduced the term "patriality". Patrial citizens were those who had a right of abode and thus were not subject to immigration control:

- Patrial CUKCs – who had acquired their CUKC citizenship in the UK (by birth, registration or naturalisation) had a parent or grandparent who had similarly acquired CUKC status in the UK, or had lived in the UK for five years or more; or CUKCs .

- Non-patrial CUKCs – all CUKCs not in the category above.

The right of abode was also withdrawn from certain British Subjects and Commonwealth citizens during this period.

In summary, the following people born pre 1983 are British Citizens:

- Those born in the UK pre 1 January 1983 (save the children of diplomats)

- Those born abroad pre 1 January 1983 whose father was born in the UK

- Those born abroad pre 1 January 1983 whose father was registered or naturalised as British before their birth

- Those adopted in the UK by a British father.

1983 onwards

With the coming into force of the British Nationality Act 1981, what mattered was parentage, rather than place of birth. The Act created three new categories of British nationals:

- British Citizens – these were people who, on 31 December 1982, were patrial CUKCs. As British citizens they retained their rights of abode, and are recognisable as the British Citizens of today.

- British "Dependent" (renamed "Overseas" in the British Overseas Territories Citizens Act 2002) Territories Citizens for people who, on 31 December 1982, were CUKCs because of their connection with a British Dependent Territory (e.g. Bermuda). Those who had the right of abode retained it.

- British Overseas Citizens for non-patrial CUKCs who did not fit into the category of British Dependent (Overseas Territories) Citizens.

Meanwhile,

- British Protected Persons retained their status.

- Commonwealth Citizens' status did not change. Those who had the right of abode retained it.

- British Subject changed its meaning. It became the new name for British Subjects Without Citizenship as defined in the BNA 1948.

Section 11 of the BNA 1981 made provision for certain CUKCs to become British citizens on passage of the Act. The principle requirements were that a person, on 31 December 1982:

- Was a citizen of the UK and colonies

- Had a right of abode in the UK

From 1 January 1983, under the British Nationality Act 1981 nationality could be obtained in three ways:

- As of right, by operation of law (this nationality will be operative regardless of any further actions)

- As of entitlement, by taking the step of registering (if the step is not taken, the entitlement can be lost; often there is a time limit which is capable of *some* extension at the discretion of the Secretary of State, or it may be the case that the application must be made whilst still a minor: it is only those born and living in the UK for the first ten years of their life who enjoy a lifelong chance to register).

- By discretion, by obtaining naturalization (or in some cases by registering, as the Secretary of State has a discretion to register any child as a British citizen if the circumstances impress him sufficiently).

2002 legislation

In 2002, the British Overseas Territories Act 2002 was passed. This Act renamed British Dependent Territories, British Overseas Territories. People became British Overseas Territories Citizens automatically on 26 February 2002 and on the 21 May 2002 they all became British Citizens with a right of abode in the UK, with the exception of those connected with the Sovereign bases.

In the same year, the Nationality, Immigration and Asylum Act 2002 was passed. It did not change the list of categories of citizen, but enlarged some and did make changes to entitlements to move between categories. It also finally abolished the partial-centric approach of previous nationality laws and in section 9 of the Act made unmarried fathers the transmitters of British nationality just as much as unmarried mothers. This provision came into force on 1 July 2006.

At the moment there are therefore a number of types of British national currently in existence:

British Citizen

British Overseas Territories Citizen

British Overseas Citizen

British National (Overseas)

British Protected Person

British Subject

This manual is intended as an introductory text and therefore focuses on British citizens.

2006 legislation

The Immigration, Asylum and Nationality Act 2006 made further changes to nationality law, widening the power to deprive a person of citizenship (s.56) or the right of abode (s.57) to include 'conducive to public good' and also removes registration as a British citizen as of right by inserting a good character test for all applicants. An Order passed in January 2010 also includes children aged 10 and over in the 'good character requirement'.

2009 legislation

Some sections of the Borders, Citizenship and Immigration Act 2009 came into force 13 January 2010. These sections are what might be described as the nice not naughty bits of the Act. The changes are as follows:

- Enables registration as British of the children born outside the UK of members of the armed forces and confirms automatic British citizenship of children born in the UK of members of the armed forces.

- Allows registration of children born outside the UK under s.3(2) of the BNA 1981 up to their 18th birthday (extended from 12 months after their birth or 6 years in exceptional circumstances).

- Permits registration of otherwise stateless BN(O)s.

- Enables registration of those born before 7 February 1961 with British mothers, if they would have become a British citizen at birth had women been able to pass on citizenship in the same way as men.

Birth or adoption in the UK

The routes by which a child born in the UK can become British by birth are as follows:

- Parent is British or settled
- Parent member of armed forces
- Abandoned minors
- Registration on parents becoming British or settled
- Early years spent in UK
- Adoption by British citizen

Parent is British or settled

The plain fact of birth in the United Kingdom does not usually create any entitlement to citizenship unless it is combined with a parental link to a person settled in the United Kingdom:

> "1(1) A person born in the United Kingdom after commencement, or in a qualifying territory on or after the appointed day, shall be a British citizen if at the time of the birth his father or mother is--
> (a) a British citizen; or
> (b) settled in the United Kingdom or that territory."

This form of acquisition of citizenship operates by law, so no registration or other forms need be completed. However, proof that a person meets the above criteria may be required to prove citizenship.

Settlement is defined in the Immigration Act 1971 as "being ordinarily resident in the United Kingdom ... without being subject under the immigration laws to any restriction on the period for which he may remain." Effectively this means that the parent in question had indefinite leave to remain or a permanent right of residence under EC law.

Until 1 July 2006, a child could establish his right to nationality via either parent so long as he was born within marriage. 'Illegitimate' children (for this was the effect of this provision) could trace entitlement only via their mother. Pursuant to section 47 of the British Nationality Act 1981, a person born out of wedlock is to be treated as legitimate for the purposes of nationality law if their parents subsequently marry.

Under a policy articulated in March 2000, Home Office practice was to register the illegitimate child of a British citizen father where (a) paternity is not in doubt (b) no reasonable objections have been lodged by those with parental responsibility; (c) there are no objections on grounds of character.

This old fashioned and discriminatory approach finally came to a partial end as of 1 July 2006 with the coming into force of section 9 of the 2002 Act. However, the change did not apply retrospectively, only to children born on or after 1 July 2006.

> **Example**
>
> Beatrice was born in the UK in 2005 to a French national mother and British father. The mother had only been present in the UK for 18 months. The parents were not married. Beatrice was not automatically therefore born British, although she could almost certainly later have been registered as British (see below).
>
> Bertie was born in the UK in 2007 to the same French mother and British father. The mother was still not resident and the parents were not married. Bertie, however, was automatically born British because of the change in the law effective from 2006.

The references to qualifying territories throughout the Act are not of great importance for our purposes, being references to specific entitlements for those born on or after 21 May 2002 in a "Qualifying territory" – which means a British overseas territory other than the Sovereign Base Areas of Akrotiri and Dhekelia in Cyprus, if a parent is a British citizen and settled in the UK or that qualifying territory.

Children born inside UK to members of the armed forces

Section 42 of the Borders, Citizenship and Nationalioty Act 2009 provides a statutory basis for the acquisition of British citizenship for children born in the UK to members of the armed forces. This removes the need to treat as settled parents of such children, which was a somewhat legally suspect 'work around' previously in place.

A new section 1(1A) was inserted into the BNA 1981, which provides that a person born in the United Kingdom or a qualifying territory on or after the relevant day shall be a British citizen if at the time of the birth his father or mother is a member of the armed forces.

Abandoned minors

Under s.1(2), a new born infant found abandoned in the United Kingdom on or after 1 January 1983 can be regarded, for the purposes of s.1(1), as having been:

- born in the United Kingdom on or after 1 January 1983; and

- born to a parent who at the time of the birth was a British citizen or settled in the United Kingdom

Unless the contrary can be proven by the Home Office. So the presumption will be that such a child is a British citizen.

Registration on parents becoming British or settled

Minors are entitled to registration under s.1(3) of the British Nationality Act 1981 if:

- they were born in the United Kingdom on or after 1 January 1983; and

- they were not British citizens at birth because at the time neither parent was a British citizen or settled here; and

- while they are minors, either parent becomes a British citizen or becomes settled in the United Kingdom; and

- they are minors on the date of application

> **Example**
>
> To continue with the example of Beatrice, above, if her mother becomes settled in the UK after five years of residence under EC law, Beatrice could be registered as British. Unlike with Bertie, this is a positive step that must be taken and it must be taken before Beatrice turns 18.
>
> Alternatively, Beatrice could probably have been registered under s.1(3) after 1 July 2006, once her father was recognised in law as her father for nationality purposes, i.e. when one of her 'parents' became British.

Registration due to early years spent in UK

Adults or minors are entitled to registration under s.1(4) of the BNA 1981 if they:

- were born in the United Kingdom on or after 1 January 1983; and

- were not a British citizen at birth because at the time neither parent was a British citizen or settled here; and

- were aged 10 years or more on the date of application; and

- have lived in the United Kingdom for the first 10 years of their life; and

- during that 10 years have not been out of the United Kingdom for more than 90 days in any one of those years

The lawfulness of residence is irrelevant for this provision. The statute (s.1(7)) gives a discretion to extend this latter requirement. This statutory discretion receives a gloss from the Nationality Instructions, which indicate that non-intentional longer absences may be permitted, and also other absences within limited parameters.

Minors adopted by British citizens

Section 1(5) of the British Nationality Act 1981, as amended, explains which children adopted on or after 1 January 1983 acquired British citizenship automatically because of their adoption. Under s.1(5), a child who is not already a British citizen becomes a British citizen from the date of an adoption order if EITHER:

- the adoption is authorised by order of a court in the United Kingdom on or after 1 January 1983 or, on or after 21 May 2002, by an order of a court in a qualifying territory; and

- the adopter or, in the case of a joint adoption, one of the adopters is a British citizen on the date of the adoption order

OR

- it is a Convention adoption under the 1993 Hague Convention on Intercountry Adoptions; and

- the adoption is effected on or after 1 June 2003; and

- the adopter or, in the case of a joint adoption, one of the adopters is a British citizen on the date of the Convention adoption; and

- the adopter or, in the case of a joint adoption, both of the adopters is habitually resident in the United Kingdom on the date of the Convention adoption

Birth outside the UK

The routes by which a child born outside the UK can become British are as follows:

At birth
- To a parent who is a British citizen otherwise than by descent

On registration
- Any time up to age of 18
- On residence in UK with British citizen parents for 3 years
- If parent is or becomes a member of the armed forces

Acquisition by descent

Section 2(1) of the BNA 1981 reads as follows:

> 'A person born outside the United Kingdom after commencement shall be a British citizen if at the time of the birth his father or mother:
> (a) is a British citizen otherwise than by descent; ...'

This form of transmission of nationality operates by law, so no registration form need be completed, but evidence may be required that the person does meet the above requirements.

Example

Chris is a British citizen who emigrates to Australia with his Australian girlfriend, Clarissa. They do not get married. They have a baby boy, Clarence, in 2005. Clarence has no entitlement to British nationality because he was born before the law changed on 1 July 2006.

Chris and Clarissa have another child, a baby girl called Carrie, who is born in 2007. Carrie is automatically born British and does not need to take any further steps to become British. She is likely to be entitled to dual nationality, depending on the nationality laws of the country in which she is born and the nationality laws of the country of the other parent.

Acquisition by registration

Some minors have an entitlement to register as British citizens (save for exceptions not relevant for this overview). The intention of sub-sections 3(2) and 3(5) is to remedy harshness created by section 2(1), with its limitation of transmission of nationality to a single generation.

Section 3(1), which is a very wide discretion, can be used to register a variety of problem cases (it is known to be used sometimes to deal with an illegitimate child where the Secretary of State accepts the relationship of the child to the British citizen father).

> '3(1) If while a person is a minor an application is made for his registration as a British citizen, the Secretary of State may, if he thinks fit, cause him to be registered as such a citizen.'

Section 3 permits registration where there is a sufficiently strong link with the UK, looking back across the generations, as to make it unfair to decline to permit access to full British citizenship. The requirements, in the normal case, are as follows:

- As of 13 January 2010, the child to be registered must be under the age of 18. The previous rule until the relevant section of the Borders, Citizenship and Immigration Act 2009 came into effect was that registration had to take place within 12 months of birth or six years in exceptional circumstances.

- The child's parent has the weak form of nationality ('by descent') but whose grandparent has the strong form of nationality (otherwise than by descent').

- The child's parent has a geographical link with the UK, in that they lived there for a three year period some time prior to the birth of the child, and did not leave the UK for more than 270 days within that period (however, for a child born stateless, this requirement is waived).

- With effect from 13 January 2010, as a result of the Borders, Citizenship and Immigration Act 2009, certain children born in the UK to a parent who becomes member of the UK armed forces before the child reaches 18, or born outside the UK to a parent serving overseas in the UK armed forces.

Section 3(5) permits of another form of registration. This does not require the grandparent connection that we saw in section 3(2), nor does it require the historic 3 year stay in the UK that that section entertains – however, it does require that the family including the child were in the UK for the 3 years leading up to the application for registration, and did not leave the UK for more than 270 days within that period. The application can only be made whilst the child is a minor.

Example

To continue with the story of the family of Chris and Clarissa, we saw earlier that Carrie was born British by descent by virtue of section 2(1) of the Act. Section 14 of the Act sets out a definition of a British citizen 'by descent' and Carrie falls within that definition.

When Carrie grows up she has a child of her own, Colin, who is born in Australia. Colin is not automatically born British citizens under the same section as Carrie, because section 2(1) states that the parent must be a British citizen 'otherwise than by descent'.

However, Colin could be registered as British citizens under section 3(2) if the proper procedures are followed, or could be registered under section 3(5) if they were later to qualify (see below).

When Colin grows up, he has two children, Claude and Cedric. They have no entitlement at all to British citizenship by descent.

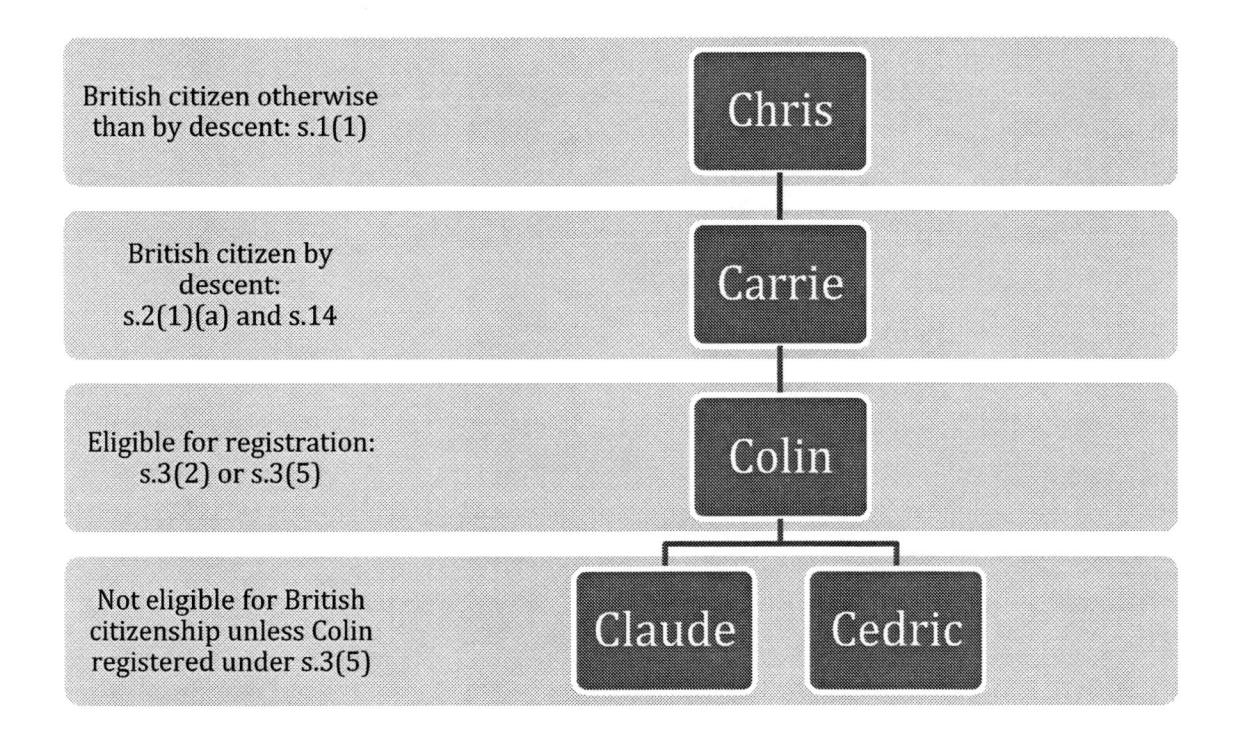

British citizen otherwise than by descent: s.1(1)	Chris
British citizen by descent: s.2(1)(a) and s.14	Carrie
Eligible for registration: s.3(2) or s.3(5)	Colin
Not eligible for British citizenship unless Colin registered under s.3(5)	Claude, Cedric

Acquisition by registration as an adult

Certain adults are also able or entitled to register as British citizens:

- A person who is a British overseas territories citizen, British National (Overseas), a British Overseas citizen, a British subject or a British protected person may register as a full British citizen if he or she meets the same residence requirement as for naturalisation and, since the advent of the 2006 Act, a good character requirement.

- There is a discretion to register as a British citizen the above persons, even if the residence requirements are not met (s.4(4) of 1981 Act).

Registration applications involve the completion of a form. There is a fee. Applications for the registration of people living abroad will normally be made through a British Diplomatic Post; consult the Foreign and Commonwealth Office website. Applications for people living in the UK are made to UKBA. Registration is evidenced by a certificate and the person can subsequently apply for a British passport.

If on receipt of an application the Home Office detect that a person does not need to register because they are already a British Citizen, they will inform the applicant of this and refund the application fee.

The Nationality, Immigration and Asylum Act 2002 amended the BNA 1981 so that those wishing to acquire British Citizenship will now do so at a public ceremony. This applies also to applicants for registration.

Naturalisation

Section 6(1) deals with naturalisation cases based on a UK connection other than marriage, and makes reference to Schedule 1 of the BNA 1981. The requirements therein are that an individual is of good character, has sufficient knowledge of the English, Welsh or Scottish Gaelic language; and that they intend to make their principal home in the United Kingdom, or, if they intend to live abroad, that they work in Crown service or for a UK enterprise.

The criteria for naturalisation are as follows:

- Minimum period of residence
- Good character test
- Knowledge of life in the UK
- Intention to live in the UK
- Oath and ceremony

Period of residence

Non spouse cases

The requirements of residence for those not applying as spouses are set out at Schedule 1 paragraph 2.

> (a) subject to subsection (3), that he was in the United Kingdom at the beginning of the period of five years ending with the date of the application and that the number of days on which he absent from the United Kingdom in that period does not exceed 450; and
> (b) that the number of days on which he was absent from the United Kingdom in the period of twelve months so ending does not exceed 90; and
> (c) that he was not at any time in the period of twelve months so ending subject under the immigration laws to any restriction on the period for which he might remain in the United Kingdom;
> (d) that he was not any time in the period of five years so ending in the United Kingdom in breach of the immigration laws.

However, there is discretion to treat these conditions as satisfied despite insufficient periods of time being accumulated.

Spouse cases

Section 6(2) deals with applications of persons "married to a British citizen". The required residence period is 270 days, with the references to 5 years replaced by 3 years, in sub-paragraphs (a) and (d).

The restriction at 3(c) is lifted, so that there is no requirement to be free from immigration control (i.e. to have indefinite leave to remain) for 12 months prior to the date of application, with the practical consequence that a spouse can apply from the grant of indefinite leave to remain without waiting for a further year.

There is no requirement to make the UK their permanent home, though they are expected to meet the good character requirement, and the language requirement or to comply with the language test.

Naturalisation is a discretionary power. There is no right of appeal against a refusal of naturalisation. However, reasons must be given and, subsequent to the amendments effected to the BNA 1981 (s.1 and s.44) by s.7 of the Nationality, Immigration and Asylum Act 2002, there is no limit on the scope of judicial review of such a refusal.

In breach of the immigration laws

Where there are qualifying periods to be met, periods spent in the relevant territory "in breach of the immigration laws" do not count. The meaning of "in breach of the immigration laws" for the specific purpose of calculating residence is set out in s.11 of the NIA 2002.

The section is not as clear as it could be, especially in subs. (3). The government has explained that subs. (3) means that periods people (usually refugees) who have not been illegal entrants or overstayers spent on temporary admission or in detention before the decision to grant their application will not be treated as periods in the UK in breach of immigration control for the calculations. The policy is that time taken from the *application* (not entry to the UK) to the Home Office decision to allow the application is not treated as time spent "in breach of the immigration laws" for the purposes of the calculation. Time spent in the UK without leave prior to making the application will not count.

EU nationals and their families used only to be treated as having been in the UK in breach of the immigration laws if they had remained here after a deportation order or removal directions had been made. From 7 November 2002 onwards, as a result of s.11, the broader grounds that they do not have either an entitlement to be here under European Community law nor permission to be here will apply.

The good character requirement

This is not tightly defined. Unspent criminal convictions, including motoring offences have to be listed. Checks are made on financial solvency and a bankrupt is unlikely to be considered of good character. Security risks will be taken into account and there can be a police check.

The good character requirement has been extended to include children aged 10 and over.

Sufficient knowledge of life in the UK

Section 1 of the NIA 2002 amended the British Nationality Act 1981 to make it necessary for all applicants for naturalisation, including those applying to naturalise on the basis of marriage, to show 'sufficient knowledge about life in the UK'. Section 2 of the NIA 2002 for the first time extended the language requirement this requirement to those applying to naturalise on the basis of marriage (from 28 July 2004).

There are two ways to fulfil the requirement to show sufficient knowledge about life in the UK:

(i) Sit and pass the Life in the UK test. This is based on a publication called *Life in the United Kingdom: A Journey to Citizenship*, focusing on chapters 2, 3 and 4. Twenty four questions have to be answered in forty five minutes at one of ninety test centres across the UK. Details are available from www.lifeintheuktest.gov.uk.

(ii) Successfully undertake an ESOL (English for Speakers of Other Languages) with citizenship course. If an applicant feels he or she does not possess the necessary language skills to sit the Life in the UK test, he or she can instead undertake this course at one of many providers across the UK.

The Home Office possesses a discretion to waive the language requirement where it would be unreasonable to expect the applicant to fulfil it because of age or physical or mental condition. The language requirement will normally be waived where the applicant is aged 65 or over.

The grounds for exemption of younger people need to be compelling, such as where the applicant:

(i) is suffering from a long term illness or disability which severely restricts mobility and ability to attend language classes; or

(ii) suffers from a speech impediment which limits ability to converse in the relevant language; or

(iii) has a mental impairment which means that they are unable to learn another language.

Intention to live in the UK

If a person is abroad or about to go abroad it may be important to explain this. For example, caring for a person overseas who is ill or dying is likely to be a temporary absence and should not be treated as evidence that a person has no intention to live in the UK.

Citizenship ceremonies

The Nationality, Immigration and Asylum Act 2002 substitutes a new s.42 to 42B and Schedule 5 into the BNA 1981 so that anyone over the age of 18 who wish to acquire British Citizenship, whether by registration or naturalisation, will now do so at a public ceremony and are required to take the Oath of Allegiance (there is an affirmation to be used by people of different religions and of none) and now a new pledge as set out in these provisions. Full details of the ceremonies can be found on a special website uknationality.gov.uk which is also a convenient portal to use to access the relevant information from the UKBA site. Ceremonies are normally held in groups, although arrangements can be made (at a price) to have individual ceremonies. People can invite guests. A fee is payable.

Some people are exempted from the requirement by Section 42(2) of the 1981 Act. These are:

   a. those not of full age; or

   b. those who are already:
   - British citizens; or
   - British overseas territories citizens; or
   - British Nationals (Overseas); or
   - British Overseas citizens; or
   - British subjects under the 1981 Act; or
   - citizens of any country of which Her Majesty is Queen (Antigua and Barbuda, Australia, the Bahamas, Barbados, Belize, Canada,

Grenada, Jamaica, New Zealand, Papua New Guinea, St Christopher and Nevis, St Lucia, St Vincent and the Grenadines, Solomon Islands and Tuvalu.)

Where an applicant is required to take an oath of allegiance s/he must normally do so within the time limit of 3 months prescribed by the British Nationality (General) Regulations 1982 (or the British Nationality (General) Regulations 2003, as appropriate). Otherwise the applicant cannot be registered or naturalised unless the Home Secretary decides to extend the period. Notification letters will advise the applicant to contact the local authority to arrange a ceremony. The Home Office will also notify the local authority.

If a person does not attend a citizenship ceremony within the time limit permitted, the Home Office should notify them that it will not be possible to become a British citizen because the Home Secretary is not able to register or naturalise a person who has not attended a ceremony and taken an oath/pledge. If the applicant still wishes to become a British citizen, and had an entitlement at the date of application, a certificate may be issued at any time on the basis of the original application on payment of the balance of fee and attending a citizenship ceremony and making an oath/pledge. In all other cases, the applicant will need to re apply under an appropriate provision of the legislation.

In exceptional circumstances an exemption may be made in respect of any or all of the following:

- the requirement to attend a citizenship ceremony
- the requirement to make an oath of allegiance and pledge
- the time limit for attending a ceremony

Challenging nationality decisions

Section 7 of the NIA 2002 amends s.44 of the BNA 1981 and the British Nationality (Hong Kong) Act 1990 so that the Home Office must now give reasons for a refusal of citizenship (in practice, its policy has been to do so since 1997) and that there are no limits on the scope of a judicial review of such a refusal. There is still no right of appeal against refusal to register or naturalise a person as a British Citizen, despite the confusing title of the section in the 2002 Act.

Thus nationality decisions are not included in the list of immigration decisions set out in s.82 of the NIA 2002 and providing an exhaustive list of appealable decisions.

There are specific rights to challenge decisions to deprive a person of their British citizenship and these are set out below under the consideration of deprivation of citizenship.

Stopping being British

The different ways in which a person can stop being a British national or citizen fall into three categories:

- Loss
- Renunciation
- Deprivation

Loss of British nationality

British Citizens cannot simply lose their nationality. However, as described above when looking at the history of British nationality law, other categories of British national have lost their status at different points in the history of nationality law. To this must be added those who have lost rights and entitlements previously attendant on their status (as for example with the abolition of special voucher quota schemes described above). As noted above, British Citizens by descent do not pass on their nationality to their children.

Other forms of British national can still lose their British nationality. A British subject who gains any other citizenship or nationality after 1 January 1983 will no longer be a British subject unless they used to be a citizen of Eire and have made a claim to remain a British subject under section 2 of the British Nationality Act 1948 or under the 1981 Act. Similarly, a British Protected Person will no longer be a British Protected Person on acquiring any other nationality or citizenship.

Renunciation of British nationality

A person can renounce their form of British nationality. People are likely to want to renounce British nationality if they wish to become or remain the national of a country that does not allow them to hold another nationality.

The requirements are that a British citizen, British Overseas Territories Citizen (see note below), British Overseas citizen, British subject, British National (Overseas) or British Protected Person may renounce that nationality if:

- s/he has a nationality other than the one it is sought to renounce; or
- can show that s/he will get another citizenship or nationality; and
- is over 18 (or under 18 but have been married); and
- is of full capacity (i.e. not of unsound mind).

The procedure is that a declaration of renunciation must be filled in. The date of registration of the declaration is the date at which nationality is lost but if the person does not obtain another citizenship within six months, the declaration does not take effect and is considered to have kept their British nationality.

If a person renounced their British citizenship or British overseas territories citizenship to keep or get another citizenship, they have a right to register and resume the citizenship they renounced. They can make use of this only once. Any subsequent attempt to resume following a second registration will be at the discretion the Home Secretary (for British citizenship) or the Governor of a British overseas territory (for British overseas territories citizenship) will decide whether you can resume it again.

Section 5 of the NIA 2002 amended the BNA 1981 to give men the (superior) rights previously enjoyed only by women, who had renounced their UK and colonies citizenship before 1983 to qualify for registration on the basis of a connection with the UK or a British Overseas Territory by marriage. It is still necessary to meet all the qualifying requirements.

All other forms of British nationality cannot be resumed following renunciation.

Deprivation of nationality

Powers to deprive people of their citizenship are set out under the Section 40 and 40A of the BNA 1981 as amended.

There are powers to deprive people of the different forms of British nationality on the following grounds:

- If the Secretary of State is satisfied that deprivation is conducive to the public good (not applicable if the person would thence be made stateless): s.40(2)

- If the Secretary of State is satisfied that nationality obtained by registration or naturalisation was in fact obtained by fraud, false representation or concealment of a material fact (there is no protection here in respect of statelessness): s.40(3)

Section 40A, inserted by the 2002 Act, gives a right of appeal against deprivation of nationality (new s.40A). This is to the immigration tribunal or to the Special Immigration Appeals Commission (SIAC), which is likely to pick up some cases given the "seriously prejudicial to the vital interests" criterion. The Secretary of State must notify a person of the intention to deprive them of their nationality and the deprivation will not take effect until any appeal has been finally determined (s.40A(6)) or the time for appealing has expired.

Checklist for Nationality

- Do I know this person's nationality?
- Have I collected enough information to check whether they might have rights under British nationality law, including information about their parents and spouses?
- Have I collected information about children, including dates of birth, where they are born, and where they lived since birth?
- Do the children have rights under nationality law even if the parents do not?
- Does it matter in this case whether the person has another nationality?
- Do the person's rights depend upon the provisions of foreign law – do I need information about foreign laws to determine whether they have another nationality?
- Is this person a European Union national?
- If they are an EU national, are there any special circumstances in the case – have immigration ever been involved in a previous departure, or proposed departure from the UK?
- Are there any national security issues in this case?
- Have I collected sufficient information to calculate whether they fill any residence requirements?
- Does the case suggest to me that the nationality laws operating in this case are discriminatory?

Cases where the person is not eligible to apply for nationality

- Will they become eligible in the future, and if so when?
- Are there any grounds for making a special application in this case?

Chapter 8: Points Based System

INTRODUCTION	297
SPONSORSHIP UNDER THE POINTS-BASED SYSTEM	298
Applying for sponsorship	298
Sponsor duties	299
DOCUMENTARY EVIDENCE AND HOME OFFICE GUIDANCE	301
OVERSTAYING AND EXTENSION APPLICATIONS	303
TIER 1: HIGHLY SKILLED	304
Tier 1 (General)	305
Eligibility for extensions of leave	305
Qualifications	306
Earnings	306
UK experience	307
Age	308
Maintenance (funds)	308
Language	309
Tier 1 (Entrepreneur)	309
Eligibility for extensions of leave	309
First time applications	310
Extension applications	311
Maintenance	311
Language	312
Tier 1 (Investor)	312
Eligibility for extensions of leave	312
First time applications	313
Extension applications	313
Maintenance	315
Language	315
Tier 1 (Post study work)	315
Eligibility for extensions of leave	315
Qualifications	316
Maintenance	316
Language	317
TIER 2: SKILLED WORKERS	317
Outline	317
Sponsorship	319
Tier 2 (General)	319
Attributes	319
Maintenance	322
English language skills	322
Extensions for Tier 2	322

    Settlement 323
  TIER 2 (INTRA-COMPANY TRANSFER) 323
  TIER 2 (SPORTSPERSON) 324
  TIER 2 (MINISTERS OF RELIGION) 324

TIER 4: STUDENTS 325

  REQUIREMENT TO HAVE A SPONSOR 325
    Licensing of sponsors 326
    Visa application process 328
  TIER 4 (GENERAL) 328
    Eligibility 328
    Funds and maintenance 331
    Length and conditions of leave 332
    Extensions 333
  CHILD STUDENT VISA 334

TIER 5: YOUTH MOBILITY AND TEMPORARY WORKERS 335

  YOUTH MOBILITY 335
  TEMPORARY WORKERS 336
    Creative and sporting category 337
    Charity worker category 338
    Religious worker category 339
    Government authorised exchange category 340
    International agreement category 341

DEPENDANTS OF PBS MIGRANTS 343

RIGHT OF APPEAL 344

RIGHT OF REVIEW 345

> **Top tip**
>
> For those sitting the LSC accreditation examinations who want to undertake publicly funded work, the 'managed migration' option must be avoided: only the immigration or asylum options can be selected for a person undertaking publicly funded work. Nevertheless, some knowledge of the managed migration options available is required for all examinees, and the Law Society Standards and Guidance for the Immigration and Asylum Accreditation Scheme must be consulted.

Introduction

The Points Based System (PBS) was announced as part of a five year strategy for asylum and immigration published in February 2005: *"Controlling Our Borders: Making Migration Work for Britain, Five Year Strategy for Asylum and Immigration"*.

The Minister introducing the changes described it as "the biggest shake-up to our border protection and immigration system for forty years". The key elements of the system are, as summarised by its propounders at the Home Office:

- it combines more than 80 pre-existing work and study routes in to the United Kingdom into five tiers;

- points are awarded on workers' skills to reflect aptitude, experience, age and also the demand for those skills any given sector, to allow the United Kingdom to respond flexibly to changes in the labour market;

- it is a fair, transparent and objective system that will enable potential migrants to assess their likelihood of making a successful application and should help to reduce the number of failed applications.

The key intentions seem to have been to simplify and consolidate the key 'managed migration' routes (as opposed to family or other forms of migration), to seek to introduce objective criteria for granting visas and leave and to reduce opportunities for abuse of immigration control. A significant part of this latter consideration was the notion of registered sponsors for some PBS migrants. Sponsors – either employers or educational institutions – would lose their capacity to sponsor future migrants if they failed to comply with extensive Home Office requirements for monitoring and reporting.

The five tiers are as follows:

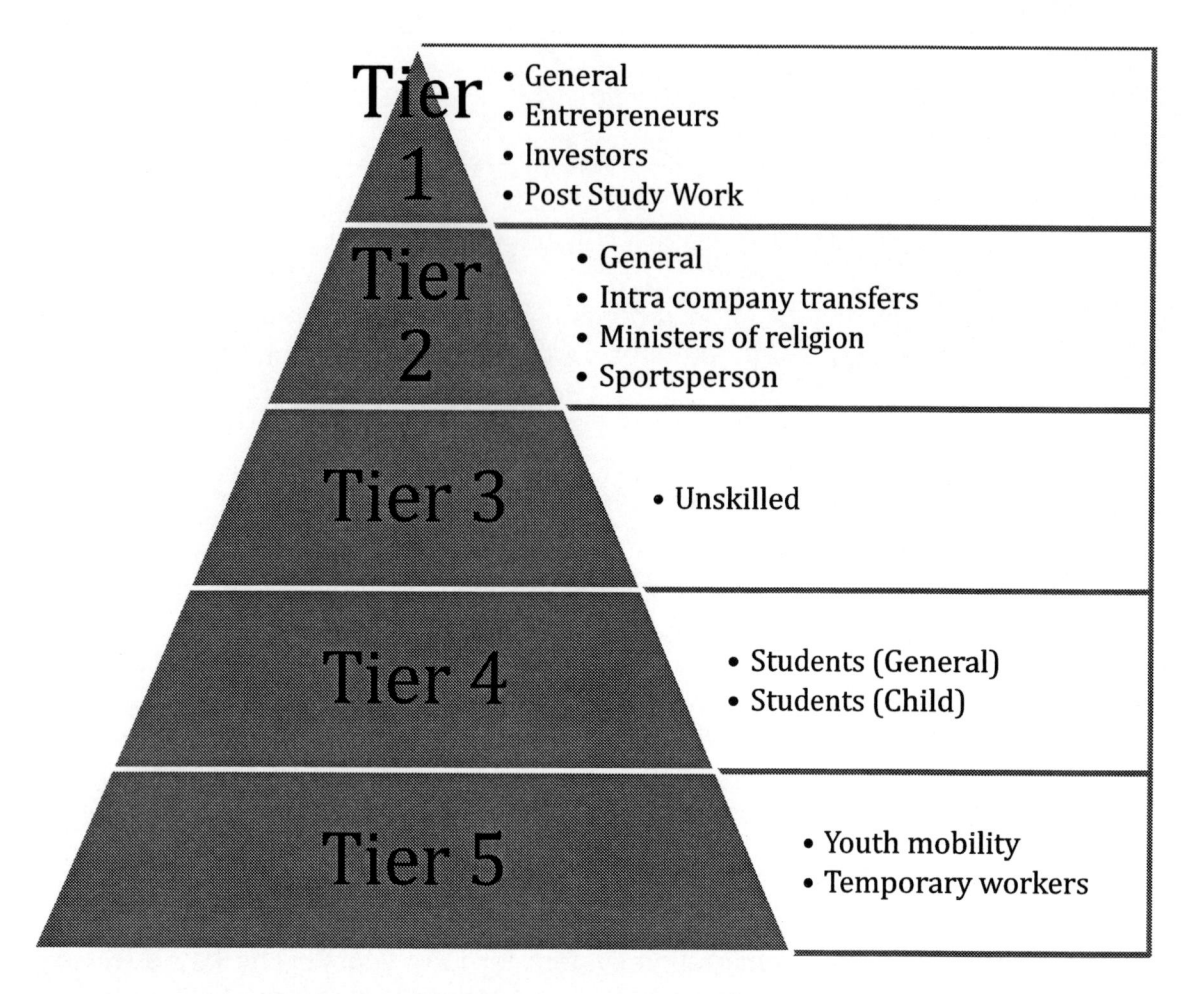

Tier 1
- General
- Entrepreneurs
- Investors
- Post Study Work

Tier 2
- General
- Intra company transfers
- Ministers of religion
- Sportsperson

Tier 3
- Unskilled

Tier 4
- Students (General)
- Students (Child)

Tier 5
- Youth mobility
- Temporary workers

Linked to the new Points Based System, the Home Office set up the Migration Advisory Committee (MAC). This is intended to provide advice to government on where labour market shortages exist. The committee has so far advised on adjusting points weighting and shortage occupations in the PBS and also on whether to relax controls for EU Accession states.

Sponsorship under the points-based system

There is now a system of sponsorship whereby prospective United Kingdom employers and sponsors must apply for a licence to employ migrant workers or to offer educational courses under tiers 2, 4 and 5 of the points-based system, and in so doing agree to meet a number of sponsorship duties.

Comprehensive guidance is available on the Home Office website and this section aims to provide a précis of only the outline of the scheme.

Applying for sponsorship

Sponsors must apply to join the register of sponsors. If awarded a licence, they are then added to the register of sponsors, and will be able to issue certificates of sponsorship when applications are taken for the relevant tiers later in the year.

An interim cap on the number of licences that may be issued was imposed by the Government from 19 July 2010. A full review will take place and a permanent policy is expected to be announced for April 2011.

The licence is valid for four years, starting from the day it is issued or the day that applications start for the relevant tier, whichever is the later.

There are three principal questions investigated on a licence application:

- Firstly, is this a genuine organisation operating legally in the United Kingdom?

- Secondly, it is trustworthy? The history and background of the organisation, its key personnel and those in control of it will be investigated. Any history of dishonesty or immigration crime will be viewed particularly seriously and can lead to refusal of the application.

- Thirdly, is the organisation capable of carrying out its sponsorship duties? This will involved an investigation of processes, like human resource practices.

Once licensed under Tier 2 and/or Tier 5 the sponsor will be able to assign certificates of sponsorship to migrants who wish to come to, or stay in the United Kingdom to work. Once licensed under Tier 4 the sponsor will be able to issue visa letters to migrants who wish to come to the United Kingdom to study. As is discussed below, Entry Clearance Officers do nevertheless retain a role in the visa application process.

Sponsor duties

Sponsors must comply with certain duties, including a duty to inform the Home Office if migrants do not turn up for their job or course, or if they are absent without permission for a significant period. Sponsors must also keep records of the migrants they have sponsored, including contact details (and, in due course, details of the migrant's ID card) and supply them to the Home Office on request.

The Home Office state they will monitor sponsors' behaviour and compliance with their duties once they are licensed. In particular the Home Office say they will:

i) set a limit on the number of certificates of sponsorship a sponsor can assign under Tiers 2 and 5, and review its performance after it has assigned a certain number;

ii) make visits, pre-arranged or not, to check compliance; and

iii) issue civil penalties where evidence is found that the sponsor has been breaching the illegal working regulations, or refer the sponsor for prosecution where appropriate.

All sponsors will be rated A or B according to the Home Office's assessment of their ability to fulfil their sponsor duties. Any sponsor that is B-rated must comply with a time-limited action plan, which will set out the steps it needs to take in order to gain or regain an A-rating. If the sponsor does not comply with this action plan, it is likely to lose its licence altogether.

Where the Home Office considers that a sponsor has not been complying with its duties, has been dishonest in its dealings with the Home Office or otherwise poses a threat to immigration control, its licence may be withdrawn or it may be downgraded to a B-rating.

A B-rating is transitional, and holders will be given a Sponsorship Action Plan. They will be expected, within a relatively short period (around three months), to have improved performance sufficiently to be upgraded to an A-rating, or risk having their licence withdrawn.

A sponsorship action plan will be drawn up, listing the steps to be taken in order fully to comply with sponsorship duties and obtain an A-rating. This might include, for example, making specific improvements to record keeping, improving control over the staff employed to issue certificates of sponsorship or improving communication between different branches of the business so it knows when a migrant has not turned up for work.

If the plan has not been met by the end of the three months the Home Office will normally withdraw the licence, though where significant progress has been made, they may instead decide to keep the organisation on a B-rating and have a new action plan drawn up. In deciding whether to draw up a new sponsorship action plan in these circumstances, they will take all the circumstances into account, including the following:

- whether genuine attempts have been made to meet the requirements of the action plan; and

- whether circumstances outside the control of the organisation prevented it from meeting the requirements.

The absolute maximum period on an action plan is 12 months. A B-rated organisation will automatically lose its licence after that time.

B-rated sponsors may be subject to additional duties. For example, a B-rated sponsor may be required to report to the Home Office when a migrant arrives for work or study, rather than simply reporting when they do not turn up. Such duties will be notified. B-rated sponsors are likely to be subject to more frequent and exacting inspections by the Home Office.

One of the key effects of A and B rating is in relation to Tier 2. Where the applicant must show that he has sufficient funds to support himself (the maintenance requirement) he may rely on an A rated sponsor to guarantee that they (the employer) will fulfil the maintenance requirement in the absence of the applicant's ability to do so.

Documentary evidence and Home Office guidance

One of the features of the new PBS is that the immigration rules set out the criteria governing whether an application will succeed, but the rules also specify that evidence specified in Home Office guidance must be submitted in order to satisfy the Home Office that the relevant criteria are met:

> 245AA. Documentary evidence
>
> (a) Where Part 6A or Appendices A to C, or E of these Rules state that specified documents must be provided, that means documents specified by the Secretary of State in the Points Based System Policy Guidance as being specified documents for the route under which the applicant is applying. If the specified documents are not provided, the applicant will not meet the requirement for which the specified documents are required as evidence.
>
> (b) If the Entry Clearance Officer or Secretary of State has reasonable cause to doubt the genuineness of any document submitted by an applicant which is, or which purports to be, a specified document under Part 6A or Appendices A to C, or E of these Rules and having taken reasonable steps to verify the document, is unable to verify that it is genuine, the document will be discounted for the purposes of this application.
>
> (c) Where Part 6A or Appendices A to C, or E of these Rules refer to the United Kingdom Border Agency guidance, this means guidance published by the United Kingdom Border Agency for use by sponsors or migrants to ensure compliance with these Rules. If the sponsor or applicant does not satisfy the requirements set out in guidance and referred to in these Rules, the applicant will not meet the related requirement in these Rules.

These paragraphs of the Immigration Rules have caused considerable controversy, largely because the policy guidance is so extremely specific. For example, to prove maintenance under the Tier 1 (Post Study Work) category, the guidance read as follows at the time of writing:

> 103. Only the following specified documents will be accepted as evidence of this requirement:
>
> i) Personal bank or building society statements covering a consecutive 90 day period: The most recent statement must be dated no more than one calendar month before the date of application.
>
> The personal bank or building society statements should clearly show:
> o the applicant's name;
> o the account number;
> o the date of the statement;
> o the financial institution's name and logo;
> o any transactions during the 90 day period;
>
> If the applicant wishes to submit electronic bank statements from an online account these must contain all of the details listed above. In addition, the applicant will need to provide either:

> o a supporting letter from his/her bank, on company headed paper, confirming the authenticity of the statements; or
> o an electronic bank statement bearing the official stamp of the bank in question will be accepted. This stamp should appear on every page of the statement.
>
> We will not accept statements which show the balance in the account on a particular day as these documents do not show that the applicant holds enough funds for the full period needed...

This is only the first of four forms of evidence that are considered acceptable. As can be seen, the requirements are extremely precise, and it is not hard to imagine what would otherwise be considered perfectly satisfactory evidence not meeting these requirements. Many immigrants who would be said to meet the substantive requirements of the PBS scheme have failed simply because they misunderstood the guidance or were unable to obtain the requisite paperwork.

In the case of *NA & others (Tier 1 Post study work funds)* [2009] UKAIT 00025 the tribunal interpreted the rules to have successfully incorporated the policy guidance, giving the policy guidance the same status as the rules. The consequence was that failure to comply with the policy guidance had the same result as failure to comply with the rules: any application or appeal was doomed to fail.

In the case of *Pankina* [2010] EWCA Civ 719 the Court of Appeal took the opposite view and held that the policy guidance is just guidance. It does not have the status of law and must therefore be interpreted sensibly and flexibly. The effect of this judgment is that only the provisions of the Immigration Rules themselves are to be given a strict statutory-style interpretation. The specific provisions of the guidance under challenge in *Pankina* was the requirement to have held the necessary level of funds for at least three months prior to making an application. This requirement featured only in the policy guidance. The Immigration Rules themselves stated only that an applicant must hold a certain level of funds. The effect of *Pankina* was that the funds must be held at the time of application, but not for the three preceding months.

A very similar judgment swiftly followed *Pankina*, in *R (on the application of English UK) v SSHD* [2010] EWHC 1726 (Admin), in which Mr Justice Foskett similarly held unlawful requirements set out in the policy guidance in respect of a mandatory minimum level of English for those wanting to study English language in the UK but which did not feature in the Immigration Rules themselves.

The Home Office responded quickly to these judgments and laid Statement of Changes HC 382. As of 23 July 2010, the three month rule on holding funds and the mandatory minimum level of English were introduced into the main Immigration Rules themselves.

One aspect of the tribunal's determination in *NA* that did survive *Pankina* was that relating to the date of assessment of the facts of the case. The tribunal held that an applicant can succeed on appeal by submitting post-decision evidence, but only if it showed that at the time of the application the applicant met the necessary criteria. It is not possible to succeed on appeal by submitting evidence that shows that at the date of the appeal the applicant meets the necessary criteria.

Section 19 of the Borders Act 2007 is designed to restrict the admissibility of post decision evidence in in-country appeal cases but this is yet to be brought into force.

> **Example**
>
> As can be seen, the guidance requires that for certain types of application three months of bank statements presented in a particular way and covering a three month period specified by reference to the date of the application must be submitted.
>
> If these documents are not included with the application, UKBA will inevitably refuse the application.
>
> On appeal, the tribunal will need to examine whether the specified documents can now be provided for the relevant dates prior to the application to UKBA. However, the tribunal is not permitted to allow the appeal on the grounds that the documents can now be provided *for the three months prior to the appeal hearing*.

Overstaying and extension applications

Overstaying is always unwise. It is a criminal offence (see chapter on criminal offences), albeit rarely one that is prosecuted, and it also leads to loss of appeal rights. Often overstaying will also leads to a loss of the right to make an in-country immigration application, as many immigration categories require the applicant to possess a particular type of leave.

Under the Points Based System, the requirements for extension applications explicitly allow for out of time applications. The relevant rules require that an application possesses *or was last granted* particular types of leave.

Before commencement of the PBS, Lord Bassam stated (Hansard, 17 March 2008, columns 97-98) that Home Office policy would be that late applications would be considered if submitted within 28 days of the expiry of leave. After that, applications would be considered if submitted up to six months late, if there were exceptional circumstances. In the event, implementation was in fact more generous than this and the Immigration Rules simply state that a person must have *or have last been granted* leave in certain immigration categories. This enables overstayers to apply for PBS visas in country, providing they were last granted leave in a relevant category. This also offers a solution to those caught out by the strict provisions of the PBS: simply re-apply.

Note that overstaying in excess of 28 days risks engaging immigration rule 320(7B) if the person departs from the UK and seeks re-entry. This provision is not applied where a grant of leave has been made subsequent to the overstaying, however.

> **Top tip**
>
> Some immigrants and advisers have found that it is possible to mitigate the effects of the stringent requirements of the PBS by lodging what may prove to be a hopeless appeal and in the time it takes the appeal to be listed ensuring that the PBS requirements are complied with, for example that the bank account never drops below £800.
>
> If the appeal fails, an out of time application can then be made within 28 days with all the documents in order. Applications cannot be made while there is an outstanding appeal: section 3C 1971 Act.

Tier 1: highly skilled

The different categories within Tier 1 are as follows:

Tier 1

General	Entrepreneur	Investor	Post Study Work
• Highly skilled individuals • Points for qualifications, attributes, age, income • No sponsor	• Setting up or taking over a business • Minimum level of investment £200,000 • Create 2 jobs	• Personal assets at least £2 million • Minimum investment at least £1 million	• UK degree

Tier 1 (General)

The highly skilled worker category of Tier 1 (General) is designed to allow highly skilled people to come to the United Kingdom to look for work or self-employment opportunities. Unlike the work permits or business people schemes, applicants do not need a job offer or detailed business plan to apply for Tier 1 (General) - highly skilled worker. On application they will be awarded points based on education, previous earnings, United Kingdom experience, age, English language, and available maintenance (funds). The applicant must score one hundred points.

The points criteria have changed several times since inception and the most recent changes at the time of writing took effect on 7 April 2010. **The information in the tables below is illustrative and relates to new first time applications on or since 31 March 2010.** Different tables, set out in the appendices to the Immigration Rules, may apply to applicants seeking extensions of stay who originally applied before 31 March 2010.

Eligibility for extensions of leave

It is only possible to apply for an extension of leave as a Tier 1 (General) migrant if the applicant possesses *or was last granted leave* in one of the following categories:

- (i) as a Highly Skilled Migrant,
- (ii) as a Tier 1 (General) Migrant,
- (iii) as an Innovator,
- (iv) as a Participant in the Fresh Talent: Working in Scotland Scheme,
- (v) as a Participant in the International Graduates Scheme (or its predecessor, the Science and Engineering Graduates Scheme),
- (vi) as a Postgraduate Doctor or Dentist,
- (vii) as a Student,
- (viii) as a Student Nurse,
- (ix) as a Student Re-Sitting an Examination,
- (x) as a Student Writing-Up a Thesis,
- (xi) as a Work Permit Holder,
- (xii) as a Businessperson,
- (xiii) as a Self-employed Lawyer,
- (xiv) as a Tier 1 (Entrepreneur) Migrant,
- (xv) as a Tier 1 (Investor) Migrant,
- (xvi) as a Tier 1 (Post-Study Work) Migrant,
- (xvii) as a Writer, Composer or Artist,
- (xviii) as a Tier 2 Migrant, or
- (xix) as a Tier 4 Migrant.

Illegal entrants are barred from applying for leave to remain.

Qualifications

Qualification	Points
Bachelor's degree	30
Master's degree	35
PhD	45

Specified documents must be provided as evidence of the qualification, unless the applicant has, or was last granted, leave as a Highly Skilled Migrant or a Tier 1 (General) Migrant and previously scored points for the same qualification in respect of which points are being claimed in this application.

Points will only be awarded for a qualification if an applicant's qualification is deemed by the National Recognition Information Centre for the United Kingdom (UK NARIC) to meet or exceed the recognised standard of a Master's degree or a PhD in the UK. Points will also be awarded for vocational and professional qualifications that are deemed by UK NARIC to be equivalent to a Master's degree or a PhD in the UK. The advice if the qualification does not appear on the points-based calculator is to contact UK NARIC directly.

If the applicant has, or was last granted, leave as a Tier 1 (General) Migrant or a Highly Skilled Migrant and the qualification for which points are now claimed was, in the applicant's last successful application for leave or for a Highly Skilled Migrant Programme Approval Letter, assessed to be of a higher level than now indicated by UK NARIC, the higher score of points will be awarded in this application too.

Earnings

Previous earnings	Points
£25,000-£29,999	5
£30,000-£34,999	15
£35,000-£39,999	20
£40,000-£49,999	25
£50,000-£54,999	30
£55,000-£64,999	35
£65,000-£74,999	40
£75,000-£149,999	45
£150,000 or more	75

In order to reflect differences in income levels across the world, the income level required to score points varies depending on where the applicant was working at the time the earnings were made. The Agency uses a series of uplift ratios to bring overseas salaries in line with their UK equivalents. The level of uplift received is dependent on the average level of income received in the country in which the earnings were made, and appears at Table 2A of Appendix A (Attributes) to the immigration rules.

The country in which the applicant has been working, rather than their nationality, determines the income bands against which the earnings will be assessed.

Earnings do not include unearned sources of income (allowances, expenses, dividends, interest, inheritance etc) but do include:

- gross salaries (includes full-time, part-time and bonuses),
- earnings derived through self-employment (pre tax),
- earnings derived through business activities (pre-tax),
- statutory and contractual maternity pay, statutory and contractual adoption pay,
- allowances (such as accommodation, schooling or car allowances) which form part of an applicant's remuneration package,
- dividends from investments, where it is a company in which the applicant is active in the day-to-day management, or where the applicant receives the dividend as part of their remuneration package,
- property rental income, where this constitutes part of the applicant's business, and
- payments in lieu of notice.

Earnings will not be taken into account if the applicant was in breach of the UK's immigration laws at the time those earnings were made.

UK experience

Applications for entry clearance and all other applications for leave to remain	Points
If the qualification was obtained in the UK	5
If £25,000 or more of the previous earnings for which points are claimed were earned in the UK	5

Points will only be awarded for UK experience in respect of qualifications obtained in the UK if:

    (a)   (i) the qualification is a Bachelor's or Master's degree or a PhD, and is deemed by UK NARIC to meet or exceed the recognised standard of a Bachelor's or Master's degree or a PhD in the UK, or
(ii) the qualification is a vocational or professional qualification and is deemed by the appropriate UK professional body to meet or exceed the recognised standard of a Bachelor's or Master's degree or a PhD in the UK,

(b) the qualification was awarded no more than 5 years before the application was made, and

(c) at least 1 academic year, or 3 consecutive terms, of the course that led to the qualification involved full-time study in the UK.

The date the qualification is awarded is the date on which the applicant was first notified in writing, by the awarding institution, that the qualification had been awarded.

The qualification for which UK experience points are claimed can be, but does not have to be, the same as the qualification for which points are claimed under table 1.

Previous earnings will not be taken into account for the purpose of awarding points for UK experience if the applicant was in breach of the UK's immigration laws at the time those earnings were made.

Age

Applications for entry clearance and leave to remain (unless the applicant falls into the boxes below)	Points
Under 30 years of age	20
30 to 34 years of age	10
35 to 39 years of age	5

Different ages apply for extension applications, otherwise an applicant might succeed in gaining entry with age as a necessary contributor only to fail in applying for an extension purely because he or she is two years older. Sensibly, for extension applications the ages are two years older than those above in order to gain the same number of points.

Maintenance (funds)

An applicant applying for entry clearance or leave to remain as a Tier 1 (General) Migrant must score 10 points for funds.

10 points will only be awarded if an applicant:

(a) applying for entry clearance has £2,800 in funds and provides the specified documents, or

(b) applying for leave to remain, has £800 of funds and provides the specified documents

The level of funds have to have been held for at least three months prior to the date of application. If the funds dip below the required level on the specified documents, the application will be refused.

Language

An applicant applying for entry clearance or leave to remain as a Tier 1 (General) migrant must have 10 points for English language.

10 points must be scored in this category by showing that the migrant is able to speak English to a basic standard. This is a mandatory requirement. This will include an ability to understand and use familiar everyday expressions, basic phrases and to be able to introduce themselves and others, and be able to answer basic personal questions.

The migrant will need to show competence in the English language by:

- passing a test in English equivalent to the appropriate level;
- coming from a majority English speaking country; or
- having taken a degree taught in English (verified using national academic recognition information centre data).

Further details on each of these routes are available in the rules themselves.

Alternatively, if applying for an extension, the migrant can score 10 points if he or she has, or was last granted, leave as a Tier 1 (General) Migrant, or has, or was last granted, leave as a Highly Skilled Migrant, if that leave was granted under the rules at a time when they included the changes which came into force on 5 December 2006.

Tier 1 (Entrepreneur)

This part of the PBS replaces the business person and innovator parts of the old immigration rules. It is to enable a migrant to come to or stay in the UK to invest in or set up a business with a substantial investment of his or her own money.

A business is defined as an enterprise as a sole trader, a partnership or a company registered in the UK.

Points are awarded for various qualities, but unlike for the Tier 1 (General) category, all of the criteria are mandatory: every available point must be obtained and there is no possibility of obtaining points in some fields but not in others. Describing it as a 'points based' application is therefore rather meaningless, in fact.

Eligibility for extensions of leave

To apply for an extension of leave as a Tier 1 (Entrepreneur) the applicant must possess or last have been granted leave in one of the following categories:

    (i)   as a Highly Skilled Migrant,

(ii) as a Tier 1 (General) Migrant,
(iii) as a Tier 1 (Entrepreneur) Migrant,
(iv) as a Tier 1 (Investor) Migrant,
(v) as a Tier 1 (Post-Study Work) Migrant,
(vi) as a Businessperson,
(vii) as an Innovator,
(viii) as an Investor,
(ix) as a Participant in the Fresh Talent: Working in Scotland Scheme,
(x) as a Participant in the International Graduates Scheme (or its predecessor, the Science and Engineering Graduates Scheme),
(xi) as a Postgraduate Doctor or Dentist,
(xii) as a Self-employed Lawyer,
(xiii) as a Student,
(xiv) as a Student Nurse,
(xv) as a Student Re-sitting an Examination,
(xvi) as a Student Writing Up a Thesis,
(xvii) as a Work Permit Holder,
(xviii) as a Writer, Composer or Artist,
(xix) as a Tier 2 Migrant, or
(xx) as a Tier 4 Migrant.

Illegal entrants are barred from applying for leave to remain.

First time applications

Migrants applying for the first time for entry as a Tier 1 (Entrepreneur) must score all of the following points:

Investment	Points
The applicant has access to not less than £200,000	25
The money is held in one or more regulated financial institutions	25
The money is disposable in the UK	25

Specified documents must be provided as evidence of any investment.

A regulated financial institution is one which is regulated by the appropriate regulatory body for the country in which the financial institution operates. For example, where a financial institution does business in the UK, the appropriate regulator is the Financial Services Authority.

Money is disposable in the UK if all of the money is held in a UK based financial institution or if the money is freely transferable to the UK and convertible to sterling. Funds in a foreign currency will be converted to pounds sterling (£) using the spot exchange rate which appeared on www.oanda.com on the date on which the application was made.

Extension applications

Migrants who possess or were last granted leave as a Tier 1 (Entrepreneur), businessperson or innovator must score all of the points from the following table:

Investment and business activity	Points
The applicant has invested, or had invested on his behalf, not less than £200,000 in cash directly into one or more businesses in the UK.	20

The applicant has:
    (a) registered with HM Revenue and Customs as self-employed, or
    (b) registered a new business in which he is a director, or
    (c) registered as a director of an existing business.
Where the applicant's last grant of entry clearance, leave to enter or leave to remain was as a Tier 1 (Entrepreneur) Migrant, the above condition must have been met within 3 months of his entry to the UK (if he was granted entry clearance as a Tier 1 (Entrepreneur) Migrant and there is evidence to establish his date of arrival to the UK), or, in any other case, the date of the grant of leave to remain.
	20

The applicant is engaged in business activity at the time of his application for leave to remain.	15

The applicant has:
    (a) established a new business or businesses that has or have created the equivalent of at least two new full time jobs for persons settled in the UK, or
    (b) taken over or joined an existing business or businesses and his services or investment have resulted in a net increase in the employment provided by the business or businesses for persons settled in the UK by creating the equivalent of at least two new full time jobs.
Where the applicant's last grant of entry clearance or leave to enter or remain was as a Tier 1 (Entrepreneur) Migrant, the jobs must have existed for at least 12 months of the period for which the previous leave was granted.
	20

Documentary evidence must be provided in all cases. Specified documents must be provided as evidence of any investment and business activity that took place when the applicant had leave as a Tier 1 (Entrepreneur) Migrant.

The investment must not include the value of any residential accommodation, property development or property management. The investment must not be in the form of a director's loan, unless it is unsecured and in favour of the business.

A full time job is one involving at least 30 hours' work a week. Two or more part time jobs that add up to 30 hours a week will count as one full time job. Where the applicant's last grant of entry clearance or leave was as a Tier 1 (Entrepreneur) Migrant, the jobs must have existed for a total of at least 12 months during the period during which the migrant had leave in that category. This need not consist of 12 consecutive months and the jobs need not exist at the date of application, provided they existed for at least 12 months during the period of leave that the migrant is seeking to extend.

Maintenance

If applying for entry clearance, the applicant must show £2,800 of personal savings, which have to have been held for at least three months prior to the date of application. This level of funds must be proven using specified documents, and the level of funds must not dip below £2,800 during the three month period.

If applying for leave to enter, the applicant must show £800 in personal savings, which has to have been held for at least three months prior to making the application. As with entry clearance applications, the funds must not drop below the specified level and specified documents must be submitted as proof of funds.

Language

As above for Tier 1 (General), the applicant will need to show competence in the English language by:

- passing a test in English equivalent to the appropriate level;
- coming from a majority English speaking country; or
- having taken a degree taught in English (verified using national academic recognition information centre data).

Further details on each of these routes are available in the rules themselves.

Tier 1 (Investor)

This category replaces the old investor immigration rule. It exists to enable very high net worth individuals to obtain leave if a substantial investment is made in various specified ways in the UK

Eligibility for extensions of leave

Migrants who have or were last granted leave in the following categories can apply for an extension as a Tier 1 (Investor):

(i) as a Highly Skilled Migrant,
(ii) as a Tier 1 (General) Migrant,
(iii) as a Tier 1 (Entrepreneur) Migrant,
(iv) as a Tier 1 (Investor) Migrant,
(v) as a Tier 1 (Post-Study Work) Migrant,
(vi) as a Businessperson,
(vii) as an Innovator,
(viii) as an Investor,
(ix) as a Student,
(x) as a Student Nurse,
(xi) as a Student Re-Sitting an Examination,
(xii) as a Student Writing Up a Thesis,
(xiii) as a Work Permit Holder,
(xiv) as a Writer, Composer or Artist,
(xv) as a Tier 2 Migrant, or
(xvi) as a Tier 4 Migrant.

Illegal entrants are barred from applying for extensions of leave.

First time applications

Those applying for the first time as a Tier 1 (Investor) must meet all of the following requirements, thereby scoring 75 points:

Assets	Points
The applicant: (a) has money of his own under his control held in a regulated financial institution and disposable in the UK amounting to not less than £1 million; or (b) (i) owns personal assets which, taking into account any liabilities to which they are subject, have a value exceeding £2 million, and (ii) has money under his control held in a regulated financial institution and disposable in the UK amounting to not less than £1 million which has been loaned to him by a financial institution regulated by the Financial Services Authority.	75

A grant of two years will be made where the criteria are fulfilled. However, the Tier 1 (Investor) rules include a specific proviso regarding curtailment. Leave to enter or remain as a Tier 1 (Investor) Migrant may be curtailed if within 3 months of the entry, the grant of entry clearance or the grant of leave to remain, the applicant has not invested, or had invested on his behalf, at least £750,000 of his capital in the UK by way of UK Government bonds, share capital or loan capital in active and trading UK registered companies other than those principally engaged in property investment.

Specified documents must be provided as evidence of investment.

Money is disposable in the UK if all of the money is held in a UK based financial institution or if the money is freely transferable to the UK and convertible to sterling. Funds in a foreign currency will be converted to pounds sterling (£) using the spot exchange rate which appeared on www.oanda.com on the date on which the application was made.

'Money of his own', 'personal assets' and 'his capital' include money or assets belonging to the applicant's spouse, civil partner or unmarried or same-sex partner, provided that specified documents are provided to show that the money or assets are under the applicant's control and that he is free to invest them.

Investment excludes investment by the applicant by way of deposits with a bank, building society or other enterprise whose normal course of business includes the acceptance of deposits.

Extension applications

Where an extension application is granted, a period of three years of leave will be granted where the applicant is already a Tier 1 (Investor) – making five years in total, so that the person is eligible to apply for settlement. A period of two years will be granted in other cases where the person is switching into this category for the first time.

Where an extension application is made by a Tier 1 (Investor), all of the following points must be obtained:

Assets and investment	Points
The applicant: (a) has money of his own under his control in the UK amounting to not less than £1 million, or (b) (i) owns personal assets which, taking into account any liabilities to which they are subject, have a value of not less than £2 million, and (ii) has money under his control and disposable in the UK amounting to not less than £1 million which has been loaned to him by a financial institution regulated by the Financial Services Authority.	30
The applicant has invested not less than £750,000 of his capital in the UK by way of UK Government bonds, share capital or loan capital in active and trading UK registered companies other than those principally engaged in property investment.	30
The investment referred to above was made within 3 months of his entry to the UK (if he was granted entry clearance as a as a Tier 1 (Investor) Migrant and there is evidence to establish his date of arrival to the UK), or the date of the grant of entry clearance as a Tier 1 (Investor) Migrant and there is no evidence to establish his date of arrival to the UK), or, in any other case, the date of the grant of leave to remain Tier 1 (Investor) Migrant and the investment has been maintained for the whole of the remaining period of that leave; or The migrant has, or was last granted, entry clearance, leave to enter or leave to remain as an Investor.	15

Where an extension application is made by an investor (the category under the old immigration rules), all of the points in the following table must be obtained:

Assets and investment	Points
The applicant: (a) has money of his own under his control in the UK amounting to not less than £1 million, or (b) (i) owns personal assets which, taking into account any liabilities to which they are subject, have a value of not less than £2 million, and (ii) has money under his control and disposable in the UK amounting to not less than £1 million which has been loaned to him by a financial institution regulated by the Financial Services Authority.	30
The applicant has invested not less than £750,000 of his capital in the UK by way of UK Government bonds, share capital or loan capital in active and trading UK registered companies other than those principally engaged in property investment.	30
The investment referred to above was made within 3 months of his entry to the UK (if he was granted entry clearance as a as a Tier 1 (Investor) Migrant and there is evidence to establish his date of arrival to the UK), or the date of the grant of entry clearance as a Tier 1 (Investor) Migrant and there is no evidence to establish his date of arrival to the UK), or, in any other case, the date of the grant of leave to remain Tier 1 (Investor) Migrant and the investment has been maintained for the whole of the remaining period of that leave; or The migrant has, or was last granted, entry clearance, leave to enter or leave to remain as an Investor.	15

Maintenance

Sensibly, there are no maintenance requirements for the Tier 1 (Investor) category.

Language

There are also no language requirements for the Tier 1 (Investor) category.

Tier 1 (Post study work)

This category replaces the International Graduates Scheme and its predecessors and the Scottish Fresh Talent scheme. It enables graduates of UK universities to apply to remain in the UK to work for up to two years. For many, this will make a later Tier 1 or Tier 2 application feasible if desired.

Those already previously granted leave under the Tier 1 (PSW), IGS or FT schemes are not eligible to apply for leave to enter. However, those who were not granted two years' leave in these categories may be eligible under the transitional arrangements for an extension of leave to remain.

Eligibility for extensions of leave

Migrants in possession of or who were last granted leave in the following categories are eligible to apply for an extension of leave as a Tier 1 (PSW) migrant:

(i) as a Participant in the Fresh Talent: Working in Scotland Scheme (but only if the applicant is a British National (Overseas), British overseas territories citizen, British Overseas citizen, British protected person or a British subject),

(ii) as a Participant in the International Graduates Scheme (or its predecessor, the Science and Engineering Graduates Scheme),

(iii) as a Student, provided the applicant has not previously been granted leave in any of the categories referred to in paragraphs (i) and (ii) above,

(iv) as a Student Nurse, provided the applicant has not previously been granted leave in any of the categories referred to in paragraphs (i) and (ii) above,

(v) as a Student Re-Sitting an Examination, provided the applicant has not previously been granted leave in any of the categories referred to in paragraphs (i) and (ii) above,

(vi) as a Student Writing Up a Thesis, provided the applicant has not previously been granted leave as a Tier 1 Migrant or in any of the categories referred to in paragraphs (i) and (ii) above, or

(vii) as a Tier 4 Migrant, provided the applicant has not previously been granted leave as a Tier 1 (Post-Study Work) Migrant or in any of the categories referred to in paragraphs (i) and (ii) above

Qualifications

75 points must be scored from the following table:

Qualifications	Points
The applicant has been awarded: (a) a UK recognised bachelor or postgraduate degree, or (b) a UK postgraduate certificate in education, or (c) a Higher National Diploma ('HND') from a Scottish institution.	20
(a) The applicant studied for his award at a UK institution that is a UK recognised or listed body, or which holds a sponsor licence under Tier 4 of the Points Based System, or (b) If the applicant is claiming points for having been awarded a Higher National Diploma from a Scottish Institution, he studied for that diploma at a Scottish publicly funded institution of further or higher education, or a Scottish bona fide private education institution which maintains satisfactory records of enrolment and attendance.	20
The applicant's periods of UK study and/or research towards his eligible award were undertaken whilst he had entry clearance, leave to enter or leave to remain in the UK: (a) as a Student or as a Tier 4 migrant, or (b) under part 8 of these rules.	20
The applicant made the application for entry clearance or leave to remain as a Tier 1 (Post-Study Work) Migrant within 12 months of obtaining the relevant qualification.	15
The applicant is applying for leave to remain and has, or was last granted, leave as a Participant in the International Graduates Scheme (or its predecessor, the Science and Engineering Graduates Scheme) or as a Participant in the Fresh Talent: Working in Scotland Scheme.	75

It is also possible to obtain 75 points by being awarded an MBA qualification from one of the institutions in Appendix A of the Immigration Rules at paragraph 58A.

Specified documents must be provided as evidence of any of the above qualifications.

A qualification will be deemed to have been obtained on the date on which the applicant was first notified in writing, by the awarding institution, that the qualification had been awarded.

A 'UK recognised body' is an institution that has been granted degree awarding powers by either a Royal Charter, an Act of Parliament or the Privy Council. 'UK listed body' is an institution that is not a UK recognised body but which provides full courses that lead to the award of a degree by a UK recognised body. To qualify as an HND from a Scottish institution, a qualification must be at level 8 on the Scottish Credit and Qualifications Framework.

Maintenance

If applying for entry clearance, the applicant must show £2,800 of personal savings, which have to have been held for at least three months prior to the date of application. This level of funds must be proven using specified documents, and the level of funds must not dip below £2,800 during the three month period.

If applying for leave to enter, the applicant must show £800 in personal savings, which has to have been held for at least three months prior to making the application. As with entry clearance applications, the funds must not drop below the specified level and specified documents must be submitted as proof of funds.

Language

As with other Tier 1 categories, the applicant will need to show competence in the English language by:

- passing a test in English equivalent to the appropriate level;
- coming from a majority English speaking country; or
- having taken a degree taught in English (verified using national academic recognition information centre data).

Further details on each of these routes are available in the rules themselves.

Tier 2: skilled workers

Outline

Tier 2 allows employers to recruit individuals from outside the United Kingdom and European Economic Area (EEA) to fill a particular job that cannot be filled by a British or EEA worker. It replaced a number of immigration categories, including:

- work permit employment (excluding temporary assignments of sportspersons and entertainers);
- ministers of religion;
- airport-based operational ground staff;
- overseas qualified nurse or midwife;
- sabbatical posts;
- seafarers;
- named researchers;
- Training and Work Experience Scheme (TWES);
- Jewish agency employees;
- overseas representatives (news media).

Tier 2 is broken down into the following four subcategories:

Tier 2

General	Intra Company Transfer	Sportsperson	Minister of religion
•Skilled workers •Sponsor necessary •Must pass resident labour test •Or fill shortage occupation	•Employees of multinational firms •Sponsor necessary •6 months prior employment with firm •Limited possibilities to stay	•Sponsor necessary •Internationally established at highest level •Must make significant contribution	•Sponsor necessary •Preaching and pastoral work, missionaries or members of religious orders

Those wishing to apply under any of the Tier 2 categories will have to have a job offer and a sponsor licensed by the Home Office supporting their application. Some additional work beyond that named in the certificate of sponsorship may be undertaken, although there are strict conditions.

Following a successful application, Tier 2 migrants are granted either a period of leave equivalent to the length of their employment contract plus one month or a period of three years plus one month – whichever is shorter.

To be eligible for Tier 2 an applicant needs to have:

(i) a job offer;

(ii) certificate of sponsorship from one of a licensed sponsor; and

(iii) scored enough points to apply.

The pass mark for points is 70 points from the three sets of criteria. These three main criteria are:

(i) attributes (50 points)

(ii) English language skills (10 points)

(iii) Maintenance (10 points)

In addition, for Tier 2 (General) there is a resident labour test, unless the job in question features on the shortage occupation list, which is regularly changed. This test ensures that resident workers have had the opportunity to apply for the job.

Sponsorship

All Tier 2 applicants need their prospective employer to have obtained a certificate of sponsorship. It is compulsory for all applicants to score points in the 'sponsorship' attributes category, and to do so the applicant will need to provide a valid Certificate of Sponsorship reference number for sponsorship in the sub-category of Tier 2 under which he is applying.

The detail of the processes through which an employer must go in order to become a registered sponsor are beyond the scope of this section but are covered in more detail above in relation to sponsorship generally under the PBS.

There are, inevitably, rules on when certificates of sponsorship are valid and invalid. For example, the certificate of sponsorship reference number must be used within 3 months of issue, the application for entry clearance must be made no more than 3 months before the commencement of employment and the reference number can potentially be cancelled by the Home Office between issue and usage, rendering it invalid at the time of use.

Tier 2 (General)

To satisfy this test, the employer must have advertised the job in JobCentre Plus or advertised the job as agreed in a sector specific Code of Practice, for at least 4 weeks. If the prospective earnings for the job are over £40,000 then there is less likelihood of undercutting the resident labour market, but even these jobs have to be advertised in JobCentre Plus or as agreed in the Code of Practice for a minimum period of one week. When a Sponsor issues a Certificate of Sponsorship on the Sponsor Management System they are required to confirm that a Resident Labour Market Test has been conducted or that it does not apply to the application.

The resident labour market test is not required where the migrant has entered under Tier 1 - Post-Study Work category, which aims to retain the most able international graduates who have studied in the UK. This is intended only as a bridge to other categories and people with Post Study Worker leave will be able to switch into Tier 2 once they find suitable employment. Such individuals, being already part of the resident labour market, will not need to meet the resident labour market test once they have been doing a job for at least six months.

Attributes

50 points must be scored in this category. There are once again three criteria. These are:
 (i) sponsorship;
 (ii) qualifications;
 (iii) prospective earnings.

Table 10 of Appendix A of the immigration rules sets out the way in which points can be earned for attributes under Tier 2:

Sponsorship	Points
Shortage occupation	50
Job Offer passes Resident Labour Market Test	30
Intra Company Transfer	25
Post Study Work	30

Qualifications	Points
None or below GCE A-level	0
GCE A-level	5
Bachelor's Degree	10
Masters or PhD	15

Prospective Earnings	Points
>£20,000	0
£20,000-23,999	10
£24,000-27,999	15
£28,000-31,999	20
£32,000+	25

Specified documents must be provided as evidence before points will be awarded.

For qualifications, an 'appropriate sub-degree level qualification' means:

(a) 1 or more passes at GCSE A level, or

(b) a qualification obtained in the UK that is deemed by the appropriate qualifications framework in the part of the UK in which it was obtained (as set out in United Kingdom Border Agency guidance) to be equivalent to, or higher than, (a) but below degree level.

A qualification has to be recognised by UK NARIC or UKBA in guidance. Points will be awarded for a vocational or professional qualification if the qualification is recognised by UK NARIC or the appropriate professional body or the qualification is below the recognised standard of or Master's degree, or a PhD, in the UK, but the applicant submits the specified evidence to prove it is an appropriate sub-degree level qualification.

In respect of earnings, the points awarded are based on the applicant's gross annual salary (including allowances specified as acceptable for this purpose in UKBA guidance). Where the applicant is paid hourly, points will only be awarded for earnings up to a maximum of 48 hours a week, even if the applicant works for longer than this.

Maintenance

10 points can be scored in this category by showing that the immigrant is able to support themselves whilst in the United Kingdom.

To score them they will need to show they have

- £800 in savings that available for use while in the United Kingdom; (Appendix C of the Immigration Rules)

- plus a further £533 for each dependant (Appendix E of the Immigration Rules)

English language skills

10 points must be scored in this category by showing that the migrant is able to speak English to a basic standard. This is a mandatory requirement. This will include an ability to understand and use familiar everyday expressions, basic phrases and to be able to introduce themselves and others, and be able to answer basic personal questions.

The migrant will need to show competence in the English language by:

- passing a test in English equivalent to the appropriate level;

- coming from a majority English speaking country; or

- having taken a degree taught in English (verified using national academic recognition information centre data).

Extensions for Tier 2

The extension test is similar to the initial entry test, which will include the certificate of sponsorship and points scoring. Table 11 of Appendix A of the rules is used to assess extension applications, and similar rules and guidance apply as for initial applications regarding providing specified documents and so forth.

Migrants with leave (or who were last granted leave) in the following categories may apply for extensions as Tier 2 (General), (Sportsperson) or (Entertainer) migrants:
(i) as a Tier 1 Migrant,
(ii) as a Tier 2 Migrant,
(iii) as a Highly Skilled Migrant,

(iv)   as an Innovator,
(v)   as a Jewish Agency Employee,
(vi)   as a Member of the Operational Ground Staff of an Overseas-owned Airline,
(vii) as a Minister of Religion, Missionary or Member of a Religious Order,
(viii) as an Overseas Qualified Nurse or Midwife,
(ix)   as a Participant in the Fresh Talent: Working in Scotland Scheme,
(x)   as a Participant in the International Graduates Scheme (or its predecessor, the Science and Engineering Graduates Scheme),
(xi)   as a Person Writing Up a Thesis,
(xii) as a Postgraduate Doctor or Dentist,
(xiii) as a Qualifying Work Permit Holder,
(xiv) as a Representative of an Overseas Newspaper, News Agency or Broadcasting Organisation,
(xv)   as a Student,
(xvi) as a Student Re-Sitting an Examination,
(xvii) as a Student Nurse,
(xviii) as a Student Union Sabbatical Officer,
(xix) as a Tier 4 Migrant, or
(xx)   as a Tier 5 (Temporary Worker) Migrant (only applies to a limited group).

Only persons with leave as a Tier 2 (Intra-company transfer) migrant or qualifying work permit holder may apply for extensions as a Tier 2 (ICT) and the person must still be working for the same employer as previously.

Settlement

A continuous period of five years in the United Kingdom must be completed before an application for settlement is possible. Time spent in Tier 2 will count towards the eligibility period.

Tier 2 (Intra-company transfer)

If the migrant is already working for a company in another country and they are transferring to a post in the United Kingdom with the same company, they can apply under the intra-company transfer category under Tier 2 - skilled worker. They must have worked overseas for the sponsoring organisation for at least twelve months and when in the United Kingdom they will earn a salary (including specific permitted allowances) appropriate for that job in the United Kingdom. The job must be at national vocation qualification level 3 (NVQ3) or above.

Rules introduced in March 2010 have tightened up the ICT route, which no longer leads to potential settlement in the UK for new entrants. In addition, shorter grants of leave were introduced for certain categories of ICT case, the Graduate Trainee and Skills Transfer categories.

Tier 2 (Sportsperson)

An applicant can score points by being sponsored by a club (or equivalent), licensed by the Home Office, to issue certificates of sponsorship under this category.

As with the rest of Tier 2, the Migrant requires a valid certificate of sponsorship.

Qualification will be for individuals who

- are qualified to do the job in question;
- intend to base themselves in the United Kingdom;
- have been approved by a governing body for the sport;
- will comply with the conditions of their permission to stay and leave the United Kingdom when their leave expires.

They must possess an endorsement from the appropriate governing body for their sport to confirm that they are:

- internationally established at the highest level; and
- will make a significant contribution to the development of their sport at the highest level in the United Kingdom.

This endorsement will also confirm that it is appropriate to fill the post from outside the European Economic Area (EEA).

Migrants in this category need the same points, and hence savings, for themselves and dependants, as set out above for this category generally.

Applicants must score points set out above for this category generally. They will need to show that they are competent in the English language by:

- passing a test in English equivalent to the appropriate level;
- coming from a majority English speaking country; or
- having taken a degree taught in English (verified using national academic recognition information centre data).

Tier 2 (Ministers of Religion)

The category is intended for ministers of religion undertaking preaching and pastoral work, missionaries or members of religious orders. Those applying under the minister of religion category need to:

- be qualified to do the job in question;
- intend to base themselves in the United Kingdom;
- intend to comply with the conditions of permission to stay and leave the United Kingdom when their leave expires.

They have the same maintenance requirements as hold generally in this category.

As to English, they must score 10 points a level of English equivalent to the Council of Europe level B2.

Tier 4: students

The key features of the scheme are set out below. It will quickly become apparent that the scheme is not properly one that can in fact be described as 'points based'. The fiction of points is maintained, but the reality is that there are inflexible requirements that must be met.

There are two types of student visa under Tier 4: child students and general students. There will continue to be student visitors and prospective students outside Tier 4, however.

Tier 4

General	Child students
• Most adult students will fall into this category • Sponsor is mandatory • Minimum course level applies • Variable maintenance depending on in or out of country application and in or out of London	• For students under the age of 18 studying at school in the UK

Requirement to have a sponsor

Before a student is eligible to apply to come to the UK to study under Tier 4, he or she must have an immigration sponsor. The sponsor is the education provider in the UK that has accepted the student on a course of study. Sponsoring education providers issue would-be students with a Confirmation of Acceptance for Studies (CAS).

The Home Office state that sponsorship plays two main roles in the application process:

(i) It provides an assurance that the education provider is confident that the student is capable of doing the particular course of study; and

(ii) It involves a pledge from the sponsoring education provider that it will accept responsibility for the student whilst he is in the UK.

Would-be students will not even be able to apply for a visa without a CAS. Education providers will not be able to issue a CAS without being licensed by the Home Office.

Licensing of sponsors

All education providers will need a UK Border Agency (UKBA) licence if they want to teach students from outside the EEA. This licensing process replaced the current Department for Innovation Universities and Skills (DIUS) Register of Education and Training Providers, which is now defunct.

To get a licence, all education providers need to show they are inspected or audited or hold valid accreditation with one of the UKBA approved accreditation bodies.

As with employers under Tier 2, there are two rankings of license:

- **A Rated Licence:** issued where the sponsor fully meets all of UKBA's licensing requirements;

- **B Rated Licence:** issued where the holder meets most of UKBA's licensing requirements but has some degree of weakness. This ranking is viewed as a temporary ranking that is intended to allow eligible sponsors to continue to sponsor migrants for visas whilst addressing their weaknesses. An action plan and timetable will be put in place when this ranking is awarded. It is expected that the sponsor will progress to an A rating if they complete this. If they fail to complete the action plan on time they will have their Licence revoked.

There are also now **Highly Trusted Sponsors** for Tier 4. Students of such institutions enjoy a slightly easier passage through the immigration application process in some respects.

The requirements to be imposed on sponsors are that they will need to:

(i) Keep a copy of all their non-EEA students' passports showing evidence of their entitlement to study;

(ii) Keep each student's contact details and update them as necessary;

(iii) Report to UKBA any students who fail to enrol on their course;

(iv) Report to UKBA any unauthorised student absences including a student who
- Fails to enrol with them by no later than 10 working days after the end of their prescribed enrolment period;
- Misses 10 expected contacts. For students in schools, Further Education (FE) and English Language Colleges this will normally be where the student has missed 2 weeks of a course. In the Higher Education (HE) sector, where daily registers are not kept UKBA will accept this reporting where the student has missed 10 expected interactions (e.g. Tutorials, submission of coursework etc);
- Stops attending either because they have withdrawn them from the course or because the student has said they are leaving, within 10 working days of this being confirmed;
- Defers their studies after their arrival in the UK. In such cases the student's permission to be in the UK will cease to be valid as they will no longer be actively studying. The sponsor will need to notify UKBA of the deferral and advise the student to leave the UK. When the student is ready to resume their studies they will need to make a fresh visa application.

(v) Report to UKBA any students who discontinue their studies (including any deferrals of study);

(vi) Report to UKBA any significant changes in students' circumstances, (e.g. if the duration of a course of study shortens);

(vii) Maintain any appropriate accreditation;

(viii) Offer courses to international students which comply with UKBA conditions;

(ix) Comply with applicable PBS rules and the law; and

(x) Co-operate with UKBA (whatever that means).

Should significant numbers of students drop out or fail to enrol with a particular education provider, this will raise concerns about the sponsor's recruitment processes and their overall suitability as a Licence holder. In these circumstances UKBA state they will investigate. If it transpires that it was due to poor administration, or deception on the part of the students, they will consider downgrading the Licence to B rated and will put in place an action plan to mitigate further abuse. If it appears that the Sponsor has been complicit in this abuse, UKBA will suspend their Licence immediately with a view to revoking it should the investigation provide satisfactory evidence to indicate this.

Visa application process

The increase in responsibilities on sponsors and tightening up of aspects of the student rules under the Points Based System is not to be balanced out with any relaxing of other requirements in the visa application process.

When the student applies for their entry clearance or visa, they will need a valid CAS from a licensed sponsor but UKBA will rigorously check all the documentation provided, including:

(i) Evidence of sufficient funds to pass a maintenance test; and

(ii) The education documents used to obtain the CAS from the sponsor, e.g. qualification certificates.

It was said in the Statement of Intent preceding the change in the rules that ECOs would concentrate on funds checks, detecting any fake or forged documents and the appropriate immigration checks to make sure the person does not have an adverse immigration history. Education providers are expected to check education certificates but ECOs verify the documents relied on by applicants.

The fingerprints of any applicants applying for a student visa will be checked and recorded. All students allowed to come to the UK will need to obtain a biometric identity card.

Visas are granted for the full duration of the course.

Out-of-country applicants can ask for one Administrative Review per application and in-country applicants can appeal, but it will be difficult for them to produce post-decision evidence (s.19 UK Borders Act 2007 once it comes into effect). However, reliance on NIAA s.85(4) which remains in force, should assist in these circumstances.

Tier 4 (General)

This is the category under which the vast majority of applications are made.

Eligibility

There are a number of general restrictions on applying under Tier 4 (General). This includes provisions for courses that are considered security-sensitive, for students in receipt of sponsorship from their home government and for post-graduate doctors and dentists.

The more commonly encountered restrictions are as follows:

- If the course is below degree level, the grant of entry clearance the applicant is seeking must not lead to the applicant having spent more than

3 years in the UK as a Tier 4 Migrant since the age of 18 studying courses that did not consist of degree level study.

- The applicant must be at least 16 years old for Tier 4 (General).

- Where the applicant is under 18 years of age, the application must be supported by the applicant's parents or legal guardian, or by just one parent if that parent has sole legal responsibility for the child.

- Where the applicant is under 18 years of age, the applicant's parents or legal guardian, or just one parent if that parent has sole responsibility for the child, must confirm that they consent to the arrangements for the applicant's travel to, and reception and care in the UK.

The immigration rules themselves specify that points have to be scored under certain paragraphs of Appendix A to the rules. However, on turning to the relevant Tier 4 section of Appendix A it transpires that 30 points are required and the points table reads as follows:

Criterion	Points awarded
CAS	30

It is therefore necessary to obtain a Confirmation of Acceptance for Studies (these documents replaced 'visa letters' in early 2010). In addition, the CAS must have been issued in the last 6 months, the offer must not have been withdrawn and the CAS has to comply with UKBA requirements.

Full time study on one of the following forms of course will be necessary:

- a full time UK degree level course or above in a publicly funded Higher Education Institution (HEI); or

- an overseas HE course which is recognised as being equivalent to a UK HE qualification at an overseas HEI; or

- a course of study involving a minimum of 15 hours per week organised daytime study; or

- a course of study which includes a workplacement element which is no more than 50% of the full course length and is at a minimum of level 3 on the National Qualifications Framework (NQF) or its equivalent (or at the equivalent of a UK degree level or above if an overseas qualification).

In addition, sandwich courses and internships are permitted, as long as the total amount of work does not exceed 50%.

The Home Office will require all such students to be enrolled on a course at Level 3 or above on the NQF or its equivalent or a course at Level A2 of the

European Common Framework of Reference for Language if they are seeking to learn English. A list of 'approved qualifications' is provided in the rules:

- validated by Royal Charter

- awarded by a recognised body on the recognised bodies list operated by DIUS

- recognised by one or more recognised bodies via a formal articulation agreement with the awarding body

- approved at level 3 or above in the National Qualifications Framework operated by the Qualifications & Curriculum Authority

- approved at an equivalent level in the Scottish Credit & Qualifications Framework

- approved at an equivalent level by the Qualifications, Curriculum and Assessment Authority for Wales

- approved at an equivalent level by the Council for Curriculum, Examinations and Assessment (CCEA) in Northern Ireland

- an overseas qualification, on which UK NARIC is able to advise on its validity, with a level equivalent to level 3 or above on the National Qualifications Framework.

As of 3 March 2010 English language students must already have attained roughly GCSE level (B2 on the Common European Framework of Reference) in order to study an English language course in the UK, although overseas Government sponsored students and 'crammer course' students studying English before commencing degree level study are exempted from this.

All other international students have had a CEFR B1 equivalent English language requirement imposed on them from summer 2010, which is a major change.

There is also a facility for studying courses outside this list. UKBA say they will also accept qualifications outside their definition where they have been assessed to offer an educational experience at NQF Level 3 or above by the Agency's own approved accreditation bodies. Education providers offering such programmes will nonetheless need to obtain independent validation for their programmes within the following 12 months in order to move to a position where all international students can be guaranteed to be studying for a formally recognised qualification.

Overseas nationals who wish to study lower level courses or to begin learning English may still do so, but they will need to qualify under the student visitor route where they will need to be able to satisfy immigration rule intentions tests.

Courses that involve a work-placement will need to contain at least 50% tuition and no more than 50% of the course length can be taken up by a work-placement.

Funds and maintenance

Students on courses of less than 12 months will be expected to show that they hold sufficient funds to cover the full costs of their course fees plus £800 per month (£600 per month for those studying outside London) for each month of the course up to a maximum of 9 months.

Students with an 'established presence studying in the United Kingdom' need only show the £800 or £600 requirement for a maximum of 2 months rather than 9 months.

A student is considered to have an established presence if:

- He/she has completed a course that was at least six months long within their last period of leave, and this leave finished within the last four months; or

- He/she is applying for continued study on a course where he/she has studied at least six months of that course and has been studying within the last four months; or

- He/she is applying to continue in Tier 4 as a sabbatical officer or as a Postgraduate Doctor or Dentist and he/she has completed a course that was at least six months long within his/her last period of leave, and this leave finished within the last four months.

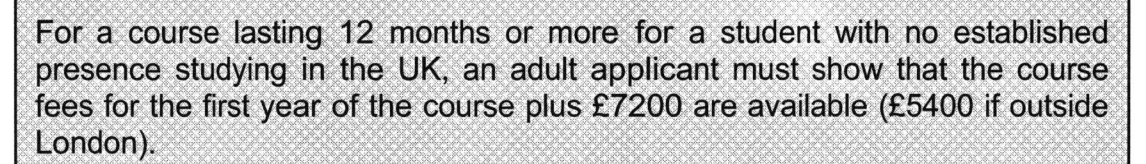

> **Example**
>
> For a course lasting 12 months or more for a student with no established presence studying in the UK, an adult applicant must show that the course fees for the first year of the course plus £7200 are available (£5400 if outside London).

The rules for extension applications are somewhat easier to satisfy. The applicant must show the full cost of fees for the first year of their continued study is available, together with 2 months' maintenance of £800 per month, i.e. £1600. For those studying outside London the figure is again £600 instead of £800 (£1200 in total plus course fees).

Study is considered to be in London if more than 50% of the applicant's study time is in any of the following London boroughs: Camden, City of London, Hackney, Hammersmith and Fulham, Haringey, Islington, Kensington and

Chelsea, Lambeth, Lewisham, Newham, Southwark, Tower Hamlets, Wandsworth and Westminster. The address given in the visa letter is used by UKBA to determine the main study site.

UKBA guidance states that the following forms of evidence 'can' prove that the necessary funds are available ('can' suggesting a less prescriptive approach than for other Tiers of the PBS):

- Cash in an account in the applicant's name (including a joint account)

- Cash in an account in an account owned by the parents or legal guardians of the student where the relationship can be proven and permission to use the funds is demonstrated

- For child students, cash in an account in their parent's name

- A loan in the applicant's name

- Official financial or government sponsorship.

Length and conditions of leave

Entry clearance is now to be granted for the duration of the course, obviating the need for expensive extension applications. The following table sets out the extra leave that is granted on top of this period:

Type of course	Period of entry clearance to be granted before the course starts	Period of entry clearance to be granted after the course ends
12 months or more	1 month	4 months
6 months or more but less than 12 months	1 month	2 months
Pre-sessional course of less than 6 months	1 month	1 month
Course of less than 6 months that is not a pre-sessional course	7 days	7 days
Postgraduate doctor or dentist	1 month	1 month

The no recourse to public funds condition will always be applied. Employment conditions are now set out in the rules rather than the IDIs. Employment is forbidden except as follows:

(1) employment during term time of no more than 20 hours per week for those studying at degree level and above

(2) employment during term time of no more than 10 hours per week for those studying below degree level (including Foundation degrees)

(3) employment (of any duration) during vacations

(4) employment as part of a course-related work placement which forms an assessed part of the applicant's course and provided that any period that the applicant spends on that placement does not exceed half of the total length of the course undertaken in the UK

(5) employment as a Student Union Sabbatical Officer, for up to 2 years, provided the post is elective and is at the institution which is the applicant's Sponsor

(6) employment as a postgraduate doctor or dentist on a recognised Foundation Programme.

Additionally, a Tier 4 (General) student may not be self employed, or employed as a Doctor in Training other than a vacancy on a recognised Foundation Programme, professional sportsperson (including a sports coach) or an entertainer, and must not fill a full time vacancy other than a vacancy on a recognised Foundation Programme.

Extensions

To apply for an extension as a Tier 4 (General) student, a person must have, or have last been granted, entry clearance, leave to enter or leave to remain in one of the following categories:
- (i) as a Tier 4 (General) Student,
- (ii) as a Tier 4 (Child) Student,
- (iii) as a Tier 1 (Post-study Work) Migrant,
- (iv) as a Tier 2 Migrant,
- (v) as a Participant in the International Graduates Scheme (or its predecessor, the Science and Engineering Graduates Scheme),
- (vi) as a Participant in the Fresh Talent: Working in Scotland Scheme,
- (vii) as a Postgraduate Doctor or Dentist,
- (viii) as a Prospective Student,
- (ix) as a Student,
- (x) as a Student Nurse,
- (xi) as a Student Re-sitting an Examination,
- (xii) as a Student Writing-Up a Thesis,
- (xiii) as a Student Union Sabbatical Officer, or
- (xiv) as a Work Permit Holder.

A visa letter must be produced, the course must meet the above requirements and the slightly more relaxed maintenance requirements described above for extension applications must be satisfied.

If the course does not involve degree level study, the grant of leave to remain the applicant is seeking must not lead to the applicant having spent more than 3 years in the UK as a Tier 4 Migrant since the age of 18 studying courses that did not consist of degree level study.

Child student visa

The following forms of study will be permitted with the following forms of assessment:

- **Residential Independent Schools**
  For a child studying and boarding at a residential independent school UKBA will require evidence of sufficient funds to pay school fees for a year plus any additional accommodation fees required by the school. Access to funds will need to be demonstrated through either money in the child's own name or money in accounts held by a parent or legal guardian.

- **Non-Residential Independent School (private foster care arrangement)**
  For a child studying at a non-residential independent school in a private foster care arrangement, UKBA will require evidence of sufficient funds to pay school fees for one year plus an undertaking from a UK resident or citizen to provide maintenance and accommodation for the duration of the course. The undertaking must set out the nature of the relationship with the child and the child's parent(s). In addition, the individual providing maintenance and accommodation will need to be able to demonstrate that they have accommodation and the funds to support a child in addition to their own existing commitments (available income of at least £500 per month will be required).

- **Independent School (Parent accompanying a child under 12)**
  UKBA will continue to allow children studying at independent schools under the age of 12 to be accompanied to the UK by a parent who will be responsible for their care. In this case, UKBA will require evidence of funds required to pay school fees for one year plus £1335 per month for each month up to a maximum of 12 months. If more than one child is studying then as well as evidence of ability to pay annual fees for each additional child, evidence of a further £535 per month will need to be shown to be available for each additional child.

The following periods of leave will be granted:

Child of primary school age at an independent feepaying school.	Leave may be granted for the duration of studies to the end of the academic year in which the child is 11, then to 31 October.
Child aged 11-16 studying pre/ for GCSEs at an independent fee-paying school.	Leave may be granted for the duration of studies to the end of the academic year in which the child is 16, then to 31 October.
Child aged 16 or over studying for A-	Leave may be granted for the duration of

levels at an independent fee-paying school.	studies to the end of the academic year in which child is 18, then to 31 October.

Tier 5: youth mobility and temporary workers

This part of the PBS collected together and replaced a range of schemes and programmes that formerly existed both inside and outside the immigration rules, most notably the working holiday maker scheme.

Entry clearance is mandatory under Tier 5.

Tier 5

Youth mobility
- Replacement for working holiday maker scheme
- Opens to Australia, Canada, New Zealand, Japan, Monaco
- Also open to British nationals who are not British citizens
- Aged 18 to 31

Temporary workers
- Creative and sporting
- Charity worker
- Religious
- Government authorised exchange
- International agreement

Youth mobility

This scheme replaced the working holiday maker scheme. It is open to nationals of the following countries:

- Australia
- Canada
- Japan
- New Zealand
- Monaco

The Japanese scheme operates on a quota basis and limitations have been placed on numbers in previous years. No similar restrictions have been imposed on nationals of Australia, Canada or New Zealand.

The scheme is also open to British Overseas Citizens, British Overseas Territories Citizens or British Nationals (Overseas), providing the requisite forms of proof of nationality are provided.

Entry clearance is mandatory and there is no facility to extend leave or switch into Tier 5 (Youth Mobility).

An applicant must also be 18 or over when his or her entry clearance becomes valid for use and under the age of 31 on the date his or her application is made. The applicant must have no children under the age of 18 who are either living with him or her or for whom he or she is financially responsible.

The applicant must show that he or she has £1600 available in funds. Specified documents bearing specified information must be used as proof of the availability of these funds.

The applicant must not previously have spent time in the UK as a Working Holidaymaker or a Tier 5 (Youth Mobility Scheme) Temporary Migrant.

If all of these requirements are met, entry clearance will be granted for a period of 2 years subject to the following conditions:

(a) no recourse to public funds,

(b) registration with the police, if this is required by paragraph 326 of these Rules,

(c) no employment as a professional sportsperson (including as a sports coach), or as a Doctor in Training, and

(d) no self employment, except where the following conditions are met:
   (i)   the migrant has no premises which he owns, other than his home, from which he carries out his business,
   (ii) the total value of any equipment used in the business does not exceed £5,000, and
   (iii) the migrant has no employees.

Temporary workers

Entry clearance will usually be required for Tier 5 temporary workers. The only exception to the requirement for entry clearance is for those who are not visa nationals, are sponsored under the creative and sporting part of the scheme and the total period of engagement (including any gaps between consecutive engagements) is no more than three months.

There is a maintenance requirement for Tier 5 (Temporary Worker). It is either that:

- The applicant has £800 or

- The applicant's sponsor is an A rated sponsor and the Certificate of Sponsorship Checking Service confirms that the sponsor has certified that the applicant will not claim public funds during his period of leave as a Tier 5 (Temporary Worker) Migrant.

The principle requirement for Tier 5 (Temporary Worker) is the obtaining of a Certificate of Sponsorship. Under each of the different temporary worker categories (see below) different types of sponsor are identified. Unlike Tier 2, the sponsor need not necessarily be the migrant's employer as such. However, the sponsor must apply to join the register of sponsors and must therefore comply with the UKBA requirements to join the register.

Creative and sporting category

This category is for migrants who want to come to the United Kingdom to work as sports people for up to 12 months, or to perform as entertainers or creative artists for up to 24 months. The requirements are then sub-divided into sporting and creative requirements.

When a sponsor assigns a certificate of sponsorship in either the creative or sporting sector, the sponsor is guaranteeing that the migrant:

(i) is seeking entry to the United Kingdom to work or perform in the relevant sector

(ii) is not intending to establish a business in the United Kingdom

(iii) poses no threat to the resident labour market and

(iv) will comply with the conditions of his/her permission to stay and leave the United Kingdom when that leave expires.

Sporting

This subcategory is aimed at sportspeople who are internationally established at the highest level in their sport and/or whose employment will make a significant contribution to the development and operation of that particular sport in the United Kingdom and for coaches who must be suitably qualified to fulfil the role in question. Whether such requirements are met is for the sponsor to decide, notably.

This category does not cover people who currently enter the United Kingdom under the permit-free concessions for entertainers (including permit-free festivals) and sports people. These concessions have been brought within the immigration rules (outside the points-based system) under the revised visitor categories.

Sporting sponsors must be a sporting body, sports club, events organiser or other organiser operating, or intending to operate in the sporting sector. An agent cannot be a sponsor under Tier 5 sporting sub-category. The prospective sponsor must submit the necessary documents as listed in Appendix A including an endorsement from the UK Border Agency recognised governing body for the sport. A governing body is one that is recognised by one of the home country sports councils (for example Sport England). A list of the approved governing bodies is on the UKBA website. If there is no recognised governing body, UKBA can be contacted.

A migrant who has already been granted leave under Tier 5 (Creative and Sport) for a job as a footballer may switch into Tier 2 (Sports people) provided they will still be employed as a footballer and he/she can meet the Tier 2 (Sports people) migrant requirements.

Creative

In order to gain a licence as a sponsor of creative and sporting workers and their entourage, the prospective sponsor must be operating, or intend to operate, in the creative or sporting sector. Examples include a national body, event organiser, producer, venue, agent or other similar organisation. Where applicable, the prospective sponsor must prior to issuing each certificate of sponsorship commit to having applied the UKBA codes of practice for taking into account the needs of the resident labour market in that field. The codes of practice will operate in three specific areas: dance, theatre, and film & television.

Charity worker category

Migrants coming to work temporarily in the United Kingdom as charity workers should only be undertaking voluntary activity and not paid employment. The migrant should intend to carry out fieldwork directly related to the purpose of the sponsoring organisation.

Migrants entering the United Kingdom under the charity workers sub-category will be given a maximum of 12 months' permission to stay. Their dependants will be allowed to work if they are accompanying or joining them in the United Kingdom.

In assigning a certificate of sponsorship, the sponsor is guaranteeing that the migrant:

(i) intends to undertake voluntary fieldwork directly related to the purpose of the charity sponsoring him/her

(ii) will not be paid or receive other remuneration for their work (with the exception of reasonable expenses outlined in section 44 of the National Minimum Wage Act)

(iii) will not take up a permanent position and

(iv) will comply with the conditions of his/her permission to stay and leave the United Kingdom when it expires.

Religious worker category

The religious worker category is for people coming to the United Kingdom to work temporarily. Religious workers can:

- do preaching, pastoral work and non-pastoral work;

- work in the United Kingdom in the same way that they are working in an overseas organisation (although their duties in the United Kingdom may be different). The job should be done in their holiday from their job overseas; or

- work in a religious order with a community which involves a permanent commitment, such as a monastery or convent. The work in a religious order must be in the order itself or be outside work directed by the order. A migrant can apply if he or she is a novice whose training means taking part in the daily community life of the order.

The work of a member of a religious order must be within the order itself, or outside work directed by the order. Teachers working in schools not maintained by their order must apply as a teacher under Tier 2 (General). Novices whose training consists of taking part in the daily community life of their order may apply under this category, but anyone studying for a qualification, on a formal full-time course of study or training in an academic institution not maintained by the order should apply as a student under Tier 4. People who are not members of a religious order, but who are working or studying within such a community, are not eligible to apply under this category and must satisfy the requirements of the relevant work or study category.

Migrants entering the United Kingdom under this category will be given a maximum of 24 months' permission to stay. Their dependants will be allowed to work if accompanying or joining them in the United Kingdom.

Sponsors wishing to apply for a licence under this category must be a bona fide religious institution, which is defined as follows:

(i) Is a registered, excepted or exempt United Kingdom charity or is an ecclesiastical corporation established for charitable purposes. Charities who are not registered according to the relevant charity legislation must explain the reason for non-registration in their application for a sponsor licence

(ii) Is the structure for a faith-based community with a common system of belief and spiritual goals, codes of behaviour and religious

practice, which exists to support and/or propagate those common beliefs and practices and where such beliefs
- include any religious belief or similar philosophical belief in something transcendental, metaphysical or ultimate
- exclude any philosophical or political belief concerned with man, unless that belief is similar to religious belief

(iii) Does not exclude from its community on the basis of gender, nationality or ethnicity

(iv) Receives financial and material support for its core religious ministry from its congregation or community on a voluntary basis only, without promise or coercion

(v) Does not breach, or encourage others to breach, any United Kingdom legislation and

(vi) Does not operate against the public interest, or in a way that has a detrimental effect on personal or family life as these are commonly understood in the United Kingdom.

When a sponsor assigns a certificate of sponsorship under this sub-category, it is guaranteeing that:

(i) The migrant is qualified to do the job in question

(ii) The migrant will not take employment except as a religious worker

(iii) The migrant will only work at the specified location, except where working under the supplementary employment provisions;

(iv) The sponsor is giving an undertaking that it will accept the responsibilities of sponsorship for the migrant

(v) The sponsor is giving an undertaking to support the migrant through funds and/or accommodation that are sufficient for them to maintain themselves throughout the duration of the certificate of sponsorship. Migrants who are unable to support themselves could face financial hardship because they will not have access to most state benefits

(vi) The migrant will not be displacing or denying an employment opportunity to a suitably qualified member of the resident labour force and

(vii) The migrant will comply with the conditions of his/her permission to stay and will leave the United Kingdom when it expires.

Government authorised exchange category

The government authorised exchange category is for people coming to the United Kingdom through approved schemes that aim to share knowledge, experience and best practice. This category must not be used to fill job vacancies or to bring unskilled labour to the United Kingdom.

Migrants entering the United Kingdom under the government authorised exchange category will be given a maximum of 24 months' permission to stay. Their dependants are allowed to work if they are accompanying or joining them in the United Kingdom.

Usually there will have to be an overarching body to administer an exchange scheme under this subcategory. This overarching body will be the sponsor and must apply for a licence. The scheme and the overarching body must have the support of a United Kingdom government department or one of its executive agencies. The overarching body will assign certificates of sponsorship to migrants who meet the requirements of the scheme.

The only exception to this is where an educational institution is recruiting a sponsored researcher. In these circumstances, the educational institution must be licensed under Tier 5 Government Authorised Exchange, and must have confirmation from the Department for Innovation, Universities and Skills (DIUS) that they support the scheme under which the researcher is being employed.

When deciding which exchange schemes to support, government departments will be expected to select schemes that meet the requirements below:

(i) The exchange scheme must not harm the resident labour market.

(ii) Any work the migrant undertakes will usually need to be skilled. Skilled work is currently defined as being equivalent to S/NVQ3 or above.

(iii) The employment must conform with all relevant United Kingdom and European legislation, such as the National Minimum Wage Act and the EC working hours directives.

(iv) The exchange scheme must include measures that protect it from being abused.

A potential sponsor has to meet various UKBA requirements in order to be registered as a sponsor for the purposes of this sub-category.

International agreement category

This category is for migrants who are coming to the United Kingdom under contract to provide a service that is covered under international law, including:

- the General Agreement on Trade in Services (GATS);

- similar agreements between the United Kingdom and another country;

- employees of overseas governments and international organisations; and
- private servants in diplomatic households.

Migrants entering the United Kingdom under the international agreement sub-category can apply for leave as follows:

- GATS and similar agreements, up to a maximum of 24 months;
- Employees of overseas governments and international organisations, up to an initial maximum of 24 months, with the option to make in-country extensions for periods of 12 months at a time up to a total maximum of 72 months
- Private servants in diplomatic households, or households of employees of international organisations, up to an initial maximum of 24 months, with the option to make in-country extensions for periods of 12 months at a time up to a total maximum of 72 months.

Their dependants will be allowed to work if they are accompanying or joining them in the United Kingdom.

To gain a licence as a sponsor of migrants under GATS or other international agreements, the prospective sponsor must show that the job or employment involved is covered by the terms of the agreement concerned.

A sponsor that assigns a certificate of sponsorship under GATS or similar will be guaranteeing that the migrant:

(i) Works for an employer or organisation, of a country that:
- is a member of the World Trade Organisation or
- has a bilateral agreement with the United Kingdom or the European Union or
- is a member of the European Union

(ii) Will be engaged in work that meets the terms and conditions of the relevant international agreement and

(iii) Where relevant, works for the employer that was awarded the contract or will provide services to the United Kingdom client.

In order to gain a licence as a sponsor of private servants in diplomatic households or households of officials working for international organisations, the sponsor must be a diplomatic mission or an international organisation recognised by the United Kingdom.

A sponsor that assigns a certificate of sponsorship to private servants in diplomatic households will be guaranteeing that the migrant:

(i) Is aged 18 or over

(ii) Will be employed as a private servant in the household of:
- a member of staff of a diplomatic or consular mission who has diplomatic privileges and immunity as defined by the Vienna Convention on Diplomatic Relations or
- an official employed by an international organisation who enjoys certain privileges and immunities under United Kingdom or international law

(iii) Intends to work full-time in domestic employment

(iv) Will not take up any other form of employment for the sponsor other than as a private servant in the specified household; and

(v) Will leave the United Kingdom when their permission to stay has expired.

To become a sponsor, the employer must apply to UKBA for a licence under Tier 5, supplying the specified evidence. Once licensed, the sponsor will be able to assign certificates of sponsorship to migrants coming to the UK to work.

Dependants of PBS migrants

Provision is made at Part 8 of the Immigration Rules for entry and for settlement for the family members of PBS migrants other than for those under Tier 5 (Youth Mobility). Relevant family members are spouses, civil partners, unmarried partners, same sex partners and children.

Students studying on courses of less than six months may no longer be accompanied by dependents, as of 3 March 2010.

Leave will be granted such as to expire on the same day as that of the PBS migrant.

Dependents of Tier 4 students entering the UK on or after 3 March 2010 are not permitted to work, although new rules were introduced to enable them to switch in-country into the Points Based System if they qualify in their own right.

The requirements for unmarried or same sex partners are that:

(i) Any previous marriage or civil partnership or similar relationship by the applicant or the PBS migrant with another person must have permanently broken down

(ii) The applicant and the PBS migrant must not be so closely related that they would be prohibited from marrying each other in the UK, and

(iii) The applicant and the PBS migrant must have been living together in a relationship similar to marriage or civil partnership for a period of at least 2 years.

Visas will usually be required for entry. Provision is made for extensions but not for switching from other categories. Apart from for family members of Tier 1 (Investor) migrants, sufficient funds must be shown to be available, as required in Appendix E of the rules:

- Where the PBS migrant to whom the application is connected is outside the UK, or has been in the UK for a period of less than 12 months, there must be £1,600 in funds.

- Where the PBS migrant to whom the application is connected has been in the UK for a period of 12 months or more, there must be £533 in funds.

Where the applicant is applying as the partner of a PBS migrant the relevant amount of funds must be available to either the applicant or the Relevant Points Based System Migrant.

Where the applicant is applying as the child of a PBS migrant, the relevant amount of funds must be available to the applicant, the PBS migrant, or the applicant's other parent who is lawfully present in the UK or being granted entry clearance, or leave to enter or remain, at the same time.

Where the PBS migrant is applying for entry clearance or leave to remain at the same time as the applicant, the amount of funds available to the applicant must be in addition to the level of funds required separately of the Relevant Points Based System Migrant.

Specified documents are required as evidence of the availability of funds.

Right of appeal

There are appeals for those applying to extend their leave to remain who are already present in the UK with leave. Out of country appeals against refusal of entry clearance are not available.

Statute now makes provision for radical restriction of the effectiveness of a right of appeal. The general ability of the immigration judge to take into account evidence he or she considers relevant to the substance of the decision, including evidence which concerns a matter arising after the date of the decision, is cut down by exceptions (although at the time of writing s.19 of the UK Borders Act 2007 which implements these changes has not itself been implemented).

In appeals against refusal of leave to enter or refusal to vary leave, where the case concerns an application under the Points Based System, and the ground of appeal is based on the immigration rules or "in accordance with the law", then there is a restriction on the materials that may be submitted. The restriction is that the Tribunal may consider evidence adduced by the appellant only if it:

- was submitted in support of, and at the time of making, the application to which the immigration decision related,

- relates to the appeal in so far as it relies on grounds such as asylum, human rights, EEA law, and race discrimination

- is adduced to prove that a document is genuine or valid, or

- is adduced in connection with the Secretary of State's reliance on a discretion under immigration rules, or compliance with a requirement of immigration rules, to refuse an application on grounds not related to the acquisition of "points" under the "Points Based System".

See generally the amended sections 84(4), 85(4)-(5) of the Nationality Immigration and Asylum Act 2002.

Right of review

For those applying from abroad, there is no right of appeal – the remedy is the right of administrative review.

This is invoked by submitting an Administrative Review Request Notice. An applicant must provide a full description of the claimed error regarding Age, Qualifications, Previous Earnings, UK Experience, English Language, Maintenance, or the General Refusal Grounds. Then the form is signed (electronic signature suffices) and handed back to the relevant Visa Application Centre or Visa Section.

An application for Administrative Review is made if the subject of the decision believes that the refusal was incorrect. An Entry Clearance Manager who was not involved in the original decision will conduct the review. In some cases, the Entry Clearance Manager may be located at a different entry clearance post to where the original entry clearance application was considered.

There is a right to apply only for one Administrative Review of the decision to refuse an application. No new or further information/documents in support of the request for Administrative Review, can be submitted, unless the refusal is under paragraphs 320(7A) or 320(7B). The objective is that, where new information or documents are available, a fresh application must be made.

Administrative Reviews are to be conducted within 28 days. Written notice will be provided if it is not possible to achieve this.

Chapter 9: Enforcement: detention and deportation

DETENTION **349**

   POWER TO DETAIN 349
   CRITERIA FOR DETENTION 352
      Presumption of liberty.. 352
      Reasons to detain 353
      Factors militating against detention 354
      Deportation cases.. 355
      Families.. 356
   DETAINED FAST TRACK 356
   DETENTION REVIEWS 357

RELEASE AND BAIL **358**

   TEMPORARY ADMISSION AND CIO BAIL 358
   TRIBUNAL BAIL 359
      Power to grant bail 359
      Sureties and recognisance... 361
      Taking instructions in bail cases 363
      Accommodation 364
      National security cases 364
   CHALLENGES TO LAWFULNESS OF DETENTION 365

ADMINISTRATIVE REMOVAL **366**

DEPORTATION **367**

   POWER TO DEPORT 367
   PROCEDURE FOR DEPORTATION 368
      Discretionary deportation 368
      Automatic deportation 369
   ASYLUM AND DEPORTATION... 371
   REVOCATION OF DEPORTATION ORDER 372
   SUBSTANTIVE CONSIDERATIONS 374

Detention

Power to detain

There are four circumstances in which a person may be detained as set down in Schedules 2 and 3 of the Immigration Act 1971 (as amended by the Immigration and Asylum Act 1999):

- During examination by an immigration officer to decide whether or not to grant leave to enter, including those previously were granted entry clearance (Schedule 2, paragraph 16(1) (1A) of the Immigration Act 1971 (IA 1971) as amended by paragraph 57, 60 Schedule 14 IAA 1999)

- Pending the giving of removal directions and removal for those refused leave to enter and for those determined to be illegal entrants (Schedule 2, paragraph 8,9 and 16(2) IA 1971 as amended by section 140(1) of the IAA 1999)

- Pending removal of those served with notice of intention to deport under s.3(5) of 71 Act, in respect of whom a deportation order has been signed and those recommended for deportation (Schedule 3, paragraph 2 of the IA 1971)

- Crew members who overstay pending the giving of removal directions and pending removal or are reasonably suspected of intending to do so (Schedule 2, paragraph 12,13 and 16(2) of IA 1971)

It can be seen that the power to detain is very extensive, in the sense that almost any person subject to immigration control can potentially be detained. However, there are limitations on the power to detain. The most important of these in a practical sense is the Secretary of State's policies on detention; exercise of the power to detain contrary to a policy is very likely to be unlawful. These policies are examined in detail below. In addition, the power to detain will lapse in lengthy detention cases if there is no realistic prospect of removal.

This principle was established by Woolf J in *R v Governor of Durham Prison ex parte Hardial Singh* [1984] 1 WLR 704:

> "First, the power can only be exercised during the period necessary, in all the circumstances of the particular case, to effect removal. Secondly, if it becomes clear that removal is not going to be possible within a reasonable time, further detention is not authorised. Thirdly, the person seeking to exercise the power of detention must take all reasonable steps within his power to ensure the removal within a reasonable time."

If it is proving impossible to actually remove or deport the person from the United Kingdom then the detention would become unlawful, something that might be demonstrated by lengthy detention whilst unsuccessful attempts are made to remove an individual: see *in re Wasfi Suleman Mahmod* [1995] Imm AR 311. In the case of R (I) v SSHD [2003] INLR 196, Dyson LJ summarised the law as follows:

> 1. The Secretary of State must intend to deport the person and can only use the power to detain for that purpose

> 2. The deportee may only be detained for a period that is reasonable in all the circumstances

> 3. If, before the expiry of the reasonable period, it becomes apparent that the Secretary of State will not be able to effect deportation within that reasonable period, he should not seek to exercise the power of detention

> 4. The Secretary of State should act with the reasonable diligence and expedition to effect removal

However, the actions of the detainee, both past and present, can have an impact on whether it is reasonable to exercise the power to detain. In R (on the application of A) v SSHD [2007] EWCA Civ 804 the Court of Appeal found that a risk of absconding was relevant to the period before which detention becomes unreasonable, as was a refusal of voluntary departure from the UK and risk of re-offending.

See further below regarding bringing a challenge to the lawfulness of detention.

> **Example**
>
> Rahul is from Algeria. He is to be deported and his appeal rights were exhausted 18 months ago. However, he has been detained now for 21 months, allegedly pending removal.
>
> The Home Office insist that they are doing everything in their power to remove Rahul, but the Algerian authorities are not co-operating. A face to face interview between Rahul and the Algerians took place 20 months ago in detention in order to obtain an Emergency Travel Document. The Algerians stated that they did not accept Rahul was Algerian. The Home Office asked Rahul to provide some written proof of his Algerian nationality. Being in detention in a foreign country, Rahul was unable to do so.
>
> A second interview was arranged and took place 15 months ago. The Algerians maintained their position. It is not clear whether any new information was submitted by the Home Office.
>
> A third telephone interview took place 3 months ago with the same result.
>
> Rahul has applied for bail five times in the last 21 months and has been refused each time because he is a high absconding risk. There is strong support for this view, as Rahul has a very poor criminal and immigration record.
>
> Rahul's detention is almost certainly unlawful and probably has been for some time; arguably since the first interview, almost indisputably since the second. AIT bail applications have failed him so he must apply for *habeas corpus* and/or judicial review. On the claim form he should also specify that he seeks a declaration of unlawful detention and damages. Quantum could easily be tens of thousands of pounds in a case such as this.

The detainee will be detained in a place in which the SSHD designates as appropriate, usually at a Detention Centre, although prisons are still used, and Reception Centres, with a less regimented environment, have been introduced. The tendency to use prisons for the detention of asylum seekers is on the wane.

The original powers regarding removal, which are the foundation for the powers to award temporary admission, or detention, are found in the 1971 Act, although subsequent legislation also addresses bail. The 2002 Act extended the rights to apply for bail to those against whom there had been a recommendation to deport or a signed deportation order, therefore filling the vacuum that had prevented universal access to release.

Prior to the 1999 Act actual illegal entry was required to give rise to the lawful power to detain. However, now where "there are reasonable grounds for suspecting that a person is someone in respect of whom directions may be given under [the illegal entry categories]," such a decision can be made.

The 2002 Act also extended the power to detain. Section 62 permits detention even where a decision is being considered as to whether or not to make removal directions. Section 67 of the Act provides for detention where an individual can not currently be removed and certain factors exist because of a legal impediment connected with the UK's obligations under an international agreement, where practical difficulties are impeding or delaying the making of arrangements, or where practical difficulties or demands on administrative resources are impeding or delaying the taking of a decision in respect of him.

Criteria for detention

The initial reasons for detention will be provided in Form IS91R; there should be regular reviews of detention (see below), the reasons for subsequent detention being given in Form IS93. These procedures as set out in the Immigration Service's Enforcement Instructions and Guidance. There is a duty promptly to provide reasons for detention and a failure to do so renders the detention unlawful (although, controversially, this is not necessarily the same as qualifying the detainee for release from detention): *Saadi v UK* 13229/03 [2008] ECHR 80.

There will be a temptation for initial reasons for detention to be built upon at a later stage should bail be sought, because at that point a bail summary will have to be prepared. Those representing detainees may therefore wish to seek disclosure of the initial reasons for detention. Sometimes the Immigration Service will reveal these on application; on other occasions, it may be necessary to seek disclosure via other measures, such as a Subject Access Bureau request under the Data Protection Act.

Guidance on detention policy can be found in the Enforcement Instructions and Guidance (EIG) on the UKBA website at chapter 55. This includes extremely useful instructions on the factors to be taken into account in assessing whether a person is to be assessed as an absconding risk and re-detention of bailees. Chapter 55 also incorporates commitments given by the Government in the 1998 White Paper and subsequently that detention is a tool of last resort and alternatives would be used whenever possible.

Presumption of liberty

There is a presumption of liberty, meaning that the starting point must be that a person should not be detained unless there are good reasons for doing so. The potential reasons for detention are explored below.

This presumption exists in common law and is also enshrined in Article 5 of the ECHR.

The presumption of liberty is also reflected, at least in theory, in Home Office policy. EIG chapter 55.1.1 states that there is a presumption of liberty and this is reiterated at other points in the EIG. However, deportation cases managed by the Criminal Casework Directorate of the Home Office, the presumption of liberty was modified for a substantial period of time and at the time of writing continues to be qualified. See EIG 55.1.2 and the section on deportation cases below.

> **Top tip**
>
> In a bail application, if the Home Office cannot prove to the civil standard that detention is necessary for one of the above reasons, the person ought to be released on bail. This is certainly how a bail application *should* work. Some immigration judges tend to require the bail applicant to prove that they are reliable, however, which can be very difficult to evidence.

Reasons to detain

The basic justifications for detention are as follows:

1. To effect removal

2. Establish identity or basis of claim

3. Reason to believe will fail to comply with conditions

These justifications are set out in Enforcement Instructions and Guidance (EIG) 55.1.1. The Home Office also exercises the power to detain in order to operate the fast track processes at Oakington, Harmondsworth and Yarl's Wood (see EIG 55.4). Detention in these circumstances is effectively for the purpose of administrative convenience but it has been upheld as acceptable by Strasbourg (*Saadi v UK* 13229/03 [2008] ECHR 80).

There are implied limitations to these justifications, which are explored below. For example, a person cannot really be detained to effect removal if there is no real prospect of their removal in a reasonable timescale.

The EIG lists the factors to be taken into account in decisions to detain at 55.3, albeit specifically stating that CCD cases are excluded from these considerations:

1. There is a presumption in favour of temporary admission or temporary release - there must be strong grounds for believing that a person will not

comply with conditions of temporary admission or temporary release for detention to be justified.

2. All reasonable alternatives to detention must be considered before detention is authorised.

3. Each case must be considered on its individual merits.

The following factors must be taken into account when considering the need for initial or continued detention:

- What is the likelihood of the person being removed and, if so, after what timescale?

- Is there any evidence of previous absconding?

- Is there any evidence of a previous failure to comply with conditions of temporary release or bail?

- Has the subject taken part in a determined attempt to breach the immigration laws? (e.g. entry in breach of a deportation order, attempted or actual clandestine entry)

- Is there a previous history of complying with the requirements of immigration control? (e.g. by applying for a visa, further leave, etc)

- What are the person's ties with the United Kingdom? Are there close relatives (including dependants) here? Does anyone rely on the person for support? Does the person have a settled address/employment?

- What are the individual's expectations about the outcome of the case? Are there factors such as an outstanding appeal, an application for judicial review or representations which afford incentive to keep in touch?

- Is there a risk of offending or harm to the public (this requires consideration of the likelihood of harm and the seriousness of the harm if the person does offend)?

- Is the subject under 18?

- Does the subject have a history of torture?

- Does the subject have a history of physical or mental ill health?

Factors militating against detention

The following factors were announced as future detention policy in the 2002 White *Paper, Fairer, Faster, Firmer – A Modern Approach to Immigration and Asylum* and have been incorporated into the EIG:

(i) Detention will normally be justified (especially where there has been a systematic attempt to breach immigration control) where there is a reasonable belief that the individual will fail to keep the terms of temporary admission; initially to clarify a person's identity and the basis of their claim; or where removal is imminent.

(ii) Evidence of torture should weigh strongly in favour of temporary admission whilst an asylum claim is being considered.

(iii) Detention of families with young children should be planned to be effected as close to removal as possible so as to ensure that families are not normally detained for more than a few days.

(iv) Unaccompanied minors should never be detained other than in the most exceptional circumstances and then only overnight with appropriate care if they, for example, arrive unaccompanied at an airport. In all cases children under the age of 18 should be referred to the Refugee Council Children's Panel. Where reliable medical evidence indicates that a person is under 18 years of age they will be treated as minors.

The EIG also incorporates at 55.1.4.1 the lawfulness factors identified in leading case law on detention, particularly from the case of *R (on the app of I) v SSHD* [2003] INLR 196 (see earlier).

Deportation cases

At the time of writing (this policy may well change under the pressure of further litigation) the modification to the presumption of liberty in deportation cases is set out at EIG 55.1.2 and is worth quoting in full:

> 'Cases concerning foreign national prisoners – dealt with by the Criminal Casework Directorate (CCD) - are subject to the general policy set out above in 55.1.1, including the presumption in favour of temporary admission or release. Thus, the starting point in these cases remains that the person should be released on temporary admission or release unless the circumstances of the case require the use of detention. However, the nature of these cases means that special attention must be paid to their individual circumstances. In any case in which the criteria for considering deportation action (the "deportation criteria") are met, the risk of re-offending and the particular risk of absconding should be weighed against the presumption in favour of temporary admission or temporary release. Due to the clear imperative to protect the public from harm from a person whose criminal record is sufficiently serious as to satisfy the deportation criteria, and/or because of the likely consequence of such a criminal record for the assessment of the risk that such a person will abscond, in many cases this is likely to result in the conclusion that the person should be detained, provided detention is, and continues to be, lawful. However, any such conclusion can be reached only if the presumption of temporary admission or release is displaced after an assessment of the need to detain in the light of the risk of re-offending and/or the risk of absconding.'

While it can be seen that the draughtsman of this policy hopes that the policy incorporates the presumption of liberty, later parts of the EIG (e.g. 55.3) suggest that in reality the presumption of liberty is not applied in deportation cases.

Families

There is specific guidance in the Enforcement Instructions and Guidance about the detention of families, at chapter 55.9.4. The guidance reiterates that there is a presumption in favour of temporary release and includes the following passage on family unity:

> 'As a matter of policy we should aim to keep the family as a single unit. However, it will be appropriate to separate a child from its parents if there is evidence that separation is in the best interests of the child. The local authority's social services department will make this decision.'

Detained fast track

The following categories of applicants should not, according to the Enforcement Instructions and Guidance at chapter 55.4, be detained in any detained fast track process:

- Unaccompanied minors (always unsuitable, see 55.9 Young Persons);

- Age dispute cases. The policy of detaining age dispute cases for the purposes of Fast Tracking was updated in February 2006 (see below);

- Disabled applicants, except the most easily manageable;

- Pregnant females of 24 weeks and above;

- Any person with a medical condition which requires 24 hour nursing or medical intervention;

- Anybody identified as having an infectious/contagious disease;

- Anybody presenting with acute psychosis e.g.: schizophrenia and requiring hospitalisation;

- Anybody presenting with physical and/or learning disabilities requiring 24 hour nursing care;

- Where there is independent evidence that the claimant has been tortured;

- Where there is independent evidence from a recognised organisation, e.g. the Poppy Project, that the claimant has been a victim of trafficking;

- Violent or uncooperative cases; for non-suspensive appeal nationalities, local enforcement offices (LEOs) should try and secure detention accommodation at an alternative removal centre and then refer to Oakington for them to be processed as a 'remote case';

- Those with criminal convictions, except where specifically authorised.

- Where detention would be contrary to published criteria.

Age dispute cases in Detained Fast Track (DFT)

Applicants claiming to be under 18 should be accepted into DFT processes only if one or more of the following criteria apply:

- There is credible and clear documentary evidence that they are 18 years of age or over;

- A full "Merton-compliant" age assessment by Social Services is available stating that they are 18 years of age or over. Please note that assessments are completed by social services

- Emergency Duty Teams are not acceptable evidence of age.

- Their physical appearance/demeanour very strongly indicates that they are significantly 18 years of age or over and no other credible evidence exists to the contrary.

Any age dispute case not falling within at least **one** of the criteria above is not suitable for DFT and it should not be referred to the AIU. If there is any room for doubt as to whether a person is under 18 they should **not** be referred to the AIU.

A failure to follow the DFT policy may render the detention unlawful, leading to a claim for damages. In the case of *R (on the application of D) v SSHD & Ors* [2006] EWHC 980 (Admin), for example, Davis J held the detention centre rules required a medical examination to take place that had not in fact taken place, that if it had taken place the Home Office would have accepted that the detainee was a victim of torture, and had this happened the detainee would have been released in accordance with policy. Damages were awarded.

Similar unlawful detention cases have been brought in respect of minors and age dispute cases, such as, *R (on the application of I & O) v SSHD* [2005] EWHC 1025 (Admin).

Detention reviews

The Enforcement Instructions and Guidance requires at 55.5 that a decision to detain or maintain detention must be reviewed at certain times and at a certain level of seniority. In the case of *R (on the application of SK) v SSHD* [2008] EWHC 98 (Admin) Munby J held that a failure to conduct these reviews properly rendered the detention unlawful, although he did not go as far as to order release as had the reviews been conducted then the decision to detain was justified. However, an enquiry as to damages was ordered.

This judgment was overturned on appeal ([2008] EWCA Civ 1204) but at the time of writing was under appeal to the House of Lords.

Reference, below, is made to various Civil Service roles. It will be useful to explain their titles to help you contextualise their functions. The UK Border Agency is split, broadly speaking, into two main functions: Enforcement and Administration, which were formerly known as the Immigration Service and the Immigration and Nationality Directorate, respectively. Since agency status was granted to this division of the Home Office, these two 'functions' have been combined into one UK Border Agency.

Managerial positions follow a grading structure for both 'functions'. An Executive Officer (EO) is a junior management grade. The equivalent in the Enforcement arm is the Immigration Officer (IO). A Chief Immigration Officer (CIO) is a middle management grade in Enforcement and the Higher Executive Officer (HEO) is the equivalent grade on the administrative arm. Her Majesty's Inspector (HMI) is a senior manager in Enforcement and the Senior Executive Officer (SEO) is the administrative equivalent. After HMI/SEO the management grades convert to Executive grades at Director level. The lowest being Assistant Director, then Deputy Director and finally Director, who will be the most senior Civil Servant at 'regional' level.

When making decisions relating to detention, the initial decision must be made by a CIO/HEO or Inspector/SEO. The requirements are for reviews to take place after:
- 24 hours
- 7 days
- 14 days by an Inspector
- 21 days
- 28 days by an Inspector

Thereafter the reviews are to take place monthly at the following levels of seniority:
- Months 1 and 2: EO
- Months 3 and 4: SEO or HMI
- Months 5, 6 and 7: Assistant Director or Grade 7
- Months 8, 9, 10 and 11: Deputy Director
- Month 12 and every three months at Director level, within intervening monthly reviews at Deputy Director level

Release and bail

There are a number of steps to be pursued in order to seek release of a client from detention:

Temporary Admission → CIO bail → Tribunal bail → Judicial review

Temporary admission and CIO bail

If a client is detained under the Immigration Acts then consideration must always be given to how they can be released. In the first place verbal communications with the Immigration Service may yield some results. This would be a request for Temporary Admission ('TA'). Then representations can be made to the Chief Immigration Officer, which is effectively a request for CIO bail. Unlike immigration tribunal bail, there is no prescribed form for CIO bail.

It is unusual for CIO bail to be granted if Temporary Admission has been refused. However, CIO bail enables some additional powers, including demand for a recognisance and sureties. A CIO bail application can be a useful tactical step; if CIO bail is agreed in principle but an unreasonably high recognisance is demanded or it is said that sureties are necessary, these are issues that can sometimes more sensibly be argued and debated with an Immigration Judge on an application for immigration tribunal bail. Once the Home Office has agreed bail in principle the only debate should be over conditions.

The office responsible for detaining the person should be contacted by phone or fax and reasons obtained if these have not already been provided and representations made as to Temporary Admission. A useful list of numbers appears in the JCWI Handbook or contact details should be on any IS96 the person has been given. If the representations are unsuccessful then the request should be followed up in writing. Written reasons are presently provided to detainees and interpreted in the form of a checklist. They are reiterated on a monthly basis.

If the detainee is released they will usually be required to comply with conditions. The usual conditions are:

1) Residence at a specified address.

2) Reporting to Police Station or /Immigration Service.

3) Sureties. These conditions can be varied by an application to an IO or immigration judge.

4) Regarding work, he can work so long as there is no restriction on this imposed by the immigration judge (the UK Border Agency do not have power to impose work conditions on an immigration judge's grant of bail).

The Immigration and Asylum Act 1999 enables the making of regulations which can prohibit those granted Temporary Admission from residing in a particular area. In addition the Home Secretary has the power to provide accommodation to those granted Temporary Admission. Where he does so, he is empowered to place conditions on their Temporary Admission requiring them to reside in that accommodation and to impose restrictions on the individual's absence from it.

Tribunal bail

Power to grant bail

The right to seek bail is contained in Schedule 2 of the 1971 Act, the 1996 and the 1999 Act. It arises in the following circumstances:

i) new arrivals detained for more than 7 days pending examination (Schedule 2 paragraph 22(1)(a)(1b) as amended by Schedule 2 paragraph 11(1)-(3) of 96 Act);

ii) those whose leave to enter is cancelled or leave to enter is refused (paragraph 22(1)(aa), Schedule 14 para 63 of the 99 Act);

iii) suspected illegal entrants and overstayers pending the giving of directions; (22(1)(b))

iv) following a decision to deport; (22(1)(b)

v) following a recommendation for deportation or a deportation order now that s.54 of 99 Act comes into force.

vi) pending appeal except where the appeal is in respect of human rights issues and the person has been recommended for deportation following criminal conviction.

vii) on an application for judicial review as part of interim relief.

viii) by the Court of Appeal on appeal from the IAT.

Bail applications may be made to a Chief Immigration Officer, or to the immigration tribunal. Therefore if the UK Border Agency refuse to grant your client temporary admission or bail, they have a right to apply for bail to the immigration tribunal.

Part IV of the Asylum and Immigration Tribunal (Procedure) Rules 2005 makes specific provision for bail applications before the immigration tribunal. The rules require detailed grounds in support, together with advanced service of a bail address and surety details (though the provision of the latter is not a pre-requisite under the rules), and similarly envisages service of the Respondent's Bail summary by 2.00pm the day prior to the bail application provided adequate notice was given.

An immigration tribunal bail application must be made on a prescribed form, a B1.

An immigration judge may release your client on bail subject to conditions similar to those an IO may impose but with the additional power to require recognisance from the client and any sureties. This will include reappearing before the immigration judge at a later hearing usually the full appeal hearing. Immigration judges can be expected to be sympathetic to clients not attending every further hearing especially where they have to travel some distance – but you may need to make clear at the hearing that your client has maintained contact with you. The exception is where the hearing is a bail variation or extension.

Scottish bail cases are very different to those in England and Wales.

Remember at the bail hearing that the burden of proof in justifying detention lies, given the presumption in favour of bail, on the Secretary of State to the balance of probabilities. The immigration judge must give a reasoned decision in writing. It should be noted that failure by the UK Border Agency to serve the Bail Summary by 2.00pm the previous day is deemed to be 'bail not challenged'.

Sureties and recognisance

Sureties are put forward as potential guarantors that a person will answer their bail.

There is no requirement in law that your client provide sureties/recognisance (*Glowacka*), nor that there be any particular sum of money, nor that the money be in especially liquid form (hence one might offer to stand on the basis of property rather than cash deposits in a bank). The UNHCR in their 1999 Guidelines on Criteria and Standards Relating to the Detention of Asylum Seekers make the point that asylum seekers should not be expected to produce sureties willing to offer prohibitively high sums of money.

The standard Bail Form, the B1, has spaces for two sureties, though there is no requirement that there are a pair: you could offer more, or none. It will be necessary to supply the immigration tribunal and UK Border Agency with their details so that the individuals in question, and their addresses, can be the subject of investigation via the Police National Computer (PNC). Two days notice should be given to the SSHD for this purpose.

Those with criminal convictions or insecure immigration status, or whose addresses have in the past been associated with absconding, are unlikely to be accepted as sureties.

The sureties should always attend court – it will rarely be the case that non-attendance will be accepted (though it is not completely unknown for a formal declaration to suffice, taken before an establishment figure). The surety should have proof of ID, address occupation, financial status, immigration status (ideally British citizenship or Indefinite Leave to Remain) and evidence of the address that is available to the detainee. Immigration judges prefer a surety who is living with or near an applicant to ensure that are able to exercise a measure of control over them. The surety should explain their relationship to the detainee, and what level of contact they have had with them in the past, and intend to maintain in the future.

Recently arrived immigration detainees are not likely to know many people in the United Kingdom. The old IAA Chief Adjudicator, alive to the likelihood that asylum seekers in particular will lack contacts in the country, specifically drew attention to this factor in his Guidance Notes for Adjudicators, published in

September 2000. This policy has not been changed, although there is no equivalent guidance currently available on the immigration tribunal website at the time of writing.

The Churches Commission for Racial Justice for this reason set up the Bail Circle, an association of people who are willing to introduce themselves to detainees and to stand surety for them in bail applications.

If bail is granted, conditions will be fixed by the immigration judge. The attendance of the sureties may be waived for the next occasion, so long as they provide letters explaining their absence and indicating their continued acquiescence in the original bail conditions. In our ethics chapter (Chapter 12, paragraph 14) we deal with the possibility of issues arising under money laundering regulations from holding money for sureties. The applicant must attend on the next occasion.

If your client doesn't attend the sureties risk forfeiting all or part of their recognisance. You must explain this to the sureties, who may be liable even though they have done their best to avoid such an event (this advice would be prudently given in writing, and care should be taken over any conflicts of interest that might ensue). Large sums have sometimes been required by immigration judges and adjudicators (or CIOs) – indeed at one time £5000 was not uncommon. In order to ascertain the surety's appreciation of the situation, the immigration judge may question the sureties to see if their confidence in the applicant meeting his bail conditions was well founded, whether they monitored compliance with bail conditions and whether they suspected any failure to comply.

Top tip

Parents and partners are often not powerful sureties. This is because of their close relationship with the applicant for bail: many immigration judges will have had the unpleasant task of conducting forfeiture hearings with such sureties and will consider them not best able to judge a bail applicant's character because of their closeness, or alternatively too much under the influence of the bail applicant or willing to do anything to get the bail applicant out of detention, including forfeit large amounts of money.

Close friends or colleagues willing to put up substantial sums and who can explain that they understand the risk may make better sureties.

Generally, Bail Circle volunteers or detention visitors are not considered good sureties by most immigration judges.

Taking instructions in bail cases

With the detainee client, ensure you cover the following ground:

- The detention criteria issues listed already, in so far as relevant to the facts of the case in hand.

- Ensure that the facts that are said to give rise to a power to detain are truly established – e.g. was the person working in breach of conditions, and/or are the UK Border Agency right to say they have overstayed their leave? Do they have an entitlement to remain in the UK under a Home Office policy?

- Ensure that any referrals are made that are shown to be necessary by the instructions – eg for mental or physical health care.

- Ensure that instructions are taken in a way that recognises any vulnerability of the client.

> **Top tip**
>
> It is an unfortunate fact that bail summaries are often woefully inaccurate and/or highly misleading. For example, the underlying facts are sometimes wrong, or important facts are omitted – such as difficulties the Home Office has had in obtaining an EDT. Sometimes a person will be accused of failing to report when in fact they did report, or were in immigration or criminal detention at the relevant time.
>
> It is crucial not to assume bail summaries are accurate and to take full instructions on them.

In addition, explain –

- a late claim for asylum and failure to approach the authorities at the border

- a failure to claim asylum from the moment contact made with the authorities

And ensure

- willingness to ensure compliance with reporting/residence conditions (and understanding that a failure to comply might have adverse implications for future immigration applications to the UK); you could suggest possible reporting regimes to clarify this

- client understands that sureties could lose their money in the event of absconding.

A criminal records check and also an address check against immigration records and past bail cases may be conducted with sureties. Therefore, it is important that sureties are aware this will happen (otherwise they will get an unpleasant surprise they will not welcome at the hearing) and that you ensure you have information regarding:

- Criminal convictions (especially offences of dishonesty or related to immigration)

- Financial situation, including expenses and income – any recent large transactions into their account should be explained. Liquidity of assets – they may have to deposit the money in question; and can they deal with its forfeiture. Evidence of support and accommodation arrangements. Ensure any money comes from sources that do not raise questions of ethics or criminal immigration offences

- Plans regarding any trips abroad or other engagements which might impact on the effectiveness of their being surety, or their ability to support subsequent extensions of bail.

- How they know, and how they intend to maintain contact with, or control over, the applicant

Accommodation

It is extremely difficult to obtain bail without an accommodation address. The main sources of accommodation currently are the organisations like Refugee Council and Refugee Action who provide accommodation prior to entry into the NASS system.

In those cases in which asylum-seekers are offering accommodation, the landlord or social service which provided the accommodation must be contacted for written agreement to accepting the bail applicant should s/he be released.

It is important to identify the nearest police station to the accommodation address as in most cases bail is granted with reporting conditions at the local police station or reporting centre.

National security cases

Under the NIA 2002, the SSHD may certify that it is believed that the person's presence in the United Kingdom is a "risk to national security" and that it is suspected that the person is connected to international terrorism. On certifying an individual is such a person the UKBA may take removal action.

The government has found it necessary to derogate from Article 5 ECHR for the duration of this legislation.

These powers have been interfered with by the ruling by Britain's highest court, the Law Lords, that the indefinite detention of foreign terrorism suspects is incompatible with the Human Rights Act and the European Convention on Human Rights (ECHR) (article 14 of the ECHR). Indefinite detention was found to discriminate on the grounds of nationality because it applies only to foreign nationals suspected of terrorism, despite a comparable threat from terrorism suspects with British nationality. They also held that the suspension of human rights was unjustified because indefinite detention powers that apply only to some of those who pose a threat cannot be said to be "strictly required". At the time of writing the Secretary of State was considering his position as to what steps to take to comply with the ruling of the House of Lords.

Applications for bail are brought before the SIAC. Under the Asylum & Immigration (Treatment Of Claimants Etc.) Act 2004, section 32 gives a right of appeal regarding the grant of bail, on a point of law, to the Court of Appeal, to which the normal SIAC processes then apply, ie an appeal may be brought only with the leave of the Commission or, if such leave is refused, with the leave of the appropriate appeal court.

Challenges to lawfulness of detention

It would be unusual directly to challenge lawfulness of detention before applying for temporary release and/or bail (bail is covered in the next section), as these are the simplest ways to secure a detainee's release from detention, which is likely to be the detainee's main priority. However, an understanding of lawfulness of detention can inform such applications, and can be important in securing compensation for a detainee after release.

Applications in such cases may be run by way of *habeas corpus* application, which is made in the Administrative Court, or in the course of judicial review proceedings. Judicial review is the more normal remedy and has the advantage of being able to pursue damages as part of the proceedings (although the case will be referred to the Queen's Bench Division or a county court for assessment). *Habeas corpus* can only be used where it is the *power* to detain that is under challenge, but it has the advantage of a quick listing in the Administrative Court.

There is judicial support for the notion that whereas immigration judges are to consider the *correctness* of the exercise of the power to detain (via the factors set out above, paragraph 3.1 onwards), the *lawfulness* of the exercise of the power is a matter for the Administrative Court alone. Thus Collins J stated in *R v Secretary of State for the Home Department ex parte Konan* [2004] EWHC 22 Admin:

> "An adjudicator in considering a bail application is not determining (indeed, he has no power to determine) the lawfulness of the detention."

However many arguments may be relevant under both the lawfulness of detention and its correctness – e.g. a lengthy detention is something which might eventually make detention unlawful, but it is also a relevant consideration as to the correctness of detention in all the circumstances and according to Home Office detention policy. Nevertheless, many immigration judges are reluctant to consider length of detention as a relevant factor and will allow detention to continue considerably beyond a reasonable period on the grounds that lawfulness is not for the immigration tribunal to decide.

In addition, unlawful detention can be grounds for compensation. See *ID and Others v The Home Office* [2005] EWCA Civ 38. Where lawfulness arises as an issue, it may be in the client's best interests to make an application for an Order to the High Court. This can be done simultaneously with an immigration tribunal bail application, as the bail application is the fastest way to try to secure release for a client, but it is not a challenge to lawfulness and is not a basis for securing compensation.

Where the issue is one of lawfulness of the detention a writ of *habeas corpus* can be applied for. This has a higher priority over judicial review with respect to listing of the hearing and a refusal of the writ is potentially appealable to the House of Lords whereas a refusal by the Court of Appeal, on a renewed application, to grant permission to apply for JR is not.

Administrative removal

Most removals from the UK of foreign nationals take place by way of 'administrative removal'. This is simply the straightforward removal of the person from the United Kingdom. Once outside the UK, the person can apply for entry under the Immigration Rules, although immigration rule 320 might present some barriers for some immigrants in this position. This distinguishes administrative removal from deportation, as a deportation order excludes the person from readmission to the UK for at least three years.

The power of administrative removal is provided for in Schedule 2 of the 1971 Act, particularly at paragraph 8. This applies to illegal entrants, as defined at s.33 of the 1971 Act.

Section 10 of the Immigration and Asylum Act 1999 extended the power to administratively remove to those who became present in the UK illegally, i.e. overstayers and others who have breached the conditions of their stay in the UK.

Before going ahead with an administrative removal, the Home Office will review all relevant factors before making such a decision, see rule 395:

> '395C. Before a decision to remove under section 10 is given, regard will be had to all the relevant factors known to the Secretary of State including:
> (i) age;
> (ii) length of residence in the United Kingdom;
> (iii) strength of connections with the United Kingdom;
> (iv) personal history, including character, conduct and employment record;
> (v) domestic circumstances;
> (vi) previous criminal record and the nature of any offence of which the person has been convicted;
> (vii) compassionate circumstances;

> (viii) any representations received on the person's behalf.'

In the case of family members, the factors listed in paragraphs 365-368 must also be taken into account.

Deportation

Power to deport

A person who is not a British citizen is liable to deportation from the United Kingdom if "the Secretary of State deems his deportation to be conducive to the public good" (section 3(5)(a) Immigration Act 1971 refers). By section 5(1) of the 1971 Act the Secretary of State may make a deportation order against a person liable to deportation order under section 3(5). A deportation order requires the person to leave and prohibits such person from entering the UK whilst such order is extant.

Section 3:

> "(5) A person who is not a British citizen is liable to deportation from the United Kingdom if-
> (a) the Secretary of State deems his deportation to be conducive to the public good; or
> (b) another person to whose family he belongs is or has been ordered to be deported.
> (6) Without prejudice to the operation of subsection (5) above, a person who is not a British citizen shall also be liable to deportation from the United Kingdom if, after he has attained the age of seventeen, he is convicted of an offence for which he is punishable with imprisonment and on his conviction is recommended for deportation by a court empowered by this Act to do so."

Section 5:

> "(1) Where a person is under section 3(5) or (6) above liable to deportation, then subject to the following provisions of this Act the Secretary of State may make a deportation order against him, that is to say an order requiring him to leave and prohibiting him from entering the United Kingdom; and a deportation order against a person shall invalidate any leave to enter or remain in the United Kingdom given him before the order is made or while it is in force.
> (2) A deportation order against a person may at any time be revoked by a further order of the Secretary of State, and shall cease to have effect if he becomes a British citizen."

Section 7 of the 1971 Act also provides for exemption from deportation for long term residents who were ordinarily resident in the UK when the 1971 came into force, on 1 January 1973, and where they have been resident in the UK for five years at the time of either a court or the Secretary of State considering whether to make a deportation order. 'Ordinarily resident' has no statutory meaning but has been held to exclude unlawful residence.

Procedure for deportation

There are two separate deportation procedures resulting in removal and exclusion from return to the UK. The following flow charts illustrate the differences between these two regimes. It is assumed for the purposes of the chart that the claimant loses at each stage of the process. It can be seen that the automatic deportation process is somewhat simpler than the discretionary process.

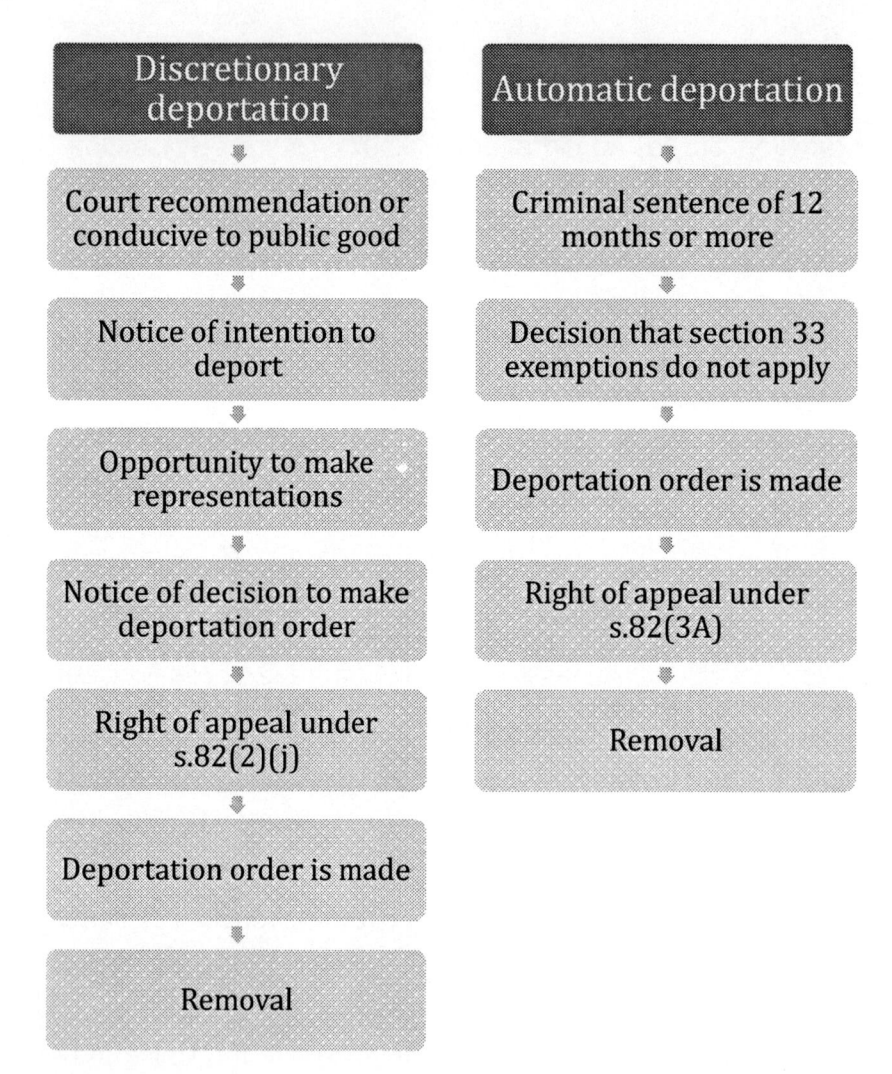

Discretionary deportation
- Court recommendation or conducive to public good
- Notice of intention to deport
- Opportunity to make representations
- Notice of decision to make deportation order
- Right of appeal under s.82(2)(j)
- Deportation order is made
- Removal

Automatic deportation
- Criminal sentence of 12 months or more
- Decision that section 33 exemptions do not apply
- Deportation order is made
- Right of appeal under s.82(3A)
- Removal

Discretionary deportation

Notification of the decision to deport and the procedure to be followed is described at rules 381 to 384:

> '381. When a decision to make a deportation order has been taken (otherwise than on the recommendation of a court) a notice will be given to the person concerned informing him of the decision and of his right of appeal.
>
> 382. Following the issue of such a notice the Secretary of State may authorise detention or make an order restricting a person as to residence, employment or occupation and requiring him to report to the police, pending the making of a deportation order.

> 383. ...
>
> 384. If a notice of appeal is given within the period allowed, a summary of the facts of the case on the basis of which the decision was taken will be sent to the appropriate appellate authorities, who will notify the appellant of the arrangements for the appeal to be heard.'

The implication that notice of a decision to deport need not be given to a person if the decision is made on the recommendation of a court misstates the true legal position. It reflects the position prior to the coming into force of NIAA s. 82 which for the first time introduced a right of appeal against decisions to deport following the recommendation of a court. The Immigration (Notices) Regulations 2003 (SI 2003/658) require written notice to be given to a person of any appealable immigration decision. A decision to deport following a recommendation of the Court is appealable and therefore a decision of which written notice must be given. The position is correctly stated in the Immigration Directorate Instruction on Deportation, Chap 13, section 1, para. 5: "If, after consideration of all the relevant facts, deportation is considered the correct course of action, a notice of a decision to make a deportation order will be served".

The deportation order may not be made while a right of appeal still exists or the appeal is pending, or, where a recommendation was made by a criminal court, the person can appeal against sentence.

The statutory bar on deportation does not apply if the SSHD certifies that the decision to make a deportation order was taken on the grounds that the person's removal from the UK would be in the interests of national security (NIAA s. 97A, inserted by IAN s. 7 with effect from 31.8.6). Such a person will be able to appeal against the decision to deport only to SIAC and only from outside the country. If the person makes a human rights claim, he or she can appeal in country unless the SSHD certifies that removal would not breach the person's human rights. In such a case, the person can appeal, in country, to SIAC against that certificate. Although some might think the out-of-country appeal unjust, fortunately it is not so, as explained by the government:

> "I do not think that appellants are disadvantaged by conducting the appeal from overseas. In the great majority of cases, much of the evidence is closed; that is, the detail is not disclosed to the appellant" (Baroness Ashton of Upholland, Hansard 7.2.6 col. 549).

Automatic deportation

So called 'automatic' deportations were introduced in the wake of the foreign prisoner scandal in 2006. In fact such deportations are far from automatic and the traditional human rights defence operates as usual. The process leading to the appeal is different, although the power to make a deportation order continues to derive from the 1971 Act.

Perhaps the most notable procedural difference, described below, is that the deportation order itself is made very early in the process without the need for a notice of intention to deport or a notice of a decision to make a deportation order. However, the making of an 'automatic' section 32 deportation order does not prevent an appeal; the appeal in such a case actually lies against the deportation order itself.

Section 32 of the UK Borders Act 2007, which came into force on 1 August 2008, places a duty on the Secretary of State to make a deportation order in respect of a person who is not a British citizen who has been convicted in the UK of an offence and sentenced to either:

(i) a period of imprisonment of at least 12 months; or

(ii) a period of imprisonment of any duration for a particularly serious offence (not in force yet).

Imprisonment for 12 months does not include where a person is serving consecutive sentences that individually are less than 12 months in duration but amount in aggregate to 12 months or more.

Section 32(4) introduces a statutory presumption that a deportation to which section 32 applies is conducive to the public good for the purpose of s.3(5)(a) 1971 Act. This duty applies to all foreign criminals except where they fall within one of the exceptions in section 33. Where an exception does apply, deportation may still be appropriate under the existing discretionary deportation provisions of the Immigration Act 1971 or, in the case of EEA nationals and their family members who are exercising Treaty rights, under the Immigration (European Economic Area) Regulations 2006.

The exceptions in s.33 are as follows:

(1) Where deportation would breach human rights or the refugee convention

(2) Age (under 18 at date of conviction)

(3) EC treaty rights would be breached

(4) Extradition – where the person is the subject of extradition proceedings

(5) Mental health grounds – but only where specific sections of the Mental Health Act 1983 apply to the person

(6) Recognised victim of trafficking – this is not yet in force but protects where the SSHD take the view removal would breach the Council of Europe trafficking convention

The applicability of one of the exceptions does not render a section 32 deportation unlawful, but can lead to revocation of the deportation order.

Section 34 governs the timing of the making of the deportation order itself and gives the Secretary of State complete discretion as to timing, other than stating that a deportation order under s.32 cannot be made while the relevant criminal sentence is under appeal (s.34(2)).

Section 35 governs the right of appeal and modifies some of the relevant primary legislation. Section 79 of the 2002 Act is modified so that the section does not apply in cases of automatic deportation orders made under s.32 2007 Act (s.79 would normally prevent a deportation order being made while an appeal is brought). Section 82 of the 2002 Act is modified to give a right of appeal against s.32(5) deportation orders.

> **Example**
>
> Mehmet was convicted of a crime and sentenced to 14 months' imprisonment. Irrespective of whether a recommendation for deportation is made by the sentencing judge, the sentence should trigger the automatic deportation process.
>
> If the Home Office take the view that none of the 2007 Act s.33 exceptions apply, Mehmet will be served with a Deportation Order at a time of the Home Office's choosing. We would expect this to occur while Mehmet is serving his criminal sentence.
>
> The serving of the Deportation Order triggers a right of appeal, because of the amended s.82(3A) of the 2002 Act. The only arguments available to Mehmet on appeal are whether any of the s.33 exceptions apply to him. In fact, this is little different to a traditional deportation case, which would in any event have turned on human rights considerations.
>
> If the appeal is successful, the Deportation Order will be revoked. If the appeal is dismissed, it will remain in force and be enforced.

Asylum and deportation

Immigration Rule 380 states as follows:

> '380. A deportation order will not be made against any person if his removal in pursuance of the order would be contrary to the United Kingdom's obligations under the Convention and Protocol relating to the Status of Refugees or the Human Rights Convention.

Section 72 of the Nationality Immigration and Asylum Act 2002 is discussed in the Chapter on asylum, under the heading "Article 33(2)". That provision essentially sets up a rebuttable presumption that certain individuals constitute a danger to the community where they have committed offences identified by statute or Order as of a certain gravity.

Revocation of deportation order

Immigration rule 390 provides as follows:

> '390. An application for revocation of a deportation order will be considered in the light of all the circumstances including the following:
>
> (i) the grounds on which the order was made;
>
> (ii) any representations made in support of revocation;
>
> (iii) the interests of the community, including the maintenance of an effective immigration control;
>
> (iv) the interests of the applicant, including any compassionate circumstances.'

Immigration rules 391-392 then go on to set out the circumstances where revocation may be appropriate and the effect of revocation:

> '391. In the case of an applicant who has been deported following conviction for a criminal offence continued exclusion
> (i) in the case of a conviction which is capable of being spent under the Rehabilitation of Offenders Act 1974, unless the conviction is spent within the meaning of that Act or, if the conviction is spent in less than 10 years, 10 years have elapsed since the making of the deportation order; or
> (ii) in the case of a conviction not capable of being spent under that Act, at any time, unless refusal to revoke the deportation order would be contrary to the Human Rights Convention or the Convention and Protocol Relating to the Status of Refugees.
> will normally be the proper course. In other cases revocation of the order will not normally be authorised unless the situation has been materially altered, either by a change of circumstances since the order was made, or by fresh information coming to light which was not before, or the appellate authorities or the Secretary of State. The passage of time since the person was deported may also in itself amount to such a change of circumstances as to warrant revocation of the order.
>
> 392. Revocation of a deportation order does not entitle the person concerned to re-enter the United Kingdom; it renders him eligible to apply for admission under the Immigration Rules. Application for revocation of the order may be made to the Entry Clearance Officer or direct to the Home Office.'

A refusal to revoke a deportation order is appealable to the immigration tribunal (see NIAA s. 82(2)(k)). Such an appeal will usually be an out of country appeal by virtue of s.92 2002 Act. However, where a fresh asylum or human rights claim is made as part of the application for revocation then the this qualifies the claimant for an in-country right of appeal under s.92(4)(a) irrespective of whether the fresh claim qualifies under immigration rule 353 (*R (on the app of BA (Nigeria)) v SSHD* [2009] UKSC 7).

If section 12 of the Immigration, Asylum and Nationality Act 2006 is ever brought into force, which would amend the definitions of asylum claim and human rights claim in s.113 of the 2002 Act, then the judgment in *BA (Nigeria)* will no longer be relevant.

Substantive considerations

The immigration rules in respect of deportation only apply to traditional discretionary deportation cases. They are not relevant in automatic deportation cases, where the only way to resist deportation is to show that one of the s.33 2007 Act exemptions applies. Usually this will mean that the claimant must rely on human rights arguments.

The old immigration rule on deportation was as follows:

> 'Subject to paragraph 380, in considering whether deportation is the right course on the merits, the public interest will be balanced against any compassionate circumstances of the case. While each case will be considered in the light of the particular circumstances, the aim is an exercise of the power of deportation which is consistent and fair as between one person and another, although one case will rarely be identical with another in all material respects. In the cases detailed in paragraph 363A, deportation will normally be the proper course where a person has failed to comply with or has contravened a condition or has remained without authority. Before a decision to deport is reached the Secretary of State will take into account all relevant factors known to him including:
> (i) age;
> (ii) length of residence in the United Kingdom;
> (iii) strength of connections with the United Kingdom;
> (iv) personal history, including character, conduct and employment record;
> (v) domestic circumstances;
> (vi) previous criminal record and the nature of any offence of which the person has been convicted;
> (vii) compassionate circumstances;
> (viii) any representations received on the person's behalf.'

This longstanding rule was changed as of 20 July 2006. The new rule is far less favourable, and includes a presumption in favour of deportation where a person is liable to such action:

> '364. Subject to paragraph 380, while each case will be considered on its merits, where a person is liable to deportation the presumption shall be that the public interest requires deportation. The Secretary of State will consider all relevant factors in considering whether the presumption is outweighed in any particular case, although it will only be in exceptional circumstances that the public interest in deportation will be outweighed in a case where it would not be contrary to the Human Rights Convention and the Convention and Protocol relating to the Status of Refugees to deport. The aim is an exercise of the power of deportation which is consistent and fair as between one person and another, although one case will rarely be identical with another in all material respects. In the cases detailed in paragraph 363A deportation will normally be the proper course where a person has failed to comply with or has contravened a condition or has remained without authority.'

Although with the passage of time fewer and fewer deportation cases are governed by the old rule, it will nevertheless be of vital importance to determine which rule is applicable. The modern rule begins with a presumption against deportation, whereas the historic rule mandated a pure balancing exercise without the scales tilted against the prospective deportee. Perhaps, absent clarification of whether an IJ has applied a presumption or not, it must be assumed, to ensure that an illegal decision is not upheld, that they applied the presumption, adversely to the Appellant. The immigration tribunal ruled in *ES (Deportation pending on 2nd October 2000) Ukraine* [2006] UKAIT 00056 (04 July 2006) (para 24 of the decision) that even an error which ostensibly favoured the appellant was a material error of law (in that case preferring a balancing exercise to the revocation test of "most exceptional circumstances"), so consideration of the wrong incarnation of the rule might demand the reconsideration of this appeal.

The relevant rule should be that in place at the date of decision.

The EIG provides some guidance as to when deportation will be considered at Chapter 12:

> "The Secretary of State may decide that a person's deportation is conducive to the public good if (amongst other things):
> - he has been convicted of a serious offence or has a series of comparatively minor convictions and where the court did not recommend deportation;
> - he has obtained indefinite leave to remain by deception
>
> ...There are many reasons why a Court may decide not to recommend deportation under section 3(6), (see Chapter 15), most commonly because its attention was not drawn to its powers in this respect or the judge decided to leave the matter to the Secretary of State. Consideration will be given to deportation on conducive grounds if the person has one conviction for a serious crime or several convictions for less serious crimes which, taken together and weighed against any compassionate circumstances, merit deportation. The fact that a court has decided not to make a recommendation does not debar the Secretary of State from taking such action himself but would be taken into account in consideration of the case."

In a case involving previous criminal offences, there is a need to address the likelihood of the Appellant's re-offending, as is stated in *N (Kenya) v Secretary of State for the Home Department* [2004] EWCA Civ 1094 (05 August 2004) at paragraph 45. However, in the same judgment it is made clear that re-offending is not the whole picture:

> "64 ... Essentially the same balance is expressed as that between the appellant's right to respect for his private and family life on the one hand and the prevention of disorder or crime on the other. Where a person who is not a British citizen commits a number of very serious crimes, the public interest side of the balance will include importantly, although not exclusively, the public policy need to deter and to express society's revulsion at the seriousness of the criminality. It is for the adjudicator in the exercise of his discretion to weigh all relevant factors, but an individual adjudicator is no better able to judge the critical public interest factor than is the court. In the first instance, that is a matter for the Secretary of State. The adjudicator should then take proper account of the Secretary of State's public interest view.
>
> 65. The risk of re-offending is a factor in the balance, but, for very serious crimes, a low risk of re-offending is not the most important public interest factor. In my view, the adjudicator's decision was over-influenced in the present case by his assessment of the risk of re-offending to the exclusion, or near exclusion, of the

> other more weighty public interest considerations characterised by the seriousness of the appellant's offences."

Where an Appellant is found not to be at risk of re-offending, this raises the question of the severity of the offence to salient importance – otherwise how can it be said that the public interest demands their departure from the UK?

In *Samaroo* the Appellant had been convicted of a very serious trafficking offence involving £400,000 of heroin (para 3): the Court paid heed to his being a "crucial part of the organisation" (para 41) and the SSHD's own policy stressed the "international dimension" (para 8 subpara 26) and "importation" (para 10). This might be in stark contrast to a case where there was a single offence that did not involve importation directly, or where the index offence is committed in the course of the offender's own drug use.

Most deportation cases will turn on Article 8 ECHR considerations, and reference can be made to that chapter of this manual. The case of *Üner V. The Netherlands* (Application No. 46410/99) is the leading judgment on the Article 8 ECHR considerations that arise in a deportation case, and the following factors are set out by the court at paragraphs 57 and 58:

1. The nature and seriousness of the offence committed by the applicant;
2. The length of the applicant's stay in the country from which he or she is to be expelled;
3. The time elapsed since the offence was committed and the applicant's conduct during that period;
4. The nationalities of the various persons concerned;
5. The applicant's family situation, such as the length of the marriage, and other factors expressing the effectiveness of a couple's family life;
6. Whether the spouse knew about the offence at the time when he or she entered into a family relationship;
7. Whether there are children of the marriage, and if so, their age; and
8. The seriousness of the difficulties which the spouse is likely to encounter in the country to which the applicant is to be expelled.
9. The best interests and well-being of the children, in particular the seriousness of the difficulties which any children of the applicant are likely to encounter in the country to which the applicant is to be expelled; and
10. The solidity of social, cultural and family ties with the host country and with the country of destination.

Uner is itself then supplemented by another later case, *Maslov v Austria* 1638/03 [2008] ECHR 546:

> '74. Although Article 8 provides no absolute protection against expulsion for any category of aliens (see *Üner*, cited above, § 55), including those who were born in the host country or moved there in their early childhood, the Court has already found that regard is to be had to the special situation of aliens who have spent most, if not all, their childhood in the host country, were brought up there and received their education there (see *Üner*, § 58 *in fine*).

> 75. In short, the Court considers that for a settled migrant who has lawfully spent all or the major part of his or her childhood and youth in the host country very serious reasons are required to justify expulsion. This is all the more so where the person concerned committed the offences underlying the expulsion measure as a juvenile.'

Maslov re-emphasises that cases involving long-settled migrants, particularly who entered the UK as children, involve very substantial interferences with Article 8 which must be properly weighed in the balance.

For further discussion of this aspect of human rights law, see the chapter on human rights and Article 8.

Top tips

It is important to consider what arguments and evidence might be available in a deportation case. It is not easy to acquire good evidence in deportation cases but this will be decisive on appeal.

Evidence to seek might include:
- Sentencing judge remarks. Ensure a complete copy is obtained and do not leave it to the Home Office to do so. The Home Office often quote very selectively and a full copy may be helpful to the client.
- Up to date probation report. Some probation officers are helpful, some are not. Whether an up to date report on risk of re-offending can be obtained might be critical.
- Copies of all pre-sentence reports. There may have been a psychological or psychiatric assessment as well as a pre-sentence probation report.
- Solid and incontrovertible evidence of family life. The Home Office will question everything in a deportation case, including even the existence of children or a partner. Whether the client can get out on bail and therefore re-establish a current and strong family life before the appeal hearing can be a critical factor.

The key case governing conduct of deportation appeals is *EO (Deportation appeals: scope and process) Turkey* [2007] UKAIT 00062. In that case the tribunal suggested there were several steps that an immigration judge should follow when assessing a case:

(i) Is the appellant liable to deportation?

(ii) If so, would deportation breach the appellant's rights under the Refugee Convention or the ECHR;

(iii) If not, consider paragraph 364 and whether the case is one where the grounds of 'exceptional circumstances' (which must logically be wider than the human rights considerations that apply) arise in the case and, if so, give careful reasons for why this is so.

Chapter 10: Race discrimination

RACE RELATIONS AND IMMIGRATION LAW AND PRACTICE 381
RACE DISCRIMINATION WITHIN THE IMMIGRATION DECISION 382
RACE DISCRIMINATION BEYOND THE IMMIGRATION DECISION 382

RACE RELATIONS ACT 1976 (AS AMENDED) 382
PROHIBITION ON DISCRIMINATION 383
DIRECT DISCRIMINATION 383
INDIRECT DISCRIMINATION 383
VICTIMISATION 385
HARASSMENT 385
EXCEPTIONS 386
DISCRIMINATION BY PUBLIC AUTHORITIES 386
Who is a public authority? 387
What functions are covered? 387
Exceptions to the duty on public authorities 387
Exceptions for immigration functions 387

RACE DISCRIMINATION IN IMMIGRATION CASES 389
NO IMMIGRATION DECISION 389
JURISDICTION OF THE IMMIGRATION TRIBUNAL 390

Race relations and immigration law and practice

Race relations legislation is of primary concern to the immigration practitioner insofar as it relates directly to procedures for dealing with applications. This chapter looks at how, and how far, race relations legislation can be used to protect the interests of clients in this context.

It should be noted that people under immigration control may be subject to race discrimination in many other areas of their lives, for example in their accommodation, access to services such as health and education, or in their employment. The Race Relations Act 1976 as amended provides a broad range of protections.

People may be subjected to attacks and actions with a racial or racist element that engage the criminal law. Besides undertaking the work within the competence of an immigration practitioner, that practitioner should be ready to refer clients to other lawyers (for example criminal law and employment law practitioners) where the matter is outside their competence and to direct clients to sources of information when they wish to know about their rights to be free from discrimination or to complain (for example against media coverage). The Commission for Racial Equality historically indicated that it wished to prioritise work on asylum and might be an early port of call for a complainant. Further calls in this regard should now be directed to the Equality and Human Rights Commission.

The Home Office, the UK Border Agency's parent government department, has a wide range of responsibilities for race relations, in particular as regards policing and crimes. Home Office policy statements made in the context of their work on race may be useful in the immigration context.

The importance that the law attributes to anti-discrimination principles received treatment by the House of Lords in *European Roma Rights Centre et ors v Immigration Officer at Prague Airport and SSHD* [2004] UKHL 55, where Lord Steyn wrote of the fact that in international law it was unlawful to discriminate on grounds of race:

> "State practice virtually universally condemns discrimination on grounds of race. It does so in recognition of the fact that it has become unlawful in international law to discriminate on the grounds of race. It is true that in the world, as we know it, departures from this norm are only too many. But the international community has signed up to it."

Paragraph 2 of the Immigration Rules HC395 requires that immigration officials "carry out their duties without regard to race, colour or religion ..."

Race discrimination within the immigration decision

Refusal notices emanating from Entry Clearance Officers (ECOs) at the British High Commission in Bangladesh frequently display stereotyped assertions. For example:-

> "I know from experience that it is common for prospective emigrants to leave their families in Bangladesh often for protracted periods, if given the opportunity of working abroad and I do not therefore, consider that the presence of families here outweighs my doubts about your intention to leave the United Kingdom after the period stated by you."

As we will see, this kind of discrimination can be fought within the appeals system. Law Centres have had success in having decisions withdrawn for such remarks. Challenges may be particularly relevant in family visitor visa and working holidaymaker appeals arising from the New Commonwealth countries.

It is not unknown to encounter more direct and personal racist remarks from immigration staff. In the case of *CS (Race discrimination, proper approach, effect) Jamaica* [2006] UKAIT 00004 an Entry Clearance Officer in Kingston, Jamaica, commented that 'some people' might think Jamaican men did not normally get married and therefore that the applicant was only interested in gaining entry to the UK by doing so. The Immigration tribunal held that it was proper to infer from this that the ECO was referring to black Jamaican men and that it was a racist remark.

Race discrimination beyond the immigration decision

Of course, racism is something that might be experienced at any point in an individual's dealings with authority in the UK. A receptionist might be racist whilst they are waiting for an appointment for an interview.

However, the complaint must be related to the immigration decision in order to trigger a right of appeal to the immigration tribunal. Where a complaint is solely about the treatment the person has received and not about the immigration decision itself, there is no right of appeal to the immigration tribunal. Instead, the complainant may take the complaint through the normal departmental complaints channels and to the County Court.

Race Relations Act 1976 (as amended)

The Race Relations Act 1976 makes it unlawful to treat a person less favourably than others on racial grounds. It provides protection from race discrimination in the fields of employment, education, training, housing and the provision of goods, facilities and services.

Prohibition on discrimination

Section 1 of the RRA 1976 (as amended – henceforth the RRA 1976 / the Act) prohibits discrimination on racial grounds. Racial grounds are defined in s.3(1) as "colour, race, nationality or ethnic or national origins'

In *Mandla v Dowell Lee* [1983] 1 All ER 1062 (HL), the House of Lords held that Sikhs constituted an "ethnic" group within the subcategories of "racial group". Lord Fraser went on to outline the characteristics of an ethnic group. Two characteristics were essential: a long shared history and a cultural tradition of its own, including social customs and manners but not necessarily associated with religious observance. Other factors would assist the case, for example, common geographical origin, a common language and literature or common religion different from neighbouring groups.

There are three forms of discrimination identified in the Act: direct discrimination, indirect discrimination and victimisation and, as we will see, there are two varieties of indirect discrimination:

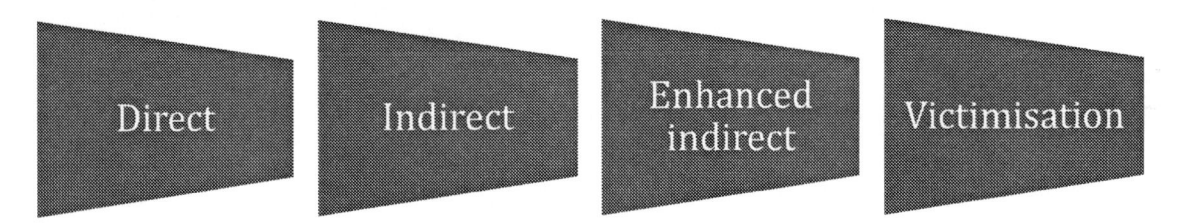

- Direct
- Indirect
- Enhanced indirect
- Victimisation

Direct discrimination

Defined in s. 1(1)(a) of the Act as "on racial grounds he treats that other less favourably than he treats or would treat other persons".

Specific different treatment of different groups falls within this definition, as do racist abuse, harassment and segregation.

It has been successfully argued, for example, that racial stereotyping by an Entry Clearance Officer constituted direct racial discrimination, and also that different treatment of certain nationals on the basis of their nationality in accordance with a declared policy amounted to direct discrimination.

Indirect discrimination

Indirect discrimination occurs when something that purports to be neutral as to race nonetheless impacts differentially on different races.

Following the amendment of the Act by the Race Relations Act (Amendment) Regulations 2003 (SI 2003/1626), two forms of indirect racial discrimination are distinguished in the Act. The original formulation continues to be available for use for all forms of discrimination, but, being narrower, is only likely to be used in circumstances which the new formulation does not catch, viz:

- all cases involving *colour or nationality*, and

- cases involving race, ethnic or national origins *outside* the fields of employment; vocational training; education; the provision of goods, facilities or services; accommodation; and any functions of a public authority in so far as they relate to any form of social security; health care; any other form of social protection; and any form of social advantage.

The original formulation, first applies to discrimination on the grounds of colour or nationality and is set out in s.1(b) of the Act

> 1(b) he applies to that other a requirement or condition which he applies or would apply equally to persons not of the same racial group as that other but –
>
> (i) which is such that the proportion of persons of the same racial group as that other who can comply with it is considerably smaller than the proportion of persons not of that racial group who can comply with it; and
>
> (ii) which he cannot show to be justifiable irrespective of the colour, race, nationality or ethnic or national origins of the person to whom it is applied; and
>
> (iii) which is to the detriment of that other because he cannot comply with it.

This can be difficult to establish. Its application is limited to a requirement or condition and thus struggles to capture informal practices. In general it will be necessary to use statistical evidence to prove indirect discrimination, and this can be very difficult to collect.

The new formulation is set out in s.1A of the Act

> A person discriminates against another if...he applies to that other a provision, criterion or practice which he applies, or would apply, equally to persons not of the same race or ethnic or national origins as that other but-
>
> (a) which puts or would put persons of the same race or ethnic or national origins as that other at a particular disadvantage when compared with other persons,
>
> (b) which puts that other at a that disadvantage and
>
> (c) which he cannot show to be a proportionate means of achieving a legitimate aim

The reference to a provision, criterion or practice institutes a broader definition. The complainant simply needs to demonstrate that the 'provision, criterion or practice' puts persons of a particular race or ethnic or national origins at a 'particular disadvantage' which may make it less necessary to provide detailed statistical evidence.

This enhanced level of protection was introduced by the Race Relations (Amendment) Regulations 2003, made to implement the Article 13 of the EC Race Directive, giving enhanced protection to those fearing discrimination on the grounds of race, ethnic or national origins (but not to those fearing discrimination on the grounds of colour or nationality) in the fields of employment; vocational training; education; the provision of goods, facilities or services; accommodation;

and any functions of a public authority in so far as they relate to any form of social security; health care; any other form of social protection; and any form of social advantage. Some commentaries suggest that stops and searches by the police, or disciplinary action in prisons could all within the ambit of 'social protection' or 'social advantage'.

Thus, in order to take advantage of the enhanced protection, you will need to show that the discrimination your client faces is as a result of his/her race, ethnic or national origins. In particular, it will be necessary to show that denial of social protection or advantage by public authorities is related to national origins, rather than nationality, and consequently, immigration status.

The Points Based System had its first casualty in indirect discrimination, in the case of *Osborne Clarke Services v Purohit* [2009] UKEAT/0305/08. The Employment Tribunal held that the law firm had discriminated indirectly on the grounds of nationality by instituting a policy of not considering applications for training contracts from non-EEA nationals.

Victimisation

Victimisation is defined in s.2 of the Act. It occurs when a person treats another less favourably because the person victimised has brought proceedings, given evidence or information in proceedings, or done anything under or by reference to the Act in relation to the discriminator, or another person. It also covers cases where the less favourable treatment is as a result of an allegation that amounts, whether this is stated explicitly or not, to an allegation that the discriminator or another person has acted in contravention of the Act. It covers cases where the discriminator knows that the person victimised intends to do any of these things, and cases where the person discriminating knows or suspects that the person victimised intends to do any of these things.

Harassment

Harassment was not specifically named in the original text of the RRA 1976. Case law had established however that harassment was undoubtedly less favourable treatment and thus a form of direct discrimination.

The 2003 Regulations amended the Act to provide a definition of harassment. The definition applies only in cases of allegations of discrimination on the grounds of race, ethnic or national origins, apply only to employment; vocational training; education; the provision of goods, facilities or services; accommodation; and any functions of a public authority in so far as they relate to any form of social security; health care; any other form of social protection; and any form of social advantage.

The regulations introduce a statutory definition of harassment as s.3A of the RRA 1976. This is:

> "(1) A person subjects another to harassment in any circumstances relevant for the purposes of any provision ... where, on grounds of race or ethnic or national origins, he engages in unwanted conduct which has the purpose or effect of —
> (a) violating that other person's dignity, or
> (b) creating an intimidating, hostile, degrading, humiliating or offensive environment for him.
>
> (2) Conduct shall be regarded as having the effect specified in paragraph (a) or (b) of subsection (1) only if, having regard to all the circumstances, in particular the perception of the other person, it should reasonably be considered as having that effect."

Exceptions

Part VI of the Act sets exceptions to the scope of the Act. It provides that nothing in Parts II to IV of the Act shall render certain Acts of discrimination unlawful. Section 41 of the Act contains an exception for acts done in pursuance of legislation or Orders in Council, and to comply with requirements imposed by Ministers in legislation. Acts that are unlawful on the grounds of race, ethnic or national origins under s.1(1B) of the amendments inserted by the Race Relations (Amendment) Regulations 2003.

Significantly under s.41(2), there is an exception which states

> "Nothing in Parts II to IV shall render unlawful any act whereby a person discriminates against another on the basis of that other's nationality or place of ordinary residence or the length of time for which he has been present or resident in the UK if that act is done..."

This is the broadest general exception in the Act. It does not rule out the possibility of showing discrimination on the grounds of race, national or ethnic origin or colour. However, it presents formidable barriers to challenging indirect discrimination on one of these grounds, where the reason for the differential treatment is nationality or place of ordinary residence or length of time in the UK.

Section 42 provides for a much more limited exception. Nothing in Part II to IV shall render unlawful an act done for the purpose of safeguarding national security, if (words added by the Race Relations Act 2000) *"the doing of the act was justified by the purpose"*.

Discrimination by public authorities

Section 19B(1) of the Act, inserted by the Race Relations (Amendment) Act 2000, into Part III of the Act, which covers non-employment cases. It states that

> "It is unlawful for a public authority in carrying out any functions of the authority to do anything which constitutes discrimination."

Who is a public authority?

Anyone exercising functions which include functions of a public nature, unless a specific exception is made.

Thus private and voluntary sector bodies are public bodies where they are carrying out a public function. An example would a private security firm contracted to the UKBA to provide escort functions, in the course of that function.

Exceptions under s.19(3) include parliament and those exercising functions in connections with proceedings in parliament; the Security Service; the Security Intelligence Service and Government Communications Headquarters.

The UK Border Agency is a public body. So is the Legal Services Commission. However the constraints that the legislation puts on their actions are limited because there are exceptions, not least to the ambit of the application of the section to UKBA. We have seen the s.41(2) exception above.

What functions are covered?

You will not find the term defined in the interpretation section of the Act. It relates to anything that a public authority does in the course of its duties. Again there are exceptions, and you have to look carefully at acts excepted from 19B to establish the full range of functions covered.

Section 27(1A) of the Act, as amended, makes special provision for s.19B to apply in relation to acts done outside the UK inn its application in relation to granting entry.

Exceptions to the duty on public authorities

Section 19C(1) provides an exception for any judicial act (whether done by a court, tribunal or any other person) or any act done on the instructions or on behalf of a person acting in a judicial capacity. This exception thus covers the High Court, and the Immigration and Asylum Chamber.

Section 19C(4) now reads *"Section 19B does not apply to any act of, or relating to, imposing a requirement or giving an express authorisation of a kind mentioned in section 19D(3) in relation to the carrying out of immigration functions"*. This is the first introduction to the specific measures set out to make exceptions in immigration cases.

Exceptions for immigration functions

Section 19D provides that it is not unlawful for a relevant person to discriminate against another person on grounds of nationality or ethnic or national origins in carrying out immigration functions".

Nothing in the section effects the position as far as discrimination on the basis of race or colour is concerned.

A relevant person is defined in s.19D(2) as a Minister of the Crown acting personally or any other person acting in accordance with a "relevant authorisation". This means (s.19D(3)) a requirement imposed or express authorisation given with respect to a particular case or class of case, by a Minister of the Crown acting personally; or an authorisation that forms part of one of the listed acts of parliament or a statutory instrument made under it.

Immigration functions are defined as those under the Immigration Acts and The Special Immigration Appeals Commission Act 1997

The Ministerial Authorisations are difficult to find. They can sometimes be located on the Home Office website (at Annexe EEff of the Immigration Directorate Instructions), which also gives details of how they are to operate.

The Race Relations (Immigration and Asylum) (No 1) Authorisation made in March 2001 came into operation on the 2nd April 2001. It allowed immigration officers to discriminate on the basis of nationality in respect of refusal of leave to enter and the exercise of powers to seek information and documents if there was statistical evidence of a pattern of breach of immigration law by persons of that nationality or if Home Office intelligence suggested that a significant number of persons of that nationality had breached or were likely to breach immigration law.

The Tamil Information Centre challenged the regulations in *R v Secretary of State for the Home Department ex parte Tamil Information Centre (2002)* Case CO/4924, Judgment 18 October 2002, TLR 30 October 2002. The Court quashed the first authorisation. It held that is was unlawful because statistical patterns or trends of breaches of control were too vague to be in accordance with the law and were not objectively justified. An interim authorisation, the Race Relations (Immigration and Asylum) Authorisation 2002 was then issued, was then issued allowing discrimination against listed nationalities. Listed, but the list was not attached to the authorisation and was not published. It does not appear on the UKBA website.

The Race Relations (Immigration and Asylum) (No 2) Authorisation 2001 which came into force on 21 November 2002 and with provision for expiry on 24 May 2003. This allowed more rigorous examination by immigration officers of Tamils, Kurds, Pontic Greeks, Roma, Somalis, Albanians, Afghans and ethnic Chinese presenting a Malaysian or Japanese passport or any other travel document issued by Malaysia or Japan.

The third order that can be seen on the Home Office website is The Race Relations (Immigration and Asylum) (No 3) Authorisation 2001 which came into operation on 25 October 2001. This gave an immigration officer power, where a person has made a claim for asylum or under Article 3 ECHR and the immigration officer *"has reason to doubt that a person is of the nationality he claims to be"* to request that person to submit to language analysis testing and take into account any refusal to submit to language analysis testing when determining whether the applicant has assisted the Secretary of State or an immigration officer in establishing the facts of the case. The authorisation was made in respect of nationals of Afghanistan, Somila and Sir Lanka. This order appears to remain in force.

An unsuccessful challenge to discrimination on the grounds of race was mounted in *European Roma Rights Centre et ors v Immigration Officer at Prague Airport and SSHD (UNHCR intervening)* [2003] EWCA Civ 666. The treatment of the Roma was found not to be prohibited by the RRA 1976 because the Roma were more likely to claim asylum in the UK.

Several other authorisations have not been published. The best place to locate recent authorisations is in the annual report of the monitor.

Race discrimination in immigration cases

Cases can be divided into those where the race discrimination is in connection with the decision on the immigration case and those where the allegation concerns discrimination in a way not connected with the decision, albeit that it originated from someone within UKBA or another public authority involved in immigration. In many cases the two will be linked: the complaint of discrimination will be alleged to have impacted on the way the decision in the immigration case. In cases where discrimination is connected with the decision, or in "mixed" cases, proceedings the RRA provides for proceedings to lie before the immigration tribunal. In cases unconnected with the decision, a person with an immigration case would make their case in the ordinary courts, just as they would if challenging discrimination by another service provider.

A complainant must prove their case on the balance of probabilities. It is recognised that claims brought under the race and sex discrimination legislation present special problems of proof for complainants, since those who discriminate on the grounds of race or gender do not in general advertise their prejudices. Thus if a claimant can show that he has been less favourably treated than comparable individuals from a different racial group, the court will look to the alleged discriminator for an explanation (which cannot be of itself on racial or sexual grounds). If no explanation is put forward or if such explanation is inadequate or unsatisfactory it will be legitimate to infer that the discrimination was on racial grounds (this is discussed in the *Roma Rights* case in the House of Lords).

No immigration decision

Section 57 of the RRA 1976 as amended by the Race Relations (Amendment) Act 2000, provides for claims of unlawful discrimination under Part III of the RRA 1976 to be brought only in a designated county court in England and Wales. This means that the county court has power to award damages.

Section 57(4) makes explicit that damages can be awarded for injury to feelings, as the sole, or one head of damages. There is an important exception. In cases of indirect discrimination under s.1(1)(b) there can be no award of damages if the respondent proves that the requirement or condition imposed was not applied with the intention of treating the claimant unfavourably on racial grounds.

If a person is complaining of race discrimination by the immigration authorities unrelated to the decision, this is the section under which the claim should be brought. Thus, for example, a person complaining of discrimination by a receptionist in the ASU, in no way held to be related to the decision on his/her asylum case, would make the complaint in the same way that the representative would if s/he was the victim of such discrimination.

In a case where discrimination by UKBA, not related to the immigration decision, is alleged, the internal complaints procedures are the first port of call (see the IDI leaflet on race relations).

Section 65 of the 1976 Act provides for a questionnaire procedure whereby an aggrieved person can question the respondent in alleged cases of discrimination. There is no time limit within which the respondent must reply but under s.65(2)(b) a court or tribunal can draw court or tribunal could draw adverse inferences from the respondent's deliberate lack of response after a reasonable period, or from an equivocal or evasive reply.

Jurisdiction of the immigration tribunal

The Race Relations (Amendment) Act, extending the RRA 1976 to cover discrimination by public authorities, including the Home Office, came into force on 2 April 2001.

Race appears at s.84(1)(b) of the 2002 Act as a potential ground of appeal – on grounds that the decision is unlawful by virtue of section 19B of the Race Relations Act 1976 (discrimination by public authorities). Provision was made for this ground of appeal to apply also in SIAC cases – see the Special Immigration Appeals Commission Act s.2(2)(e)

A finding of discrimination may vitiate the decision, but is unlikely to provide, in and of itself, a reason to allow the substantive claim. You were discriminated against, but does that mean you should be granted entry clearance? Or recognised as a refugee? It is not uncommon for an appeal to be allowed on racial discrimination grounds but dismissed on the substantive immigration case, as occurred in the case of *CS Jamaica* [2006] UKAIT 00004 (although it is worth noting that the appellant in this case was entitled to a compensation claim that would almost certainly tip the balance in favour of adequate maintenance for a future application).

This makes s.85(2) of the Nationality, Asylum and Immigration Act 2002 particularly important in discrimination cases. The section provides that the immigration tribunal must determine any matter raised as a ground of appeal or which it is required to consider by s.85 of the 2002 Act. Thus, whether the appeal is allowed or dismissed, a ruling must be made on the discrimination ground. The ruling is needed by the appellant if s/he is to be able to seek damages for discrimination in the county court as described above, although where there is a failure to make such a finding and the situation cannot be remedied within the immigration tribunal (for example the appeal is treated as abandoned following a grant of leave to enter) then the county court remedy can be pursued.

The need to make findings on racial discrimination claim is reinforced by the current immigration tribunal Practice Direction:

> '20. Discrimination
>
> 20.1 Section 84(1)(b) makes it a ground of appeal against an immigration decision that that decision is unlawful by virtue of section 19B of the Race Relations Act 1976 (discrimination by public authorities).
>
> 20.2 In cases where there is a finding of discrimination, the person affected can bring a claim in the County Court. On that claim, both the claimant and the court are bound by the decision in the immigration appeal (section 57A of the Race Relations Act 1976).
>
> 20.3 Accordingly, in a case where discrimination is raised as a ground of appeal, it is particularly important that the Tribunal is aware of its duty under section 86(2)(a) to determine any matter raised as a ground of appeal and that it makes a finding on that ground, even if the alleged discrimination is not relevant to the ultimate outcome of the appeal (see *Bibi* [2005] EWHC 386 (Admin)).'

If there is no race discrimination finding in a determination in which it was raised as a ground of appeal, consideration must be given to applying for reconsideration on this ground.

As is stated in the practice direction above, where a finding of racial discrimination is made at the immigration tribunal, a claim for compensation can then be pursued in the county court. Problems arise if the immigration tribunal fails to make a finding, but this does not prevent a compensation claim being pursued. The Tribunal has given guidance on the issues in a case called *VE (Racial discrimination) Nigeria* [2005] UKIAT 00057, which went to the Court of Appeal and was reported as [2005] EWCA Civ 1002.

It is also worth noting that another problem arising in some racial discrimination claims will be solved by the 2006 Act once s.9 of that Act is brought into force. At present, an appeal is treated as abandoned under s.104(5) of the 2002 Act if leave to enter is granted. This has led to situations where a claimant was successful on immigration grounds but may have appealed further on racial discrimination grounds (perhaps because no finding was made). If the claimant is granted leave by the Home Office or enters the UK having been granted entry clearance, the outstanding appeal currently falls away.

Chapter 11: The law of appeals

RIGHT OF APPEAL 395
   DECISIONS ATTRACTING A RIGHT OF APPEAL 395
   LIMITATIONS ON THE RIGHT OF APPEAL 398
   IN-COUNTRY AND OUT-OF-COUNTRY APPEALS 400

GROUNDS OF APPEAL 401
   STATEMENT OF ADDITIONAL GROUNDS 401

APPEALS STRUCTURE 403
   DIAGRAM 403
   SOURCES OF LAW, PRACTICE AND PROCEDURE 404

FIRST TIER TRIBUNAL 410
   OVERRIDING OBJECTIVE 410
   LODGING APPEALS 410
      Method of lodging 410
      Deadline for appeal 411
      Extension of time for lodging notice of appeal 412
   IMMINENT REMOVAL CASES 412
   CASE MANAGEMENT REVIEW HEARINGS 412
   BEST PRACTICE IN BUNDLES 413
   DIRECTIONS 414
   SUMMONING A WITNESS 416
   DOCUMENTS TO BE SENT TO TRIBUNAL 416
   VARIATION OF GROUNDS OF APPEAL 416
   ADJOURNMENTS 416
   CONDUCT OF THE APPEAL 417
      Concessions by the Home Office 418
      Natural justice 419
      Public hearing 419
      Hearing in the absence of a party 420
      Determination without a hearing 420
      Combined hearings 421
      Evidence 421
      Forgery and authenticity of documents 421
      Evaluating country reports 422
   ABANDONMENT OF APPEALS 423
   AUTHORITY TO REPRESENT 423
   IRREGULARITIES AND CORRECTIONS 424
   SECOND OR SUBSEQUENT APPEALS 424
   SPECIAL PROCEDURES AND TIME LIMITS IN ASYLUM APPEALS 425

SEEKING PERMISSION TO APPEAL FROM THE FTT 425
   BASIS OF APPLICATION 426

APPLICATION TO THE FIRST TIER TRIBUNAL	426
REVIEW PROCESS	427
FTT considers whether to review the decision	427
FTT self review	428
Decision set aside by FTT following self review	429
Decision not set aside by FTT following self review	429
PERMISSION TO APPEAL IN THE FTT	430
SEEKING PERMISSION TO APPEAL FROM THE UT	**430**
APPEALING WITH PERMISSION FROM THE FTT	431
RENEWED PERMISSION TO APPEAL APPLICATION	431
STATUS AND RACE RELATIONS APPEALS	431
PURSUING AN UPPER TRIBUNAL APPEAL	**431**
NON-COMPLIANCE IN THE UT	432
RESPONDENT'S RESPONSE TO APPEAL	432
FURTHER EVIDENCE	433
INITIAL HEARING	434
REMITTAL TO FTT	435
ONWARD APPEAL	**436**
SEEKING PERMISSION FROM THE UT	436
UT SELF REVIEW	437
TRIBUNAL DETERMINATIONS AS PRECEDENTS	**438**
STARRED APPEALS	438
REPORTED TRIBUNAL CASES	438
'COUNTRY GUIDELINE' DECISIONS	438

Right of appeal

It is not always entirely straightforward to determine whether there is a right of appeal, what the grounds of appeal might be and whether the appeal should be determined inside the UK or outside. These three issues provide the framework for the first part of this chapter:

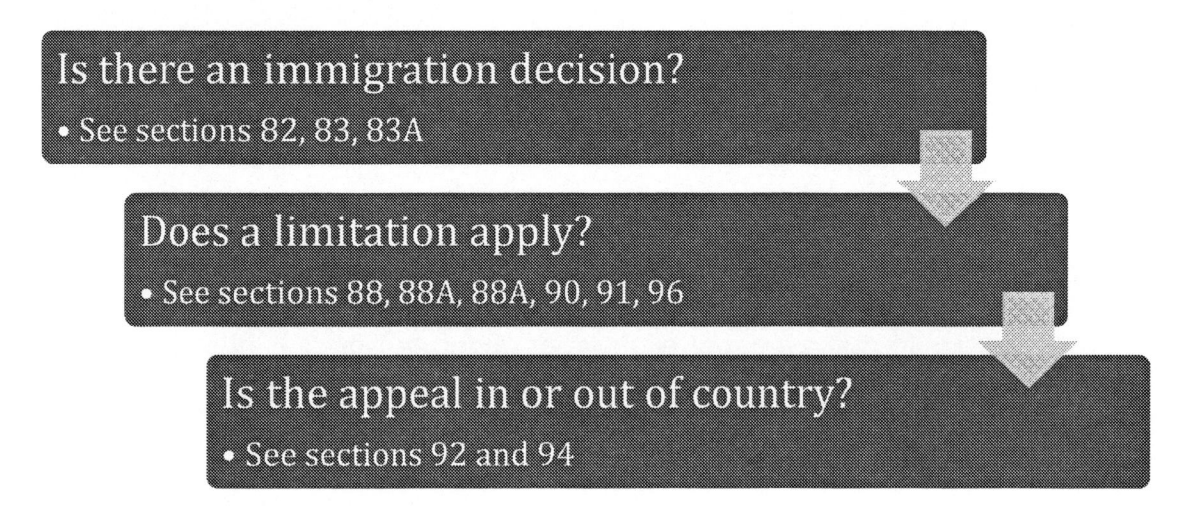

> **Is there an immigration decision?**
> - See sections 82, 83, 83A

> **Does a limitation apply?**
> - See sections 88, 88A, 88A, 90, 91, 96

> **Is the appeal in or out of country?**
> - See sections 92 and 94

Decisions attracting a right of appeal

The Nationality, Immigration and Asylum Act 2002 came into force on 1st April 2003. It provides the foundation of most rights of appeal – i.e. the question of when there is a right of appeal. Previously it also set out the framework of the appeal system, albeit through heavy amendments by the Immigration and Asylum (Treatment of Claimants Etc) Act 2004. As of 15 February 2010 the appeal structure is dictated by the Tribunals, Courts and Enforcement Act 2007 (TCEA 2007). The changes to the tribunal appeal system have not affected the right of appeal, however, which remains the same as in previous years.

Section 82 of the 2002 Act outlines the main rights of appeal generated under the 2002 Act. Sub-section 82(2) exhaustively defines which immigration decisions are potentially appealable under s.82:

a) refusal of leave to enter the UK

b) refusal of entry clearance

c) refusal of certificate of entitlement under section 10 of this Act

d) refusal to vary a person's leave to enter or remain in the UK if the result of the refusal is that the person has no leave to enter or remain;

e) variation of a person's leave to enter or remain in the UK if when the variation takes effect the person has no leave to enter or remain;

f) revocation under section 76 of this Act of indefinite leave to enter or remain in the UK;

g) a decision that a person is to be removed from the UK by way of directions under section [10(1)(a), (b), (ba) or (c)]** of the IAA 1999

h) a decision that an illegal entrant is to be removed from the UK by way of directions under paragraphs 8-10 of Schedule 2 to the Immigration Act 1971 (control of entry: removal)

[ha) a decision that a person is to be removed from the United Kingdom by way of directions under section 47 of the Immigration, Asylum and Nationality Act 2006 (removal: persons with statutorily extended leave)]**

i) a decision that a person is to be removed from the UK by way of directions given by virtue of paragraph 10A of that schedule (family)

[ia) a decision that a person is to be removed from the United Kingdom by way of directions under paragraph 12(2) of Schedule 2 to the Immigration Act 1971 (c. 77) (seamen and aircrews)]*

[ib) a decision to make an order under section 2A of that Act (deprivation of right of abode)]**

j) a decision to make a deportation order under section 5(1) of that Act, and refusal to revoke a deportation order under section 5(2) of that Act (i.e. the decision to make a deportation order following a court recommendation (Section 82(2)(j)).

* amendments by the Asylum and Immigration (Treatment of Claimants etc) Act 2004
** amendments by the Immigration, Asylum and Nationality Act 2006

A right of appeal is also generated by section 83 and 83A of the 2002 Act, the latter of which being amended into the 2002 Act from 31 August 2006 by the 2006 Act. These rights of appeal are specific to asylum appeals and are addressed in greater detail below.

Some decisions which used to attract appeal rights do so no longer:

- Refusal of asylum where leave to enter or remain is granted for one year (Section 83(1)). However once successive grants in combination succeed one year, they will attract an asylum appeal right from the grant that will ultimately lead to a period exceeding 12 months;

- Decisions taken outside the rules (Section 88 - Ineligibility). Where there is an existing appeal right it may still be possible to appeal on this ground.

- Destination specified in the Removal Directions;

- Validity of removal directions (section 66(2) IAA 1999).

- Refusal of entry clearance under the PBS – see limitations on right of appeal, below

> **Top tip**
>
> It is crucial to understand that the list of immigration decisions that generate a right of appeal is exhaustive. If a decision does not appear on the list, there is no right of appeal. For example, there is no right of appeal against an out of time application for leave to remain. It cannot be considered an application to vary leave (which might in some circumstances attract a right of appeal under s.82(2)(d)) as there is no current leave that could be varied.
>
> As a further example, there is not necessarily a right of appeal against a decision to refuse leave to remain even where the applicant relies on human rights grounds. At the time of writing it had become commonplace for human rights applications to be refused but for no immigration decision to be made, such as the making of a decision to set removal directions, thereby depriving the applicant of a right of appeal and leaving judicial review as the only potential remedy.

In practice UKBA issues a decision with an accompanying statement declaring whether that decision is an immigration decision or not. If UKBA has in fact made an immigration decision under the terms of section 82 an immigration judge will have jurisdiction to deal with the appeal (subject to the other conditions in the Act). This is the case regardless of whether UKBA recognises that he has made an immigration decision or not. Therefore even if a document is issued stating that it is not an immigration decision and there is no right of appeal, the judicial decision maker will have jurisdiction if the decision that was made is one of those defined in section 82(2).

Similarly, even if UKBA wrongly assert that there is a right of appeal when in law there is not and the case proceeds to the appeal stage, the immigration tribunal must decline to hear the case if there was in truth no right of appeal in the first place.

> **Example**
>
> A particular problem has arisen in relation to those who arrive in the UK as visitors and then claim asylum. On arrival such people will usually have been granted 6 months leave to enter/remain as a visitor. If they still possess such leave at the time of the refusal, they are not in the position described in section 82(2)(d) - because they still have current leave to remain. Home Office practice is to curtail the existing leave. The right of appeal in such a situation is actually against the curtailment (a variation of leave) rather than the original refusal to vary leave. If the Home Office do not curtail leave and do not set removal directions, however, there would be no right of appeal.
>
> It would not be acceptable to advise an applicant to delay applying for asylum in such circumstances because the delay in claiming could then be held against them when assessing the credibility of their account, it may also have implications for their eventual ability to access support and accommodation through NASS pursuant to the requirement in section 55 NIAA 2002 that asylum applicant's claim 'as soon as reasonably practicable' or risk losing access to support.

Limitations on the right of appeal

Before moving on, it is useful to record that there are miscellaneous exceptions to the right to appeal. This is now an unnecessarily complex area of law because the Home Office has somehow contrived to have two different sections 88A to the 2002 Act in force at the same time in respect of different types of application. In addition, Phelan and Gillespie's *Immigration Law Handbook* only includes one of the current sections 88A, so it is convenient to set out the law in detail.

The problem has arisen because the latest s.88A (the version to be seen in the 5th and 6th editions of *Phelan*), introduced by s.4 of the 2006 Act, has only commenced in respect of applications under the Points Based System. See the Immigration, Asylum and Nationality Act 2006 (Commencement No. 8 and Transitional and Saving Provisions) Order 2008 (SI 2008/310), paragraph 4.

The latest, 2006 Act version of s.88A prevents appeals against refusals of entry clearance in Points Based System cases. There is provision to make regulations to exempt some classes of person from this limitation on appeals rights, but no such regulations have been laid. It therefore amounts to a blanket ban on PBS entry clearance appeals. Section 4 of the 2006 Act also scraps sections 90 and 91 of the 2002 Act *but only in PBS cases*, because of the terms of the commencement order.

In fact, therefore, the old s.88A and sections 90 and 91 remain in force in respect of all non PBS cases. These are only relevant to visitors and students and their dependants. Thus the following categories of persons seeking entry clearance or leave to enter have no recourse to the immigration tribunal:

- Visitors or students without entry clearance (save for on grounds in 82(1)(b), (c) and (g)): see s.89

- Non-family visitors (save for grounds in 82(1)(b) and (c)): see s.91

- Students seeking entry for a period of less than six months or who have not been accepted for a course (save for grounds in 82(1)(b) and (c)): see s.92

- The dependant of a student as above.

The old section 88A is now irrelevant even if it does theoretically remain in force for non PBS cases. It relied on regulations being laid to become effective and regulations have never been laid. Given that sections 90 and 91 are not at the time of writing available in *Phelan* it is useful for them to be set out here:

> **90 Non-family visitor**
>
> (1) A person who applies for entry clearance for the purpose of entering the United Kingdom as a visitor may appeal under section 82(1) against refusal of entry clearance only if the application was made for the purpose of visiting a member of the applicant's family.
>
> (2) In subsection (1) the reference to a member of the applicant's family shall be construed in accordance with regulations.
>
> (3) Regulations under subsection (2) may, in particular, make provision wholly or partly by reference to the duration of two individuals' residence together.
>
> (4) Subsection (1) does not prevent the bringing of an appeal on either or both of the grounds referred to in section 84(1)(b) and (c).
>
> **91 Student**
>
> (1) A person may not appeal under section 82(1) against refusal of entry clearance if he seeks it—
> (a) in order to follow a course of study for which he has been accepted and which will not last more than six months,
> (b) in order to study but without having been accepted for a course, or
> (c) as the dependant of a person seeking entry clearance for a purpose described in paragraph (a) or (b).
>
> (2) Subsection (1) does not prevent the bringing of an appeal on either or both of the grounds referred to in section 84(1)(b) and (c).

There are also general grounds of ineligibility for an appeal, which are set out at section 88 of the 2002 Act. These apply where a potential appellant:

(a) does not satisfy a requirement as to age, nationality or citizenship specified in immigration rules

(b) does not have an immigration document of a particular kind (or any immigration document)

(ba) has failed to supply a medical report or medical certificate in accordance with a requirement of the immigration rules (amended in by 2006 Act)

(c) is seeking to be in the United Kingdom for a period greater than that permitted in his case by immigration rules, or

(d) is seeking to enter or remain in the United Kingdom for a purpose other than one for which entry or remaining is permitted in accordance with immigration rules.

'Immigration document' is specifically defined to mean entry clearance, a passport (or similar) and a work permit or other immigration employment document.

The section 88 exemptions do not prevent the bringing of an appeal on the grounds of s.84(1)(b), (c) or (g), i.e. on human rights or race relations grounds.

Section 96 of the NIAA 2002, as amended, provides that the right to further appeals is limited once an individual has been through the system. We deal with this in the chapter on asylum.

In-country and out-of-country appeals

Section 92 establishes a presumption that an appeal can only be pursued from outside the UK. The trigger for the hearing of the appeal from inside the UK is either (or both) the type of decision appeal against and/or the ground of appeal relied on:

Immigration decisions

- refusal of certificate of entitlement
- refusal to vary leave if refusal leaves person with no leave
- variation of leave if variation leaves person with no leave
- revocation of ILR under s.76 2002 Act
- decision to make deportation order under s.5(1) 1971 Act

Ground of appeal

- asylum grounds
- human rights grounds
- EEA grounds

In addition, there is an in-country right of appeal where a person with entry clearance is refused leave to enter on arrival in the UK, unless the refusal is for an attempt to enter for a purpose other than that specified in the entry clearance.

Perhaps the most arresting feature of the modern appeal system is that some asylum seekers do not enjoy a right of appeal from within the UK at all. These are those subject to 'clearly unfounded' certification procedures, set out at s.94 of the 2002 Act. We deal with this phenomenon in our asylum chapter.

Grounds of appeal

The potential grounds of appeal are set out at section 84 of the 2002 Act as follows:

a) not in accordance with immigration rules

b) that the decision is unlawful by virtue of 19(b) Race Relations Act 1976 (discrimination by public authorities)

c) decision is unlawful by virtue of section 6 Human Rights Act incompatible with A's convention rights;

d) appellant is EEA national or family member and decision breaches the appellant's rights under Community Treaties in respect of entry to or residence in the UK;

e) decision otherwise not in accordance with the law;

f) person taking decision should have exercised differently a discretion conferred by immigration rules;

g) removal of A from UK in consequence of the immigration decision would breach UK's obligations under the Refugee Convention or would be unlawful under section 6 HRA.

At least one of these grounds of appeal must be relied upon. Slightly strangely, where an appeal right arises, any or all potential grounds of appeal may then be relied upon. For example, the appeal may arise through a decision to make a deportation order, but asylum grounds can be relied upon. See *AS (Afghanistan) v SSHD* [2009] EWCA Civ 1076.

The exception to this is in s.83 appeals, which are limited to Refugee Convention grounds other than in cases raising issues of Humanitarian Protection (see *FA (Iraq) v SSHD* [2010] EWCA Civ 696).

Statement of additional grounds

The one stop procedure is a key element of the appeals system. Section 120 of the 2002 Act (contained in Part 6 - Immigration Procedure) requires an appellant to declare any additional grounds for their application. This applies if a person has made an application to enter or remain or in circumstances where an immigration decision under the terms of Section 82 has been taken in respect of him.

The person must state:

- His reasons for wishing to enter or remain

- Any grounds on which he should be permitted to enter or remain in the UK, and

- Any grounds on which he should not be removed from the UK

The statement need not repeat reasons or grounds set out in the application or an application to which the immigration decision relates.

It is absolutely essential to keep up to date with a client's circumstances and take full and detailed instructions when matters arise. The client, if refused, will have one chance to put arguments before an immigration judge. If this chance is lost it will be almost impossible to have the arguments considered at all before or after the person is removed.

Preparation for appeals MUST include consideration of:

- Any human rights issues arising pre or post decision;

- Any home office policy or concession applicable to the case;

- Any immigration rule applicable

Appeals structure
Diagram

```
                    ┌─────────────────────┐
                    │ Immigration Decision │
                    └──────────┬──────────┘
                               ▼
                    ┌─────────────────────┐
                    │      Appeal to       │◄──────┐
                    │  First Tier Tribunal │       │
                    └──────────┬──────────┘       │
                               ▼                   │
                    ┌─────────────────────┐       │
                    │    Seek PTA from     │       │
                    │  First Tier Tribunal │       │
                    └──────────┬──────────┘       │
                               ▼                   │
                    ┌─ ─ ─ ─ ─ ─ ─ ─ ─ ─ ─ ┐      │
                    │  First Tier Tribunal │ ─ ─ ─┤
                    │        review        │      │
                    └─ ─ ─ ─ ─ ─┬─ ─ ─ ─ ─ ┘      │
                               ▼                   │
                    ┌─────────────────────┐       │
                    │    Seek PTA from     │       │
                    │    Upper Tribunal    │       │
                    └──────────┬──────────┘       │
                               ▼                   │
                    ┌─────────────────────┐       │
                    │      Appeal to       │─ ─ ─ ─┘
                    │    Upper Tribunal    │
                    └──────────┬──────────┘
                               ▼
                    ┌─────────────────────┐
                    │    Seek PTA from     │
                    │    Upper Tribunal    │
                    └──────────┬──────────┘
                               ▼
                    ┌─ ─ ─ ─ ─ ─ ─ ─ ─ ─ ─ ┐
                    │    Upper Tribunal    │
                    │        review        │
                    └─ ─ ─ ─ ─ ─┬─ ─ ─ ─ ─ ┘
                               ▼
                    ┌─────────────────────┐
                    │    Seek PTA from     │
                    │   Court of Appeal    │
                    └──────────┬──────────┘
                               ▼
```

Decided by judge of the UT

One review only, on a procedural error of law

Decided by selected judge of the UT

Remittal to FTT from UT is intended to be far less common than in past but can be repeated, unlike reconsideration process

Public interest test for appeals to the Court of Appeal

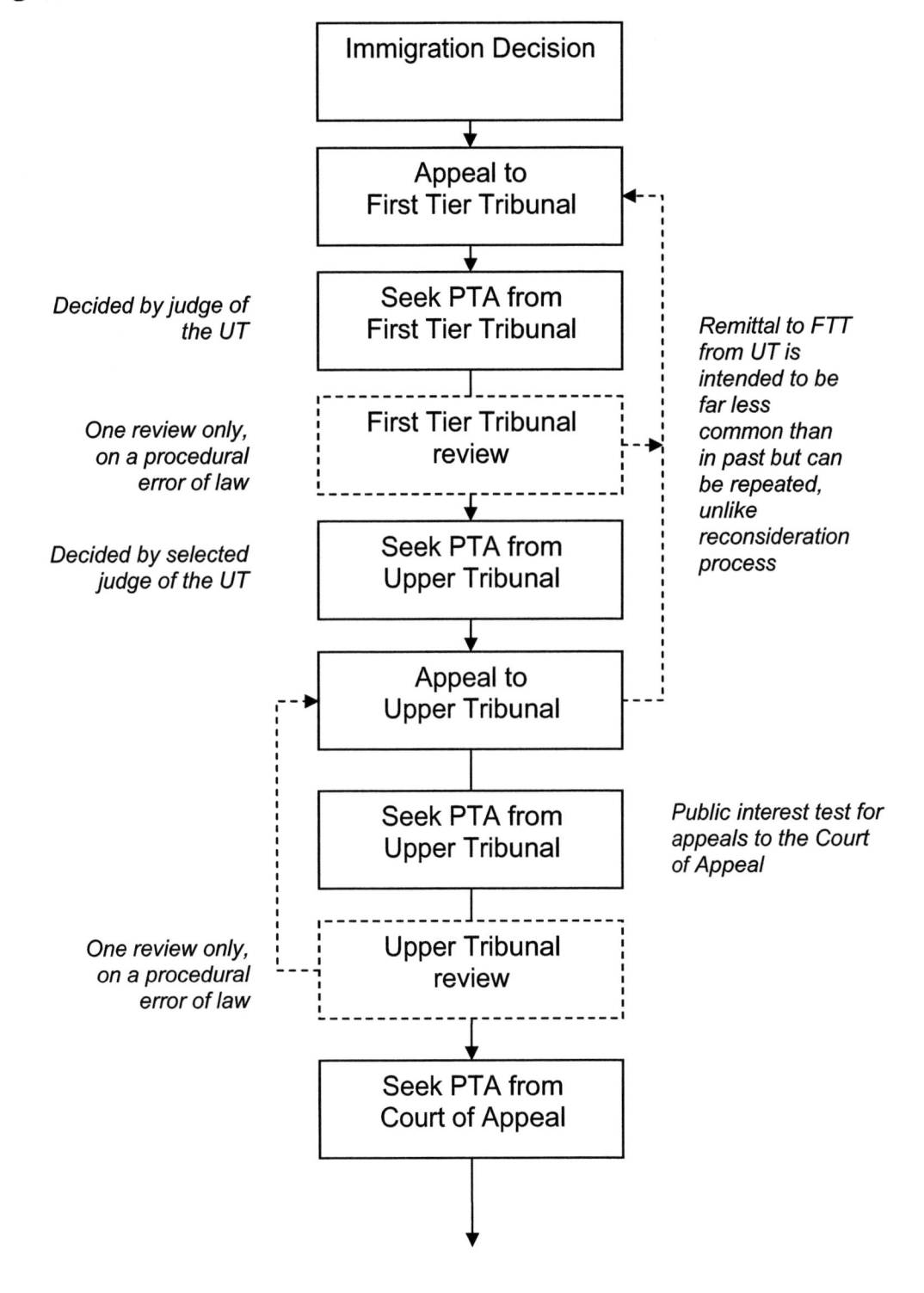

One review only, on a procedural error of law

Sources of law, practice and procedure

Because the relevant legislation setting out the process for immigration appeals is now the Tribunals, Courts and Enforcement Act 2007, which is not included in the most recent edition of Phelan, it is convenient to set out the relevant law:

> **9 Review of decision of First-tier Tribunal**
>
> (1) The First-tier Tribunal may review a decision made by it on a matter in a case, other than a decision that is an excluded decision for the purposes of section 11(1) (but see subsection (9)).
>
> (2) The First-tier Tribunal's power under subsection (1) in relation to a decision is exercisable—
> (a) of its own initiative, or
> (b) on application by a person who for the purposes of section 11(2) has a right of appeal in respect of the decision.
>
> (3) Tribunal Procedure Rules may—
> (a) provide that the First-tier Tribunal may not under subsection (1) review (whether of its own initiative or on application under subsection (2)(b)) a decision of a description specified for the purposes of this paragraph in Tribunal Procedure Rules;
> (b) provide that the First-tier Tribunal's power under subsection (1) to review a decision of a description specified for the purposes of this paragraph in Tribunal Procedure Rules is exercisable only of the tribunal's own initiative;
> (c) provide that an application under subsection (2)(b) that is of a description specified for the purposes of this paragraph in Tribunal Procedure Rules may be made only on grounds specified for the purposes of this paragraph in Tribunal Procedure Rules;
> (d) provide, in relation to a decision of a description specified for the purposes of this paragraph in Tribunal Procedure Rules, that the First-tier Tribunal's power under subsection (1) to review the decision of its own initiative is exercisable only on grounds specified for the purposes of this paragraph in Tribunal Procedure Rules.
>
> (4) Where the First-tier Tribunal has under subsection (1) reviewed a decision, the First-tier Tribunal may in the light of the review do any of the following—
> (a) correct accidental errors in the decision or in a record of the decision;
> (b) amend reasons given for the decision;
> (c) set the decision aside.
>
> (5) Where under subsection (4)(c) the First-tier Tribunal sets a decision aside, the First-tier Tribunal must either—
> (a) re-decide the matter concerned, or
> (b) refer that matter to the Upper Tribunal.
>
> (6) Where a matter is referred to the Upper Tribunal under subsection (5)(b), the Upper Tribunal must re-decide the matter.
>
> (7) Where the Upper Tribunal is under subsection (6) re-deciding a matter, it may make any decision which the First-tier Tribunal could make if the First-tier Tribunal were re-deciding the matter.
>
> (8) Where a tribunal is acting under subsection (5)(a) or (6), it may make such findings of fact as it considers appropriate.
>
> (9) This section has effect as if a decision under subsection (4)(c) to set aside an earlier decision were not an excluded decision for the purposes of section 11(1), but the First-tier Tribunal's only power in the light of a review under subsection (1) of a decision under subsection (4)(c) is the power under subsection (4)(a).

(10) A decision of the First-tier Tribunal may not be reviewed under subsection (1) more than once, and once the First-tier Tribunal has decided that an earlier decision should not be reviewed under subsection (1) it may not then decide to review that earlier decision under that subsection.

(11) Where under this section a decision is set aside and the matter concerned is then re-decided, the decision set aside and the decision made in re-deciding the matter are for the purposes of subsection (10) to be taken to be different decisions.

10 Review of decision of Upper Tribunal

(1) The Upper Tribunal may review a decision made by it on a matter in a case, other than a decision that is an excluded decision for the purposes of section 13(1) (but see subsection (7)).

(2) The Upper Tribunal's power under subsection (1) in relation to a decision is exercisable—
(a) of its own initiative, or
(b) on application by a person who for the purposes of section 13(2) has a right of appeal in respect of the decision.

(3) Tribunal Procedure Rules may—
(a) provide that the Upper Tribunal may not under subsection (1) review (whether of its own initiative or on application under subsection (2)(b)) a decision of a description specified for the purposes of this paragraph in Tribunal Procedure Rules;
(b) provide that the Upper Tribunal's power under subsection (1) to review a decision of a description specified for the purposes of this paragraph in Tribunal Procedure Rules is exercisable only of the tribunal's own initiative;
(c) provide that an application under subsection (2)(b) that is of a description specified for the purposes of this paragraph in Tribunal Procedure Rules may be made only on grounds specified for the purposes of this paragraph in Tribunal Procedure Rules;
(d) provide, in relation to a decision of a description specified for the purposes of this paragraph in Tribunal Procedure Rules, that the Upper Tribunal's power under subsection (1) to review the decision of its own initiative is exercisable only on grounds specified for the purposes of this paragraph in Tribunal Procedure Rules.

(4) Where the Upper Tribunal has under subsection (1) reviewed a decision, the Upper Tribunal may in the light of the review do any of the following—
(a) correct accidental errors in the decision or in a record of the decision;
(b) amend reasons given for the decision;
(c) set the decision aside.

(5) Where under subsection (4)(c) the Upper Tribunal sets a decision aside, the Upper Tribunal must re-decide the matter concerned.

(6) Where the Upper Tribunal is acting under subsection (5), it may make such findings of fact as it considers appropriate.

(7) This section has effect as if a decision under subsection (4)(c) to set aside an earlier decision were not an excluded decision for the purposes of section 13(1), but the Upper Tribunal's only power in the light of a review under subsection (1) of a decision under subsection (4)(c) is the power under subsection (4)(a).

(8) A decision of the Upper Tribunal may not be reviewed under subsection (1) more than once, and once the Upper Tribunal has decided that an earlier decision should not be reviewed under subsection (1) it may not then decide to review that earlier decision under that subsection.

(9) Where under this section a decision is set aside and the matter concerned is then re-decided, the decision set aside and the decision made in re-deciding the matter are for the purposes of subsection (8) to be taken to be different decisions.

11 Right to appeal to Upper Tribunal

(1) For the purposes of subsection (2), the reference to a right of appeal is to a right to appeal to the Upper Tribunal on any point of law arising from a decision made by the First-tier Tribunal other than an excluded decision.

(2) Any party to a case has a right of appeal, subject to subsection (8).

(3) That right may be exercised only with permission (or, in Northern Ireland, leave).

(4) Permission (or leave) may be given by—
(a) the First-tier Tribunal, or
(b) the Upper Tribunal,
on an application by the party.

(5) For the purposes of subsection (1), an "excluded decision" is—
(a) …
(b) …
(c) …
(d) a decision of the First-tier Tribunal under section 9—
 (i) to review, or not to review, an earlier decision of the tribunal,
 (ii) to take no action, or not to take any particular action, in the light of a review of an earlier decision of the tribunal,
 (iii) to set aside an earlier decision of the tribunal, or
 (iv) to refer, or not to refer, a matter to the Upper Tribunal,
(e) a decision of the First-tier Tribunal that is set aside under section 9 (including a decision set aside after proceedings on an appeal under this section have been begun), or
(f) any decision of the First-tier Tribunal that is of a description specified in an order made by the Lord Chancellor.

(6) …

(7) …

(8) The Lord Chancellor may by order make provision for a person to be treated as being, or to be treated as not being, a party to a case for the purposes of subsection (2).

12 Proceedings on appeal to Upper Tribunal

(1) Subsection (2) applies if the Upper Tribunal, in deciding an appeal under section 11, finds that the making of the decision concerned involved the making of an error on a point of law.

(2) The Upper Tribunal—
(a) may (but need not) set aside the decision of the First-tier Tribunal, and
(b) if it does, must either—
 (i) remit the case to the First-tier Tribunal with directions for its reconsideration, or
 (ii) re-make the decision.

(3) In acting under subsection (2)(b)(i), the Upper Tribunal may also—
(a) direct that the members of the First-tier Tribunal who are chosen to reconsider the case are not to be the same as those who made the decision that has been set aside;

(b) give procedural directions in connection with the reconsideration of the case by the First-tier Tribunal.

(4) In acting under subsection (2)(b)(ii), the Upper Tribunal—
(a) may make any decision which the First-tier Tribunal could make if the First-tier Tribunal were re-making the decision, and
(b) may make such findings of fact as it considers appropriate.

13 Right to appeal to Court of Appeal etc

(1) For the purposes of subsection (2), the reference to a right of appeal is to a right to appeal to the relevant appellate court on any point of law arising from a decision made by the Upper Tribunal other than an excluded decision.

(2) Any party to a case has a right of appeal, subject to subsection (14).

(3) That right may be exercised only with permission (or, in Northern Ireland, leave).

(4) Permission (or leave) may be given by—
(a) the Upper Tribunal, or
(b) the relevant appellate court,
on an application by the party.

(5) An application may be made under subsection (4) to the relevant appellate court only if permission (or leave) has been refused by the Upper Tribunal.

(6) The Lord Chancellor may, as respects an application under subsection (4) that falls within subsection (7) and for which the relevant appellate court is the Court of Appeal in England and Wales or the Court of Appeal in Northern Ireland, by order make provision for permission (or leave) not to be granted on the application unless the Upper Tribunal or (as the case may be) the relevant appellate court considers—
(a) that the proposed appeal would raise some important point of principle or practice, or
(b) that there is some other compelling reason for the relevant appellate court to hear the appeal.

(7) An application falls within this subsection if the application is for permission (or leave) to appeal from any decision of the Upper Tribunal on an appeal under section 11.

(8) For the purposes of subsection (1), an "excluded decision" is—
(a) ...
(b) ...
(c) ...
(d) a decision of the Upper Tribunal under section 10—
 (i) to review, or not to review, an earlier decision of the tribunal,
 (ii) to take no action, or not to take any particular action, in the light of a review of an earlier decision of the tribunal, or
 (iii) to set aside an earlier decision of the tribunal,
(e) a decision of the Upper Tribunal that is set aside under section 10 (including a decision set aside after proceedings on an appeal under this section have been begun), or
(f) any decision of the Upper Tribunal that is of a description specified in an order made by the Lord Chancellor.

(9) ...

> (10) ...
>
> (11) Before the Upper Tribunal decides an application made to it under subsection (4), the Upper Tribunal must specify the court that is to be the relevant appellate court as respects the proposed appeal.
>
> (12) The court to be specified under subsection (11) in relation to a proposed appeal is whichever of the following courts appears to the Upper Tribunal to be the most appropriate—
> (a) the Court of Appeal in England and Wales;
> (b) the Court of Session;
> (c) the Court of Appeal in Northern Ireland.
>
> (13) In this section except subsection (11), "the relevant appellate court", as respects an appeal, means the court specified as respects that appeal by the Upper Tribunal under subsection (11).
>
> (14) The Lord Chancellor may by order make provision for a person to be treated as being, or to be treated as not being, a party to a case for the purposes of subsection (2).
>
> (15) Rules of court may make provision as to the time within which an application under subsection (4) to the relevant appellate court must be made.
>
> **14 Proceedings on appeal to Court of Appeal etc**
>
> (1) Subsection (2) applies if the relevant appellate court, in deciding an appeal under section 13, finds that the making of the decision concerned involved the making of an error on a point of law.
>
> (2) The relevant appellate court—
> (a) may (but need not) set aside the decision of the Upper Tribunal, and
> (b) if it does, must either—
> > (i) remit the case to the Upper Tribunal or, where the decision of the Upper Tribunal was on an appeal or reference from another tribunal or some other person, to the Upper Tribunal or that other tribunal or person, with directions for its reconsideration, or
> > (ii) re-make the decision.

In addition to the primary legislation itself there are several other sources of practice and procedure, as follows:

In summary the main provisions relating to practice and procedure in immigration appeals are now as follows:

Asylum and Immigration (Procedure) Rules 2005

- These have been further amended and now stand as the procedure rules for the Immigration and Asylum Chamber of the First Tier Tribunal
- http://www.tribunals.gov.uk/Tribunals/Documents/Rules/Consolidated_AI_ProcedureRules2005.pdf

Tribunal Procedure (Upper Tribunal) Rules 2008

- The Asylum and Immigration Chamber of the Upper Tribunal will operate under the main Upper Tribunal rules, although these have been amended in places in order to accommodate particular features of immigration appeals procedure:
  - http://www.tribunals.gov.uk/Tribunals/Documents/Rules/Consolidated_UT_Rules_15Feb10.pdf

IAC Practice Directions

- The AIT Practice Directions have been replaced with a single set of Practice Directions for the Immigration and Asylum Chambers of both the First Tier and Upper Tribunals. These can be found here:
  - http://www.tribunals.gov.uk/Tribunals/Documents/Rules/IAC_UT_FtT_PracticeDirection.pdf

Child, vulnerable adult and sensitive witness PD

- One of the pre-existing Practice Directions of the First Tier and Upper Tribunals is relevant to immigration and asylum appeals. This is the PD relating to child, vulnerable adult and sensitive witnesses, and can be found here:
  - http://www.tribunals.gov.uk/Tribunals/Documents/Rules/Childvulnerableadultandsensitivewitnesses.pdf
- This Practice Direction is noteworthy, as it creates a presumption that children and vulnerable adult and sensitive witnesses should not give evidence and also creates a welfare test which must be satisfied if they are to give evidence.

IAC Practice Statements

- The Practice Directions are now supplemented by Practice Statements, again in the form of a unified document for both the Immigration and Asylum Chambers of both the First Tier and Upper Tribunals, which can be found here:
  - http://www.tribunals.gov.uk/Tribunals/Documents/Rules/IAC_UT_FtT_PracticeStatement.pdf

AIT Guidance Notes

- Most of the old AIT Guidance Notes have been retained on the Tribunals Service website and continue to be relevant to the hearing and determination of immigration and asylum appeals in the new system. The retained Guidance Notes can be found here:
- http://www.tribunals.gov.uk/ImmigrationAsylum/RulesLegislation.htm

First Tier Tribunal

Immigration tribunal appeals in the Immigration and Asylum Chamber of the First Tier Tribunal continue to be governed by the Asylum and Immigration Tribunal (Procedure) Rules 2005, which stand as the procedure rules for the First Tier Tribunal by virtue of the Transfer of Functions of the Asylum and Immigration Tribunal Order 2010 (SI 2010/21). The Asylum and Immigration Tribunal (Fast Track Procedure) Rules 2005 continue to be the operative regime for accelerated procedure cases in the First Tier Tribunal. Both sets of AIT rules have been amended, however, principally by the Tribunal Procedure (Amendment No. 2) Rules 2010 (SI 2010/44).

Immigration tribunal appeals to the Immigration and Asylum Chamber of the Upper Tribunal are governed by the amended Tribunal Procedure (Upper Tribunal) Rules 2008, addressed below.

Consolidated, amended versions of both main sets of rules can be found on the website of the Tribunals Service.

The procedure rules are supplemented by both Practice Directions and also Practice Statements.

Overriding Objective

The overriding objective is that proceedings before the tribunal are handled as fairly, quickly and efficiently as possible and, where appropriate, that members of the tribunal have responsibility for ensuring this, in the interests of the parties to the proceedings and in the wider public interest

Lodging appeals

Method of lodging

The notice of appeal is usually to be sent to the Immigration tribunal itself. However, detainees can serve their notice of appeal on their custodian if in detention and those who are outside the UK appealing against decisions of ECOs can serve the appeal on the ECO, in which case the latter must forward the papers to the tribunal within 10 days.

The notice of appeal must, if reasonably practicable, be accompanied by the notice of decision against which the appellant is appealing, or a copy of it.

Under rule 8, the notice of appeal must be in the appropriate prescribed form and must -

(a) state the name and address of the appellant; and

(b) state whether the appellant has authorised a representative to act for him in the appeal and, if so, give the representative's name and address;

(c) set out the grounds for the appeal;

(d) give reasons in support of those grounds; and

(e) so far as reasonably practicable, list any documents which the appellant intends to rely upon as evidence in support of the appeal.

Any document filed with the tribunal must be in English or be accompanied by a translation into English signed by the translator to certify that the translation is accurate.

Deadline for appeal

The deadlines are specified at rule 7:

> 5 business days from receipt of notice of decision if detained

> 10 business days if at liberty

> 28 calendar days from receipt of the decision in other cases

The distinction between business and calendar days does not actually appear in rule 7 itself but is provided for at rule 57, which states that a period of 10 days or less excludes non-working days.

However, calculation of the time limit requires appreciation of another rule, that on service, at rule 55. This is a deeming provision and its consequences can be rebutted by evidence (hence "unless the contrary is proved", rule 55):

- Decisions are deemed served 2 days later if posted to a UK address
- Decisions are deemed served 28 days later if posted to a place abroad
- Decisions are deemed served on receipt if delivered personally

The relevant deadline will be calculated by excluding the day on which time begins. Hence for a decision regarding an asylum seeker who is at liberty and who has a right of appeal in-country, promulgated Monday 10 May 2010: it will be deemed received Wednesday 12 May 2010.

If a bank holiday or the Christmas period was involved, the time period would be extended by the period of the holiday (see the interpretation clause on the meaning of "business day").

Extension of time for lodging notice of appeal

There is a distinct procedure for appeals which are out of time with good reason for the oversight, or where the allegation of late service is being contested, i.e. where the appellant provides evidence that they *did* serve the notice in time. There *must* be an explanation for the lateness (rule 10(1)(a)) supported by evidence, provided either with the notice of appeal, or upon the Tribunal noticing the lateness (rule 10(2)(3)). Presumably exceptionally, one might benefit from the largesse of the Tribunal exercised "on its own initiative" (rule 10(2)).

The appellant has 3 days to provide a response in an in-country case, 10 days if out-of-country (rule 10(4)).

There is no hearing of the matter: all is decided by exchange of written submissions (rule 10(6)), after which an immigration judge determines the issue based on the material before the tribunal and "any other relevant matters of fact within the knowledge of the Tribunal" (rule 10(6)(c)).

Where the appellant is in the UK and the tribunal declines to extend time, it will notify the Home Office of the decision, who will arrange for service on the appellant (rule 10(8)).

Imminent removal cases

Under rule 11, which deals with "Imminent Removal" cases, where the respondent informs the tribunal that it is proposed to remove the individual within 5 days of the date on which notice of appeal was given, the procedure is to be expedited, and the tribunal may even receive evidence via the telephone.

This rule has, as far as the authors are aware, never been used in practice.

Case Management Review Hearings

These may be arranged in any case (rule 45(4)(d)(ii)) but will normally only be listed where the tribunal so directs and the appellant is present in the UK and has a right of appeal in the UK (Practice Direction 7). In practice they are mainly used in asylum appeals.

Practice regarding CMRHs now varies between hearing centres and there is little consistency. At some hearing centres, CMRHs have ceased to exist as hearings but a pre-hearing review may be held on the papers by an immigration judge in chambers. Directions may be issued in advance of a CMRH or such a paper pre-hearing review requiring documents and information to be sent to the tribunal.

Non-compliance with direction always risks adverse consequences and in the case of CMRHs and pre hearing reviews, procedure rule 15(2)(c) might in theory be invoked by the tribunal:

> (2) The Tribunal may determine an appeal without a hearing if—

> ...
>
> (c) a party has failed to comply with a provision of these Rules or a direction of the Tribunal, or to provide a satisfactory explanation under rule 8(2)(b), and the Tribunal is satisfied that in all the circumstances, including the extent of the failure and any reasons for it, it is appropriate to determine the appeal without a hearing...

In asylum cases the CMRH will often take place after two weeks and the full hearing after four weeks, unless there is an adjournment or a variation of the standard time limits.

At these hearings, the appellant should provide:

(a) particulars of any application for permission to vary the grounds of appeal;

(b) particulars of any amendments to the reasons in support of the grounds of appeal;

(c) particulars of any witnesses to be called or whose written statement or report is proposed to be relied upon at the full hearing; and

(d) a draft of any directions that the appellant is requesting the Tribunal to make at the CMR hearing.

The respondent must provide the Tribunal and the appellant at the CMR hearing with:

(a) any amendment that has been made or that is proposed to be made to the notice of decision to which the appeal relates or to any other document served on the appellant giving reasons for that decision;

and

(b) a draft of any directions that the respondent is requesting the Tribunal to make at the CMR hearing.

It will be at the CMRH that the tribunal gives notice of any intention to hear the appeal before a panel rather than before a single immigration judge, or that the case is being considered as a Country Guideline case.

The tribunal will give written confirmation of any agreed issues and concessions at this point.

Best practice in bundles

This is Practice Direction 8.2:

> The best practice for the preparation of bundles is as follows:

(a) all documents must be relevant, be presented in logical order and be legible;

(b) where the document is not in the English language, a typed translation of the document signed by the translator in accordance with rule 52 (language of documents) to certify that the translation is accurate, must be inserted in the bundle next to the copy of the original document, together with details of the identity and qualifications of the translator;

(c) if it is necessary to include a lengthy document, that part of the document on which reliance is placed should, unless the passages are outlined in any skeleton argument, be highlighted or clearly identified by reference to page and/or paragraph number;

(d) bundles submitted must have an index showing the page numbers of each document in the bundle;

(e) the skeleton argument or written submission should define and confine the areas at issue in a numbered list of brief points and each point should refer to any documentation in the bundle on which the appellant proposes to rely (together with its page number);

(f) where reliance is placed on a particular case or text, photocopies of the case or text must be provided in full for the Tribunal and the other party; and

(g) large bundles should be contained in a ring binder or lever arch file, capable of lying flat when opened.

Further encouragement is given in the Practice Directions to parties to comply with the spirit of the requirements, although it is explicitly stated that the tribunal is aware of the constraints under which representatives operate.

Parties should avoid sending documents (such as replies to directions) at the last moment or they risk not having them accepted as having arrived in time to be acted upon.

Directions

The standard directions issued with the first notice of hearing sent to the parties will usually be as follows:

(a) not later than 5 working days before the full hearing (or 10 days in the case of an out-of-country appeal) the appellant shall serve on the Tribunal and the respondent:
(i) witness statements of the evidence to be called at the hearing, such statements to stand as evidence in chief at the hearing;
(ii) a paginated and indexed bundle of all the documents to be relied on at the hearing with a schedule identifying the essential passages;

(iii) a skeleton argument, identifying all relevant issues including human rights claims and citing all the authorities relied upon; and
(iv) a chronology of events;

(b) not later than 5 working days before the full hearing, the respondent shall serve on the Tribunal and the appellant a paginated and indexed bundle of all the documents to be relied upon at the hearing, with a schedule identifying the relevant passages, and a list of any authorities relied upon.

Practice Direction 7.7 slightly softens the steer given regarding witness statements standing as evidence in chief:

> Although in normal circumstances a witness statement should stand as evidence-in-chief, there may be cases where it will be appropriate for appellants or witnesses to have the opportunity of adding to or supplementing their witness statements.

The power of the tribunal to issue directions was circumscribed by the Court of Appeal in *Mwanza v SSHD* (C/2000/0616; 3rd November 2000), which ruled that directions could be given only pursuant to "the conduct of the appeal" – this ruled out orders that the Secretary of State re-interview someone, or make a new decision with a new refusal letter, for these were matters that were prior to the appeal process, and substantive rather than procedural in nature.

Under Rule 51(4), an immigration judge must not consider any evidence which is not filed or served in accordance with time limits set out in the Rules or directions given under them unless satisfied that there are good reasons to do so. However, this does not apply to oral evidence: see *MA (rule 51(4) - not oral evidence) Somalia* [2007] UKAIT 00079.

Under Rule 15(2)(c), failure to comply either with the rules themselves or directions given pursuant to them may lead the tribunal to determine the appeal without a hearing. Such a step should be taken only where required, 'in all the circumstances ... [including] the extent of the failure and any reasons for it,' no doubt having regard to the overriding objective in rule 4.

The tribunal may also make directions pursuant to the outcome of an appeal, in order to give effect to that appeal. Those directions form part of the determination and if the respondent is discontented with the directions, they must be appealed as normal (*LS (Gambia)* [2005] UKAIT 00085).

In *R v SSHD (ex parte Boafo)* [2002] 1 WLR 1919 the Court of Appeal held that the Secretary of State is bound by the factual findings of the tribunal and must normally give effect to an appeal, irrespective of whether directions have been given at the conclusion of that appeal. There are, however, some limited circumstances where the Secretary of State might re-open a decision.

Summoning a witness

At the time of writing there appears to be a policy at some Presenting Officer Units to request a direction that an expert attend the hearing if an expert report is to be adduced.

There is a specific procedure rule that deals with summoning witnesses: rule 50. While rule 45(4)(d)(iv) states that the tribunal may 'provide for' witnesses, if any, to be heard, this does not extend to directing that a specific witness attend court; this would be to sidestep the summoning rule at rule 50.

If the Home Office want a witness summons, they may request it and may pay the expenses of their witness, and arrange that the hearing date takes place when the witness is available. The Home Office will also be barred from cross examining their witness, unless an application is made to treat their witness as hostile.

The tribunal does not have a power to dictate to an appellant how to present his or her case or what evidence must be relied upon. Applications by Presenting Officers for this type of direction should be resisted, not least because any such direction is unlawful. However, where the Home Office has expressed an interest in cross examining a witness, it would be wise to seek to ensure that the witness can be present; if the Home Office will not consent to an adjournment for this purpose or the tribunal will not co-operate with a realistic listing then that cannot rationally be held against the appellant, however.

See correspondence from the then Asylum and Immigration Tribunal President to ILPA, 12 June 2008.

Documents to be sent to tribunal

Rule 13(1) requires the Home Office to produce all interview records and SEFs, and to provide unpublished documents "referred to" in the notice of decision and more importantly in the refusal letter. This gives some power to the tribunal to extract documents from the Home Office.

Variation of Grounds of Appeal

Grounds of appeal to an immigration judge may be varied only with their leave (Rule 14). In practice, it can be difficult to prompt the tribunal to respond to such a request unless it is made prior to or at a CMR (and there is a CMR, i.e. it is an asylum case).

Adjournments

Adjournments are to be given only if necessary in the interests of justice. Rule 21(2) says "unless satisfied that the appeal or application cannot otherwise be justly determined." They will be rarely granted: as Justice Collins stated once, "The whole tenor of our rules is that we should get on with it."

In the past, the considerations raised in the *Martin* case (*R v Kingston-upon-Thames Magistrates ex parte Martin* [1994] Imm AR 172) have been recommended as being relevant matters to be taken into account.

> '1. The importance of the proceedings and their likely consequences to the party seeking the adjournment.
> 2. The risk of the party being prejudiced in the conduct of the proceedings if the application were refused.
> 3. The risk of prejudice or other disadvantage to the other party if the adjournment were granted.
> 4. The convenience of the court.
> 5. The interests of justice generally in the efficient dispatch of court business.
> 6. The desirability of not delaying future litigants by adjourning early and thus leaving the court empty.
> 7. The extent to which the party applying for the adjournment had been responsible for creating the difficulty which had led to the application.'

On an adjournment application, under rule 21 the applicant must:

(a) if practicable, notify all other parties of the application;

(b) show good reason why an adjournment is necessary; and

(c) produce evidence of any fact or matter relied upon in support of the application.

Such applications are made with respect to the obtaining of further evidence, rule 21(3) will permit their being granted only where the evidence is relevant, the interests of justice require its admission, and where a satisfactory explanation is provided if evidence has not been produced in compliance with directions.

Applications must be made not later than 17:00 hours one full working day before the hearing – that is to say, more than 24 hours before the hearing (Practice Direction 9.1, 9.2). Later applications require the attendance of the applicant at the hearing.

Although the term "closure date" is now vanquished from the rules, rule 21(4)) requires the most minimal adjournments to be given with postponements greater than 28 days being permitted only exceptionally in the interests of justice.

Conduct of the appeal

The tribunal is free to regulate procedure as it sees fit (Rule 45) no doubt having regard to "the overriding objective" identified above (Rule 4). The Rules particularise the matters upon which directions may be made, although the list is not exhaustive. The directions are now standard in nature. Parties must provide the other party copies of any documents served under directions. Where a party is unrepresented, the tribunal may only give directions with which it is satisfied that the person is capable of compliance (Rule 45(5)).

The order of proceedings is normally approximately as follows:

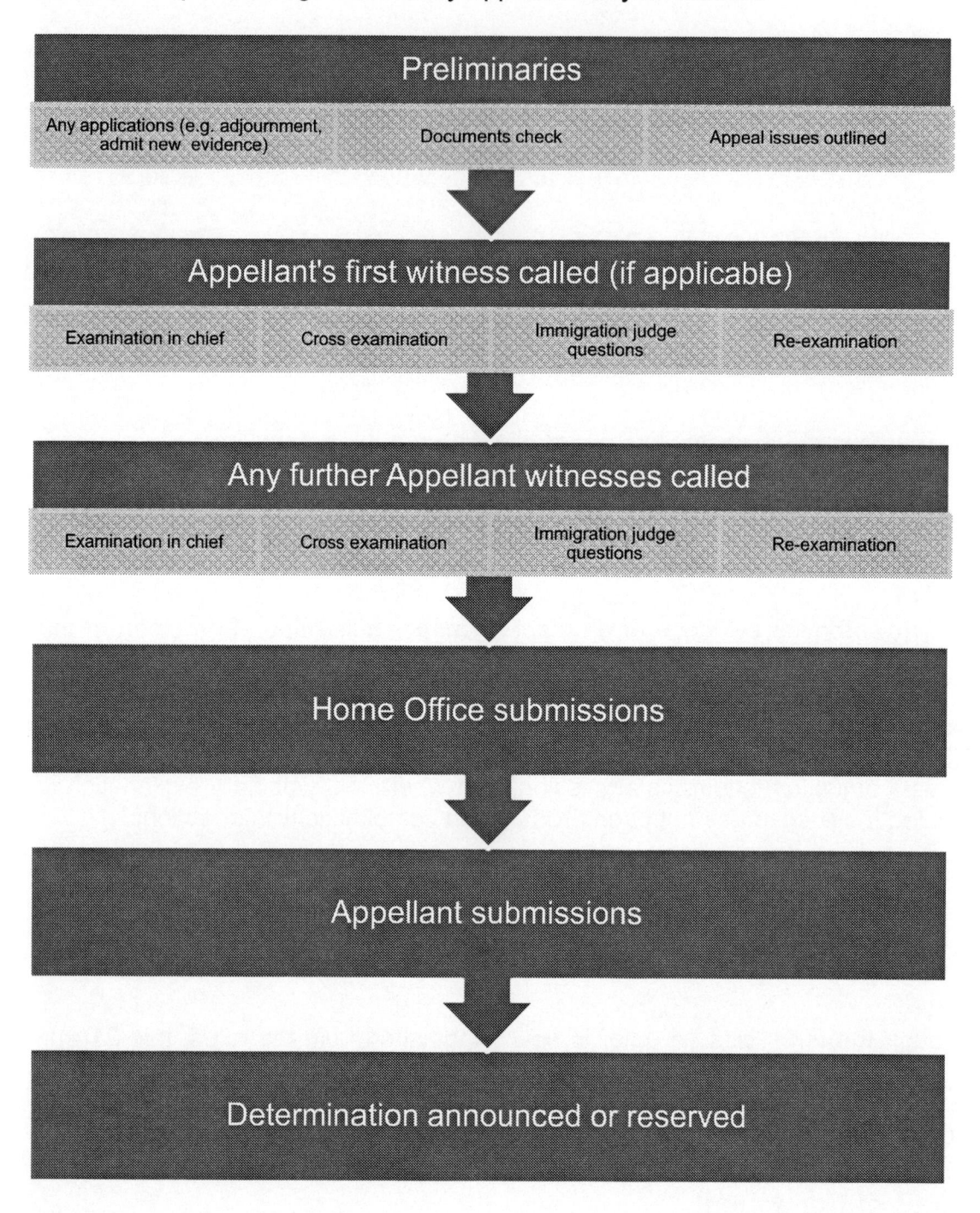

Preliminaries
- Any applications (e.g. adjournment, admit new evidence)
- Documents check
- Appeal issues outlined

⬇

Appellant's first witness called (if applicable)
- Examination in chief
- Cross examination
- Immigration judge questions
- Re-examination

⬇

Any further Appellant witnesses called
- Examination in chief
- Cross examination
- Immigration judge questions
- Re-examination

⬇

Home Office submissions

⬇

Appellant submissions

⬇

Determination announced or reserved

Concessions by the Home Office

In a determination intended to be followed in preference to any others on the issue, the Tribunal in *Carcabuk & Bla* (00/TH/01426; 18 May 2000) authoritatively ruled that an immigration judge should not seek to go behind concessions of fact ('for example that a particular document is genuine or that an event described by the appellant or a witness did occur') although the immigration judge might wish to raise doubts as to the correctness of a concession. The issue of withdrawing concessions was revisited in the case of *NR (Jamaica) v SSHD* [2009] EWCA Civ 856. It was held that the Tribunal had discretion to permit withdrawal but that it should not prejudice the affected party: an adjournment may well be necessary.

It is to be noted that Practice Direction 7.8 states that concessions and agreed issues are to be recorded at the Case Management Review Hearings, suggesting that these interlocutory hearings may be used to steer the proceedings.

Natural justice

Asylum appeals are supposed to receive 'the most anxious scrutiny'. Thus an immigration judge should give the parties a chance to make submissions upon any researches the immigration judge themselves might enter upon, or upon the immigration judge's own accumulated specialist knowledge of a particular country's history; so too the immigration judge should give an opportunity to be addressed upon decisions of factual relevance of which the immigration judge is aware, including their own, and equally upon authorities the immigration judge considers relevant. The general rule is that an opportunity should be given to address any material said to be adverse to the appellant's case.

An immigration judge is entitled to probe evidence where it contains apparent improbabilities in order to satisfy themselves of the account's reliability. The immigration judge should enter the arena, however, only where it is absolutely necessary to enable them to ascertain the truth and without giving any impression of being partisan.

For a rare example of a challenge to the conduct of proceedings by an immigration judge being seriously entertained by the higher courts, see *R (on the application of AM (Cameroon)) v Asylum and Immigration Tribunal* [2007] EWCA Civ 131.

Public hearing

In general, hearings take place in public (Rule 54). Where allegations of forgery are made with respect to which it would be contrary to the public interest if the detection methods were exposed, then that element of the proceedings which addresses this must be carried out in the absence of the appellant and their representatives; any members of the public must also be excluded. This procedure is provided for at s.108 of the NIAA 2002 and is also addressed in the case of *OA (Alleged forgery; section 108 procedure) Nigeria* [2007] UKIAT 00096:

1. Each application on behalf of the respondent for the section 108, Nationality, Immigration and Asylum Act, 2002 procedure to be invoked must be decided on its own merits.

2. Immigration Judges should first consider whether it is being alleged that the document concerned is a forgery, or whether it is simply asserted that it is a document which cannot be relied upon (T*anveer Ahmed* [2002] UKIAT 00439*).

3. Applications must be heard in camera, in the absence of the appellant and the appellant's representatives.

4. The Home Office Presenting Officer should be ready to identify precisely what documents the respondent contends are forged and the evidence which it is claimed relates to the detection of the forgery and which is to be the subject of the section 108 application. Explaining why disclosure of this evidence would be contrary to the public interest.

5. A careful note should be taken by the judge. The respondent may, if he wishes to, withdraw the allegation and in doing so withdraw the evidence relied upon.

6. Clear evidence will be necessary; if *RP (Proof of Forgery) Nigeria* [2006] UKAIT 00086 is not satisfied, then the application will fail.

7. If the judge grants the application, he should say so in public and clearly identify which document or documents or other evidence is the subject of the section 108 application.

The public may also be excluded in certain circumstances, where in the opinion of the tribunal 'it is necessary in the interests of public order or national security,' 'or to protect the private life of the parties or the interests of a minor;' and also, 'in exceptional circumstances, ... to ensure that publicity does not prejudice the interests of justice, but only if and to the extent that it is strictly necessary to do so.'

Hearing in the absence of a party

Where appropriate, the tribunal may hear the appeal in the absence of a party, namely where: they are represented at the hearing, not in United Kingdom, are suffering from a communicable disease or there is a risk of him behaving in a violent or disorderly manner, by reason of illness, accident or some other good reason cannot attend the hearing, it is impracticable to give them notice of the hearing and the party is unrepresented at the hearing, or they have notified the tribunal that they do not wish to attend the hearing (rule 19(2)).

Aside from those scenarios, a hearing *must* be held in the absence of a party (or his representative) if the tribunal is satisfied that, in the case of that party, notice of the date, time and place of the hearing, or of the adjourned hearing, has been given, and that no satisfactory explanation of his absence has been put forward (rule 19(1)).

Determination without a hearing

Rule 15 sets out that every appeal must be considered at a hearing before an immigration judge, except where

- the appeal lapses due to certification for reasons of abuse of the one stop process, national security or other public good (section 99 of NIAA 2002);

- the appeal is treated as abandoned because the Appellant has left the country or been granted leave to remain (section 104(4) of NIAA 2002);
- the appeal is treated as finally determined because of the making of a deportation order against the Appellant (section 104(5) of NIAA 2002); or
- the appeal is withdrawn by the appellant; or
- where a provision of these Rules or of any other enactment permits or requires an immigration judge to dispose of an appeal without a hearing.

An appeal may be determined without a hearing where all the parties consent, where the party appealing against a relevant decision is outside the United Kingdom or it is impracticable to give him notice of a hearing and, in either case, he is unrepresented, where, having given the parties an opportunity to make written representations, the tribunal is satisfied (vis-à-vis the nature of the issues raised and the material before it) that the appeal could be disposed of justly; or, as discussed above, where a failure to comply with directions or the 2005 Rules themselves causes the tribunal to conclude that, bearing in mind the overriding objective of just, effective and timely disposal of appeals, it should so determine the appeal.

Combined hearings

The tribunal may determine that two or more pending appeals are to be heard together, having given all parties an opportunity to be heard on the point, in three circumstances: where some common question of law or fact arises in both or all of them; where they relate to decisions or action taken in respect of persons who are members of the same family; or where for some other reason it is desirable to so proceed with the appeals.

Evidence

Immigration appeals are intended to be an informal procedure, in which the forms of material which may constitute evidence of facts (especially in asylum and human rights cases regarding the well-foundedness of the appellant's fears) are broader than might support a case in other jurisdictions, see Rule 51(1): 'The Tribunal may receive oral, documentary or other evidence of any fact which appears to that authority to be relevant to the appeal, even though that evidence would be inadmissible in a court of law.'

Forgery and authenticity of documents

Given the variety of documents that face the tribunal, it is difficult to contend that all are entitled to a presumption of genuineness. The approach now is that the asylum seeker bears the burden of proof (albeit to the same low standard as regards the rest of their claim) in establishing the genuineness of documents in support of their appeal; where such a person does so, which they might do so either on account of their intrinsic cogency or via extraneous evidence, the Secretary of State bears the burden of showing that they are nevertheless forged. This has the consequence that is permissible for an immigration judge to make findings on the documents based on findings on the oral evidence

(*Tanveer Ahmed* [2002] UKIAT 00439 (20 February 2002; starred), at least so long as they do not rule out the chance that the documents themselves would have an impact on their initial credibility assessment.

Where the respondent alleges forgery, it for the respondent to make out this allegation. See *RP (proof of forgery) Nigeria* [2006] UKAIT 00086:

> '14. In judicial proceedings an allegation of forgery needs to be established to a high degree of proof, by the person making the allegation. This is therefore a matter on which the respondent bears the burden of proof. Immigration Judges decide cases on evidence, and in the absence of any concession by the appellant, an Immigration Judge is not entitled to find or assume that a document is a forgery, or to treat it as a forgery for the purposes of his determination, save on the basis of evidence before him. In the present case the evidence was limited to the Entry Clearance Officer's assertion of his own view and the defect in the document identified in the notes on the application form – that is to say, the mismatch between the run date and the date stamp on one of the remittance documents. That evidence is wholly insufficient to establish that that document is a forgery. There is no reason to suppose that it is not a simple mistake. As it happens, "petroleum" is misspelt in the Notice of Refusal. Although we would be inclined to suppose that Entry Clearance Officers can spell this word, we do not automatically assume that the Notice of Refusal is a forgery: there is no reason to suppose that it was not simply a mistake.'

See *OA (Alleged forgery; section 108 procedure) Nigeria* [2007] UKIAT 00096, above, regarding the section 108 procedure for excluding the appellant from a hearing while certain forms of evidence regarding forgery are considered by the tribunal.

Burden and standard of proof in allegations

When an allegation is made by an ECO or the UK Border Agency, the burden proof shifts to them, under the principle of 'he who asserts must prove'. See also *JC (Part 9 HC395- burden of proof) China* [2007] UKAIT 00027. The standard of proof is the 'preponderance of probabilities' which amounts to a standard between civil and criminal. For detailed guidance see *Khawaja v SSHD* [1983] UKHL 8.

Evaluating country reports

The Country Guideline case of *TK (Tamils – LP updated) Sri Lanka CG* [2009] UKAIT 00049 represents the tribunal's considered view on the assessment of country reports and expert evidence. The tribunal urges judges to adopt the approach of Strasbourg in *NA v UK* App. no. 25904/07:

> '5. ...it seems to us that, at least within the context of Article 3 jurisprudence, judges should now be assessing COI by the standards set out by the Court at paras 132-135 of NA (which can be summarised as accuracy, independence, reliability, objectivity, reputation, adequacy of methodology, consistency and corroboration). Indeed, within the closely related context of asylum and humanitarian protection claims, very much the same standards have now become, by virtue of EU legislation, legal standards: see the Refugee Qualification Directive (2004/83/EC),

> Article 4(1), 4(3)(a), 4(5),4(5)(a) and 4(5)(c) and the Procedures Directive (2005)85/EC), Article 8(2)(a)and (b) and 8(3).'

The tribunal then goes on to decry the use of the term 'objective evidence':

> '7. The emphasis we place on assessment based on objective merit prompts us to make one further comment. It is still widespread practice for practitioners and judges to refer to "objective country evidence" when all they mean is background country evidence. In our view, to refer to such evidence as "objective" obscures the need for the decision-maker to subject such evidence to scrutiny to see if it conforms to the COI standards just noted. This practice appears to have had its origin in a distinction between evidence relating to an individual applicant (so-called "subjective evidence") and evidence about country conditions (so-called"objective evidence"), but as our subsequent deliberations on the appellant's case illustrate (see below paras 153-9), even this distinction can cause confusion when there is an issue about whether an appellant's subjective fears have an objective foundation. We hope the above practice will cease.'

Abandonment of appeals

The tribunal possesses the power to declare an appeal abandoned where the statute deems it to be so, (rule 15(1)(a)(ii), rule 18), referring to the Nationality, Immigration and Asylum Act 2002, ss 104, 105, where an appeal is deemed abandoned due to the appellant having left the UK or being granted leave to remain in the course of the appeal), in which case it is to issue a notice to that effect and to take no further action in relation to the appeal. Parties are under an obligation to notify the tribunal of such events (rule 18(1)).

It is important to note that the regime governing abandonment of appeals has been altered by the 2006 Act, which allows racial discrimination appeals and upgrade Refugee Convention appeals to continue despite leave to enter being granted or the appellant leaving the UK (s.9 of 2006 Act, amending s.104 of 2002 Act).

Authority to represent

At appeal, the Secretary of State may be represented by any person authorised to act on his behalf. The appellant may be represented by any person not prohibited from providing legal services under the Immigration and Asylum Act 1999; the right to legal representation has, by authority of statute, to be given by the Rules. Representatives are entitled to 'do anything relating to the proceedings that the person whom he represents is by these Rules required or authorised to do'. There is a positive duty on the parties to maintain contact with their representatives and to notify them of any changes of address, and on the representative to enter onto the record as soon as they are instructed. Upon a change of representation, both the party in question and the outgoing representative are under a duty to notify the tribunal of the fact, and of any new representative, where known; until notification is made, the tribunal is entitled to continue to serve the last notified representative, and such service will be valid.

Historically, a party has been considered fixed with the errors of his or her representative. In *FP (Iran) v SSHD* [2007] EWCA Civ 13, in which in two linked cases, the appellant had lost touch with the tribunal through fault on the part of the appellant's representative and the immigration judges had in both cases proceeded to hear the appeals in the absence of the parties, as was required by the procedure rules, the Court of Appeal held that (i) there is no general principle of law that a party is fixed with the faults of his representative and (ii) the procedure rules were unlawful because of the absence of discretion not to proceed without a party being present.

Irregularities and corrections

An error of procedure prior to the determination of an appeal, such as a failure to comply with a rule, does not of itself invalidate any step taken in the proceedings. Faced with such an irregularity, 'an adjudicator or the Tribunal may make an order, or take any other step, that he or it considers appropriate to remedy the error.

Clerical errors, accidental slips and omissions in a determination may be corrected by the tribunal. In such cases time for appealing runs from service of the corrected determination (rule 60(3)).

Second or subsequent appeals

At least prior to the one stop regime, persons may have more than one appeal before the old Appellate Authority: where persons had their original appeals on Refugee Convention grounds determined well before 2 October 2000 (i.e. before the Immigration and Asylum Act 1999 came into effect), they will have an appeal against removal directions in which they can raise human rights points; persons with appeals pending at 2 October 2000 will be in a similar position on account of the *Pardeepan* concession; and, given the period of time for which many persons remain in the UK even after an initial unsuccessful appeal, there will be cases where their removal substantially later poses different threats to their human rights.

The Tribunal in *Devaseelan* gave guidance on this situation (referring to adjudicators at the time). The second immigration judge should have regard to the determination of the first immigration judge where the earlier decision is unchallenged, or not successfully challenged.

The first immigration judge's determination should always be the starting-point for consideration of a later application, for it is the authoritative assessment of the appellant's status at the time it was made – there is at yet no judicial answer to the question of how to approach a decision which stands unchallenged yet is on its face in error of law, though there has been some circumspection expressed about the wisdom of adopting unclear reasoning.

Facts happening prior to the original determination, but of no relevance to the issues it decided, and facts happening since the original determination, can be considered by the second immigration judge afresh.

Facts said to have been relevant to the original determination, but not raised, should be treated with circumspection in so far as they are particular to the individual appellant; country material tending to undermine the original determination will be of limited relevance to the later appeal.

Where there is no material difference between the facts relied upon at the second appeal to the first, the immigration judge charged with the later consideration of the case should treat matters as settled by his predecessor. The later decision-maker should only countenance an allegation that an error of a representative undermines the earlier decision where satisfied that such is genuinely the case, and should ensure that such a state of affairs is reported to those responsible for the regulation of immigration advice. Lack of representation on the first occasion is not determinative.

This approach was approved by the Court of Appeal in *AA (Somalia) v SSHD* [2007] EWCA Civ 1040, and it is clear that although *Devaseelan* concerned one specific set of subsequent appeals (so-called *Pardeepan* appeals), the same principles can be applied in other subsequent appeal situations and even between appeals of a witness, e.g. where a witness was found credible in a previous appeal that witness must still be evaluated on giving evidence in a later appeal, which necessarily may mean their evidence might not be accepted, even though the earlier determination should be a starting point.

Special procedures and time limits in asylum appeals

There are particular time limits for the determination of asylum appeals when the appellant is in the UK.

The hearing is to be fixed not later than 28 days from the date on which the tribunal receives notice of appeal (rule 23(2)(a)(i)) and the determination is to be served not later than 10 days after the conclusion of the appeal hearing (rule 23(4)(a)).

Service of the determination in asylum appeals (i.e. relating in whole or in part to a Refugee Convention claim) is on the Home Office, which is then charged with serving the determination on the appellant.

Seeking permission to appeal from the FTT

Since 15 February 2010, the date of commencement of the current tribunal appeals structure, the process for challenging a decision of the First Tier Tribunal has been to apply for permission to appeal to the Upper Tribunal. The process chart earlier in this chapter sets out the various stages in applying for permission to appeal and pursuing such an application further.

Basis of application

Applications for permission to appeal are made only on the basis of an error of law. Such errors might consist of:

(i) Making perverse or irrational findings on a matter or matters that were material to the outcome ("material matters");

(ii) Failing to give reasons or any adequate reasons for findings on material matters;

(iii) Failing to take into account and/or resolve conflicts of fact or opinion on material matters;

(iv) Giving weight to immaterial matters;

(v) Making a material misdirection of law on any material matter;

(vi) Committing or permitting a procedural or other irregularity capable of making a material difference to the outcome or the fairness of the proceedings;

(vii) Making a mistake as to a material fact which could be established by objective and uncontentious evidence, where the appellant and/or his advisers were not responsible for the mistake, and where unfairness resulted from the fact that a mistake was made.

See *R (Iran) & Ors v SSHD* [2005] EWCA Civ 982. The Court of Appeal in *E v SSHD* [2004] EWCA Civ 49 explains the circumstances in which error of fact could be an error of law:

> "First, there must have been a mistake as to an existing fact, including a mistake as to the availability of evidence on a particular matter. Secondly, the fact or evidence must have been 'established', in the sense that it was uncontentious and objectively verifiable. Thirdly, the appellant (or his advisers) must not have been responsible for the mistake. Fourthly, the mistake must have played a material (not necessarily decisive) part in the Tribunal's reasoning."

Application to the First Tier Tribunal

An application form is provided on the Tribunals Service website:

> IAFT–4: Application to the First–tier Tribunal for permission to appeal to the Upper Tribunal

The deadline is 'no later than 5 days after the date on which the party making the application is deemed to have been served with written reasons for the decision' or, 'where an appellant is outside the UK, the time limit for that person sending or delivering an application [for permission to appeal] is 28 days'.

Deemed receipt provisions have not been altered, nor have the rules on business and calendar days. This means that the 5 days normally runs from 2 days after the decision under appeal was sent and the days are working days. The 28 days, however, are calendar days. 28 days is still allowed for postage in out of country cases in the FTT rules.

There is nothing in the procedure rules that refers to a prescribed form, so it would appear that use of the form is not in fact compulsory. Rule 24(5) details the necessities of an application, which must

- (i) identify the decision an appeal is pursued against,
- (ii) identify the alleged errors of law and
- (iii) state the result that the party seeks.

These rules appear more relaxed than the previous requirements of CPR 54.29, which required certain documents to be filed and required that grounds and reasons in support of the grounds also be filed. The requirement to state the result sought is a new feature, though.

As will be seen below, there are two different possible routes to a FTT decision being overturned: self-review and appeal. The same application form appears to be used for both and it is unclear to what extent a dissatisfied party can try and steer the FTT towards either review or appeal as a mechanism. If the party does have a preference, submissions could be made on this point in the grounds of appeal.

Decisions made in the First Tier Tribunal on review and permission to appeal are in fact made by Senior Immigration Judges rather than ordinary or garden Immigration Judges. Senior Immigration Judges have a dual existence as members of both the First Tier and Upper Tribunals.

If an application to the FTT fails and is renewed to the Upper Tribunal, it is there decided by a select group of eight Senior Immigration Judges selected by the President or by Deputy or full High Court Judges sitting in rotation in the Upper Tribunal.

Review process

FTT considers whether to review the decision

There is no separate or distinct mechanism for applying for a review (see below) rather than permission to appeal. In all cases, the way to challenge a decision of the FTT is simply to make an application to the FTT for permission to appeal to the Upper Tribunal.

The first thing the FTT then has to do on receipt of an application for permission to appeal is decide whether the FTT should itself review the decision against which an appeal is sought. This is provided for at new rule 25(1), and the review procedure is detailed at new rule 26. The statutory authority to review a decision of the FTT is contained in section 9 of the TCEA 2007. If the FTT decides not to review or having reviewed the decision decides to leave it substantively the same, the FTT then has to itself go on and decide whether to grant permission to appeal to the UT.

We refer hereafter to 'self review' in order to distinguish the new review procedure for both the FTT and the UT at sections 9 and 10 of the TCEA 2007 respectively from the old 'opt-in review' procedure whereby a party dissatisfied with a reconsideration decision could request a High Court review of that decision. The processes are very different and although the term 'self review' appears nowhere in statute, rules or practice directions or statements, it is hoped that its use assists in avoiding confusion for veteran practitioners familiar with the Asylum and Immigration Tribunal procedures.

It is unclear to what extent a party can seek to persuade the FTT to self review the decision rather than considering granting permission to appeal to the UT. The way the rules are framed appears to suggest this is a matter for the tribunal, but it would obviously be possible to address this issue in grounds of appeal.

From the point of view of a representative or appellant, there is no necessity to be concerned about the review process because it is something the tribunal undertakes for itself: the representative or appellant will be unaware of what internal machinations are taking place within the tribunal. There is certainly no need to 'renew' an application for permission to appeal to the FTT as the FTT must automatically go on to consider whether to grant permission to appeal to the UT.

In order to undertake a self review, the FTT has to be satisfied that there was an error of law in the decision. In a departure from the old procedure rules, there is no requirement in the rules for there to be a realistic prospect of success or 'a real possibility that the tribunal would make a different decision' (old CPR 54.33(5)(b) test).

FTT self review

If the FTT does decide to self review the FTT decision, no detail is provided as to the mechanisms for that review or test to be applied in the procedure rules themselves. This is found instead in the Practice Statements document, which at section 4 provides as follows:

> 4 Review of decision of First-tier Tribunal
>
> 4.1 On an application to the First-tier Tribunal for permission to appeal under section 11 of the 2007 Act (right to appeal to Upper Tribunal) on a point of law arising from a decision, the First-tier Tribunal may review that decision pursuant to First-tier rule 26, only if it is satisfied that there was an error of law in that decision.
>
> 4.2 Following such a review, the First-tier Tribunal may (subject to section 9(10)) set the decision aside under section 9(4)(c) and re-decide the matter concerned under

> section 9(5)(a). The First-tier Tribunal is, however, likely to adopt this course only if it is satisfied that:-
> (a) the effect of any error of law has been to deprive a party before the First-tier Tribunal of a fair hearing or other opportunity for that party's case to be put to and considered by the First-tier Tribunal; or
> (b) there are highly compelling reasons why the matter should be re-decided by the First-tier Tribunal. (Such reasons are likely to be rare.)
>
> 4.3 Nothing in this Practice Statement affects the operation of First-tier rule 60 (correction of orders and determinations).

The references to section 9 are to section 9 of the TCEA 2007:

- Section 9(10) provides that there can only be one review of a FTT decision

- Section 9(5)(a) enables the FTT to 're-decide the matter concerned'. Interestingly, there is no apparent mention of section 9(5)(b) which enables the FTT to refer the matter to the UT.

- Section 9(4)(c) enables the FTT to set the decision aside, presumably as a prelude to re-deciding the matter. Sections 9(4)(a) and (b) enable the FTT to correct accidental errors or amend reasons given but are not mentioned in the Practice Statement.

It can be seen that the perception of an error of law acts as a gateway but is not the test the FTT will apply in practice in deciding whether to set a decision aside and/or re-decide the matter. The test is whether the error of law deprived a party of a fair hearing or other opportunity to put their case OR there are 'highly compelling reasons' why the matter should be re-decided by the FTT, which is explicitly stated to be unlikely to occur often.

It remains to be seen how these narrow-sounding tests will be interpreted in practice, but it appears that a self-review by the FTT will be comparatively rare. An appeal to the UT looks like it will be the most likely avenue for seeking to overturn a decision of the FTT.

Decision set aside by FTT following self review

Logically, if the FTT does set a decision aside after self reviewing it then there would have to be a re-hearing of the FTT appeal. However, this is not explicit in the Act, Procedure Rules or the Practice Statements.

There can only ever be one FTT self review, so if either party is dissatisfied with the outcome of the 're-decided decision' then the only remedy is an appeal to the UT.

Decision not set aside by FTT following self review

If the FTT does self review the decision but decides not to set the decision aside, it must go on to decide whether to grant permission to appeal to the UT.

Alternatively, leading to the same outcome, the FTT appears to have the option of not deciding to self review the decision and simply jumping straight to considering whether to grant permission to appeal. This will always be the case if there has already been a review earlier in the same proceedings.

The criteria for self review and permission to appeal are not identical but do bear considerable similarities, in that an error of law must be detected. For self review to lead to the setting aside of the decision, though, the error of law appears to have to affect fair hearing of the FTT appeal. If the error of law is a different sort of error of law, it is entirely possible for review to be refused but permission to appeal to be granted.

Permission to appeal in the FTT

The FTT will consider whether to grant permission to appeal to the UT in the following situations:

(i) There has already been a previous FTT self-review, in which case there can be no further reviews and the FTT must consider PTA

(ii) Following a review the FTT decides not to set aside the FTT decision

(iii) If the FTT decides not to review a FTT decision at all.

The right of appeal to the UT is derived from s.11(1) TCEA 2007, which so far as is relevant provides as follows:

> 'For the purposes of subsection (2), the reference to a right of appeal is to a right to appeal to the Upper Tribunal on any point of law arising from a decision made by the First-tier Tribunal...'

There are no further restrictions imposed in procedure rules or elsewhere and no references have yet been detected to a 'reasonable prospect of success' requirement or similar, although this is likely to form part of the consideration of both the FTT and UT in determining whether to grant permission to appeal. Both tiers of tribunal have a broad discretion whether to grant permission, as long as there is an appeal on a point of law.

Seeking permission to appeal from the UT

Procedure in the UT does vary from that in the former AIT and the rules governing UT proceedings are a completely different set of procedure rules, as discussed above.

It should be noted that permission cannot be sought from the UT without having first sought it from the FTT: UT rule 21(2). Any such application to the FTT must have been either refused or not admitted, which suggests that an out of time application can be made to the FTT and then on refusal renewed to the UT, even if the FTT application was out of time. This is how appeals to the Court of Appeal have operated in the past.

Appealing with permission from the FTT

For the purposes of the UT in immigration and asylum cases, where the FTT has granted permission the notice of appeal delivered to the FTT stands as the notice of appeal to the UT: see UT rule 23(1A). No appellants' notice or similar appears to be required. It therefore appears that the FTT will without further intervention by the appellant communicate with the UT to inform the UT that permission has been granted and on what grounds.

Renewed permission to appeal application

If the FTT did not grant permission, the application to the UT must be made 7 working days after the date on which the FTT's refusal of permission was sent to the appellant (or 4 days in fast track cases). The time limit is 56 days where the appellant is outside the UK. See UT rule 21(3)(aa).

Different time limits apply where a decision is sent electronically or delivered personally.

The previous AIT rules on deemed service have been replaced by hard rules running from the date of sending. However, rule 5(3)(a) imparts the UT with total discretion to vary any time limits, so if an application is made late reasons should be included.

The form provided (although not specified as compulsory in the rules) for applications to the UT for permission to appeal to the UT is:

> IAUT–1 Application to the Upper Tribunal for permission to appeal to the Upper Tribunal

If permission to appeal to the UT is granted by the UT, written notice must be given to both parties.

Status and race relations appeals

There is a specific procedure laid out at UT rule 17A and Practice Direction 5 for pursuing an appeal even where leave has been granted, i.e. refugee status and race relations appeals.

Pursuing an Upper Tribunal appeal

Procedure in the UT is dictated by the amended Tribunal Procedure (Upper Tribunal) Rules 2008 in combination with the joint Practice Directions and Practice Statements of the FTT and UT Immigration and Asylum Chambers.

Non-compliance in the UT

Non-compliance with UT rules is explicitly dealt with at UT rule 7 and also rules 8 (strike out of case), 10 (wasted costs) and 5 (case management). However, rules 8 and 10 do not apply in immigration and asylum cases, leaving the UT with very limited powers.

In a speech to the new tribunal shortly before commencement, President Mr Justice Blake said as follows regarding compliance with directions:

> We must expect that the legal profession and UKBA representatives will respond to these directions and be imaginative in sanction if they don't. Although this chamber of the UT may not have the power to strike out cases for non-compliance, there are other measures available in terms of identifying the issues and how they will be determined that may sorely disadvantage defaulting parties [whoever] they are.

It may prove to be the case that the UT proves more robust than the AIT in the face of UKBA non-compliance. This may, of course, be a two edged sword.

Respondent's response to appeal

Rule 24(1A) states that, subject to any directions from the tribunal, the respondent 'may' (not must) lodge a response to a notice of appeal. However, the information required in such a response strongly suggests that these responses will considered important documents and failure to lodge one may have consequences for a respondent:

(a) the name and address of the respondent;

(b) the name and address of the representative (if any) of the respondent;

(c) an address where documents for the respondent may be sent or delivered;

(d) whether the respondent opposes the appeal;

(e) the grounds on which the respondent relies, including [(in the case of an appeal against the decision of another tribunal)] any grounds on which the respondent was unsuccessful in the proceedings which are the subject of the appeal, but intends to rely in the appeal; and

(f) whether the respondent wants the case to be dealt with at a hearing.

Subrule 24(4) suggests by its very existence that non-compliance may be taken seriously:

> 'If the respondent provides the response to the Upper Tribunal later than the time required by paragraph (2) or by an extension of time allowed under rule 5(3)(a) (power to extend time), the response must include a request for an extension of time and the reason why the [response] was not provided in time.'

Further evidence

The Upper Tribunal may consider fresh evidence not previously relied on in the FTT. A specific provision was inserted into the general UT procedure rules to deal specifically with immigration and asylum appeals, however, at rule 15(2A):

> '(2A) In an asylum case or an immigration case
>
> (a) if a party wishes the Upper Tribunal to consider evidence that was not before the First-tier Tribunal, that party must send or deliver a notice to the Upper Tribunal and any other party
> (i) indicating the nature of the evidence; and
> (ii) explaining why it was not submitted to the First-tier Tribunal; and
>
> (b) when considering whether to admit evidence that was not before the First-tier Tribunal, the Upper Tribunal must have regard to whether there has been unreasonable delay in producing that evidence.'

Practice Direction 4 addresses evidence in the UT and emphasises that rule 15(2A) must be complied with in every case where a party wishes to rely on further evidence. In addition, the Practice Directions specifies that a party seeking to adduce new evidence must make it clear in the rule 15(2A) notice whether the evidence is:

(a) in connection with the issue of whether the First-tier Tribunal made an error of law, requiring its decision to be set aside; or

(b) in connection with the re-making of the decision by the Upper Tribunal, in the event of the First-tier Tribunal being found to have made such an error.

In asylum and human rights cases where the facts have to be decided at the date of hearing, it will be normal for fresh country information evidence to be admitted. Evidence as to other matters will normally be subject to the test set out by the Court of Appeal in *E v SSHD* [2004] EWCA Civ 49:

> 'The *Ladd v Marshall* principles are, in summary: first, that the fresh evidence could not have been obtained with reasonable diligence for use at the trial; secondly, that if given, it probably would have had an important influence on the result; and, thirdly, that it is apparently credible although not necessarily incontrovertible. As a general rule, the fact that the failure to adduce the evidence was that of the party's legal advisers provides no excuse: see *Al-Mehdawi v Home Secretary* [1990] 1AC 876.'

As the Tribunal recognized in the starred appeal of *MA (Fresh evidence) Sri Lanka* [2004] UKIAT 00161 (21 June 2004):

> 'Of course there may be exceptional factors in an asylum or human rights case, which mean that evidence which could and should have been before the Adjudicator can be admitted on appeal.'

Hence the test for admission of fresh evidence has three stages:

(1) Prior availability taking into account the need for reasonable diligence;

(2) Materiality;

(3) Apparent Credibility;

With a fourth, doubtless rare, get out clause:

(4) With a residual possibility of exceptional factors being present in an asylum and human rights case albeit that the above criteria are not met.

The tribunal cannot give permission to appeal, nor consider whether to allow an appeal, on the grounds of fresh evidence, unless an error of law is present in the determination of the immigration judge, see the Court of Appeal in *CA v Secretary of State for the Home Department* [2004] EWCA Civ 1165.

Initial hearing

The first issue to be decided in the Upper Tribunal will be whether there was in fact an error of law in the decision of the First Tier Tribunal. This test is a prerequisite to an appeal to the UT and must be satisfied in all cases, whether permission was granted by the FTT or the UT.

The possible grounds for asserting that there is an error of law are addressed briefly above.

It will be unusual for new evidence to be relied on at this stage in the proceedings because the focus must be the material that was before the decision maker who it is contended committed an error of law.

The procedure to be followed on appeal is set out in Practice Direction 3. There is a clear steer towards the UT retaining cases for final decision rather than remitting them to the FTT.

Since the inception of the Asylum and Immigration Tribunal in 2005, representatives have faced considerable difficulties in assessing whether full evidence should be prepared in advance of an initial error of law hearing. This is because any such preparation could be a colossal waste of time and money because the tribunal might decided there was no error of law, meaning the evidence would not be called upon.

This dilemma very much continues in the TCEA 2007 tribunal structure. Practice Direction 3 provides as follows:

> '3.2 The parties should be aware that, in the circumstances described in paragraph 3.1(c), the Upper Tribunal will generally expect to proceed, without any further hearing, to re-make the decision, where this can be undertaken without having to hear oral evidence...

> 3.3 In a case where no oral evidence is likely to be required in order for the Upper Tribunal to re-make the decision, the Upper Tribunal will therefore expect any documentary evidence relevant to the re-making of the decision to be adduced in accordance with Practice Direction 4 so that it may be considered at the relevant hearing; and, accordingly, the party seeking to rely on such documentary evidence will be expected to show good reason why it is not reasonably practicable to adduce the same in order for it to be considered at that hearing.'

It therefore seems safe to assume that where the error of law asserted is such that oral evidence would be necessary for a re-decision, witnesses need not attend the initial UT hearing and full up-to-date evidence need not be prepared. In all other cases, representatives have to assess whether it is 'reasonably practicable' to prepare and adduce any necessary further evidence.

It is impossible to give firm guidance. Commonsense and experience will be required in assessing whether to prepare on the basis that the Upper Tribunal may immediately re-hear the case.

Consider the following examples:

Credibility challenge in asylum case
- It is unlikely that the case can be re-decided without oral evidence, adjournment very likely

Failure to consider relevant evidence
- Oral evidence may not be needed, adjournment unlikely

Legal error such as Convention reason
- Oral evidence unlikely to be needed, adjournment very unlikely

At the time of writing it was the relatively early days of the new tribunal structure. It appears that it is increasingly common for the tribunal to grant permission to appeal, dispose of the oral hearing in relation to whether there is an error of law and progress straight to a re-hearing of the appeal. The parties have an opportunity to request an oral hearing if they so wish. Where an oral hearing is held, it appears to be the case that the Senior Immigration Judge who hears the initial argument about whether there is an error of law will reserve the case to him or herself and sit on any adjourned hearing.

It is implicit in all of the above that the emphasis is on the UT retaining cases for itself and making a final decision itself, as opposed to remitting cases to the FTT.

Remittal to FTT

In addition to the clear steer given in the Practice Directions to the UT determining appeals itself rather than remitting to the FTT, the Practice Statements confirm this at section 7:

> 7 Disposal of appeals in Upper Tribunal
>
> 7.1 Where under section 12(1) of the 2007 Act (proceedings on appeal to the Upper Tribunal) the Upper Tribunal finds that the making of the decision concerned involved the making of an error on a point of law, the Upper Tribunal may set aside the decision and, if it does so, must either remit the case to the First-tier Tribunal under section 12(2)(b)(i) or proceed (in accordance with relevant Practice Directions) to re-make the decision under section 12(2)(b)(ii).
>
> 7.2 The Upper Tribunal is likely on each such occasion to proceed to re-make the decision, instead of remitting the case to the First-tier Tribunal, unless the Upper Tribunal is satisfied that:-
>> (a) the effect of the error has been to deprive a party before the First-tier Tribunal of a fair hearing or other opportunity for that party's case to be put to and considered by the First-tier Tribunal; or
>> (b) there are highly compelling reasons why the decision should not be re-made by the Upper Tribunal. (Such reasons are likely to be rare.)

It is certainly envisaged by those responsible for managing the Immigration and Asylum Chamber of the Upper Tribunal that remittals to the FTT will be rare.

It should be noted that consent orders are now specifically provided for, at UT rule 39. This would obviate the need for an error of law hearing where the error is clear – should UKBA prove to be capable of responding to correspondence.

Onward appeal

Seeking permission from the UT

As previously, an application to the UT for permission to appeal to the Court of Appeal must first be made before seeking permission to appeal directly from the Court of Appeal.

The deadline is set out at UT rule 44(3B) and is 12 days from the sending of the determination, or 7 working days if the person is detained or 38 days if the person is outside the UK. Different time limits apply where the person was served personally or by electronic means.

An appeal to the Court of Appeal must be on a point of law (s.13 TCEA 2007) and must also satisfy a new hurdle created by the TCEA 2007 and show:

(a) that the proposed appeal would raise some important point of principle or practice, or

(b) that there is some other compelling reason for the relevant appellate court to hear the appeal.

Lord Justice Buxton, after his retirement, was commissioned by JCWI to give an opinion on how this test might be applied in immigration and asylum cases. He suggested that cases involving UK international obligations (i.e. refugee and human rights cases) would very often pass this test. However, how it operates in practice remains to be seen.

UT self review

The possibility of the UT reviewing its own decision is allowed for in detail at section 10 of TCEA 2007, either of the UT's own initiative or on application by a party with a right of appeal.

This is dealt with at UT rules 41 to 47, although not all of those rules will be relevant in immigration and asylum cases.

Unlike some previous historic slip rules in immigration cases, s.10 allows the UT to set aside its own decision. However, there are limited circumstances in which the UT can review an UT decision, however. UT rule 45(1) provides that a review can only occur on receiving an application for permission to appeal (this may allow review in the unlikely scenario that an application for permission to appeal is not made) where either

(a) when making the decision the Upper Tribunal overlooked a legislative provision or binding authority which could have had a material effect on the decision; or

(b) since the Upper Tribunal's decision, a court has made a decision which is binding on the Upper Tribunal and which, had it been made before the Upper Tribunal s decision, could have had a material effect on the decision.

In addition, the decision can only be set aside where the UT considers that it would be in the interests of justice to do so AND one of four conditions applies:

(a) a document relating to the proceedings was not sent to, or was not received at an appropriate time by, a party or a party's representative;

(b) a document relating to the proceedings was not sent to the Upper Tribunal at an appropriate time;

(c) a party, or a party's representative, was not present at a hearing related to the proceedings; or

(d) there has been some other procedural irregularity in the proceedings.

A time limit of 12 days from the sending of the notice by the tribunal applies, or 38 days where the appellant is outside the UK.

Tribunal determinations as precedents

Starred appeals

In recent years the Tribunal introduced the practice of elevating certain determinations to prominence and near-binding effect by 'Starring' them. In such cases, a legal panel, chaired by the President or his Deputy (and sometimes featuring both) will sit together, to determine issues upon which authority is split, or otherwise of general importance. Speaking as supervising Lord Justice in relation to immigration cases, Laws LJ in *Sepet and Bulbul* endorsed the system, stating that adjudicators should consider themselves bound by such decisions and other divisions of the Tribunal should depart from them only if satisfied that they were clearly wrong. Since then, the system of starred determinations and now Country Guideline cases has been accepted by the higher courts.

Reported tribunal cases

As of May 2003 a practice direction came into effect which ended the era of universal promulgation of Tribunal determinations, so that the senior tribunal judiciary identify those decisions which are 'reportable'. These are also anonymised. Only reported decisions can be cited before the tribunal (aside for a caveat for the determinations of family members and for proceedings to which the present appellant was a party), though exceptionally a party may manage to persuade the decision maker of the authoritativeness of a non-reported decision through a predefined, and rather onerous, mechanism (see Practice Direction).

There will be no bar on citing Tribunal decisions from the era before the new regime, though from 1 May 2004 those relying on them must be able to certify there is no more modern authority on the point.

'Country Guideline' decisions

Unusually in the legal field, because of the need for consistency in determining asylum appeals, it is necessary to recognize some need for factual precedent, see Laws LJ in the Court of Appeal in *S and Others* [2002] EWCA Civ 539:

> 'While in our general law this notion of a factual precedent is exotic, in the context of the IAT's responsibilities it seems to us in principle to be benign and practical. Refugee claims vis-à-vis any particular State are inevitably made against a political backdrop which over a period of time, however long or short, is, if not constant, at any rate identifiable. Of course the impact of the prevailing political reality may vary as between one claimant and another, and it is always the appellate authorities' duty to examine the facts of individual cases. But there is no public interest, nor any legitimate individual interest, in multiple examinations of the state of the backdrop at any particular time. Such revisits give rise to the risk, perhaps the likelihood, of inconsistent results; and the likelihood, perhaps the certainty, of repeated and therefore wasted expenditure of judicial and financial resources upon the same issues and the same evidence.'

In the light of decisions such as *S and Others*, the Tribunal has also begun issuing 'Country Guideline' decisions on country situations to supplement

'Starred' decisions: "a small sub-set of reported cases, intended to indicate the Tribunal's present view on constantly recurring general matters of fact and they will complement starred cases." The Country Guideline (CG) case system has grown increasingly important and it is now essential to be familiar with relevant CG cases. Indeed, the tribunal states in the Practice Directions that it expects practitioners to be familiar with relevant CG cases.

Chapter 12: Criminal offences

INTRODUCTION	443
IMMIGRATION OFFICERS AND POLICE POWERS	443
EFFECTS OF A CRIMINAL CONVICTION	444
Recommendation for deportation	444
Citizenship applications	445
Eligibility for Home Office policies	445
Criminal convictions for refugees	445
ARTICLE 31 DEFENCE AGAINST PROSECUTION	446
TRAFFICKING	446
OFFENCES UNDER THE IMMIGRATION ACT 1971	447
Illegal entry and stay: s.24 to 24A	448
Assisting: s.25 to 25D	448
General offences: s.26	450
Registration cards and immigration stamps	451
Offences connected with ships or ports	451
Powers of entry and search	451
OFFENCES UNDER THE 2004 ACT	452
Immigration document offence: s.2	452
Duty to co-operate: s.35	452
OFFENCES IN NATIONALITY ACTS	453
EMPLOYER AND FINANCIAL INSTITUTION OFFENCES	453
Civil penalties	453
Sections 135 to 139 of the 2002 Act	453
GIVING IMMIGRATION ADVICE: THE OISC	454
Section 91 of the Immigration and Asylum Act 1999	454
Section 84 of the Immigration and Asylum Act 1999	455
OFFENCES CONNECTED WITH SUPPORT	455
False and dishonest representations, delay or obstruction	455
Section 107 of the 1999 Act	456
Failure of a sponsor to maintain	456
Offences under Schedule 3 of the NIA 2002	456

Introduction

Immigration legislation contains a plethora of offences. In addition the practitioner will find a range of other penalties, for examples the fines and civil penalties that can be imposed upon carriers under Part II of the Immigration and Asylum Act 1999. It is also important to note that the new Asylum and Immigration (Treatment of Claimants etc) Act 2004, increases the range of offences considerably, for example creating a new offence of failure to cooperate, without reasonable excuse, in one's documentation for removal or deportation; or failing to possess a valid passport or similar document without reasonable excuse on arrival.

It is also important to be aware that there are general offences of aiding and abetting the commission of a criminal offence, which can broaden the scope of who can be caught by an offence.

> **Top tip**
>
> If sitting the accreditation examinations, it is important to bear in mind that criminal offences will be examined, but questions raising such issues may not be immediately obvious. As with the ethical dimension to the exams, practitioners are expected to identify when problems might arise without a specific 'pointer' to this effect.

Immigration officers and police powers

Part VII of the Immigration and Asylum Act 1999, modelled to a large extent of the Police and Criminal Evidence Act 1984, amended the Immigration Act 1971 to give immigration officers powers of arrest and search, previously the sole province of the police force. These powers have been extended by subsequent legislation. Section 145 of the 1999 Act provides for immigration officers to have regard to Codes of Practice in exercising these powers. Code of Practice Directions have been issued. These take as their starting point the PACE codes, and take the form of a series of instructions modifying those Codes. However it is also notable that some safeguards that apply to police officers do not apply to them, for example the requirement to give one's name when conducting certain searches.

Section 14 of the Asylum and Immigration (Treatment of Claimants, etc) Act 2004 considerably broadens the powers of arrest, and ancillary powers of entry, search and seizure, of immigration officers. Once in force, they will possess powers of arrest when in the course of exercising a function under the immigration acts they form a reasonable suspicion that one of a wide range of offences under the general criminal law have been committed, including conspiracy to defraud under the common law, bigamy under the Offences Against the Person Act 1861, offences under s.3 or s.4 of the Perjury Act 1911, as well as aiding and abetting offences; a range of offences pertaining to obtaining by deception, false accounting and handling stolen goods under the Theft Acts and a range of offences under the Forgery and Counterfeiting Act. Perhaps this represents the development of a separate policing of persons under immigration control.

The Act also contains proposals to allow the DPP to give immigration officers advice on criminal offences.

Effects of a criminal conviction

While a person under immigration control faces trial and conviction in the ordinary courts, and would serve their sentence in prison, a criminal conviction may have more consequences for them than it would have for a British citizen.

Recommendation for deportation

Under s.3 of the Immigration Act 1971, where any person over 17 convicted of an offence for which he is punishable with imprisonment the sentencing court can recommend deportation. Section 6 of the Act specifies how the provision is to operate.

Section 7 provides that Irish or Commonwealth citizens who were lawfully ordinarily resident in the UK at the commencement of the 1971 Act (ie 1973) for more than five years at the time of sentence, exclusive of any periods they have spent in prison following conviction, are protected from such recommendations.

Section 5 of the 1971 Act provides for the Secretary of State to make a deportation order against such a person; it is, ultimately, a matter for the Secretary of State. Subject to limitations, including of time, orders can also be made against family members. People affected by these provisions are liable to detention under immigration act powers as provided in Schedule 3 of the 1971 Act at the end of their criminal sentence.

The Asylum and Immigration (Treatment of Claimants etc) Act introduces a provision whereby release on bail by a court will no longer prevent the detention under immigration powers of a person who is the subject of deportation action.

Section 82(2)(j) of the Nationality Immigration and Asylum Act 2002 provides for a right of appeal against the Secretary of State's decision to make such an order. Previously the only route to challenge was to appeal against the recommendation as part of an appeal against sentence in the criminal courts. This ends the distinction between these cases and cases where it is decided to make a deportation order on the basis that deportation is conducive to the public good.

Citizenship applications

Citizenship applications can also be affected. One requirement for naturalisation as a British citizen is that a person be of good character, and a criminal record will tell against them in this respect.

Eligibility for Home Office policies

The recent backlog clearance/amnesty for families seeking asylum provides another example of how a criminal conviction may affect the exercise of discretionary powers. While a large number of families who claimed asylum before October 2000 have benefited from this exercise and been granted ILR, it has not been automatic. They have had to fill in a form which enquiries as to any criminal convictions. Recent refusals to allow people to benefit from the amnesty have included refusals where the basis of the conviction was travelling on someone else's bus pass. The rules on "Spent" convictions apply – both to UK convictions and those received abroad.

Criminal convictions for refugees

The Nationality, Immigration and Asylum Act 2002 changed the consequences of a criminal conviction for a refugee. Article 33 of the 1951 UN Convention relating to the Status of Refugees 1951 provides refugees with protection from refoulement. That protection may be lost however where 'there are reasonable grounds for regarding as a danger to the security of the country in which he is, or who, having been convicted by a final judgment of a particularly serious crime, constitutes a danger to the community of that country.'

Section 72 of the 2002 Act provides that anyone who has been sentenced to two years or more imprisonment, or sentenced to a crime specified in regulations made under the section, has been convicted of a "particularly serious crime" within the meaning of Article 33(2). The person will also be presumed to constitute "a danger to the community". The presumption is rebuttable. If the person fails to rebut the presumption, the risks of persecution cannot be taken into account in deciding that the person can be returned (subsection (8)). However, the section will not affect the prohibition on *refoulement* to torture, inhuman or degrading treatment or punishment contained in Article 3 ECHR and therefore whether this section will lead to removals is in doubt.

The section would also cover sentences imposed abroad. But only where a person is first recognised as a refugee in the United Kingdom, leaves the UK, and commits a crime abroad... and returns to the United Kingdom.

People of any age could be affected by this provision and subsection (11) envisages people placed in young offender institutions, as well as people placed in mental institutions, following conviction, being removed under this provision.

Article 31 defence against prosecution

During the passage of the Immigration and Asylum Act 1999, judgement was given in *R v Uxbridge Magistrates Court ex p Adimi* [1999] INLR 490, [1999] EWHC Admin 765, [2001] QB 667. The case examined the United Kingdom's obligations under Article 31 of the UN Convention on the Status of Refugees. Article 31(1) states:

> "The contracting States shall not impose penalties, on account of their illegal entry or presence, on refugees who, coming directly from a territory where their life or freedom was threatened in the sense of Article 1, enter or are present in their territory without authorisation, provided they present themselves without delay to the authorities and show good cause for their illegal entry or presence".

As a result, s.31 was introduced into the 1999 Act. Section 31, by contrast, requires the refugee to have:

- presented him/herself to the authorities in the UK without delay

- made a claim for asylum as soon as was reasonably practicable after his arrival in the UK (interesting cases have arisen where refugees have been deemed to have presented early enough not be caught by the denial of support for late claims under s.55 of the NIA 2002 but have nonetheless been prosecuted with the view being taken that they delayed in presenting themselves to the authorities)

- shown good cause for the illegal entry or presence

The *Adimi* case has lead to successful applications for compensation for those imprisoned in violation of the UK's obligations under Article 31. Such cases are brought by first quashing the conviction and then making a claim for compensation, which has been paid for the Home Office's *ex gratia* scheme.

In *R v Afsaw* [2008] UKHL 31 the House of Lords considered the extent to which Article 31 and section 31 IAA 1999 afford protection against prosecution. The majority held that it was an abuse of process to prosecute offences not explicitly covered by the section 31(3) exclusions from prosecution but which nonetheless fell within the scope of Article 31. The minority took a narrow approach to the interpretation of Article 31, doubted the correctness of *Adimi* and held that the offence in question did not fall within Article 31 in any event.

Trafficking

Criminalising of trafficking straddles immigration legislation and other laws.

In sections 145 (and 146) of the Nationality, Immigration and Asylum Act 2002, the offence of Traffic in Prostitution was created. This criminalised those who arranged or facilitated the arrival in the UK, or departure from the UK, of a person intending that the trafficker, or another person, would exercise control over the prostitution of the person moved, whether in the UK or in another country. It also criminalised arranging or facilitating travel within the UK of a person who had been brought into the country, where it was intended that the trafficker, or another person, would exercise control over the person moved. The maximum penalty is 14 years.

In the Sexual Offences Act 2003, the government revisited the 2002 Act and produced a whole part of the Act on trafficking (sections 57 to 60). Section 57 criminalised trafficking into the UK for sexual exploitation; section 58 trafficking within the UK, section 59 trafficking from the UK. Sexual exploitation is defined by reference to criminal offences within UK law. Intentionally arranging or facilitating travel were criminalised. The maximum sentence was again 14 years.

Section 4 of the Asylum and Immigration (Treatment of Claimants, etc.) Act criminalises other forms of trafficking: acts in contravention of Article 4 of the European Convention on Human Rights (slavery or forced labour); trafficking in human organs, and the use of force, threats or deception to induce a person to provide services, provide another person with benefits of any kind or to enable another person to acquire benefits of any kind. Again the maximum penalty is 14 years.

Section 4 was amended as of 10 November 2009 whereby a person is exploited under AITCA 2004, s 4(4)(d) in circumstances where a person uses or attempts to use him for any purpose listed in s 4(4)(c)(i)–(iii), having chosen him for that purpose on the ground that:

i. he is mentally or physically ill or disabled, he is young or he has a family relationship with a person; and
ii. a person without the illness, disability, youth or family relationship would be likely to refuse to be used for that purpose.

Offences under the Immigration Act 1971

This is one of the main sources of offences under immigration law. The key offences are as follows:

- Illegal entry and stay
- Assisting
- General offences
- Registration cards and immigration stamps
- Ships and ports

Illegal entry and stay: s.24 to 24A

Section 24 criminalises entry into the UK in breach of a deportation order or without leave; overstaying and failing to comply with the conditions on which leave if granted without reasonable excuse. By s.24(1A) an overstayer is committing an offence throughout the period of overstaying, but can only be prosecuted once in respect of overstaying the same leave. It is for the defence to prove that the person did in fact have leave, or that a stamp in a passport or travel document is wrong.

The s.24 offence as a whole is subject to an extended time limit for prosecution as set out in s.28. The offence can be tried if information is laid within 3 years of the commission of the offence provided that a senior police officer certify that this is within 2 months of the date on which there is sufficient evidence to justify proceedings. Otherwise, the more usual 6 month time limit for trial in the magistrates' court applies.

Section 24A, inserted by the Immigration and Asylum Act 1999, again applies to a person who is not a British citizen. It criminalises obtaining or seeking to obtain leave to enter or remain, or securing or seeking to secure avoidance postponement or revocation of the giving of removal directions, making a deportation order, or actual removal, by deception. It can be tried either way and before the Crown Court the maximum penalty is two years imprisonment and a fine.

Assisting: s.25 to 25D

These offences were substantially amended by the NIAA 2002. Section 25 means that it is an offence to do anything

- to facilitate

- the entry, transit or stay in the UK

- of a person who is not an European Union national

- in breach of the immigration law of any member State of the EU (the Asylum and Immigration (Treatment of Claimants etc) Act gives the Secretary of State powers to add states to the list covered if it is necessary to do so to comply with UK obligations under EU law)

- if you know, or have reasonable cause to believe that the person is not an EU national

AND

- if you know or have reasonable cause to believe that your act facilitates a breach of immigration law.

Anyone can be prosecuted for an act done in the UK. All forms of British nationals can be prosecuted for acts done outside the UK and so can corporate bodies incorporated under UK law. The maximum penalty is 14 years in prison and a fine.

It is not an offence to make an application to regularise a person's status where that person is an overstayer, or has entered illegally. Such an application would assist the person to attempt to stop being in the UK in breach of immigration law. Nor does the section override normal duties of confidentiality. If a person comes to you and you advise them that they are, or may be, in the UK in breach of immigration law, you have not facilitated their stay by giving them that advice. Nor would you do so if you took action on behalf to regularise their stay. Nor would you do so if you gave your advice and they said "thank you very much" and disappeared. Where you would be in trouble would be if you took steps to facilitate their remaining in the UK in breach of immigration law.

Section 25A makes it an offence to

- facilitate the arrival in the UK of a person
- knowingly
- and for gain
- if you know or have reasonable cause to believe that the person is an asylum-seeker (the definition of an asylum seeker also covers those who say that their removal would be contrary to the Human Rights Act 1998).

There is an exception to 25A. To benefit from the exception you must be

- acting on behalf on an organisation
- which aims to assist asylum-seekers and
- and which does not charge for its services.

Gain is not limited to financial gain. The exception is narrowly drafted. It will not help a person who is working for a "not for profit" organisation if they are not acting in the course of their employment, and it will not help a person who works for an organisation existing to help people seeking asylum if the organisation charges for its services.

Section 25B means that it is an offence to do anything

- to facilitate a breach of a deportation order
- by an EU national

- if you know or have reasonable cause to believe that your act facilitates a breach of a deportation order.

OR

- to assist a person who has been excluded from the UK
- on the grounds that this is conducive to the public good
- to arrive in, enter, or remain in the UK
- if you know or have reasonable cause to believe that your act assists the person to arrive in, enter or remain in the UK
- and if you know or have reasonable cause to believe that the person is excluded from the UK because this is considered conducive to the public good.

All three offences carry a maximum sentence of 14 years in prison. Section 25D deals with related powers to detain ships aircrafts and vehicles.

General offences: s.26

Section 26 lists a whole series of offences, all of which carry a maximum sentence of six months imprisonment and a fine, and to all of which the extended time limit for prosecution (s.28) applies (see note above to s.24). The offences are all linked to the administration of the immigration acts.

Those under examination under Schedule 2 to the 1999 Act (i.e. clients) are criminalised if:

- they fail to submit to such examination without reasonable excuse
- they fail without reasonable excuse, or refuse, to produce documents in their possession or control which they are under examination to produce
- they fail to complete and produce a landing or embarkation card in accordance with an order made under Schedule 2 of the 1971 Act
- without reasonable excuse they fail to comply with reporting restrictions (or certificates of registration or payment of fees for same – ie requirements of regulations made under s.4(3) of the IA 1971).

The last two offences in the section could catch anybody:

- Altering without lawful authority a certificate of entitlement, entry clearance, work permit or other document issued or made under or for the purposes of any of the Acts named; or (this later part for clients and third parties, probably under immigration control) using or having in one's possession for a document for such use which one knows or has reasonable cause to believe to be false.

- Obstructing an immigration officer or other person acting lawfully in the execution of one of the named Acts, without reasonable excuse.

Registration cards and immigration stamps

Section 26A provides for a whole range of criminal offences in connection with ARC (Asylum Registration Card) issued to people seeking asylum including forgery etc. Penalties vary with the offence to a maximum of two years in prison or a fine.

Section 26B criminalises having in one's possession an "immigration stamp" – not the impression it leaves in a passport or on a document, but the device used to make that impression – or a replica of the same, without reasonable excuse. The maximum penalty is two years in prison and a fine.

The Asylum and Immigration (Treatment of Claimants etc) Act proposes corresponding amendments to the Forgery and Counterfeiting Act 1981.

Offences connected with ships or ports

Criminalising captains, owners and agents of ships or aircraft for offences in connection with embarkation and disembarkation, including making arrangements in connection with a removal: highly specialist work.

Powers of entry and search

As detailed above, there are broad powers for both the police and immigration officers, of arrest and to enter and search premises, with or without a warrant, in connection with immigration offences. These are broad powers but there is a protection for items subject to legal privilege. However, there is no protection for a solicitor's firm, voluntary organisation or other body, from searches for people taking place, and arrests being made, on the premises.

The Asylum and Immigration (Treatment of Claimants) etc Act extends the search powers of immigration officers, providing powers under sections 28C, 28E, 28F and 28I in relation to the general criminal offences for which immigration officers will now have powers of arrest.

S.28G (inserted by the IAA 1999 s.134) allows searches, excluding strip searches but including searches of a person's mouth, at places other than a police station.

Failure to comply with a written notice to attend for fingerprinting makes a person liable to arrest without warrant under s.142 of the Immigration Act 1999, and although no provision is made for a corresponding offence the person could no doubt be caught by the provisions of Part III of the IAA 1971, for example s.26.

Offences under the 2004 Act

Immigration document offence: s.2

There are a new set of criminal provisions regarding those who (or whose dependants) are unable to produce an "immigration document" (passport or document of similar function) at an interview on arrival; for those already within the UK, they have three days grace to produce such a document (see section 2 of the Asylum & Immigration (Treatment Of Claimants Etc.) Act 2004).

There are defences: *viz* being an EEA national; or having a reasonable excuse for so doing, or proving that the document was used as an immigration document for all purposes en route to the UK, or proving that no immigration document was used on the journey at all.

Reasonable excuses will not include the fact that a document has been deliberately destroyed or disposed of, unless the disposal or destruction was for a reasonable cause or beyond the control of the person charged with the offence. Reasonable excuses do not include following an agent's instructions, unless in the circumstances of the case it is unreasonable to expect non-compliance with the instructions or advice. The burden of proof is on the applicant in these cases.

In *Thet v Director of Public Prosecutions* [2006] EWHC 2701 (Admin) the Lord Chief Justice held that the section applies to genuine immigration documents, and if a genuine document is not held then the person has a reasonable excuse for not possessing it and can make out the defence at s.2(6)(b). This decision drastically curtailed the number of s.2 prosecutions.

Duty to co-operate: s.35

The government says that currently more than 60 per cent of asylum seekers have no documents and this is the single biggest barrier to dealing with their claim and, if their claim is rejected, to returning them to their country of origin.

There is provision for certain steps to be taken to facilitate removal, by an enforced duty of co-operation with endeavours to obtain travel documents: see Asylum & Immigration (Treatment Of Claimants Etc.) Act 2004 section 35. Under this section a person commits an offence if he fails without reasonable excuse to comply with a requirement of the Secretary of State relating to arrangements for removal, including making arrangements with third parties, the provision of information, complying with identification procedures.

In *R v Tabnak* [2007] EWCA Crim 380 the Court of Appeal held that the 'reasonable excuse' had to render a person unable to comply with requests, rather than simply unwilling, and that fear of the consequences of removal was not sufficient to render the person unable to comply.

Offences in Nationality Acts

Section 46(1) makes it an offence for a person, for the purpose of procuring anything to be done or not done under the Act, to:

- make a statement which s/he knows to be false in a material particular

- recklessly make a statement is false in a material particular

The offence carries a maximum penalty of three months imprisonment and a fine. It is subject to extended time limits for prosecution on the same terms as those contained in the IA 1971 s.28.

Section 46(2) criminalises failure without reasonable excuse to comply with requirements the Act imposes on delivering up certificates of naturalisation. The maximum penalty is a level 4 fine, and there is no extended time limit for prosecution.

Employer and financial institution offences

Civil penalties

Sections 15 to 25 of the 2006 Act introduced a scheme of civil penalties for employers on a similar basis to the old s.8 1996 Act offence (i.e. employing a person without permission to work unless certain documents have been copied and kept), with a criminal offence of knowingly employing someone who does not possess permission to work. There is a system of appeals first to the government then to the county court against the level or imposition of a fine.

A number of penalties had been issued of either £5,000 or £10,000 at the time of writing and the Home Office had started to publish defaulting employers on the Home Office website. Most affected employers appeared to be small businesses, usually take away food restaurants.

The Points Based System has radically increased the risk to persons involved with immigrants, namely education providers and employers. There is a concerted drive to transfer responsibility for policing migrants to these categories of person. It is now possible to be sentenced to up to two years for failure to make proper checks and keep records on non-EEA employees/ students. Employers and education providers also risk breaching discrimination legislation if they target foreign workers only, for record keeping purposes. See the Chapter on Race Discrimination, above, for information about a recent decision at the Employment Tribunal.

Sections 135 to 139 of the 2002 Act

Employers or financial institutions can be required to provide information relevant to determining whether a person has committed an immigration offence, or an offence of fraud in relation to asylum support. Section 136 provides that employers or banks must reply to a notice issued by the Secretary of State requiring the information. Failure to do so, without reasonable excuse, is made a criminal offence under s.137 for which a range of responsible people in the company (see s.138) can be held responsible.

Information provided in a response to a s.136 notice could be used in a criminal prosecution for a s.137 offence. However, it cannot be used in other criminal proceedings against the person providing the information

Giving immigration advice: The OISC
Section 91 of the Immigration and Asylum Act 1999

Section 91 states as follows:

> "91(1) A person who provides immigration advice or immigration services in contravention of s.84 or of a restraining order is guilty of an offence"

Immigration advice" is defined in s.82 as advice which:

- Relates to a particular individual

- Is given in connection with one or more relevant matters

- Is given by a person who knows that he is giving it in relation to a particular individual and in connection with one or more relevant matters

- By a person in the UK (wherever the client is)

- In the course of a business carried on whether or not for profit, by him or another

AND

- Is not given in connection with representing an individual before a court in criminal proceedings or in matters ancillary to criminal proceedings.

Immigration services are defined as the making of representations on behalf of a particular individual:

- In connection with one or more relevant matters

- In civil proceedings before a judicial decision maker in the United Kingdom or

- In correspondence with a Minister of the crown or government department

- By a person in the UK (wherever the client is)

- In the course of a business carried on whether or not for profit, by him or another

Section 84 of the Immigration and Asylum Act 1999

Section 84 provides that no person may provide immigration advice or immigration services unless s/he is a qualified person. Qualified people are defined in s.84 to include those registered with the Immigration Services Commissioner, or employed by them or working under their supervision. They also include those authorised by a "designated professional body" to and those working under their supervision. The bodies designated in the Act are the Solicitor Regulation Authority, ILEX and the Bar Council.

The Asylum and Immigration (Treatment of Claimants, etc) Act inserts a new s.92A into the 1999 Act to give the OISC a power to enter and search premises, with a warrant where there are reasonable grounds for suspecting that immigration advice or services are being provided by someone thereby committing a criminal offence under s.91 of the 1999 Act and that material likely to be "of substantial value (whether by itself or together with other material) to the investigation of the offence" is on the premises. Material subject to legal privilege is expressly *included*.

The Act also creates, by inserting a new s.92B into the 1999 Act, a new offence of advertising or offering to provide immigration or services when unqualified, with a maximum penalty of a fine.

Offences connected with support

Provisions connected with asylum support can fall within the general scope of offences relating to all immigration acts, as detailed in the discussion of Part III of the IA 1971 above. However, there are also specific offences related to asylum support.

False and dishonest representations, delay or obstruction

Sections 112 and 113 of the 1999 Act address the means by which the Secretary of State may recover expenditure on support following misrepresentation or a sponsor's failure to support and maintain.

Section 105 provides that a person is guilty of an offence if with a view to obtaining support under Part VI of the 1999 Act for him/herself and any other person s/he:

- makes a statement which s/he knows to be false in a material particular

- Gives or causes to be given to a person exercising functions under Part VI a document s/he knows to be false in a material particular

- Fails, without reasonable excuse to notify a change of circumstances when required to do so in accordance with support provisions or knowingly causes another person so to fail.

Section 106 relates to a more serious offence. It contains all the same provisions as s.105, but with the aggravating circumstance that the person does what they do dishonestly. In this case the maximum sentence is seven years imprisonment, or a fine. The provision is modelled on the Social Security Administration Act 1992. Although they are not part of the statute or an official statement of the law, it is interesting to note that the Explanatory Notes to the Act specify:

> "This section is directed at cases of serious and calculated fraud, such as where a person makes a plan to extract as much from the Home Office as possible by deception."

Section 107 of the 1999 Act

Section 107 provides that a person is guilty of an offence if without reasonable excuse s/he intentionally delays or obstructs a person exercising functions conferred by or under Part VI refuses or neglects to answer a question, give any information or produce a document when required to do so in accordance with support provisions. The maximum penalty is a level three fine. The provision is modelled on s.111 of the Social Security Administration Act 1992.

As far as we are aware, no prosecutions of NASS or Home Office employees have taken place under this section.

Failure of a sponsor to maintain

Section 108 criminalises a sponsor who, having given a written undertaking to support and maintain under the immigration rules "persistently refuses or neglects" without reasonable excuse, to maintain the person in accordance with that undertaking, where a consequence of that refusal or neglect is that support under Part VI of the 1999 Act has to be provided for that person.

Offences under Schedule 3 of the NIA 2002

Schedule 3 of the NIA 2002 makes provision for withdrawal of support for different categories of person under immigration control. Its overriding philosophy is "if you cannot afford to support yourself here and you can leave – please leave". There are provisions to assist people to leave the UK, and to accommodate them pending their departure. Paragraph 13 of the Schedule makes it an offence to leave the UK in accordance with arrangements made under the Schedule and then return to ask for assistance in leaving again, or for support during the period pending departure. It is also an offence to request such support without disclosing that one has made a previous request. The penalty is 6 months in prison.

Chapter 13: Professional ethics

GENERAL DUTIES 458
BASIC PRINCIPLES 458
FALSE REPRESENTATIONS 459
APPEALS 459
COSTS AND CLIENT CARE 460
    ADDRESSING STATUS OF THE FEE EARNER IN THE CLIENT CARE LETTER 461
SUPERVISION 461
LIENS – RETENTION OF DOCUMENTS 462
STANDARD OF WORK 462
SUPERVISION OF STAFF 463
CONFLICT OF INTEREST 463
CONFIDENTIALITY 467
    BASIC DUTY 467
    EXCEPTIONS TO THE RULE ON CONFIDENTIALITY 469
MONEY LAUNDERING 470
    TERRORISM, MONEY LAUNDERING AND CONFIDENTIALITY 470
DUTIES TO THE COURT 471
COMPLAINTS PROCEDURES 474
    RESPONSIBILITY FOR COMPLAINTS 474
    PRACTICAL SOLUTIONS 474
    THIRD PARTY INSTRUCTIONS 475

General duties

The following is an extract from the Guidelines for Immigration Practitioners issued by the Law Society and approved by its immigration law committee in June 2001. Its salient requirements are to:

- Be aware of vulnerability of clients;

- Use appropriate interpreters;

- Avoid deceit or active misleading of the immigration authorities;

- Limit work in terms of competence and capacity;

- Maintain records.

> *General duties*
>
> 1. Solicitors are expected to maintain the highest traditions of professional service in the conduct of activities as advisers and representatives in the field of immigration, nationality and asylum law and practice related matters. In particular:
> (a) They should give sound advice having familiarised themselves with the relevant law, the immigration rules (including details of any published concessions outside the rules), and the principal published materials that relate to the issue in question (e.g. the best practice guides published from time to time by the Immigration Law Practitioners' Association/the Law Society/Refugee Legal Group, and the published determinations of the Immigration Appeal Tribunal, etc).
> (b) They should at all times show sensitivity to the particularly vulnerable position of those seeking immigration advice. Practitioners should pay due regard to the related difficulties faced by such a client, and should ensure that the client fully understands the implications for his or her position of any decision or proposed course of action, making full use of an appropriate interpreter, who should be appropriately monitored and used for translation purposes only, as necessary.
> (c) They must not deceive or deliberately mislead the immigration authorities or the courts or knowingly allow themselves to be used in any such way.
> (d) They should consider whether, by virtue of their knowledge, skills and experience, they are competent to act in the particular case, and must not take on cases outside their area of competence or beyond their caseload capacity.
> (e) They must maintain proper records of their professional dealings, including records of the matters set out below [costs and appeals]."

Basic principles

This is rule 1 of the Solicitor Regulation Authority Code of Conduct:

> **'1.01 Justice and the rule of law**
>
> You must uphold the rule of law and the proper administration of justice.
>
> **1.02 Integrity**
>
> You must act with integrity.

> **1.03 Independence**
>
> You must not allow your independence to be compromised.
>
> **1.04 Best interests of clients**
>
> You must act in the best interests of each client.
>
> **1.05 Standard of service**
>
> You must provide a good standard of service to your clients.
>
> **1.06 Public confidence**
>
> You must not behave in a way that is likely to diminish the trust the public places in you or the legal profession.'

The guidance to the code states that 'where two or more core duties come into conflict, the factor determining precedence must be the public interest, and especially the public interest in the administration of justice. Compliance with the core duties, as with all the rules, is subject to any overriding legal obligations.' The guidance as to the meaning of best interests specifically refers to the duty of confidentiality, obligations with regards to conflicts of interest and not taking unfair advantage of the client.

The professional advisor may be forced to withdraw in a case where the client's conduct threatens compromise or impairment of any of the foregoing. On the other hand, so long as the client accepts advice that will prevent the problem arising, there will be no difficulty in continuing to act.

False representations

Where a client indicates that they wish to represent a state of affairs to the Home Office which is not correct, the advisor will find their duty not to mislead to be in conflict with the usual duty to act in accordance with the client's instructions. It is the duty of honesty which prevails. This may also be relevant where it is apparent to the advisor from the client's general conduct or from other information which comes to light that the facts of the case are not in truth consistent with the client's express instructions. In this scenario you should advise the client that you are unable to act unless you can be satisfied that their instructions accord with the reality of the situation. There will be no obligation to inform the immigration authorities of dishonesty as this is not one of the scenarios which attracts the waiver of confidentiality (see generally below): the solution for the professional advisor is to cease acting.

Appeals

This too emanates from the Guidelines for Immigration Practitioners issued by the Law Society and approved by its immigration law committee in June 2001:

- Take all reasonable steps to comply with Rules and Directions of the tribunal;

- Determine the retainer only for good reason and with reasonable notice;

- Deal with issues surrounding merits tests, funding, arrangements for the advocate, in good time before the hearing - it is unacceptable to end the retainer shortly before an appeal hearing.

> *Appeals*
>
> 5. In the conduct of appeals a solicitor must take all reasonable steps to comply with the rules of procedure and with practice and court directions both to protect the interests of the client and to meet obligations to the court which includes the immigration appellate authorities.
>
> 6. A solicitor must not terminate a retainer except for good reason and upon reasonable notice, recording the reasons for terminating the retainer. Where, for good reason, whether the client has Community Legal Service funding or otherwise, the solicitor determines his/her retainer, it must be with as much notice to the client as possible in all the circumstances. Issues of merits, funding and arrangements to provide advocacy must be addressed at the earliest possible date so as to avoid damage either to the client's interests or to the effective operation of the court. Such advice as may be appropriate should be given to the client for alternative representation. Notice of withdrawal from representation must be promptly given to the court in such manner as to minimise prejudice to the client and to avoid misallocation of resources to the court.
>
> 7. If a practitioner is without funds to cover a hearing it is unacceptable for the solicitor to terminate the retainer so close to the date of the hearing as to prevent the client having any opportunity of seeking to find alternative representation, or to hinder the court in adequately disposing of matters pending."

Costs and client care

The same June 2001 guidance note has this to say about costs, in essence:

- Costs information and complaints handling should be given out at the outset of taking instructions;

- Public funding eligibility should be addressed and the availability of free legal advice mentioned;

- Costs estimates should be given, and revised, throughout the proceedings, including VAT and disbursements.

> *Costs information*
>
> 2. Solicitors must observe Practice Rule 15 and the Solicitors' Costs Information and Client Care Code in relation to the giving of advance costs information, general information for clients and complaints handling (see Chapter 13 p.265 - 275 in 'The Guide to the Professional Conduct of Solicitors 8th edition' - the Guide).

> 3. At the outset, the question of whether the client is eligible for any level of Community Legal Service funding (Legal Help/Controlled Legal Representation/Legal Representation) must be explored and discussed with the client. It is good practice to make the client aware of the existence and range of any services for free representation.
>
> 4. Where a charge is to be made to a client for the provision of legal services, a written estimate of the costs should be supplied to the client at the outset of the matter to which the charge relates, with a description of the work to be done to a specified stage and the method of calculation of such fee (unless the fee is fixed) and the likely overall cost including disbursements and VAT. Where the fee is likely to exceed the estimate given or requires variation, a written revision of the estimate and mode of calculation should be given as soon as it becomes apparent that the original estimate is likely to be exceeded or requires revision, and in any event before it is in fact exceeded.

Addressing status of the fee earner in the client care letter

There is a specific requirement to inform the client of the status (especially of unqualified staff) of the fee earner who would be carrying out their work and to give the name of the supervising principal where the fee earner is not a partner.

Supervision

There follows an extract from the Law Society's note of September 2002 regarding Supervision and Obtaining Work, in which it warns against providing nominal supervision to non-solicitor businesses:

> 3.1 The Society is concerned by reports of solicitors being requested to supervise the work of non-qualified immigration advisers in circumstances where it appears that this is merely a device to avoid the immigration adviser needing to register with OISC. The Society considers that the purpose of the Act was to exempt from a requirement to register with OISC solicitors and staff supervised as part of their practice. It was not intended to allow solicitors to provide nominal supervision to non-solicitor businesses. Supervision of immigration work for the purpose of the Act must be an internal function and form part of the management structure of the firm. It is not possible for a supervisor to fulfil this task properly unless that person works as a part of the firm. The Society takes a similar view regarding the provision of other "reserved" activities – e.g. conveyancing, and probate.
>
> 3.2 Solicitors need to be aware, therefore, that this kind of involvement with a non-solicitor organisation is likely to involve a breach of the Solicitors' Practice Rules 1990, in particular:
>
> - practice rule 1 (basic principles)
> - practice rule 4 (employed solicitors) and/or
> - practice rule 5 (providing services other than as a solicitor).
>
> Practice rule 1 sets out a solicitor's fundamental duties which include preserving his or her integrity and the good repute of the profession. Practice rule 4, broadly, prevents a solicitor working in a non-solicitor firm doing, or taking responsibility for, work for the public. Practice rule 5 prevents a practising solicitor from becoming involved in the running of a non-solicitor business which provides legal services.

Liens – retention of documents

A client is entitled to the papers on his file which belong to him unless the solicitor can exercise a lien for unpaid costs.

- However, best practice is that the solicitor should transfer papers even though financial issues remain unresolved, obtaining undertakings from the new representatives as appropriate;

- The client should, if now acting for themselves, be given copies of material on file at their own expense, and be given access to the file.

> *Lien (privately funded)*
>
> 8. If the client terminates the retainer just before a hearing date and a successor solicitor is appointed, the Society recommends the papers be released to the successor solicitor, subject to a satisfactory undertaking as to costs being given in lieu of the exercise of a lien.
>
> Lien (CLS funded)
>
> 9(a) Subject to the need to comply with the requirements of the General Civil Contract in relation to Legal Help and Controlled Legal Representation, a solicitor who has acted in a CLS funded matter may call for an undertaking from a successor solicitor either:
>
> to return the papers promptly at the end of the matter to enable a bill of costs to be drawn up; or
>
> that the successor solicitor will include the former solicitor's costs in a bill to be assessed, collect those costs and then pay them over to the former solicitor.
>
> (b) If the client subsequently acts for himself or herself, it is not misconduct for a solicitor to retain the file to get a bill drawn and assessed, but the client must be allowed access to the file and to take copies of the papers at the client's expense.

Standard of work

In an urgent case, it is permissible to take on a client simply for the purpose of seeking an adjournment. However if that is refused, and if continuing to act will do more harm than good, then representation at the hearing should be curtailed (which is not to say that the firm should not continue to act).

> *Standard of work*
>
> 10. A solicitor should not normally agree to represent a client where adequate preparation of a case is not possible, but in cases of urgency the solicitor may agree to act or continue to act for the purpose of applying for an adjournment. Where an adjournment is refused, the solicitor must consider whether continuing to act compromises effective standards of representation. If so, the solicitor should then not participate further in the hearing.

This is therefore a limited caveat to the general rule 12.03 of the Professional Conduct rules which states:

> "A solicitor must not act, or continue to act, where the client cannot be represented with competence or diligence."

The Rules stipulate that this applies where a solicitor has insufficient time, experience or skill to deal with the instructions.

Supervision of staff

There follows an extract from the Law Society's note of September 2002 regarding Supervision and Obtaining Work:

> 4. Supervision of staff in a solicitors' practice
>
> 4.1 The Society is also asked, from time to time, for advice concerning the supervision requirements when a solicitors' practice employs staff, whether qualified or unqualified, who deal with immigration work. The staff may be employed under a contract of service or a contract for services. Solicitor principals must comply with practice rule 13 with regard to the supervision and management of their practice. See also principle 3.07 and Annexes 3C and 21G in The Guide to the Professional Conduct of Solicitors (8th edition, 1999). Solicitor principals, as a matter of professional conduct, must ensure that staff (whether employed under a contract of service or a contract for services):
>
> - are competent to carry out the work; and
> - are appropriately supervised.
>
> 4.2 "Supervision" in the context of practice rule 13 refers to the professional overseeing of staff and the professional overseeing of clients' matters. Operationally, supervision may be delegated within an established framework for reporting and accountability. However, ultimate responsibility remains with the principals. The Society acknowledges that work may properly take place away from the office (e.g. when staff visit clients, attend court etc., or if a person normally works away from the office, such as a teleworker) but it is important that systems of supervision and management encompass these situations.
>
> 4.3 Practice rule 13, however, also prohibits a non-solicitor immigration practitioner from operating, as a member of a solicitors' practice, from a separate office, unless a solicitor who is qualified to supervise is employed at that office.
>
> 4.4 In addition, solicitors should be aware that unqualified staff working on immigration matters must be supervised by a solicitor (or by an RFL principal or by a person registered with OISC) in order to comply with the requirements of the Act. This can only be done if the unqualified staff, even if employed under a contract for services, are working within the firm's practice, and not if they are working independently."

Conflict of interest

The relevant parts of rule 3 of the Solicitor Code of Conduct reads as follows:

'3.01 Duty not to act

(1) You must not act if there is a conflict of interests (except in the limited circumstances dealt with in 3.02).

(2) There is a conflict of interests if:
(a) you owe, or your firm owes, separate duties to act in the best interests of two or more clients in relation to the same or related matters, and those duties conflict, or there is a significant risk that those duties may conflict; or
(b) your duty to act in the best interests of any client in relation to a matter conflicts, or there is a significant risk that it may conflict, with your own interests in relation to that or a related matter.
(3) For the purpose of 3.01(2), a related matter will always include any other matter which involves the same asset or liability.

3.02 Exceptions to duty not to act

(1) You or your firm may act for two or more clients in relation to a matter in situations of conflict or possible conflict if:
(a) the different clients have a substantially common interest in relation to that matter or a particular aspect of it; and
(b) all the clients have given in writing their informed consent to you or your firm acting.

(2) Your firm may act for two or more clients in relation to a matter in situations of conflict or possible conflict if:
(a) the clients are competing for the same asset which, if attained by one client, will make that asset unattainable to the other client(s);
(b) there is no other conflict, or significant risk of conflict, between the interests of any of the clients in relation to that matter;
(c) the clients have confirmed in writing that they want your firm to act in the knowledge that your firm acts, or may act, for one or more other clients who are competing for the same asset; and
(d) unless the clients specifically agree, no individual acts for, or is responsible for the supervision of, more than one of those clients.

(3) When acting in accordance with 3.02(1) or (2) it must be reasonable in all the circumstances for you or your firm to act for all those clients.

(4) If you are relying on the exceptions in 3.02(1) or (2), you must:
(a) draw all the relevant issues to the attention of the clients before agreeing to act or, where already acting, when the conflict arises or as soon as is reasonably practicable, and in such a way that the clients concerned can understand the issues and the risks involved;
(b) have a reasonable belief that the clients understand the relevant issues; and
(c) be reasonably satisfied that those clients are of full capacity.

3.03 Conflict when already acting

If you act, or your firm acts, for more than one client in a matter and, during the course of the conduct of that matter, a conflict arises between the interests of two or more of those clients, you, or your firm, may only continue to act for one of the clients (or a group of clients between whom there is no conflict) provided that the duty of confidentiality to the other client(s) is not put at risk.

> **3.04 Accepting gifts from clients**
>
> Where a client proposes to make a lifetime gift or a gift on death to, or for the benefit of:
> (a) you;
> (b) any manager, owner or employee of your firm;
> (c) a family member of any of the above,
> and the gift is of a significant amount, either in itself or having regard to the size of the client's estate and the reasonable expectations of the prospective beneficiaries, you must advise the client to take independent advice about the gift, unless the client is a member of the beneficiary's family. If the client refuses, you must stop acting for the client in relation to the gift.'

Additional guidance is given on conflict of interests between clients. While it is clearly aimed principally at criminal law solicitors the principles are clearly transferrable:

> 'Co-defendants
>
> 23. In publicly funded cases, regulations require that one solicitor be appointed to act for all co-defendants in a legal aid case unless there is, or is likely to be, a conflict. The purpose of this is to ensure economy in the use of public funds by ensuring that a single solicitor represents co-defendants where it is proper to do so. The professional conduct obligations which deal with conflicts of interest have always prevented a solicitor or firm acting for two or more clients where there is a conflict or significant risk of a conflict arising between the interests of two or more clients. A solicitor can act, however, for co-defendants where conflict is not a factor. The difficulty often lies, however, in spotting potential conflict and deciding whether it is sufficiently real to refuse instructions.
>
> 24. Your starting point should always be your fundamental professional obligation to act in each client's best interests. Can you discharge this obligation to each client? This means first asking each client if they are aware of any actual or potential conflict between them and then, if they indicate that there is no such conflict, asking yourself whether you feel there are any constraints on the advice you would want to give to one client, or on the action you would want to take on that client's behalf, which are likely to arise because you act for another co-defendant.
>
> 25. A conflict of interest arises wherever there is a constraint of that sort, for example where it is in the best interests of client A:
> (a) to give evidence against client B;
> (b) to make a statement incriminating client B;
> (c) to implicate client B in a police interview;
> (d) to provide prejudicial information regarding client B to an investigator;
> (e) to cross-examine client B in such a manner as to call into question his or her credibility;
> (f) to rely upon confidential information given by client B without his or her consent; or
> (g) to adopt tactics in the course of the retainer which potentially or actually harm client B.

26. If these obligations actually come into conflict when acting for two or more clients you will have to cease to act for one and often both. This can cause considerable disruption and expense, which is why the rules require that you should not accept instructions if there is a significant risk of this happening.

...

29. When considering accepting instructions from more than one client in the same matter you need to assess not only whether there is a conflict at the outset, but whether events are likely to arise which will prevent you from continuing to act for one or both at a later stage in the proceedings. In almost all cases there will be some possibility of differences in instructions between the clients but the rules do not prevent you acting unless the risk of conflict is significant. Assessing the risk is often not easy. It is also important that where you have accepted instructions from co-defendants you remain alert to the risk of conflict arising as the case progresses.

30. When considering whether there is an actual conflict there are obvious indicators such as whether the clients have differing accounts of the important relevant circumstances of the alleged crime or where one seems likely to change his or her plea. There are also less obvious indicators. These would include situations where there is some clear inequality between the co-defendants which might, for example, suggest that one client is acting under the influence of the other rather than on his or her own initiative. If you are acting for both this may make it difficult for you to raise and discuss these issues equally with them. In trying to help one, you might be undermining the other. If you believe you are going to be unable to do your best for one without worrying about whether this might prejudice the other you should only accept instructions from one.

31. The risk of future conflict can be an even more difficult issue to assess. It may be that you have two clients who are pleading not guilty and who are apparently in total agreement on the factual evidence. Should they both be found guilty, you need to consider at the outset whether you would be able to mitigate fully and freely on behalf of one client without in so doing harming the interests of the other. It may be that one has a long list of convictions and is considerably older than the other. If so, it may be that the younger client with a comparatively clean record was led astray or pressurised into committing the crime and would want you to emphasise this in mitigation. If there is a significant risk of this happening you should not accept instructions from both.

32. Even where care is taken when accepting instructions from more than one client in the same matter there will inevitably be situations where a conflict subsequently arises. This will commonly happen where one defendant changes his or her plea or evidence. A decision will then have to be taken as to whether it is proper to continue to represent one client or whether both will have to instruct new firms. In making this decision you need to consider whether in the changed circumstances your duty to disclose all relevant information to the retained client will place you in breach of your duty of confidentiality to the other client. In other words, you need to decide whether you hold confidential information about the departing client which is now relevant to the retained client. If you do have such information then you cannot act for either client.

...

34. For the avoidance of doubt, you cannot resolve a conflict by instructing another firm or counsel to undertake the advocacy on behalf of one client. Neither can you

> pass one of the clients to another member of your firm. The rules make it quite clear that your firm cannot act for clients whose interests conflict.
>
> 35. Any decision to act, or not to act, for co-defendants should be recorded with a brief note of the reasons.
>
> Your interests conflicting with the client's – 3.01(2)(b)
>
> 39. There are no circumstances where you can act for a client whose interests conflict with your own interests. The situations outlined in 3.02 where you can act for two or more clients whose interests conflict have no application in this situation. This is because of the fiduciary relationship which exists between you and your client which prevents you taking advantage of the client or acting where there is a conflict or potential conflict of interests between you and your client...
>
> ...
>
> 54. Where you discover an act or omission which would justify a claim against you, you must inform the client, and recommend they seek independent advice. You must also inform the client that independent advice should be sought in cases where the client makes a claim against you, or notifies an intention to do so. If the client refuses to seek independent advice, you should not continue to act unless you are satisfied that there is no conflict of interest. See 20.09 (Dealing with claims).'

In the case of *Kaur* (01/TH/02438; 26 September 2001) the tribunal noted that in the case of a solicitor whose firm practises in the same centre as that in which he or she is an Adjudicator, actual interest, not merely appearance of interest, arises if a member of the firm appears before him or her. It is essential that in such cases the Adjudicator disqualifies himself or herself at once. For that reason it is no doubt better if the centre where the Adjudicator sits is not the one at which the firm practises, thus avoiding possible problems of last-minute relisting.

Confidentiality

Basic duty

The duty of confidentiality is fundamental to the relationship of solicitor and client. It exists as an obligation both in law, having regard to the nature of the contract of retainer, and as a matter of conduct. See rule 4 of the solicitors code of conduct:

> 4.01 Duty of confidentiality
>
> You and your firm must keep the affairs of clients and former clients confidential except where disclosure is required or permitted by law or by your client (or former client).
>
> 4.02 Duty of disclosure
>
> If you are a lawyer or other fee earner you must disclose to a client for whom you are personally acting on a matter, whether individually or as one of a group, or

> whose matter you are personally supervising, all information of which you are aware which is material to that client's matter regardless of the source of the information, subject to:
> (a) the duty of confidentiality in 4.01 above, which always overrides the duty to disclose; and
> (b) the following where the duty does not apply:
> (i) where such disclosure is prohibited by law;
> (ii) where it is agreed expressly that no duty to disclose arises or a different standard of disclosure applies; or
> (iii) where you reasonably believe that serious physical or mental injury will be caused to any person if the information is disclosed to a client.
>
> 4.03 Duty not to put confidentiality at risk by acting
>
> If you are a lawyer or other fee earner and you personally hold, or your firm holds, confidential information in relation to a client or former client, you must not risk breaching confidentiality by acting, or continuing to act, for another client on a matter where:
> (a) that information might reasonably be expected to be material; and
> (b) that client has an interest adverse to the first-mentioned client or former client, except where proper arrangements can be made to protect that information in accordance with 4.04 and 4.05 below.

The rule receives is supplemented by the following guidance:

> 3. Rule 4.01 sets out your fundamental duty to keep all clients' affairs confidential. It is important to bear in mind the distinction between this duty and the concept of law known as legal professional privilege. The duty of confidentiality extends to all confidential information about a client's affairs, irrespective of the source of the information, subject to the limited exceptions described below. Legal professional privilege protects certain communications between you and your client from being disclosed, even in court. However, not all communications are protected from disclosure and you should, if necessary, refer to an appropriate authority on the law of evidence.
>
> 4. The duty of confidentiality continues after the end of the retainer. After the client dies the right to confidentiality passes to the personal representatives, but note that an administrator's power dates only from the grant of the letters of administration.
>
> 5. Information received in the context of a joint retainer must be available between the clients. They must, however, all consent to any confidential information being disclosed to a third party. Information communicated to you when acting for one of the clients in relation to a separate matter must not be disclosed to the other client(s) without the consent of that client.
>
> 6. If you obtain information in relation to a prospective client you may still be bound by a duty of confidentiality, even if that prospective client does not subsequently instruct your firm. There may be circumstances, however, where you receive information where there is no real or genuine interest in instructing your firm and that information is unlikely to be confidential.

In summary:

- Even aside from legal professional privilege (which applies to communications between solicitor and client), there is a duty to maintain confidentiality;

- It applies regarding any source of information;

- It applies after the client's death or the end of the retainer;

- A duty may arise even regarding a prospective client.

Guidance specifically states that a client's address should not be disclosed without the client's consent.

Exceptions to the rule on confidentiality

This is the Solicitor Regulation Authority's guidance on this issue:

> '12. You may reveal confidential information to the extent that you believe necessary to prevent the client or a third party committing a criminal act that you reasonably believe is likely to result in serious bodily harm.
>
> 13. There may be exceptional circumstances involving children where you should consider revealing confidential information to an appropriate authority. This may be where the child is the client and the child reveals information which indicates continuing sexual or other physical abuse but refuses to allow disclosure of such information. Similarly, there may be situations where an adult discloses abuse either by himself or herself or by another adult against a child but refuses to allow any disclosure. You must consider whether the threat to the child's life or health, both mental and physical, is sufficiently serious to justify a breach of the duty of confidentiality.
>
> 14. In proceedings under the Children Act 1989 you are under a duty to reveal experts' reports commissioned for the purposes of proceedings, as these reports are not privileged. The position in relation to voluntary disclosure of other documents or solicitor-client communications is uncertain. Under 11.01, an advocate is under a duty not to mislead the court. Therefore, if you are an advocate, and have certain knowledge which you realise is adverse to the client's case, you may be extremely limited in what you can state in the client's favour. In this situation, you should seek the client's agreement for full voluntary disclosure, for three reasons:
> (a) the matters the client wants to hide will probably emerge anyway;
> (b) you will be able to do a better job for the client if all the relevant information is presented to the court; and
> (c) if the information is not voluntarily disclosed, you may be severely criticised by the court.
> If the client refuses to give you authority to disclose the relevant information, you are entitled to refuse to continue to act for the client if to do so will place you in breach of your obligations to the court.
>
> ...
>
> 16. Occasionally you may be asked by the police or a third party to give information or to show them documents which you have obtained when acting for a client.

> Unless the client is prepared to waive confidentiality, or where you have strong prima facie evidence that you have been used by the client to perpetrate a fraud or other crime and the duty of confidence does not arise, you should insist upon receiving a witness summons or subpoena so that, where appropriate, privilege may be claimed and the court asked to decide the issue.'

In summary:

- A solicitor should not permit themselves to be used as an instrument of crime or fraud;

- The client may consent to the duty being waived;

- Information can be passed on if relevant to a reasonable belief that the client or a third party will commit a criminal act resulting in serious bodily harm.

- Information can be passed on where there is a threat to a child's physical or mental health.

Money Laundering

The Solicitor Regulation Authority warns that if solicitors do not take steps to learn about the provisions of the Criminal Justice Act 1993, they may commit criminal offences, by assisting someone known or suspected to be laundering money generated by any serious crime, by telling clients or anyone else that they are under investigation for an offence of money laundering, or by failing to report a suspicion of money laundering in the case of drug trafficking or terrorism.

Accordingly, attention should be paid to: Unusual settlement requests, unusual instructions, large sums of cash, secretive clients (particularly where you do not meet them in person) and dealings with suspect territories where production of drugs or drug trafficking may be prevalent.

As at late 2004, the Law Society indicated that the problems that might ensue from the Home Office demanding that the lodging of the surety money is a condition of bail, given that the Proceeds of Crime Act 2003 can disadvantage a bail applicant who is unrepresented and can pose problems for solicitors with regard to the Law Society's conduct rules. The Home Office is therefore issuing revised instructions to staff that indicate that they should no longer impose a condition of bail requiring the lodging of monies and that they should not seek such a condition from an adjudicator.

Terrorism, Money Laundering and Confidentiality

It is an offence to provide assistance to a money launderer to retain the benefit of funds if that person should have known or suspected that those funds were the proceeds of terrorism. It is also an offence for any person who acquired knowledge or a suspicion of money laundering of terrorist funds in the course of their profession, not to report it.

Section 19 of the Terrorism Act 2000 creates a duty to disclose to the police any information where a person suspects that another person has committed a terrorist offence outlined in sections 15 to 18 (involving funding terrorist purposes and money laundering). This section is triggered where the belief or suspicion is based on information gathered "in the course of a trade, profession, business or employment". The duty comprises disclosing (a) the belief or suspicion in question and (b) the information on which it is based. The maximum penalty for the failure to disclose such information is five years imprisonment. There is a defence if the person charged establishes he had a "reasonable excuse" for not disclosing the information. The Anti-Terrorism Crime and Security Act 2001 has introduced a further level of liability by developing this offence so as to require disclosure of "information about acts of terrorism" in general. It is now an offence if the individual does not disclose "as soon as reasonably practicable" information which can be of "material assistance" in preventing an act of terrorism, or lead to the apprehension, prosecution, or conviction of a person involved in acts of terrorism. Once again there is a defence of "reasonable excuse."

Duties to the Court

There is a fundamental duty not to deceive or mislead the court (Rule 11):

> **'11.01 Deceiving or misleading the court**
>
> (1) You must never deceive or knowingly or recklessly mislead the court.
>
> (2) You must draw to the court's attention:
> (a) relevant cases and statutory provisions;
> (b) the contents of any document that has been filed in the proceedings where failure to draw it to the court's attention might result in the court being misled; and
> (c) any procedural irregularity.
>
> (3) You must not construct facts supporting your client's case or draft any documents relating to any proceedings containing:
> (a) any contention which you do not consider to be properly arguable; or
> (b) any allegation of fraud unless you are instructed to do so and you have material which you reasonably believe establishes, on the face of it, a case of fraud.
>
> **11.02 Obeying court orders**
>
> You must comply with any court order requiring you or your firm to take, or refrain from taking, a particular course of action.
>
> **11.03 Contempt of court**
>
> You must not become in contempt of court.
>
> **11.04 Refusing instructions to act as advocate**
>
> (1) You must not refuse to act as an advocate for any person on any of the following grounds:

> (a) that the nature of the case is objectionable to you or to any section of the public;
> (b) that the conduct, opinions or beliefs of the prospective client are unacceptable to you or to any section of the public; or
> (c) that the source of any financial support which may properly be given to the prospective client for the proceedings is unacceptable to you.
>
> (2) You are not required to act as an advocate:
> (a) under a conditional fee agreement; or
> (b) if you reasonably consider that you are not being offered a proper fee having regard to:
>   (i) the circumstances of the case;
>   (ii) the nature of your practice; or
>   (iii) your experience and standing.
>
> **11.05 Appearing as an advocate**
>
> If you are appearing as an advocate:
> (a) you must not say anything which is merely scandalous or intended only to insult a witness or any other person;
> (b) you must avoid naming in open court any third party whose character would thereby be called into question, unless it is necessary for the proper conduct of the case;
> (c) you must not call into question the character of a witness you have cross-examined unless the witness has had the opportunity to answer the allegations during cross-examination; and
> (d) you must not suggest that any person is guilty of a crime, fraud or misconduct unless such allegations:
>   (i) go to a matter in issue which is material to your client's case; and
>   (ii) appear to you to be supported by reasonable grounds.
>
> **11.06 Appearing as a witness**
>
> You must not appear as an advocate at a trial or act in the litigation if it is clear that you, or anyone within your firm, will be called as a witness, unless you are satisfied that this will not prejudice your independence as an advocate, or litigator, or the interests of your client or the interests of justice.'

The duty encompasses;

- advising the court of cases or provisions that state the law;

- advising the adjudicator of relevant materials filed in the proceedings that would assist the opponent;

- calling a witness whose evidence is untrue to their knowledge (not belief);

There is specific guidance on the distinction between misleading the court and deceiving the court and how to reconcile one's duty to the client and duty to the court:

> 12. Rule 11.01 makes a distinction between deceiving the court, where knowledge is assumed, and misleading the court, which could happen inadvertently. You would not normally be guilty of misconduct if you inadvertently misled the court. However,

if during the course of proceedings you become aware that you have inadvertently misled the court, you must, with your client's consent, immediately inform the court. If the client does not consent you must stop acting. Rule 11.01 includes attempting to deceive or mislead the court.

13. You might deceive or mislead the court by, for example:
(a) submitting inaccurate information or allowing another person to do so;
(b) indicating agreement with information that another person puts forward which you know is false;
(c) calling a witness whose evidence you know is untrue;
(d) not immediately disclosing a document you have become aware of during the course of a case, which should have been, but was not, disclosed;
(e) attempting to influence a witness, when taking a statement from that witness, with regard to the contents of their statement; and
(f) tampering with evidence or seeking to persuade a witness to change their evidence. To avoid such allegations it would be wise, when seeking to interview a witness for the other side, to offer to interview them in the presence of the other side's representative.

14. Whilst a person may call themselves by whatever name they choose, you must (in the context of court proceedings) be satisfied that the client is not adopting a different name or date of birth to avoid previous convictions becoming known to the court, or to deceive the court in any other way.

15. If you are acting for a defendant, you need not correct information given to the court by the prosecution or any other party which you know may allow the court to make incorrect assumptions about the client or the case, provided you do not indicate agreement with that information.

16. Where a client admits to having committed perjury or having misled the court in any material matter relating to ongoing proceedings, you must not act further in those proceedings unless the client agrees to disclose the truth to the court.

17. If, either before or during the course of proceedings, the client makes statements to you which are inconsistent, this is not of itself a ground for you to stop acting. Only where it is clear that the client is attempting to put forward false evidence to the court should you stop acting. In other circumstances it would be for the court, and not for you, to assess the truth or otherwise of the client's statement.

18. There are some types of information which you are obliged to disclose to the court, whether or not it is in the best interests of the client to do so. Failure to disclose such information could amount to a breach of 11.01. For example:
(a) The advocates on both sides must advise the court of relevant cases and statutory provisions. If one of them omits a case or provision or makes an incorrect reference to a case or provision, it is the duty of the other to draw attention to it even if it assists the opponent's case.
(b) Except when acting or appearing for the prosecution, if you know of facts which, or of a witness who, would assist the adversary you are not under any duty to inform the adversary, or the court, of this to the prejudice of your own client. However, if you know that a relevant document has been filed in the proceedings and is therefore notionally within the knowledge of the court, you must inform the judge of its existence.

Complaints procedures

The LSC give certain guidance on complaints. A complaint should be defined as any expression of client dissatisfaction, however it is expressed. This might be in writing, over the telephone or in person.

The firm's approach to complaints should be positive, as they alert you to problems that your clients have about the service and thereby provide an opportunity for service.

Practice Rule 15, the "client care" rule provides that all private firms must operate a complaints system and must make their clients aware of it. Although the client does not need to be advised of the entire system when given one-off advice (including police station advice and court duty solicitor advice), they must at least be advised of the name of the person with whom they should raise any problems. Compliant practice would therefore include telling the client whom to approach in the event of dissatisfaction and/or providing them with a prepared letter/leaflet containing a brief explanation, and supplementing that with a more detailed written explanation if/once a file is opened and further work is done for them.

The Solicitor Regulation Authority has recommended that firms consider having face to face meetings earlier in the process to discuss concerns given the potential needs of immigration clients.

Responsibility for complaints

Ensure that the client is aware of the *names of individuals who are authorised to handle complaints* (e.g. those to whom specific training has been given), or the level at which all complaints should first be handled (e.g. by the caseworker initially, with guidance from the supervisor or a manager). This will include the name of *the individual who has ultimate responsibility* in the organisation for tracking and monitoring complaints (this is often, but not always, the same person to whom complaints escalate if they cannot be resolved initially).

It is imperative that the firm has a system to report and record centrally every complaint made: so ensure complaints are passed onto this system, for analysis and review of all complaints at least annually by an appropriate person.

Ensure that you respond appropriately to any complaint. This will include identifying the cause of any problem of which a client has complained, offering any appropriate redress and correcting any unsatisfactory procedure.

Practical solutions

Make sure that you explain the circumstances behind any problem clearly to a client, and explain what practical steps are available to remedy whatever problems have arisen (obtaining statements from delinquent interpreters or colleagues or third parties, writing representations, admitting one's error to the immigration authorities).

Third party instructions

The client is the individual for whom you are providing legal services. This is from the old Law Society Professional Conduct Guide:

> '12.05 Third party instructions
>
> Where instructions are received from a third party, a solicitor should obtain written instructions from the client that he or she wishes the solicitor to act. In any case of doubt the solicitor should see the client or take other appropriate steps to confirm instructions.
>
> 1. This principle applies to a joint retainer, e.g. when acting for a husband and wife in a conveyancing transaction.
>
> 2. The solicitor must advise the client without regard to the interests of the introducer. See also 11.05 (p.224), 11.07 (p.227) and the Solicitors' Introduction and Referral Code (Annex 11B, p.238).
>
> 3. When acting for a client who has language or other communication difficulties, and instructions are given through an interpreter, the solicitor should take reasonable steps to ensure that the interpreter is appropriate for the client's needs. Guidelines for solicitors dealing with immigration cases are set out in Annex 12C, p.262.
>
> 4. In the case of elderly clients, a solicitor is sometimes put under pressure by the client's family to accept instructions which are not in accordance with the client's own intentions. In this case the solicitor should see the client.'

There is no obvious equivalent in the new Code of Conduct. Rule 2 (client relations) touches on the subject as follows:

> **2.01 Taking on clients**
>
> (1) You are generally free to decide whether or not to take on a particular client. However, you must refuse to act or cease acting for a client in the following circumstances:
> (a) when to act would involve you in a breach of the law or a breach of the rules of professional conduct;
> (b) where you have insufficient resources or lack the competence to deal with the matter;
> (c) where instructions are given by someone other than the client, or by only one client on behalf of others in a joint matter, you must not proceed without checking that all clients agree with the instructions given; or
> (d) where you know or have reasonable grounds for believing that the instructions are affected by duress or undue influence, you must not act on those instructions until you have satisfied yourself that they represent the client's wishes.
>
> (2) You must not cease acting for a client except for good reason and on reasonable notice.
>
> **2.02 Client care**
>
> (1) You must:

(a) identify clearly the client's objectives in relation to the work to be done for the client;
(b) give the client a clear explanation of the issues involved and the options available to the client;
(c) agree with the client the next steps to be taken; and
(d) keep the client informed of progress, unless otherwise agreed.

(2) You must, both at the outset and, as necessary, during the course of the matter:
(a) agree an appropriate level of service;
(b) explain your responsibilities;
(c) explain the client's responsibilities;
(d) ensure that the client is given, in writing, the name and status of the person dealing with the matter and the name of the person responsible for its overall supervision; and
(e) explain any limitations or conditions resulting from your relationship with a third party (for example a funder, fee sharer or introducer) which affect the steps you can take on the client's behalf.

(3) If you can demonstrate that it was inappropriate in the circumstances to meet some or all of these requirements, you will not breach 2.02.'

Top tip: accreditation exams

If there is a question with an ethics dimension to which you are unsure of the answer in the exam, you may wish to indicate that you would consult a supervisor and/or the Solicitor Regulation Authority Professional Conduct telephone line. A note on examination technique previously posted on the CLT website suggested this was a possible way of trying to extract a mark and it would seem particularly apposite for ethics questions.

Also bear in mind the possibility of a criminal offence dimension to a particular exercise as well as a conduct/ethics dimension, as where conduct which is unethical, such as representing a false situation to the Home Office, might also bring liability in terms of seeking to obtain leave to remain via deception.

The question of how non Solicitor Regulation Authority regulated LSC examinees are tested on ethics is an unresolved one. Practice so far has been to make ethical issues non-specific to the Solicitor Regulation Authority Code of Conduct. Nevertheless, the code provides extremely useful general ethical guidance and the principles therein are certainly examinable.

Chapter 14: Practical skills

ASYLUM APPLICATIONS **478**

    TAKING INSTRUCTIONS 478
    SUBSTANCE OF INSTRUCTIONS 479
    SUBSTANCE OF INITIAL ADVICE 479
    DEALING WITH INTERPRETERS 480
    MINORS 481
    UNACCOMPANIED ASYLUM SEEKING CHILDREN 482
    DISPUTED MINORS 482
    WOMEN 482
    VULNERABLE CLIENTS 483

PROFESSIONAL CONDUCT REGARDING ASYLUM CLAIMS **484**

EXPERT EVIDENCE PRACTICE DIRECTION **485**

COMMISSIONING MEDICAL EVIDENCE **487**

    IDENTIFYING THE ISSUES 487
    CORROBORATION 487
    CREDIBILITY 488
    REVIEWING THE MEDICAL REPORT 488
    CHECKLIST FOR MEDICAL EVIDENCE 489
    SUBMITTING THE MEDICAL REPORT TO THE COURT 490
    REFERRAL ONWARDS 490
    PRACTICALITIES 490

COMMISSIONING COUNTRY EXPERT EVIDENCE **491**

    WHEN TO COMMISSION COUNTRY EXPERT EVIDENCE 491
    EXAMPLES OF THE ASSISTANCE THAT EXPERT EVIDENCE CAN GIVE 491
    FINDING AN EXPERT WITNESS 492
    TESTING THE EXPERT WITNESS 492
    DUTIES OF EXPERT WITNESSES 493
    DOCTRINE OF ULTIMATE ISSUE 494
    LETTER OF INSTRUCTIONS 494
    THE REPORT 495
    REUSING EXPERT REPORTS 496

Asylum applications

Taking instructions

It is recommended that you are familiar with the ILPA Making an Asylum Application as to the best practice to follow throughout asylum applications, although we summarise most of the important points in this section – for example making sure you take instructions on other basis than asylum on which an application for leave to remain could be made (and indeed whether an article 8 human rights claim is a realistic option to going abroad and applying under the immigration rules), immigration history, the status of other family members, and ensuring you are aware of all relevant documents held by the client (eg documents going to the basis of stay of relatives and witnesses in the United Kingdom be it ILR on the basis of refugee status, or lesser forms of leave to remain, and accompanying statements).

> **Top tip**
>
> HJT strongly recommends reading the following ILPA best practice guides, which are essentially skills guides. They are written by skilled, experienced practitioners who have distilled their learning into readable and accessible form. Aspiring practitioners would be mugs to pass by the opportunity to learn from them! Contact ILPA for details.
>
> *Best practice guide to asylum and human rights appeals*, Mark Henderson (2003). The second edition was published in 2003 but an updated version was at the time of writing soon to be made available electronically via the Electronic Immigration Network
>
> *Making an asylum application: a best practice guide*, Jane Coker, Garry Kelly, Martin Soorjoo (2002)
>
> *Challenging immigration detention: a best practice guide*, Emily Burnham (2003)
>
> *Working with children and young people subject to immigration control: guidelines for best practice*, Heaven Crawley with Gaenor Bruce, Jane Coker, Nadine Finch, Susan Rowlands, Sue Shutter and Alison Stanley (2004)
>
> *Representation at immigration appeals: a best practice guide*, Jane Coker, Jim Gillespie, Sue Shutter, Alison Stanley (2005)
>
> *The detained fast track process: a best practice guide*, Matthew Davies (2008)

Ensure you investigate whether there have been any other encounters with the authorities such as visa applications or other applications to remain in the United Kingdom.

Applications for asylum must be made in person, and are often followed directly by the screening interview. It is useful to send clients along with written materials confirming that the firm is on the record. Give your client's name, firm's reference number for client, date of birth, and nationality, confirm you are instructed. After a claim has been lodged, confirm that the Home Office have recorded these details, confirm the temporary admission address (and that it is the correct and permitted address), and that a SEF has been issued, and the return date (if applicable), or the interview date set if no SEF has been issued. It should be noted that SEF forms are no longer issued under the NAM model. See the asylum process and practice chapter for further details.

Where a non-compliance refusal is issued which is inaccurate (ie there has been compliance, overlooked or lost by the Home Office), an appeal should still be lodged, although it is possible the Home Office will recognise their oversight and issue a substantive decision in due course. Remember that on appeal, an Immigration judge may take into account the reasons for the non-compliance, but their overriding duty is to determine whether the immigration decision being carried out would breach the Refugee Convention, which requires they determine whether your client is a refugee or not, something as to which the non-compliance issue may be neutral (*Haddad* (starred) (00/HX/00926) 13 March 2000).

Substance of instructions

Ensure you deal with issues such as:

- Internal relocation and State protection issues

- Delay in leaving country of origin

- Time in third countries

- Family members left behind

- Delay in claiming asylum

- Possession of a national passport

Substance of initial advice

Ensure you deal with issues such as

- Possessing a nationality (or kind of case) liable to fast tracking, be that non-suspensive appeals with detention at Oakington or accelerated appeals with detention at Harmondsworth, or third countrying

- Liability to treatment as illegal entrant

- Being ready for the interview and the general non-readback policy, and the absence of clerks

- Entitlement to ARCs

Re witnesses, ensure that you know their:

- Immigration status (and have advised them of any possible adverse consequences of giving evidence, for example, whilst it is no doubt very unlikely indeed, there is a power to revoke ILR available to the SSHD)

- If they are refugees or otherwise made applications to the SSHD, that you have details of those applications (it can be a disaster if a SEF turns up on the SSHD's file at court showing claims inconsistent with those already available)

Dealing with interpreters

Ensure that:

- The interpreter is competent to interpret both in the client's language to English and back again

- Interpreters do not interpolate information into questions or answers, nor summarise them, nor render "comprehensible" answers that if not so decoded would indicate mental health issues.

- Interpretation is in the first person

- The interpreter is conversant with the client's dialect as well as language, and does not intimidate them

The Best Practice Guide (BPG) advises of the possibility of errors resulting from the use of an under-qualified interpreter, or one who is inappropriate because he speaks a different dialect or because his cultural or ethnic background or gender inhibit communication

Practitioners should not proceed to use an interpreter who is inadequate. It will be preferable to make alternative arrangements even if this risks antagonising the client: it is better to explain the need for professional interpretation than to follow a client's wishes to proceed speedily by using a well-meaning friend. Using an inadequate interpreter runs a risk of acting incompatibly with the fundamentals of Solicitor Regulation Authority rules on acting in the best interests of the client and working on the case with due diligence.

Minors

Regarding claimants who are under 18:

- If unaccompanied they should be referred to the Refugee Council's Children's Panel of Advisors.

- Counselling

- Psychiatric report

- More attention should be afforded objective indications of risk. Just because the child is too young to understand their situation does not mean they do not have a well founded fear in the sense of an objective risk of persecution that a third party would be able to determine whatever the child's own apprehension of future events (see the immigration rules).

A child is less likely to be interviewed re their asylum claim although the present immigration rules state:

> "352. An accompanied or unaccompanied child who has claimed asylum in his own right may be interviewed about the substance of his claim or to determine his age and identity. When an interview is necessary it should be conducted in the presence of a parent, guardian, representative or another adult who for the time being takes responsibility for the child and is not an Immigration Officer, an officer of the Secretary of State or a police officer. The interviewer should have particular regard to the possibility that a child will feel inhibited or alarmed. The child should be allowed to express himself in his own way and at his own speed. If he appears tired or distressed, the interview should be stopped."

Consideration of a child's asylum application should be prioritised and be determined within 6 months (ILPA Best Practice Guide *Making an Asylum Application* 2002).

Medical evidence is one form of material that might assist in demonstrating minority, although there is significant margin for error (often said to be two years).

Remember in making appointments for children to ensure they attend with an appropriate adult who is responsible for the child's welfare (e.g. panel adviser, foster parent or social worker). Try to avoid appointments that will disrupt school. Have breaks as often as required. Ensure you use appropriate language and pace of delivery. Information should be sought from other sources where possible: from parents, adults, or objective material regarding the country.

Section 55 of the Borders, Citizenship and Immigration Act 2009 introduced an obligation on the Secretary of State to make arrangements to ensure that specified functions are discharged having regard to *the need to safeguard and promote the welfare of children* who are in the United Kingdom. In so doing it aligns the duty imposed with that imposed on public authorities under the Children Act 2004, s.11(2).

The duty applies to UKBA and also to those performing immigration functions, broadly defined. It only applies to children present in the UK, although the guidance (see below) encourages officials abroad to act compatibly.

By section 55(3), a person exercising any of the specified functions must, in so exercising them, have regard to any guidance given to the person by the Secretary of State for the purpose specified in BCIA 2009, s 55(1). The statutory guidance *Every Child Matters: Change for Children* was issued in November 2009.

Unaccompanied Asylum Seeking Children

The Secretary of State makes particular provision for unaccompanied asylum seeking children (UASCs):

An unaccompanied asylum seeking child is a person who, at the time of making the asylum application:

- is, or (if there is no proof) appears to be, under eighteen;
- is applying for asylum in his or her own right;
- and has no adult relative or guardian to turn to in this country (guardian is here used in a technical sense).

The policy of the Secretary of State is not to remove UASCs unless there are adequate reception facilities in the country of origin. They will receive discretionary leave (which we address in our chapter on the European Convention on Human Rights, under the provisions for "discretionary leave").

Disputed minors

These are extracts from the Home Office website regarding disputed minors:

> 6.1 Where an applicant claims to be a child but his/her appearance strongly suggests that he/she is over 18, UKBA's policy is to treat the applicant as an adult and offer NASS support (if appropriate) until there is credible documentary or medical evidence to demonstrate the age claimed. These applications are flagged as 'disputed minors' and they are treated as adult cases throughout the asylum process, or until we accept evidence to the contrary. In borderline cases UKBA gives the applicant the benefit of the doubt and treats the applicant as a minor.

Although it is rare, where social services disagrees with UKBA's assessment of age, it is UKBA's policy to accept the social services department professional assessment.

Women

The Home Office have now incorporated elements of the best practices contained in the old IAA Gender Guidelines and elsewhere in their APIs.

Thus they recognise that various sorts of ill-treatment that may particularly affect women may be persecution. They name marriage-related harm; violence within the family or community; domestic slavery; forced abortion; forced sterilisation; trafficking; female genital mutilation; sexual violence and abuse; and rape.

They also recognize that women may be subjected to discriminatory treatment that is enforced through law or through the imposition of social or religious norms that restrict their opportunities and rights. This can include, but is not limited to: Family and personal laws; Dress codes; Employment or education restrictions; Restrictions on women's freedom of movement and/or activities; and Political disenfranchisement.

The Convention reasons apply to women as men, although there are general considerations to be borne in mind in assessing the former's cases. There are cases where women are persecuted solely because of their family or kinship relationships, for example, a woman may be persecuted as a means of demoralising or punishing members of her family or community, or in order to pressurise her into revealing information. Whilst many women will be involved in such conventional political activities and raise similar claims this does not always correspond to the reality of the experiences of women in some societies. The gender roles in many countries mean that women will more often be involved in low level political activities for instance hiding people, passing messages or providing community services, food, clothing or medical care. "Low-level" political activity does not necessarily make it low-risk. The response of the state to such activity may be disproportionately persecutory because of the involvement of a section of society, namely women, who because of their gender it is considered inappropriate for them to be involved at all.

In terms of establishing the facts of their cases, it should be remembered that women who have been sexually assaulted may suffer trauma. The symptoms of this include persistent fear, a loss of self-confidence and self-esteem, difficulty in concentration, an attitude of self-blame, a pervasive loss of control and memory loss or distortion. Beware of inhibitors to taking instructions – the presence of family members, for example.

Vulnerable clients

Ensure that you create a suitable atmosphere for the interview. Seek a rapport, using body language, eye contact and tone of voice (though it will be appreciated that these devices may not survive cultural divides).

Make sure the client understands they can have another interpreter or even representative so long as that choice is made on grounds that are not themselves discriminatory.

Be aware of body language as a clue to distress.

Be aware of the possibility that the interview will be the first opportunity the individual has to relate the events to another person: this may lead to a release of pent-up emotion.

Be alive to the possible need to refer to a health care professional in extreme cases where there is a concern that the interview is threatening the health of the client. It would not be impossible for the account to be provided via a statement or summary produced by such a professional absent any other alternative.

Determine whether the client wishes to commit self harm, and seek professional help for them if you judge there to be a real risk of this eventuating.

Advise them on the possibility of support and counselling from specialists.

Bear in mind the difficulties occasioned by recent arrival: disorientation, and fatigue.

Watch out for language that may imply sexual ill treatment (eg "I found myself naked in the street"). Late disclosure of this is to be expected; but it still needs to be dealt with (watch out for relying on explanations such as gender of interviewer or interpreter only to discover that the sought-for combination was available earlier in the process). Do not probe unnecessarily for details, but nor should you fail to obtain clear instructions unless the client's well being is threatened by this.

Be alive to behaviour that suggests PTSD, such as extreme symptoms of, or a combination of: recurrent recollections (including nightmares) of past trauma; fear of figures of authority or other cues to past trauma; irritability; memory failure and poor concentration; fatigue.

Do not underestimate the impact on yourself of a traumatic interview.

Checklist regarding vulnerable clients

(i) Where the client is an adult with a history of torture consider:
- Counselling
- Psychiatric Report
- Physical injuries report

(ii) Where the client is disabled consider:
- Their current health (e.g. are they well enough to attend an interview with us)
- Whether they will require assistance to attend our offices or any appeal
- Whether they will expect third parties to attend the interview
- Whether they will have special access requirements (eg parking close to the building, use of lifts, wheelchair access)

Professional Conduct Regarding Asylum Claims

Advise your client of the need for prompt disclosure, this will be in their interests, however upsetting they find it. If they cannot disclose details of their case for reasons of mental health, medical evidence should be sought to explain this on an objective basis.

Ensure that all relevant asylum claims are brought forwards – women or other dependants may have independent claims which are prejudiced by a failure to explore them sufficiently early on.

Bear in mind issues that might ensue from a conflict of interests – this may lead you to have to stop acting from one or more of your clients (the latter situation might arise where you are privy to information that could assist one or other to succeed in their case, where you have come into possession of the information due to the confidential lawyer/client relationship). There is a duty to keep your client's case confidential, however you receive information in relation to it – and this continues after you stop acting.

As to confidentiality more generally, an Appellant client might wish to give evidence in private (what used to be called *in camera*), Immigration and Asylum Appeals (Procedure) Rules 2003,r 50(4). Nevertheless, once an appeal has been made, the determination is in the public domain. *Tabores and Munoz* (17819; 24 July 1998). The Secretary of State expressly tells asylum seekers that there are some foreign and domestic agencies to which he may reveal details of their asylum claim – however, in so doing, he may create additional risks which can be taken into account in any appeal - *Bouamama* (18630; 28 September 1998).

Expert evidence practice direction

It is important to be familiar with the practice direction on expert evidence in the tribunal. In particular, note the parts of the direction referring to the instructions to the expert and the contents and structure of the expert report.

> 10 Expert evidence
>
> 10.1 A party who instructs an expert must provide clear and precise instructions to the expert, together with all relevant information concerning the nature of the appellant's case, including the appellant's immigration history, the reasons why the appellant's claim or application has been refused by the respondent and copies of any relevant previous reports prepared in respect of the appellant.
>
> 10.2 It is the duty of an expert to help the Tribunal on matters within the expert's own expertise. This duty is paramount and overrides any obligation to the person from whom the expert has received instructions or by whom the expert is paid.
>
> 10.3 Expert evidence should be the independent product of the expert uninfluenced by the pressures of litigation.
>
> 10.4 An expert should assist the Tribunal by providing objective, unbiased opinion on matters within his or her expertise, and should not assume the role of an advocate.
>
> 10.5 An expert should consider all material facts, including those which might detract from his or her opinion.
>
> 10.6 An expert should make it clear:-
> (a) when a question or issue falls outside his or her expertise; and

(b) when the expert is not able to reach a definite opinion, for example because of insufficient information.

10.7 If, after producing a report, an expert changes his or her view on any material matter, that change of view should be communicated to the parties without delay, and when appropriate to the Tribunal.

10.8 An expert's report should be addressed to the Tribunal and not to the party from whom the expert has received instructions.

10.9 An expert's report must:-
(a) give details of the expert's qualifications;
(b) give details of any literature or other material which the expert has relied on in making the report;
(c) contain a statement setting out the substance of all facts and instructions given to the expert which are material to the opinions expressed in the report or upon which those opinions are based;
(d) make clear which of the facts stated in the report are within the expert's own knowledge;
(e) say who carried out any examination, measurement or other procedure which the expert has used for the report, give the qualifications of that person, and say whether or not the procedure has been carried out under the expert's supervision;
(f) where there is a range of opinion on the matters dealt with in the report –
   (i) summarise the range of opinion, so far as reasonably practicable, and
   (ii) give reasons for the expert's own opinion;
(g) contain a summary of the conclusions reached;
(h) if the expert is not able to give an opinion without qualification, state the qualification; and
(j) contain a statement that the expert understands his or her duty to the Tribunal, and has complied and will continue to comply with that duty.

10.10 An expert's report must be verified by a Statement of Truth as well as containing the statements required in paragraph 10.9(h) and (j).

10.11 The form of the Statement of Truth is as follows:
"I confirm that insofar as the facts stated in my report are within my own knowledge I have made clear which they are and I believe them to be true, and that the opinions I have expressed represent my true and complete professional opinion".

10.12 The instructions referred to in paragraph 10.9(c) are not protected by privilege but cross-examination of the expert on the contents of the instructions will not be allowed unless the Tribunal permits it (or unless the party who gave the instructions consents to it). Before it gives permission the Tribunal must be satisfied that there are reasonable grounds to consider that the statement in the report or the substance of the instructions is inaccurate or incomplete. If the Tribunal is so satisfied, it will allow the cross-examination where it appears to be in the interests of justice to do so.

10.13 In this Practice Direction:-
"appellant" means the party who is or was the appellant before the First-tier Tribunal; and
"respondent" means the party who is or was the respondent before the First-tier Tribunal.'

Commissioning medical evidence

Identifying the issues

The legal professional, when setting out on the medical aspect of the case, must first evaluate what the Medical Expert can do for the case's presentation.

Medical evidence can be of use in a number of scenarios.

(i) In establishing the facts of the case independently of the client's oral evidence, e.g. by showing that there is scarring present, and perhaps also that it does not have any obvious explanation than that offered by the Appellant (e.g. bullet wounds, blade wounds to the back);

(ii) In showing physical evidence of past problems that might exacerbate risk on return to the country of origin, or in showing that present health questions may attract discrimination (e.g. HIV in some countries);

(iii) In establishing why the client cannot themselves give a coherent account, e.g. because they have mental health problems following serious ill treatment, or because it would be unusual for a victim of trauma to be able to give details of certain episodes in their life;

(iv) In establishing that the client has health problems counting against their return to their country of origin, where this would amount to a breach of ECHR Article 3 or Article 8 – this will be particularly relevant where they cannot access health care at all.

Before setting out to write your letter of instructions, you should determine which of these functions you hope that the evidence will serve.

Corroboration

Whilst there is no absolute requirement for corroboration, bear in mind that a lack of medical evidence that is in principle capable of being obtained is sure to raise doubts in the mind of a decision maker.

The tribunal will often say that the existence of an injury is not probative of its alleged causation. But the more particular the injury, the greater the argument for saying that it could not have an alternative history (contrast cigarette burns on the back with scarring on the knee).

In cases where the account of torture is, or is likely to be, the subject of challenge, Chapter Five of the United Nations Document, known as the Istanbul Protocol, submitted to the United Nations High Commissioner for Human Rights on 9 August 1999 (Manual on the Effective Investigation and Documentation of Torture and Other Cruel, Inhuman or Degrading Treatment or Punishment) is particularly instructive.

At paras 186-7, under the heading "*D. Examination and Evaluation following specific forms of Torture*" it states:

> 186... For each lesion and for the overall pattern of lesions, the physician should indicate the degree of consistency between it and the attribution
> (a) Not consistent: the lesion could not have been caused by the trauma described;
> (b) Consistent with: the lesion could have been caused by the trauma described, but it is non-specific and there are many other possible causes;
> (c) Highly consistent: the lesion could have been caused by the trauma described, and there are few other possible causes;
> (d) Typical of: this is an appearance that is usually found with this type of trauma, but there are other possible causes;
> (e) Diagnostic of: this appearance could not have been caused in anyway other than that described.
>
> 187. Ultimately, it is the overall evaluation of all lesions and not the consistency of each lesion with a particular form of torture that is important in assessing the torture story (see Chapter IV.G for a list of torture methods).

This is known as the Istanbul Protocol and medical reports documenting torture and scars should follow the language of the protocol. Its use was approved by the Court of Appeal in the case of *SA (Somalia) v SSHD* [2006] EWCA Civ 1302.

Credibility

Beware the expert commenting on credibility without good reason. However expert the expert may be, immigration judges remain jealous of their independence on assessing truthfulness. If the expert has good reason to make a judgment on credibility, they should provide clear justification.

A recent decision in the Scottish courts reaffirms the judicial view that a Doctor's role is not to assess credibility, which remains the exclusive role of the decision maker at the tribunal; see M.E. v SSHD [2009] CSIH 86

Reviewing the medical report

The work is not finished with the arrival of the newly commissioned report. It is also necessary to determine whether the report requires further work. Always ask yourself: Why did I commission this report? And then review the report to determine whether your objectives have been met.

Sometimes the doctor gives an account that the asylum seekers have themselves given to them. Remember to check the account that the doctor receives is consistent with that which appears in the statements – there are lots of reasons why they may differ (the doctor may have less time than the solicitor to go into the story, and may have less experience of the pitfalls of working through interpreters, or does not attach quite the same weight to accuracy).

Bear in mind the chance that the witness will be found to lack credibility by the immigration judge who hears oral evidence. In such a case, the value of the report may be significantly diminished. Consider if it is possible to preserve some aspects of its value, e.g. comments on the impact of return on a traumatised individual may retain relevance even if the reasons for the trauma are rejected.

Checklist for medical evidence

The very best doctors, unless they have a great deal of experience of medico-legal report writing, are likely to be unaware of the strictures by which the Tribunal recommends medical evidence is to be assessed. Whilst it may be tempting to dismiss much of the Tribunal's guidance as neurotic or anti-expert, it remains the case that they are the ultimate arbiter of the weight to be given reports, and in order for your report to be taken seriously, it is advisable that it takes into account their approach.

(i) Has the doctor commented on credibility? If so, have they given reasons for their conclusions? For example, is there a careful analysis of the patient's manner of telling their story as well as the doctor's own expertise of assessing the truthfulness of patients?

(ii) Is the doctor, by their use of language, liable to be criticized by an immigration judge for seeming to become an advocate for the patient, or in commenting on matters that go beyond their actual *medical* expertise (e.g. making generalized comments on the availability of medical treatment in a country without having expertise on that issue), or beyond their own area of medical expertise (e.g. a physician making statements regarding PTSD)?

(iii) Has the doctor made judgments based on the truthfulness of the appellant's account? If so, does this mean the value of the report will be wholly lost if an adverse credibility finding is made based on the evidence "in the round", and is there anything that can be done about this (e.g. is it possible to isolate some elements of the report from the acceptance of the story)?

(iv) Has the doctor commented on the possible causes of the client's physical and mental presentation, if it is realistic to do so, and have they given the basis for their expertise in determining causation?

(v) Is there any reason to make the doctor available for cross examination, so as to be able to answer specific questions from an immigration judge?

(vi) Has the doctor provided their methodology including any relevant diagnostic criteria (Dr Storey wishes to see this, in *P (Yugoslavia)*, above)?

(vii) Has the doctor explained the reasons for their diagnosis and prognosis and any other conclusions, and is it clear how their conclusions are reached based on the presentation of the patient to them?

(viii) Is the doctor liable to criticism from an immigration judge for not having spent sufficient time with the patient to justify their conclusions?

Submitting the medical report to the court

It is advisable to submit your letter of instructions together with the report, because then the immigration judge can be certain of what the expert was asked; and it avoids any chance that the report will be given diminished weight on account of a lack of clarity over precisely what instructions were given to the expert.

As with any evidence that is specific to the case in hand, it is better to submit it in good time before the hearing, serving it on the Home Office as well as the court. Then any failure to grapple with its contents will be something that the Home Office representative has to address without being able to fend off the report's implications with a suggestion that the Secretary of State has had no effective opportunity to consider its contents. The Best Practice Guide to Asylum and Human Rights Appeals recommends that a direction be sought (at the First Hearing stage) that the Home Office expresses any challenge to the report in advance of the full hearing.

Make sure that the doctor has provided details of their qualifications, emphasizing weighty aspects of their curriculum vitae such as official appointments, and any experience that is particularly relevant to the case in hand.

Sometimes it may be desirable to submit photographic evidence of the scarring or other injuries of the appellant. It may be distressing, and inappropriate, for the appellant to be expected to display their scarring at court, which after all is a public hearing. Medical photography is available from the Photography & Illustration Department, University College London, tel: 020 7380 9079.

Referral onwards

Remember that, even if, or once, the medical "evidence" aspect of the health professional's work is done, there may remain an issue of desirable referral onwards for therapeutic reasons. Do not neglect this. Experts will not necessarily perceive their role as bringing with it a need to arrange treatment (the Medical Foundation is an exception to this).

Practicalities

Always check when instructing –

- Fees (clarify with the expert)

- Timing of report (almost inevitably there is a degree of urgency, and in any event you should agree a timetable)

- Availability for giving oral evidence

And ensure that you

- Enclose all relevant documentation (a schedule is advisable for clarity)

- Explain the purpose of the report, succinctly and without legal-ese.

- Have asked all relevant questions, psychiatric and physical (including the impact of each on the other), dealing with future prognosis, present diagnosis, present and future treatment.

Commissioning country expert evidence

When to commission country expert evidence

To show that events are credible in the sense of being plausible

If there is a dearth of general material about an unfamiliar country; or if, re a more familiar country, the issues in question are not dealt with by the existing publicly available materials.

Examples of the assistance that expert evidence can give

There is an excellent section in the ILPA/RLG Best Practice Guide on Asylum Appeals which itemises various forms of assistance that might be derived from expert evidence.

However, in short, expert evidence will potentially be available to prove any aspect of the case.

- The likely reaction of the authorities or other agencies to any aspect of your client's circumstances (including whether your client is "Low-level" and whether this matters) including whatever activities they have undertaken, and whether her sexuality or ethnicity will place her at risk;

- whether the criminal offence for which she is wanted may put her at risk of ill-treatment during interrogation, detention conditions that will be inhuman or degrading, or an unfair trial;

- the consequences of future actions that the client proposes on a return;

- whether she will be at risk of ill-treatment as an expelled asylum seeker;

- whether dissident activities abroad are monitored, and whether your client's activities in the UK may place her at risk.

- Any aspect of the case as to which evidence that you have to hand is lacking – eg parties or groups unmentioned in the country evidence.

- Questions of protection - whether the Government's statements on human rights are contradicted by its deeds and how effective are its investigations into human rights abuses by its security forces.

- You may be assisted in determining whether the relevant tests for the availability of internal location are met: (a) accessibility of safe haven; (b) safety in reaching the safe haven, or living there; (c) undue harshness in reaching the safe area, or living there; (d) discriminatory breaches of socio-economic rights.

- *Where such matters are in dispute*, it can be advisable to seek expert evidence on whether language and accent/dialect, behaviour, knowledge of local areas, are consistent with the client's account of their own background.

Human Rights Cases

- The likelihood of destitution (availability of social services, family networks, discrimination in access to human rights) may benefit from expert input. So too can expert input on medical treatment: remember, there is little reason to suppose that most doctors have knowledge of the state of medical care abroad, as opposed the consequences of removal on health.

- The level of stigma nationally and in local communities are relevant, eg regarding rape or HIV victims.

- You might wish for expert evidence as to the situation if family members were to relocate – medical treatment, discrimination or dangers aimed against Westerners, health and educational facilities for children.

Finding an expert witness

The ILPA Directory of Expert Witnesses, now available on the EIN, is one source. The School of Oriental and African Studies (SOAS) is also a useful resource, and the searchable Refugee Legal Group website can be very helpful (contact Kahiye Alim at Asylum Aid for details).

Testing the expert witness

Ensure that they are not partisan so as to give the appearance of a lack of objectiveness. Bear in mind the possibility that they give evidence in camera. Obtain a CV, bearing in mind the following indicia of expertise:

- Publications, especially recent and relevant ones.

- Journalism, particularly for media with a reputation for impartiality.

- Advising national or international bodies, and reputable NGOs. Obviously if an expert has at any stage advised the Foreign Office, or if the Home Office has relied upon their work, that will be of particular interest. The Canadian independent documentation centre, DIRB, is among foreign organisations perceived by the tribunal as reliable.

- Academic discipline, postings and research, and work with research organisations and think tanks.

- Relevant work with reputable NGOs, particularly human rights monitoring but also in the aid and development fields.

- Time spent in the country (but see the next paragraph)."

Determine whether the expert has given evidence in legal proceedings previously – and specifically whether they have done so in the immigration courts. Also always check:

- Fees

- Timing of Report

- Availability for giving oral evidence

Bear in mind the words of the BPG:

> "Consult your client about choice of expert if she is to be interviewed by him, but distinguish between legitimate concession to her vulnerability and illegitimate discrimination."

Duties of expert witnesses

The impact of expert evidence can be seriously damaged by failing to take account any of the following common faults, taken again from the BPG:

- Expert evidence presented to the court should be and should be seen to be the independent product of an expert uninfluenced as to the form or content by the exigencies of litigation.
- An expert witness should provide independent assistance to the court by way of objective unbiased opinion in relation to matters within his expertise.
- An expert witness in the High Court should never assume the role of advocate (ie they should not argue the case for the asylum seeker).
- An expert witness should state the facts or assumptions on which his opinion is based. He should not omit to consider material facts which detract from the concluded opinion.
- An expert witness should make it clear when a particular question or issue falls outside his expertise.

- If an expert's opinion is not properly researched because it considers that insufficient data is available then this must be stated with an indication that the opinion is no more than a provisional one.
- If after exchange of reports, an expert witness changes his view on a material matter, such change of view should be communicated to the other side without delay and when appropriate to the court.
- Where expert evidence refers to photographs, plans, calculations, survey reports or other similar documents, they must be provided to the opposite party at the same time as the exchange of reports.

The Civil Procedure Rules (Pt 35) provide further guidance on expert evidence in civil litigation which in light of their citation by the old Immigration Appeal Tribunal in the Starred determination of *Slimani* should be followed (and is reflected in the guidance given below).

The expert should address his report to the Court rather than taking the form of a letter addressed to the person commissioning it.

Doctrine of ultimate issue

It is advisable to avoid the expert stepping on the toes of the judicial decision maker by expressing conclusions on "ultimate issues" – ie by stating a fear of persecution is "well founded"; by saying that a particular form of harm is "persecution" or "inhuman or degrading treatment or punishment"; or by stating that protection is not satisfactory to the standard required by international law. It is preferable for the expert to give their opinion in their own words without using legal terms of art.

Experts should steer clear of stating that a claim is credible, although it is not inappropriate for them to comment on its consistency with country conditions, ie its plausibility.

Letter of instructions

This should ensure the expert understands the issues above, and that they are clear as to the ambit of their instructions (eg as to whether or not to comment on the plausibility of certain events):

Whilst your letter to the expert is privileged, beware asking loaded questions which will diminish the report's value:

> "You should obviously ensure, regardless of the risk of disclosure, that your questions to the expert are fair and cannot be characterised as slanted or misleading: pose the question in a manner that you would not be embarrassed to have disclosed to the adjudicator."

Consider whether you wish to seek opinions in the alternative, e.g. on the basis of the account being found credible by an immigration judge, and upon the basis that the appellant is only considered to be a failed asylum seeker.

An expert can advise you as well as act as an expert, but beware crossing boundaries between those roles:

> "23.14 An expert can advise you on your preparation and conduct of the case as well as providing a report for disclosure. You might, for example, seek his comments on a document which your client has obtained from the country of origin and which you are unsure whether to submit (see further chapter 16). Traditionally, communications with an expert are privileged to the extent that he is acting in an advisory capacity rather than an expert witness. The CPR require an expert to state only the '*substance of all material instructions... on the basis of which the report was written*' [emphasis added]. If the expert who produces a report could not also advise privately on other issues, that would encourage the practice of solicitors instructing a second '*shadow expert*' to avoid the risk of his advice being disclosed. However, the matter is not free from doubt. Any issue on which you ask your expert to act in an advisory capacity should be clearly differentiated from those issues that he will address as an expert witness."

The expert should receive all documentation relevant to the matters in hand.

The expert may wish to meet the client. This will be of doubtful utility in cases other than nationality disputes, where face-to-face meetings can be vital.

The report

This is the BPG's summary of the key components of an expert report:

- An account of the expert's qualifications, training and experience, such as are relevant to his ability to assist the court reliably on the issues raised by his instructions.

- A statement setting out the substance of his material instructions (whether written or oral). The statement should summarise those facts and instructions provided to the expert which are material to the opinions expressed in the report or upon which those opinions are based (see by analogy *CPR rule 35.10(3)*).

- What documentation he has considered.

- His conclusions upon each question posed in his instructions, separating facts, inferences drawn from facts, and opinion.

- An explanation of how the expert arrived at each answer, including particular aspects of his qualifications, training, experience or research which led him to the answer, and the sources upon which he has relied (see below).

- The declaration that the expert has complied with his duty to the Court and a 'statement of truth')."

Always check the report for consistency against the versions of the appellant's account that you have, to ensure that the expert has not overplayed discrepancies, or given the appearance of a discrepancy when none truly exists.

Watch out for emotive language.

Reusing expert reports

Here is the BPG guidance on this topic:

- The IAT expressed consistent concern about 'recycling' of expert reports and preferred to receive a report specifically directed to the appellant, and this has not changed under the AIT or the unified tribunal system.
- It will not consider a 'recycled' report at all unless the expert has given permission for it to be reused.
- Always obtain an individual report where possible.
- If that is impractical, strive to obtain the expert's consent to the use of a previous (relevant) report and ensure that it is anonymised.
- Consider obtaining a report that is expressly issue-based rather than client-based to deal with issues that arise repeatedly in the same form."

Also see the BPG on professional conduct and experts:

> "Although you can and should ask your expert to make necessary changes to his report, you must be careful not to overstep the mark into writing it for him. Expert reports must not be 'settled' by the lawyers."